Fearing the Dark

Fearing the Dark

The Val Lewton Career

by

EDMUND G. BANSAK

with a foreword by
ROBERT WISE

McFarland & Company, Inc., Publishers
Jefferson, North Carolina, and London

This book is written partly to
honor the memory of
Arthur Lewis (1908–1991),
a friend, a gentleman, and a scholar.

The present work is a reprint of the library bound edition of Fearing the Dark: The Val Lewton Career, *first published in 1995.*

LIBRARY OF CONGRESS CATALOGUING-IN-PUBLICATION DATA

Bansak, Edmund G., 1950–
Fearing the dark : the Val Lewton career / by Edmund G. Bansak: with a foreword by Robert Wise.
p. cm.
Includes bibliographical references and index.

ISBN-13: 978-0-7864-1709-4
(softcover : 50# alkaline paper) ∞

1. Lewton, Val — Criticism and interpretation. 2. Horror films — United States — History and criticism. I. Title.
PN1998.3.L469B36 2003
791.43'0232'092 — dc20 94-23271

British Library cataloguing data are available

Manufactured in the United States of America

McFarland & Company, Inc., Publishers
Box 611, Jefferson, North Carolina 28640
www.mcfarlandpub.com

Dedicated with love and appreciation
to Bernice,
Sarah and Amber,
and to my parents,
Ed and Helen,
and to my sister, Joan

ACKNOWLEDGMENTS

A special thanks to several people who were instrumental in the creation of this book:

Gary Svehla, who got the ball rolling by saying, "That sounds like a good idea, Ed; why *don't* you write an article on Val Lewton for *Midnight Marquee?*" After my article, "Fearing the Dark: The Val Lewton Legacy," began to grow to tremendous proportions, it was Gary who suggested I turn it into a book. Thanks Gary, for your friendship and advice.

Joel E. Siegel, whose marvelous 1973 volume, *Val Lewton: The Reality of Terror,* provided the backbone for this book. I cannot thank Mr. Siegel enough for his interest, encouragement, assistance, and cooperation, all of which were essential in turning my dream into a reality.

Robert Wise, who not only wrote the foreword to this volume, but also took the time to grant me some terrific interviews.

Val Edwin Lewton, who was warm, helpful, and most informative. His personal remarks about his father were much appreciated.

Ruth Knapp Lewton, for her time and trouble and her wonderful story about how she first met Val Lewton.

Lucy Olga Lewton, for her cooperation in my use of her fond and colorful memoir, *Val Ivan Lewton: Writer and Film Producer—My Brother.*

Tom Weaver, for his help, encouragement, and friendship. Thanks for showing me around New York, Tom.

And Greg Mank, whose fabulous 1981 book, *It's Alive: The Story of the Frankenstein Saga,* inspired me to try and write a horror movie book of my own.

Others who have lent their invaluable services include Greg Hill, Steve Bissette, Stanley Wiater, Robert Clarke, John McCarty, Mark Martucci, Kelly Astukewicz, Mark Miller, Russ Tamblyn, Paul Jensen, Bryan Senn, Ted Okuda, Alice Birney, George Koch, Delbert Winans, Barbara Rice, Susan Svehla, and Allen Koszowski (aka Allen K.).

I would like to offer thanks to some special friends for their encouragement and support: Robert Bombard, Peter MacDonald, Joan Walter, Dexter Newton, Kenneth Blake, Roger Charette, Francis Simanski, David Roach, Dale Ploski, David Modugno, and Tony Dunne.

Additional thanks to: Forrest J Ackerman, James Allen, Pat Ballard, Barbara Barron, Ron and Margaret Borst, John Brunas, Michael Brunas, Bob and Andrea Brunelle, Brian Burns, Robert Burns, Roger Charette, Dick Chase,

David Cidorowich, Joe Citro, Alan M. Clark, Bill Conroy, Matthew Costello, Sarah Coty, Les Daniels, Karl Decker, Mike Dube, Mary Duff, Scott Duggan, Joe Earls, William Emrich, Leo Farrand, Matthew Fertel, Beth Freedman-Hawley, Craig Shaw Gardner, Christopher Golden, Charles L. Grant, Dick Green, Rick Hautala, Nancy Holder, John Johnston, John Keenan, Ron Koslowski, Charles and Wendy Lang, Arthur and Diana Lewis, Joe Lieberman, Mary Ligouri, Jessie Lilly, Tim and Donna Lucas, Deb McKinstry, Elizabeth Massie, Tom Monteleone, Kathy ("Seymour") Moore, Bill Munster, Garfield Norton, Phil Nutman, John Parnum, Christina Pelouze, David Pollack, Kit Randall, Mary Remian, Gerald Sawyer, Nancy Sawyer, Dr. John Scott, David Skal, Don G. Smith, Steven Spruill, Ted Steenson, Linda Stevens, Steve ("Rocky") Thompson, Don Ulrich, Tom Weldon, Jim White, Iris Wiater, Roland Wilson, F. Paul Wilson, all the folks at *FANEX* and *NECON*, and everyone at the Tantasqua Regional Schools.

Some final words of appreciation:

To my wonderful wife, Bernice, for her numerous contributions to the shaping of this book, for her encouragement and her love.

To my daughters, Sarah and Amber, for being wonderful human beings.

To my parents, Edmund and Helen, for letting me stay up late to watch monster movies on television.

To my sister Joan, for her terrific sense of humor, my brother-in-law, Bill, for that mountain we climbed, and my two nieces, Cheryl and Kristin, for being themselves.

To my mother-in-law, Ethel M. Freedman, for her help, encouragement, and boundless energy.

To my cousins, Ronnie and Nancy, for fostering my interest in comic books and horror movies. Thanks, Ron, for those first issues of *Famous Monsters of Filmland.*

To my uncle, Joseph Kielbus, the first adult in my life to help cultivate my interest in horror/sci-fi/fantasy films.

TABLE OF CONTENTS

FOREWORD

by Robert Wise

If only for the fact that he gave me my first opportunity to direct a feature film, one could understand why Val Lewton has always for me held a special place of esteem, respect, and appreciation.

My feelings are generated, however, by more than my gratitude for that first opportunity. They come from the warm and highly stimulating creative experience I had working with Val. He taught me so much about directing and filmmaking in general.

Val Lewton was one of that fairly rare species, a truly creative producer. As such, he was able to achieve an outstanding reputation for the high quality, unusual, and interesting "B" pictures he produced at RKO Studios starting in the early 1940s. He brought something new to the so-called horror films. They were a rare breed—the "psychological" horror film where the tension and fear were generated not by monsters and special effects but by suggestion, *the fear of the unknown.* As such they are chilling and frightening films.

Val was a writer himself and was responsible for creating most of the stories he produced. He worked closely with the scriptwriters on the scripts. He was vitally interested in the visual look of his pictures and worked closely with the director and the art directors, cinematographers, and costumers. Yet he never imposed himself heavily on the director and was most supportive of him in the making of his films.

Edmund Bansak's book is a most welcome addtion to the shelf of books about outstanding creative talents in films. In an all-too-brief period of time (Val died when he was only 46), Lewton gained national and international attention for the quality of his films. He was written up in our national magazines, an almost unheard of accomplishment for a "B" pictures producer. The reader will be introduced to one of the most creative talents in the history of Hollywood, one to whom many of us have always been indebted.

Los Angeles
March 1994

PREFACE

Our story begins at night, in Central Europe, sometime during the Middle Ages. Around us we see a deep-rooted atavistic fear of the dark, the unseen. Superstition reigns as mankind's accepted protection against the forces of darkness. Widespread superstition, fueled by man's dread of the unknown and seasoned with personal and communal misfortune, gives rise to witch hunts and inquisitions; folktales of demons and magic are carried over distance and time. Even the most accurate accounts of local violence and distant wars are tinged with hysteria and unchecked by critical media. What spreads before us is a fertile field, one tilled and harvested only in the dead of night.

As the years pass, we see the Germanic folktales flourish, providing an archetypal foundation for our deepest fears, the tales themselves persisting longer than anyone would have dreamed. We see the Renaissance come and go, Marlowe and Shakespeare with it, along with an uncountable horde of storytellers exploring the nature of evil.

Enter Horace Walpole and Goethe, the latter evincing an uncanny interest in Germanic occult literature, ironically during an era known as the Age of Reason. Curiously, these enlightened times also pave the way for the Gothic novel, a form which—modifications notwithstanding—would prove as immortal as the spirits inhabiting its pages. Ushered in by Walpole's *The Castle of Otronto,* the Gothic novel becomes the rage in England and France, the trend continuing through the years of the French Revolution, when real-life horror, on a grand scale, eclipses the imaginary terrors and fanciful dementias conjured up by "Monk" Lewis and his Gothic associates.

Soon would follow Mary Shelley, arm-in-arm with two Romantic poets, Percy Bysshe Shelley and Lord Byron; in turn, their fanciful visions would be shared by John Keats, Samuel Taylor Coleridge, William Wordsworth, and a ghostly host of others. Looking east, we see two brothers named Grimm gathering up well over one hundred typically morbid folktales in and around Germany and publishing them in one volume.

An interest in horrific folklore abounds, even in the New World. With Charles Brockden Brown's *Wieland,* the Gothic novel is neatly transplanted to American soil. Washington Irving, a New York writer of narrative sketches, uses European folktales as a basis for his numerous flights of dark fantasy. Edgar Allan Poe treads his own ground, creating his own mythos of of dementia and death and stamping his manias onto our collective consciousness.

Meanwhile, back on the other side of the globe, the Germanic horror tradition also extends east into Russia, the land that gives us the horror tales of Gogol and Chekhov, the horrific tone poems of composer Modest Mussorgsky, and the private psychological hell of Dostoevski's *Crime and Punishment.*

With the birth of psychology comes the acknowledgment of the "power of suggestion," a concept well suited to the flood of British Victorian ghost stories which put suggestion to good use. Robert Louis Stevenson, Oscar Wilde, and Henry James reveal vivid glimpses of the dark underside of the human soul. Bram Stoker takes the characteristics of Lord Byron (via John Polidori's *The Vampire*) and turns the lord into a count. By the time Stoker's *Dracula* is published in 1897, a Frenchman named Georges Méliès has already made close to a hundred examples of a novelty called the motion picture.

The lights go out and it is movie time. As the twentieth century unfolds, we see early experiments in cinematic horror and the rise and fall of the silent German horror film, rich with its European folklore. We also see German expressionism embodied in the film direction of Paul Wegener, Fritz Lang, Robert Wiene, F.W. Murnau, and Paul Leni and in the cinematography of Karl Freund. Back in Hollywood, we witness the chameleon-like career of Lon Chaney, the first of a long line of American horror film stars. German cinema responds with its own horror star, Conrad Veidt.

With the advent of sound, we see a landmark of German film noir, Fritz Lang's subtle exercise in terror: *M.* Around this time we see the German filmmakers pulling up stakes, coming to Hollywood, fleeing before the goose-stepped march of paranoia, the mob-crazed tactics of the Nazi movement.

Hollywood studios, especially Universal, provide refuge for Central European filmmakers and their expressionistic visions. By giving sanctuary to myriad Germanic talents, Universal's atmospheric horror films become the rage, fully equipped with expressionistic flourishes and two new figureheads of horror: Bela Lugosi and Boris Karloff. Other studios take their cues from Universal, releasing intermittent genre entries in hopes of giving the "Home of Horror" a run for its money, but nothing shakes Universal's stature as the major trendsetter of Hollywood horror . . .

. . . until RKO's release of a terrifying little film called *Cat People.*

ONE

Rites of Passage: Lewton's Early Years

He had a folk fear — an atavistic kind of fear of something going way, way back. Of course, he knew better — he was a very intellectual man and not a superstitious person — and so he was both frightened and fascinated by his fear.

— Ruth Lewton
(from *Val Lewton: The Reality of Terror*, by Joel E. Siegel)

The story of Val Lewton begins in Yalta, Russia, during the last decades of the nineteenth century. Yalta, the southernmost tip of the Crimean Peninsula on the Black Sea bore little resemblance to the typical Ukrainian countryside. Although Yalta's latitude placed it further north than Boston, Massachusetts, this Crimean paradise had been blessed with an extremely warm climate, stately mountains, and exotic tropical flora, including native palm trees.

The Crimea had been populated by Tartars before Czar Alexander III targeted the area as an ideal vacation spot, turning it into a Russian colony for certain privileged citizens of St. Petersberg. Jacob (Yacov) Leventon, a renowned chemist, was one such privileged personage. He had served the czar and knew a number of influential people in the arts as well as in the sciences. He had once filled prescriptions for the tubercular Russian playwright Anton Chekhov.

Jacob was one of Yalta's first settlers, arriving there in 1873. In short time, as Yalta's reputation as a resort paradise steadily climbed, the community became a mecca for a number of well-known Russian writers and composers and attracted high society from St. Petersberg, Kiev, Odessa, and Moscow. Yalta's cultural environment was soon ripe with literature, music, theater, and art.

At this time, Russia, and especially the Ukraine, was filled with superstition, something which affected the lives of all classes, all cultures. Accounts of ghosts, witches, vampires, and werewolves circulated among people of every village, town, and city in the Ukraine, and certainly beyond. Every child growing up there heard stories of Baba Yaga, the witch who ate little children who ventured too far into the woods. Because of its envious location on the Black Sea, Yalta had become a melting pot of folktales from an array of cultures. In fact, west of the Crimea, crossing the northern portion of the Black Sea, was Romania and the Transylvanian Alps; in geographic miles, Yalta was closer to Transylvania than to either Moscow or St. Petersburg.

It was within this environment of art and superstition that the Leventon family lived. There were three children, Volodya, Nina, and Adelaide, all of whom showed considerable flair and ambition in literature and the fine arts. The Leventons, a prosperous, well-traveled family, took great pride in their sophistication and culture.

Volodya, Jacob Leventon's only son (of whom the least is known), was sent to law school, but instead of entering the field of law, he sought a career in journalism, becoming a successful foreign correspondent in Berlin, where he eventually settled.

Adelaide, the youngest of the Leventon children, was the one to watch. Born on May 22, 1879, Adelaide was recognized as a gifted child early in her life; when she was 12 her parents sent her to Geneva, Switzerland, to study violin. Her musical interests soon gave way to her desire to act upon the stage; a year later she returned to Russia in hopes of getting a foothold in the theater. In 1892, believing that drama offered the "noblest opportunity for women to rise in the world of art," the 13-year-old Adelaide studied dramatics at the conservatory at Odessa.

Meanwhile, Nina, the middle sibling, was involved in an extensive regimen in piano and voice in a music conservatory in Dresden, Germany. On one fateful day Nina was informed of her father's sudden stroke and felt compelled to come home, giving up her studies. Nina's return was not a happy one; relinquishing her career to tend to home matters was a sacrifice difficult to endure, and her frustration eventually led to some hasty decisions. Nina's chosen lot, as the years progressed, was not made any sweeter by sister Adelaide's rising good fortune.

After winning the gold medal upon graduation from the conservatory, Adelaide Leventon changed her name to Alla Nazimova and began to create sparks with her professional theater career in the city of Kostrome. Her rise was meteoric; by her early 20s she had already become a star in St. Petersburg and was engaged to play the title roles in *Trilby, Camille,* and *Hedda Gabler*.

Back in Yalta, Nina was proud of her sister's stage success, though this tended to accent the drudgery in her own life. However idyllic it may have been to tourists, Yalta seemed extremely provincial to Nina after she had lived and studied in Dresden. She could scarcely be blamed for seeking excitement

Val in Yalta, 1907 (courtesy of the Val Lewton Collection, Library of Congress).

and finding it in a tall, handsome young military man named Maximilian who pursued life with reckless abandon. Nina and Maximilian were married in 1889. On June 23, 1900, a daughter, Lucy Olga, was born. Ninety years later, Lucy would publish "A Fond Memoir" called *Val Ivan Lewton: Writer and Film Producer—My Brother*. According to this privately funded publication (which will hereafter be called *My Brother*), "Maximilian Lewton was a British Navy officer whose ship had sailed to Yalta to pay the British government's respects to Czar Nicholas II, then resident in Livadia." (Differing sources also claim that Maximilian was a Russian soldier [last name unknown] and that the surname "Lewton" was an Americanization of Nina's maiden name, Leventon.)

The marriage was not a good one, and the responsibilities of being a parent did not curb Maximilian's two favorite pursuits, gambling and beautiful women. The birth of a son, Vladimir Ivan, on May 7, 1904, only added more strain to the relationship, as Lucy Lewton notes in *My Brother*: "After eight years of an unhappy marriage, Nina Leventon Lewton left Yalta in 1906. Her husband had died of pneumonia in England where he had gone to be posted in the Admiralty for a land job. So Nina Lewton . . . found herself penniless, as her husband had gambled away her inheritance from her father."

While Nina's marriage was dissolving, her economic security growing bleaker by the day, the career of Alla Nazimova was soaring to unprecedented heights. The year her nephew was born, Nazimova left her country, finding the Russian theater too restrictive for her talents. First she went to Berlin, then London.

In the fall of 1905, Alla Nazimova arrived in New York, where she hoped to gain success upon the Broadway stage. Although her journey to America was accompanied with little fanfare, Nazimova quickly established a reputation based on her electrifying stage presence. After spending her first months in New York's Third Street Russian colony, where she appeared in a variety of unknown plays for Russian-speaking audiences, she turned her attention to the mastery of English and became proficient in the language within the remarkably short span of six months.

Within a year of her arrival, the dynamic Russian actress appeared on the legitimate Broadway stage in English-speaking starring roles. Her reputation rose as she performed in a number of Ibsen plays, including *Hedda Gabler, The Doll House,* and *The Master Builder.* Soon the name Nazimova was a buzzword among New York critics, who claimed her as the "major exponent of Ibsen's work in America." With her success insured, Nazimova bought a Revolutionary War–era country estate in King Street in Port Chester, New York, dubbing the domain "Who-Torok" (Russian for "Little Farm").

While doors opened for the dazzling Russian actress, sister Nina found things growing ever more grim back home. In 1905 social discontent and the harbingers of revolution, combined with Russia's participation in a losing war with Japan, made Nina's homeland a place of dwindling opportunities. Following the examples of her brother and sister, Nina and her children searched for stability in Berlin. Upon arriving there in 1906, Nina struggled to support her family by doing clerical work for which she was overqualified. Her brother, Volodya, the journalist, helped in any way he could, but Lucy

Val Lewton's mother, Nina Anna Leventon (courtesy of the Val Lewton Collection, Library of Congress).

Lewton reveals in *My Brother* that he had little to offer: "[Volodya] had married Frieda von Schatten, an impoverished countess. They lived beyond their means, as he had given her to understand he was a wealthy man, and inherited half of his father Jacob Leventon's estate. Actually he had subsidized Maximilian Lewton's gambling and was himself almost penniless."

Nina would spend three difficult years trying to eke out a living in Berlin. Occupying a cheap top-floor apartment, Nina endured unaccustomed hardship, and, understandably, grew depressed. In 1909 opportunity appeared, however.

Alla Nazimova, enjoying her American success (and sudden solvency), wrote to Nina describing the Who-Torok estate; she also offered Nina a job as "housekeeper and theater maid." A prepaid ticket for a second-class cabin was sent to the Lewton family, who, on Easter Eve 1909, boarded the S.S. *Amerika* out of Bremen. Because sister Alla arranged to have them sponsored, Nina and her children were able to avoid Ellis Island. The children, Lucy and Val, had a happy time aboard the boat, bringing their dog, Mopsy, and a straw hamper of children's books.

Upon their arrival at Who-Torok, the children were ushered into a room all their own, fully equipped with toys, dolls, and clothes: "Truly their fairy godmother Aunt had thought of everything to delight a child's heart," notes Lucy Lewton in *My Brother*. Nazimova soon became, if not the "fairy godmother," at least the guiding force behind this unique family arrangement. Nina trusted her younger sister's business sense and followed her advice implicitly, even when it extended beyond matters of business.

This outspoken, highly opinionated actress relished her control over the Lewton family, but Nina and her children surely profited from their Nazimova connections. Nina quickly learned English while becoming her sister's secretary/companion and doubling as the manager of household affairs. Nina was a strong woman by any standard, only seeming subdued next to Alla Nazimova, who defied standards altogether. While Nina fulfilled Alla's needs, she managed to find time to take up writing fiction in the English language. Confidence and intelligence ran strong in the Leventon family, and Nina's efforts were soon rewarded when one of her short stories appeared in *Harper's Monthly*. Nina had found her niche; whether she was writing unproduced plays for the sake of art or translating engineering texts for the profit it afforded, Nina provided a strong career model for her son.

Nina's daughter Lucy did very well in a convent school before she moved on to Port Chester High School, where she continued to excel. Unlike Lucy, Nina's son had trouble adjusting to authority; the boy's eccentric behavior caused consternation and embarrassment within the matriarchal household. Val told wildly imaginative stories detailing his confrontations with dangerous animals in the woods and did his best to amuse, and at times annoy, Nazimova's coterie of friends. In *My Brother*, Lucy Lewton notes that Val once warned his elders of "a black tiger with yellow eyes behind Dr. Sand's barn" and asserted that Dr. Sands "actually did keep exotic animals in his barn for experiments." The memoir also tells of Lewton's photographic memory and how he infuriated a group of Nazimova's friends by refusing to desist in his rote line-by-line recitation of "The Life of the Grizzly Bear."

Two particular phobias of Lewton's youth—two that would remain with him for the rest of his life—were his fear of cats and his extreme aversion to being touched. Even during his halcyon Who-Torok days, young Lewton was already haunted by personal demons. Lewton escaped from his woes and fears through reading, and he exhibited a remarkable ability to retain accurate details of whatever he read. In *Val Lewton: The Reality of Terror,* author Siegel tells us:

> More than anything else, Lewton wanted to have a pony, but his aunt refused. Instead she got him an elaborate mechanical horse covered with real horsehide. When he was good he was permitted to play with it, but whenever he did anything to cause the slightest displeasure it was locked away.

After prolonged frustration in trying to control the boy, the two women thought it a good idea to send him to a private school in New Rochelle. When he continued to be a behavior problem, Nina was told to take her son elsewhere. The only solution, the two women deemed, was to send the boy to a military school, where he would learn the rigors of discipline. The Classon Point Military Academy, however, provided only a meager portion of the discipline that Alla and Nina felt he needed. In her memoir, Lucy mentions that the youth picked up bad habits from "a lot of Irish tough boys there."

In 1913 Nazimova married her leading man, Charles Bryant. Plans were drawn to tear down Who-Torok's main building and replace it with a villa, as well as to tear up the garden and replace it with a tennis court. As these plans were being executed, the married couple moved to an apartment, while Nina and her children moved to a Manhattan apartment on 141st Street. Lewton was sent to public school, where he picked up more bad habits, when he chose to attend at all.

Nazimova and Bryant sold off a portion of the farm and deeded a cottage to Nina. After a long string of heralded stage performances, Nazimova made her celebrated film debut in the very timely *War Brides* (1916). After Nazimova broke into motion pictures, the level of power she wielded in her film projects was enormous and the success she achieved with her new medium had a great impact upon the Lewton family. In a June 1982 *Films in Review* article, "Nazimova," Maeve Druesne calls her "a liberated woman long before the term became fashionable," and says that she "expressed ideas about motherhood and children that were no doubt regarded as radical at the time." Druesne notes that she was an aggressive businesswoman who "owned her own production company, overseeing virtually every phase of production herself: scripting, titling, editing, casting and acting."

As she kept abreast of the course of World War I in Europe, a war involving her native Russia, Nazimova signed a contract with New York's Metro Studios where, pulling some strings, she got Nina a job as a reader in the story department. Young Lewton, while entertaining romantic notions about the war, continued to be a handful, as Lucy Lewton illuminates in *My Brother:*

"Going in and out of the porch, [Val] would bang the screen door, and when Nina asked him to make up his mind whether to stay in or out, he would swear at her, using the awful swear words he had learned at Classon Point Academy. Bryant was shocked and decided Val had to have a man's hand to control him. Therefore, he arranged to send the boy to New York Military Academy on the Hudson and he was to stay there the year round." Lewton's behavior improved this time around, and though he still was not a model student, he made cadet captain.

In *My Brother,* Lucy Lewton suggests that things were not dull at the academy:

> A fellow student fell into the icy waters of Hudson River; in a quixotic gesture Val plunged in after him and saved him. He got pneumonia. Nina was sent for as it was thought Val would die. . . . Nina was frequently sent for; one time Val had broken his arm playing football. . . . Another time Val was about to be thrown out of the Academy because during chapel he had passed along the pew a roll of toilet paper with a serial story written on it. However, Val did graduate.

Lewton spent his summers at Who-Torok, in spite of Charles Bryant's previous decision to make him stay at school year-round. During summer vacations from the academy, he continued to be a nuisance. Author Joel Siegel, in *The Reality of Terror,* provides numerous anecdotes of Val's flamboyant behavior, including the young boy's penchant for fabricating stories of his past, his insistence (at age fourteen) upon dressing up as Villon and reciting poems at a neighborhood bus stop and, later, his predilection for reciting speeches from *Cyrano* during intervals in local basketball games.

While Val was flexing his eccentricities, the film career of Alla Nazimova was enjoying a critical reception of unparalleled dimensions. Her autonomy increasing with each film, Nazimova made a number of well-received movies—*Revelation, Toys of Fate* (both 1918), *The Red Lantern, The Brat* (both 1919), *Stronger Than Death,* and *The Heart of a Child* (both 1920)—before she earned the distinction of being declared the highest paid film performer in Hollywood history. In 1920 she was earning in the whereabouts of $13,000 per week. Although she swept most of the critics off their feet, there were Nazimova bashers; film reviewers either loved her madly and went overboard with grandiose praise or wrote her off as being too flamboyant and bizarre. In Maeve Druesne's *Films in Review* article on Nazimova, one critic's gushing appraisal of the actress strikes a significant chord in the study of Val Lewton: "You will notice that Madame Nazimova's eyes are meditative—somewhat visionary. . . . She is highly intuitive. . . . She is interested in the 'things unseen.'"

When *Motion Picture* magazine asked Nazimova, "Do you believe in having children?" Nazimova responded: "Not for creative women. A woman living a creative life is bound necessarily to do things sometimes defiant to convention. In order to fulfill herself, she should live freely. Children bring fear, and in that way arrest personal development."

During his summers off from the academy, a teenage Val Lewton developed a growing friendship with a neighborhood girl, Ruth Knapp, whom he would eventually marry. In a 1992 interview with the author, Ruth Knapp Lewton reminisced about the first time she cast her eyes upon her future husband:

> I had an older sister, five or six years older than I, and she was a friend of Val's sister and went to high school with her. I was invited one day to a tea to meet Nazimova. I was thirteen years old with braids down my back and that sort of stuff, and I had no idea who Nazimova even was, just that she was an actress. I only went along for the ride. Then Val came in as we were having tea, and I thought to myself, "That's the best-looking guy I've ever seen!" We were introduced, but I didn't see him again until about four or five years later. It was at a block party in the town where we lived—we lived on the same street, only two miles apart. I'd gone to the block party with friends, and he came up and introduced himself. He wrote me a letter when he got back to the New York Military Academy, asking permission to write to me, which I thought was kind of funny since he was already writing. I was thrilled. I was thrilled to death. By that time I really had fallen quite in love with him.

The long-term relationship between Val Lewton and Ruth Knapp would be frowned upon by her straightlaced parents. But however conservative the Knapps may have been, they could hardly be blamed for feeling disconcerted by Lewton's off-center behavior; his peculiar penchant for public recitations had not gone unnoticed by the town's populace.

Two artistocratic families dominated Port Chester: the Knapps and the Burdsalls. Ruth Knapp was "officially" being courted by one of the sons of the Burdsall family, and this suited her parents perfectly. In their eyes, Lewton, whom they called "the flamboyant foreigner," was interfering with Ruth's carefully planned future; at one point Mrs. Knapp took Ruth to Europe for an extended visit designed to break up the unwanted relationship.

Viewing Ruth Knapp's parents as snobs, Val researched the town's history, and after finding that Port Chester and Greenwich were "founded by a drunken sailor who had been thrown off his ship which was buying timbers to build houses in New York City," he made a demonstrative disclosure of this to Ruth's genteel parents. Despite her parents' remonstrations, Ruth was captivated by Lewton and his uniform; his wild imagination did not seem to deter her affections, as Lucy Lewton recounts in *My Brother*: "He kept Ruth fascinated relating how he had walked through the sewers of Port Chester. He had just read *Les Miserables* and, as always, cast himself in the main role."

One summer Lewton worked as an elevator operator at Steiger and Schicks department store, though as Lucy relates in her memoir, he was fired when he told the owner's corpulent wife, "Sorry Madam, this elevator takes only one person." After reading the Russian poet Lermontov, Val began writing his own verse under the pseudonym Toison d'Or. In Port Chester Square, he would hand out his poetry to passing commuters. He gave public readings of his poems and even a few private readings, once going so far as to perform, uninvited, at a Russell, Burdsall and Ward employees' meeting.

For a while, Lewton worked as a reporter at a New York night court, an experience which undoubtedly gave him material for his later fiction. In 1920 Lewton, not yet 17, got a job as a society reporter for the *Darien-Stamford Review*. He was fired when the editor found out that he had fabricated an article about a "truckload of kosher chickens dying in a New York heat wave."

The unemployed reporter then entered Columbia University's School of Journalism, where he met Herbert Kerkow, a kindred spirit who would years later collaborate with him on two novels. Kerkow's sister Polly was one of Lucy's best friends. While Lewton courted his "respectable" girl, he also began seeing Port Chester's Olive Aldred, a "fast girl" who drove a flashy car and wore the latest fashions. According to Lucy Lewton's *My Brother,* Olive would later provide the inspiration for characters who would appear in Lewton's fiction and films. Lewton often took his sister to the theater and insisted on arriving in a cab even though their destination was only a block away. "Let's arrive in style," Lucy remembers him saying. "People in the lobby will think it's John Barrymore arriving in a taxi."

Lewton spent two years at Columbia before dropping out of the journalism program but viewed the experience as "a waste of time." Before turning 20, he saw the small-press publication of his book of romantic verse bearing a rather prophetic title, *Panther Skin and Grapes* (Poynton Press, 1923). He began to find work with various newspapers. On the subject of his newspaper career (which included jobs with *The Bridgeport Herald, The New York Morning World,* and *The New York American*), Lewton said, "I was fired from each of the newspapers listed above and acquired a reputation as one of the world's worst reporters" (Siegel, *The Reality of Terror*).

Ruth Lewton told the author: "I went away to college, and Val would write me at least one letter a day, sometimes two. My family did not want me to marry him, and I promised them I wouldn't marry him until after I finished college and worked for a year."

Undaunted by his lack of competence as a newspaper reporter, Lewton continued to write, turning to fiction, a move no doubt influenced by his friendship with Donald Henderson Clarke, who was both a reporter and a novelist. Lewton submitted fiction, articles, and verse to a variety of periodicals. As the years progressed, he would see some of his work published in *Cosmopolitan, Redbook, Adventure, Biography, American Mercury, The Mentor,* as well as the *New York Times Magazine.*

Val and his Model T Ford, 1920 (courtesy of the Val Lewton Collection, Library of Congress).

In 1924 Lewton finished his first novel, *Improved Road,* which was published the next year in Edinburgh, Scotland. The novel by the 21-year-old author was never published in the United States. In 1926 the same Scottish publishing house, Collins and Sons, picked up his second book, an historical novel set in Russia called *The Cossack Sword.* Despite their status as lightweight popular fiction, these novels gave evidence that Lewton was, indeed, a gifted storyteller. Rather than shoot for the "great American novel," Lewton seemed more comfortable avoiding such pretentions and worked in realms more closely associated with pulp fiction. Within the next seven years, Lewton would try his hand at detective fiction, exotic adventure, sultry woman-on-the-skids Depression fiction, and a variety of other pulp genres. He also would write two pornographic novels for under-the-counter sales in New York City.

In 1926, with two published novels under his belt, Lewton secured a position as a publicity writer at Metro's New York office (his mother was now already a 10-year veteran with the studio). He was placed under the supervision of Howard Dietz, the noted lyricist of Tin Pan Alley. Nina offered further assistance by training her son for the job, focusing particularly upon story analysis and synopsis writing. Lewton proved himself to be a prolific writer who could be used in an all-purpose way. He would later state in a portfolio of his working credentials that as a Metro publicity writer: "I inaugurated and was in charge of the serialization and radio departments for Dietz. This required me to write, with the assistance of a 19-year-old boy, a full-length serialization of 50,000 words each week of the year and also make a radio dramatization of every other film MGM produced."

As Lewton worked for MGM's New York office, writing his novels on the side, he and Ruth decided they were ready for marriage. Despite the prospective groom's "literary" success and apparent economic security, so opposed were Ruth's parents that they threatened to disown her. So adamant was Ruth's position in remaining with Lewton that the threat was eventually carried out. The Knapps virtually cut all ties with their daughter.

Lewton and Ruth Knapp were married in St. John's Church (on Perry Street) on April 19, 1929, with Herbert Kerkow as the best man. The weather was grey, and there was no wedding trip. The Knapps did not attend the ceremony, and "The morning after the wedding, Mrs. Knapp phoned them at six o'clock. She said, 'You've made your bed, now sleep in it.'" (Lucy Lewton, *My Brother*).

The Lewtons took an apartment in Greenwich Village, New York. While they were adjusting to their roles as husband and wife, Nazimova announced her retirement from the motion picture screen and hailed her long-delayed return to the stage. She raised a few eyebrows when she publicly confessed, "I wish I could burn every inch of my films. I'm ashamed of them." Although the actress's official retirement came in 1929, it had been four years since she made her last film. Her enthusiasm for the medium had dwindled when her heir apparent, Greta Garbo, made her 1924 American film debut.

Lewton found himself engaged in an exhaustive burst of writing, a good portion of which was done in his Greenwich Village quarters. It has been said that the style and substance of Lewton's fiction was influenced by Emile Zola, but Lewton's journalistic background, his penchant for naturalism, and his unorthodox behavior ran closer parallels to American writer Stephen Crane (1871–1900), whose work was enjoying a revival in the 1920s, especially among journalists.

With the Great Crash of October 1929, Val and Ruth Lewton, along with the rest of the country, began to feel the apprehensions of a new era, one characterized by breadlines and unemployment. To compound matters, Ruth was expecting a child. Motivated to survive the Depression years by exploiting whatever writing talents he had, Lewton pounded the typewriter in his Greenwich Village flat till all hours of the morning. When Ruth Nina was born to the Lewtons on May 7, 1930, it only added extra weight to the shoulders of the 25-year-old aspiring author. The birth of Ruth Nina (whose name was dropped to Nina) was a difficult one that endangered her mother's life. Lewton had to give his daughter a direct blood transfusion to keep her alive.

By this time the Lewtons had moved into a small apartment in Rye, New York. Val wrote at the office, he wrote at home, he wrote on business trips.

Left: Picture of himself sent to Ruth in 1928 (courtesy of the Val Lewton Collection, Library of Congress). _Right:_ The engagement picture of Val's wife, Ruth Elliot Knapp, 1928. She is 22 (courtesy of the Val Lewton Collection, Library of Congress).

One of his better short stories from this period has survived, thanks to the cult following of its pulp source, Farnsworth Wright's *Weird Tales* magazine. Val Lewton's "The Bagheeta," which appeared in the July 1930 issue of Wright's magazine, was reprinted in *Weird Tales: The Magazine That Never Dies,* a 1988 anthology edited by Marvin Kaye. Although Kaye notes how much Lewton's story resembles Gustave Flaubert's "St. Julian the Hospitaller" (which had been reprinted in *Weird Tales* two years before), "The Bagheeta" shows considerable evidence that Lewton had developed his cinematic politics of terror long before his associations with RKO. Today "The Bagheeta" stands as a seminal work of fiction from the man who would later produce *Cat People, The Leopard Man,* and *Curse of the Cat People.*

Set in the Ukraine, probably during the seventeenth century, "The Bagheeta" is the rite-of-passage story of Kolya, a 16-year-old boy who helps his uncle forge armor. When someone comes to town bearing a slaughtered sheep and claiming to have seen a Bagheeta, the black leopard that changes into a beautiful woman, the town is alerted. Only one person, we are told, can kill a Bagheeta: a virgin male, at least one who can resist her seduction. If he is seduced, the woman will turn into a black leopard and eat him.

Kolya volunteers for the task and journeys into the dark forest, accompanied by two hunters and a band of able men. One hunter, Davil, is well known and highly celebrated for having killed a Bagheeta many years before; the other hunter, Rifkhas, is a skeptic who doesn't believe in "were-beasts." Although the men can offer Kolya some much-needed advice, they remind him that he has to meet the creature alone, after the moon sets, and that their purpose on this expedition is merely to help flush the creature in his direction. Kolya carries his uncle's best sword, his only protection against the lycanthrope, but he becomes increasingly apprehensive, and his confidence ebbs with his horse's every step. Davil sings verses of a song he composed, glorifying his own long-past confrontation with the creature.

Finally the time has come. Kolya goes off on his fearful solo journey to meet the creature and, taking Rifkhas's advice, plants himself on the bank of a stream, the Bagheeta's drinking spot. After a long wait, a black leopard appears on the other side of the stream. While the creature drinks, Kolya hurls a large rock behind it, causing the leopard to run forward, right into Kolya's ambush. As the leopard jumps over Kolya to gain the precipice above, the boy buries the sword into the creature's neck, killing it.

But Kolya is confused over the ease of the kill, and since there was no beautiful woman to resist, he decides that the legend of the Bagheeta is all a pack of lies. With his horse dragging the leopard carcass, Kolya makes his way back to the camp, thinking how foolish Davil will feel when the boy reports that there is no such thing as a Bagheeta. After so easily debunking this great legend, Kolya begins to wonder whether Christianity itself is a sham.

As Kolya rides back, his faith in God deeply shaken, he begins to consider his own fate among the villagers. His reputation as a great hunter of a leopard would last a mere month or two, but his reputation as the boy who killed the Bagheeta would last many years, just as it had with Davil.

Kolya changes his game plan:

> "I shall tell them that I first saw the Bagheeta as a beautiful maiden, bathing at the water hole, her body surrounded by white light. That she called me by name and spoke to me courteously—and that, enchanted by her beauty, I had forgotten all warning and bent to kiss her. Then I shall say that an arrow of fire sprang through the sky. Knowing it for the sign of Ilya the Archer, I will say that I took warning from this and, springing away from the maiden, drew my sword. So fast that I could not even see the change, the Bagheeta transformed herself again into a leopard and sprang at me. I shall tell them that we fought for an hour and then, just as I was ready to drop my sword from weariness, a great strength surged through me and I killed the beast."

"The Bagheeta" is a marvelous precursor to Lewton's first horror film, *Cat People,* about a beautiful Serbian woman named Irena who dreads falling in love in her belief that such passion would transform her into a ferocious black leopard. In Irena's apartment, there is a statue of Serbia's King John; he is in armor, on horseback, raising his sword high in the air, and impaled on the sword is a large cat.

But it is not only the short story's feline-lycanthropic content that allies it to *Cat People* and Lewton's other horror films. "The Bagheeta" takes the same kind of ambivalent stance toward the supernatural (is there is, is not there, a Bagheeta?) and its narrative is written with a cinematic prose that exemplifies the terror techniques that would become synonymous with Lewton's name. "The Bagheeta" reveals that Lewton had already set the cinematic groundwork for the horror films he would produce more than a decade later.

The fear of the dark is central to the story's effectiveness, and certain passages are very characteristic of Lewton's later horror film approach. Two examples show this theme particularly well:

> The lad shuddered. He could well imagine the sinuous body of the beast, black as the night it walked through, creeping through the tree trunks in the forest. How dark the forest would be after the moon had gone down! Kolya's horse quivered. It was as if his master's agitation had been conveyed to her too, and that she also knew of the trial ahead of them. . . .
>
> A restive horse in the darkness of the midnight forest; a silent and unseen foe, waiting to leap from ambush, to strike one down with huge paws, to rend one with enormous teeth.

> On whispering feet, darkness came stealing into the little glen in which they had halted. The beech leaves, quivering in the evening wind, lisped a plaintive song of nervous fear to Kolya's heart. The same breeze, straying though the pine boughs, struck deep soughing chords. . . .
>
> The trees rustled in the light night currents. Each falling leaf, each snapping twig, brought sharp ice to the skin of Kolya's back. Clumps of deeper darkness—some fallen tree or jagged stump—denser than the overflowing night, caused Kolya to tighten his reins and grip fast the hilt of his sword. . . . It would be just so softly, and with just such lack of warning, that the Bagheeta would spring upon him from the dark thickets at either side of the path. . . .
>
> Again he rode through the wood. Again he peered right and left for some sign of the beast, fearful always of seeing golden eyes glow at him from the pitch blackness of the night. Every rustle of the wind, every mouse that scampered on its way, flooded his heart with fear, and filled his eyes with the lithe, black hulk of the Bagheeta, stalking toward him on noiseless paws. With all of his heart he wished that the beast would materialize, stand before him, allow him opportunity to slash and thrust and ward. Anything, even deep wounds, would be better than this dreadful uncertainty, this darkness haunted by the dark form of the were-beast.

This last paragraph sums up the basic tenet of the Lewton approach to cinematic terror, that it is the unseen menace that is the most frightening menace of all.

Although Kolya meets eye-to-eye with the leopard during the kill, Lewton's characteristic approach to the unseen is chillingly executed when the boy, from his niche near the bank of the stream, first senses the creature's presence:

> Even as he settled himself in a comfortable position, the falling of a pebble attracted his attention to the other bank of the stream. He could distinguish nothing. The water was as dark as the night. But from the water came a lapping sound. Something was drinking there at the edge of the creek. Kolya strained his eyes. He could see nothing. But as he continued to stare into the darkness he caught a gleam of eyes, yellow, round and burning as the burnished brass of the alter rail. Again Kolya heard the sound of water being lapped up by the rough tongue of the animal. The round, golden eyes were hidden as the creature drank.

Passages such as these make mincemeat of the popular notion that Val Lewton was somehow not the prime force behind the less-is-more approach taken by his horror films. Lewton's characteristic phobia of cats and his fear-the-dark horror techniques are to be found, intact, in "The Bagheeta."

In 1930, apart from his tremendous workload at MGM, Lewton produced two more novels. The first was a mystery, *The Fateful Star Murder* (based on the Starr Faithful murder case), that was begun and completed during a marathon 48-hour stretch in a hotel room, in collaboration with friend Herbert Kerkow. Lewton's new publisher, Mohawk Press, also picked up his earlier novel, *The Cossack Sword,* for its first U.S. publication (altering its title to the more sensational *Rape of Glory*). Both books were released in 1931, while Lewton, on an obvious roll, poured his energies into finishing a fourth novel, an exotic adventure called *Where the Cobra Sings,* which would be published (under the pseudonym Cosmo Forbes) early the next year by Macaulay Publishing Company.

By the middle of 1932, while Universal Studios was riding high on its first wave of sound-era horror films, the prolific Lewton found himself navigating his own course of good fortune by examining the economic horrors of the present day. A major publishing outfit, Vanguard Press, had bought his just-finished Depression-era novel, *No Bed of Her Own.* Written in a small house in Cos Cob (near Greenwich, Connecticut) which the Lewtons had rented, *No Bed of Her Own* had the distinction of being the first of the 1930s Depression novels, even beating Steinbeck to the punch. The book became an overnight success. According to Lewton, "*No Bed of Her Own* was translated into nine languages and published in twelve different countries. It was particularly popular in Germany, where it appeared as *Rose Mahoney: Her Depression.* It was also included on the list of books burned by Hitler's orders" (Siegel, *The Reality of Terror*).

The novel's success, however, was largely the result of its shockingly liberal sexual attitudes rather than its exploration of a timely subject. But it was timely; so much so, in fact, that Heckschar Flour Co. did a radio serial of it (sanitized, of course). A plot concerning out-of-work stenographers turning to prostitution showed that Lewton had a flair for sensationalism.

In spite of its dubious potential as a film, *No Bed of Her Own* caught the attention of Paramount Studios, which purchased the rights to the novel for a possible film. Paramount's story editors discovered, upon further examination, that Lewton's candor with taboo themes had rendered the book virtually unfilmable. Finally, Paramount's front office decided that it would throw out Lewton's story entirely and use only his novel's racy title, which would be a drawing card, given the book's popularity. Ironically, and to Lewton's further chagrin, even the title was scrapped when the Hays Office squawked. The resulting film, impressively cast as a Clark Gable/Carole Lombard vehicle, finally hit the marquees near the end of 1932 as *No Man of Her Own* and bore absolutely no resemblance to its Lewton source.

It is unfortunate that Lewton's book has been doomed to obscurity; even its late-1940s Triangle Books reissue qualifies as a rare find. *No Bed of Her Own* is a surprisingly frank book and a very readable one. Unexpectedly, its dated slang works in its favor, documenting the times in its quasi-exposé fashion. For fans of Lewton's RKO films, this tale of Rose Mahoney and her coterie of hard luck friends gives further definition to the female roles that turned up repeatedly in Lewton's RKO films. Film critics who have alluded to hints of prostitution, lesbianism, and kinky sex in such Lewton films as *The Seventh Victim, I Walked with a Zombie, Cat People, Mademoiselle Fifi,* and *Youth Runs Wild,* appear to be on the money after a reading of *No Bed of Her Own* (or its even saucier follow-up, *Yearly Lease*).

Theodore Dreiser's *Sister Carrie* and the early works of Emile Zola have been cited as influences upon Lewton's *No Bed of Her Own,* but the primary inspiration for the novel was probably Stephen Crane's *Maggie: A Girl of the Streets.*

Emulating Crane and Zola, Lewton did not moralize upon the events of his narrative; like his models, he chose an objective, almost cinematic, point of view, allowing his story's ironies to speak for themselves. In the true naturalist tradition, Lewton delineated his characters with the use of dialogue and the manner in which they behaved toward one another, especially during a crisis. He presented a world where even the most heroic are hopelessly flawed individuals. It may be a grade "B" pulp noir potboiler, but *No Bed of Her Own* is a rummage through Val Lewton's closet that is not otherwise afforded by the viewing of his films.

Rose Mahoney is a plucky, no-nonsense stenographer who loses her job in the Depression. At first the self-centered overly confident Rose thinks her savings of $40 will hold her over until she gets another job; she spends a few days going to the movies, treating her termination as if it were a well-deserved vacation. But all too quickly, things become grim. Rose has been around the block once or twice and is no stranger to fast times; she sleeps with her boyfriend of the month as a matter of course. But despite her hard-boiled attitudes and improper behavior, she is more admirable than the majority of those around her.

Rose's workmates are also on the skids, one by one joining the masses of the unemployed. One of these unfortunate women, Mildred, is a marvelously realized prototype of the kind of doomed female the censorship-bound Lewton films could only suggest (in such films as *The Seventh Victim* and *Youth Runs Wild*). A habitual whiner, Mildred is not very likeable; she has our pity, but not our respect. Early on she talks of her boyfriend dropping her because she did not "put out," but when the chips are down and Mildred becomes hungry, she takes to prostitution like a duck to water. Unfortunately, this particular pond is small and crowded, and it is doubtful that the plain-looking Mildred will prove herself to be a swan. Rather, she gains weight and becomes a punching bag for her pimp lover.

From one dwelling to another Rose moves, all the while finding time for some modest good deeds. She has nothing against sex with the right partner, but there are limits. Although she has no compunctions about posing nude for a modeling agency, she refuses to participate in the main event: a stag film. Later, when she is down to her last 50 cents, Rose donates half of it to a starving woman; this act of charity is witnessed by a stout young woman who has just finished complaining about being down to her last $100. As the novel progresses, we become aware of Rose's strength of character, of her ability to take risks and follow her instincts; in short, we recognize her ability to survive in a world devoid of meaning. Although she does not campaign for sainthood, Rose's humble benevolence adds meaning to her bleak world.

At times Lewton's narrative is amusingly crude. Consider his description of Fanny Wise, Rose's haughty superior in the corporation where Rose works before her job is terminated:

> She turned and stalked out of the room with long, swinging strides in imitation of her favorite motion picture actress, a lank Swedish person to whom such a gait was well suited. As Fanny Wise was short, thick-hipped and had long, pendulous breasts which Arthur, the office boy, had labelled "belly blankets" among his confreres, this striding walk made her ludicrous. It was as if a side of bacon had suddenly taken up aesthetic dancing.

Oddly, our sympathy for the hard-boiled Rose Mahoney as she continues her downward plunge is evoked by her ignorance of the seriousness of her plight. Pitted against the dark forces of poverty and despair, this woman of questionable repute becomes the most likeable character in a world of hypocrisy and selfishness, very much a female version of the antihero prototype who would become a permanent fixture in 1940s films noir. Most importantly for Rose, the compromises she makes do little to undermine her humanity; like Nell Bowen in *Bedlam* (Val Lewton's last RKO film), Rose Mahoney will find her redemption by surviving in a world gone mad.

At times, *No Bed of Her Own* suggests the twisted world of Lewton's contemporary, Nathaniel West. When Rose seeks shelter at a movie theater, an usherette kicks her out, fearing (incorrectly) that Rose is soliciting upon the premises. This same usherette, however, performs two dollar "quickies" for sailors in the dark recesses of the balcony.

Because Rose uses her money wisely and keeps up her appearance, knowing it is the only card she has left, people believe she is either a woman of means or a whore. The Y.W.C.A. is skeptical of "her kind" taking quarters in a Christian enterprise, and charity groups do not think she looks wretched enough to receive assistance. Furthermore, Rose refuses to stand in breadlines, which, for her, would be the ultimate evidence of her ruination. When she tries for legitimate work, her male employers expect additional services rendered.

Although there are some perks along the way—Rose assisting a friend with the raising of a child, Rose striking up a warm live-in relationship with a struggling writer (the most sympathetic male in the book, of course), Rose befriending a pair of warm-hearted prostitutes—most of Lewton's book is indeed a dark journey. When Rose obtains enough money to visit her family on Christmas, she finds a dearth of familial comfort:

> To help pay the rent of their little house, the Mahoneys had been forced to take in a boarder, a milk man. . . . As Rose's father was away in the daytime, and the milkman home, he had taken advantage of this situation to seduce Rose's mother, a fat, slatternly woman with a weak will. Mrs. Mahoney lived in dread of her boarder, and yet could not seem to say no. This was the first time in twenty-five years of an unhappy married life that she had been unfaithful to her husband, and the whole situation was too much for her. Whenever she could, she ran off to the corner grocery, operated by her crony, Mrs. Wichnefsky, to drink. The grocery store peddled liquor. Most of the time Mrs. Mahoney went about the house drunk and weeping, except when she suffered the milkman's embraces, and then Rose could hear her gusty sighing and passionate ejaculations even through the closed door.
>
> Rose's brother, Pat, had also been hurt by the depression. In 1928, he had been expelled from the police force for accepting bribes from speeders. Since then he had worked as a brush salesman and his Irish good looks and quick tongue had won him a ready following of housewives. Brushes went best when he supplied bed service as well. But now that so many men were out

> of work and staying home, Pat's activities were greatly curtailed. He hung about the house all day, grumbling and cursing his bad luck.
>
> The Mahoneys had a dreary Christmas. The handbag Rose had purchased for her mother was the only present. There was no tree, no holly, none of the cheer and good will traditionally allied with the Christmas festival. Mr. Mahoney spent the day at the dining room table, scribbling figures on scraps of paper, trying to find some way to save his business from bankruptcy. At five o'clock he gave up the task and, crying, went off to bed.

This may not be great literature, but it *is* compelling prose.

No Bed of Her Own ends with a stirring, if contrived, sequence involving Rose's desperate attempt to get prescription money for a child dying of pneumonia. Rose runs down Third Avenue accosting any adult male in sight: "I'll do anything for four dollars, if you'll only hurry." After repeating her offer a number of times, she finally gets a taker. However, by the time she reaches the child, medicine in hand, he is dead. As a result, Rose is resolved to give up her humanity. The final paragraph:

> She would be inhumanely cruel, self-assertive, immoral, industrious—anything; whipping herself on to become rich and secure. That was what mattered. And poverty was the crime of crimes. Tomorrow the new job. She would never let it go until she had a better one.

This tack-on ending, which intends to bring the novel to its shattering close, unfortunately has little impact. Rose's hollow words of determination have the firmness of a drunk's sobriety pledge on New Year's Eve. In spite of its numerous shortcomings, however, *No Bed of Her Own* offers a revealing look at Val Lewton the storyteller and provides several of the archetypes that would later turn up in his films.

With the success of *No Bed of Her Own* behind him, Lewton signed a contract with Vanguard Press which called for the delivery of five novels in one year (*No Bed of Her Own* counting as the first). The demands of this whirlwind contract suggest that Lewton was not preparing to distinguish himself as an American man of letters. Fast and furious, Lewton worked to honor his agreement and to bring in the money. Although he would obviously be compromising his artistic integrity, Lewton's willingness to work hard through difficult times shows that the young man possessed the very spirit of survival he extolled in his fiction and his films. As Val Edwin Lewton, Jr., told the author in a 1992 interview, "[My father] was a kind of hack, but he enjoyed the challenge that came with turning hack work into something special, to take an impossible thing and do something with it. There is a sort of pride in being a whore. He saw a certain honesty in being able to make a living."

As Lewton attempted to fulfill his destiny as a successful novelist, some adjustments in his life-style had become necessary. With the Vanguard contract, as well as a commission to write a New York radio serial, Lewton believed there was no alternative but to give up his job at MGM, which he did in 1932.

At their house in Cos Cob, Lewton now fancied himself an outdoorsman, somewhat in the Hemingway mold. Buying a boat, he took up sailing which, almost overnight, turned into an obsession. So attached did he become to this particular sporting activity that rather than remain at home and inevitably give in to its lure, he would rent cheap hotel rooms where, without interruption or temptation, he could work on his novels. Although Val's love for sailing would be a lifelong preoccupation, close friends and family noted that he seldom appeared comfortable or relaxed on his own boat.

With compulsive deliberation, Lewton continued to write, ignoring most other things whenever it was possible. By the end of 1933, Vanguard Press would publish Lewton's remaining four contractual obligations: *Four Wives, Yearly Lease, A Laughing Woman,* and *This Fool Passion.* Like *No Bed of Her Own, Yearly Lease* was published under Lewton's own name; the other three were tagged with the pseudonym Carlos Keith, a moniker that would later reappear in his screenwriting credits. In addition to fulfilling the Vanguard contract, Lewton wrote the thrice-weekly radio serial called *The Luck of Joan Christopher.*

Of all the Lewton novels, it is likely that *Yearly Lease* was the most autobiographical. We can even find hints of prophecy in its lively prose. *Yearly Lease* is actually the story of a house and the people who occupy it. The house is a massive 55-room structure built just after the turn of the century by "Lucky" Larry Bishop and intended as a present to his faithless wife, Lily, and shy, retiring daughter, Laura. Larry gets a rise from his daughter by telling her of the pony that awaits her at their new home. Unfortunately, the Phillistine sensibilities of "Lucky" Larry are not unlike those of the theater moguls who encouraged the ostentatious designs of movie palaces of the 1920s and 1930s. Flamboyance becomes the rule of the day as the mansion incorporates, willy-nilly, the styles of many disparate cultures. When Lily takes her first look at the structure, she pronounces it an atrocity and orders the coach to return to the city. As Lewton tells it:

> Laura, who had followed them about, silent, unnoticed and very happy at the thought of the pony, began to cry quietly. . . . The child wanted to say something, to tell [her mother] about her love of green lawns and her desire for this pony, but she said nothing. She did not stop crying until they reached the station and took the train back. . . . The child tried to visualize the pony she had not seen. Getting out at the station she asked:
>
> "Was it a black pony?"

Amidst the many characters in *Yearly Lease,* we see a composite of details from Lewton's own life. The novel takes a sudden leap ahead; some 20 years later the small town of Chester Manor (read Port Chester) seems to have little use for "Lucky's" estate (now known as "Bishop's Folly") until its disreputable new owner, Dr. Faber, proposes to turn the structure into an apartment complex. After the stuffy town officials veto the idea, Faber craftily withdraws his plan and tells the locals of his new proposal: turning the estate into a hospital for "colored orphans." The townspeople suddenly become enthusiastic about the original plan, and there are soon advertisements for vacancies in the Bishop Arms Apartments.

Laura Bishop, fully grown and troubled, still scarred from a neglectful upbringing, makes a belated return visit to her father's architectural labor of love: "I missed a pony all my life," she says to her lesbian lover, Reynardine Field, who accompanies her on the trip. The passage below contains a quality of candor that was shocking in 1932:

> Laura had long ago forgotten. Two marriages, two divorces, lovers in drove, and now Reynardine, had been her antidotes for unhappy memories of childhood. . . . Since that time she had kept herself always drugged with love of one sort or another. The two husbands and the drove of lovers that had passed through her life had left her satiated. In her boredom she had turned to Reynardine and her little coterie of strange friends. Now she was growing tired of them. . . . She had grown tired of Reynardine. There was no doubt of that. She felt a loathing for that masculine profile, that short-cropped yellow hair and the mannish ensemble of tweeds, shirt and tie.

Laura rents—but does not occupy (reminding us of Jacqueline in *The Seventh Victim*)—the smallest, cheapest apartment of Bishop Arms and leaves it empty, but paid for, for the next six months. "She don't live here, but every month, regular as clock-work, I get a check from a lawyer in the city," explains the manager.

Meanwhile, a budding writer, Hans Fife, and his pregnant wife, Helen, quit their two-room Greenwich Village apartment and move into the Bishop Arms, an apartment house inhabited by many newlyweds (presumably Lewton's Rye, New York, apartment). Lewton clearly describes himself, as Fife is given to reflection:

> He saw no clear way in which to earn more money, but he knew that the fifty dollars a week he received as the associate editor of *The Projectionists' Journal,* was not enough to enable him to live in the country. His short stories were not selling well. Yet there must be some way in which he could amass the money necessary. He'd work hard; strain to the last ounce of mental energy, succeed. . . . To work hard, work even when you felt ill or tired. From now on, no matter what happened, even if his eyes were so tired he could hardly see, he would work and write; no set schedule, no given time, all the time. . . . He reviewed his past life. He was already twenty-five. He had accomplished nothing.

These are words from the heart.

What the Fifes do not know is that Hans's ex-flame, Berenice Laidlaw, has also (along with her self-centered husband, Bill) taken residence in the Bishop Arms. Forward and aggressive, Berenice pays the Fifes a visit. She behaves in a bitchy fashion, not letting Hans forget about his past relationship with her. Berenice carries a black kitten in her arms. Note the cattiness in the following dialogue:

> "Isn't it funny how one always smokes the cigarettes of the man one goes out with. I used to smoke Luckies. Remember, Hans? But not now. Bill smokes an English cigarette. I've gotten quite used to it."
>
> "I don't smoke," Helen told her.
>
> "Don't you? That's strange. I remember Hans always used to say that it felt so companionable to smoke together—afterwards."

A short time later, the Fifes meet their neighbor, Mrs. Meadows, a retired actress of the stage and silent films: "Her voice had been heard with rapture from the stages of London and New York, and which, in ten years of private life, had lost none of its theatrical quality. . . . 'She was a great actress,' Hans said. 'One of the old duffers around the office remembers her, says she was more beautiful than Greta Garbo, Constance Bennett and all the other movie queens rolled into one.'"

The character of Mrs. Meadows is portrayed in a sympathetic light, giving insight into Lewton's more accepting adult relationship with his aunt. Mrs. Meadows functions primarily as the giver of sagely advice, and just about all of the young tenants adore her.

Meanwhile, Laura Bishop discovers that her estate has gone into bankruptcy. Reynardine, confessing that she was once a bookkeeper, offers her services:

> "But how in the world were you ever a bookkeeper?"
>
> "I kept the books and sometimes I modeled for Madame Aldine when she first started her dress house. It was while I was there that I met Mrs. Hays and became her companion."
>
> Laura nodded.
>
> "And now I don't know what you'd call me," Reynardine concluded.
>
> "No. It would be hard for me to give your profession a name."
>
> "But I'm good at it, darling?"
>
> "You are."
>
> Reynardine drew the arm she had about Laura's neck tight and kissed her on the mouth.

Laura asks her lover for some money to tide her over, and Reynardine refuses (in spite of her bank account consisting of payments given to her by Laura for "services" rendered). The two have a falling out, and Laura out of necessity must occupy the room she has been renting in absentia.

When Laura moves into Bishop Arms, she finds Hans Fife occupying the vacant room she has rented; with the landlord's permission, he had been using it as a hideaway for himself and his typewriter. When he finds that the unknown boarder has finally come to claim her living space, Hans embarrassedly retreats to his own quarters.

Then our final major character takes an apartment at Bishop Arms, quickly becoming Laura's close friend. Athletic and tanned, the 19-year-old Jean Pomeroy is a wholesome, spirited girl whose purity is incongruous with her background; her mother, formerly a member of the Floradora Sextette, is so coarsely man-crazy that she frowns upon her daughter's inactive sex life. Mrs. Pomeroy takes pleasure in describing her many adulterous exploits to her daughter. Another female predator, Mrs. Pomeroy boasts: "I'm just like a little cat. I love the heat." But Jean is unimpressed by the world of sex. She would rather play tennis than be pawed by the type of males her mother takes as lovers. Mrs. Pomeroy shows a picture of Jean Harlow to her daughter:

> "But you'd look exactly like this girl if you had that white blonde hair."
>
> "Yeah, I'd look like something, but I wouldn't look much like her, Ma. I'm not the type. I'd rather be a homely and a permanent brunette than a temporary blonde."
>
> "Why, Jean, you'd look elegant—the boys would be wild about it."
>
> "One vamp in the family is enough," Jean answered.
>
> "You've got to bleach your hair."
>
> "But, Ma, I don't want to look like her. I don't care much about being pretty that way."
>
> "Jean, you listen to reason. You've got to have the men like you, and they don't seem to like you now—not in the right way."
>
> Jean did not say anything but went right on preparing luncheon. Mrs. Pomeroy kept up her attack.
>
> "You ask your friend upstairs, that Laura, if you wouldn't look better with bleached hair. She's a woman who's seen something of the world—she'll tell you."
>
> "But, Ma, she hasn't bleached her hair."
>
> "She don't need to. She's got jet black hair. But you've got mouse-brown hair. There's no flash to it."
>
> The discussion went on all through luncheon. Then Mrs. Pomeroy shifted to another tack.
>
> "Now take Mr. Peterson," she said, "he hasn't any use for brunettes. He says they haven't enough life to them. That's one of the reasons he loves me so much. I'm a blonde—so far as he knows."

After weeks of this prodding, Jean finally agrees to bleach her hair, just to get her mother off her back, and she hates the results. Now the boys—even those with whom she formerly had good platonic relationships—do nothing but make passes.

Hans Fife, meanwhile, has been feverishly pounding the typewriter. He needs the cash to pay the hospital bill when the time comes for his wife's delivery. Desperate for money, he finally agrees to ghost write a book for the oily Mr. Fischer, a man who wants his numerous love affairs turned into a pornographic novel. Fischer is amazingly generous with the amount he offers to pay, but it is easy to be generous when he has no intention of making good his word.

In *Yearly Lease,* all major characters seem to be at the mercy of their frustrations, all of which eventually lead to their questionable behavior. For some, like Hans Fife and Laura Bishop, lack of money seems to be the source of the frustration. But the real issue here, the demon haunting every character, is rejection. The novel's very first incident—the rejection of Bishop Mansion by the person for whom it was built—sets the tone for this dominant theme. Laura as a girl is rejected by her mother; the pony she never had is only a symbol of her loss. Her turn to lesbianism may be interpreted as her belated attempt to get the feminine love she never received as a child.

Hans Fife works on stories that, again and again, are rejected; when he gets an opportunity with some promise, ghost writing, he is never paid for his efforts. When Hans does not wish to face his wife, Helen, after having not been paid for his work, he rejects her and takes up with Berenice, who has been rejected by her own husband. Round and round we go. Later, Hans rejects Berenice and goes back to his wife. Mrs. Pomeroy rejects both her husband as well as her daughter Jean (who is not good enough as a brunette). After accepting a marriage proposal from one of the local boys, Jean faces further rejection when she walks into her apartment to find her fiancé making love to her mother, the incident that ultimately drives her away from men and into Laura Bishop's loving embrace.

Before *Yearly Lease* comes to a close, Helen goes into labor and has a baby boy, but complications result and Hans must give a blood transfusion to save the infant's life. At one point in the novel, Lewton plugs himself, poking fun at his career in the process. Mrs. Pomeroy is described "lolling on the sofa, deeply absorbed in *Four Wives,* a novel by Carlos Keith which had been recommended to her by her hairdresser."

Lewton's career as a novelist would come to a quick end. There were better things ahead. Someday he would become embarrassed by the blatant sensationalism of his novels and their refusal to remain buried in his past. Potboilers they may have been, but Lewton's novels are extremely engaging. *No Bed of Her Own* and *Yearly Lease* are surprisingly unconventional and were obviously designed to transcend their pulpish origins; anyone professing an interest in Lewton the film producer would be both entertained and enlightened by the flamboyant, yet naturalistic, prose of Lewton the novelist.

TWO

Emigrés and Icons: Dark Visionaries and Hollywood Wonders

It took root in Germany following the First World War. It started as an attitude and spread into a movement. German Expressionism, as it was called, carried disillusionment and despair into all the arts; nothing suited it better than a film genre fueled by the fear of death and the realization of nightmare.

Germany was the true holy land of the horror film. The country had long had associations with horror literature. Very popular were the "Schauerromane" (shudder novels); with origins in Teutonic folk tales and word-of-mouth ghost stories, German horror literature featured black magic, werewolves, vampires, ghosts, and all things supernatural. It comes as no surprise that German cinema should play a significant role in shaping the horror film.

Before the start of World War I, Germany had already made some notable horror films, including *In the Shadow of the Sea* (1912), *The Student of Prague* (1913), and *The Golem* (1915). *In the Shadow of the Sea* is an ambitious 40-minute excursion into dark territory. A shadowy personification of Death rises from the sea, enters a fisherman's hut and beckons an unhappy woman to take her life and thereby follow the spectre of Death into a watery grave. The title character of *The Student of Prague* (loosely based upon Edgar Allan Poe's story "William Wilson") makes a deal with the devil, signing away his mirror image in return for riches and power. *The Golem* was inspired by the Jewish folktale about a clay statue summoned to life to defend a Hebrew community. The "body without a soul" concept of *The Golem* runs a close parallel to themes found in Shelley's *Frankenstein*, which was itself the inspiration for the popular *Homunculus* (1916), a six-hour/six-part film about an artificially created superman who becomes a malevolent creature when he learns of his origins.

Although horror films were not a novelty in prewar Germany, they underwent a dramatic change at the war's end by allying themselves with the expressionism movement. Like Paris, with its postwar assortment of cultural outcasts and expatriots, Germany had its own manner of "lost generation." In his landmark 1967 *Illustrated History of the Horror Film,* Carlos Clarens told of how the malcontents of Germany rallied under the banner of expressionism.

> Unrestrained, violently emotional, and often pessimistic, the new movement sought to restore man to the center of things. . . . Accordingly, everything—objects, light, the universe itself—had to be reshaped according to man's individual vision. . . . The German film had found in Expressionism the style required to render in black and white the reawakened fantasies of the darkly romantic soul.

The Cabinet of Dr. Caligari (1919) was, and still is, the most flamboyant example of German expressionism in the cinema. Set in a small Dutch village, *The Cabinet of Dr. Caligari* chronicles the tale of a fairground magician named Caligari (Werner Krauss), whose main attraction is Cesare (Conrad Veidt), an anemic-looking somnambulist who goes around town in a black bodystocking murdering people on Caligari's command. Forget the story, *Caligari*'s vaulted reputation lies largely upon its set design. The bizarrely painted canvas scenery rendered an atmosphere of insanity and nightmare and provided the distorted effects director Robert Weine desired for the simulation of derangement, a world seen through the eyes of a lunatic. *Caligari*'s twisted landscapes—the out-of-proportion angles in the shapes of houses, buildings, and carnival tents, the eccentric windows and doorways, the misshapen lamp posts lining the sinister streets—all give the impression that everything is quite wrong.

In *Caligari's Children,* S.S. Prawer tells us:

> Within its stylized settings *Caligari* introduces a multitude of visual motifs that later terror-films were to elaborate. The huge staring eyes of Veidt's Cesare, filling the screen in the most intimate close-ups of the whole film, matched by the glare of Caligari's spectacles; the shadow of a murderer, showing his nefarious work without showing his body; the clutching, warding-off hands of a murder victim. . . .
>
> Commenting, in 1920, on Wiene's imaginative use of shadows on a wall to make murder visible, Kurt Tucholsky singled out an aspect of *Caligari* which is worth recalling in face of the ever greater explicitness that audiences and film-makers have demanded in recent years. "This demonstrates again," Tucholsky writes, "that what is guessed at is more terrible than anything that can be shown. No film can come up to our imagination." The thoughts *Caligari* here inspires in Tucholsky were later to be restated, and put into practice, by Fritz Lang and Val Lewton.

Of course, numerous other German expressionistic horror films were to follow in *Caligari*'s wake: F.W. Murnau's *Nosferatu* (1921), Robert Wiene's *The Hands of Orlac* (1924), Paul Leni's *Waxworks* (1924) and *The Man Who Laughs* (1928), as well as expressionistic remakes of *The Golem* (1920) and *The Student of Prague* (1926). By the 1920s, however, expressionism was no longer the province of the set designers. Rather than continue to use painted canvas backdrops, filmmakers sought natural ways to distort reality, primarily through their use of innovative lighting and camera placement.

Ironically, the bond between Hollywood horror and German expressionism (for which the term "Caligariesque" was coined) owes more to the rise of the Third Reich than it does to any American trend founded upon the deliberate imitation of the Germanic style. With Nazism gaining strength and force, Central and Eastern European filmmakers, a vast number of them German, found good reason to relocate to Hollywood; the film industry there was being controlled by an earlier generation of their fellow countrymen.

Hollywood icons such as Marcus Loew (b. Austria), Louis B. Mayer (b. Russia), Samuel Goldwyn (b. Poland), Adolph Zukor (b. Hungary), William Fox (b. Hungary) and, especially, Carl Laemmle (b. Germany)—the men who played leading roles in building Hollywood empires—had emigrated to North America before the turn of the century as teenagers. As they set up businesses in the mercantile trade, the farthest thing from their minds was the type of opportunity that would later turn up in the motion picture business. The vast majority of them Jewish, they saw in the film trade the absence of anti-Semitic barriers, barriers which stood before them if they aspired to, say, the high society of the American theater.

These founders of Hollywood first purchased nickelodeons, and the booming film market allowed them to become entrepreneurs in motion picture exhibition in very short time. They added one theater after another to their new stock in trade, branching out from city to city until they came up with the idea of making their own pictures and cutting out the middleman. The middleman was a filmmaking monopoly called the Motion Picture Patents Corporation; incorporated in 1908, the MPPC had come to be known simply as the Trust.

In 1909 one of these entrepreneurs, a maverick independent named Carl Laemmle, thumbed his nose at the Trust and began producing films under his own company banner (IMP—Independent Motion Pictures), an action the Trust viewed as illegal. Since the film companies supported by the Trust ran their operations, including production, on the East Coast, Laemmle established his production company as far away from the Trust as possible, setting up his operations on the West Coast. Laemmle built a studio in the small California town of Hollywood.

By keeping an ever watchful eye on his stronger rival's product and putting his dollars to good use, Laemmle, the boy with the slingshot, managed to lure Florence Lawrence and Mary Pickford away from Biograph Pictures (a member of the Trust). By 1912 Laemmle bought another independent film company, which he merged with his own, resulting in the birth of Universal Pictures.

Laemmle's success story spurred the advances of other independents who entered the fray by setting up their own Hollywood production outfits and suing the Trust for "conspiracy in restraint of trade." By 1915 a federal court would rule against the monopoly formed by the Trust. This gave William Fox the official nod to form his own Fox Film Corporation. Adolph Zukor, who had founded his Famous Players production company in 1912, would also, the next year, set his base of operations in Hollywood. By 1916 Zukor would merge his production company with those owned by Jesse Lasky and Samuel Goldwyn to create Paramount Pictures. A short time later, Goldwyn would break away to inaugurate another independent Hollywood production company. Splinter groups would abound. Marcus Loew would acquire Metro Pictures, another Hollywood outfit, one officiated by Louis B. Mayer until he left to head his own production group. In 1924 Metro Pictures would merge with Goldwyn Pictures and Louis B. Mayer Productions to form Metro-Goldwyn-Mayer. And on and on we go.

Although the studio moguls were not particularly zealous in the practice of their religion, looking upon themselves as "100 percent American," they opened up the Hollywood gates for the exodus of Central and Eastern European filmmakers who wished sanctuary from the Third Reich during the late 1920s and early 1930s. Carl Laemmle, the founder of Universal, would live by a code of nepotism, hiring any German relative who wanted a job, at times even hiring those who only claimed to be distant relatives. Zukor, Fox, Mayer, and others would offer a similar red carpet to European filmmakers. Certainly Laemmle, the most notoriously indiscriminate of the lot, was easy game for foreign filmmakers with talent and hope. In *The Genius of the System*, author Thomas Schatz tells us:

> Laemmle signed scores of European filmmakers during his annual trips abroad. Many of those recruits were German . . . and were schooled not only in the European tradition of gothic horror, but also in the German Expressionist cinema of the late teens and the 1920s. They brought a fascination for the cinema's distinctly unrealistic qualities, its capacity to depict a surreal landscape of darkness, nightmare logic and death. . . . The dark, foreboding atmosphere of Universal's horror pictures cut the costs and complexity of lighting and set design—indeed, it became standard practice to construct only the portion of a set that would be visible through the shadows or fog.

Some German filmmakers—Erich Von Stroheim, Ernst Lubitsch, F.W. Murnau, Paul Leni—had successfully emigrated to Hollywood in the late

1920s, prior to the impending threat of Nazism. Others had closer calls with disaster.

Fritz Lang had been a gifted painter, studying art in Paris, before he went to Berlin to begin writing for films; by the mid-1920s he had become Germany's most highly acclaimed film director. Born in Vienna in 1890, Lang studied architecture and then traveled the world and established a noteworthy painting career before he began taking an interest in motion pictures. After establishing himself as a screenwriter, Lang began to direct his own film projects, scoring success with *The Spiders,* a popular and lengthy serial about a secret society of criminals. His producer, Erich Pommer, was so impressed that he offered Lang the directing helm for *The Cabinet of Dr. Caligari,* also a Pommer production. But Lang preferred to stay on the *Spiders* project.

Lang's direction became more impressive with each film: *The Moving Image* (1920), *Four Around the Woman* (1921), *Destiny* (1921), *Dr. Mabuse the Gambler* (1922), *Die Nibelungen* (1924), *Metropolis* (1927), *Spies* (1928), *Woman in the Moon* (1929). By the mid-1920s, his reputation was known internationally. Because Lang laced his contemporary thrillers with the expressionistic flourishes of the German horror film, it could easily be argued that he singlehandedly invented the genre that would come to be called "film noir." He also invented the spy film and, with *Metropolis* and *Woman in the Moon,* shaped the science fiction film into a serious cinematic form. One of Lang's films, *Destiny,* inspired a young Alfred Hitchcock to become a film director.

The Fritz Lang film most relevant to a study of Val Lewton is *M.* Released in 1931, *M* defied conventions and broke taboos in its depiction of a sympathetic child murderer (brilliantly played by Peter Lorre). Set amidst the dark and rainy city streets of Berlin, *M* foreshadows the noirish style of hundreds of Hollywood films of the 1940s, including those produced by Val Lewton. Lang's film also made striking use of the horror aesthetic Lewton would adopt as his own. Justly famous is *M*'s opening sequence, where the murder of a little girl is frighteningly conveyed purely through a series of suggestive visuals. In an interview with Peter Bogdanovich, Lang offered his views:

> If I could show what is the most horrible for *me,* it may not be horrible for somebody else. *Everybody* in the audience—even the one who doesn't dare allow himself to understand what really happened to that poor child—has a horrible feeling that runs cold over his back. But everybody has a *different* feeling, because everybody imagines the most difficult thing that could happen to her. . . . In this way, I force the audience to become a collaborator of mine; by *suggesting* something I achieve a greater impression, a greater involvement, than by showing it.

In 1933, after completing his covertly anti-Nazi *The Last Will of Dr. Mabuse,* Lang was summoned by Goebbels, who, speaking on behalf of Hitler, wished to secure the director as the lead filmmaker for the Nazi party. Lang feigned an interest and left Germany that same night; the banks being closed, he had just enough money for a ticket to Paris, where he arrived penniless. After meeting Pommer, who had also recently fled to Paris, Lang made enough money directing a French film, *Liliom,* to insure his trip to Hollywood. Lang's wife and writing collaborator, Thea Von Harbou, willingly remained in Germany to serve in the ranks of the Third Reich film industry.

Other East European filmmakers who secured jobs in Hollywood during the rise of the Third Reich included John Brahm, Michael Curtiz, William Dieterle, Karl Freund, Anatole Litvak, Joe May, Curt and Robert Siodmak, Douglas Sirk, Edgar Ulmer, Billy Wilder, Frank Wisbar, Fred Zinnemann, and a good many others. Outside of this assortment of present-and-future film directors, the list of additional European émigrés who secured Hollywood positions as composers, cinematographers, scriptwriters, editors, art directors, and set designers would comprise an equally formidable who's who of the Hollywood film.

The horror cinema of Germany would be a fundamental influence upon the Lewton films, but there were other influences as well. Maurice Tourneur, a pioneer French director, had a considerable impact (however indirectly) upon the formularized look of Lewton's RKO films. Tourneur, the great pictorialist, would teach his mastery of composition to his son Jacques, who would be destined to direct the first three Val Lewton films, *Cat People* (1942), *I Walked with a Zombie* (1943), and *The Leopard Man* (1943), setting the tone for the remaining films in the RKO series. Jacques Tourneur's third Lewton film springs to mind when we consider one of his father's early French horror films, the 1912 *Le Système du Docteur Goudron et du Professeur Plume* (aka *The Lunatics*), a loose adaptation of an Edgar Allan Poe story, "The System of Dr. Tarr and Professor Feather." In his *Encyclopedia of Horror Movies,* Phil Hardy informs us that Maurice Tourneur's film is about

> a visitor making a tour of inspection of a lunatic asylum who finds to his discomfiture that it has been taken over by the inmates after a mutiny. . . . As with all Grand Guignol productions, subtlety is beside the point, but Tourneur manages to inject some in the film's most notorious scene, where the supposed director of the asylum is describing for the benefit of the visitors his new cure for insanity: first cutting out an eye, then slitting the throat. Interrupted by noises off-screen, he rushes into the next room and reappears with bloody hands while blood slowly oozes under the door from the next room and begins to arouse feral instincts in the inmates surrounding the visitors.

The blood-under-the-door motif would reappear, again in notorious fashion, some 30 years later in *The Leopard Man.*

By 1915 Maurice Tourneur had emigrated to Hollywood, where he directed *Trilby,* the first movie version of the often filmed George du Maurier novel/play. The du Maurier narrative concerns a deranged hypnotist who governs the behavior and fate of his subject, in this instance a beautiful female vocalist. (Note that *Trilby* used the sinister hypnotist angle years before *Caligari.*) Maurice Tourneur's 1915 thriller was a major success, and his American reputation grew with each film. By the early 1920s Hollywood had come to look upon Maurice Tourneur as a national treasure.

One significant trend in Hollywood horror of the 1920s was the development of the old house thriller, a form that took its inspiration from the Broadway stage. After 867 record-breaking performances of *The Bat* in 1922, Broadway fell prey to numerous old house thrillers, including *The Cat and the Canary, The Charlatan, The Night Call, Drums of Jeopardy, The Last Warning,* and *The Monster.* Eventually all of these plays were adapted for the screen. Although the repetitious elements soon made this subgenre the subject of derision, the old house thriller was instrumental in the evolution of the Hollywood horror film cycles to come. Simply put, the old house thrillers were the first horror films to exploit an audience's fear of the dark.

A study of the Val Lewton films would not be complete without an understanding of the kind of film producer Lewton aspired to be. To achieve this, we must direct our attention to a second generation of Hollywood moguls. Although born in America, these new motion picture luminaries shared the heritage of their elder counterparts in that they too were Jews of Central and Eastern European lineage. The industry's new blood included Jack L. Warner, Harry Cohn, Irving Thalberg, Darryl Zanuck, and David O. Selznick.

Jack Warner (president/founder, in 1923, of Warner Bros. Pictures) and Harry Cohn (production chief/founder, in 1923, of Columbia Pictures) were more like the movie moguls of the old school, closer in both spirit and intellect to Louis B. Mayer, Adolph Zukor, William Fox, and Carl Laemmle. Warner and Cohn were clever businessmen, but they were also known to be coarse and vulgar; their get-'em-out-quick filmmaking philosophy revealed a greater interest in the creation of capital than in the creation of art.

But Irving Thalberg, Darryl Zanuck, and David O. Selznick were part of an entirely different breed; they believed in making tasteful films, films with dignity. Because they were young men when they launched their careers, the Hollywood press labeled them "boy wonders." Thalberg, Zanuck, and Selznick became the heads of production for major studios, all three of them proving successful in carrying their studios through the difficult transition to the sound era and creating, in the 1930s and 1940s, what is now called the "classical Hollywood style." They were preoccupied with quality and prestige and appalled by its absence. All three wunderkind supervised production with a fastidiousness that approached obsession. They displayed upward mobility, moving from one studio to another to achieve the fame and power they desired: Thalberg moved from Universal to MGM, Zanuck moved from Warners to 20th Century–Fox, and Selznick moved from Paramount to RKO and then to MGM. Being intelligent and extremely literate, they reworked scenarios and rewrote scripts. They were present during shooting, and they observed editing. They were involved in nearly every aspect of their films' creations. They were, in fact, what Val Lewton would dream of becoming.

Irving Thalberg had been the first of the boy wonders. In 1918 Carl Laemmle hired the 19-year-old Thalberg as a $25-per-week secretary at Universal's New York office; before Thalberg turned 20, he was appointed to the position of Laemmle's private secretary.

Thalberg was driven to excel by the knowledge that he would die prematurely. Since he was a "blue baby" with an imperfect heart, the doctors had little hope that he would survive through his teens. His mother, however, became his private nurse and taught him to live each day as if it were his last. He read voraciously, wasting not a minute of his time or education. He taught himself to type and studied Spanish and shorthand at a commercial college before going to work for Laemmle. At age 20, he left his New York home to travel to Universal City. While Laemmle was abroad, hiring more "relatives" from Germany, Thalberg took it upon himself to make a study of the studio. He scrutinized the operations, took copious notes, and jotted down his own ideas. When Laemmle returned, Thalberg showed him his findings; Laemmle immediately appointed him studio manager, giving him the responsibility of overseeing all day-to-day operations.

Within six months, the 20-year-old Thalberg was in complete command of Universal Pictures, Laemmle's position of president little more than that of a figurehead. Laemmle took Thalberg's advice implicitly, and the boy wonder was suddenly the talk of Hollywood. In *Movieland,* author Jerome Charyn gives us a colorful picture of Thalberg's relentless dedication to his profession:

> He was five feet six and never weighed more than a hundred and twenty pounds. . . . He worked nineteen hours a day. He could juggle the content and the shooting schedules of half a dozen films in his head. He wouldn't greet dignitaries, like a normal prince, or give interviews. Irving didn't have the time. He was too busy killing himself for some infernal ideal that few people could ever understand. The clock he ran to was a movie clock. He was like an incarnation of the movies themselves. A silver shadow that couldn't stop. He held story conferences in limousines and funeral parlors. And when he took visiting executives around to a bordello, "he would sit in the hallway, in a rocking chair, reading *Variety.*"

In 1922 Lon Chaney, the master of makeup, had captured Thalberg's attention. He had been very impressed by Chaney's role as Fagin in First National's *Oliver Twist,* a vehicle for the young Jackie Coogan. Even at this early stage of his career, Thalberg favored prestige productions, often adaptations of classical works, and his current ambition was to film an adaptation of Victor Hugo's *The Hunchback of Notre Dame.* It would be a well-mounted production, a spectacle with elaborate sets and a cast of thousands. There was no question of whom he would choose for the title role.

Thalberg approached Laemmle, who was reticent about the project, and told him of his plan to construct on the Universal lot a huge square, complete with a replica of Notre Dame. Laemmle was still feeling gun-shy about expensive productions, particularly after two Erich von Stroheim fiascos. Nonetheless, Thalberg had yet to steer him wrong, so he was given the green light.

An entire year was required for the construction of the massive sets. Thalberg spared no expense in the building of the great facade of the cathedral (so well constructed was it that it stands in Universal City to this very day). The shooting time was scheduled to last no less than four months; the cast of 3,500 supporting players and extras was so unwieldy that former armed services officer Charles Stallings was called in to mobilize the mob with the use of military tactics. Military commands had to be issued just to get everyone costumed, loaded on trucks, and ready for location shooting. Public address speakers, placed every 25 feet, were connected to one radio transmitter. From a high platform, director Wallace Worsley shouted orders into a microphone to the thousands spread out before him, a mob that occupied nearly a square quarter mile.

Thalberg's gamble paid off; *The Hunchback of Notre Dame* became a massive hit, the biggest Universal had had up to that time, and it elevated Lon Chaney to the status of a superstar. After putting Universal on the map with the Lon Chaney epic, Thalberg left for the greener pastures of MGM, where his official title was "supervisor of production."

But boy wonders like Irving Thalberg were born, not made, as Carl Laemmle would eventually discover. One day in 1928, Laemmle's office of general manager of Universal Studios was handed down, father-to-son, as a "coming of age" present. A 21-year-old Julius Laemmle so wanted to be cast in his father's image that he changed his name to Carl Laemmle, Jr., and was suddenly running a movie studio. In passing the studio down to his son, Laemmle hoped the young man would magically acquire Thalberg's golden touch. Thus, Junior Laemmle (as he was called by Universal employees) was forced to reign in Thalberg's shadow, an unenviable position if there ever was one.

Thalberg had gone on to unprecedented success at MGM; in fact, he made the small studio into a megagiant within the first year of his tenure. Employing the no-holds-barred approach he used at Universal with *The Hunchback of Notre Dame,* Thalberg masterminded the success of the most extravagant motion picture of its time: *Ben Hur* (1926). Despite Mayer's nervousness as the costs kept piling higher, Thalberg's second literary epic was an unqualified critical and box-office success.

Doing his best to stand up to the obvious pressures that came with the job, Junior Laemmle took pride in his new role as Universal's top man. At the dawn of the sound era, he became interested in the successful London and New York stage versions of Bram Stoker's *Dracula* (adapted by Hamilton Deane and John L. Balderston, respectively), and this seemed an ideal property for a feature film. Junior even hoped to lure Chaney back to Universal City for the title role. But Universal's success with *The Hunchback of Notre Dame, Phantom of the Opera,* and *The Cat and the Canary* did not reflect an affinity for the horror film on the part of the elder Carl Laemmle. David Skal's magnificently researched volume, *Hollywood Gothic* (which traces the evolution of *Dracula,* from novel to stage to film), informs us that the elder Laemmle did his best to discourage his son's purchase of the Stoker property: "'I don't believe in horror movies,' insisted Uncle Carl to an interviewer. 'It's morbid. None of our officers are for it. People don't want that sort of thing. . . . Only Junior wanted it.'"

The Crash of 1929 was reason enough to give pause to many of Hollywood's upcoming projects, but *Dracula* was especially beset by innumerable fits and starts, as Skal details in *Hollywood Gothic.* Finally, late in June 1930, Universal acquired the rights for *Dracula.* The studio announced that the director would be Tod Browning (Lon Chaney's favorite director), but by the summer of 1930, there was little hope that Universal, or any other studio, could obtain the talents of Lon Chaney himself. In July the silent king of horror had taken ill; closer examination showed malignant cells. The course of the condition was mercifully quick and within a month he would be dead. On August 25, 1930, just after the release of MGM's sound remake of *The Unholy Three,* the "man of 1,000 faces" died of throat cancer.

When *Dracula* went into production in late September 1930 with Broadway's star vampire, Hungarian-born Bela Lugosi, in the lead role, Universal was already drawing notices with the release of the studio's most critically acclaimed movie ever, *All Quiet on the Western Front.* For a short while, it looked like Junior might surprise them all and actually fill the vacuum left by Thalberg's departure. In an odd sort of way, he did.

Although only a would-be boy wonder, one who was not a particularly active force upon the projects he oversaw, Carl Laemmle, Jr., made enough of the right decisions to at least be hailed the Irving Thalberg of the horror film. Junior hired Karl Freund, the German cinematographer of *The Golem* and Fritz Lang's *Metropolis* and an innovative force in the German expressionism movement, to photograph *Dracula.* For a production which cost in excess of $400,000, Junior Laemmle authorized expensive and highly evocative interior and exterior sets for art director Charles D. Hall. *Dracula*'s strong opening reel reveals the elaborate lengths in art direction to which Junior was prepared to go in making *Dracula* a success.

When *Dracula* hit the theaters on February 14, 1931, there was a resounding audience turnout that helped make it one of the five top grossing Hollywood films of 1931. Its highly publicized success would usher in a wave of horror films from rival studios. *Dracula* marked the beginning of a trend and delivered, in Bela Lugosi, a newly crowned king of horror.

While *Dracula* was being ballyhooed, Junior Laemmle already had *Frankenstein* on the drawing board, having assigned the project to director Robert Florey, who had written a treatment for the film. With Lon Chaney's demise and Bela Lugosi's overnight fame, the Hungarian actor seemed the logical choice for the monster in *Frankenstein.* Junior Laemmle had his publicity department run a full-page magazine spread advertising their upcoming project and announcing the names of their proposed director and star, Robert Florey and Bela Lugosi. But this, of course, was not to be.

Despite some misgivings, Lugosi eventually accepted the role of the monster, though he had yet to discover that Florey had eliminated all of his dialogue. Universal arranged the shooting of a Florey-directed test reel with Lugosi (made up as the monster) to give Laemmle an idea of the final product. The test reel proved to be a fiasco. It was not a promising prelude for a film Junior hoped would be a worthy successor to *Dracula.* Laemmle reevaluated his *Frankenstein* plans, causing the course of horror film history to be forever altered when he took both Florey and Lugosi off the picture and replaced them with two British wild cards: James Whale and Boris Karloff.

Whale's talents as a director of stage and screen had been highly applauded on both sides of the Atlantic. He had come to prominence in 1928 with his direction of R. C. Sheriff's stage hit, *Journey's End,* which focused upon the ravages of the First World War; in 1930 he directed a critically hailed screen adaptation of the play for Tiffany Studios. During the time of the ill-fated *Frankenstein* screen tests, Whale had been putting the finishing touches on his first assignment for Universal, *Waterlook Bridge.*

Boris Karloff, born William Henry Pratt, had been in the acting business for 21 years when Whale, noticing him in the Universal commissary, asked him to take the monster role in *Frankenstein.* After several years on the stage, Karloff had appeared in his first motion picture in 1919, the year Lon Chaney stunned the movie-going public with *The Miracle Man.* Although Karloff never achieved the star power of Chaney in a similar career of silent screen heavies, he surely got the exposure; by 1930 he had already played character roles in close to 80 films. Now, at the age of 43, he was about to be discovered.

Released on November 21, 1931, *Frankenstein* drew the kind of crowds that elevated a motion picture's success to the level of a national phenomenon. Boris Karloff was suddenly a household name. The rest, as they say, is horror film history.

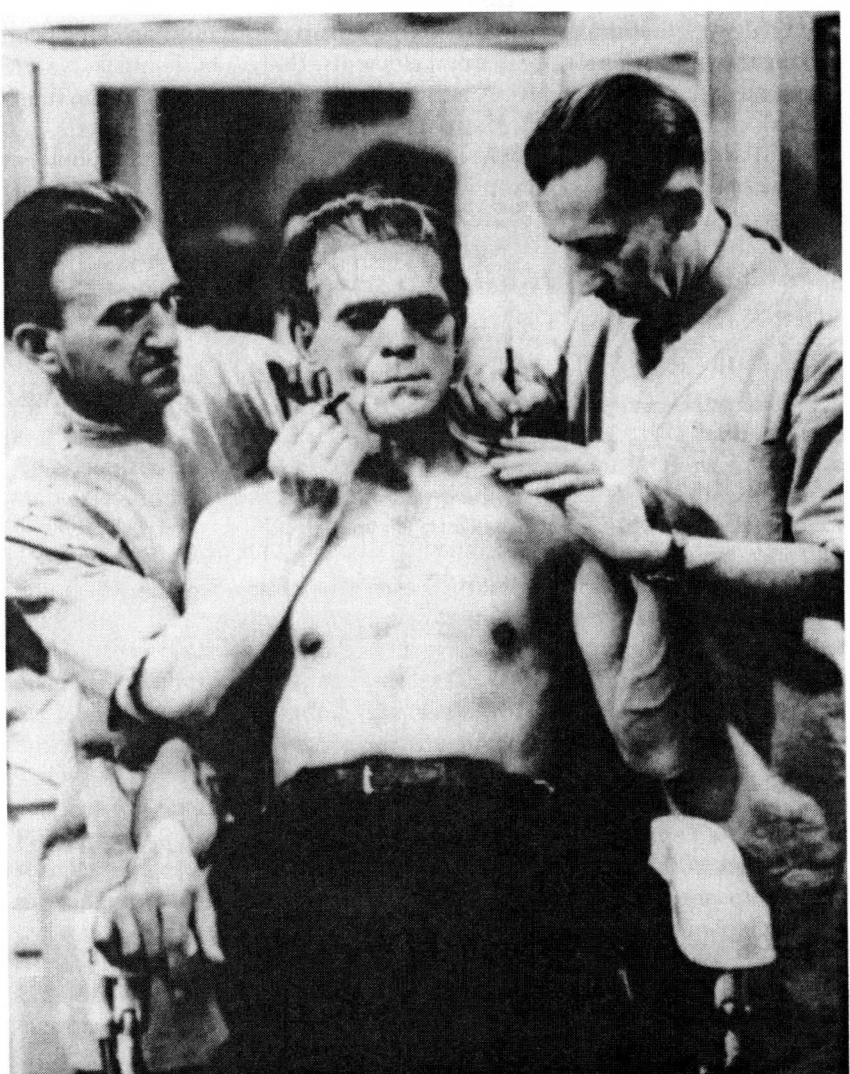

Jack Pierce (left) applying the monster makeup for Frankenstein.

In their exploitation of supernatural elements, *Dracula* and *Frankenstein* were nothing short of revolutionary. Prior to their release, the Hollywood horror film had been locked into the formula-bound traditions of the old house thriller. Although designed and marketed as horror films (which, indeed, they exemplified at the time), the old house thrillers were merely trumped-up mysteries which, by the final reel, trundled out rational explanations for seemingly supernatural events. Although German horror films had long been making use of "genuine" supernatural elements, Hollywood filmmakers were apparently reluctant to believe American audiences would accept the unexplained.

But as it turned out, *Dracula* and *Frankenstein* spearheaded a sound-era horror cycle, one that would run its course and nearly fizzle to a close, only to be given a renewed burst of life by Val Lewton's own celebrated contributions to the genre.

THREE

Apprenticeship: Selznick and Lewton

Lewis J. Zeleznick, born in the Ukraine (Kiev) on May 2, 1870, came to Pittsburg, Pennsylvania, when he was still in his 20s. Before seizing a foothold in the motion picture business, he had been a jeweler. In 1912, with his name Americanized to Selznick, he claimed a nonexistent working position at Universal Film Manufacturing Company in New York, literally hiring himself. "Arriving at the Universal studio to peddle jewelry," say authors Stephen Farber and Marc Green in *Hollywood Dynasties*, "[Lewis Selznick] found an empty desk and sat down, announcing that he was a new employee; before long he promoted himself to general manager."

By 1915 Selznick had joined up with Arthur Spiegel, and the two produced silent films for their World Sales Corporation, signing a number of rising Hollywood stars, including Alla Nazimova. That same year Selznick and Spiegel were also responsible for the production of Maurice Tourneur's *Trilby*.

Lewis Selznick later teamed with Adolph Zukor and formed the Select Film Corporation. It was Selznick who, after the furor of the Fatty Arbuckle scandal, suggested Will Hays as the head of Hollywood's self-contained censorship program, the Motion Picture Producers and Distributors of America.

Louis B. Mayer was born on July 4, 1885 (or so he claimed) in Minsk, Russia, and after a stretch as a successful junk man in New Brunswick, Canada, he moved to Haverill, Massachusetts, and later Boston, where he became a movie theater entrepreneur. His securing of prints of D.W. Griffith's *Birth of a Nation* (1915) brought him much success and gave him the solvency to establish the Orpheum Theater chain in Boston.

Selznick and Mayer got to know one another when Mayer was the New England distributor for Selznick's Select Film Corporation. In spite of their similar background, both being Russian Jews, Selznick and Mayer held antithetical points of view. Selznick was loud and brassy, a showman and a notorious gambler. "Selznick the Jester," as he was called, premiered his movies with a flamboyance that rivaled P.T. Barnum. Louis B. Mayer, on the other hand, glorified wholesome, all–American virtues and held motherhood as the most sacred of all human duties. As told by Farber and Green in *Hollywood Dynasties:*

> Selznick brought his two older sons, Myron and David, into the business at an early age. The two participated in story conferences at their father's studio while still in their teens. . . . Even in public school, the boys were given allowances of several hundred dollars a week and told, "Spend it all. Give it away. Throw it away." Their father encouraged them to live beyond their means, so that they would be impelled to work that much harder.

But good things came to an end when Lewis Selznick overextended himself and declared bankruptcy in 1923, just as the 24-year-old wonder boy, Irving Thalberg, was defying all odds with his production of *Hunchback of the Notre Dame* at Universal. Selznick's old partner, Adolph Zukor, had become a bitter enemy when Selznick broke up their corporation and lured its stars away. Zukor saw some manner of divine justice in Selznick's bankruptcy and would not lift a finger to help. Neither would Mayer, who deplored Selznick's extravagance and vulgarity. Between these two there was little sympathy shared over the concerns of a recklessly flamboyant has-been.

Selznick traded in his 17-room $18,000-a-year Park Avenue apartment and moved his family into a tiny three-room flat. Selznick's wife was forced to sell all her jewelry and take up cooking for the first time in her life. For 10 years Lewis Selznick tried for a comeback, but by his death in 1933, he had become a forgotten force of the silent era.

The riches-to-rags descent of Lewis Selznick had a lasting impact upon his sons, both of whom became obsessed with avenging their father's name through their own work within the film industry. Myron became an agent who, by the mid–1930s, had assembled the most star-studded roster of talents in Hollywood, from performers (Hepburn, Lombard, Astaire, Fonda, Cooper, Olivier, et al.) to directors (Capra, Lubitsch, McCarey, et al.).

Both boys wanted their father vindicated, but while Myron wanted to get even, David wanted to rebuild the Selznick filmmaking empire. David O. Selznick made his move in 1926 (the same year Val Lewton became a reader for the story department back at MGM's New York office). Selznick envisioned himself as every bit the boy wonder that Thalberg had recently proven himself to be. Although his only credential was a tainted family name, Selznick sought work with MGM. His confidence was a wonder to behold, considering that the 25-year-old had never held a job in his life.

When David Selznick walked onto the MGM lot looking for work, Mayer remembered his conflicts with the young man's father and refused to offer a position. Not to be stopped by this rebuff, David went over Mayer's head, calling upon Nicholas Schenck, president of E.M. Loew's (which owned MGM). Old connections worked their magic, and Selznick, after becoming a reader for MGM's story department, was soon given a job as an assistant in the studio's "B" production unit, where he proved his capabilities with a number of Western quickies. Within months, his weekly salary rose from $100 to $3,000. He even managed to gain some of Mayer's respect.

But the studio already had a boy wonder with Thalberg, and he was a difficult figure to topple. The chronically ill Thalberg no doubt saw his would-be rival's driving behavior as a form of challenge. Selznick was jockeying for a major position within studio ranks, and the series of standoffs that ensued between him and Thalberg, as well as the personal and economic barriers erected by Mayer, caused enough friction for Selznick to go elsewhere to prove himself.

David Selznick found some pleasure in accepting a higher paying job at Paramount in 1927; it was, after all, another victory over a past Selznick family nemesis, Adolph Zukor. His credentials were good enough to secure him a position as assistant to the general manager, B.P. Schulberg. As a producer, Selznick became involved in a number of Paramount films during the next three years: *Forgotten Faces* (1928), *Betrayal* (1928), *The Dance of Life* (1929, in which he experimented with two-color technicolor), *For the Defense* (1929), *The Four Feathers* (1929), *Honey* (1930), *Sarah and Son* (1930), and *Street of Chance* (1930). All of these were well-mounted "A" budget productions in which Selznick already showed some of his characteristic style and good taste. He also met a number of filmmakers with whom he would collaborate in the future: George Cukor, John Cromwell, Merian C. Cooper, and Ernest Schoedsack, to name a few.

The Four Feathers, in particular, became a notable coup for Selznick. In *Genius of the System,* Thomas Schatz reveals Selznick's capacity as a fixer-upper: "[After] a disastrous preview of *The Four Feathers* . . . Selznick conducted a massive salvage job on the adventure drama, reconstructing the story and setting up a program of retakes, and then he personally supervised the reediting. The picture was a mild success, and it put codirectors Merian Cooper and Ernest Schoedsack on the industry map; it also fueled Selznick's desire to get out from behind a desk and onto the lot, making movies rather than administrative decisions."

During his stay at Paramount, Selznick's three-year dalliance with Louis B. Mayer's daughter Irene had blossomed into something serious. When the couple finally approached Mayer with the intent to marry within six weeks, the man was aghast, but the united front put on by Irene and David was more than a match for him, as he had always been a somewhat indulgent father. Mayer reluctantly accepted the match but wanted to postpone the ceremony. The couple wanted none of this, and the April 1930 wedding was what Mayer might have termed a rushed production. Mayer spoke to neither bride nor groom on the day of the wedding.

Soon after his marriage, Selznick planned to leave Paramount for greener pastures. What he truly wanted to do was to start his own production company and have the major studios like MGM, Paramount, and the ever-growing First National/Warner Bros. distribute his films. His plans were to make only important films; no low-budget programmers for the Selznick company. In essence, Selznick envisioned himself as a jazz-age variation of Samuel Goldwyn, complete with airs of self-importance and unimpeachable sophistication. However, unlike the uneducated Goldwyn, who promoted literary productions primarily because it gave him an edge of class, Selznick loved literature, read it, cherished it, understood it. Selznick hobnobbed with the literati from Hollywood to New York. He was well versed in modern writing as well and was especially impressed with F. Scott Fitzgerald, particularly with *The Great Gatsby*.

However dazzling Selznick's aspirations may have been, they were premature; the major Hollywood moguls supported each other in their refusal to buy into Selznick's independent productions. Mayer, in particular, was very vocal, saying such an enterprise would set a dangerous precedent which would ultimately bring the collapse of studio hierarchy.

Overcoming his disappointment, Selznick worked his way into a new studio, one that was not well established. Such an approach had once worked for Thalberg, who used his keen business acumen to turn the small production units Universal and MGM into major forces. And so, using his resentment of the established moguls as a driving motivation, Selznick allied himself with an underdog studio, a veritable Johnny-come-lately: the Radio-Keith-Orpheum film company, otherwise known as RKO.

The first RKO films had appeared in 1929, and none of them were very successful. By 1930 things had improved, but only because the novelty of talking pictures guaranteed box office; virtually every studio making sound features was in the black in 1930. When the Depression took a more severe bite out of the industry in 1931, the studio began to flounder. What it needed was the involvement of an educated filmmaker, one with a youthful energy and an aggressive spirit. David O. Selznick was its man. In November 1931 he was appointed RKO's vice president in charge of production, meaning, essentially, that he was given the reins to the entire studio. He was finally wearing Irving Thalberg's shoes.

Thomas Schatz tells us, in *The Genius of the System:*

> Selznick immediately merged the two West Coast studios [RKO Radio and RKO Pathé] and went to a supervisory system, though he hoped to use a few of RKO's top filmmakers as unit producers within another year or so. He established the RKO-Radio facility as the base of filmmaking operations, with Pathé serving as a rental facility when it wasn't required by RKO. He assembled a staff of seven associate producers, two of whom, Pandro Berman and Merian Cooper, also served as his executive assistants.

Together, Berman, Cooper, and Selznick reevaluated the structure of the merged studios, laying off a sizeable number of RKO employees from both. Selznick had great faith in the remarkable talent of Merian Cooper and his equally daring partner, Ernest B. Schoedsack, a man Cooper insisted Selznick sign for RKO. Irene Mayer Selznick, in her autobiography, *A Private View,* recalls: "Merian Cooper . . . had a project up his sleeve that I never took seriously because it was so preposterous. It was *King Kong.* I thought he was kidding. Anyone would but David, who promised to scrounge for funds if Coop could work out the problems." In an effort to raise money for the *King Kong* project and other "A" budget features, Selznick cut corners on modest pictures.

Two productions in particular put Selznick on the cutting edge in 1932: *What Price Hollywood* and *A Bill of Divorcement,* both directed by George Cukor. *What Price Hollywood* is a surprisingly good film for its time and is in some ways superior to its three remakes (as *A Star Is Born*). The suicide that ends the film is extremely disquieting and plays like an expressionistic nightmare. *Bill of Divorcement* made a star out of the outspoken Katharine Hepburn. The film's popularity with both critics and public made it an enviable hit for any studio, let alone a second rater like RKO. Even John Barrymore's performance, as Hepburn's mentally ill father, was uncharacteristically restrained. When Hepburn discovers her family is shrouded with insanity, her relationship with her fiancé (played by David Manners) disintegrates because she lives in dread of passing her imminent madness on to a future generation. If we substitute a supernatural curse for the fear of inherited insanity, we have a plot not unlike that of *Cat People.*

The story behind *King Kong* may be the greatest of all Hollywood production tales. (It perhaps eclipses the two other obvious candidates for the prize: Selznick's *Gone with the Wind* and Welles's *Citizen Kane.* Several volumes have been written on the subject. Perhaps the best is Goldner and Turner's *The Making of King Kong.*) Early in 1930, before Selznick came aboard, RKO had bought Willis O'Brien's new animation project (a follow-up to his 1926 dinosaur fest, *The Lost World*), which by that time had been dubbed *Creation.* It would never get past a few test reels before Selznick, Merian Cooper, and Ernest Schoedsack scrapped O'Brien's plan and drew up their own for *King Kong.*

It was because of Selznick's belief in the project and its three mentors—Cooper, Schoedsack, and O'Brien—that *King Kong* was ever allowed to get off the ground. And it was precisely the work Willis O'Brien had already done on *Creation* that gave Cooper, Schoedsack, and Selznick reason to believe that RKO could handle the *Kong* picture.

Originally, RKO's front office was reluctant to take the chance on another jungle picture, especially after their 1932 fiasco, *Bird of Paradise,* which even Selznick couldn't save. But Selznick managed to keep his word with Cooper, giving *Kong* the green light as well as initiating a companion jungle film, *The Most Dangerous Game,* which, produced simultaneously, would make use of *Kong*'s cast and sets.

(*King Kong* and the films of Val Lewton are admittedly worlds apart, yet *Kong*'s highly successful 1942 rerelease would become one of the reasons that would prompt RKO to initiate the horror film series that Lewton would produce. In 1952 *King Kong* would see another rerelease, this time double-billed with *The Leopard Man*; yet another *Kong* rerelease in 1956 would pair it with *I Walked with a Zombie.*)

While Cooper and Schoedsack were busy with the production of their two jungle adventures, David Selznick was pondering his recent discontent. Merlin ("Deac") Aylesworth had recently been appointed studio president. The meddlesome Aylesworth was an abrasion to Selznick's ego and autonomy. When he began tampering with Selznick's casting and script supervision, the situation became intolerable for the boy wonder of RKO. What's more, Aylesworth started to meddle in areas into which even Selznick did not care to trespass. However large his ego, Selznick at least believed in delegating power and responsibility to his subordinates, people like Merian C. Cooper, Pan Berman, and George Cukor, once he had hand-picked them, and he supported a surprising number of decisions from below, offered by individuals he respected enough to hire.

Louis B. Mayer knew of Selznick's plight at RKO and how it must have rankled his son-in-law. Irving Thalberg had been working too hard, and as 1932 was drawing to a close, the strains and demands had begun to take their toll. When Thalberg suffered a heart attack after a Christmas party, forcing him to take a European vacation for the sake of convalescence, Mayer made an offer. Selznick had already proven his worth at RKO, and in spite of the potential animosity between the two men, Mayer's business sense held sway over any objections of an emotional order. Selznick accepted Mayer's appointment as Thalberg's immediate replacement, and the press, with whom Thalberg's name was gold, had a field day with snide remarks concerning Mayer's thinly veiled nepotism. *The Hollywood Spectator* responded with the immortal and oft-repeated play-on-words: "The son-in-law also rises."

In February 1933, one month before the release of *King Kong,* Selznick went on the MGM payroll; *The Hollywood Spectator* soon saw the folly of its cynicism. Selznick convinced his past associate, director George Cukor, to come aboard for *Dinner at Eight,* Selznick's follow-up to the previous year's MGM success, *Grand Hotel.* Assembling some of the same cast, John Barrymore, Lionel Barrymore, Wallace Beery, Jean Hersholt, as well as a similar narrative structure, *Dinner at Eight* proved a winner all the way. This coup, on top of the massive success of RKO's *King Kong* (for which Selznick was credited executive producer), made the new boy wonder the talk of the town.

Even Thalberg, when he came back to work, congratulated Selznick on his success with *Dinner at Eight.*

Selznick continued with two additional moneymakers for 1933, *Night Flight,* an adaptation of the St. Exupery novel, featuring Clark Gable, and *Dancing Lady,* the historic first pairing of Gable and Joan Crawford. In 1934 Selznick successfully salvaged *Viva Villa,* a film initially to be shot in Mexico and directed by Howard Hawks. The production a shambles, Selznick moved the Wallace Beery vehicle back to Hollywood, and despite the inflated budget, the film made money. Next Selznick tested his mettle in budget filmmaking with *Manhattan Melodrama,* a film capitalizing on Warner Bros./First National's current success with gangster movies. *Manhattan Melodrama* was shot in three weeks for only $300,000. How to make a modestly budgeted film look expensive was a lesson Selznick had learned at the beginning of his career. The film, which starred Clark Gable and provided the first screen pairing of William Powell and Myrna Loy, would prove enormously popular, paving the way for the "Thin Man" series. *Manhattan Melodrama* would further be immortalized as the movie that John Dillinger attended the night he was shot down coming out of a Chicago movie palace.

In comparing the MGM works of Irving Thalberg and David O. Selznick, one can easily see similarities in the tastefulness and deliberate splendor of their film productions. But aside from their mutual love for literature, there were some marked contrasts between MGM's rival princes. Thalberg's leanings were slightly more sophisticated than Selznick's, perhaps a bit self-consciously so; his projects were often those of a more genteel nature. Selznick, on the other hand, avoided anything too high-minded or precious; his choices in literature appeared to reflect an affection for the common and the coarse, at times even the vulgar. Unlike Thalberg, Selznick was not crusading to elevate the public's cultural tastes.

It is difficult to imagine Selznick selling Shakespeare to his movie audiences, as Thalberg did. For the most part, Selznick had a keener eye for public tastes, especially when it came to romance, and he gave his audiences what he believed they already wanted. Selznick also had the edge on Thalberg when it came to casting. While Thalberg was indeed capable of expert casting, one example of misjudgment speaks volumes: Clark Gable as the proposed lead for Thalberg's adaptation of *Romeo and Juliet.* Even Gable knew better and told Thalberg (according to Jerome Charyn's *Movieland*): "I don't look Shakespeare, I don't talk Shakespeare, I don't like Shakespeare, and I won't do Shakespeare."

Although it is probable that there were times each wished the other would drop into a deep hole, Selznick and Thalberg shared a mutual, albeit slightly grudging, professional respect for one another's work. Thalberg was the more private of the two: forceful, but never really trying to please anyone but himself (with whatever time he had left). But Selznick's personal Hollywood vendetta—his crusade to restore the family name—necessitated a high profile. Thalberg made it a point not to have his name included in the opening credits of any of his films; Selznick, like Sam Goldwyn, not only wanted his name listed—he wanted it to appear first, before the title. Another profound difference was that most employers (aside from Erich Von Stroheim) liked Irving Thalberg; the tyrannical Selznick, on the other hand, resorted to bullying tactics to achieve his goal and as a result made enemies easily.

Enter Val Lewton.

When Selznick gained his new MGM position, he sent out numerous feelers for more writers. In the spring of 1934, he sent a request to MGM's New York office, whose scripting department was still being managed by Nina Lewton. Selznick knew of Nina's long-term position with the department, and her relationship to the great Nazimova (whom his father had once employed) only increased his respect for the cultured and very literate MGM employee. In particular, he felt Nina's Russian background could be instrumental to his upcoming project, an adaptation of Nikolai Gogol's *Taras Bulba*.

Although born in America, Selznick was of Ukrainian descent, and he wished to dignify his heritage with a movie founded upon a Russian work of literature. He knew Nina had been educated in Russia and, with faith in her expertise, asked her to search for a Russian-born writer for the Gogol project. Nina took the request seriously, but could not help but include one Russian-born writer she knew very well, one who had left the MGM story department to fulfill an exhausting book contract with Vanguard Press.

In *The Reality of Terror*, Joel E. Siegel tells us that Nina Lewton had sent Selznick a list of five "well-known writers of Russian extraction" and included, as a sixth candidate, the name of her son. After the other five writers showed a lack of interest, Val Lewton—author of the 1926 pulp epic, *The Cossack Sword*—was hired to write a treatment (but not a scenario) for the Gogol project. The job was expected to take two or three months at a weekly salary of $200. Lewton, who had recently complected his contractual obligations with his submissions of *A Laughing Woman* and *This Fool Passion* (both penned under his favorite pseudonym, Carlos Keith), saw opportunity beckon on the western horizon.

Lewton made the move to California by train, his wife and daughter following a month later after their house was sold. In *My Brother*, Lucy informs us: "So it was that Val and Ruth came to Hollywood with Baby Ruth Nina in June 1934. They left behind all their furniture, many antiques which Ruth had saved from her family."

The Lewtons rented a Mexican-style house with a nice location in Pacific Palisades. Although the house was by no means palatial, it had some unique features, such as a patio and fountain, which, combined with the gorgeous climate, made the Lewtons feel they had found some degree of luxury in their lives. They vowed to remain in California as long as the work held out. In *My Brother*, Lucy Lewton details this period as a rather bleak one:

> Val sat in a small office alone writing the script for *Taras Bulba;* no one came to ask him how he was getting along. When the month was up and he had finished the script [actually just a treatment] he received his check and a notice that his services were no longer required. Having burned all his bridges in the East . . . he sat in the studio commissary quite depressed.

After Lewton fulfilled his obligation on *Taras Bulba*, Selznick shelved the project. Lewton had hoped for a hand in the script and was dismayed by the sudden disintegration of his sole reason for coming to California. Now that he and Ruth were happily settled, the uncertainty of his employment was unbearable.

Fortunately, Selznick had seen something he respected in Lewton. Perhaps it was because Lewton presented a docile mirror-image of himself. Like Selznick (who was older by two years), Lewton started out as a reader for MGM; both men, worshipping literature and sharing a Russian heritage, came from families that achieved and then lost tremendous power in the motion picture trade. According to Lucy Lewton in *My Brother*, "David Selznick asked Val if he wanted to join as his secretary and assistant at $75 per week. Val was most happy to accept and so started their long association."

Because Selznick respected Lewton's intelligence and literary sensibilities, much use was made of his employment. Since they both loved to read, especially the classics, Lewton had become a good sounding board for Selznick's ideas about literary adaptations. Selznick was also impressed by Lewton's having published eight novels before turning thirty, while holding down an additional full-time job at Metro's New York offices. He knew that Lewton was from a cultured family with a background in the high arts, something toward which he himself aspired. Lewton was also the fastest reader Selznick had ever met.

Selznick knew how to spend money on movies and how to lose exhaustive amounts on gambling sprees, but he valued economy and took pride in getting his money's worth. With Val Lewton, Selznick got much for his dollar. Joel E. Siegel tells us that Lewton "became Selznick's Man Friday, advising on properties and the selection of actors, patching up rough places in screenplays and checking production designs and set dressings for historical authenticity" (*The Reality of Terror*). According to Lucy Lewton, "Whenever Selznick had to come East on business he took Val along. . . . Val, at every train stop, would have to buy books and relate the story to Selznick" (*My Brother*).

When Lewton began his apprenticeship with Selznick, the big project in the works was *David Copperfield;* its release in December 1934 would elevate its producer to new heights. This Charles Dickens adaptation was a bold stroke, even for MGM, with a genuinely inspired cast and an exceptional script. Although the film included an incredible number of familiar faces—Lionel Barrymore, Roland Young, Basil Rathbone, W.C. Fields (ingeniously cast against type), Edna May Oliver, Maureen O'Sullivan, Lewis Stone, Elsa Lanchester, Una O'Conner, and Arthur Treacher—Selznick decided to give the title role to two virtual unknowns, Freddie Bartholomew and Frank Lawton. George Cukor was again called in to direct.

David Copperfield met all audience expectations and pleased the Dickens scholars as well. It is with this film that Selznick founded his policy of making literary adaptations as faithful to their sources as was humanly possible. *David Copperfield* would become the most well-respected release of 1934 and would even be held in high esteem in Great Britain, where Hollywood adaptations of British works were often met with scorn.

Lewton was happy to see Selznick basking in the acclaim, but was discouraged by the lack of acknowledgment given to his (uncredited) scripting contributions. Perhaps such anonymity would have been easier to bear if Lewton had not been treated so shabbily. In *The Reality of Terror*, Joel E. Siegel reports a characteristic episode:

> Lewton, like all of Selznick's employees, was often forced to bow terribly low to serve his master. Just after Selznick had produced *David Copperfield*, he called Lewton at home and asked how well he knew *Oliver Twist*. Lewton said he knew the novel fairly well and was told to be at Selznick's home at ten the next morning. Feeling sure it would be just Selznick's style to trip him up on some obscure piece of information, Lewton spent the night poring over Dickens. He drove twenty miles to Selznick's house, arrived on time and was shown into the bathroom where Selznick was seated on the toilet. "How old is Oliver Twist when the story opens?" Selznick asked. Lewton told him. "Freddie Bartholomew's too old for that," Selznick responded and told Lewton to go home.

The year 1935 got Selznick off to a onerous start with a couple of back-to-back disappointments: *Vanessa: Her Love Story*, a soaper/weeper starring Helen Hayes, and *Reckless*, a combination of music, dance, and comedy—all tidily wrapped together with a suicide theme (the latter turning up with great regularity in Selznick films). Selznick's stock had been lowered with these two misfies, but just before leaving MGM at the end of 1935, he delivered two literary adaptations, *Anna Karenina* and *A Tale of Two Cities*, that quickly reestablished his credibility as a premiere film producer.

With *Anna Karenina*, Selznick tapped the resources of his Russian literature authority, Val Lewton. Lewton's familiarity with Tolstoy's work designated him as the valuable sounding board upon which Selznick tested his own ideas, though Lewton's script contributions once again remained uncredited. The screenplay credits went to Clemence Dane and Salka Viertel;

the latter quickly became a friend of Lewton's. In fact, Selznick had just appointed Salka's son, the 18-year-old Peter Viertel, as Lewton's assistant. (Thanks to Lewton's encouragement, Peter Viertel would become a novelist, publishing his first book, *The Canyon*, at the age of 19.)

With *Anna Karenina*, Selznick once again strove for absolute fidelity in his adaptation of a literary classic, an attitude Lewton had no trouble sharing: both men respected the purity of the classics and neither thought it wise to improve upon a masterpiece. Selznick and Lewton could not avoid alterations made to appease the censors, but even this was done with considerable reluctance. Casting, which by now had become a Selznick speciality, once more was a major concern. From the first, Selznick saw Greta Garbo as the ideal choice for the title role of Anna (she had already played the role in the 1928 *Love*, a silent version of the novel), and for the role of Vronsky, her lover, he considered Clark Gable, before arriving at his final choice, Fredric March.

It was typical of Selznick to treat *Anna Karenina* with the integrity he knew it deserved. A sense of opulence pervades the film from the start: an incredible tracking shot, in close up, of an impossibly long banquet table dressed and ready for the feast, the remarkable visuals of this impeccably arranged repast feeling not unlike a moving aerial shot of some distant planet. With this peculiar bird's-eye-view of culinary extravagance, Selznick sets the tone for his spare-no-expense production, complicated camera setups having already become a tradition with the producer, in part providing what the public was coming to recognize as the "Selznick touch."

The critics were pleased with *Anna Karenina*, and the downbeat ending somehow did not drive away its audience. The heartstopping climax that ended in Anna's suicide was horrific enough to rival any terror scene from a Universal Studios monster opus. It remains among the most frightening death scenes ever put upon the screen. Clarence Brown's direction of this memorable set piece likely had an impact upon Lewton's approach to cinematic terror. Brown had learned his craft well, having spent many fruitful years as assistant (and later scriptwriter and codirector) to Maurice Tourneur. In *The Movie Director's Story*, Joel W. Finler tells us: "In spite of his lack of experience, Brown managed to talk himself into the job by pointing out to Tourneur the advantage of hiring a 'fresh brain' whom he could influence in his own way."

The power of *Anna Karenina*'s climactic sequence is derived from Clarence Brown's vibrant interplay of light and dark, a technique highly characteristic of his mentor. Robert J. Kern's editing, combined with Herbert Stothart's driving score and William Daniels's marvelous photography, works the sequence to a crescendo pitch.

Having lost everything (her husband, her lover, and her son), Anna sits upon a bench at the train station. It is dark, and she is alone, the fog-shrouded night occasionally punctuated by angry bursts of engine steam and the accompanying clinking sounds of railroad men hammering the train wheels, insuring the friction between track and wheel. There is minimal score music. Anna's resolved, almost catatonic, facial expression already suggests what she is about to do, and we follow her as she walks near the edge of the track, waiting for the railroad men to leave. Cut to the train whistle blasting out a head of steam and a shrill hell-bent cry. Cut to the engineer's hand pulling the switch. The tension builds with each progressive puff of the engine, as the train makes its leadeningly slow departure. Next comes a dynamic repetition of cuts: medium shots of Garbo (her face reflecting the pulsation of light caused by the passing of the cars) interwoven with close shots of moving train wheels. The intensity of this repetition builds with the speed of the train, the sound of the grinding wheels, the staccato puffs of the engine. By this time the gradually building musical score sounds like it's out of control, like a runaway train. In our last shot of Anna, her frozen expression changes to one of desperation, and she lurches forward, at which point we cut to a long shot of the train pulling out of the station into the night. The soundtrack is suddenly quiet as the score comes to a halt, and so jarring is this silence that the sounds of the massive locomotive seem to linger on, adding a sense of doom that is entirely personal.

Although it was an elaborately produced, well-mounted film, the 95-minute *Anna Karenina* did not have the epic scale of Selznick's next feature: *A Tale of Two Cities.* The Dickens novel detailed a broad canvas of events, the French Revolution being the all-pervasive background. The film called for spectacle, which is exactly what Selznick gave it. He arranged to build a set that was a reasonable facsimile of the towering French Bastille, and he hired literally thousands of extras to give the crowd scenes the degree of verisimilitude he sought. Certainly much of his motivation for epic scale was spurred by his desire to outdo Irving Thalberg's French epic of the previous decade, *The Hunchback of Notre Dame.*

While Jack Conway was enlisted to direct the principal scenes derived from the novel, Selznick needed a second-unit production team to take charge of what would be the film's most memorable moments: the Revolutionary sequences. The economic and physical hazards of these mob scenes, particularly the storming of the Bastille, would prove an arduous task to those in command of this second unit. Like the crowd scenes in *The Hunchback of Notre Dame,* the extras would have to respond to supervisors' militarylike commands, and yet make the action look like that of a completely disorganized mob. The scale of these sequences was enough to make Louis B. Mayer wince, especially when he considered his son-in-law's penchant for high-risk stakes.

Selznick may have, on other occasions, treated Lewton rather brusquely, but his decision to put him in charge of these key Revolutionary sequences was ample evidence of his faith in the man. With *A Tale of Two Cities,*

Lewton's name would even be included among the film's opening credits. According to Selznick's plan, Lewton would function as producer of the second unit, while another appointee would serve as that unit's director. In circumstances paralleling his hiring of Lewton, Selznick sought someone whose ethnic background would add an air of authenticity to the proceedings. For the Revolutionary sequences, he wanted someone with a French background, and there was no budding film director on the MGM payroll whose name sounded more French than Jacques Tourneur.

Born in France in 1904 (the same year as Lewton), Jacques Tourneur had a first-hand view of the motion picture business. His father, Maurice Tourneur, had been a major director in his day. He remains one of the silent era's great pictorialsts, and his sense of composition was as innovative as it was influential. Lewis Jacobs, in *The Rise of the American Film,* claimed: "[Maurice Tourneur's] importance in the history of American films, like the importance of some other pioneers, lies not . . . in the work he left but in his suggestiveness to the industry. Much of the atmosphere, design, and pictorial beauty of pictures today are due indirectly to Tourneur's influence."

After coming to America in 1915 to direct *Trilby,* the elder Tourneur worked in Hollywood for 11 years, making a large number of successful films, including *The Blue Bird* (1918), *The Great Redeemer* (1920, codirected by Clarence Brown), *The Last of the Mohicans* (1920, codirected by Clarence Brown and featuring Boris Karloff), *Treasure Island* (1920, featuring Lon Chaney), *Foolish Matrons* (1921, codirected by Clarence Brown and inspired by Stroheim's *Foolish Wives*), *Lorna Doone* (1923), *Jealous Husbands* (1923, inspired by Stroheim's *Blind Husbands*), *While Paris Sleeps* (1923), *Aloma of the South Seas* (1926), and many others. While making *Mysterious Island* for MGM in 1926, Maurice became involved in such a dispute with studio executives that he walked off the picture, pulled up stakes, and moved himself and his family back to France. The film Tourneur abandoned was left in such disorganized state that it would not be released until 1929, with extra sound footage and color sequences added.

In 1923, Tamer Lane wrote, in *What's Wrong with the Movies:*

> [Maurice] Tourneur is the leader of the artistic school of directors and in many respects is five years ahead of the rest of the pack. . . . Huge sets, mob scenes or any of the other forms of lavishness mean little or nothing to Tourneur. . . . He can get more drama and beauty out of a small two-walled set representing an underworld den or a close-up of a small Mexican hut, than other studio skippers can get through the burning of Rome. . . . Tourneur's scenes are often exquisite compositions of light and shade painted with photoplay ingredients [Stanley Hochman, *American Film Directors*].

Like father, like son.

It was in France that Maurice's son began his own film career. As his father continued to direct films in his native land, Jacques began to assist as a script clerk and editor. In 1932, after gaining inestimable experience with his father, the 28-year-old Tourneur was given a $50-a-week contract with Pathé-Natan to direct his first film, *Tout Ça ne Vaut pas l'Amour.* In 1934, after helming three more films for the French studio and noting the number of European film directors emigrating to America, Tourneur traveled to Hollywood. The move was likely inspired by Fritz Lang's highly publicized Hollywood contract. At the time, Lang was working in France, having recently taken leave of his homeland with little more than the shirt on his back. In 1934 it was David Selznick who, traveling to France to do research for *A Tale of Two Cities,* signed Lang for a one-picture deal with MGM. It was obvious to any young filmmaker who courted opportunity that Hollywood was clearly the place to be.

His respectable film credentials notwithstanding, Tourneur discovered that in the midst of the Great Depression, it was more difficult breaking into the Hollywood system than he imagined it would be. After some disheartening experiences in his efforts to obtain employment, he finally landed a $100-a-week job at MGM, where he was put to work directing shorts. According to Tourneur:

> My career in Hollywood really began when I was working on *A Tale of Two Cities* at Metro for David O. Selznick. I was on contract to Metro on a week-by-week basis and doing very small B and C class pictures. Selznick put me in charge of the second unit on *A Tale,* which involved handling all the Revolution scenes. He introduced me to the writer Val Lewton, who was to be a major presence in my career [Charles Higham and Joel Greenberg, *The Celluloid Muse*].

The Lewton/Tourneur team did give these sequences staggering authenticity. *A Tale of Two Cities* was nominated for an Academy Award as Best Picture, but apart from its stunning Revolutionary sequences, impressive cast, and respectable performances, this Dickens adaptation was, on the whole, a rather stodgy affair. Even Lewton and Tourneur's brilliant sequences (lasting about five minutes, total) were nearly ruined by Selznick's decision to place epigraphic messages over the spectacular visuals, turning these marvelous moments into something akin to a cinematic comic-book.

Nevertheless, the dynamics of the Lewton/Tourneur sequences are breathtaking and must be seen to be believed. We see accelerated montages of angry faces and unspeakable acts; we witness victims trampled by soldiers' horses; we observe the results of a cannon being fired into the massive crowd and the carpet of corpses left in the line of cannon fire when the crowd retreats. We see death, destruction conflagration, ending with a macabre tilt shot of the guillotine looming against a flaming sky. The thousands of extras move like a sea of madness through the streets of Paris as Tourneur's exalted crane shots capture this tableau of chaos with a staggering air of authenticity.

After Lewton and Tourneur had completed their second-unit production work, Selznick announced his resignation from MGM. He had grown disenchanted with the studio, especially after seeing how MGM publicity was handling the promotion of his films. He made some studio enemies with his departure, but in view of his upcoming plans, this phased him little; the path ahead led to the achievement of a dream. David O. Selznick was about to form his own production company. Seeing the value of Lewton's talent, Selznick insured him a position at Selznick-International, his newly named independent studio. It was difficult to refuse being part of the Selznick dream, and Lewton was wise to maintain his apprenticeship.

MGM realized the full impact of its loss when *Anna Karenina* and *A Tale of Two Cities* made a combined profit of $4 million. Irving Thalberg's steadily declining health only accentuated the gap left by Selznick's departure.

Selznick knew he would have to work hand-in-hand with United Artists to get Selznick-International Studios off the ground. By 1935, UA had become the releasing company for a wide variety of independent films, including those produced by Samuel Goldwyn, Darryl Zanuck, Howard Hughes, Edward Small, Alexander Korda, Walter Wanger, and many others.

Selznick had little trouble coming up with the $3 million needed to finance his production studio because of his track record. Some of the capital came from smaller investors, including Irving Thalberg, but most of the funding came from John Hay Whitney, president of Pioneer Pictures and a close associate of Merian C. Cooper.

The time was right. Selznick managed to set up a lucrative deal with UA, which was hard-pressed for films since Darryl Zanuck had just pulled his 20th Century Pictures from their roster. Selznick promised to provide 10 films per year for United Artists; in addition, he was appointed chief executive of all UA releases and coordinated the schedules of the number of independent productions released through the studio. Although he fulfilled his responsibilities as chief executive, his 10-film-per-year deal was merely wishful thinking; it would take Selznick five years to deliver his 10 independently produced films.

The RKO-Pathé studios, which had years before been built by pioneer filmmaker Thomas Ince, became the official headquarters for all Selznick-International operations. The front edifice of the white-columned Thomas Ince building became the logo for SIP, Selznick-International Pictures.

Selznick spent the first six months of 1936 working on two lavish costume dramas: *Little Lord Fauntleroy*, another vehicle for Freddie Bartholomew, and *The Garden of Allah*, an exotic romance which ran like a hodgepodge of every cliché imaginable. Although *Fauntleroy*, directed by Jack Conway, was a blatant attempt to duplicate the success of *David Copperfield*, the public was not put off by a second helping of Freddie Bartholomew supported by an expert cast. Whatever credibility *Fauntleroy* established, however, was almost dashed by the leaden opus which followed.

Despite the quality casting of Marlene Dietrich, Charles Boyer, Basil Rathbone, Joseph Schildkraut, and John Carradine, *The Garden of Allah* was in general panned by the critics. Even the novelty of its being the first feature film to use the three-color Technicolor process proved to be little inducement to ticket buyers. However forgettable the film, the irony of its title was not lost on Lewton; during the 1920s, "The Garden of Allah" had been the name of Alla Nazimova's famous Sunset Boulevard estate, a mecca for Bohemian gatherings and alternative life-styles.

It was around the time of the Selznick-produced *Fauntleroy* and *Allah* that Lewton and his wife began rubbing elbows with a vast variety of Hollywood notables and distinguished literati. At the time, the Lewtons lived across the street from William Faulkner. In a 1992 interview, Ruth Lewton told the author: "Mr. Faulkner's daughter and our daughter were very little and became quite close. Our maids would take them down to the beach in Santa Monica Canyon every day. The Faulkners came to dinner at our house, and we would often go there for dinner as well. Mr. Faulkner was a tremendously interesting man, but he was a heavy drinker. He enjoyed my husband, though, and my husband enjoyed him. One late night, though, I remember, Mr. Faulkner's maid came knocking on my door, scared to death, screaming, 'Mr. Lewton! Mr. Lewton! Mr. Faulkner done gone owly!' I tried to calm her down while my husband went to see what he could find out. I was worried that [Faulkner] may have tried to commit suicide. He was an unhappy man, and I thought he might have gone down to the ocean. They got the police and found him two miles away, huddled up in a chicken coop."

In *The Reality of Terror*, Joel E. Siegel informs us, "Although they did not go out a great deal, the Lewtons began to attend the salons of Salka Viertel, where they met Chaplin, Garbo, Mann, Brecht, Zweig, Isherwood, and Auden."

All manner of Hollywood festivities, however, were interrupted on September 14, 1936, when the 37-year-old Irving Thalberg died of pneumonia. Hollywood displayed a sense of grand tragedy rivaled only by the death scene of Thalberg's *Camille* and grieved with a degree of sincerity seldom afforded the death of a Hollywood dignitary. Thalberg had earned everyone's respect in the way he lived his years, resisting a lifetime of impending doom. He may have been the weakest of the litter of Hollywood's wunderkind, but he demonstrated the kind of courage the industry could not resist. Tributes poured in from, among others, Louis B. Mayer ("the finest friend a man could ever have"), Samuel Goldwyn ("my dearest friend"), Darryl Zanuck ("more than any other man, he raised the industry to its present world prestige"), and Cecil B. De Mille ("the greatest conceivable loss to the motion picture industry"). And from David O. Selznick: "Irving Thalberg was beyond any question the greatest individual force for fine pictures." (All quotes are from Bob Thomas's *Thalberg.*)

Perhaps as a result of his heightened sense of mortality—the direct result of Thalberg's demise—Selznick began to develop a sense of urgency in his filmmaking. He was already in the initial stages of a project that would prove to be the biggest blockbuster in movie history. According to Thomas Schatz in *A Genius of the System:*

> [*Gone with the Wind*] first came to Selznick's attention via Kay Brown, SIP's East Coast story editor. In May 1936, a month before its publication, Brown sent Selznick a copy of Mitchell's manuscript and a fifty-seven-page condensation of the novel. "I am absolutely off my nut about this book," she wrote Selznick. "I beg, urge, coax, and plead with you to read it at once." With *The Garden of Allah* still in production, Selznick had no time to read the novel, so he read the condensed version and passed the manuscript to Val Lewton, his West Coast story editor. Lewton dismissed Mitchell's novel as "ponderous trash," but Selznick was taken with the story.

Shortly after Selznick purchased Mitchell's novel, Lewton began to feel an increasingly dislike for his East Coast rival, Kay Brown. His ego was slighted (he had been pushing for an adaptation of Tolstoy's *War and Peace*), but Lewton was usually not prone to broadcast his disgruntlement. Rather, he tended to curb his sentiments, keeping them bottled-up, until he found some surreptitious way of expressing them. William Wright, Selznick's production associate, who, like Lewton, left MGM to continue his work with Selznick at SIP, told Joel E. Siegel an anecdote which the latter recounted in *The Reality of Terror:*

> Wright knew of Lewton's antipathy [toward Selznick's East Coast story editor, Kay Brown], and was surprised to discover that Lewton had met Miss Brown at the railroad station during one of her Hollywood visits, and had moreover presented her with a bouquet of gardenias and a card reading "Welcome to Hollywood." Wright asked Lewton if he had revised his opinion of Miss Brown, but Lewton replied that he liked her less than ever. He explained that the utter banality of the gift of gardenias was only exceeded by the banality of the card's inscription, and that if Miss Brown had any intelligence at all she would know he had no respect for her. Then he removed his coat and showed Wright his necktie. "See this?" he said. "I wore my 'dog puke' tie which I only wear to insult people. Anybody who looks at this tie and doesn't realize that I'm insulting him is a fool anyway." Wright told Daniel O'Shea, Selznick's lawyer, about Lewton's mauve paisley "dog puke" tie; O'Shea liked the story and said he'd ask Lewton about it at their next meeting. Several days later Lewton arrived in O'Shea's office for a business conference, and just as he was about to ask, O'Shea noticed the necktie in question on proud display.

Although *Gone with the Wind* became Selznick's pet project, three years would pass before it would actually hit the big screen. In the meantime, SIP would pave the way with the release of seven carefully crafted productions: *A Star Is Born* (1937), *The Prisoner of Zenda* (1937), *Nothing Sacred* (1937), *The Adventures of Tom Sawyer* (1938), *The Young at Heart* (1938), *Made for Each Other* (1939), and *Intermezzo* (1939), all of which would be released by UA. Selznick quickly came to realize that it took more than one person to run a production studio, however independent that studio may have been. According to Thomas Schatz in *The Genius of the System:*

> [Selznick] could handle the creative end, with his support staff keeping the wheels turning. His essential technicians were art director Lyle Wheeler, editor Hal Kern, and color cameraman Howard Greene. His chief studio administrators were production manager Ray Klune and assistant director Eric Stacey. Story editors Val Lewton and Kay Brown were also important, with Brown keeping Selznick abreast of the East Coast theater and publishing scenes and Lewton acting as an in-house script consultant and story editor, and handling all communications with the Breen office.

The Joseph Breen office was an extension of Will Hays's censorship board. Much of the smoothness of SIP's operations hinged upon the rapport between Lewton and Breen. Lewton's deceptively nonabrasive personality did wonders in opening doors that would have remained closed in the faces of more aggressive emissaries. In Breen, Lewton found an ally, one who would be willing to forego the conventions of his office by slipping Lewton vital bits of information concerning films being made by rival studios, like Warners' own Civil War drama, *Jezebel.*

In assisting with the seven SIP productions released prior to *Gone with the Wind,* Val Lewton gained tremendous experience but was given little acknowledgment for his contributions. Never again did Selznick appoint him to a position as second-unit producer; apparently, he found Lewton too valuable as his "Man Friday" and wanted him close at hand. Perhaps he reasoned that production responsibilities would limit Lewton's capacity as a script consultant/story editor and pull him away from his position as courier of good will between SIP and the Breen office. In spite of his role as Selznick's underling, Lewton made his share of contributions to SIP. According to Joel Siegel in *The Reality of Terror:*

> It was [Lewton] who saw *Intermezzo* at a Los Angeles art theatre and persuaded Selznick to purchase the rights and bring the star, Ingrid Bergman, to Hollywood. It was he who stopped Victor Fleming from shooting a dinner-table set-up in *Gone with the Wind,* in which he had framed Vivian Leigh with two large grapefruit just below and in front of her breasts. It was he who, according to his own account, wrote several scenes for *Gone with the Wind,* including the famous Atlanta depot sequence, the climax of the first half of the

> film. [The scene had been written by three or four different teams of writers but was still not satisfactory to Selnick. As a joke, knowing nobody could ever afford to shoot such a scene, Lewton wrote it to end with the elaborate elevator shot of hundreds of wounded soldiers. Selznick liked it and it went into the film.] And it was he whom Selznick placed outside the men's room at the *Gone with the Wind* preview with a stop-watch to time how long it took men to relieve themselves so that the length of the intermission could be determined.

It was also Lewton who (according to Bob Thomas's recent Selznick biography) directed Selznick's attention to James H. Street's novel, *Letter to the Editor,* which became the inspiration for *Nothing Sacred.* In a 1992 interview with the author, Ruth Lewton confirmed that her husband had a hand in most of the Selznick scripts ("He often wrote part of the scripts. I know he worked on *David Copperfield, Anna Karenina, A Tale of Two Cities*—which was when he met his dear friend, Jacques—*Nothing Sacred* . . . oh, there were so many of them, even *Gone with the Wind.*") All of Lewton's contributions to Selznick scripts remained uncredited.

Despite his relative anonymity, Lewton took pride in his connections with the body of work produced at SIP. But working for Selznick was a taste of heaven and hell for any employee, primarily because of the way Selznick played the game. Although Lewton was vastly underpaid, he felt, with Selznick, a sense of importance. At the time, Selznick was so well regarded in the Hollywood industry that Lewton could envision himself as the unsung hero behind Hollywood's greatest living boy wonder. Such fancies, however, did not put bread on the table. The birth of a son, Val Edwin Lewton (May 23, 1937), further accentuated Lewton's need for a more impressive paycheck.

Lewton's ego wasn't helped by Selznick's high regard for his East Coast story editor, Kay Brown. It was Brown who maneuvered Alfred Hitchcock's emigration to Hollywood, and it was she who played a principal function in bringing him to Selznick. The pairing of Selznick and Hitchcock would become a mixture of water and oil, with both men vying to rise to the top. Selznick's parents had been excessive, living their lives with broad strokes of the brush, encouraging their sons, Myron and David, to adopt a similarly expansive life-style. Hitchcock, on the other hand, lived a life of restriction, his Catholic parents providing the epitome of caution and frugality.

Born in London on August 13, 1899, to William and Emma Whelan Hitchcock, Alfred Joseph Hitchcock found himself a lone child in a strict Catholic family. His father was a poultry dealer and fruit importer, and the family ate a steady diet of potatoes to keep from going hungry. William Hitchcock was rigid in his beliefs and occasionally exhibited a cruel streak, while mother Emma was overbearing and demanding. In 1962 Hitchcock related this incident to François Truffaut: "I must have been about four or five years old. My father sent me to the police station with a note. The chief of police read it and locked me in a cell for five or ten minutes, saying, 'This is what we do to naughty boys.'" Hitchcock claimed the experience scarred him for life. His biographer, Anthony Spoto, in *Dark Side of Genius* informs us: "Asked if he were ever really frightened about anything, Hitchcock would reply simply: 'Always!'" Hitchcock's fears of isolation and darkness—combined with his phobia of being unjustly convicted of a crime—would become essential to his brand of cinema.

Hitchcock's birth roughly coincided with the birth of cinema, and his determination to break into the motion picture business came with the advent of German expressionism. In 1919 *The Cabinet of Caligari* captured the imagination of the young draftsman, and when he heard the next year that Jesse Lasky's Famous Players was opening a studio in nearby Islington, he quit his job and applied for a position in the studio's title department, submitting some of his drawings as evidence of his qualifications. For two years, he worked for the studio, where he quickly became the head of the department. The German directors—Robert Wiene, Fritz Lang, Ernst Lubitsch—became his new sources of inspiration. When the studio folded, it was picked up by another investor, who registered it as the home of Gainsborough Pictures. From 1925 to 1927, Hitchcock directed five films for Gainsborough; his third, *The Lodger,* established his reputation for terror and suspense.

Hitchcock moved to a larger English studio, British International, where from 1927 to 1932, he directed four silent and six sound features, the latter crop including the successful *Blackmail* (1929), *Murder* (1930), and *Rich and Strange* (1932). By 1934, his reputation now preceding him, Hitchcock joined ranks with Gaumont-British pictures, where he directed the six most lauded films of his British period: *The Man Who Knew Too Much* (1934), *The Thirty-Nine Steps* (1935), *Secret Agent* (1935), *Sabotage* (1936), *Young and Innocent* (1937), and *The Lady Vanishes* (1937).

Lewton was not particularly eager to see Hitchcock on the Selznick payroll; part of his reluctance was no doubt colored by Kay Brown's key position in the Hitchcock negotiations. As quoted in Anthony Spoto's *Dark Side of Genius,* Lewton wrote: "I think the Hitchcock-type of story fundamentally wrong, and that we need something better and more substantial than the old-fashioned chase pictures which he turns out when left to his own devices."

When Hitchcock came to America in August 1937, he first went to New York, where he and Kay Brown hit it off so well he stayed for several days at her home, accompanied by both his wife, Alma Reville, and his scenarist, Joan Harrison. Major SIP investor Jock Whitney had been disappointed in Hitchcock's latest film, *Young and Innocent,* and wanted Selznick to hold up negotiations. Kay Brown, however, was so insistent upon obtaining the British director that she encouraged Selznick not to do a thing until he viewed Hitchcock's next film, *The Lady Vanishes.* With Kay Brown, Hitchcock shared his plans for his next production, an adaptation of *Jamaica Inn,* written by a young British novelist named Daphne du Maurier.

Daphne du Maurier was the granddaughter of George du Maurier, the Victorian illustrator and author of the plays *Trilby* (the thriller that added the word "Svengali" to the world's vocabulary) and *Peter Ibbetson.* Continuing a family tradition, Daphne began writing prolifically at an early age, publishing her first novel, *The Loving Spirit,* in 1931 at the age of 25. The setting for the novel was her home, Cornwall, England, and this location became the predominant setting for many of her works.

While *Jamaica Inn* was still in its dream stages and Hitchcock was enjoying the remainder of those pleasant first days in Kay Brown's Long Island home, he let Brown see a manuscript of du Maurier's latest novel, *Rebecca,* a dark romance which would have made the Brontë sisters proud. She was overwhelmed by the potential of the property.

Brown sent Selznick the *Rebecca* manuscript, and he forwarded it to the story department. After they assessed the property, they sent Selznick a synopsis of the novel. One thing was certain: a faithful adaptation would cause friction with the Breen office. In the novel's dénouement, the protagonist, Max de Winter, remains unconvicted for the crime of killing his fiendish first wife, Rebecca, and he presumably goes on to live a fruitful life with his second wife (who remains unnamed). However, the most pervasive fetish held by the Breen and Hays offices during the late 1930s was the notion that every film should end with "just and moral retribution." Working within such strictures would prove a challenge for Lewton, Selznick's key Breen office go-between.

By June 1938, Lewton and Brown were chosen to collaborate (each from their separate headquarters) upon an alternative ending. Brown suggested that Rebecca commit suicide, while Lewton tried to sell the "mental anguish as moral retribution" angle to the Breen office, accepting Brown's alternative only as a backup if all else failed.

When Hitchcock brought the galleys of the still unpublished du Maurier novel to Hollywood, Selznick forwarded them to Lewton. In *The Genius of the System,* Thomas Schatz tells us:

> At that point Lewton had only read the reader's synopsis, and his attitude toward the project changed quite literally overnight once he read the novel. The following morning Lewton reported to Selznick that du Maurier's novel was "superb"—far better than anything indicated in the readers' reports. . . . Selznick received another memo from Val Lewton. "The more I think of it," wrote the SIP story editor, "the more I feel that we have got ourselves a tiger. It is as good as *Jane Eyre* and I think that women will be wild about it."

In response to Lewton's constant urging, Selznick finally got around to reading *Rebecca* himself, but by that time the novel had already been published and was on its way to becoming a best-seller. Because of his reticence in purchasing the property forthright, Selznick now found himself in a bidding war with rival Samuel Goldwyn. In September, Brown closed the deal with du Maurier at $50,000, the same price spent for the property rights of *Gone with the Wind.*

In November, Selznick sold the *Rebecca* rights to Orson Welles for a "Mercury Theatre of the Air" radio adaptation, which came on the heels of Welles's infamous *War of the Worlds* broadcast.

Selznick sent a short letter to Kay Brown, suggesting an interesting bit of casting that would never come about: "I am very interested in the idea of having Nazimova play Mrs. Danvers [the menacing housekeeper of *Rebecca*]. She had previously communicated her desire to play this role to me through George Cukor. . . . I think that Nazimova is one of the greatest actresses in the world and, despite her accent, I think she would be magnificent" (Richard Behlmer, *Memos from Selznick*).

Hitchcock took a flat fee of $5,000 for working out the *Rebecca* screenplay, the first draft of which was finished by April 1939. Hitchcock wanted to begin production in July, even though *Gone with the Wind* was scheduled to wind up its shooting around that time, going almost round the clock, with three separate production units rotating about the SIP studio.

With *Gone with the Wind*'s busy production barreling to a conclusion, the initial days of *Rebecca*'s production would have been strained even if Selznick had been happy with Hitchcock's treatment. But he was not. In a memo to Hitchcock, one which ran several thousand words, Selznick announced: "I am shocked and disappointed beyond words by the treatment of *Rebecca.* I regard it as a distorted and vulgarized version of a provenly successful work." Hitchcock's script (written in collaboration with Joan Harrison) included a more menacing Max de Winter and a spunkier heroine. Hitchcock acceded to Selznick's wishes and called for a revision.

Surprisingly, it was Samuel Goldwyn who influenced the shaping of the first Selznick/Hitchcock collaboration. After he had lost his bid for the *Rebecca* rights, Goldwyn was so determined to make a great Gothic romance that he rushed Emily Brontë's *Wuthering Heights* into production. Selznick soon made up his mind that Lawrence Olivier, cast as the quintessential Heathcliff in Goldwyn's *Wuthering Heights,* would make the ideal Max de Winter. Hitchcock had seen *Wuthering Heights* and, knowing Olivier would play a similarly dark hero in *Rebecca,* he patterned much of the Max de Winter character upon Olivier's earlier Gothic role. He remained, however, within the framework of du Maurier's intent in order to mollify Selznick's demands for fidelity to the novel.

In late June, Hitchcock handed over a revised treatment of *Rebecca,* assuring Selznick of its fidelity. That same week Selznick closed shooting for *Gone with the Wind.* He hired playwright Robert E. Sherwood to turn Hitchcock's revised treatment into a script. Just as he had done with the casting of Scarlet O'Hara, Selznick took time in his well-publicized search for *Rebecca*'s leading lady. Although he considered Margaret Sullavan, Anne Baxter, Anita Louise, Bette Davis, Loretta Young, Joan Crawford, even Vivian Leigh, for the skittish second Mrs. de Winter, he chose the relatively unknown Joan Fontaine (the sister of actress Olivia De Havillnd, who was also considered for the role).

When *Rebecca* went into production in September 1939, Selznick became disturbed by Hitchcock's work habits. The celebrated English director preferred to edit "in the camera" (having already conceived—in minute detail—every shot and angle before shooting started), and this left a hands-on producer like Selznick with very little to do. His original intent had been to make *Rebecca* a modest effort, a breather in the aftermath of *Wind*, but Selznick's perfectionism prohibited *Rebecca*'s "quickie" stature. He wanted his fingerprints deep into the finished work. He made sure that all of *Rebecca*'s ads included: "By the maker of *Gone with the Wind!*"

In October, Lewton helped Selznick and Hitchcock fine tune the script's ending with the additional implication that Rebecca had provoked Max to kill her because she knew she was dying of cancer. Lewton, in conference with the Breen office, managed to have Rebecca's self-destructive intent worked into the film. Again, Lewton showed his tact and expertise in handling censor Joseph Breen and his associate, Geoffrey Sherlock. Somehow Lewton worked wonders with these powerful men, causing them to cooperate remarkably well and respond in a manner that made one believe they wished to assist SIP, rather than stand in its way.

Production for *Rebecca* closed on November 20, 1939, nearly a month behind schedule and more than $400,000 over budget. Selznick's preoccupation with *Wind* had given Hitchcock the room to work at his preferred pace. After some trimming of Hitchcock's own rough cut and some additional retakes, *Rebecca* was ready for a sneak preview in February.

Just before *Rebecca*'s general release, Selznick got the ball rolling on a project very much in the same vein: Charlotte Brontë's *Jane Eyre*, the novel that in fact gave du Maurier her main source of inspiration for *Rebecca*. Lewton had done some demographic research on the popularity of classic novels and discovered that *Jane Eyre* ranked high, not only in his own heart, but also on the list of most-read classics in public libraries. Lewton had evaluated Orson Welles's Mercury Theater radio adaptation of the Brontë classic, and though he liked much of what he heard, he believed Orson Welles was all wrong for the part of Rochester: "far below his very good rendering of *Rebecca* . . . Welles played [Rochester] as if [he] were the Hunchback of Notre Dame" (Thomas Schatz, *The Genius of the System*).

The way it turned out, *Rebecca* (released in the early spring, 1940) preceded *Gone with the Wind* in general release, the bigger film not making it to many areas until the midspring and summer. *Intermezzo* (released in late 1939) was also a huge hit, one whose popularity continued to guarantee theater play dates through the first months of 1940. Selznick may have been guilty of unrealistic expectations in promising 10 films per year, but he had indeed provided Hollywood with his own retelling of the David and Goliath myth. According to Thomas Schatz in *The Genius of the System:*

> In 1940 SIP had only three pictures in release—*Wind, Rebecca,* and *Intermezzo*—while the five major studios along with Columbia and Universal were releasing roughly one feature per week. But none of those massive production companies took in anywhere near the $10 million in net profits that Selznick International earned that year. Only MGM, at $8.7 million, was even close, and half of its profits came from the deal with SIP to distribute *Wind.*

Gone with the Wind won a record-breaking 10 Academy Awards, including Best Picture of 1939, and an Irving Thalberg Award for Selznick. *Rebecca* won Best Picture the following year. Selznick's gambling had finally paid off; he won the biggest jackpot in Hollywood history. In 1940 there was no motion picture producer more successful than David O. Selznick.

Although he had become Hollywood's newfound king, one whose efforts had eclipsed even those of the beloved Thalberg, Selznick would not maintain his throne for very long. Schatz tells us, "The enormous effort he put into *Wind* and *Rebecca* left him physically, mentally, and emotionally spent, and the two pictures did in SIP as well. As the profits from *Wind* and *Rebecca* poured in, it became evident that the company was the victim of its own success. Without either a massive facility or a full program of productions, the profits could not be amortized, reinvested, or otherwise defrayed, so the tax bite was enormous." By August, SIP investors decided to dissolve the company and have their profits be taxed as capital gains rather than corporate or personal income. Selznick announced to the press that he was taking indefinite leave from active production.

Witnessing the dramatic rise and fall of SIP was a learning experience for Val Lewton, a man who had dreams of being a film producer in the Selznick mold. By tagging along with Selznick for eight years, he had seen many sides of the film production business: how a major studio like MGM could interfere with productions, how an independent enterprise could vault a film producer to a supreme position over the major studios, and how too much independence became its own unwieldy burden, a burden capable of breaking the back of even the most powerful producer in the industry. Now that Selznick announced an indefinite leave from active production, Lewton's career opportunities seemed even bleaker than before.

After Selznick liquidated SIP, Lewton still had a job at David O. Selznick Productions, a company founded the same year SIP went under. But the new company, as lucrative an enterprise as it would become, was merely Selznick's way of keeping a hand in the business. In many ways, Selznick's new venture was an attempt to best his Hollywood agent brother, Myron, at his own game. Although SIP was gone, Selznick still held a handful of pending contracts. He had under exclusive contract stars like Joan Fontaine, Ingrid Bergman, Gregory Peck, Dorothy McGuire, and Gene Kelly. He also had his ace-in-the-hole director, Alfred Hitchcock, as well as top-of-the-line cameramen like George Barnes and Stanley Cortez. While still not actually producing pictures, Selznick would continue to draw contracts for new talent like actress Phyllis Walker (later to become Jennifer Jones) and British director Robert Stevenson. David O. Selznick Productions became primarily a "rental" service for those held under contract, the company reaping cash rewards that actually exceeded the salary Selznick would pay if his contractees were making films for him.

For example, Hitchcock signed a multipicture contract with Selznick guaranteeing the English director a minimum of $40,000 per picture, which was a good rate in early 1939. Following the *Rebecca* fanfare, however, Selznick contracted Hitchcock to independent producer Walter Wanger, who was using UA as his distributor. As a result of this transaction, Hitchcock made *Foreign Correspondent* ("In Arrangement with David O. Selznick" of course), and Selznick, charging Wanger an amount of $5,000 per week for Hitchcock's services, wound up with a purse equal to Hitchcock's $40,000. Within the next three years, Selznick assigned Hitchcock to RKO (*Mr. and Mr. Smith* and *Suspicion*), Universal (*Saboteur* and *Shadow of a Doubt*), and 20th Century–Fox (*Lifeboat*). Each time he made a bundle.

With the end of the Depression, Hollywood was willing to pay top dollar for what it wanted. And what it wanted was part of Selznick's glory. The "Selznick touch" would be associated with any film bearing his signature and "In Arrangement with David O. Selznick" followed the name of many a Selznick contractee appearing in a wide variety of out-of-house productions. Since the Selznick name signified quality, this practice was considered highly marketable, and the major studios were only too pleased to include Selznick's name in opening credits as a form of endorsement.

Another feature of Selznick's new company was the packaging of ready-to-go productions, complete with star, director, cameraman, and film property rights, sometimes even a script. This is precisely what was done with *Jane Eyre*. Selznick bought the rights to the novel, cast contract player Joan Fontaine, assigned Robert Stevenson as director, W.L. Pereira as production designer, and sold the whole package to 20th Century–Fox for a quarter of a million dollars. Once he sold the package, Selznick also had an option to become an unofficial adviser for the production.

Selznick felt some dismay when *Jane Eyre* went into production in 1942 and Orson Welles took on the role of Rochester. Welles's obligation was merely to play the character, but his uncredited influence (coscripting, codirecting, and having a hand in producing the film) was considerable. The presence of actress Agnes Moorehead, composer Bernard Herrmann, and scriptwriter John Houseman—all members of Mercury Theatre Productions—is a further indication that Orson Welles had a far greater impact upon the production than Selznick would have liked. Welles's aggressive involvement tended to defeat the entire purpose of Selznick's prepackaging process.

By 1942 Val Lewton had little to gain from Selznick's new order. His jack-of-all-trades role resembled that of a lackey, albeit a valuable one. Lewton was hardly a known commodity in Hollywood, and not being under any sort of contract, he could not be subject to Selznick's intrastudio transactions. He was paid a weekly salary, and one of the things he hated most was to approach his boss for a raise. He may not have been the kind of man it took to become a Thalberg, a Zanuck, or a Selznick, but then again, he would never discover what capabilities he possessed as a film producer if he continued putting wraps on film packages.

Lewton's last major job before leaving Selznick was working on the *Jane Eyre* package. Although the details of Lewton's leave-taking will become clearer in later chapters, for now let it suffice that after having spent eight years as Selznick's apprentice, Lewton was about to take the biggest gamble of his career. Selznick had gained everything by taking risks, and Lewton was finally ready to follow suit.

Selznick was unhappy to see Lewton go, but understood his desire to advance himself. They wished each other well and remained on cordial terms for the rest of their lives. However, one can only wonder what crossed Lewton's mind when, four years later, in the Selznick-produced 1946 epic, *Duel in the Sun,* he discovered his cinematic namesake in the film's evil lothario, Lewton McCanless, played Gregory Peck. Lewton signed with RKO, the studio his boss had put on the Hollywood map; indeed, had it not been for David O. Selznick, it is unlikely that there would still have been an RKO studio in 1942. RKO needed rescue again, and in his own way, Lewton would be the one to save the studio from bankruptcy. Although his time in the spotlight would be short, his few moments of near-glory were enough to alter the course of cinema history.

Lewton's apprenticeship may have had its share of thorny paths and unrealized ambitions, but the value of the experience cannot be denied. Had Lewton not worked those eight years under Selznick, it is doubtful that he would have been offered the position that awaited him at RKO. Furthermore, Lewton's films are precisely what they are because of his Selznick experience. He learned the ropes of film production from Hollywood's most illustrious boy wonder and, while Lewton was not nearly as overtly aggressive as his senior partner, he would nonetheless follow Selznick's example as a hands-on producer. He would develop a "Lewton touch," a "B" scale version of the Selznick signature, and he would take the same refined, literate approach in his filmmaking. Like Selznick, he would provide his films with strong female roles; sometimes his films would even seem to borrow ideas from the Selznick pictures. For instance:

• The climactic scene in *A Star Is Born,* when Norman Maine (March) commits suicide by walking into the ocean, would make something of a reappearance in *I Walked with a Zombie.*

• The grave-robbing scene in *The Adventures of Tom Sawyer* would, loosely speaking, be expanded to its own feature in *The Body Snatcher.*

• *Gone with the Wind*'s panorama of the dead would turn up, on a meager scale, in the beginning of *Isle of the Dead.*

• *Rebecca*'s first-person female voice-over would find its unmistakable parallel in *I Walked with a Zombie.*

• *Anna Karenina*'s bleak ending would transform itself to the dark fatality of *The Seventh Victim*'s conclusion.

Surely there are other such Selznick connections to be found in Lewton's body of work. Although Selznick's name is seldom associated with horror film, he did have a morbid side, and this was not lost on a novice producer who would soon portray death with a similar degree of unflinching fear and respect.

It is fitting that Orson Welles should have taken over the *Jane Eyre* project that Lewton helped design, because Welles was the boy wonder who, quite inadvertently, cleared Lewton's path to RKO. As we shall see, Orson Welles was a significant piece of the Lewton puzzle.

FOUR

Out of Left Field: The Orson Welles Connection

When George Orson Welles was two years old, his mother Beatrice read to him from Charles Lamb's *Tales from Shakespeare*. Within a year, the young child, not satisfied with the watered-down versions, demanded that the Bard's plays be read in their entirety. By now the precocious tot was familiar with the musical scores of Heifetz, Casals, Wallenstein, and Mischa Elman. His Shakespeare diet had also been supplemented with readings from Whitman, Rossetti, Tennyson, Keats, and Swinburne. After learning the alphabet, the boy taught himself to read.

Before turning four, George Orson Welles became a professional actor in the Chicago Opera Company, where he played several child roles. His tremendous size and weight began to strain the muscles of those performers whose on-stage tasks included carrying him about. At the age of four, he wrote, designed, and produced original plays for his puppet theater, presenting them to family and friends. He hated school. At seven, Welles considered himself an authority on poetry and drama; he had all of the major speeches in *King Lear* memorized. After convincing his father to buy him a typewriter, he began writing papers and critiques—everything from the history of world drama to an assessment of Nietzche's *Thus Spake Zarathustra.* At 10, his IQ registering 146, he became the subject of a nationally known psychological study. The next year, he "eloped" with nine-year-old Marjorie Watson, the daughter of the family with whom he was then living. He had begun drinking wine at the age of five, had consumed mixed drinks three years later, and by age 10 had taken up smoking cigars.

Welles wanted desperately to be an adult. When he presented himself in public, he applied makeup to his face, adding hollows to his cheeks and creases to his forehead. Attempting to add further credibility to this affectation of age, he lowered his voice and feigned the resonant tones of someone years older. His physical form seemed to follow suit, adhering to the demands of his desires; by the time he was 13 he was already over six feet tall and weighed over 180 pounds. The next year he was nearly arrested when, posing as a Greek scholar, he sold a mainly plagiarized translation of a Sophocles play for $300.

Of course Welles was a misfit among his peers. When he was 10, he would bring his theater makeup to school. One day, when an older boy punched him in the nose, Welles ran into the bathroom and, using gore makeup, turned his face into a bloody mess. He then confronted the bully, who ran home screaming at the spectacle of his victim's gore-smeared features.

Despite his youthful eccentricities, Welles had his coterie of admirers, both male and female, who were held spellbound by his storytelling abilities. Some adults voiced complaints of how he terrified the local children with ghost stories and horror tales. Yet the children kept coming back for more.

Orson Welles's family lineage was a notable one, with descendents dating back to the Mayflower's John and Priscilla Alden. His father, Richard Hodgdon Welles, was a lucrative inventor, engineer, and businessman who owned factories and hotels and manufactured one of the earliest auto lights. Orson's mother, Beatrice Ives Welles, was not only a respected and talented musician, but also a vehement advocate of women's rights. Beatrice had a wide circle of friends and admirers—many of them celebrities cultured in the fine arts. Richard and Beatrice Welles settled in Kenosha, Illinois, where their two sons, Richard Jr. (1904) and George Orson (1915), were born.

The home where the Welles children grew up was a turbulent one. Their father, Richard, eschewed the high arts, preferring popular culture to the esoteric tastes of his cultured wife. While Beatrice expressed an interest in the avant-garde, her husband's tastes reflected what was to her a more common—perhaps vulgar—set of interests. Beatrice loved art museums, classical music, and the opera; Richard favored jazz, the stage (legitimate theater as well as vaudeville), and the motion picture (which, by Orson's birth, had just come of age with Griffith's *Birth of a Nation*). Such differences in taste between man and wife became a considerable source of friction in the Welles household. While Richard held fast to his love of films, Beatrice campaigned against them, hoping to have them banned for their allegedly immoral content.

Unfortunately for this married couple, their incompatibility did not stop with their disparate cultural interests. During the Prohibition, Richard's affection for the bottle led him to frequent a number of illegal drinking establishments, both local and distant, where the effects of alcohol, often as not, led to an adulterous escapade. Invariably, Beatrice would hear about it.

But all familial disruptions aside, what had the most profound impact upon Orson Welles's childhood was his firsthand knowledge of death. One of the boy's earliest memories was the lingering illness and agonizing death of his aunt, Lucy Ives, who, living in their guest room, suffered a long bout with cancer. Her screams of agony, filling the entire house, gave young Orson a terrifying introduction to death.

A youthful Russian-born physician, Dr. Maurice Bernstein, had been called in to look after Mrs. Ives. Bernstein's frequent visits brought him close to the family, and he took a particular interest in the young prodigy, Orson. Becoming something of a fixture in the Welles household, Bernstein began making advances toward Beatrice. Relishing their like-minded cultural interests, the two of them eventually became lovers. Aware of Beatrice's skills as a talented pianist, Bernstein encouraged her to break into the musical society of Chicago. His renowned reputation within high society opened many doors, and Beatrice began giving recitals.

Meanwhile, Richard's drinking escalated. With the advent of her modest musical success, Beatrice left her husband and took Orson to live with her in a classy Chicago apartment, at which point Dr. Bernstein became Orson's unofficial guardian, a position he would maintain for years to come.

In 1924, when Orson had turned nine, his mother, stricken by a severe case of hepatitis contracted the year before, would talk to her youngest son from her death bed. According to Charles Higham in his *Orson Welles: The Rise and Fall of an American Genius:*

> In the large and handsome apartment at 150 East Superior Street, Beatrice spoke to him of her approaching end, quoting Shakespeare, her shining eyes appearing dark by the light of the candles on his birthday cake. Eyes that had been green were now almost black with suffering; her flesh was yellow and flabby with sickness. She told Orson to blow out all the candles on the cake, and as he did so, for there was no other light in the room, it became utterly dark. In this charged and symbolic way, she told him what death was, and he may never have recovered from that terrifying moment.

Years later Welles would confess that he never forgave himself for not making a particular wish—that his mother's life be spared—with the customary blowing out of birthday candles.

Welles would later claim that his paternal grandmother, Mary Head Welles (a self-avowed witch with a great interest in Aleister Crowley), put a curse on his parents' marriage. Indeed, there was ample evidence that Orson's parents lived a cursed existence.

Although there are conflicting accounts of Richard Welles's death (one that he committed suicide, another that he had drank himself to death), the coroner's report lists the death as a case of chronic mythocarditis and nephritis. Welles was 15 at the time. He later declared that his grandmother had performed satanic rites at his father's funeral.

With the premature passing of his aunt, mother, and father, it should not surprise us that Orson Welles's career in theater, radio, and film should reflect a morbid fascination with death.

In the summer of 1931, the 16-year-old Welles journeyed to Ireland, where in Dublin he gained a foothold in the Irish theater. His first night, playing the Duke in *Jew Suss,* was nearly a disaster, but so intense was his eccentric performance that he received good notices. In his death scene, the desperate young actor, looking for any way to salvage what he believed to be a fiasco, deliberately took a tumble down a set of steps. The audience was so impressed by his dangerous-looking (and entirely unplanned) plunge that they gave him a standing ovation. Thus begins Welles's career as one of the performing arts' most flamboyant risk-takers.

Success followed success in a number of productions, Welles all the time gaining experience in a wide variety of roles. With his fascination for the macabre, he took a surprising number of roles that are relevant to aficionados of dark fantasy. After receiving good notices in *The Dead Ride Fast,* Welles went on to play Duke Lamberto in *Death Takes a Holiday.* He gave such a startling performance as the Ghost in *Hamlet* that the critical praises he garnered were heard across the Atlantic.

Returning to the States, Welles found work in a number of different theatrical companies, his more macabre roles including Svengali in du Maurier's *Trilby,* the lead in Marlowe's *Doctor Faustus,* as well as the lead in *Ten Million Ghosts,* the latter an apocalyptic vision of a dark future foreshadowing the development of the atomic bomb. By this time, he was also writing his own plays and taking an ever-growing part in direction and production. His first full-length production as a playwright was *Bright Lucifer,* which included a major character who was unhappy about being typecast in horror movies.

In 1934 Welles also made a short film called *Hearts of Age,* which was influenced by Jean Cocteau's film *Blood of a Poet.* Inspired in part by the early 1930s Hollywood horror boom, *Hearts of Age* boasted a Caligariesque flair and provided images of grave-stones, tombs, lighted candles, and skulls. Evidently, the German expressionism that permeated Hollywood's early 1930s horror cycle held a firm grip upon Welles's imagination.

Proof of this could be found in a particularly significant Orson Welles stage production, one which not only raised the eyebrows (and no doubt dropped the jaws) of every theater critic in New York City, but also caught the attention of theater critics across the nation. We speak of Welles's bizarre 1936 production of *Macbeth,* presented on stage in Harlem.

By this time Welles had joined forces with John Houseman, the two of them collaborating on ways to develop their own theater group, one which would eventually be dubbed "The Mercury Players." The Harlem production of *Macbeth* was a daring venture, but it met with resounding applause, heralding Welles as a major creative force in the theater world.

What set it apart from other Shakespeare interpretations was that the production was an all-black voodoo variation of the Bard's classic, set in Haiti. It is likely that Welles had been influenced by William B. Seabrook's 1929 book about Haitian voodoo, *The Magic Island,* as well as its cinematic follow-up,

Hollywood's 1932 low-budget horror sleeper, *White Zombie*. In *Citizen Welles*, biographer Frank Brady informs us: "Welles visualized this *Macbeth* with voodoo priestesses as the witches and scenes that would capture the frenzy and magic of the occult, combining the rhythms of beating drums, blood, and mayhem, an expressionistic combination of the shadows and violence and chantings of Haiti, Scotland, and Manhattan all rolled into one."

For this production Welles also experimented with chiaroscuro-styled stage lighting, long before this expressionistic technique became a regular staple in 1940s film noir. Biographer Charles Higham further describes Welles's voodoo–*Macbeth*: "Again and again, the director [Welles] emphasized the corruptions of power; the atmosphere of thunder, lightning, jungle, mountain, and witchcraft evoked a world in which everything was saturated with evil."

To insure a degree of verisimilitude, Welles hired a troupe of dancers from the west coast of Africa. Among them was a dwarf named Abdul, acquired for his expertise in witchcraft and voodoo. Abdul, sporting gold and diamond teeth, was a genuine witchdoctor, and Welles hired him to make the voodoo ritual as authentic as possible. On the first day of rehearsal, Abdul demanded the use of 12 live goats. When Welles inquired as to their use, Abdul answered that their skins were needed to make "devil drums." Welles complied; the goats were obtained, slaughtered, skinned, and turned into drums. A backstage legend soon followed: anyone touching the drums would be doomed. The story spread past the stage doors and was even mentioned in local papers. When a reluctant stagehand moved a drum, shortly thereafter he fell from some scaffolding and broke his neck, escalating the notoriety of the already controversial production.

Incorporating voodoo witchcraft into a play that already had an infamous reputation for mishap only heightened backstage superstitions. Percy Hammond of the *Herald Times* wrote a scathing (and rather racist) review of the production. Abdul approached Welles, asking him, "You want we make beriberi on this bad man?" Welles may have believed it a joke, but he offhandedly answered in the affirmative; Abdul then assured Welles that Hammond would be dead in 23 hours. As biographer Frank Brady reports (in *Citizen Welles*):

> After the performance, as Welles left the theater, he noticed that the drumming by the witch doctors continued, and there were later reports throughout Harlem that it went on all through the night. Hammond did not die twenty-three hours later; however, he did contract pneumonia. Within forty-eight hours, as predicted by the men of magic, he was dead. Welles has said that on reflection the story is "hard to believe, but it is circumstancially true," and its accuracy has been corroborated by journalists and theater people many times over the years.

Whatever manner of bad luck may be associated with it, Welles's *Macbeth* brought just the kind of publicity critics and gossips thrive upon. And one day

Welles's concept—a voodoo variation of a literary source—would provide the impetus for a Val Lewton film.

Despite his high profile in stage productions and his more than passing interest in motion pictures, Orson Welles found in radio a medium well suited to his sonorous, highly theatrical voice. An early appearance on NBC radio's production of *Panic,* a Depression drama, brought him the right kind of recognition. The national broadcast elevated his reputation, and Welles continued in radio, his career soaring from the exposure. After a stint with the news-oriented *March of Time,* his voice was soon to become familiar to the American public via the success of a revamped version of *The Shadow.* The new leading character, Lamont Cranston (played by Welles), would by 1937 become a national hero. At the same time that he did his weekly radio shows, Welles continued working on the stage, at times having only minutes to spare in traveling between theater and broadcast studio.

By the beginning of 1937, Welles possessed a working schedule so tight one would have thought he enlisted the aid of a doppelganger. Now, at the age of 22, his radio career had already reached unprecedented heights. He was appearing weekly on both *The Shadow* and *The March of Time,* making guest appearances in classical plays broadcast on Federal Theater Radio, voicing commercials, reading poetry over the air, reading passages of the Bible on a CBS program, appearing in "Roses and Drums" (a weekly Civil War series), and narrating (as well as performing in) the "Wonder Show" series. Apart from this, he was appearing several times a week on stage in *Doctor Faustus,* functioning as its director and star, and he commuted to Chicago once a week to do a radio show broadcast from there. In the midst of this impossible schedule, he still managed to find some spare time to invest in the planning of forthcoming projects.

His megalomaniacal ambitions aside, Welles did turn down a number of notable offers, particularly those which came from the motion picture industry. Warner Bros. wanted him to play Friar Tuck or King Richard in their upcoming Michael Curtiz/Errol Flynn opus, *The Adventures of Robin Hood,* but Welles, not quite ready for Hollywood, declined. One of the more fascinating Hollywood offers he received, as far as the story of Val Lewton is concerned, was that which came from David Selznick. In 1937 Selznick wanted Welles as the head of his story department, a prospect that would have put Val Lewton in a highly precarious position. In *Citizen Welles,* Frank Brady describes the proposed offer in no uncertain terms:

> Welles would be given the power (although not unlimited) to select new properties and to adapt, or assign adaptations of, novels, short stories, and plays. The idea of Welles becoming one of Selznick's directors or actors was not entirely ruled out for sometime in the future, but it was implicit that Selznick's interest in Welles was literary and editorial: he saw him neither

> behind nor in front of a camera, but in an office, making deals, securing rights, and transforming classical stories into money-making films.

Although Welles was flattered by Selznick's offer, we can be grateful that he refused. The magnitude of the audience he was able to captivate on radio was staggering and the power Welles wielded over the airwaves was heady stuff indeed; he was not yet ready to give it up.

By the next year, in addition to two new radio series (including *First Person Singular,* which he produced, directed, and starred in), Welles's reputation gained even higher ground with his similarly multifaceted involved in the "Mercury Theatre on the Air" series, again in collaboration with John Houseman. In the two mentioned programs, Welles presented a wide variety of literary works, among them Dickens's *A Tale of Two Cities,* Brontë's *Jane Eyre,* Conrad's *Heart of Darkness,* Stevenson's *Treasure Island,* and an adaptation of Saki's ghost story, "The Open Window."

Welles also reappeared onstage, coproducing, directing, and starring in a number of ambitious stage productions, including Shaw's *Heartbreak House* (for which the 23-year-old Welles, playing an octagenarian, would make the cover of *Time*), William Gillette's *Too Much Johnson,* George Buechner's *Danton's Death,* and William Archer's *The Green Goddess.*

But between 1938 and 1939, Welles's largest coup would be the reputation he garnered through his radio exposure, his wide variety of radio adaptations of literary works (broadcast coast-to-coast) during this time accounting for no less than 60 separate productions (which he produced, directed, and starred in).

Welles's production of Bram Stoker's *Dracula* satisfied the most jaded of horror fans. With the emphasis on audience imagination, many found the effect of Welles's radio adaptation to be superior to that of the 1931 Bela Lugosi film. In *Dracula,* Welles supplied the voices for both Jonathan Harker and the Count, a difficult task as the two characters played off one another in the opening scenes. Frank Brady, in *Citizen Welles,* tells us: "Welles as Jonathan Harker was convincing. As Count Dracula, however, he was masterful."

Of course the most infamous broadcast of that or any radio season was yet to come. Welles's decision to adapt the H.G. Wells novel, *The War of the Worlds,* for his CBS "Mercury Theatre on the Air" radio show resulted in a broadcast that would soon ensnare the imagination, and in many cases the rational thinking, of an entire nation.

After scrapping an earlier script for "War of the Worlds," Welles enlisted the aid of lawyer-turned-playwright Howard Koch for a revision, all within six days of the scheduled broadcast. Welles wanted a modernized and localized version to replace the original draft which had been faithful to the British setting of the Wells novel. The script would be in a state of continual revision as each day passed, changes being made even minutes before the broadcast.

Taking their lead from a recent radio play called "Air Raid," Welles and Koch developed a script that mocked reality by simulating a program of dancehall music only to have it interrupted by a series of emergency news bulletins detailing a Martian attack. Upon first being given the assignment, Howard Koch closed his eyes and lowered his pencil point until it touched the map of New Jersey laid out before him, and as chance would have it, the authentic small community of Grovers Mill was targeted as the Martians' first area of attack.

Thus begins the inception of a radio program that would make the front pages of every daily newspaper in the nation. According to a study made by Princeton University shortly after the notorious broadcast (as reported in the ABC television series "Our World"), six million listeners had heard portions of "War of the Worlds," and an approximate one million had believed the broadcast to be real.

Although reams have already been written about the broadcast, a brief glimpse at this remarkable case of audience manipulation is significant to our study. A broadcast which terrified listeners through aural suggestion—with imagination serving as the major special effect—is indeed relevant to an understanding of Val Lewton's fear-the-dark techniques.

On Sunday, October 30, 1938, Orson Welles downed a bottle of pineapple juice and stepped up to the podium. It was 7:58 P.M. The Mercury Player had been rehearsing for eight hours, and there was no turning back.

After the CBS announcer's introduction and 20 seconds of the show's theme music, courtesy of the Bernard Herrmann orchestra, Welles voiced his prologue: "We know now that in the early years of the twentieth century this world was being watched closely by intelligences greater than man's and yet as mortal as his own." This was followed by a mock weather report and then a few minutes of dance music before the interruption of an emergency "news" bulletin concerning "gas explosions from the planet Mars" and a short time later, a report from Princeton Observatory of a crashed meteorite of sizeable proportions that had fallen at nearby Grovers Mill, New Jersey. The meteor, it was said, probably had no connection with earlier reported gas explosions, and the program of dance music was resumed "in progress."

By this time it was 8:12, and a vast audience of radio listeners had just tuned in to the Welles broadcast; a huge portion of station-switchers had been listening to NBC's very popular Edgar Bergen/Charlie McCarthy program and, as was their custom, went dial searching when Bergen and McCarthy introduced "this week's musical guest" (who, for the record, happened to be Nelson Eddy). When NBC listeners switched over to CBS, the Welles's broadcast was in one of its "dance music" phases. The Hooper rating system concluded that some four million people switched to CBS to hear the dance music suddenly interrupted by an authentic-sounding newscaster, direct from Wilmuth Farm in Grovers Mill, describing the projectile that had landed, half buried, in a pasture. Soon the purported newscast announced that the top of projectile had begun to unscrew and that some sort of strange creature was emerging. In *Citizen Welles,* Frank Brady tells us: "The reporter, with great dramatic sincerity, continued to describe what he saw then, his voice rising in terror as he screamed into the microphone that the whole field had burst into fire. Then, mysteriously the eyewitness description suddenly stopped, 'due to circumstances beyond our control.'"

In *Orson Welles: The Rise and Fall of an American Genius,* Charles Higham gives a pithy account of the listeners' reactions:

> Thousands panicked. In Newark, New Jersey, twenty families fled their homes, covering their heads with towels and pressing handkerchiefs to their faces. In New York City several hundred people jammed railroad stations and bus terminals in search of an immediate exit from the city. One woman called up a terminal to obtain a schedule, screaming, "Hurry, please, the world is coming to an end!"
>
> In Harlem hundreds more swept into the churches, seeking sanctuary and calling for prayer because of "the end of the world." One woman described how she ran up to her roof to look for signs in the sky and in her anxiety almost plunged to her death when she slipped and fell. In Rhode Island people stormed the switchboard of *The Providence Journal.* Electric light companies were asked to disconnect all power so the Martians would have no light to guide them. In Pittsburgh one man found his wife in the bathroom, holding a poison bottle and yelling, "I'd rather die this way than that!" As far away as San Francisco switchboards were swamped, and one woman shouted over the line to her local operator, "How can I volunteer to stop this awful thing?"
>
> In Birmingham, Alabama, people rushed into the streets en masse; at one college the women in the sorority houses, weeping and trembling over the broadcast, lined up at the telephones to speak to their parents or other loved ones for the last time. The streets leading from almost every city in New England were filled with refugee cars. Parties stopped dead as the hysteria spread. No one seems to have listened to the end of the broadcast, when Welles explained that a dramatic presentation was all it was.

The aftermath of this broadcast brought forth a deluge of repercussions. The press condemned the irresponsibility of the heretofore illustrious CBS radio network for allowing such a prank to occur. The Federal Communications Commission even got into the act, and rumors of a possible disciplinary action were being tossed about.

But CBS had covered itself; they had, after all, listed the "War of the Worlds" broadcast in all the newspapers and announcements at the beginning and end of the broadcast confirmed that the show was a fictional adaptation of the H.G. Wells novel. Unfortunately, those who panicked had missed the beginning, and a vast number did not stick around to hear the end. A clause in the CBS contract absolved the Mercury Players from "all legal liability resulting from the content of the show." Welles himself was very apologetic in his words to the press, but over the years his remarks about the broadcast have suggested amusement rather than contrition.

In addressing his own countrymen, Hitler used the example of "The War of the Worlds" example to show how Americans would flee in panic at the slightest hint of any invasion.

Orson Welles's radio career was not impaired by the controversial Halloween broadcast; if anything, the tremendous amount of press ink he received further bolstered his reputation. All radio networks, as well as independent stations, carried the story of the near-disastrous panic. Despite rumors to the contrary, no one had actually died because of the hoax, and the outcome was exactly the kind of grand-scale publicity that fueled Welles's less than diminutive ego.

It was just after the Halloween hoax that David Selznick decided to sell Welles the rights for Daphne du Maurier's *Rebecca*; Val Lewton was appointed to investigate the resulting "Mercury on the Air" radio adaptation. Obviously, the Halloween controversy in no way acted as a stumbling block for the boy wonder of radio. In fact, over the following year Welles would display his multifaceted creative involvement in close to 40 different radio broadcasts of literary adaptations.

It was in 1939 that Welles finally succumbed to a motion picture offer. RKO Pictures had been interested in obtaining the talents of Orson Welles as early as 1937, when the studio's East Coast story editor encouraged RKO head, Leo Spitz, to see Welles's New York production of *Julius Caeser*. Nothing immediate resulted, but the seeds of interest were sown. On October 21, 1938, less than ten days before the airing of "War of the Worlds," George J. Schaefer replaced Spitz as RKO's president. Nine days later Schaefer would not be one of those listeners who would come to the "War of the Worlds" broadcast by way of Nelson Eddy; he would be tuned in from the start. And he would be impressed, not only by the broadcast, but also by the publicity that dogged Welles's heels. Clearly, Welles generated the kind of fanfare Hollywood executives dreamed about.

In an attempt to follow the path taken by David Selznick during *his* RKO days, Schaefer hoped to reinstitute units of independent production within the studio and believed the Mercury Players would make an ideal choice to get the ball rolling. The eyes and ears of the nation had been captured by Orson Welles, and the acquisition of such a celebrity, Schaefer reasoned, would do the studio no harm. RKO was planning a remake of the Lon Chaney favorite, *The Hunchback of Notre Dame,* as one of the biggest and most expensive productions of the studio's history, and the title role was their first serious offer to Welles. The directors who were being considered for the Hugo adaptation included Alfred Hitchcock and James Whale.

Although he was both tempted and flattered by the offer of the Quasimodo role, Welles eventually turned it down for fear of being typecast as a horror actor. Soon other offers came from Schaefer, including the chance to direct, but Welles adamantly stated, as he did with David Selznick the year before, that he wanted a position in Hollywood on his own terms. He wanted the opportunity to call the shots, something that would parallel the degree of autonomy he had found in radio.

Other Hollywood studio offers were made to Welles, including those from Paramount, Samuel Goldwyn, and MGM. Paramount wanted to give some competition to MGM's success with the Andy Hardy series and hoped that Welles would give MGM a run for its money by involving himself with Paramount's forthcoming series of Henry Aldrich comedies. But Welles was not interested in such lighthearted fare. Far more intriguing was MGM's offer involving the filming of Sinclair Lewis's *It Can't Happen Here,* a story of a totalitarian United States, a theme which paralleled Hitler's rise to power.

Not willing to take Welles's initial turndown as his last word, Schaefer dangled another carrot: the starring role in a remake of *Dr. Jekyll and Mr. Hyde.* The thought of such a dual role was enticing to an actor with Orson's range, but again, he did not want to be typecast with horror. Schaefer persisted in his attempts to win over Welles, and his efforts eventually succeeded. Like the quarry that he struggled to capture, Schaefer prided himself in being a man of refined cultural tastes, and under his aegis, he wanted to turn RKO into a "prestige" studio. More and more, the prestige factor began to appeal to Welles's artistic sensibilities.

Much has been said and written about the contract Schaefer gave to the 24-year-old boy wonder. A carte blanche, if one believed the whispers floating around at the time. As far as autonomy was concerned, the only other filmmaker allowed to wield this kind of power had been Charlie Chaplin. Welles, it was said, had been given an unprecedented privilege: "having control over the final cut" and answering only to himself for the form in which the film would be released. The contract was exceptional, but it was not the carte blanche some believed it to be. There were fine lines.

There were restrictions on the content of the proposed films that stated they could be neither "political" nor "controversial." The studio also reserved the right to edit, cut, dub, or change the film if it in any way did not fall in accordance with the Production Code. Furthermore, Welles also had to comply with the execs' desires to see and confer upon daily rushes.

The contract was signed July 22, 1939. For his first picture, RKO pushed for a film version of *War of the Worlds,* but Welles wanted his film debut to be something entirely different, not a revamped previous success. Eventually a number of projects were proposed. Welles's choices included, among others, *Cyrano de Bergerac,* Conrad's *Heart of Darkness,* and C. Day Lewis's *A Smiler with a Knife.* Some of RKO's suggestions included *Man from Mars, Vigil in the Night* (eventually picked up by George Stevens), and *Brave New World.*

The many delays in settling upon a choice of project must have tested the frustration levels of all those involved, especially with the eyes of the Hollywood press peering over their shoulders. By August 1939, Welles had come up with a suitable project, Joseph Conrad's *Heart of Darkness,* but clouds of indecision still hovered above his head. He took weekly trips back to New York to continue with his radio work: again, a vast variety of literary adaptations, including Booth Tarkington's *The Magnificent Ambersons* and Charlotte Brontë's *Jane Eyre.* (The latter production was assessed by Val Lewton as he investigated the potential of *Jane Eyre* as a Selznick property.) By now it was early 1940, and there was still no Orson Welles movie in sight.

Meanwhile, RKO was more than a little embarrassed by Welles's slow results, especially on the heels of such a highly publicized contract. Everyone wondered why it took so long for *The Heart of Darkness* to materialize.

For the most part, the delay was the result of Welles's examination of his new medium. Before he made any real stratagems, he began an extensive study of the motion picture, screening films by the dozens. In connection with *Heart of Darkness*'s tropical locale, Welles viewed scores of films set in the jungle, including both narrative films and documentaries. He then viewed the works of particular directors: Fritz Lang, Rene Clair, Alfred Hitchcock, King Vidor, Jean Renoir, Frank Capra, and especially John Ford. Years later, when asked to name the three directors who influenced him most, Welles would reply, "John Ford, John Ford, and John Ford." During this period of absorption, Welles claimed to have viewed Ford's *Stagecoach* no less than 40 times.

Welles also began an extensive examination of film technique and style, cataloguing hundreds of film terms in a herculean effort rivaling preparation for a bar exam. After Welles gave some serious thought to casting his film with legitimate movie "stars," he realized he would save much expense by flying his own troupe, the Mercury Players, to Hollywood. The proposed budget for his first production was at this time $400,000.

Still, the project continued to be plagued with problems. Welles hoped to shoot on location in the Louisiana bayous, and the estimated production costs began to grow. He wanted to import 3,000 African natives as extras because he was dissatisfied with the "light-skinned blacks" used by Hollywood at this time. He considered covering his light-skinned extras with dark grease-paint, but doing so would elevate the costs even higher. As each extra had to be paid $11 a day, the total budget had more than doubled, running very close to the $1,000,000 bracket.

Eventually, the Conrad adaptation was scrapped, as were a number of other proposals which followed. By the spring of 1940, Welles had already been under contract nearly a year, and the press was not kind. Typical was the response of one *Detroit News* reporter: "Orson Welles, the boy wonder who was expected to revolutionize the whole movie-making map, is still around town and still waiting for the right story. With his retinue of actors, he's been attached to one studio for nearly a year, without even starting a movie." Another reporter quipped, "They say Orson Welles has increased his production schedule. Instead of *not* making three pics for RKO, he'll *not* make five."

Of course, the Orson Welles film that came to fruition amidst all this chaos was surely worth the wait, for we speak of *Citizen Kane,* one of the greatest motion pictures ever made. Volumes of criticism and analysis have been written about this undisputed masterpiece, and our purpose here will not be to rival the coverage already given but, rather, to show how *Citizen Kane* paved the way for Val Lewton's RKO films.

Exactly when the editing team of Robert Wise and Mark Robson came into the *Citizen Kane* project has been the subject of some dispute. In *Citizen Welles,* Frank Brady asserts that in September 1940, when the shooting for *Citizen Kane* neared its end, the original editor, George Crone, was replaced by the 26-year-old Robert Wise. In his biography, *Orson Welles,* Charles Higham implies that Wise came upon the scene later than that: "Once *[Citizen Kane]* was completely shot . . . [Welles] turned the film over to Robert Wise."

Yet in Charles Higham's 1969 *The Celluloid Muse,* a series of interviews with Hollywood directors, Mark Robson is quoted as saying:

> Robert Wise and I, who formed a sort of team in those days—he was film editor and I was his assistant—went to work at RKO on *Heart of Darkness.* Time went on, shots came in, and then one day we found ourselves looking at some film that took place inside a projection room. "What the hell does this have to do with *Heart of Darkness?*" we wondered.
>
> We found out within a few days that this was a totally different film.

In an attempt to clear this up, the author asked Robert Wise for his side of the story. He responded:

> Everyone is wrong a bit, including Mark. I don't ever remember having anything to do with *Heart of Darkness.* I had just finished editing *My Favorite Wife.* Mark was my assistant on that. We had just shipped the film on Saturday and were celebrating that event. I walked into the studio on Monday and had a call from my boss, Jimmy Wilkinson, saying the following: "You know this Orson Welles fella kind of pulled a fast one on the studio. He got an okay to go ahead and make two or three tests for *[Citizen Kane].* . . . Now Orson's done about three of those and the studio's realized he's actually shooting his film, that these are actual scenes from the film, so they've given him the green light to go ahead and make the picture."
>
> One of those "tests" was the projection room scene for the "News on the March" people . . . another was the scene, going through the skylight, for Dorothy Comingore's, Susan's, interview.

> He had a hack editor named George Crone assigned to those so-called tests, but now that he was into production, Orson wanted someone else, someone younger. I was free.
>
> I had never met Orson, had never seen him around the lot, to my memory. I was sent down to RKO-Pathé in Culver City where Orson was shooting. He was actually shooting the scene in the tent, where they all went down to the beach in that caravan. Orson's assistant told him that I was down there to see him and a few minutes later he came out to tell me that when he got a break in the shooting he'd see me. And so I first saw Orson as the old, old Kane, the old man.
>
> We chatted for a few minutes, and he liked the fact that I had a fairly good record of films I'd edited by this time, and I was obviously his age. I got back to the studio and my boss said Orson had called and said I was on the picture. And that started our whole experience, Mark and I, with Orson, on both *Kane* and *Ambersons*. That's the story and the other people are quite wrong about that. I have no recollection of having anything to do with *Heart of Darkness*, or even seeing any of the tests on that.

No one can deny that working on *Citizen Kane* offered both Wise and Robson editing challenges of unprecedented scope. In an interview with Frank Brady (in *Citizen Welles*), Wise recalls: "I would put several sequences together from the rushes and then project them for [Welles]; he would ask for changes, suggest improvements, ask me to re-change and then change again. It was a constant process of molding and building. We both learned from each other, but he overwhelmed me with his radio background and his masterful use of sound, stretching the boundaries of how I thought sound could be used."

Charles Higham points out, in his Welles biography:

> Wise was especially effective in preparing the newsreel, "News on the March," in which he created an impression of a vast mass of film footage drawn from many periods; in some cases he even scratched the film deliberately by dragging it over the cement floor of the editing room to give it a look of age and wear and tear. He did a fine job with Susan's disastrous opera tour, ending it on a shot of a fading cue light. This crude but effective symbol terminated a montage that owed everything to Wise's talent. . . . Wise also gave the movie much of its extraordinary fluency by using brilliant radiolike linking devices that at one stroke overcame a decade of clumsiness in the narrative form of many talking pictures.

The teamwork of Welles, Wise, and Robson was responsible for a large portion of *Citizen Kane*'s magic. Such avant-garde editing techniques may not have been invented for the film, but seldom had they been employed with such verve. Consider that stunning sequence, spanning years, where Kane and his first wife have their progressively clipped and fleeting table discussions. Or the different perspectives we get while viewing Susan Alexander's opera debut a second time. The lap dissolves alone make *Kane* a notable work, especially those in the prologue where the lighted window of the Kane mansion remains frozen on a particular spot of the frame, regardless of the numerous dissolves that follow. The extremely long lap dissolves during Leland's flashbacks are also noteworthy, the background dissolving to a different scene while Leland remains in the foreground until finally his image too evaporates.

In spite of all he cinematic wonders one can behold in Welles's auspicious debut film, the story of *Citizen Kane* was not a happy one for RKO. Over budget and behind schedule, *Kane* was finally released under a banner of controversy in 1941. The subject matter of Welles's debut film bore an undeniable resemblance to the life of William Randolph Hearst, a man who was widely regarded as the colossus of the publishing world, the mere mention of his name chilling the hearts, if such a thing were possible, of Hollywood's most powerful moguls.

Hearst newspapers had been responsible for unleashing the most scathing exposé of Hollywood, the infamous Fatty Arbuckle scandal that spearheaded a 1920s muckraking trend that was gone but not forgotten. The last thing any RKO executive needed was to have "wonder boy" Welles stir the ire of the sleeping dragon. But RKO was not the only studio to fear a retaliation from Hearst; bigwigs from several other majors pooled together close to a million dollars in the hopes of getting the film away from Welles and into the nearest incinerator.

Before the film opened, George J. Schaefer was summoned to New York. A man representing MGM offered Schaefer $842,000 if he would destroy all prints and the negative. He refused on behalf of Welles. This was not a sum sponsored by Hearst himself, but "fear money" gathered by several studios in an effort to placate the publishing magnate. Schaefer refused the payment without even conferring with his board of directors (who likely would have agreed to drop the film). Although Hearst was not actively involved in this attempted payoff, the powerful arm of the Hearst machine could and would squelch any box-office success *Citizen Kane* had coming.

The premiere of *Kane* had been scheduled for Radio City Music Hall, owned by the Rockefellers and the Chase National Bank. Quite suddenly, Radio City reneged on the premiere. Schaefer phoned Nelson Rockefeller to inquire about the cancellation and discovered that Hearst spokesperson Louella Parsons had phoned Rockefeller to "warn him off the picture," saying (according to Pauline Kael's *Citizen Kane Book*), "How would you like to have an *American Weekly* magazine section run a double page spread on John D. Rockefeller?" She had also called RCA magnate David Sarnoff, another large investor at RKO, and threatened him.

In mid–February, the Hearst papers blasted RKO and Schaefer in front page stories: an unmistakable public warning to all advocates of Welles and

Citizen Kane. Schaefer was left stranded and had to scrounge for theater openings. Owners of the nation's film palaces were afraid that if they showed *Citizen Kane,* Hearst would refuse to run ads from the various theater chains indefinitely. Thus, Schaefer could not get bookings except in the theaters RKO owned outright.

Forced into a corner, Schaefer threatened to sue Warners, Fox, Paramount, and Loew's MGM on a charge of conspiracy. Reluctantly, Warner Bros. caved in and very halfheartedly booked the picture, and the other theater chains followed suit with the expected dearth of enthusiasm. In many cases, the theaters would book the film to avoid lawsuit, but they did not have to, by law, actually show the movie. This "fine print" tactic was chosen by many theaters simply to avoid the wrath of Hearst (whose papers did, in fact, ban publicity on all RKO productions).

Well before *Kane* was actually released, George Schaefer had clearly seen the writing on the wall and suspected Welles's debut project was too esoteric for popular tastes. While *Kane* was on the drawing boards, Schaefer encouraged Welles to do what he thought would be a profitable, yet inexpensive, thriller: an adaptation of Eric Ambler's espionage novel, *Journey into Fear.* Welles did not resist the idea entirely, although it was not one of his priorities at the time. He did appreciate Schaefer's concern over profit making, but he was unconvinced that he needed to compromise his artistic integrity by complying with box-office demands.

When *Citizen Kane* was completed and scheduled for its upcoming May 1941 release, the film was already a hot topic of controversy. If Schaefer wished to continue holding his job, he had to persuade Welles to venture into safer cinematic territory. On April 3, Welles was given a copy of Ambler's novel, and Schaefer pressed the young director to make a film that would guarantee a profit. In *Citizen Welles,* Frank Brady tells us: "Virtually overnight, Welles made up his mind to get involved, and this is when he made an unofficial deal with Schaefer to do *Journey into Fear* if he was first allowed to do Booth Tarkington's *The Magnificent Ambersons.*"

The Ambler thriller was dangled, carrotlike, before the studio executives, and they reluctantly accepted Welles's proposal. Welles did some preproduction work on the Ambler adaptation, but his heart was in the *Ambersons* project. Unfortunately, by then the Hearst pressure was in full bloom, and it appeared that RKO was going to take an awful loss on *Kane.* With sweaty palms, RKO's front office executives knew their self-indulgent boy wonder had better start concentrating on matters that were more profitable than artistic integrity.

Welles decided to live to the wire and work on three film projects at once. Moreover, he maintained the nightlife and the high spirits he thought typical of a man-of-the-hour, all amid sensationalized press coverage of his marriage, infidelity, and imminent divorce. By the time *Ambersons* went into production, Welles had gained 40 pounds. Halfway through the shooting, the Japanese bombed Pearl Harbor. Plainly, it was a time for caution and deliberation, but Welles's ambition knew no bounds.

Welles worked on the script of *Journey into Fear* while *Ambersons* was about to go into production. By the time he got around to shooting *Journey,* he was going back and forth between Hollywood and Mexico, where he was filming the first part of an ill-fated documentary called *It's All True.* He supervised the editing (via telephone) for *The Magnificent Ambersons* from Rio de Janeiro, where he shot further segments for *It's All True,* all the while being involved in a new weekly radio program sponsored by Lady Esther cosmetics.

Because *Ambersons* and *Journey* were for a time overlapping productions, Welles had to relinquish the director's helm on *Journey* to Norman Foster, formerly the director of Fox's two "B" budget detective series, "Mr. Moto" and "Charlie Chan." Thus during the day Welles directed (but did not star in) *The Magnificent Ambersons,* while during the night he starred in (but did not direct) *Journey Into Fear.* Although Foster was *Journey*'s credited director, Welles oversaw all of Foster's work. In *The Films of Orson Welles,* Charles Higham tells us, "The two men discussed every scene in detail together, and although Foster did the actual direction, Welles undoubtedly controlled every one of his effects until he left for Rio."

When Welles flew down to South America after the shooting of *Ambersons,* he left Robert Wise and Mark Robson (the team that had just completed *All That Money Can Buy*) to edit from virtually miles of takes. *Ambersons* became an excruciating ordeal for the editing team. While Welles was in Rio phoning and wiring in his editing directions, Wise and Robson became exasperated trying to piece the film together according to his instructions. Said Wise, "I didn't know what the hell was going on half the time. . . . We tried for clarification over the telephone, and the problems were enormous, just getting through. Then when we reached him, we usually could not hear him because of the connections. It was a nightmare." When Welles's final cut, lasting 148 minutes, was tested on a Pomona preview, Schaefer's response (via a special airmail delivery to Welles) was as follows:

> Never in all my experience in the industry have I taken so much punishment or suffered as I did at the Pomona preview. . . . They laughed in the wrong places, talked at the picture, kidded it, and did everything that you can possibly imagine. . . . It was like getting one sock in the jaw after another for over two hours [Frank Brady, *Citizen Welles*].

After another test audience had a similar lack of patience with *Ambersons*'s leisurely pace, Welles authorized an edited print of 131 minutes and then was forced to fulfill obligations elsewhere. While Welles busied himself on location sites in South America, RKO executives, not satisfied with Welles's fix-up, initiated a further degree of "paring down" without the director's authorization. According to Charles Higham's biography: "Robert Wise and his assistant, Mark Robson, had left their families and holed up in a motel, working 24-hour shifts to, in Robert Wise's words, 'keep the audiences in the theater.' Scene after scene was sliced through, transposed or replaced in order to make the picture tighter, speedier, more understandable." Before the job was done, the team was split up, with Robson reassigned to *Journey into Fear*, which he edited single-handedly.

Wise finally brought the million-dollar-budgeted film down to a total running time of 88 minutes. It was the unfortuate fate of *The Magnificent Ambersons* to wind up on the lower half of a double bill, playing second fiddle to a second-rate Lupe Velez opus called *Mexican Spitfire Sees a Ghost.*

The *Ambersons* fiasco was not Hollywood's best-kept secret. Most of the executives at RKO were sorry they ever heard the name "Orson Welles." George Schaefer's head was on the chopping block, and it rolled with his resignation. Joseph Breen (the Production Code censor) had been called to step into Schaefer's position until RKO found, in March, a more appropriate replacement: Charles Koerner. Koerner took charge until Schaefer's resignation was made official in July 1942. One of the first things Koerner did was evict the Mercury Productions team from its RKO offices.

Welles had wreaked havoc with RKO, but Koerner believed there was still some life in the studio. For one thing, the "B" budget series films, like the "Saint" and "Falcon" movies, were still turning a profit. Koerner noticed that horror films had made a big comeback at Universal, especially with an assortment of monster movie sequels: *Son of Frankenstein* (1939), *The Mummy's Hand* (1940), and *The Invisible Man Returns* (1940). But the biggest monster hit of all was *The Wolfman* (1941). Koerner reasoned RKO could do the same with a "B" unit specializing in horror.

Meanwhile, at David O. Selznick Productions, a 38-year-old Val Lewton was becoming increasingly disillusioned with his job.

FIVE

Staking the Territory

Lewton's grand opportunity, his chance of a lifetime, was dependent upon a chain of events that took place within the structure of RKO studios during those first months of 1942. Orson Welles had put the studio dangerously in the red by failing to draw appreciative audiences to his top-heavy film productions; RKO desperately needed to recoup its losses and could no longer afford to obey the whims of the champion risk-taker Welles had become.

With the arrival of Charles Koerner, attitudes began to change around the RKO lot. Esoteric properties like the Welles pictures, as well as another recent box-office flop, William Dieterle's *All That Money Can Buy* (also edited by the Wise/Robson team), would be discouraged. Koerner was running a new RKO, and he was determined to please the public and the bank.

There was extensive housecleaning. Scores of people were fired (in addition to Welles and his Mercury Theatre Players), and many RKO workers resigned of their own accord. If the studio was unable to fire all the employees associated with the Welles projects, then it would at least demote several of them to "B" unit production, almost as a form of punishment. Lew Ostrow was appointed the new superintendent of all "B" unit productions, and he assisted in the housecleaning.

Koerner meanwhile turned his gaze to Universal Studios, where *The Wolf Man,* still playing in some theaters close to four months after its release, continued to turn over a profit. And now, as if in swift pursuit, one monster after another, came the March 13 release of *The Ghost of Frankenstein.* Koerner knew there was money to be made in the horror market, and RKO's front office began calling Universal's horror excursions "Midas productions."

According to Ruth Lewton, Koerner approached her husband at a dinner party and offered him the position of horror-unit producer, even giving him the proposed title—*Cat People*—of the initial entry. (Joseph Breen, Lewton's longtime ally and George Schaefer's temporary replacement, had probably suggested Lewton's name to Koerner.) Lewton was initially reluctant to accept Koerner's offer because he feared Selznick would be angry. He mulled over the idea for many days. His job with Selznick had become stagnant, making him feel as if he were in a state of hibernation. Finally, Ruth convinced her husband that Selznick would probably be pleased over his advancement and would perhaps even convey his blessings. Lewton called Koerner and accepted the job.

(Later, after his RKO success was insured, Lewton fabricated a story that he was approached because of a misunderstanding: "I write novels for a living, and when RKO was looking for producers, someone told them I had written horrible novels. They mistook the word *horrible* for *horror* and I got the job.")

In March 1942, Val Lewton ended his eight-year employment with David O. Selznick and walked into RKO Studios to begin his new career as a film producer. The trepidation he must have felt over the prospects of a new beginning probably paralleled the "politics of terror" he was soon to develop in his films; fear of the unknown had a palpable grip upon his confidence.

At RKO, Lewton was authorized to set up a production unit for the series of horror programmers which, as proposed, actually were not as inexpensive as some of the "B" horrors over at Universal (and they were surely miles above the paltry budgets of the Poverty Row horror offerings that were then being made at minor studios like Monogram and PRC).

In accordance with front office demands, Lewton's films would cost no more than $150,000 each, and none of them could exceed 75 minutes in length. In addition, he would be obliged to work from a series of "pre-tested" titles which would be supplied by his superiors. As long as Lewton conceded to these stipulations, he could fashion the films as he pleased. He went on the RKO payroll at $250 per week.

Lewton was introduced to Jesse Ponitz, a young stenographer who was appointed to his unit; in addition to being his secretary, she was to help familiarize him with the studio.

While he busily pondered the possibilities of his first project, Lewton began his careful search for team players. One of the first of many talented people to be drafted to the Lewton unit was screenwriter DeWitt Bodeen. Months before, while Lewton was working on the *Jane Eyre* Selznick package, he had come across a play written about the Brontë sisters; the play's author had been DeWitt Bodeen. Lewton contacted the playwright and managed to secure him as a research assistant to Aldous Huxley, who was then writing the screenplay for *Jane Eyre*. Lewton and Bodeen, who worked together on period authenticity, developed a good relationship, the two of them seeing eye-to-eye on a great number of things. Upon leaving Selznick for RKO, Lewton told the young playwright to contact him as soon as his work on the Selznick package was completed.

As Lewton accustomed himself to his new job, he began screening a large number of 1930s horror films. George Turner (in "Cat People," an article in the May-June 1982 *Cinéfantastique*) tells us, "[Lewton and DeWitt Bodeen] . . . screened numerous successful horror films, mostly made by Universal, with the idea of eliminating as many cliches of the genre as possible." Although George Turner interviewed Bodeen for the article, the latter mentioned only one of the titles screened: Paramount's *Island of Lost Souls* (1932). Since Bodeen passed away in the late 1980s, it is anyone's guess exactly which 1930s horror films Lewton and Bodeen watched. (Neither Ruth Lewton nor Lewton's son, Val Edwin Lewton, could come up with any titles.)

Perhaps it is fitting that these films remain a mystery; our reliance upon mere speculation allows us to examine an entire decade of horror films as they may, or may not, relate to Lewton's body of work. What we do know is that the screening of previous horror features had an impact on Lewton's cinematic formula, even if they only provided examples of the kinds of things Lewton and Bodeen wished to avoid. In all probability, however, Lewton also discovered many things of which he approved.

Although he discarded many of the trappings of 1930s horror, what is most surprising about Lewton's films is how much they do reflect what had come before. Some safe, albeit very general, assertions can be made: Lewton was partial to the German expressionism that permeated a major portion of Hollywood horror in the 1930s; Lewton, whose job was to produce films which were recognizably part of the genre, found little wisdom or satisfaction in discarding all horror film conventions; and, finally, Lewton was already familiar with several of the landmark horror films—*Dracula, Frankenstein, King Kong, Dr. Jekyll and Mr. Hyde*, et al.—before he ever thought of producing his own examples of the form.

Moreover, and perhaps contrary to popular belief, Lewton had a genuine interest in the horror genre both in literature and in film. If he felt some disdain for what may be termed "monster movies," this is no indication that he rejected the genre in its purer forms. Lewton's fond appreciation for the Gothic novel and the Victorian ghost story, with their accent upon the unseen, appears to also have had a considerable influence upon the tactics of terror that the Lewton films would ultimately adopt. One reading of Lewton's *Weird Tales* contribution, "The Bagheeta," is ample evidence of his appreciation of the understated techniques employed by the British masters. With Lewton's voracious appetite for literature, we can probably assume that he was familiar with the work of Mary Shelley, Bram Stoker, Sheridan Le Fanu, Edgar Allan Poe, Nathaniel Hawthorne, Arthur Machen, E.F. Benson, M.R. James, Ambrose Bierce, Algernon Blackwood, William Hope Hodgson, and—given that Lewton had contributed to *Weird Tales*—perhaps even A. Merritt and H.P. Lovecraft.

As we examine the relationship between 1930s horror and Lewton's RKO films, there will be much guesswork. The reader should not assume our slightly meandering survey of the possible antecedents of the Val Lewton films to be a chronicle of cause and effect. We have no real way of knowing whether we speak of influences or parallels; the best we can offer is a series of possibilities.

The appropriate starting point in any examination of 1930s horror should, of course, be Tod Browning's *Dracula*. Although the film does not bear much in common with the typical Val Lewton entry, we should at least recognize that Browning made a conscious effort to accent the unseen. Much of the film's horrific content takes place offscreen, sometimes to good effect (the shipboard scene, the victim in the alley), sometimes not (the hero pointing out the window and announcing that the Count has just turned into a wolf). We also can see that *Dracula*'s chillingly silent female vampires are the ancestral soul sisters to Lewton's ghostly women in white (in *I Walked with a Zombie* and *Isle of the Dead*). But if any sustained portrait of *Dracula* could be likened to the less-is-more approach championed by the Lewton films, it would have to be the opening scenes in Dracula's Transylvanian castle, the pervasive silence, the undercurrents of terror. The disquieting atmosphere of the drafty web-and-vermin-infested Castle Dracula—an effect achieved through camera shots, set design, lighting, and a healthy portion of audience imagination—maintains its power, even today. The absence of score music, characteristic of many early sound films, works to the movie's advantage during these moments.

When Browning moved back to MGM, Irving Thalberg gave the green light to *Freaks*, even though Mayer felt the project, a horror movie using real carnival freaks for actors, overstepped the boundaries of good taste. For once, Mayer proved to be a better barometer of public reaction than Thalberg. The 1932 release outraged audiences, and the film was immediately banned in England. *Freaks* was pulled from distribution and shelved by MGM, only to be picked up again a few years later by Dwain *(Maniac)* Esper, who packaged and distributed it as one of his exploitation films.

Freaks has an emotional core, pity for the outcast, that is significant to a wide range of classic horror films, Lewton's included. In the way *Freaks* evokes our sympathy for the misfits, Browning's film provides an emotional subtext that would appear again and again in horror films of the 1930s and 1940s. The outcast theme is, in fact, one of the cornerstones of cinematic horror, one that connects the Lewton films to the classic horror prototypes: Quasimodo, the monster, the werewolf, and a hoary host of others.

Most of the pathos we feel for Lewton's doomed characters comes from their inability to remain in step with the rest of the human race. Such characters see themselves as misfits and outcasts, freaks with normal bodies, and virtually every one of Lewton's 11 RKO films makes strong use of this theme of rejection. It is not the thread, but the cord that runs through the entire series. Whether they be villains, victims, or heroes, there is a staggeringly high number of square pegs in Lewton's work. Our sympathy for the outcast accounts for much of the depth and poignancy Lewton was able to develop with so many of his screen characters. In many instances, Lewton's portrayal of sympathetic, but off-center, human beings established the same

The "wives" of *Dracula*. The one in the middle looks like an early incarnation of Jessica Holland from Lewton's *I Walked with a Zombie*.

commentary on society as did Browning's *Freaks*. Lewton's misfits often have more humanity than their persecutors, the "well-adjusted" strata of society.

The most obvious example of the above would be the portrayal of the "loonies" in Lewton's *Bedlam*. In fact, *Bedlam*'s climactic scene—where the lunatics revolt against their cruel captor, Master Sims (Boris Karloff)—is only a stone's throw away from the horrifying finale of Browning's *Freaks*, where the title characters wreak their revenge upon the "normal" villains (played by Olga Baclanova and Henry Victor).

Some elements of James Whale's work prefigure Lewton's less-is-more approach to the raising of goose bumps: a reliance upon atmosphere and setting, shadow and light, sound and silence. Once a set designer himself, Whale's extraordinary sense of composition within the milieu of artificial scenery reveals a much more dramatic evocation of the spirit of German expressionism than any film of Browning's. *Frankenstein*'s opening reel gives ample evidence of this ability, hinting at a quality of visual splendor that would reach near perfection with the marvelous soundstage sets of Whale's sequel, *The Bride of Frankenstein.*

The much-heralded introduction of Karloff's Monster in *Frankenstein* is a genuine highlight of horror filmmaking. By having the Monster make a slow entrance through a shadowy threshold, Whale teases his audience; when we discover that the creature is emerging backwards, his face yet unseen, our apprehensions are relieved, though our curiosity is frustrated, and these mixed feelings put us off guard. Until the Monster turns around....

Whale delivers three quick telescopic jump cuts to an extreme close-up of the Monster's face, and our curiosity gives way to terror. Such an inspired moment characterizes Whale as a director who, like Hitchcock and Lang, relishes the manipulation of his audience. With a dark sense of humor reminiscient of Hitchcock, James Whale would in film after film exhibit a bleak neurotic vision that took glee in its own morbidity.

The scenes of Dr. Frankenstein (Colin Clive) and Fritz (Dwight Frye) involved in their various charnel activities—the two of them exhuming the recently buried dead, Fritz climbing the hangman's gallows to cut the rope of a dangling specimen, Fritz stealing the wrong brain from the medical college—have their obvious parallels in Lewton's ghoulish masterpiece, *The Body Snatcher,* the latter having enough dark humor to put it squarely in the James Whale tradition.

The famous scene of the Monster reaching towards the skylight, trying to grasp the descending rays, is only one example of the kind of visual poetry at work in Whale's genuinely inspired direction. Whale's rich compositions, a signature of his directing style, closely anticipate the dark mysticism and pictorial splendor for which the Lewton films would be praised.

Whale's film direction is much more dynamic than Tod Browning's; Whale reaches levels of poignance and humor that seem to be infinitely out of reach for the other director. Compare Browning's forced humor in *Mark of the Vampire* with the hilariously eccentric quirks of Whale's *The Old Dark House,* and we can plainly see what sets these directors apart. When Whale's direction became excessive, which it sometimes did, its excesses were so adventurous that they could easily be forgiven. Like Browning, Whale was awkward with his romantic scenes and altogether too pedestrian with scenes of exposition, but unlike Browning, Whale compensated for these lulls by creating shots, scenes, and entire sequences which, once seen, were impossible to forget. The narratives of Browning's films are a blur to the memory, containing few of the numerous cinematic "hooks" that are typical in James Whale's horror efforts.

Consider the boldness of having the Monster in *Frankenstein* kill a little girl. With the notable exception of Fritz Lang's *M*, released that same year, the killing of children was (and still is) a rarity in horror films. For its time, the inclusion of such a scene was extremely shocking. But Whale takes it in an unanticipated direction by playing the scene for its charm and innocence, turning what would be in another director's hands merely horrific into something unexpectedly sublime.

In this famous scene, little Maria warmly accepts the Monster (like young Amy in Lewton's *Curse of the Cat People*, she is in need of a playmate). Maria is as much an outcast as her newfound friend, both abandoned, so to speak, by their fathers. They play by the sun-dappled pond, taking turns throwing flowers onto the water's surface, watching them float. We understand what the Monster is thinking: that little Maria would also look so pretty floating on the water just like the flowers. With the accidental drowning of the girl, the Monster seals his own doom. The sense of tragedy we feel (the Monster displays considerable anguish over the girl's loss) is much more profound than it would have been had the scene been played for sheer terror.

No one forgets *Frankenstein*'s climax: the baying of hounds and the angry shouts of the torch-carrying mob, the doctor and his creation locked in the windmill, engaged in a cat-and-mouse waltz around the creaking rotating shaft, silently gazing into one another's eyes through the gaps in the shaft's protective structure, the villagers finally setting fire to the windmill, the Monster's desperate terror at the sight of the growing flames, and the final long shot of the burning, crumbling mill. Compare such dynamics as these with the limp climax of Browning's *Dracula*. Whale supplies the kind of imagery that transcends genre expectations, lifting the horror film out of the realm of exploitation and turning it into art. Like Lewton, Whale was a cultured intellectual who just happened to be making horror films; as long as that was his assignment, however, he was determined to make them his own way.

Whale's sequel, *The Bride of Frankenstein* (1935), contains all the notable characteristics of its predecessor and, in many ways, improves upon them. The portrayal of the Monster as a sympathetic outcast (a Christ figure, in fact) is given a degree of poignancy seldom achieved in the genre. Still looking for a friend, he saves a girl from drowning (feeling his anguish, we suspect, over his misdeed in the previous film), befriends a blind man, and at last becomes corrupted by a effete villain, Dr. Pretorious (Ernest Thesiger). Once again, Whale's sense of composition, amidst such atmospheric soundstage sets as the primeval forest and the barren cemetery, is unfailingly provocative. *The Bride of Frankenstein* is rich with symbolism and imagery, and while it is not as frightening as its predecessor, it is surely more eloquent in its approach. Clearly, it was not the kind of horror film the studio was anticipating when they handed the assignment to Whale.

Supernatural horror, exemplified by *Dracula* and *Frankenstein,* only accounted for a fraction of the 1930s horror cycle. Far more frequent were the marketed-as-horror "old house" thrillers, an extremely prolific trend of forgettable programmers that were the staple of the genre during the late twenties, early thirties, and even beyond. Spooky as they may have been, the final reels, almost without exception, exposed the "supernatural" elements as a sham orchestrated by greedy human culprits who served to benefit by scaring or killing off the other principal characters. In these formulaic outings, the supernatural threat is often given credibility by the presence of some form of spiritualist, be it a mindreader, fortune-teller, clairvoyant, astrologer, medium, or hypnotist. Red herrings abound. So do clutching hands. Seances are par for the course, and murders in the dark are almost a prerequisite. Many an old house thriller offered a death scene where the screen was plunged in darkness, thereby allowing the audience to hear only the screams (or gurgles) of murder victims; this technique mimicked the horror radio shows which were quickly gaining popularity during the 1930s. Such a "fear the dark" device also has a substantial connection, at least in theory, to Lewton's RKO films.

The Old Dark House (1932) was James Whale's wickedly eccentric contribution to the subgenre. It is considered a quintessential example of the form, but Whale's decision to break free of many of the conventions of the formula makes *The Old Dark House* a singular work. Although the opening scenes are typical of the form, once our trio of "normal" protagonists walk into the Femm family mansion, they have bidden farewell to sanity and logic. Whale presents *The Old Dark House* as a deranged lark, a fun-filled frolic through a kaleidoscope of dementia which includes the unlikeliest chain of events that should ever befall a group of travelers who escape a raging storm by finding shelter in a house occupied by maniacs.

The Old Dark House (reputedly a faithful, though more humorous, adaptation of J.B. Priestley's British novel, *The Benighted*) nearly defies description. Unlike the typical old house thriller, there is no apparent motivation (nor any attempted explanation) for the behavior exhibited by its menacing characters. We are given Ernest Thesiger as the skeletal Horace Femm, a man who, as effeminate as his last name suggests, looks as if his main perception of the world is through his nostrils. His religious fanatic sister, Rebecca (Eva Moore), is an old hag who delights in exhibiting behavior calculated to make her guests as uncomfortable as possible. No illusions of etiquette here, with Rebecca continually reminding all within earshot that the guests can have "No beds! No beds!" Add to this eccentric pair an alcoholic mute butler,

Morgan (Boris Karloff), a 102-year-old bedridden patriarch named Sir Roderick, and a cackling, face-biting pyromaniac, brother Saul, who, locked away in his top-floor room, comes across like a refugee from an H.P. Lovecraft story.

Aside from its marginal connections with *Bedlam,* the one pervading aspect of Whale's film that ties it to the Lewton oeuvre is its use of lighting. As its title clearly implies, *The Old Dark House* is a very darkly lit film, more so than any other horror film of the 1930s. The interior of the Femm mansion is illuminated by an electric generator that is continually on the brink of malfunction. This extremely erratic source of dim light ebbs and flows through the first half of the film before breaking down completely in the second half. After that, the film's only onscreen illumination is provided by flickering light from the burning hearth, an occasional candle or two (these apparently being in short supply), and frequent bursts of lightning from the ongoing storm. When characters grope about to explore the mansion's murky recesses, the darkness is so palpable as to be almost suffocating.

In one memorable scene, the heroine, left alone in the dining room, uses her hands to make shadow animals on the flickering wall, her comical whistling-in-the-dark actions merely an attempt to bolster her courage. As she steps closer to the candle source, and thus out of the frame, the silhouette of her body becomes enlarged upon the wall. Suddenly, another shadow, unmistakably that of Rebecca Femm, intrudes upon the wall space and pokes the heroine's silhouette in the chest. The heroine screams, but when we cut back to her real form she is shown turning about, trying to locate the source of the other shadow. To her bafflement, there is no one else in the room. As is the case with several peculiar events in the Femm mansion, there is no forthcoming explanation.

No study of unseen terrors would be complete without giving brief mention to *The Invisible Man* (1933), probably Whale's most fully realized venture into the dark fantasy genre. *The Invisible Man* has it all: a gripping story, wonderful old-world atmosphere, a dynamic score, an intoxicating lead performer, wild black comedy, a searing screenplay, wondrous special effects, spectacular sets, and a good share of chills.

Although it may not be immediately apparent, *The Invisible Man* shares some things in common with Lewton's *The Body Snatcher:* the complete illusion of a British setting with plenty of pub atmosphere and local color, intelligent dialogue sprinkled with liberal doses of macabre humor, a totally amoral, but nonetheless endearing, murderer as the title character. Like *The Body Snatcher,* Whale's film is also about a doctor who sacrifices his humanity for the pursuit of science, thereby giving way to his own dark underside.

The Invisible Man is often remembered for its comic touches, but fear of the unseen is exploited to chilling effect in a number of scenes. Most noteworthy is the sequence that leads to Kemp's death. The character of Dr.

Griffin (Claude Rains, in the title role) swears revenge upon his traitorous friend, Kemp (William Harrigan). Although Kemp is an unlikeable creep, we cannot help but sympathize with his fears as his final hour approaches. Because Griffin is invisible, he might be anywhere, so the very air surrounding Kemp becomes charged with menace.

The film careers of James Whale and Val Lewton had some profound similarities. In a manner of speaking, both men backed into the film genre that brought them fame. Then, having found their true cinematic niche with horror films, they did everything they could to break out of the genre for which they were best suited. James Whale had as much influence upon the horror films of the 1930s as Val Lewton had upon the horror films of the 1940s. Although Whale and Lewton performed different creative functions in the making of their respective films (Lewton, remember, was a producer, not a director), the two filmmakers shared other things in common. Neither of them possessed a university education, but both were erudite, highly cultured, and remarkably well-read men, just like actor Boris Karloff, with whom they each shared a close association (Karloff starred in three Whale films and three Lewton films).

Tod Browning and James Whale were not the only fish in the pond. Cinematographer-turned-director Karl Freund made two horror entries relevant to our study. Born in Koenigshof, Bohemia (now the Czech Republic), in 1890, Karl Freund found a career in the German film industry, where he worked with the best of the expressionistic directors: Robert Weine, F.W. Murnau, Fritz Lang, even Paul Wegener. Freund was a highly influential cinematographer during Germany's pioneer film days, eschewing the static theater-seat perspective for experimentation with a fluid camera to incorporate an assortment of very smooth moving shots and pans. The seemingly effortless flow of Freund's camera movement was often accented by low-key lighting and chiaroscuro effects. Freund emigrated to Hollywood in 1929 and established himself at Universal, where he was given the assignment of shooting an ending for *All Quiet on the Western Front*, the result being the film's celebrated "butterfly finale."

The Mummy, Freund's directorial debut, is a slow but entirely sustained film of horror, romance, and mysticism; like Lewton's *I Walked with a Zombie*, Freund's film achieves a somber beauty in its presentation of dark tragedy. The less-is-more approach that Lewton would later embrace as his own horror aesthetic, can here be found in good supply. The film's opening reel, like those of *Dracula* and *Frankenstein*, is a notable addition to horror film history. Im-ho-tep's resurrection has the kind of kinetic power we would see in Lewton's own resurrection scene in *Isle of the Dead*. In both cases the directors take great relish in forestalling the inevitable and manipulating audience tension. Although *The Mummy* is graced with a marvelous musical score, Freund refrains from using it in the classic resurrection set piece, prefiguring Lewton's own tendency to intentionally dispense with score music during key fright sequences. It is not what we see but what we *do not* see which gives this opening sequence its harrowing edge.

A young archeologist (played by Bramwell Fletcher), left alone in the recently opened tomb of Im-Ho-Tep, tries to occupy himself with his work, but his attention is continually drawn to the mysterious scroll he has been told not to touch. Finally, he opens the small box containing the scroll and, taking a moment to wipe his sweaty palms against the front of his shirt, gingerly lifts it out. He carefully pulls off the decomposed ribbon wrap (it seems to take forever) and unravels the ancient document. Securing a pad and pencil, he mumbles the sacred words as he translates.

The camera smoothly pans left to the rigid figure of Im-Ho-Tep (Boris Karloff), a 3,000-year-old mummy within his upright sarcophagus, and without a hitch pans right back to the mumbling archeologist deep in his work. Soon we see a close shot of Im-Ho-Tep; this time the shot holds. The mummified face is absolutely immobile. Until we see a glimmer behind one of the eyelids. The camera tilts down as one of the bandaged arms slips from its crossed position upon the chest and falls to the mummy's side, seemingly by its own weight. We cut back to the archeologist, too busy with his translation to know that anything is amiss. Finally, as we look over his shoulder as he writes, an ancient hand comes into the corner of the frame and touches the scroll.

There is one bloodcurdling yell before the man collapses into mad paroxysms of laughter which continue unabated for the remainder of the sequence. We never see the mummy, just his hand and some unraveled leg bandages dragging past the doorway, and yet the effect is more terrifying than if we had. The young archeologist, forever mad, continues his hysterics, stopping his crazed laughter only once to quip, "He went for a little walk!" The scene is a classic, and Bramwell Fletcher's unexpectedly mirthful reaction bears an intensity seldom attained, before or since, by the standard scream-of-the-victim horror film cliché.

The Mummy remains a mesmerizing excursion to a mystical, exotic realm. Its powerhouse opening notwithstanding, Freund's debut is one of the most subtle and sublime horror films of the period and makes a fitting double bill with Lewton's *I Walked with a Zombie.*

In 1935 MGM assigned Karl Freund to do a remake of the German film *The Hands of Orlac,* a project he was ready to tackle with style and panache. Freund's film, which became *Mad Love,* is one of the more sumptuous horror film productions of the 1930s; no one was cutting corners on the MGM lot. *Mad Love* glows with high production values and boasts three fine performers: Peter Lorre (in his American debut), Colin Clive (playing the tormented title character), and Frances Drake (one of the more strikingly beautiful actresses to ever grace a horror film, playing Orlac's wife).

The plot concerns a pianist (Clive) who, injured in a train wreck, has a murderous knife-thrower's hands grafted onto his wrists. The surgeon in charge of this dubious operation is Dr. Gogol (Lorre), who performs the deed in an effort to win the affections of the pianist's wife (Drake). The grafted hands, however, have a life of their own and get into the habit of throwing knives whenever they find them lying about.

It is likely that Lewton was familiar with *Mad Love,* as it was being produced at MGM while he and Jacques Tourneur were doing second-unit work on *A Tale of Two Cities,* and both Selznick employees had been very impressed by Peter Lorre's performance in *M.* But aside from its possible relevance to the Lewton films, *Mad Love* has a peculiar connection with Orson Welles. Gregg Toland, who was the cinematographer for Freund's film, was the same man who would six years later photograph *Citizen Kane.* In the early 1970s, in her series of articles (and subsequent book) on *Citizen Kane,* Pauline Kael stated the following:

> I recently looked at a print of *Mad Love,* and the resemblances to *Citizen Kane* are even greater than my memories of it suggested. Not only is the large room with the fireplaces at Xanadu similar to Lorre's domain as a mad doctor, with similar lighting and similar placement of figures, but Kane's appearance and makeup in some sequences might be a facsimile of Lorre's. Lorre, who had come out of the German theatre and German films, played in a stylized manner that is visually imitated in *Kane.* And, amusingly, that screeching white cockatoo, which isn't in the script of *Kane* but appeared out of nowhere in the movie to provide an extra "touch," is a regular member of Lorre's household.
>
> . . . [Toland] probably responded to Welles' penchant for tales of terror and his desire for a portentous mythic look. . . . It's the Gothic atmosphere, partly derived from Toland's work on *Mad Love,* that inflates *Citizen Kane* and puts it in a different tradition from the newspaper comedies and the big bios of the thirties. . . . The dark, Gothic horror style, with looming figures, and with vast interiors that suggested castles rather than houses, formed the basis for much of Welles' later visual style [*The Citizen Kane Book*].

Horror films set in modern urban America were a rarity in the 1930s. Lewton is often credited with providing the first examples of localized, up-to-date, urban horror, but this distinction really belongs to Hungarian émigré Michael Curtiz for his creation of three near-classic forerunners of urban horror-noir: *Doctor X* (1931), *Mystery of the Wax Museum* (1933), and *The Walking Dead* (1936), each of them set in contemporary New York City and released by Warner Bros.

All three films reveal Curtiz as a visionary director (in the Fritz Langian mold) working in a noirish milieu well before the release of Lang's American debut, *Fury* (1936). Because of Curtiz's later associations with Errol Flynn epics and other crowd pleasers (*Casablanca* and *Yankee Doodle Dandy* among the latter), there is a tendency to dismiss his contributions to the horror genre. But Curtiz's three chillers anticipate the look of such 1940s horror noir classics as *Stranger on the Third Floor* (1940), *Among the Living* (1941), *The Face Behind the Mask* (1941), *I Wake Up Screaming* (1941), *Cat People* (1942), and *The Seventh Victim* (1943).

Bolstered by a strong cast (Lionel Atwill, Fay Wray, and Preston Foster), *Doctor X* has some wonderfully ghoulish moments. The plot, which follows the exploits of a scalpel-wielding "moon killer" who cannibalizes his victims, provided a gruesome edge that never would have passed the Production Code had the movie been released a couple years later. The ever-nefarious Atwill plays Dr. Xavier, a suspicious surgeon whose red herring status is dispelled a little too early in the film. The film's biggest liability is the hero, a wiseacre reporter played by Lee Tracy. Tracy is obnoxious rather than funny, and it's difficult to believe that even *Doctor X*'s contemporary audiences felt otherwise. Nonetheless, the wisecracking-reporter-in-love role was to become, rather unfortunately, a staple of the genre throughout the decade.

Doctor X's noirish overtones can found in waterfront streets murky with fog and shadow or a dimly lit city morgue where pathologists engaged in their work display faces distorted by low-key lighting. At other times we are transported to futuristic sets within a stately mansion, the interior design of which appears to draw equal inspiration from Fritz Lang's *Metropolis* (1926) and—with its lopsided lines and unlikely shaped secret doorways—*The Cabinet of Dr. Caligari*.

Although *Mystery of the Wax Museum* is not nearly as unconventional as *Dr. X*, it is generally more satisfying. Not only does it boast a superior role for Lionel Atwill (perhaps the best of his career) and another good performance from champion screamer Fay Wray, but its comic relief, via a wisecracking female reporter, this time actually works. Glenda Farrell offers unexpected appeal in her role as the spunky, streetwise reporter, years ahead of highly acclaimed similar girl reporter roles played by Jean Arthur in *Mr. Deeds Goes to Town* (1936) and Rosalind Russell in *His Girl Friday* (1940).

Glenda Farrell's plucky performance as the streetwise (and rather coarse) reporter prefigures the kind of strong, resilient females that would find their way into many a Val Lewton film. Farrell's machine-gun delivery and flippant persona may be trying at times, but we recognize her vitality and her sexuality; for those reasons alone, we hope she survives through the last reel. Glenda Farrell would have been perfectly cast as Rose Mahoney had there ever been a genuine film adaptation of Lewton's 1932 novel, *No Bed of Her Own*.

The plot of *Mystery of the Wax Museum* (by now known to most horror fans as a result of its extremely successful 1953 Vincent Price remake, *House of Wax*) concerns a wax sculptor (Atwill) who becomes crippled and disfigured in a fire when his unscrupulous business partner decides to burn down their wax museum and claim the insurance. Years pass and the sculptor relocates to New York, where he plans the grand opening of his new museum. Because of the extent of his afflictions, however, he must take some shortcuts, namely graverobbing and murder to provide deathmask models for a more expedient method of sculpting.

The burning of the wax museum and the grotesque melting of the sculpted figures therein is a grisly prelude for the horrors to come. The scene in the morgue, where a shrouded female corpse sits up (a normal reaction from the embalming fluid, so the coroner tells us), accompanied by a dead woman's involuntary sigh, still raises some hackles. Like *Doctor X*, *Wax Museum* is full of urban noir touches and a few effective shocks. Rainy streets, a noir staple, saturate the film's opening, and three distorted human shadows pass before the morgue entrance in grand expressionistic style. Interestingly, the two-color technicolor process used in both *Doctor X* and *Mystery of the Wax Museum* seems to suit the noir style almost as well as a black-and-white medium.

The Walking Dead (1936) was Curtiz's last, and probably best, horror film. The plot chronicles the unfortunate fate of John Ellman, a concert pianist framed on a murder charge by a gang of mobsters, electrocuted, and then brought back to life, whereupon he makes a little visit to each of the men who framed him. Karloff's John Ellman is played for optimum sympathy, and it is the revived Ellman who continues to haunt the memory of those who have seen the film. Simultaneously tragic and creepy, the mute walking corpse confronts his enemies without actually having a hand in their subsequent deaths; the sight of the spectral figure is enough to insure the rash actions that lead to the mobsters' well-deserved misfortunes.

The scene where the revived Ellman stares down his enemies one by one, while playing piano in a bizarre postmortem concert, is a premiere showcase for Karloff's prowess as the most subtle of physical actors. Like his mute portrayal of the Monster in *Frankenstein*, his role in *The Walking Dead* affords him the opportunity to show that less is more, a concept that seemed to have been lost altogether on his fellow horror star, Bela Lugosi.

Although the connections of *The Walking Dead* with our subject are slight, there is a subtlety at work that recalls the dark tragedy of several of the Lewton films. Karloff's creepy catatonic state also shares something in common with the two examples of the living dead in Lewton's *I Walked with a Zombie*.

If Curtiz's horror films fell short of masterpiece status, one shouldn't wonder, since they were made during his most prolific Hollywood period; *Mystery of the Wax Museum*, for instance, was only one of seven features that Curtis directed in 1933. Had he continued in the horror vein with the expanded budgets and shooting schedules of his mainstream films, the results could have been wondrous. Consider his 1941 adaptation of Jack London's

Fredric March and Miriam Hopkins in *Dr. Jekyll and Mr. Hyde* (1931).

The Sea Wolf, a film which bears several thematic connections to Lewton's *Ghost Ship.* Although not a horror film, *The Sea Wolf,* with its story of a psychopathic sea captain (brilliantly played by Edward G. Robinson) aboard a renegade ship called *The Ghost,* is certainly horrific. Moreover, its evocative, fog-laden sea imagery contains enough haunting atmosphere for several horror features.

MGM led the 1930s parade as Hollywood's most prestigious studio, but Paramount marched closely behind. Paramount films were known for their European flair, their exotic locales, their sophistication, and—dating back to Cecil B. DeMille and, more recently, Ernst Lubitsch and Josef von Sternberg—their reputation for surprisingly steamy sex scenes. Paramount pictures looked different from those of their rival studios; they had a glow, a sheen. The studio presented a world of soft misty edges, a world where white clothing looked absolutely radiant, and where the glint of an eye sparkled like a reflection in cut glass.

Although the studio was never really associated with the horror trade, during the early 1930s Paramount made four horror films, *Dr. Jekyll and Mr. Hyde, Island of Lost Souls, Murders in the Zoo,* and *Supernatural,* which prefigured the sex-triggers-the-beast motif which was central to Lewton's *Cat People* and *The Leopard Man.*

The 1932 release of *Dr. Jekyll and Mr. Hyde* seemed to indicate that Paramount was about to give Universal some fierce competition. Directed by Armenian-born Rouben Mammoulian, *Dr. Jekyll and Mr. Hyde* is a class-A production all the way. Mammoulian made an effort to play-up the Victorian moralities of its characters, as if to make sure 1930s audiences were able to recognize how old-fashioned the 1800s were. Seen today, the film is seriously impaired by the exaggerated propriety of several drawing room scenes, especially the romantic interludes between Jekyll and his fiancée (played by Rose Hobart). But whenever actor Fredric March becomes the primitive Hyde (and he, indeed, resembles a primate), the film shifts into high gear.

The role is an astonishing tour de force for March; so complete is the transformation that nothing of the actor can be seen in Hyde. In fact, Hyde's body language differs so drastically from Jekyll's that we almost suspect that another actor has stepped in for March. His twitchy countenance and simian mannerisms are quite unlike anything done before or since. Because the makeup gets progressively more grotesque with each transformation, our earliest glimpses of Hyde, which rely less on makeup and more upon March's quirky mannerisms, are absolutely inspired. When Hyde looks into the mirror and takes in his first view of his twitching face, expressing sudden bursts of rapture and narcissistic glee ("Free! Free!" he chants), we know that sex is the primary thing on his mind, a Freudian element which foreshadows Irena Dubrovna's transformations in *Cat People* and Dr. Galbraith's psychopathic murders in *The Leopard Man.* (To some extent, all of Lewton's RKO films, including his two nonhorror entries, *Mademoiselle Fifi* and *Youth Runs Wild,* exhibit a preoccupation with man's dual nature, revealing that there is both a Dr. Jekyll and a Mr. Hyde in every one of us.)

Fredric March's simian Mr. Hyde would actually fit in rather nicely with the "manimals" in *The Island of Lost Souls* (1932). Based on the H.G. Wells novel, *The Island of Dr. Moreau,* this Paramount adaptation was at the time

Lota, the panther woman (Kathleen Burke), in *Island of Lost Souls* (Paramount, 1932).

of its release panned by the critics for being lurid and tasteless; author Wells himself reportedly disliked the film. Like *Freaks,* which it somewhat resembles, *The Island of Lost Souls* was banned in England. According to William K. Everson's *Classics of the Horror Film,* "Despite being billed by Paramount as 'H.G. Wells's surging rhapsody of terror,' and ballyhooed by a spectacular stunt advertising campaign built primarily around the Panther Woman, for whom a well-publicized search had been conducted, *The Island of Lost Souls* was a comparative commercial failure at the time."

Compared to present Hollywood standards, *The Island of Lost Souls,* directed by Erle C. Kenton, is a subtle, if not exactly tame, excursion into horror and depravity. Charles Laughton plays Dr. Moreau, a vivisectionist who, banished from his English homeland, finds an ideal location for his unwholesome practices on a tropical island which is inhabited by a vast array of humanoid animals; apemen, dogmen, wolfmen, bearmen, pigmen, and assorted other grotesque hybrids, all of them the handiwork of Moreau's experimental surgery. The bestial makeup is imaginative, convincing, and genuinely frightening, especially when these grotesques revolt against Moreau like refugees from a George Romero movie. The dogman, M'ling, when hit by a drunken sea captain shakes his head like a canine recovering from a bath; the extreme close-up we get of his pointed ear provides a memorably chilling moment.

When Edward Parker (Richard Arlen) finds himself stranded on the island and consequently under Moreau's bidding, the doctor tries to bring about a romantic match between Parker and Lota (Kathleen Burke), the panther woman. The most successful of Moreau's animal-to-human experiments, Lota looks appealingly human; knowing nothing of her feline origins, Parker has tremendous difficulty resisting her seduction. After kissing her, he voices his regrets and confesses he is already engaged to be married. Once his fiancée conveniently manages to find her way to the island (via a sympathetic boat captain), Lota's jealousy causes her to regress; on the ends of her fingers she begins to sport curved panther claws.

The Island of Lost Souls is the only film that has been verified as one of the many that Lewton and Bodeen (and perhaps, by then, even Jacques Tourneur and Mark Robson) screened during those first months at RKO. Although obvious parallels to *Cat People* abound, the horrifying climax of *The Island of Lost Souls*—when Moreau is ruthlessly attacked by his suddenly fearless victims—resembles (as does the climax of *Freaks*) the ending of another Lewton film: *Bedlam*. While Moreau takes caged animals and transforms them into something resembling human beings, *Bedlam*'s sadistic villain, Master Sims (Boris Karloff), takes human beings and transforms them into something resembling caged animals. In either case, Moreau and Sims—men who play God in a most merciless fashion—were destined to see the tables of justice turned upon themselves.

Speaking of sadists and animals in cages, we have Paramount's third horror offering, *Murders in the Zoo* (1933). This rarely seen film is notorious for its opening sequence, where Lionel Atwill, playing the insanely jealous big game hunter/zoologist, Eric Gorman, sews together the lips of one of his wife's suitors (we are given a shockingly gruesome close-up of Gorman's rudimentary stitchwork), and leaves him stranded, bound and tied, in the middle of the African jungle. When Gorman reunites with his wife (played by Kathleen Burke, previously Lota, the panther woman, in the Kenton film), she inquires of her paramour's whereabouts; Gorman casually tells her that the man in question has departed from the expedition. When asked if he left any sort of message, Gorman glibly responds, "He didn't say anything."

Although most of *Murders in the Zoo*, directed by Edward Sutherland, is not particularly subtle in its approach, as this opening sequence attests (having more in common with the Herman Cohen's 1963 sadistic thriller, *The Black Zoo*, than anything in the Lewton catalog), its city zoo location is used to evoke some genuine atmosphere that is highly reminiscient of *Cat People*'s city zoo scenes. During the day, the zoo is bright and festive with people and children milling about, drawing wonder and amusement from the sights therein. During the off hours, however, when the sun is down and the patrons have vanished, the zoo is a different place entirely. The baleful cries of its caged specimens, the haunting bleakness of its empty walkways, the distorted moonlit shadows that cover the grounds, and the myriad patches of darkness that greet the eye in every direction all work to make the zoo a less-than-desirable place for a midnight stroll.

Supernatural (1933) is about executed astrologer/murderess, Ruth Rogen (Vivienne Osborne), whose passion for revenge refuses to remain buried in her grave. In a variation on the doppelganger theme, the spirit of Rogen takes possession of innocent bystander Roma Courtney (Carole Lombard) in order to get back at Nicky Hammond (William Farnum), the man who wronged her. The possessed Roma ducks her boyfriend (played by Randolph Scott) in order to seduce Hammond; when she has him in her fond embraces (with his hand squeezing her breast, believe it or not), she goes for the kill. *Supernatural*'s terrific opening montage promises more than the rest of the film delivers but this Paramount effort is a fascinating and very erotic minor entry to the genre. Its sexual content (which never would have made it through the censors had it been released a year later) kept it off television for a number of years (a fate it shared with *Island of Lost Souls* and *Murders in the Zoo*). Even today it is rarely telecast.

Like the horror films of Michael Curtiz, *Supernatural* is set in a modern urban environment, again New York City, and it also displays some of the expressionistic flourishes to be found in the Curtiz films (and, later, in the urban thrillers of the 1940s). *Supernatural* foreshadows *Cat People* in its use of a female predator whose killing instincts are triggered by sexual passion. It was the second horror feature by the Halperin brothers, a pair of Poverty Row filmmakers whose one-picture contract with Paramount was a result of their staggeringly successful low-budget horror film called *White Zombie,* itself a most significant predecessor to another Lewton film.

Most Poverty Row horror films of the 1930s avoided the admission of ghosts or monsters; it was cheaper and safer to utilize the tried-and-true formula of old house thrillers. *White Zombie* (1932), one of but a handful of supernatural Poverty Row horror films, probably had some direct influence upon Lewton's *I Walked with a Zombie* (and possibly upon Orson Welles's voodoo *Macbeth*). Directed by Victor Halperin and produced by his brother Edward, *White Zombie* was a fish out of water from its inception. The Halperins chose to do away with the staccato dialogue so characteristic of the early talkies and, instead, to treat the entire production more or less as a silent film with a few speaking parts.

Bela Lugosi, fresh from his performance in Robert Florey's critically panned *Murders in the Rue Morgue,* is given a meaty role here as Murder Legendre, though many critics responded by identifying the variety of meat as ham. *White Zombie* was shot at two different studios, both rented for the occasion: the RKO-Pathé lot (where the Halperins had to shoot around *The Most Dangerous Game* and *King Kong*) and the Universal lot (where *The Old Dark House* and *The Mummy* were being put under wraps). Independently produced by the Halperins, *White Zombie* was released by United Artists. It was enormously popular and according to Richard Bojarski's *The Films of Bela Lugosi,* "made Phil Goldstone, the producer, a multi-millionaire."

In *White Zombie,* a young couple, Madeline Short (Madge Bellamy) and Neil Parker (John Harron), have been invited to Haiti in order to be wed on the plantation of island aristocrat Charles Beaumont (Robert Frazer). This is merely a ploy, as Beaumont, in love with Madeline, wants her for himself. After she resists his advances, Beaumont enlists the aid of the Murder Legendre, another plantation owner, but one who uses zombies as workers. Using a drugged corsage, Legendre casts a spell that causes Madeline to drop dead on her wedding day; the unrequited groom, overcome with grief, stays on the island to become a drunken derelict. Meanwhile, Legendre works his spell, and Beaumont is given his bride: a beautiful wide-eyed zombie wife who can play piano marvelously but can do little else. Because Beaumont's idea of a honeymoon was more than hearing a series of cadenzas, he complains to Legendre that he would rather have Madeline dead than a soulless bride. But Legendre has his own designs on the beautiful Madeline and drugs Beaumont's drink, an initial step in the zombie process. Neil sobers up and calls upon Dr. Brunner (Joseph Cawthorne), a missionary who has made a study of native superstitions and thus serves as a Van Helsing prototype for the rest of the film. The two heroes are off to the rescue.

White Zombie was the first of its type and introduced the word "zombie" to America's movie-going public. The first widespread application of the term came about through William B. Seabrook's 1929 book about Haitian voodoo, *The Magic Island.* Early in 1932, a play called *Zombie,* by Kenneth Webb, opened on the New York stage. A month after the play's debut, Webb brought suit against the Halperin brothers, who had announced plans to make the film called *White Zombie.* Of course, Webb did not invent the word, so he lost the case.

For all the shortcomings of *White Zombie,* including its nod to the outmoded techniques of the silent era, the film is visually rich. The Halperins believed, and rightfully so, that sound films of the early 1930s were too talky. The Halperins may have been out-of-step with the industry in their insistence on minimal dialogue (they wanted to keep it down to 15 percent), but they were ahead of their time in allowing an early sound film some room for visual narrative.

Good use is made of wipes, split screens, double exposures, and superimpositions as storytelling devices. The Halperins were also progressive in their use of sound; instead of filling the soundtrack with endless chatter, they intermixed pregnant pauses with innovative sound effects. In *Forgotten Horrors* (a study of Poverty Row horror films from the early 1930s), authors George E. Turner and Michael H. Price make their own assertions concerning *White Zombie's* relevance to our subject: "Fine use is made of long silences punctuated with sudden noises and occasional bursts of music. In this respect, *White Zombie* proves an ancestor of the unusual handling of sound in the Val Lewton productions *The Cat People* (1942) and *I Walked with a Zombie* (1943)."

We have no way of knowing whether Val Lewton or Jacques Tourneur ever viewed *White Zombie,* but there are a number of striking parallels between the Halperins' film and *I Walked with a Zombie.* The two films include uncannily similar tilt shots to give us our first look at a zombie. In both cases the camera starts with a close-up of the immobile zombie's bare feet, and then, very gradually, the camera begins its upward climb—all this accompanied by absolute silence—until, finally, we stare face-to-face into the creature's lifeless eyes and hold. Admittedly, this manner of camera direction necessitates no great leap of imagination, but this type of moving tilt shot was not at all a common practice in horror films of the 1930s and 1940s.

Both films deal with a white woman being turned into a zombie to keep her from loving a particular man, who as a result becomes a drunk; moreover, each film includes a cafe scene designed to show the man in question drowning his grief in drink. A missionary figure open to voodoo beliefs is a pivotal character in each of the films (though their functions and sexes differ). Furthermore, both films make use of authentic voodoo ritual chants. While the catchy voodoo chants in *White Zombie* and *I Walked with a Zombie* are by no means identical, they *are* very similar (sounding as if they could be the A and B sides of a record on the voodoo "top ten").

If *I Walked with a Zombie* is lauded for its poetic images and haunting use of a soundtrack, we can easily give similar praise to *White Zombie.* Visually, *White Zombie* offers some breathtaking examples of sophisticated composition; camera setups often show taste and style. Despite a primitive production and a number of choppy transitions, the film shows an unusual amount of imagination. William K. Everson, in *Classics of the Horror Film,* accurately addresses this aspect of the film:

> There is a meticulous, almost ornamental composition of the frame throughout: Zombies parade silently behind latticed windows, scenes that are almost Dreyer-like in their pace and design. Lugosi and Madge Bellamy frequently move into a scene by being framed through apertures in masonry, or staircase bannisters, the resulting scenes being almost literal equivalents of the old, laboriously handwritten books, where the first letter of the first word of a new chapter would be elaborately enlarged and illuminated.

One shot in particular pulls back through the aperture of an ornate gate, in spite of there being no evidence of the gate in the first part of the shot; it is the kind of trick camerawork one identifies with Welles's *Citizen Kane.* A number of shots capture the silhouettes of zombies walking down the hilly slopes, predating a similar composition in Ingmar Bergman's *The Seventh Seal;* a hooded zombie coachdriver (resembling Death incarnate) also anticipates the Bergman film. When Neil grieves in the cafe, we see only the shadows of other cafe patrons on the wall behind him, figures dancing, conversing across tables; although the device is primitive (while, at the same time, self-consciously artistic), it informs us that Neil is living in a world of shadows. The matte shots of the magnificent exterior of Legendre's cliff-top castle, with the waves lapping the shore beneath, possess the hypnotic majesty and fairy-tale atmosphere befitting a narrative about a young bride falling into a trance on her wedding day. Equally impressive are the interior mattes of the castle's cavernous room where the soulless Madeline plays her piano.

The sugar mill scene, with its unbearable creaking of the zombie-powered cane-crushing machine (a sound that resembles the gut-wrenching moans of lost souls), is just one example of how the Halperins made effective use of their soundtrack. One unfortunate specimen of the living dead falls into the machinery without uttering the expected scream, and the wheels just keep on turning, business as usual, the victim's silence letting us know the extent of Legendre's power. Meanwhile, the low, groanlike creaks of the machine aptly serve to represent the victim's pain. Other sounds punctuate the thick atmosphere of the Haitian countryside: squawks from birds of prey, voodoo drum rhythms (credited to Guy Bevier Williams), and numerous screams in the night. When the drunken Neil stumbles toward Madeline's crypt, crying out her name with every step, the camera stays behind as he enters her tomb and the audience knows that he will find an empty coffin. There is absolute silence as we wait . . . and wait . . . until, finally, from the echoing depths of the crypt, we hear Neil's unbridled scream. Fade out.

White Zombie is not an unqualified masterpiece. The acting is stilted, the timing is off, and certain aspects of the film are haphazard and sloppy. John Harron, miscast as Neil, is so awkward and insipid one would be happy to have him replaced with any of the bland romantic leads who waltzed through Universal's horror films. Madge Bellamy makes an outstanding zombie, but when she's her normal self, gangway and head for the lobby. Robert Frazer, as Beaumont, is not bad if you are up for a character with the behavior of a villain and the looks of Liberace. Joseph Cawthorne, as Dr. Brunner, would be slightly more convincing if his Christian missionary character did not speak with a Yiddish accent. Even Lugosi is off the mark now and then; the silent pauses between his lines last entirely too long. Although *White Zombie* is a film with courage, a film difficult not to admire, its ambitions overstep the competence of its principal players.

It is worth noting that the vaulting success of this Poverty Row feature also prefigures the "low-budget-film-makes-good" phenomenon that is so essential a part of the Val Lewton mystique. Whether RKO's own voodoo venture, *I Walked with a Zombie,* was a deliberate rehashing of the elements of *White Zombie* (mixed, of course, with liberal doses of *Jane Eyre*) or whether Lewton and company had in fact paid any attention to the earlier film does not matter. Regardless of where the truth of this matter lies, the Lewton film is a direct descendent of the Halperins' pioneer effort.

In 1932, when *Murders in the Rue Morgue* was in postproduction, Universal announced plans for a follow-up Poe film, *The Black Cat.* The bad reviews and poor box office of *Murders,* however, made them think twice, and the follow-up Poe project was temporarily shelved. A young Austrian-born art director named Edgar Ulmer, who had once worked in Berlin with F.W. Murnau (the director of *Nosferatu*), eventually found himself working at Universal. It was he who dusted off the second Poe adaptation and eventually, in 1934, made it his own; the result marked the first time Boris Karloff and Bela Lugosi were paired together in the same film. Their last of eight filmic pairings would be Lewton's *The Body Snatcher.*

Because *The Black Cat* deals with a satanic cult, it begs comparison with Lewton's own satanic cult film, *The Seventh Victim.* Films about satanism were rare during the 1930s and 1940s, so the two mentioned films are apt to be paired together though their approaches to the subject are quite different. Ulmer, who had a hand in the script, modeled the character of Hjalmar Poelzig (Boris Karloff) upon the notorious British master of the black arts Aleister Crowley, reputedly the "most evil man of the 20th century." According to *The Penguin Encyclopedia of Horror and the Supernatural* (edited by Jack Sullivan):

> [Aleister Crowley] was reputed to be a cannibal, a murderer, a child sacrificer, a traitor—in short an evil being who had performed every wicked deed known to man. . . . Crowley's life was a prolonged experience with drugs, sexual orgies, and strange magical practices, all to acquire supernatural powers and advancement. He believed that he had revelations from higher beings and wrote them down as new sacred texts; in the name of these documents he underwent unspeakable degradations and drove his wives and associates to madness or suicide. He accepted the mission of destroying Christianity and setting up in its stead worship of the devil. . . . He had been a German agent in the United States during World War I. . . . Yet Crowley was an intelligent, well-educated man, and, oddly enough, one of the best chess players in England.

To some degree, *The Black Cat* plays like a reworked version of *The Old Dark House* (or a number of other old house mysteries), where, in the midst of a terrible storm, a young couple is forced to seek shelter in an ominous dwelling (except, in this case, it's a new house). At other times, Ulmer's film, with its newlywed couple whose honeymoon is cut short by the interference of two sinister men, one worse than the other, bears some similarity to *White Zombie*. To be sure, Lugosi's Murder Legendre and Karloff's Hjalmar Poelzig are fashioned from the same bolt of cloth, both of them looking like nothing less than alternate interpretations of the devil incarnate.

Over the years, *The Black Cat* has achieved a film cult reputation, not only for Ulmer's direction and outstanding visuals, but also because of the ripe performances of its two horror stars. Although loosely based on an Edgar Allan Poe story, the only things it has in common with the work are its title, its ailuraphobia (fear of cats), and its pervasive dementia. Since the film was made over to accomodate the overriding demands of the studio and the censors, *The Black Cat*'s narrative makes little sense. In *Cult Movies* 3, Dan Peary underscores the erratic nature of the plot when he says, "It's a film where a man marries, murders, and embalms his friend's wife, then marries his stepdaughter and kills her, too, and then is skinned alive by his father-in-law."

Giving an in-depth analysis of *The Black Cat* would be like untangling a massive length of garden hose only to find, once it has been unraveled, that we have been handling a serpent. *The Black Cat* is the kind of film where continuity appears deliberately abandoned. Edgar Ulmer claimed that his primary influence for the nightmare texture of his film was Robert Weine's *The Cabinet of Dr. Caligari*. Certainly the art deco set design presents an otherworldly atmosphere, and the lack of logic does resemble the "anything goes" fabric of a disturbing dream. (Actually, a dream sequence in Ulmer's film would have been terribly redundant.)

The Black Cat's obvious connection with Lewton is its relationship with *The Seventh Victim*. It is true that both films portray devil worshippers as otherwise ordinary people (Karloff's character being a glaring exception), but the films are really quite dissimilar. The ailuraphobia of Ulmer's film is in abundant supply in *Cat People*, but, oddly enough, the Lewton film that most resembles *The Black Cat* is *Isle of the Dead* (Lewton's own variation of the old house Boris Karloff thriller). While Karloff's villainous roles differ in the two works, both films are unremittingly morbid in their preoccupation with war, treachery, battlefields, revenge, and death. They make a great double bill.

A 1935 film that shared some qualities with Lewton's final three RKO films was Columbia's *The Black Room*, a literate thriller that gave Boris Karloff the opportunity to show the kind of sterling performance he was capable of giving. *The Black Room* is, for Columbia, an atypically stylish and elaborate-looking period piece. Karloff has the dual role in this variation of the evil twin theme. While there is nothing novel about the basic plot gimmick of *The Black Room*, Roy William Neill (who would later direct *Frankenstein Meets the Wolfman* and a number of Sherlock Holmes entries at Universal) meets the occasion with an incredible degree of verve. On the one hand, *The Black Room* has the look and feel of the Lewton/Karloff films; on the other, it shares some things with the James Whale films, particularly the expressionistic set design (drafty castles, painted skies, twisted trees, and a spooky cemetery) which deliberately vaults style over realism.

The Black Room opened to lukewarm reviews in 1935 and even to this day remains an underrated film. For Karloff fans it is sheer delight, holding up quite well after several viewings. The dual roles are nicely delineated: Gregor, the eldest twin, revels in debauchery and sadism, while the younger, Anton, is kindhearted and righteous. What makes *The Black Room* particularly fascinating is that it includes in one film the good/evil screen personas that Karloff alternately drew upon through his entire career. One is tempted to say Karloff carries the show, but the direction and production are also exemplary in this well-mounted costume melodrama. *The Black Room* is a tasteful, literate production, one which has enormous faith in Karloff's acting ability. Perhaps this is why it seems like such a close cousin to *The Body Snatcher* and *Bedlam*.

The year 1935 had been a halcyon one for Hollywood horror, but difficult times were ahead. Universal's *The Raven* (1935), the Karloff/Lugosi follow-up to *The Black Cat,* signaled the sudden end to the horror craze. Because of its torture theme, which incited considerable outrage in England, *The Raven* initiated a virtual ban on all horror films shown in the British Isles. Universal, the only major studio to depend on horror as its stock-in-trade, had never established a reputation for brisk, economic production. Unlike most of the other majors, it did not own a chain of movie theaters as a supplementary source of income, so the British market was vital to the Laemmles. The insistence of the British Board of Censors upon rating horror films with an "H" (horror) certificate was the kiss of death to Universal's horror exports. The studio's resulting losses could not have been much worse if horror films had been banned outright.

In the spring of 1936, Universal was headed toward imminent bankruptcy, and the Laemmles were forced to sell the longtime family business to Charles R. Rogers and the Standard Capital Corporation. Universal's would-be boy wonder, Junior Laemmle, at the ripe age of 28 had already seen the last of his glory days; he would never produce another film. By the time the last Carl Laemmle, Jr., horror film, *Dracula's Daughter,* was released in 1936, the studio had already changed hands. *Dracula* had launched the Universal horror boom, and now its belated sequel, *Dracula's Daughter,* was bringing the cycle to a close.

Dracula's Daughter, loosely based on the Bram Stoker short story "Dracula's Guest," was a deliberately paced, provocative, and intelligently scripted film that fell several notches short of being the classic sequel it could have been. Much of its originally hefty budget was forfeited as the result of misfortune and mismanagement but, as Val Lewton would soon prove, quality films with intelligent scripts could be delivered on a low budget, and *Dracula's Daughter* aspires to similar virtues.

Future Lewton art director, Albert S. D'Agostino, may be another reason for drawing such a comparison. D'Agostino's efforts are put to good use in *Dracula's Daughter*; his redressing of Charles D. Hall's 1931 Castle Dracula set is thoroughly satisfying, and the look of earlier scenes—the fog-shrouded funeral pyre, the murky London streets, the misty bridge, and the title character's studio apartment—are appropriately eerie and tastefully rendered.

But it is the film's theme, content, and pervasively dark mood that make it such a close cousin to the Lewton entries. Directed by Lambert Hillyer, *Dracula's Daughter* is the first of many Hollywood films to treat vampirism as an addiction; as a result of this slant, Hillyer's film has many things in common with *Cat People*. Its title character, going under the name of Countess Marya Zaleska, does not want to be a vampire; in fact, she makes numerous efforts to cure herself of her curse.

Like Irena Dubrovna in *Cat People*, Countess Zaleska (Gloria Holden) is not a monster but a tragic woman plagued by a sinister heritage over which she has no control. Like the doomed and guilt-ridden heroine of the Lewton film, the Countess is an artist with an exotic old-world background; she is out of her element in the modern urban setting in which she currently resides. Although both women win our sympathy, we see the folly in the way they cling to a hopeless delusion. Try as they may, they are not capable of leading normal lives. In the hopes of ridding themselves of their torment, both women consult urbane but incredulous psychiatrists, but these preventative measures, by the final reel, only serve to seal their doom.

Like Lewton's films, *Dracula's Daughter* shies away from heavy-handed supernatural elements; there is a noticeable scarcity of bats, rats, crosses, holy water, and the range of other gimmicky trappings associated with the vampire film. Instead, Countess Zaleska acts like a real person; she paints pictures, uses telephones, listens to the radio, and travels in automobiles and airplanes. When her romantic rival lies about the whereabouts of the psychiatrist, the Countess's anger is entirely convincing because her reaction is human, not vampiric. Because she is a sympathetic and complex human being—even if she is one of the undead—vampirism is made to seem like a genuine calamity, allowing us to identify with the soul of the monster. Such identification is also a primary source of *Cat People*'s effectiveness.

In the opening reel, the police cell in which Dracula's body is kept is appropriately dark and dire; even the unfunny comic relief of the policemen does not entirely ruin the dreadful feeling of the place. We hear noises in the cell and see something rippling underneath the dirt floor; we see the floor beginning to crack open. That such phenomena remain unexplained evokes a lingering feeling of unease, a sense of undisclosed horror that is difficult to dismiss for the remainder of the film. The haunted foggy moor where Dracula's body is burned is perfectly captured by George Robinson's camera;

it's a moody, expressionistic vision with mystical overtones. The stark and penetrating cries of a wolf, coupled with this dense and misty atmosphere, suggest the kind of dark poetry for which the Lewton films would be praised. Glory Holden is appropriately aloof and ethereal as Countess Zaleska; adding class to the entire production, she is throughout a welcome counterpart to Bela Lugosi.

Unfortunately, the film's virtues, however enterprising they may be, are seriously undermined by its rushed ending. In its final reels, when the entire cast seems to be boarding airplanes, the whole thing takes a silly turn. There is no real reason for everyone to hightail it to Transylvania except to make use of the existing Charles D. Hall sets. The villagers are glimpsed in a laughably short scene, apparently thrown in to give the costume department something to do before the new management came in with hatchet men and plans for reorganization.

During the 1937–1938 horror dry spell, a new breed of cinematic thriller was beginning to evolve. A coterie of British playwrights—Frank Vosper, Barre Lyndon, Emlyn Williams, Patrick Hamilton, and a few others—were writing stage thrillers that harked back to the spirit of George du Maurier's *Trilby* and Tod Slaughter's numerous British melodramas. Gone were the clutching hands, the bizarre masquerades, the contrived gimmickry; they were replaced by cultured, charming, or handsome men (often all three) whose specialty was psychological terror. These suave villains relished the power they held over their distressed heroines; though more subtle than the likes of Svengali, this new model of psychological terrorist wove webs which were just as binding.

The British film *Love from a Stranger* (1937), directed by Rowland V. Lee and adapted for the stage by Frank Vosper from a story by Agatha Christie, provided a chilling alternative to the horror film. Even better was an American film, *Night Must Fall*, an MGM adaptation of an Emlyn Williams play. *Night Must Fall* (1937), which for the time was an uncharacteristically gruesome thriller, is often overlooked when surveys of the genre comment upon the dearth of horror entries during the 1937-1938 hiatus. The refusal to regard *Night Must Fall* as a horror film is curious; it is true that it contains no supernatural elements, but if Lang's *M*, Whale's *The Old Dark House*, Hitchcock's *Psycho*, and Demme's *The Silence of the Lambs* are considered influential films in the horror genre, then surely the same must apply to *Night Must Fall*, a film about a charming psychopathic rapist who decapitates his victim and proceeds to carry her head about in a piece of luggage.

Although Richard Thorpe's film signaled no immediate cinematic trend, it set the stage for the kind of Hollywood thriller that would dominate the 1940s, influencing the films of a wide variety of directors, including Alfred Hitchcock, John Brahm, Val Lewton, Orson Welles, George Cukor, Robert Siodmak, and many others. Like so many of the 1940s thrillers it heralds,

Night Must Fall is a classy "A" picture, with powerful performances by all its principal players. Robert Montgomery, against Louis B. Mayer's advice, fought for the role of Danny, the psychopath; Mayer thought it would ruin the actor's image and possibly his career. Instead, the role brought Montgomery his only Best Actor Academy Award nomination, at the same time giving his career a much needed boost. His performance is superb and quite unlike anything else Hollywood had to offer at the time or for many years to come. Rarely has an American actor done so well with a British role.

Montgomery is given marvelous support by Rosalind Russell and especially Dame May Whitty (absolutely glorious in her film debut). Russell's Olivia is the niece of the wealthy but garrulous hypochondriac, Mrs. Branson, played by the 72-year-old Whitty. Although Olivia lives with her aunt, presumably to take care of her needs, it is obvious that the two do not get along. Soon a charming but irreverent young man named Danny (Montgomery) comes upon the scene and gloms onto Mrs. Branson, showing concern for her imaginary illnesses. Soon replacing Olivia in responding to Mrs. Branson's every need, Danny develops what appears to be a wonderfully warm relationship with the elderly woman. Soon the neighborhood is humming with the news of another murder as a woman's body (at least most of it) is found very close to the Branson estate.

Night Must Fall is almost entirely dependent upon dialogue, and yet, thanks to the richness of the Emlyn Williams play, the film never fails to capture the viewer's full attention. The final reels are memorable, manipulating the audience into a state of white-knuckled tension. Although Richard Thorpe was never among the pantheon of great directors, he does a superior job here. It is certain that Alfred Hitchcock (who immediately used Dame May Whitty for the title role in his 1937 *The Lady Vanishes*) admired the film; elements of it pop up in numerous Hitchcock opuses, including *Rebecca* (1940), *Suspicion* (1941), *Shadow of a Doubt* (1943), *Dial M for Murder* (1953), *Rear Window* (1954), *Psycho* (1960), and *Frenzy* (1972). In fact, the character of Olivia is only a stone's throw from the reticent but resilient Gothic heroines embodied by Joan Fontaine in Hitchcock's *Rebecca* and *Suspicion*. (Appropriately, Fontaine would also be the heroine in Robert Stevenson's *Jane Eyre* [1943], playing opposite Orson Welles's Rochester.)

Night Must Fall is not only a 1930s macabre classic of the first rank, but it is also an important link between the horror genre and the literate Gothic thrillers that characterized the 1940s: *Ladies in Retirement, Rebecca, Gaslight, The Spiral Staircase, Hangover Square, Experiment Perilous, A Double Life*, and many others.

As influential as Thorpe's film was to the shaping of 1940s thrillers, the Lewton films would probably not have been made had it not been for Universal's late-summer 1938 double bill of two vintage films, *Dracula* and *Frankenstein*, which drew record business in theaters across the country. Universal announced its plans for *Son of Frankenstein* and rather suddenly, 1939 Hollywood was back in the horror business. Once again, most major studios wanted to get a finger in the pie. Paramount released another version of *The Cat and the Canary*. Columbia started a "mad doctor" series with Boris Karloff. Warner Bros. made *The Return of Doctor X* (a sequel in name only). RKO released its remake of *The Hunchback of Notre Dame*, an elaborate, masterfully produced film.

Among all the films in the first wave (1939–1942) of the new cycle, the one that was most instrumental in motivating Charles Koerner's proposal for an RKO horror unit was Universal's December 1941 release of *The Wolf Man*. Hitting the theaters just five days after the bombing of Pearl Harbor, *The Wolf Man* was disparaged by many critics who deemed it inappropriate fare for the times; a country at war, it was believed, had its own nightmares with which to contend and little time for fanciful old-world legends concerning werewolves and gypsies. But Americans attended *The Wolf Man* in droves, according to Michael Brunas, John Brunas, and Tom Weaver's *Universal Horrors*: "The studio made millions off the picture and Chaney reportedly received more fan mail than any other star on the lot."

The Wolf Man was both directed and produced by George Waggner, who would become the studio's new resident expert in classy horror productions. Waggner did a commendable job; with a modestly respectable $180,000 budget, the film looks glossier than its price tag indicates and easily gives the appearance of being a more handsome production than *The Invisible Man Returns*, whose budget tally amounted to $270,000.

Waggner's cast is also impressive, reinforcing the notion that no expense was spared. In addition to leading players Lon Chaney, Jr. and Evelyn Ankers, the film is sprinkled with such "A" supporting performers as Claude Rains, Warren William, Ralph Bellamy, Patric Knowles, Bela Lugosi, and Marie Ouspenskaya. If the cast were not enough to give the film dignity, Curt Siodmak insured further quality with his excellent original screenplay, perhaps the best of his career.

The werewolf movie, at least as Hollywood has chosen to film it, is actually a descendant of the Jekyll-and-Hyde theme, as can be seen in *The Werewolf of London* (1935), which mixed science and legend. A thread that links *Dr. Jekyll and Mr. Hyde, The Werewolf of London, The Wolfman,* and *Cat People* is that the shape-shifter in each film is part of a romantic triangle (though the nature of that triangle varies from film to film). What is more, in each case, the tragic central character lives in fear of harming the one he or she loves.

Rather than attempt to draw science into the plot, *The Wolf Man* plays its supernatural mysticism straight. Siodmak's script displays a pleasing simplicity; everything hinges upon the doomed hero's silver-handled wolf's-head cane, which provides the film's unifying symbol and linking device.

(Oddly, a cane of some sort serves as the deadly weapon in the demise of both Talbot and *Cat People*'s Irena Dubrovna.)

According to authors Michael Brunas, John Brunas, and Tom Weaver in *Universal Horrors,* "Siodmak admitted that he unconsciously duplicated the structure of Greek drama in his script by featuring a hero who cannot escape his fate." Concerning *The Wolf Man*'s connection with Val Lewton, Brunas, Brunas, and Weaver tell us:

> In spite of the popularity of *The Wolf Man,* it still hasn't received its due in certain critical quarters. To many, the '40s was the decade of Val Lewton and, compared to his highly imaginative thrillers wherein the focus was on the unseen presence of terror, *The Wolf Man* seems extremely conventional. It's a rather unfair assessment, considering the fact that RKO ... didn't jump on the horror bandwagon until *The Wolf Man* drew record crowds. It's worth noting, too, that Lewton's first horror movie, *Cat People,* while excellent, smacks of imitation. In fact, Curt Siodmak's unrevised original script clearly anticipated Lewton's subtle approach, keeping the monster out of camera range throughout most of the movie. But concealed horrors just didn't fit in with Universal's formula.

Although the two films were fashioned from separate bolts of cloth, the theme of *Cat People* was obviously inspired by its successful lycanthropic predecessor. But *Cat People* differs (as do all the Lewton films) from its genre antecedents in its provision of well-drawn, more realistic characterizations that one would expect to find among the brilliant scientists, European aristocrats, and bands of gypsies that populated the conventional horror film.

While Universal kept the monster shows coming, Alfred Hitchcock and Fritz Lang were busy making thrillers that avoided genre stereotyping and exotic period locales. A movement toward a new kind of dark thriller was just beginning to take shape.

While most critics acknowledge Fritz Lang's *You Only Live Once* (1937) as a seminal example of what came to be called "film noir," a surprising number of noir elements were already present in the horror genre. The noir protagonist, almost always a down-on-his-luck male, was a tragic hero with a tragic flaw, a character usually beset by hasty decisions, obsessive behavior (often entwined with the lure of a femme fatale), and well-intended ambitions that go awry, a man in a trap of his own making. The noir form was further characterized by both its narrative and visual style; often flashbacks were used, sometimes with accompanying voice-overs, and there was usually an abundance of night scenes characterized by expressionistic camerawork and chiaroscuro lighting.

We can see some elements of this genre in a wide variety of horror films, especially those where men tread the path reserved for the divine. *Dr. Jekyll and Mr. Hyde, The Invisible Man, The Invisible Ray,* and innumerable other

Lobby poster for *Stranger on the Third Floor* (1940—directed by Boris Ingster), the film that anticipates the "look" of the Lewton series.

"mad doctor" films make use of this kind of antihero. Noir elements can also be found in horror films whose protagonists are the innocent victims of misadventure (*The Walking Dead* and *The Wolf Man,* to name but two).

The Lewton RKO films have strong associations with the early 1940s examples of noir melodrama, which is what sets them apart from the horror fare of the previous decade. The prototypical film noir is a modified horror film, one which exploits adult concerns and discards the fantastic elements. Human monsters replace the likes of Boris Karloff and Bela Lugosi, and laws of fate supercede the intervention of mystic powers or scientific experiments gone awry. Most important is that both genres are the stuff of nightmares.

Authors Alain Silver and Elizabeth Ward (in *Film Noir: An Encyclopedia Reference to the American Style*) bring up "the interesting speculation that RKO developed the quintessential noir style of the 1940's due to a unique synthesizing of the expressionistic style of [Orson] Welles and the moody, Gothic atmosphere of Lewton."

Boris Ingster's *Stranger on the Third Floor* (1940), the film that bridged the gap between horror and noir, is especially noteworthy to Lewtonphiles because it combines the RKO house style with the talents of an ace expressionist photographer, Nicholas Musuraca, who would go on to shoot five of the Lewton films. The presence of Peter Lorre as a furtive psychopath in a dark urban environment recalls Fritz Lang's *M.* Lorre plays an escaped lunatic who kills only when threatened. Unfortunately, his paranoia makes just about anyone a potential threat and, thereby, a potential victim. When the story's well-intentioned hero (John McGuire) wrongly implicates a man (played by Elisha Cook) for a murder committed by Lorre, the innocent man is tried in a most incompetent manner, found guilty, and sentenced to death. The hero has no real reason to doubt the court's decision, but feels the pangs of guilt that come with providing the case's most damning evidence.

Here begins a long and extremely effective voice-over as the hero ruminates over the tenuous nature of circumstantial evidence. When he goes home, he finds a stranger lurking the halls of his apartment building, chases him out, and then realizes his neighbor's apartment is strangely silent, devoid of the usual raucous snoring that penetrates the protagonist's thin apartment wall. The hero is almost certain that his neighbor has been killed, but he doesn't want to investigate because he has had a history of confrontations with the neighbor—even threatened to kill him once—and he knows that circumstantial evidence would make him a prime suspect. Locking himself in his room, the hero eventually falls asleep. What follows is a hair-raising nightmare montage by Vernon L. Walker and Nicholas Musuraca, no doubt influenced by *The Cabinet of Dr. Caligari.*

Tom Flinn, in *Kings of the Bs,* discusses the film's pièce de résistance:

> The dream sequence itself is so completely expressionistic in style . . . with strong contrasts in lighting, angular shadow patterns, and distorted, emblematic architecture, in short, a kind of total stylization that manages to be both extremely evocative and somewhat theatrical. The use of a tilted camera destroys the normal play of horizontals and verticals, creating a forest of oblique angles that recalls the unsettling favorite device of horror director James Whale. . . . In *Stranger on the Third Floor* the Germanic influence, so important in the creation of the film noir style, is quite obvious, and not confined to the dream sequence. Throughout the film the lighting by Nick Musuraca is very much in the baroque 1940s manner, with numerous shadow patterns on the walls.

In *Film Noir,* Alain Silver and Elizabeth Ward add:

> *Stranger on the Third Floor* is the first true film noir; and it represents a distinct break in style and substance with the preceding mystery, crime, detection, and horror films of the 1930s. To begin with, there is the oneiristic blurring of the distinction between dream and reality. But more significantly, this unheralded "B" film noir, made a full year before *Citizen Kane,* demonstrates the most overt influence yet of German expressionism on American crime films to that time. . . . [Its] story and script stresses paranoia and claustrophobia. . . . Ingster's Germanic direction is given additional force through the heavily gestured performance of Peter Lorre. . . . [The film]

exploits the Baroque photography of Nick Musuraca, whose mannered style would later be further refined in films made by Orson Welles and Val Lewton.

We will probably never know which films discussed in this chapter were actually screened by Lewton (and company) during those first months at RKO but judging from what was available, we can safely assume that the celebrated Lewton approach was a synthesis of many things that came before. As we shall see in the following chapters, the 11 films in the Lewton/RKO cycle were also the products of team effort, group dynamics, and pure happenstance.

SIX

Cat People

December 14, 1942

Mr. Val Lewton
RKO Pictures, Inc.
780 Gower St.
Hollywood, California

Dear Val:

I saw *Cat People* last night, and I am very proud of you. I think it is an altogether superb producing job, and is in every way a much better picture than ninety percent of the "A" product that I have seen in recent months. . . . Indeed, I think it is one of the most credible and most skillfully worked out horror pieces in many years. . . . I am sending a copy of this wire by mail to Mr. Koerner, who I am sure feels as I do, that RKO is fortunate to have made such a ten-strike as the acquisition of your services as a producer. Other studios hopefully have extended such opportunities to would-be producers by the score without getting a result such as you have delivered at the outset.

Sincerely,
David O. Selznick

An important lesson Lewton learned as a child was that a single folktale could be told and retold, its quality of interpretation dependent upon the person doing the telling. Some storytellers embellished the tale with gore and lingered upon the morbid details; others used darkness, the unseen, the unstated, to mine their chills. Val Lewton, a born raconteur, would take this knowledge to heart.

Now he and his screenwriter, DeWitt Bodeen, were about to prove their worth as storytellers. In Joel E. Siegel's *The Reality of Terror,* Bodeen recalls his early days with Lewton. After the latter left for RKO, Bodeen remained with Selznick an additional two weeks, putting some finishing touches on the *Jane Eyre* Selznick package that would eventually be sold to Fox. Meanwhile, Lewton arranged to have Bodeen hired by RKO at $75 a week. Once reunited, Lewton and Bodeen embarked upon an extensive study of the cat in literature. For a time, the two men dallied with the notion of adapting Algernon Blackwood's short story, "Ancient Sorceries," for the big screen. Two other short stories were also considered: Ambrose Bierce's "The Eyes of a Panther" and Margaret Irwin's "Monsieur Seeks a Wife." Ultimately, Lewton vetoed these proposals and decided to do an original story set in contemporary New York. In *My Brother,* Lucy Lewton tells us that Val's contemporary story was inspired, in part, "by a series of French fashion designs . . . drawings of gowns worn by models with the heads of cats."

Lewton then began thinking of a director, his first choice being his *A Tale of Two Cities* partner, Jacques Tourneur. Remaining on the MGM lot after Selznick and Lewton left, Tourneur had made a series of dramatic shorts (covering everything from adaptations of famous short stories to realistic "crime does not pay" shorts. In 1939 Tourneur directed his American feature film debut, *They All Come Out.* Although it was a low-budget production, the first half of this film is a striking precursor to the film noir style that would dominate the 1940s. Tourneur also directed lively "B" budget "Nick Carter" entries like *Nick Carter, Master Detective* (1939) and *Phantom Raiders* (1940), showing considerable directing flair with the programmer material he had been given.

Over the years, Lewton and Tourneur remained in touch with one another, indulging in occasional boating weekends with their combined families. When Lewton asked his friend to direct *Cat People,* Tourneur was available and happy to comply. Lewton arranged to have him signed on at RKO.

In the spring of 1942, while Robert Wise was still struggling over the monumental task of a final edit for *The Magnificent Ambersons,* his former assistant, Mark Robson, was sent over to the horror production unit as Lewton's adviser and cutter. Robson had just finished editing the Orson Welles/Norman Foster collaboration, *Journey Into Fear.*

Lewton's first business was to put into practice the experience he had gained working under Selznick, though he was not inclined to exploit his employees the way Selznick had exploited him. Mark Robson once characterized Lewton as "a benevolent David Selznick."

Jacques Tourneur later told Charles Higham and Joel Greenberg (in *The Celluloid Muse*):

> [Lewton] would originate the ideas for our films, and then call in the writers, myself, and the editor, Mark Robson, and we were encouraged, over cups of tea, to say anything "wild." . . . Val was so conscientious! I'd go to a film or a theatre downtown, and my wife and I would be driving back . . . at half past one or two in the morning. And always, as we passed the studio, we'd see a light in that corner office of his, and he'd be alone working, correcting what the writer had written; he could only work at that time of night. Next day he'd hand the work to us.

Lewton's own phobia of cats added a degree of resonance to the *Cat People* project. Years earlier he had written the effective "cat werewolf" story,

RKO Publicity poster for *Cat People.*

"The Bagheeta," for *Weird Tales* magazine. Anecdotes of Lewton's unnatural fear of felines are numerous. In 1934, while Lewton crossed the country by train, scouting out his new Hollywood job with Selznick, his sleep was troubled by recurring nightmares involving cats (Siegel, *Reality of Terror*). Ruth Lewton recently told the author that if her husband was keeping a late night writing vigil and a neighborhood cat began to howl, he would hurry into her room so as not to face his fear alone. One can easily understand Lewton's discomfort during the gestation of *Cat People* when he was writing and rewriting the script in those wee hours of the morning as he was prone to do.

Lewton's original story was set to open in a snowbound Balkan village recently occupied by a Nazi Panzer division. By day the village inhabitants are docile and cooperative; by night they become carnivorous beasts who reduce German soldiers to shredded uniforms. After the slaughter, a girl flees the village, travels to New York, and falls in love. At the time, Lewton's idea was to have the girl's words remain unintelligible to the audience, her lines spoken in long shots. According to Lewton, "You hear the murmur of her voice, you never hear what she is saying and, if it is necessary to give her words meaning to the audience, I think we can always contrive to have some other character tell what the girl said" (George Turner, "Val Lewton's *Cat People*," *Cinéfantastique*, vol. 12, no. 4).

Lobby poster, "It's Super Sensational!"

Turner also quotes Lewton as having several interesting ideas that never made it into the film:

> Most of the cat werewolf stories I have read and all the werewolf stories I have seen on the screen end with the beast gunshot and turning back into a human being after death. In this story I'd like to reverse the process. For the final scene I'd like to show a violent quarrel between the man and woman

> in which she is provoked into an assault upon him. To protect himself, he pushes her away, she stumbles, falls awkwardly, and breaks her neck in the fall. The young man, horrified, kneels to see if he can feel her heart beat. Under his hand black hair and hide come up and he draws back to look down in horror at a dead black panther."

Most of Lewton's original ideas so defied convention that Lew Ostrow, who disliked some of Lewton's pretentions, was ready to throw in the towel and perhaps seek a more appropriate producer for horror programmers. Fortunately, Charles Koerner went to bat for Lewton who, though encouraged to revise along more conventional lines, managed to retain some of his original ideas. Koerner was impressed by some of Lewton's notions, and the two men had an appreciation for one another.

Eventually, Lewton discarded the exotic Balkan setting when he hit upon the idea of bringing the entire film closer to home. He reasoned: "The characters in the run-of-the-mill weird films were usually people very remote from the audiences' experiences. European nobles of dark antecedents, mad scientists, man-created monsters, and the like cavorted across the screen. It would be much more entertaining if people with whom audiences could identify were shown in contact with the strange, the weird, and the occult" (Turner, "*Cat People*").

In an attempt to create this sense of normalcy, Lewton would plan sets that looked lived in. If characters occupied an apartment, props would be typically arranged to reflect the tastes of the apartment's owner; if a workplace was shown, the environment would reflect work in progress. To create an illusion of normalcy, Lewton would avoid the pristine, tidied-up interior sets so common at the time.

Jacques Tourneur came up with an idea for a terror sequence that was based on an experience he had had some years earlier while swimming alone in a friend's pool. The friend, whose pool Tourneur frequented, kept two pet cheetahs. Tourneur tells us:

> And one day I'll be damned if one of the cheetahs wasn't out of his cage and starting to prowl around and growl in a low way, and I thought, "Oh my God, here I am feeling naked, I can't scream," and I was going around in circles in the nude. . . . Luckily, the cheetah was afraid of the water. And eventually, from way back on the property somewhere, the gardener came with a rake and shooed the cheetah back. [Higham and Greenberg, *The Celluloid Muse*].

A matter of pressing importance during Lewton's first month on the *Cat People* project was obtaining the appropriate actress for the title character. Lewton told Lew Ostrow: "I took a look at the Paramount Picture *The Island of Lost Souls* and after seeing their much publicized 'panther woman,' I feel that any attempt to secure a cat-like quality in our girl's physical appearance would be absolutely disastrous" (Turner, "*Cat People*").

Then, while Lewton was screening RKO's *All That Money Can Buy* (1941), a coquettish French actress, Simone Simon, caught his eye: "I'd like to have a girl with a little kitten-face like Simone Simon, cute and soft and cuddly and seemingly not at all dangerous," he wrote Ostrow (Turner, in "*Cat People*").

Simone Simon, born in 1910, had made her screen debut in *Le Chanteur Inconnu,* a 1931 French film. She came to America in the mid–1930s, starring in *Girl's Dormitory* and *Seventh Heaven* before going back to her native France in 1938. In 1941 Simon returned to Hollywood for William Dieterle's *All That Money Can Buy,* which inspired Lewton to acquire her talents. Although Simon had already journeyed back to her native home, Lewton was able to talk his superiors into offering her the lead role.

After Lewton and DeWitt Bodeen worked out their basic storyline for *Cat People,* Lewton assigned Bodeen to write a complete treatment in short story form. Lewton called for a first-person narrative written by Alice, the character in love with the "cat woman's" husband. Lewton then instructed Bodeen to model the Irena Dubrovna "cat woman" role upon the actress Simone Simon, which he did. Bodeen, already in tune with Lewton's aesthetics of terror, included dark, shadowy passages suggesting, rather than displaying, the presence of horror. When the piece was finished, it was sent to Simone Simon, who read the treatment and quickly accepted the role.

While Bodeen prepared the treatment, Lewton received some sage advice from RKO "B" veteran, producer Herman Schlom, who revealed ways of cutting preproduction costs by writing around preexisting sets and dressing them up a bit so that they would not be readily recognized. Lewton found he could make use of a Central Park set from an Astaire/Rogers musical as well as an office workplace from the 1941 Jean Arthur film, *The Devil and Miss Jones.* A standing cafe set was dressed and redressed to function as a coffee shop, a pet shop, and a restaurant.

After scouting the flexibility of set locations, Lewton had to concentrate on the remainder of his cast. For the wholesome male lead, an ex–Broadway leading man named Kent Smith had captured Lewton's attention. Although Smith had been under contract to RKO since 1941, he had done little work except for some Army training films. Lewton saw Smith commuting back and forth to the studio every day on his bicycle, and the neophyte producer was taken by his solid good looks and healthy appeal. Lewton moved quickly, obtaining Kent as *Cat People*'s leading male character, Oliver Reed.

The second female lead, Oliver's working associate, Alice, was not as easily secured. Lewton sought the talent of a new Selznick discovery, Phyllis Isley. Although Isley had worked in films before, being taken under Selznick's wing, it was Lewton who suggested she change her name to Jennifer Jones. Selznick, who was convinced of his protegée's genuine star potential, accepted the new moniker but nixed the idea of her taking part in a "B" film.

Mark Robson may have been of some help in securing Jane Randolph for the role of Alice. Robson had just recently finished editing an entry in RKO's "Falcon" series, *The Falcon's Brother,* which starred a pert and likeable Randolph in the female lead. Although Lewton initially had another choice in mind for psychiatrist Dr. Louis Judd, his screening of the "Falcon" picture convinced him that Tom Conway, who had just replaced his brother (George Sanders) as the lead in the series, would be an ideal choice for the role of an articulate and debonair heel.

The rest of the players were mostly contract actors handpicked from the RKO rosters by Lewton and Tourneur. One very significant small role came about when Lewton, at a cocktail party, bumped into a statuesque model and sometime actress named Elizabeth Russell. Lewton did not want an actress who resembled a cat to carry his lead role, but he could not resist using Russell's austere feline beauty in a key scene. Although lasting only moments, the economy of Russell's cameo is wondrous and it remains etched in viewers' memories long after the more essential concerns of plot and character have been all but forgotten.

Lewton surrounded himself with the best technicians the studio had to offer. Nicholas Musuraca, the cinematographer from *Stranger on the Third Floor,* was advised to continue his expressionistic style for *Cat People*; his photography became instrumental in establishing the film's classic set pieces. The estimable talents of house art directors Albert S. D'Agostino and Walter E. Keller were also put to good use.

For *Cat People*'s musical score, the front office urged Lewton to use the generic canned music RKO had in its vaults, including its oft-used pastiches of Max Steiner scores. However, even before the actual screenplay was prepared, Lewton consulted composer Roy Webb and musical director Constantin Bakaleinikoff for a proposed original score. Like the musical leitmotifs Franz Waxman prepared to correspond with characters and situations in *The Bride of Frankenstein,* Lewton wanted to link his visuals with music, but this again raised eyebrows at the front office. Roy Webb was assigned the task of writing the score and would do the same for the vast majority of Lewton's RKO efforts. For *Cat People,* Webb scored seven separate themes (including a lovely lullabye), each centering around the main character, Irena Dubrovna.

Webb, a graduate of Columbia University (and composer of the university's "fight song") was a cofounder of ASCAP in 1914. He came to Hollywood in 1929, near the beginning of the sound era, and joined RKO in 1935, becoming assistant to Max Steiner. Although he did some supervisory work for other composers in *Gunga Din, Citizen Kane,* and *Kitty Foyle,* Webb's first original score was for *Alice Adams* (1935). He also composed the score for *The Stranger on the Third Floor* (1940).

On July 6, 1942, *The Hollywood Reporter* announced that even before shooting had begun on *Cat People,* RKO had already assigned Lewton a property called *I Walked with a Zombie.* Elsewhere, the periodical mentioned that

Simone Simon had just arrived in America for her "personal tour in the East which she will cut short to report at the studio for a July 21 start."

Under Jacques Tourneur's direction, Nicholas Musuraca's cameras began to roll on July 28, 1942, for Val Lewton's production of *Cat People*. Four days later, things got shaky when Lew Ostrow viewed the rushes and, not liking the results, threatened to replace Tourneur with a studio contract director. Lewton managed to stay Ostrow's hand until Charles Koerner, who was away on business, returned and could be consulted. The next day, Koerner looked at the rushes and could not understand what Ostrow was complaining about; he declared that Tourneur was doing just fine and should be left to his own business. Ostrow offered little interference after that.

The August 3 *Hollywood Reporter* announced that *Cat People* was six days into production and that two units were "shooting round-the-clock," a night unit shooting with animals and a day unit shooting with the major performers.

Lewton felt a need to impress his superiors with the speed of his production, thinking it would improve his chances of gaining some degree of autonomy, but Koerner and Ostrow could not be so easily mollified by economy of production. Koerner voiced a few complaints concerning Lewton and Tourneur's tendency to leave too much to the imagination, and the filmmakers had to comply (minimally) with their superiors' wishes.

George Turner, in his article "Val Lewton's *Cat People*," comments upon the meticulous efforts afforded the sound track and records the front office's reaction to such tomfoolery:

> When the cost accounting office demanded to know why John Cass's recording crew worked an extra three days on *Cat People*, it was explained that they spent one day at Gay's Lion Farm recording the growls and roars of the big cats and two days at the indoor swimming pool of the Royal Palms hotel recording reverberation effects. A vocal effects actress, Dorothy Lloyd, was hired to create the cat noises. The studio bosses regarded all this as unusually extravagant for a "B" picture.

Except for the expected amount of friction from the front office, *Cat People*'s production was smooth sailing. Shooting ended on August 21, ahead of schedule. Although the original proposed budget ($118,948) had been revised to $141,659 shortly after production had begun, Lewton managed to bring the film in at $134,959. Some of the department heads believed Lewton was taking an undue amount of care with postproduction particulars on what they felt was, after all, just another "B" programmer, but Lewton stood his ground.

Finally, Lewton and Tourneur ran the completed film for their studio bosses. After the screening, there was dead silence. Koerner refused to speak to either of them and left in a hurry. Only Ostrow stayed behind to nag the filmmaking duo about *Cat People*'s profound lack of horrific content.

Lewton was not encouraged by this cold reception, especially since he was by this time already deeply enmeshed in his second production and about ready to begin his third. Several weeks later, the Lewton unit attended the first public preview at the Hillside Theatre, a Los Angeles movie house known for its rowdy clientele. In Joel E. Siegel's *The Reality of Terror*, Bodeen recalled the Hillside Theatre preview, telling us that "Val's spirits sank lower and lower" when the preceding cartoon, an animated Disney short featuring "a little pussycat," provoked the audience into catcalls and mewing sounds. Things took a more disturbing turn when *Cat People*'s title hit the screen, "greeted with whoops of derision and louder meows." Fortunately, the film thereafter worked its dark magic upon the audience and the latter, having become intrigued by the credible story and sympathetic characters, responded well to the film's terror highlights, emitting gasps and screams in all the appropriate places.

The press began to unleash their reviews on Friday, November 13, 1942, and they were mixed. Some were wildly favorable; others were caustic, calling the movie "fantastic and unhealthy" or "morbid and unproductive." None of the reviews, even those partial to the film, prepared anyone for the forthcoming "sleeper" status of *Cat People*. Word of mouth escalated the film's worth by the time of its general release in December (when it was inexplicably paired with the misleadingly titled nonhorror film *Gorilla Man*), and it began playing to sellout crowds.

The bewildered critics went back to see it a second time and admitted their initial hastiness in not recognizing the film's obvious value. It played a record 13-week engagement at Hollywood's Hawaii Theater and by the end of its general nationwide release, had earned enough money to bring RKO back from the dead. Most available estimates credit an international gross exceeding $4,000,000.

Suddenly Lewton and Tourneur were the critics' darlings and the talk of RKO. The esteemed film critic Manny Farber called *Cat People* "the best Hollywood film in three years." Tourneur was given a bonus and a contract provision enabling him to go onto "A" pictures as soon as he finished his third Lewton film (by now already in production). Lewton's meager $250-a-week salary remained just as it was, however.

Following *Cat People*'s opening credits, an epigraph reads: "even as fog continues to lie in the valleys, so does ancient sin cling to the low places, the depressions in the world's consciousness." The source offered is *The Anatomy of Atavism* by Dr. Judd (a fictitious volume purportedly written by one of the film's principal characters, though the quote bears all the earmarks of having been penned by Lewton).

The scene is autumn in Manhattan's Central Park Zoo. Joyous cries of

Example of a Lobby display for *Cat People.* The display announces, "You'll shiver . . . you'll shake. . . . You'll shudder and shrivel!" and promises "stark shockery . . . killing chillery!" (from the Val Lewton Collection, Library of Congress).

children are heard over the buoyant tones of an organ grinder. Oliver Reed (Kent Smith) spots a pretty woman (Simon), apparently an artist, drawing something in her sketchbook as she stands near a caged panther. Oliver watches as the woman, dissatisfied with her sketch, wrinkles it into a ball and aims for a trash receptacle. When she misses, Oliver picks up the paper, points to the no littering sign, and uses the occasion to approach her.

This brief, seemingly uneventful, episode speaks volumes about the rest of the film. It reveals the woman's dissatisfaction with herself (she disposes of several sketches), it demonstrates Oliver's fetish for order, it introduces a location instrumental to the story (the Central Park Zoo), and it provides us with our first look at the film's unifying symbol—the black panther. In addition, since we see one of the woman's torn sketches, a panther impaled by a sword, we are given a significant foreshadowing of how the film will end. All of this information is conveyed without a word of dialogue.

Oliver and the woman, whose name is Irena (pronounced ear-RAY-nuh), seem to hit it off; he walks her to her nearby apartment, where she invites him in for tea. They enter the apartment lobby and climb the elaborate staircase

Oliver (Kent Smith) and Irena (Simone Simon) in *Cat People*.

(a leftover set from *The Magnificent Ambersons*), as Oliver remarks, "I never cease to marvel at what lies behind a brownstone front." He thus voices for the first time a motif which runs through the entire Lewton series: that things are seldom what they appear to be. As Irena opens her apartment door, Oliver is inundated with the fragrance of her favorite perfume which he says "smells warm."

After Irena comments that she has never had a man in her apartment, she closes the door to the camera. A dissolve to a darkened apartment reveals that Oliver's visit has been a long one. When the couple hear the cries of the nearby zoo animals, Irena describes their sounds as "soothing." She begins humming a haunting lullaby, happy to be sitting in the dark with her new friend, Oliver. Suddenly Irena becomes tense; she switches on a light, apologizing for not doing it earlier. She forgets, she says, because she likes the dark, "it's friendly."

The lighted apartment now reveals its decor. It is adorned with many feline artifacts: statues, paintings, flowers, and a folding screen (the kind behind which a lady "changes") upon which is painted a mural-sized art deco black panther. Oliver inquires about a statue of a king on horseback, his sword upraised, the body of a large cat impaled upon it. His query prompts Irena to explain about her Serbian heritage, how cats in her homeland were the sign of evil (transformed versions of the dreaded enemy, the Mamelukes) and how her national hero, King John, rid Serbia of the dreaded felines. Irena is plainly proud of her heritage but offers no explanation why, if cats are so evil, they should provide the main decorating motif of her living quarters.

Oliver buys her a kitten the next day during lunchbreak (he is a draftsman by trade) because her apartment decor seemed to bear evidence of her fondness for cats. But it turns out that the kitten is petrified of Irena. As they enter the pet shop to make an exchange, every animal raises a raucous cry, creating a din that is entirely the result of Irena's presence. Oliver exchanges the kitten for a bird while Irena waits outside in the rain.

Weeks pass and Oliver has long declared his love for Irena, though he finds it strange that he has never once attempted to kiss her in all the time they have been together. When he proposes marriage, Irena admits her love for him but is frightened by the dark curse that haunts her soul. She confesses her apprehensions about physical contact (reminding us of Lewton's own affliction) and implies that sexual intimacy would transform her into something evil. Oliver buys none of this.

The next thing we know, Oliver and Irena are having their wedding party at a Serbian restaurant (a peculiar choice, considering Oliver's long-winded efforts to debunk her native superstitions). Falling snow is visible through the restaurant windows as the participants, all of them Oliver's workmates, wish the bride and groom a happy marriage. As we realize that there is no one at the party on Irena's behalf, a Serbian catlike woman (Elizabeth Russell) walks into the room, plunging the spirited chattering of the wedding party into silence (a nice counterpoint to the pet-shop scene). The strange woman stares at Irena and in her native tongue declares the frightened bride "her sister."

This seemingly minor incident puts a strain on the wedding night which, oddly enough, is little more than Oliver giving up his quarters to move in with Irena. Begging him to be patient, Irena goes to her bedroom alone, gently closing the door behind her; within, she slides to the floor to lean against the door panel as she weeps.

Time passes. Irena works in her apartment, making fashion design sketches. Bored, she goes over to the birdcage, sticks her hand in the little door, and obviously enjoying herself, teases the bird. Her smile evaporates when the bird drops dead of fright. That she is visibly distressed about this event only makes it more shocking when she takes the dead bird to the zoo to throw it into the panther's cage.

When she confesses her behavior to Oliver, he, running out of patience, begins to believe Irena is suffering from psychological problems. He sets up an appointment for her with Dr. Judd (Tom Conway), a pretentious psychiatrist who believes all mental illness can be cured with the application of reason or, in this case, a little lecherous attention. Irena is unmoved by his alternately flirtatious and bombastic manner. Judd offers his solution: forget about the past and live in the present (worth every penny of the cost of that office visit, we may be sure). Irena believes her soul to be sick, not her mind.

Jealousy begins to darken Irena's mood (Jane Randolph) as she becomes aware of the amount of time Oliver is spending with Alice, his coworker. Irena's contempt for the other woman becomes apparent when Oliver reveals that he and Alice have been discussing his "marital problems." Irena tells Oliver, "There are some things a woman doesn't want another woman to understand."

A rift forms between the married couple; Oliver sometimes goes to the office at night and on at least one occasion has bumped into Alice. One particular night Irena discovers the two of them in a restaurant together. She bides her time, out of sight, until the two take leave of one another. When Alice, walking alone, takes a shortcut through Central Park, Irena begins to follow several steps behind.

As Alice treads the concrete walk that runs through the wooded park, she grows apprehensive about what she thinks she hears, but hopes it is only the echo of her own high heels. (The Roy Webb score is suddenly quiet.) Soon, amidst her own click-clacking footsteps, Alice hears the sound of another pair of high heels, sounding much like her own, only moving at a faster rate. (Editor Robson alternates shots of the pursuer and the pursued—their legs only—in genuinely unnerving fashion, tightening the distance between the two women with each progressive cut.) Alice's pace has quickened, but she still refuses to run. Suddenly the menacing footsteps, last heard moving far too quickly to signal a change of intent, vanish without an echo, leaving Alice (and the audience) to speculate why the pursuer would suddenly find a need to follow barefoot. Alice halts, looking back into the darkness, and seeing nothing but the terrors of her own imagination, she finally breaks into a run.

Just as she approaches the safety of a city street, making her way to a curb just outside the park wall, we hear a loud, breathy hiss of what sounds like a gigantic cat . . . only to be jolted out of our seats when a bus lurches into the entire foreground of the frame, the noisy air brakes bringing the vehicle to an abrupt stop in front of Alice. Her heart in her throat, Alice climbs aboard. (When Lewton attended a sneak preview audience for the film, he sat in the back and witnessed an entire audience jumping in unison at the appropriate time. Because this highly manipulative bus sequence delivered a rousing scare, similar false jolts in subsequent Lewton films were to be dubbed "buses.")

Meanwhile, a man discovers a dead sheep in the park apparently butchered by some animal. Seeing paw prints, he follows them until they turn into what appear to be the prints of high heel shoes. This is followed by a shot of Irena walking out of the park, gently dabbing her mouth with her handkerchief.

Irena takes a taxi home, looking very downtrodden as she walks into her apartment and avoids a confrontation with Oliver. She goes to the bathroom

Alice (Jane Randolph, right) discovering that her robe has been torn to shreds.

and starts filling the tub. We dissolve to a shot of Irena bathing; we see only her naked back, speckled with beads of moisture, as she hunches over, wracked with sobs, adding tears to the bath water.

As days pass, Irena becomes withdrawn and finds solace near the panther cage at the zoo. On this day the absentminded zookeeper, after throwing a large chunk of meat to the animal, leaves his key in the cage door. Irena removes it and hands it to the zookeeper. Turning around, she is accosted by Dr. Judd, who commends her self-control and wonders why she has not been keeping her appointments. She knows Judd can not help her and tells him so.

That night Irena has a surrealistic dream (shades of *Caligari* and *The Stranger on the Third Floor*) in which a series of angular cats (via some nicely expressionistic cartoon animation) come prowling toward the foreground, replaced with an image of Dr. Judd, who, in the knighted attire of King John, holds his sword before him while his voice-over spouts theories of Irena's secret desire to unleash evil upon the world through the use of "the key . . . the key . . . the key," at which point the sword turns into a gigantic key. The next morning Irena steals the key to the panther cage (presumably because Judd put the idea into her head) and carries it home with her.

Meanwhile, the bond between Oliver and Alice grows stronger. Irena sees more evidence of this when she accompanies them to the museum and is made to feel like a third wheel. Oliver makes things worse by patronizing her.

After Alice returns to her YWCA apartment late that evening, she goes for a lonely swim in the basement pool. Meanwhile, Irena strolls into the lobby and asks the desk clerk where Alice is. We cut back to Alice, who, having finished her swim, has already turned off the lights and is about to make her way up the stairs. The room is suddenly too quiet. A low, slinking shadow is seen descending the staircase. Thinking fast, Alice jumps back into the swimming pool. Shimmering reflections move about the walls and ceiling, accompanied by the splashes of Alice desperately treading water as she looks about the pool's darkened perimeter. She hears a low growling sound; it could be a truck passing on the street or maybe the heavy scrape of furniture being moved on the floor above. But that would not explain the large shadow moving near the pool's edge. We think we hear a loud feline shriek, but Alice's shrill cry of terror is so quickly forthcoming that we can't be sure. In the blink of an eye, Irena appears, seemingly out of nowhere; stepping out of the shadows, she turns on the light. She is menacingly aloof, perhaps even slightly amused, standing there at the poolside. Only when Irena leaves the premises does Alice finally get out of the pool; it is then that she discovers that her robe has been torn to shreds.

Alice meets with Dr. Judd to tell him she knows of Irena's obsessions and that she now believes in her feline transformations. Dr. Judd brushes this off and, showing he is armed for danger, reveals the secret of his cane: a thin sword sheathed within.

Irena, worried about her blackouts, consults Dr. Judd, who, using the opportunity to make romantic advances, consistently proves himself to be a meager source of comfort. When Irena shows no interest, he alludes to the distinct possibility of bringing her case up to the board to have her institutionalized.

Returning home, Irena is resolved to make another go of her marriage, but Oliver gloomily admits that he is no longer in love with her, that he loves Alice. Absolutely deflated, Irena tells Oliver to leave the apartment; when he does, she runs her nails over the sofa cover, tearing through the fabric.

Judd meets with Oliver and Alice to discuss their options. Judd suggests that Oliver have his marriage annulled because divorce would not be possible after the commitment proceedings. Oliver decides to have Irena committed but refuses to have the marriage annulled, Alice halfheartedly agreeing, "it's the only right thing to do." When the three of them go to Irena's apartment for a confrontation with her, she is nowhere to be found.

That night Alice and Oliver are working late at the office (the otherwise dark room eerily lit by the soft glow of the drafting table lights). When they are about to leave, they find the exit door, which was open moments before, is closed and locked. The snarling presence of a stalking animal makes itself felt in the room.

(Although it is hardly recognizable, we do catch glimpses of an actual panther. This was one of Lewton's concessions to the front office. The "cat" shadow in swimming pool sequence, however, was nothing more than an amorphous shadow made by Jacques Tourneur's fist.)

The couple back into a corner of the office as the panther comes closer. Oliver grabs a T-square from the wall and holds it aloft in self-defense. When the makeshift weapon casts the shadow of a cross on the wall behind them, the panther departs (somehow unlocking the door). Alice smells Irena's perfume as she and Oliver walk out into the foggy street.

Meanwhile, Dr. Judd awaits Irena's return, making himself at home in her apartment. When she arrives, he does little more than make lecherous advances, but this time Irena gives into his efforts to kiss her, despising him enough not to be concerned over the probable consequences of his action. In a tight close-up, Irena's face darkens, her eyes sparkle like cut glass, and her head sinks below the frame. Judd's reaction shot reveals everything. The next thing we know, he is grappling with a fierce feline, as much of the rough-and-tumble battle is displayed through shadows on the wall.

Judd uses his sword cane to good advantage, impaling the beast, though he is killed in the process. Mortally wounded, Irena's human form steals down the stairway and escapes into the night. She arrives at the zoo and clutching her wound—the broken sword blade still in her chest—she unlocks the panther cage. The beast lunges from the cage, knocks her over, and clears the park wall to meet its offscreen death under the wheels of a passing car. Oliver and Alice discover Irena's lifeless form and hang their heads low as Oliver remarks, "She never lied to us." The film ends with a quote from John Donne's "Holy Sonnets": "But black sin hath betrayed to endless night / My world, both parts, and both parts must die."

In today's horror film climate, *Cat People* may seem like a tame and surprisingly ordinary film, but its approach was incredibly daring for its era. By design, *Cat People* was made to appear ordinary; Tourneur's understated direction makes the film feel commonplace and uneventful, but underneath the apparent calm, the veneer of normalcy, run numerous sinister undercurrents.

Cat People has its share of flaws. Its ending is rushed and contrived, and a few scenes are difficult to swallow. The numerous meetings with Dr. Judd in the last half hour tax the viewer's patience, especially when it should appear plain to any sensible human being that aside from being a probable quack, Judd is both a nuisance and a nemesis. The drafting office scene is effectively lit, but for such a climactic moment, it is curiously unsatisfying. The T-square business is such a horror cliché that for a moment we feel we are in the middle of a Universal vampire opus.

For all of its shortcomings, however, *Cat People* still works wonderfully well, never seeming like the cheap exploitation film that RKO intended it to be (judging from the studio's misleadingly lurid newspaper ads and lobby posters). Instead, we get a well-conceived and carefully produced little film, one which possesses enough ambition to ably transcend its budgetary limitations. Lewton's fear-the-dark approach—drawing equal measures of inspiration from Victorian ghost stories and Depression-era radio plays—struck a primal chord of fear with audiences across the nation.

It is remarkable how much care was given to the film, considering it was shot within three weeks and brought in under budget. Notice the amount of attention given to the weather; we get sun, wind, rain, snow, and fog. Unlike the standard "B" budget programmer (which was usually designed for the "shirt sleeve" crowd), Lewton's film strives to be artistic; as a result, it is loaded with provocative images—swords, keys, doors, walls, cages, staircases, water, birds, felines, and so on. Belying its modest budget, the film has an unusually rich sound track; Roy Webb's score is very effective, never obtrusive. And yet so many memorable scenes rely upon silence punctuated with haunting sound effects: the clicking of high heels, the distant noises of zoo animals, the echoes in the swimming pool, and the hissing of air brakes. Mark Robson's experience with the former boy wonder of radio, Orson Welles, is at least partly responsible for the peerless execution of the sound editing in *Cat People*. Many fans of the Lewton films credit the invention of the "Lewton bus" to Jacques Tourneur, but it was actually Mark Robson's contribution. In *The Celluloid Muse*, Robson told authors Charles Higham and Joel Greenberg:

> The "bus" [was] an editing device I had invented by accident, or possibly by design. . . . I put a big, solid sound of air brakes on it, cutting it in at the decisive moment so that it knocked viewers out of their seats. This became the "bus," and we used the same principle in every film.

Another significant way that *Cat People* defied genre conventions was its inclusion of so many ambiguous characters. Irena is not the only predator on the loose in this film; she is just the only one with any real sense of conscience. Like Larry Talbot in *The Wolf Man* or Countess Zaleska in *Dracula's Daughter*, Irena doesn't want to be a murderer; she just can't help herself. Her prized statue of King John impaling a cat and her drawings of panthers vanquished with swords show how much she wishes to defeat her dreaded curse. She is a female version of the classic noir protagonist: obsessed, alienated, haunted, ill-advised, and doomed. So strongly do we sympathize with Irena's agonized plight that we forgive her for her actions, even for something as questionable as feeding a dead canary to a panther. Irena remains the character for whom we feel the most genuine concern, even after we know how dangerous she has become. The RKO poster art may characterize Simone Simon's character as the ultimate female predator, but she is really the film's ultimate victim, the only one for whom we will finally grieve.

Each of the secondary characters, Oliver, Alice, Judd, exhibits questionable motives and behavior. Oliver Reed is appealing at first, but the more we see, the less we like. Halfway through the film, Oliver admits to Alice that until he married Irena, he had "never known the meaning of unhappiness." He is a callow, overgrown boy who is used to having his own way. Oliver aggressively goes after Irena, getting everything he sets his sights upon. He hounds Irena into marriage, barreling his way through all her fears, calling them superstitious nonsense, and somehow manages to have her put aside a lifetime of self-doubt to agree to become his wife. The only thing he cannot get Irena to go along with is having sex.

Oliver is a draftsman, a designer, a man who likes to build things. He may be something of a square, but he is just the sort of square society seems to like, stiff upper lip and all that. He seems to take all his meals in restaurants, and he is forever being served apple pie (the waitresses know him well and deliver this dessert before he puts in his order). Imagination to Oliver is a tool for work, something to be left behind at the office. For all his expertise at his job, he seems a dullard around the house, never doing much besides putting a new mast on his model boat or pacing around Irena's apartment pretending to be patient. He may be a survivor, but we should not rule out the "blind luck of fools" as a considerable portion of Oliver's survival gear. Kent Smith may have been a limited actor, but his performance in *Cat People,* often denounced as wooden and bland, is misunderstood primarily because audiences expected something more rousing from the all–American hero Oliver Reed appeared to be. He looks like a hero, so he must act like a hero, and because Oliver's ambiguous character falls short of being heroic, Smith's "bland acting" is often blamed. But Oliver, as written, is a stalwart, shallow, and self-serving character who is only posing as a film hero.

Jane Randolph's Alice, with whom Oliver shares an "above-board" relationship, is an equally ambiguous character. Alice professes a tremendous concern for Oliver and Irena and appears to be (thanks to Oliver's candid day-by-day reports) quite an authority on the history of Oliver's failed marriage. Alice seems to encourage Oliver's marriage, but her various "slips" in front of Irena seem deliberate, and the conspicuous time she spends with another woman's husband outside of work is at best reckless and insensitive, given the situation. Unless Alice is plain stupid (which is obviously not the case), she is entirely aware of the way she is undermining Oliver's marriage. Alice is clever enough to know what she is doing, and Oliver doesn't just happen to fall in love with her. One of her tactics—shedding tears when Oliver confesses unhappiness—is older than Greek drama.

Lewton and Bodeen were able to undermine the appeal of Oliver and Alice with such subtlety that one can easily, upon first glance, mistake them for admirable human beings. But, as Oliver remarked earlier, one never ceases "to marvel at what lies behind a brownstone front."

Although no viewer mourns his passing, Judd provides a distinct purpose; he is the voice of reason, the debunker of superstition. But when we have someone this unlikeable speaking on behalf of reason, the audience feels inclined to refute logic and accept the supernatural instead. When Judd makes jokes about silver bullets, it only makes the viewer wish to see him be attacked by a werebeast all the sooner. By making Judd such a disreputable authority, Lewton and Bodeen have provided a voice of reason with no credibility.

J.P. Telotte, in his volume on Lewton, *Dreams of Darkness,* points out an intriguing facet of the "normal" characters in *Cat People*: none of them have homes of their own. It's true. Irena's apartment is the only example of personal "living quarters" in the entire film, and yet, being a foreigner who can't forget her origins, Irena is the character who is farthest from her home. Alice takes a room at the YWCA, but we never see it. Dr. Judd lives in a hotel room (which we never see) when he's not at his office. And Oliver's home (prior to his moving in with Irena) remains an absolute mystery.

It is true that *Cat People* owes a debt to *The Wolf Man,* and it is probable that many members of the Lewton unit had seen Waggner's film. (By the time *Cat People* went into production, *The Wolf Man*'s screenwriter, Curt Siodmak, had already been secured for the scripting chores of *I Walked with a Zombie.*) Irena's lullaby has the same old-world effect as *The Wolf Man*'s gypsy verse ("Even a man who is pure at heart. . .") and the love triangle in the Waggner film is uncomfortably similar to the romantic triangle in *Cat People* (though the genders are reversed). Larry Talbot's pursuit of Evelyn Ankers also exhibits the same blindly aggressive drive we see in Oliver's whirlwind courtship of Irena; neither of these stereotypical All-American males will take no for an answer.

Cat People may have lost some of its edge over the years and what remains may be a bit tarnished, but it is infinitely better than Paul Schrader's 1982 remake. Schrader's *Cat People* should have been just fine, considering the talent behind it, but it was hardly inspired, the participants having apparently learned no appreciable lessons from their sources of inspiration (Lewton, Tourneur, Robson, Bodeen, Musuraca). Schrader's attempt at duplicating Lewton's "bus" is particularly limp, but at least it proves that the filmmakers had seen the original, something we wouldn't have otherwise known, given the rest of the picture. Schrader and company drew more inspiration from *The Howling* and *American Werewolf in London* than they did from the Lewton original. With Lewton's film, Irena's dual existence remained open to debate; with Schrader's film the only thing that was open to debate was how many more state-of-the-art transformation scenes we would see before the ending credits.

It would be unfair to say that the 1982 *Cat People* is completely without merit, but too much of the film is a depressing showcase of lost opportunities. Schrader's film, in spite of the hype which accompanied it, didn't have a fraction of the impact of Lewton's modest feature. It was Lewton's film that became a national phenomenon, its simplicity and subtlety delivering an impact that Schrader, even with his top notch cast and expensive effects, could not come close to repeating. Three years later, in a *Life* magazine interview (Feb. 25, 1946), Lewton aptly expressed the reason for his success when he said:

> I'll tell you a secret: if you make the screen dark enough, the mind's eye will read anything into it they want! We're great ones for dark patches. . . . The horror addicts will populate the darkness with more horrors than all the horror writers in Hollywood could think of.

SEVEN

I Walked with a Zombie

> ***He had a Russian background, and he was a dreamer and an idealist. I am a realist: I always brought him back to earth. You need that in a partnership. He'd go off into flights of fancy and I'd say, "Well, look, this can't be done." I'd pull him down and he'd bring me up. That was good. Without me he would have been out of the business: he was so impractical. He was a sort of Danny Kaye fey character out of Papavili, and lived in another world. Every afternoon we'd have tea and stop everything! For an hour we'd talk about everything except the film: Pushkin and the old steppes and the snow.***
>
> —Jacques Tourneur (from *The Celluloid Muse,* by Charles Higgam and Joel Greenberg)

Because RKO's horror unit had been designed for quick production, Lewton's superiors grew impatient with his meticulous attention to details and his erratic working habits. Lewton's commitment to quality did not waver, however, regardless of the lightning crank-'em-out pace of "B" budget production. Before the cameras rolled on *Cat People,* the Lewton unit was already enmeshed in the preproduction of *I Walked with a Zombie.* By the time *Cat People* hit the theaters, members of the RKO unit had already completed shooting their second film and were beginning the production of their third *(The Leopard Man).* When their second film was released, Lewton and company were wrapping up their fourth *(The Seventh Victim).* And on and on it went, making us wonder how they ever found time to break for tea.

Lewton may not have been happy with the rapid pace he was forced to keep, but this tight schedule tested the resourcefulness of his horror unit and, rather ironically, provided the conditions under which he did his best work.

After working with Orson Welles, a filmmaker who was allowed the indulgences of slow production, editor Mark Robson must have felt taxed by the assembly-line grind of Lewton's regimen. Ever the perfectionist, Lewton would compound the pressures of his rigorous workday by ignoring the routes of efficiency taken by other "B" producers. According to Mark Robson in *The Celluloid Muse,* "He wasted time and seldom could accomplish anything without the pressure of a deadline on his head."

Then, when his employees went home to live their lives and relax with their families, Lewton (an insomniac) would work around the clock to make up for the lost time, rewriting the script and mulling over new ideas; often decisions made the previous day were scrapped. As his new ideas were being implemented, Lewton would ask his workers for their opinions on the matter; trusting their judgment, he would make further alterations. When Jessie Ponitz, Lewton's secretary, was typing up the final script for *Cat People,* he would stay by her side, asking her for further advice on characterization and plot development.

However democratic Lewton appeared to be, his brand of democracy did nothing to make him relinquish the tight control he held over every one of his films. It is one of Hollywood's great paradoxes that Lewton, a man who encouraged extensive collaboration, would end up producing the most personal body of work in horror film history.

DeWitt Bodeen, screenwriter for *Cat People* (as well as later Lewton films), made the following observations to author John Brosnan (in *Horror People*):

> The whole arrangement could have worked out fine because in the beginning Val was a marvelous producer, but then he attempted to do too much. He tried to move into every department, which was unfortunate. Val was the only producer, in the American sense of the word, to whom the credit *producer* really applied. People give him credit for the whole thing and in a way they're right. It's just that it became impossible for Val to work with anybody, and he couldn't do it *all* by himself. It would have been marvelous if he had just stayed as producer and father to the whole project but he wanted his hands on everything. He became very difficult to work with, and very nervous, and a story session became a trial instead of the joy it once was. You had to be, eventually, a very patient person to work with him.

Lewton's frustrations with RKO's front office were an ever-present source of antagonism; in order to maintain a semblance of artistic integrity, Lewton would find ways to circumvent the often ludicrous advice of his superiors. This took some delicate juggling, as Lewton walked the tightrope from one production to another, his job always in the balance.

The spark of discontent between Lewton and his superiors had been there from the beginning. A lengthy article on horror films in the May 23, 1942, issue of *The Saturday Evening Post* (while *Cat People* was still in its preproduction stages) did not further the credibility of Lewton's maverick approach to the horror film. The article itself, "Scare 'Em to Death—and Cash In" (by Richard G. Hubler), had obviously taken its cues from the staggering success of both *The Wolf Man* (which "cracked an all-time record at Bridgeport") and *The Ghost of Frankenstein* ("in Cincinnati it outgrossed *Dumbo*"). Obviously, the article had a strong bias towards Universal horror films. Hubler spotlighted Curt Siodmak (who had scripted the two Universal films), George Waggner (the producer of both), and Lon Chaney, Jr. (who, as Universal's new horror man, starred in both). The six-page spread also announced the next Siodmak/Waggner/Chaney vehicle: *The Wolfman Meets Frankenstein* (the title would be inverted upon its release the next year).

While extolling the virtues of the Universal horror formula, Hubler's article included George Waggner's seven-ingredient recipe for horror films:

> 1) They must be once-upon-a-time tales.
> 2) They must be believable in characterization.
> 3) They must have unusual technical effects.
> 4) Besides the major monster, there must be a secondary character of weird appearance, such as Igor.
> 5) They must confess right off that the show is a horror film.
> 6) They must include a pish-tush character to express the normal skepticism of the audience.
> 7) They must be based on some pseudoscientific premise.

Although this tried-and-true formula made a lot of sense to the RKO executives, Lewton was determined to ignore most of Waggner's recipe and develop a formula he could call his own. Lewton told his unit: "They may think I'm going to do the usual chiller stuff which will make a quick profit, be laughed at, and be forgotten, but I'm going to make the kind of suspense movie I like" (Danny Peary, *Cult Movies*).

After the *Cat People* script was completed, Lewton acquired another secretary. Jessie Ponitz had to leave California for Georgia to be with her husband who was drafted into the service and stationed in the South. Jessie's replacement was the ever-capable Verna De Mots (who would faithfully serve Lewton almost until the time of his death).

Shortly before *Cat People* went into production, Charles Koerner called Lewton into his office and announced the title of the second RKO horror film: *I Walked with a Zombie* (to be based upon an *American Weekly* article of the same name by Inez Wallace). Koerner also informed Lewton that Curt Siodmak, Universal's horror scriptwriter of the hour, had been selected to write the screenplay. There was little Lewton could do but stand there and wonder what encounters lay ahead with a writer whose last project was the yet-unreleased *Frankenstein Meets the Wolfman,* and whose previous writing credits included *The Invisible Man Returns, The Wolf Man, The Ghost of Frankenstein, Man-Made Monster,* and *The Invisible Woman.* Apparently, Hubler's *Saturday Evening Post* article spotlighting Curt Siodmak had left a lasting impression upon Lewton's superiors.

Post-production ad for *I Walked with a Zombie*.

A pre-production publicity ad for *I Walked with a Zombie.*

In Siegel's The Reality of Terror, Mark Robson recalled the day Lewton returned from his meeting with Koerner, characterizing Lewton as "impossibly gloomy." However gloomy he may have been, the next morning, according to Robson, Lewton came to work in an exuberant mood and announced that his unit would make a "West Indian version of *Jane Eyre.*"

It is probable that Lewton spent that particular night brooding over the ludicrous title, trying to think of some way to make a zombie movie respectable. In his reveries, he may have recalled Orson Welles's 1936 voodoo stage version of *Macbeth,* a production that, though having its share of controversy, had been well received by the critics. If Lewton was thinking of Orson Welles, he couldn't help but think about Welles's current project, *Jane Eyre,* the very same package that Lewton helped prepare before leaving Selznick for RKO. Moreover, since Daphne du Maurier's *Rebecca* had been a modernized reworking of *Jane Eyre,* there was no reason why Lewton couldn't do his own variation of the Charlotte Brontë classic, one of his favorite novels. Although the above is mere speculation, it would certainly account for Lewton's jubilation the following day.

The "nonfiction" Inez Wallace article, "I Walked with a Zombie," had appeared in the Sunday supplement of a popular Hearst newspaper. According to Danny Peary's *Cult Movies:* "[Inez Wallace, a *Cleveland Plain Dealer* film columnist] wrote that she had been skeptical about the existence of zombies until she ran into one while walking across a Haitian plantation. These beings, she discovered, were not 'dead,' but their minds and vocal cords had been utterly destroyed from poison (or drugs). As they could understand simple orders, which they obediently carried out, they were put to work in the fields and lived in slavery."

Ardel Wray had been involved in RKO's Young Writers' Project. Lewton reportedly took notice of Wray's work and hired the young woman to do voodoo research and possibly to collaborate with Curt Siodmak. In Tom Weaver's 1989 interview with Siodmak (from *Interviews with B Science Fiction and Horror Movie Makers*), the German screenwriter revealed: "Nobody helped me with *I Walked with a Zombie.* Of course, Lewton and I discussed scenes, and if he objected to something, I came up with an alternative suggestion. Ardel Wray came on the picture after I left; I never met her. Maybe Lewton had had enough of me, and that was why he hired somebody else."

Siodmak describes Lewton as "brilliant, constructive and intelligent—much more interesting than any of those Universal guys." When Weaver asked if Siodmak's work with Universal had caused any "initial tensions," the screenwriter replied, "Oh, no. Why would he engage me if he had so little respect?" (Perhaps Siodmak should have taken a look at the color of Lewton's tie.) Later in the interview Siodmak admits: "There was . . . a kind of friction between us because he liked people he could dominate. He couldn't do that with me because I was independent."

Maybe Lewton saw something of a rival in the erudite Siodmak. When Siodmak gave Lewton a copy of his novel, *Donovan's Brain,* he read it and responded, "It is not a good book," as if his own potboiler novels from the previous decade had made him a peerless man of letters. *Donovan's Brain* was apparently good enough for Orson Welles, who adapted it for radio around this time.

Most likely, the friction between Siodmak and Lewton stemmed from Lewton's aversion to what Siodmak represented: Universal's horror formula. Siodmak stood for everything Lewton wished to avoid. He had Ardel Wray rewrite Siodmak's script, after which Lewton rewrote Wray's script. By the time Lewton began the final revision, Siodmak was already off the lot.

It is difficult to pinpoint Siodmak's contributions to the finished screenplay of *I Walked with a Zombie*. Dennis Fischer, in an interview with Siodmak (*Filmfax,* issue 13), inquired about the *Zombie* script. Siodmak answered: "[Lewton and Ardel Wray] made some changes. My idea was a little different. I started with the beautiful wife married to a plantation owner who every year went to Paris. He wants to keep her forever, so when he finds out that she wants to run away, he will not let her go. So he makes her into a zombie—then he can keep her, have her whenever he wants. But she has no reactions toward him. That's why she walks around. She was in a living death. But I don't know if he (Val Lewton) kept it this way. I never saw the picture afterwards." Actually, Siodmak's version sounds less like *Jane Eyre* and more like *White Zombie.*

Ardel Wray's memories of *I Walked with a Zombie* in Siegel's *The Reality of Terror* celebrate the spirit of collaboration between Lewton and his coworkers. According to Wray, Lewton and company sought all the information they could possibly find on the subject of Haitian voodoo. Soon they hired Sir Lancelot, an influential pioneer of calypso music, as well as a number of "genuine voodoo musicians." Wray recalls: "Everything had to be cheap because we really were on a shoestring. That was another thing about Val—a low budget was a challenge to him, a spur to inventiveness, and everyone around him caught the fever."

Shooting began on October 26, 1942 (roughly two months before the release of *Cat People*). Again, Tourneur directed, Robson edited, Roy Webb scored the music, and Albert S. D'Agostino/Walter E. Keller lent their consistently invaluable services as art directors. Nick Musuraca was not available, but cinematographer J. Roy Hunt was (and it is safe to say, in this one instance, that Musuraca's talents were not sorely missed).

On October 29, *The Hollywood Reporter* announced: "LeRoy Antoine, who is one of the country's leading authorities on Haiti and Haitian folk music and voodoo, will be the technical advisor on *I Walked with a Zombie*. Antoine will also teach the negro actors Haitian rhythms for use in voodoo ceremony."

If anything, *Zombie* boasts an even better cast than its Lewton predecessor. Paul Holland, the lead male role, was assigned to Tom Conway (Dr. Judd in *Cat People*), while Holland's half-brother, Wesley Rand, was played by James Ellison (who received top billing). Christine Gordon was chosen for the pivotal role (a nonspeaking part) of Jessica Holland, the zombie wife. The role of Betsy (the nurse hired to tend to Jessica's needs), originally slated for Anna Lee, went to Frances Dee. Smaller, though nonetheless memorable roles, went to Edith Barrett (Mrs. Rand), James Bell (the doctor), Sir Lancelot (the calypso singer), and, of course, Darby Jones (Carrefour, the zombie).

The exotic musical soundtrack of *Zombie* is particularly evocative. No doubt musical director C. Bakaleinikoff had his hands full with a diverse assortment of musical sources. Reportedly, *Zombie* is the first movie to include calypso music (courtesy of singer/actor Sir Lancelot) as part of its musical score. Sir Lancelot, accompanying himself on the guitar, sings two numbers: "British Grenadiers" and "Fort Holland"; the latter, written by Lancelot in collaboration with Lewton, functions as a narrative device in advancing the plot. In Tourneur's own words, "we used [Sir Lancelot] as a Greek chorus, wandering in seven or eight times and explaining the plot."

"Fort Holland" is a catchy ditty that led many viewers to mimic its chorus ("Ah, woe / Is me / Shame and sorrow for the family") upon leaving the theater. In the 1950s, folk singer Odetta would do a cover of "Fort Holland" on one of her record albums. Apart from the calypso music, there are the three chants performed by authentic voodoo musicians: "O Marie Congo," "O Legba," and "Walee Nan Guinan." In addition, the soundtrack is dominated by the pulsating rhythms of voodoo drum beats, often accompanied by native vocals. At one point, as we hear one of the main characters perform Chopin's "E Minor Etude" on the piano, we hear simultaneously the omnipresent voodoo drums providing an eerie counterpoint to the piano number, a technique that ingeniously accents the disparate nature of St. Sebastian's two cultures. Roy Webb's orchestral scoring is by necessity briefer than his work in the previous Lewton film.

Lewton's final draft of the script fully illustrates the producer's obsessive attention to detail. Here is a portion of Lewton's description of Jessica Holland's bedroom:

> It is a beautiful woman's room, feminine but with no suggestion of the bagnio; elegant rather than seductive, and reflecting a playful yet sophisticated taste. The furniture is Biedermeier. There is a large bed, a trim chaise longue, a little slipper chair and, in one corner of the room, that hallmark of great vanity, a triple-screen, full-length mirror, also in Biedermeier style. Before it is a tabouret, the surface of which is literally covered with expensive-looking perfume bottles and cosmetic jars. . . . There is one picture in the room. It is Boecklin's "The Isle of the Dead," framed in a narrow frame of dark wood [Siegel, *The Reality of Terror*].

One wonders just how much of this was lost upon an audience looking for the cheap thrills anyone would expect from a movie called *I Walked with a Zombie*. The above description of Jessica's room — which is shortened from the script's full description — should convince readers that props and decor in a Lewton film were not haphazardly thrown together. The studio set decorators must have wondered whether or not Lewton was on the level. One description caused considerable puzzlement: "Outside the nightjars whistle softly, the cicadas twitter, and the Hammer tree frogs make drowsy, somnolent little croaks; it is a tropic lullaby of bird, batrachian and insect sound." The set decorators, Siegel tells us, didn't know what a nightjar was and brought Lewton a chamber pot.

Shooting ended on November 19, 1942, and trade press screenings took place in early March; their reviews were very positive. By this time, Lewton's reputation had been bolstered by the resounding success of *Cat People*. The latter film was still playing some of the lesser theaters when *I Walked with a Zombie* went into public release in April 1943.

Unfortunately, *Zombie*'s lurid title put off any viewers not interested in the horror trade; the title of Universal's March release, *Frankenstein Meets the Wolfman*, had already done much to cheapen the name of the genre. While Lewton and his cohorts were trying to keep their monsters in the dark, Universal had upped the ante by including two monsters for the price of one, providing the first of the studio's four monster rallies.

Universal may have taken some of the respectability away from the horror trade, but the success of *Cat People* attracted a new legion of fans. While Universal's early-1940s horror films had begun to pander to the juvenile trade, *Cat People* and *I Walked with a Zombie* drew adult audiences.

As we might expect, in *I Walked with a Zombie* nothing is as it appears to be. This is a world where horror always lurks beneath the calm. After the credits, we see a gorgeous long shot of two distant human figures walking along the water's edge; the beach seems endless and the shot is mostly sky. We hear Frances Dee's pleasant, gently self-mocking, voice-over: "I walked with a zombie . . . [she laughs]. It does seem an odd thing to say. If anyone said that to me a year ago, I'm not at all sure I would have known what a zombie was." The mirthful tone of the voice and the soothing visual imagery carry a sense of well-being, but this is just the first of the film's many deceptions.

The story is told through a flashback that, strangely, never makes a completed loop to its point of origin, so the identity of the two people walking on the beach remains a mystery. Moreover, the film's narrative form causes further confusion when Betsy's occasional voice-over (it is her flashback, remember) is dropped halfway through the film, never to be heard again, while the remainder of the story takes an omniscient narrative approach.

After a short scene in Ottawa, Canada—where Betsy (Frances Dee), a nurse, is appointed to her new charge, the wife of the wealthy Caribbean sugar plantation owner—we shift to warmer climes. It is evening and Betsy is on a large commercial sailboat; the star-filled sky and shimmering ocean obviously hold our heroine in a state of awe. Her reveries are interrupted by another boat passenger, Paul Holland (Tom Conway), the wealthy plantation owner: "It's not beautiful," he reads her thoughts, ". . . everything seems beautiful because you don't understand. Those flying fish—they're not leaping for joy; they're jumping in terror. Bigger fish want to eat them. That luminous water—it takes its gleam from millions of dead bodies, the glitter of putresence. There's no beauty here, only death and decay." Following a shot of the sky and a falling star, he adds, "Everything good dies here, even the stars."

Betsy arrives at her destination, the island of St. Sebastian, where a native coachman fills her in on the legend of the island martyr, Ti Misery (Saint Sebastian). Near the Holland estate is a carved wooden figure of Ti Misery—riddled with arrows—formerly the figurehead of a large slave ship. This figurehead becomes *Zombie*'s central recurring image; like Christ, Ti Misery bore pain and degradation for the cause of his people. When the coachman talks about his ancestors chained beneath the decks of slave ships, Betsy rather insensitively chimes in, "Well, they brought them to a beautiful place." To which the coachman stoically replies, "If you say, miss, if you say."

As Betsy inspects her room at Fort Holland, the blinds cast bars of light against the walls, a continuing visual motif in subsequent Fort Holland interiors that suggests bars of captivity. Betsy's voice-over continues, commenting that Fort Holland is starkly desolate and the beautiful garden paths are absolutely barren, with not a soul around.

In the dining room Betsy meets the charming Wesley Rand (James Ellison), Paul's half-brother. Adding to the air of desolation around the estate, Wesley and Betsy sit at a dining table surrounded by empty chairs; Wesley introduces Paul and his mother (both in absentia) via their empty places at the table. There is cynicism in his tone as he talks about the "Byronic" Paul, who is "so very sad." Wesley remarks that his mother feels more comfortable living at the village dispensary; he explains that she was the wife of an island missionary and that after her husband died she stayed on to serve in his place, caring for the islanders' needs. While they dine and talk, we hear the jungle drums.

Paul appears and Wesley makes an uncomfortable exit. Paul is his usual stoic self; he carries a tray to his wife's room (in the stone tower in the courtyard). Betsy wishes to meet Jessica (Christine Gordon), but Paul, mysteriously reluctant, puts off the meeting until the next day. Betsy can not help feeling that Fort Holland and its inhabitants share a deep, dark secret.

That night, after she douses her bedroom light, Betsy looks out the window and sees the ghostly form of a woman dressed in a white flowing gown walking through the moonlit courtyard; this is accompanied by mournful female sobs, amplified by the still night air. Betsy goes into the courtyard to investigate. Bravely, she seeks the source of the soulful lament and heads for the stone tower where Jessica resides. Within, we see a darkened chamber whose stone staircase is bathed in moonlight. The light accents the edges of the steps, making them look like nothing more than a precarious stack of rectangular stones.

As Betsy ascends the steps, the sobbing echoes louder within the chamber. Upon reaching the top landing, she sees the ghostly woman in white enter the tower. In a slow, gliding gait, the woman moves to the steps and begins her climb. As the half-lit form of Jessica Holland, catatonia-in-motion, comes nearer, Betsy screams and runs to the other side of the landing, where she becomes cornered against the opposite wall. Betsy's cries of alarm have no effect upon Jessica's fluid but deliberate movement as she continues to make her way toward the young nurse. In the dense atmosphere of the stone tower, Jessica (now clearly lit by the moon's rays) is a perambulating nightmare, resembling one of the vampire women in the opening scenes of Browning's *Dracula*.

Betsy's rising terror is dismantled by the arrival of Paul Holland and several servants. The eerie sobbing, which has nothing to do with Jessica, is explained. It was Alma (Teresa Harris), a black servant living in the tower's bottom room, who was responsible for the mournful sounds because her sister had "gone a-birthing." Paul explains that on St. Sebastian, where pain and sorrow have been the native's constant companions, bringing a child into the world is a reason to mourn, which is why the natives "make merry at a burial." On the island of St. Sebastian, things are seldom what they appear to be. For example, the next morning at breakfast Betsy tells Alma that she couldn't possibly do justice to the huge puff pastry given her, but when she presses her fork down upon it, it flattens to pancake proportions.

Paul has second thoughts about Betsy; he doesn't want an easily frightened nurse. Betsy tells him a frightened nurse wouldn't have left her room that night and points out that no one told her Jessica was a "mental case." Not offended, Paul takes the opportunity to warn her not to place any stock in tales of voodoo and magic.

Betsy stays on and takes an interest in Jessica's illness. (Or could it be that her selfless dedication to Jessica is an unconscious ruse to cover her feelings for the patient's husband?) Attending physician Dr. Maxwell (James Bell) explains that Jessica had a tropical fever that resulted in her present state. She can sleepwalk and obey simple commands, but that is about it for her social life. "She makes a beautiful zombie, doesn't she?" Dr. Maxwell jokes. He mentions that a zombie is also a drink, which Betsy knows because she once tried one, "but there wasn't anything dead about it."

Wesley chances upon Betsy in town, and the two of them attend a cafe given some local color by a calypso singer (Sir Lancelot). When the singer, not knowing Wesley is in the vicinity, breaks into the "Fort Holland" song, it causes some embarrassment, as its lyrics include the personal misadventures of the Holland/Rand family. When Wesley recognizes the song, he talks louder to drown it out. Betsy, not having yet caught on to the nature of the song, shushes him and hears a verse detailing a love triangle between Paul, his wife, and his half-brother Wesley. The singer notices Wesley sitting among the tables and brings the song to an abrupt halt. He apologizes to Wesley, who begins to escalate his drinking as Betsy takes notice.

Wesley becomes belligerent and makes insulting remarks about Paul: "He's playing the noble husband," he says, "but he uses words like other men use their fists." After a few more drinks, Wesley passes out. Now that Betsy's companion is unconscious, the calypso singer approaches with some new verses of the "Fort Holland" song.

Lancelot's character is frightening because his behavior defies all social etiquette. Moments before, the singer was warm and humble; his apologies over his previous blunder quite genuine. But now he has the effrontery to approach Betsy with additional verses, singing and strumming and staring directly into her eyes, making us think of Jessica that night in the tower. We notice how empty the cafe suddenly is; there's just an unconscious man, a frightened nurse, and a frightening man with a guitar. It's a special Lewton moment, and its brilliance lies in the way it is underplayed; Lancelot does nothing particularly menacing, but his insistent approach is so terrifying that even his song scares us. With this scene, Lewton and Tourneur prove that a strong atmosphere of impending menace need not require a dousing of the lights.

The ascending terror of the cafe scene is interrupted by the first appearance of Mrs. Rand (Edith Barrett), who has come to help take Wesley home; she is obviously used to this. They heave him onto his horse and let the animal engineer the way home. "Give [Wesley] a horse, and he'll ride to his own funeral," says the older woman.

The sounds of drumbeats are heard by Betsy, Paul, and Wesley during dinner. The brothers have a heated argument, and Wesley starts baring the sordid details of the past. Paul, as tactfully as possible, brings him to a sudden halt and sends Betsy out of the room to finish her dinner elsewhere.

Later, Paul almost opens up to Betsy, until the sound of voodoo drums puts him in check and he says, "I think it would be better for all of us if this subject were never mentioned again."

In her last voice-over in the film, Betsy confesses she has fallen in love with Paul. It is the unselfishness of her love, she believes, that drives her to make Jessica well; she is motivated by the prospect of Paul achieving a long-sought inner peace. Knowing that all else has failed, Betsy becomes desperate enough to consider voodoo magic. Alma persuades her to bring Jessica to the Houmfort (voodoo temple) and offers Betsy a "voodoo patch" to ward off danger.

The central set piece of *I Walked with a Zombie* is, of course, Betsy's walk with Jessica through the moonlit cane field en route to the Houmfort. Perhaps the most lauded of Lewton's "walks," this sequence is noted for its mysticism and visual poetry. The walk through Central Park in *Cat People* captured the urban noir style exemplified by Germanic directors like Fritz Lang *(M)* and

Boris Ingster *(Stranger on the Third Floor). Zombie's* walk, however, has tighter connections with the lush pictorialism of Maurice Tourneur or his countryman director Jean Renoir.

There will be no sudden jolts or Lewton "buses" during this fluid and hypnotic walk through the cane fields; Tourneur chooses to sustain, rather than interrupt, the mystical flavor of this spooky journey. Betsy's mute companion, Jessica, being oblivious to everything around her, only enhances the effectiveness of the sequence; Jessica is poor company for moral support, just dead weight to slow Betsy down in a crisis. Hand in hand, Betsy leads Jessica to an uncertain destination. There are numerous sights and sounds along the way.

Rather than implement a musical score to highlight terror, Lewton wanted the sounds of the night to speak for themselves. In *Zombie*'s walk, we hear what Betsy hears: the hooting of an owl, the shifting of the wind, the rustling of the sugar cane, the baleful sound of a hanging hollow gourd filled with holes so it will sing in the breeze.

In addition to the subtle chills of the sound track, the visuals captured by Roy Hunt's photography and Tourneur's direction (in a series of lateral tracking shots through the cane fields) are exquisite. Seldom do we have such scenes of rare beauty in a genre designed to terrify.

En route, Betsy's "voodoo patch" is snagged off by a tree branch, and we presume this means there's trouble ahead. Oddly, the loss of the badge makes not a single bit of difference. This kind of "foundless" manipulation feels like a cheat, but J.P. Telotte contends in *Dreams of Darkness* that it ties in with the film's unifying theme: "all appearances are deceptive . . . the low-key lighting and strategically placed shadows work upon our generic expectations to *suggest* some threat which never materializes . . . even the highly atmospheric walk through the cane fields seems almost an exercise in deception."

The walk sequence is finally punctuated by a chilling vision of Carrefour (Darby Jones). Betsy, pointing her flashlight down as she walks, comes to an abrupt stop when the narrow radius of her beam reveals a pair of naked feet standing motionless on the path before her. The beam follows a long slow upward path, and we see the unforgettable face of Carrefour (the closest we will ever come to finding a Hollywood monster in a Lewton film). Although subtle in its application, the makeup is extremely effective, much better than the clown makeup used in *White Zombie* (where the leader of the walking dead looks like Mack Swain, the villain from Chaplin two-reelers).

The Houmfort scenes, taking place in the native camp, are inspired, and the voodoo chants and dances are quite provocative. Betsy and Jessica simply walk around the zombie guard, and with the music of the ceremony growing louder with each step, they arrive at the Houmfort, where they are ignored by the natives.

Betsy (Frances Dee) and Jessica (Christine Gordon) meet Carrefour the zombie (Darby Jones).

Eventually, when the ceremony begins to die down, Betsy goes into the hut, where she finds Mrs. Rand. The Holland/Rand matriarch begins to tell Betsy the story of her life, saying that it all started when she discovered that the natives were more cooperative when she pretended to accept their beliefs. Instead of saying, "Boil the water, and you will kill the germs," she learned to say, "Boil the water, and the gods will take away the evil spirits."

We cut to the outside of the hut, where Jessica has captured the natives' attention. A man with a sword approaches her and impales her forearm with his weapon: "She doesn't bleed!" they announce in awe and unison, "Zombie! Zombie!" Mrs. Rand tells Betsy to take Jessica back to Fort Holland immediately, before trouble starts.

When Paul finds out about Betsy and Jessica's pilgrimage to the Houmfort, he scolds Betsy, "There's no telling what you might have started with this insanity!" Then he becomes tender: "You think I love Jessica and want her back. I wish it were true if only for your sake." The next day the police commissioner informs Paul Holland that the natives want Jessica back—to do to her what must be done—or they will neglect their work in the cane fields. The commissioner suggests Jessica be institutionalized somewhere off the island; like Oliver in *Cat People,* Paul is willing to have his wife committed. Wesley, however, objects vehemently. Paul wants Betsy to leave the island to extricate herself from the mess, but she refuses. Intercut with the Fort Holland scenes are scenes at the Houmfort, where we see the preparation of a voodoo doll rendered in the image of Jessica.

Later that night, while Betsy sits with Jessica in the tower, the silhouette of Carrefour intrudes upon the latticework of shadows on the interior wall. Betsy sees his form move away, hears the accompanying sounds of shuffling feet, and goes into the courtyard to investigate (resulting in an abbreviated Lewton "walk"). A bullfrog, croaking and jumping into a pond immediately followed by the abrupt screech of a bird provide us with the "bus"-like jolts that were missing in the walk through the cane field.

Only Carrefour's shadow can be seen as it moves along the patio stones; again, we hear his shuffling feet. After being alerted, Paul enters the courtyard, where he watches the zombie (finally visible) advance upon him. In an effective shot from Paul's point of view, we see Carrefour's frightening form heading toward the camera, his arms poised in a strangling gesture, his frightening face eventually filling the frame in extreme close-up. All that viewers tend to remember, however, are those gaping lifeless eyes. Rather conveniently, Mrs. Rand (who seems to have some control over Carrefour) once again comes to the rescue.

The commissioner becomes nervous about the zombie's aggressive behavior and tells the Fort Holland residents that he has been forced to make a legal investigation, meaning that all the details of the dark past will be made a public spectacle. Encouraged to come to the fore, Mrs. Rand tells them there will be no need of an investigation and explains that she was to blame for Jessica's condition. Mrs. Rand confesses that when she discovered Wesley and Jessica were in love and planning to go away together, she went to the Houmfort and pretended to be possessed by a voodoo spirit. Then she actually found herself under the spell of native magic. While in a trance (she claims), she ordered the natives to put a spell upon Jessica: "I kept seeing her face smiling because she was beautiful enough to take my family in her hands and tear it apart." Mrs. Rand's confession is given no credence; just the result of strain and overwork, the commissioner believes.

We see a ritual with Jessica's voodoo doll that evening; the Houmfort is ablaze with excitement as a witchdoctor pulls the doll upon a string, making the standing figure glide slowly toward him. We cut back to Fort Holland, where Jessica is seen walking through the courtyard in response to the voodoo magic. She is apprehended by Paul and Betsy as she is about to reach the outer gate.

This scene is followed by a shot of the St. Sebastian figurehead, with running water splashing over its arrow-ridden form. Wesley stands by the gate, presumably to keep guard over Jessica. In a cut to the ceremony, the witchdoctor pulls the string; when the camera cuts back to the courtyard, we see Jessica returning to the gate. Wesley opens it and lets her pass. He pulls one of the arrows out of the St. Sebastian figurehead and follows Jessica. Back at the Houmfort we see the doll lying in a prone position as the witchdoctor's hand hovers above with a thin sword which he now plunges into the doll. We cut to Wesley to see him pulling his arrow out of Jessica's prostrate form.

Better seen than described, *Zombie*'s closing scenes display a visually rich, almost mythic, quality that provides an elegance rare in horror films. Carrefour arrives, his extended arms showing he wishes to claim the body. Without saying a word, Wesley picks up Jessica and heads down the path, making his way toward the raging waves of the Caribbean shore. Carrefour follows several yards behind. Wesley carries Jessica into the water, deeper and deeper, until they are engulfed by a huge wave. (Wesley's suicide was probably inspired by Fredric March's death scene in Selznick's *A Star Is Born.*) The screen is almost pitch black, accompanied by the sound of crashing waves and Roy Webb's soaring score. As the white foam of a huge wave creeps into the black frame, it defines Carrefour's silhouette, undetectable before the rush of foam. A sublime shot.

We dissolve to another night scene that reveals a series of spear-fishermen knee deep in water, combing the shallows for their catch. We hear their dirgelike chant as they come upon the form of Jessica, floating face-up in the water. Another voice-over, this time from an unknown native source, comes as an aural epitaph: "O Lord God mostly holy. Deliver them from the bitter pain of eternal death. The woman was a wicked woman, and she was dead in her own life. Yea, Lord, dead in the selfishness of her spirit. And the man followed her. Her steps led him down to evil. Her feet took hold on death. Forgive him, O Lord, who knowest the secret of all hearts. Yea, Lord, pity them who are dead and give peace and happiness to the living."

I Walked with a Zombie succeeds in its ability to transport *Jane Eyre*'s Gothic elements from a gloomy British estate to the sunny climes of the Caribbean without sacrificing the stasis and decay inherent in the novel's mood. The Holland/Rand estate, like the family itself, is dark and twisted within, despite a fairly normal looking exterior. The tropical sun does nothing to cheer things up; it only accents the film's "deceptive appearances" theme. Most interior shots are compositions of light and shadow, the light source seeping in through curtains, blinds, lattices. One gets the impression that a similar darkness exists within each member of the Holland/Rand family, all of them living their lives through closed shades.

Because threads of influence exist between *Jane Eyre* and *Rebecca* (and because Lewton contributed to the film adaptations of both), it is not surprising to see something of an amalgam of the two novels in *I Walked with a Zombie.* Paul Holland is an equivalent to *Jane Eyre*'s Rochester and *Rebecca*'s Maximilian; Fort Holland has the same function as Thornfield Manor in *Eyre* and Manderley in *Rebecca.* In Brontë's novel, the Byronic hero's wife is insane; in du Maurier's novel the wife is dead, but her memory is kept alive by the housekeeper. Jessica Holland's character in *Zombie* is an intriguing combination of both doomed women; some say Jessica is insane or brain damaged, while others believe she is dead and actually a zombie.

In *Hollywood from Vietnam to Reagan,* Robin Wood calls Lewton's second film, "one of the finest of all American horror films." Wood goes on to state:

> *I Walked with a Zombie* explicitly locates horror at the heart of the family, identifying it with sexual repressiveness in the cause of preserving family unity. . . . It is built on an elaborate set of apparently clear-cut structural oppositions: Canada-West Indies, white-black, light-darkness, life-death, science-black magic, Christianity-Voodoo, conscious-unconscious, etc.—and it proceeds systematically to blur all of them. Jessica is both living and dead; Mrs. Rand mixes medicine, Christianity, and voodoo; the figurehead is both St. Sebastian and a black slave; the black-white opposition is poetically undercut in a complex patterning of dresses and voodoo patches; the motivation of all the characters is called into question.

I Walked with a Zombie, unlike *Cat People,* is constructed as a mystery rather than as a horror film. In *Cat People,* the supernatural elements are linked to Irena, the sympathetic central character. In *Zombie,* the "supernatural" character, Jessica Holland (wonderfully played by Christine Gordon), is minor and about as sympathetic as the Ti Misery figurehead. Cheerful, good-natured Betsy, presented as a healthy contrast to the family's morbid nature, is the heroine of *Zombie.* Although Betsy initially scoffs at superstition, her skepticism is shaken by the abnormal events around her. Betsy may finally accede to the possibility of mystical forces, but the horrors she uncovers are born of human weakness, not supernatural intervention.

As in the classic mystery setup, the audience knows only what its main character knows. Although we easily identify with Betsy (the film's unofficial detective, well played by Frances Dee), her healthy persona does not elicit the kind of sympathetic concern we felt for the doomed heroine of *Cat People.* Actually, Betsy's role is more similar to Jane Randolph's Alice in the above film. Like Alice, Betsy is an intelligent, resourceful character who stirs the affections of another woman's husband. Although Alice and Betsy are hardly sinister, their intrusions upon the two marriages indirectly lead to the deaths of the respective wives.

Lewton's female characters have been strangely neglected by feminist critics, who more often gravitate to heroines like Rosalind Russell in *His Girl Friday* or Katharine Hepburn in *Sylvia Scarlett* as exemplar models of the career woman of their respective eras. Russell and Hepburn, in the above films, however, are women managing in a man's world by proving themselves capable of male standards. The female roles in Lewton's films are admirable on their own terms and closer to the kind of "liberated" feminine film roles we expect today.

Lewton's films appeared to generate two special feminine archetypes:

survivors and victims. The survivor is a resourceful, often professional, woman who, playing by her own rules, shows intelligence and courage in a crisis. In *Cat People,* it was Alice who had the resourcefulness to jump into a swimming pool immediately upon sensing danger; in *Zombie,* it is Betsy who trusts her instincts and acts quickly and accordingly. These are not the prototypical horror film females reduced to tears and hysteria at the first sign of a threat.

Lewton's victims, on the other hand, are tragic women who have lost their pride (though not their underlying decency) by making concessions against their better judgment; these are women caught in traps, but traps only partially of their own design. Lewton's feminine victims possess a sense of shame or a burden of guilt, sometimes a burden forced upon them. *Cat People*'s Irena Dubrovna is the quintessential Lewton victim, but other examples of varying significance appear in subsequent films in the Lewton cycle. They do not always die; they may survive the final reel, but they will probably remain victims for the rest of their lives. In *Zombie* we have two women who serve as victims, Jessica Holland and Mrs. Rand; the latter, played by Edith Barrett, gives an outstanding, yet understated, performance. Mrs. Rand's feigned good cheer is increasingly undermined by her sense of irreversible doom as her emotional fatigue erodes her last vestiges of dignity.

We can see an interesting dichotomy in the first two Lewton/Tourneur films: *Cat People*'s central character (Irena) is a victim; *Zombie*'s central character (Betsy) is a survivor. These distinctions make a world of difference in how the two films work. Examples of both female archetypes will appear repeatedly in Lewton's 11-film cycle.

There are those who consider *I Walked with a Zombie* to be an unqualified classic, the best of Lewton's 11 films for RKO. One can easily appreciate the film's moody atmosphere and poetic beauty, the handsome production values, the intelligent script, the multilayered soundtrack and tasteful score, the good performances, and, among other things, the Tourneur/Hunt team's unerring eye for composition.

And there are those who find the film strangely inaccessible and unsatisfying. For all its strengths, *I Walked with a Zombie* is often a disappointment to first-time viewers; repeated viewings make *Zombie* more enjoyable but, even then, one may question the film's lofty reputation.

Most viewers approach a horror movie expecting a straightforward plot progression, which is where *Zombie* fails to be accommodating. Some viewers miss important narrative details in lines that are either thrown away or spoken too softly. Much of this was intentional, as Tourneur explained to Charles Higham and Joel Greenberg in *The Celluloid Muse:* "In *[I Walked with a Zombie]*, as in others, I made the people talk very low, as I think this indicates sincerity . . . it makes for the effect I want. I'll have an actor replay a whole scene as though he's just talking to me in a normal voice, and it's effective."

Viewers may be disappointed by the uneventful outcome of the Houmfort walk. If this is the famous walk indicated in the title, it is admittedly anticlimactic. Moreover, the scenes of exposition that immediately follow are fairly pedestrian, causing some viewers to tune out during stretches of underplayed dialogue significant to the unraveling of the mystery. *Zombie* is so elliptical in its storytelling, however, that some of its audience did not know there was a mystery to solve.

Tourneur often uses his visuals to bewilder or even mislead his audience, while the important details of plot progression are given mere lip service in quiet discourses between characters. Most of *Zombie*'s actual story is told aurally, while the film's outstanding visuals reach for ambience and ambiguity. The creepy tower scene in the first half hour, however well executed, is merely gratuitous, as are several other of the film's fright scenes, because it is made clear that St. Sebastian's walking dead do not go around killing people.

It is characteristic that Lewton makes little provision for the "monster" in his script. The rising terror of three similar scare scenes, each with the menacing approach of a different zombie (Jessica, the calypso singer, and Carrefour), is so quickly deflated by convenient arrivals from the Holland/Rand family that when our chills subside, we feel a little cheated by such half-hearted, obligatory, and merely manipulative horror film tactics. The front office urged Lewton to come up with a monster, but the producer was reluctant to make significant, or at least more conventional, use of the zombie. Lewton's reticence to turn Carrefour into a typical horror movie monster has also been a source of disappointment for some first-time viewers. (It is interesting to note that since Tourneur and Lewton were both fans of Jean Renoir, the name of the film's zombie may well have been inspired by Renoir's 1932 film *La Nuit de Carrefour*.)

Sometimes *Zombie*'s visuals are disorienting. Our sense of place is extremely vague during the Fort Holland scenes: Are they inside or outside the house? Does that door go to the main dwelling or does it go to the spooky tower? We never get an idea of where things are. Why does Jessica's tower room look cheerful and well lit from the inside when the tower was previously revealed to be a dark, damp structure short on windows? If Fort Holland's ambiguous layout was supposed to suggest the qualities of a maze, then not much use is made of it as a dramatic device.

For some viewers, *Zombie* may be too "artistic" for its own good. Sir Lancelot's Greek chorus function may be a nifty idea for lovers of classical literature, but its easy to understand why people have missed the significance of the lyrics (thinking the song just a pleasant bit of local color) only to become lost when they see Wesley's reaction to the tune. The verses concerning the "Holland man" and his half-brother, the "man called Rand," may go right over viewers' heads, especially so early in the film, when names have been mentioned too offhandedly for them to stick. After Wesley passes out and the singer reprises his song, what follows is so unnerving that we tend to ignore the lyrics in the expectation that some sort of mayhem is about to occur.

Some aspects of the film are less that convincing. The romance between Paul and Betsy has little credibility and even less screen chemistry. Clearly, a plucky heroine like Betsy deserves better than a stuffed shirt like Paul Holland. Another unconvincing aspect of the film is Wesley's former infatuation with Jessica. Although we are repeatedly told how beautiful Jessica is (was), there is nothing in Christine Gordon's ferretlike countenance that gives substance to the numerous declarations of her loveliness. It is also curious that Wesley appears to have absolutely no interest in the bedridden Jessica.

Zombie's plot elements are at times a bit suspect. Why all the fuss about the legal investigation? What are the Holland/Rands afraid of? Is the adulterous love triangle really such a big deal in a world where native islanders can raise the dead? Other plot holes present themselves. There is no reason why Paul Holland needed to hire Betsy if Alma would have done just fine, having provided excellent care for Jessica in the past. Not only does Alma enjoy this task, but she also makes it plain that she is reluctant to give it up. If Paul was so determined to avoid at all costs public knowledge of Fort Holland's dark secret, it is odd that he would arrange to have a Canadian nurse shipped down to the Caribbean.

Another puzzling detail concerns the natives' surprise when they recognize Jessica as a zombie. Although they take part in frenzied rituals to get her back to the Houmfort, weren't they the ones who, with Mrs. Rand's assistance, orchestrated the voodoo curse in the first place? When Betsy brings Jessica to the Houmfort, the witchdoctor's reaction, after impaling Jessica's arm, is one of awe and fear. This is tantamount to a baker being terrified by a loaf of bread. If the natives are so afraid of Jessica, why aren't they bothered by the bug-eyed Carrefour, a far more intimidating example of their work? Why do they want to destroy Jessica and not Carrefour? Is Carrefour's zombie state more acceptable than Jessica's? Questions, questions, questions.

I Walked with a Zombie is a far more daring film than its Lewton/Tourneur predecessor, and it remains surprising that it was such a box-office hit (though it did not score as well as *Cat People*). The film caused critics of *The New Republic* and *The Nation*, Manny Farber and James Agee respectively, to heap praise upon the Lewton team, which undoubtedly meant more to the producer than the film's box-office clout. Still, it is not difficult to understand how RKO's front office must have felt when it viewed *Zombie* for the first time. Even today, it remains a highly unconventional horror film.

Near the end of his impressive directing career, Jacques Tourneur called *I Walked with a Zombie* "the best film I've ever done in my life." Lewton's wife, Ruth, recently told the author that she still considers it her favorite among all the films her husband produced. *The Penguin Encyclopedia of Horror and the Supernatural* (edited by Jack Sullivan) calls it Lewton's "most satisfyingly oblique piece of supernatural poetry. . . . The film's refreshing seriousness of approach and the director's almost effortless skill in suggesting a supernatural world just out of reach are more than enough to compensate for the slight traces of cultural pretension." In his *Encyclopedia of Horror Movies,* Phil Hardy describes it as "a haunting nightmarishly beautiful tone poem of voodoo drums, dark moonlight and somnambulist ladies in floating white brought to perfection by Tourneur's direction, Hunt's camerawork, and Wray's dialogue. . . . Tourneur's best film." Danny Peary writes in *Cult Movies,* "The lyrical quality of the long silent passages, the shadows, the lighting, the music, the settings . . . is what makes *I Walked with a Zombie* so fascinating, and so different from the typically brutal horror film."

Unfortunately, the success of Lewton's first two films did not deliver the kind of mainstream recognition the producer was hoping for. It is probable (considering Lewton's later career) that had he been vaulted to the ranks of a top studio producer, he would have fallen on his face. Lewton tended to gripe about the injustices of his profession; Mark Robson said, "He knew he was good, and still he had a habit of pleading poverty. . . . In a way, I think he was a man who needed an enemy." Perhaps the studio executives looked upon the horror genre with such disdain that it naturally carried over to their feelings toward Lewton, but he preserved their livelihood and they treated him with deference.

EIGHT

The Leopard Man

I remember him staying up until all hours of the night working on screenplays. He enjoyed having his hand in the writing. I used to think that he went out of his way to pick inept writers so that he'd have to redo their work. He used to write on a Royal typewriter; he used only two fingers but he was very fast. He'd talk out the different parts as he wrote them and, since my bed was just on the other side of the wall, I'd fall asleep listening.

—NINA LEWTON DRUCKMAN
from *The Reality of Terror*, by Joel Siegel

On February 8, 1943, *The Leopard Man* went into its first day of production. *Cat People* had been playing the theaters for a little over a month, and it was still at the peak of its success. The phenomenal box office of his debut production was the only weapon Lewton had to keep his superiors at bay. *I Walked with a Zombie* still had two months before its April release, and though the front office executives were not enthusiastic about its commercial potential, they had little reason to balk, given that *Cat People* had put the studio back in the black.

The Leopard Man was announced in the trade papers as early as November 1942. It was to be Lewton's first (official) adaptation of a previously written work, in this case Cornell Woolrich's dark thriller, *Black Alibi*. Ardel Wray was secured as the screenwriter (though Lewton would be responsible for the final revision, uncredited as usual), with "additional dialogue" being supplied by Edward Dein. The title change to *The Leopard Man* was devised by the front office to make the thriller more marketable as a horror film. Because the story was set in New Mexico, Lewton assigned Ardel Wray to do some preliminary field work by visiting that geographical area and taking some photographs of the locale.

A Cornell Woolrich novel was the perfect source for a Lewton production. Of all the hard-boiled mystery writers of the era (Dashiel Hammett, Raymond Chandler, James M. Cain), Cornell Woolrich was the one who most embodied, in literary form, the style and substance of film noir (his name will turn up many times in this volume). In *Film Noir: The Dark Side of the Screen,* author Foster Hirsch tells us:

> The Woolrich world is a maze of wrong impressions as the author sets traps for his luckless protagonists and then watches as they fall into them. Filled with pitfalls and sudden violence, the landscape in Woolrich is the kind of place where a single wrong turn, a mere chance encounter, triggers a chain reaction in which one calamity follows another. . . .
>
> Night, darkness, the menacing streets of the city at night, the city as a landscape of doom: these supply the inevitable *mise en scène* for Woolrich's taut stories of black deeds, sudden eruptions of foulness, grisly twists of fate. . . . Many of his characters are plagued by self-division, by conflicts between their rational daytime selves and their night-time alter egos, just as the typical Woolrich fable customarily begins in the ordered, daytime world before it plummets into darkness. The Woolrich canon is rife with visual and psychological doubleness, as day is contrasted with night and sanity teeters on the edge of darkness.

In this third outing, Lewton retained the same production team as in the previous effort, with the exception of Robert de Grasse, who replaced J. Roy Hunt as director of photography. Tourneur again directed (his last in the series), and Mark Robson again edited (his last credit as an editor). All principal shooting was done within a month's time; the budget came in at around $150,000.

The Leopard Man sports a larger cast than either of the previous Lewton films. Dennis O'Keefe gets star billing, and his romantic interest is played by Jean Brooks in her first of a trio of Lewton film performances. To cast the approximately 40 speaking parts, Lewton made an effort to secure as many Mexican/Hispanic performers as possible to enhance the credibility of the convincing "New Mexico" sets. The film's pivotal role, that of the spunky flamenco dancer, Clo-Clo, went to actress Margo (the aging beauty in *Lost Horizon*), an inspired casting choice. Other significant roles went to James Bell, Margaret Landry, Isobel Jewell, Abner Biberman, Ben Bard, and Kate Lawson.

Thanks to Robson's expert editing, *The Leopard Man* is a veritable sound collage. Clo-Clo's castinets provide the chief pulse of this film, though other percussive elements—rhythms of banging pans, echoing footsteps, the rattling of passing trains, plunking waterdrops, chanting processions—permeate the soundtrack. The lively Spanish-flavored Roy Webb score enhances these elements of the soundtrack.

The Leopard Man is often characterized as a horrific mystery thriller without the supernatural shadings of its predecessors, but this is not entirely true. Although *The Leopard Man*'s characters are quick to dismiss the supernatural elements in their lives, the narrative's seemingly disjointed structure is unified by a fortune-teller's prophecy of doom. The ill-fated woman Clo-Clo, in dismissing the prophecy, unknowingly taints the lives of those in her community. In *The Leopard Man,* doom is as contagious as poison ivy, and Clo-Clo's destiny has random repercussions upon the rich and the poor, the guilty and the innocent, the sane and the insane.

Because of the credence given the fortune-teller's numerous readings (at least five on-screen occasions, all ending with the death card) and the odd way Clo-Clo's dark destiny appears to rub off upon innocent females, *The Leopard Man* is not quite the straight mystery thriller people think it is. Actually, the only way to find unity within its rambling narrative is to acknowledge the presence of a supernatural force.

The Leopard Man's mazelike narrative structure is actually more daring than *Zombie*'s ambiguous flashbacks. Here the decision was not to focus on a single character but to make abrupt shifts, using Clo-Clo's pivotal role as a transitional device. Various sounds, particularly her castanets, are also used to provide continuity for a number of transitional detours. Clo-Clo is instrumental in holding the film together, for she functions as its central "supernatural" figure; it is she who, quite literally, unleashes evil upon her small New Mexican town.

With the opening credits, Roy Webb's score breaks into what sounds like a standard mystery theme, only to be magically transformed into a bolero-styled composition accompanied by the cricketlike staccato of castanets. Under the credits, we see a dark, labyrinthian street accented by the glow of a globe streetlamp. After Tourneur's name fades, the music comes to an abrupt halt; the castanets make a slow rhythmic return, picking up pace (and volume, it seems) as de Grasse's fluid voyeuristic camera pulls ahead to the open threshold of a small apartment where we see Clo-Clo (Margo) pirouetting, castanets in hand.

The camera tracks to the immediate right, to another open door (in a motellike battery of apartments) where Kiki Walker (Jean Brooks), fed up with Clo-Clo's racket, complains loudly, bangs on the wall, and slams the door to the camera. It is a masterful opening, one which not only introduces its two high-spirited females (one a victim, the other a survivor) but also establishes the friction in their relationship. Since she is the narrative's binding force, it is fitting that Clo-Clo is the first character we see.

Kiki's press-agent boyfriend, Jerry Manning (Dennis O'Keefe), wants to put some spice into her nightclub act, which is why he brings a black leopard into her dressing room. The leopard is rented as a publicity stunt in the hope that as an addition to Kiki's act, it would add a few more dollars to the till.

We dissolve to a scene in the cafe, our first image being a fountain with a hollow ball perched atop a vertical stream of water. Like the statue of St. Sebastian in *Zombie,* the cafe fountain will function as *The Leopard Man*'s

Jean Brooks and her dark companion in *The Leopard Man*.

recurring symbol, with the floating ball representing the lack of control man has over the forces that keep him in motion.

Accompanied by the sound of castanets, one of the cafe dancers, Clo-Clo, finishes her number. It is plain that the Latino dancer does not approve of Kiki's new act when her rival appears on the floor with the leopard on a leash. Clo-Clo approaches the docile animal, harassing it with her chattering castanets; the frightened animal bolts out the door, leash and all.

A nocturnal street scene follows, crowded with police and townspeople; they are roaming about with flashlights, banging pots, shouting, generally doing everything they shouldn't do, according to Charlie "How-Come," the leopard's owner. Charlie (Abner Biberman) is near his wagon, upon which we see his advertising sign: "The Leopard Man." He explains that all the commotion will scare the cat, making him dangerous.

We hear the sound of castanets coming from the direction of a length of darkened sidewalk. Clo-Clo steps into our view, cheerful and animated amid the surrounding turmoil, feeling little guilt over her responsibility in the matter. But Clo-Clo has unleashed the curse that will turn the town upon itself and ultimately consume her. One her way home, Clo-Clo passes her fortune-teller friend, Maria (Isobel Jewell), who, leaning out the door, tells Clo-Clo to pick a card from the fanned deck. Clo-Clo picks the ace of spades (the death

Mrs. Delgado (Kate Lawson), about to shoo her frightened daughter Teresa (Margaret Landry) out the door.

card), gives it back and laughs, calling Maria a "faker," and continues on her way. For most of the film, Clo-Clo appears perpetually undaunted by dark streets and mounting hysteria; she holds her head high, walks with a determined, confident stride, and bids cheerful greetings to the people she passes. If she doesn't like what someone has to say, she chatters her castanets in his direction (a repetition of her earlier action with the leopard), smiling brazenly all the while. Everyone seems to know Clo-Clo, and we get the impression that they enjoy her sense of bravura. She is not a bad person, really, and she bears many of the earmarks of the plucky "Lewton survivor" . . . for a time.

Clo-Clo passes the house of the Delgado family, where daughter Teresa (Margaret Landry), not yet 20, leans out her window, greeting Clo-Clo as she passes. "Hello, Chiquita," Clo-Clo responds, continuing on her merry way. But here, instead of the camera continuing to track Clo-Clo, it remains with Teresa. The sound of castanet recedes into the distance as the camera follows Teresa into her house.

Teresa's domineering mother (Kate Lawson) insists that the girl go out to buy corn meal; when Teresa confesses that she is afraid of being attacked in the dark streets by the escaped leopard, Señora Delgado scoffs. Teresa's sadistic younger brother takes joy in creating large catlike hand shadows on the wall, scaring his sister by saying, "Leopards are big and they jump on you!"

Looking like an even match for any leopard, Señora Delgado offers no sympathy: "Did you ever meet one of them on your way to the store before? . . . Then you won't meet them now!" Whereupon the woman pushes her daughter out the door with a broom (as one would shoo out a cat) and locks the door from the inside, vowing not to open it until the corn meal is delivered. Intuition already tells us Teresa is in for a hair-raising journey, but this is no real preparation for the visceral terror of what follows, one of the most frightening sequences in the history of the genre.

As Teresa reluctantly walks along, blending into the night as she goes, she arrives at the nearest market, which has just closed for the evening. The woman storekeeper is still inside and could just as easily have opened the door to admit one last customer, but she tells Teresa, "It means taking off the lock again, turning on the light, measuring the meal; it's too much trouble."

And so Teresa must walk across town, cutting through alleys, across arroyos and river beds, and under train trestles, to find an open store. A tumbleweed rolling across her path in the dark frightens her. We hear the wind, a distant train whistle; nothing more. Teresa makes it to an open store, but the proprietors, recognizing her as the "little girl afraid of the dark," make jest of her dreaded return trip. Teresa looks at some mechanical songbirds in a birdcage near the store's counter. As is often the case with a prototypical Lewton victim, Teresa receives little help from the people who know her.

On her return route, the girl retraces her steps, once again going through the train trestle. A stream flows underneath, casting shimmering reflections upon the surfaces all around her (shades of the swimming pool scene in *Cat People*). In lieu of score music, we hear the steady sound of water drops plunking into surrounding puddles from the trestle above. At the moment that Teresa, looking up, locks her gaze upon a pair of glowing eyes, a train screams by on the above trestle (a jolting Lewton "bus"). The train passes on but the glowing eyes remain. The leopard moves out of his shadowy perch underneath the trestle. He is large and terrifying and now looks nothing like that tabby-on-a-leash we met in Kiki's room. The cat's eyes continue to shine as it crouches to spring. Teresa runs and in her haste falls upon and breaks the sack of corn meal (which reminds us that a locked door still awaits the girl). Finally, Teresa makes it to her house and pounds on her door, screaming, "Mamacita, let me in! It's coming! Let me in! I can see it! It's coming!"

Señora Delgado, annoyed over her daughter's tardiness, refuses to rush, answering, "Just what she needs: something to nip at her heels to hurry her up." After hearing the extremity of Teresa's bloodcurdling shrieks, Senora Delgado makes a frenzied attempt to open the door, but the lock breaks and it can't be budged. Gutteral sounds come from the opposite side of the door, the creature thumping against the wood, gnawing on something. Then a large trickle of human blood seeps under the locked door, along the floorboard groove, near the feet of Senora Delgado and her son.

A typically lurid RKO ad for *The Leopard Man*.

At Teresa's wake, Dr. Galbraith (James Bell), the local museum curator and resident "cat expert," confirms the cause of death (a leopard attack) to Chief Robles (Ben Bard) and Jerry Manning. Although Robles holds Jerry partially to blame for the tragedy, the latter remains detached, cynical, and unperturbed, causing the chief to become angry when he refuses to join the leopard posse.

While Señor and Señora Delgado grieve at their daughter's wake, their son makes hand shadows of a cat upon the interior wall of the church.

We go back to Clo-Clo, our narrative thread, and find her visiting her friend Maria, who reluctantly tells Clo-Clo that numerous rereadings on her friend's behalf have all ended with the death card. Clo-Clo is unperturbed by this and asks the spiritualist to tell her of important financial matters: "For what was I born if it wasn't for money?" Maria, reading her cards, says, "You will get money . . . and then," she lifts another card. The ace of spades.

Eventually, Jerry joins Galbraith in a failed leopard posse. Galbraith informs Jerry, "To know where that leopard went, you'd have to be a leopard and think like a leopard." At the cafe, Galbraith joins Jerry and Kiki for a drink. The ball remains atop the fountain spout, giving Galbraith the opportunity to make some seemingly profound remarks about humanity and "the forces that move us."

The next day Clo-Clo's confident stride carries us through the morning streets, giving us a day-by-day look at human activity. She passes her friend Rosita, who is carrying a bouquet of roses, a birthday gift for the daughter of the wealthy Contrera family for whom Rosita works as a maid. Clo-Clo takes one of the roses from Rosita's bouquet (her action reminding us of her fortune readings) and goes on her way, as the camera stays behind to follow the maid back to the Contrera household (a narrative gesture quite similar to that which preceded the Teresa sequence).

Rosita goes into Consuelo's bedroom and puts the roses on the sleeping girl's pillow. The camera shot, framing the roses and her face, looks uncomfortably like the image of death (at Teresa's funeral, moments before, Kiki had commented that all flowers reminded her of death).

Consuelo (Tula Parma) is roused and an intimate birthday party follows. When things are breaking up, Consuelo tells her mother: "I must go to the cemetery. It's my birthday." The girl says she wishes to put flowers on her father's grave, but she really wants to meet her boyfriend, Raoul Belmonte (Richard Martin), by using the cemetery as their meeting place. Because Raoul is poor, Consuelo fears her mother will not approve. Finally, after some considerable urging, Senora Contreras relents. "I'll hurry," says Consuelo, "I'll be right back."

By the time she arrives at the cemetery, Consuelo has apparently just missed Raoul, although this is a bit vague (if not altogether baffling). The gatekeeper (Brandon Hurst) warns that it is almost closing time. Consuelo says, "It'll only take a moment," to which the gatekeeper cryptically replies, "Time is strange; a moment can be as short as a breath or as long as an eternity." (It is a safe bet that Lewton penned that one.)

Consuelo visits her father's grave for an indeterminate amount of time, and her lingering presence suggests that she believes Raoul is merely late. She appears concerned over his whereabouts and goes back to their meeting place near a stone bench upon which she sees some cigarette butts. One cigarette appears to be lit. (Some significance is made of this, but its meaning is rather obscure, especially when Consuelo remains inert and a lap-dissolve signals that time has passed and the sun has set.) The caretaker blows his whistle, warning that the gates are going to be closed and locked. Consuelo is clearly in earshot of the warning whistle, but by the time she makes an effort to leave, it is already too late. She runs to the gate, but like Teresa, she stands face to face with a locked door.

Thanks to director Tourneur and photographer Robert de Grasse, this sequence is wonderfully evocative; the spooky cemetery is replete with claustrophobic mazes, creepy statues, and freshly dug open graves. The gatekeeper's dying wood fire, flickering through the latticework above the heavy double doors of the cemetery gate, also produces an eerie effect; there are some great shots of the moon past the high cemetery wall. Some subtle but chilling Roy Webb music, ending nicely in midscene with a single sustained organ note, is finally overpowered by the sounds of the wind and the silence of the dead.

Consuelo hears a car start outside the cemetery wall (the suddenness of its engine serving as a mild "bus"); the girl screams to alert the driver and his screech of brakes tells us he has heard her cries for help. We remain with Consuelo, never seeing the car or its driver, and this carries an unnerving effect. All we hear is a disembodied voice (courtesy of Lewton's future performer, Russell Wade), sounding like a some benevolent spirit of the night coming in answer to Consuelo's prayers.

One would hope for better service, however. The voice we hear could be anybody, but it seems to express genuine concern. In a Lewton film, though, even good samaritans seldom provide any real help to a victim in distress. Although the terrified Consuelo pleads for the man to stay, he insists on leaving to get a ladder, remaining offhandedly casual in his reassurance. He says, "I'll be back before you know it!" Consuelo's terror builds as she waits and waits. She hears a rustling noise and looks up to see a tree branch bending toward the cemetery wall, weighed down by some frightful presence. We cut to her terrified face as she screams.

The good samaritan said he would be right back, but the discovery of the body after daybreak, with a clear view of the ladder still leaning against the wall, would suggest that our helpful stranger took in a movie, a full night's sleep, and maybe even some breakfast, before making his return. When the police gather around the scene of the crime, significance is made of deep scratch marks on the tree, a broken claw, and some animal fur: "It's the leopard, all right," announces Chief Robles. Jerry, who is present, begins to suspect that this time a human may be responsible. Jerry's belief, supported by Charlie "How Come," is that the leopard had no reason to come to the cemetery when it could have been miles into the desert. Galbraith says, "Caged animals are unpredictable—they're like frustrated human beings."

Seeing Charlie, Galbraith remarks, "He'd have to know about leopards and have access to claws and hair," the insinuation growing clearer as he inquires about Charlie's drunken blackouts. The good-natured Charlie falls for it and, suspecting himself of murder, insists that Robles lock him up for a day or two. That night, while he is in jail, Charlie hears castanets and looks out the cell window. The camera, like a predator, leaves the cell behind and tracks Clo-Clo, presently on her way to the cafe.

Upon entering she meets a wealthy older man, a sugar daddy who will be fleeced of some cash, we suspect, but things are not quite as they seem. The man is one up on the situation; he knows Clo-Clo is a gold-digger, and, frankly, he does not care because he is lonely and knows no better way to spend his loot. Finding the man's honesty appealing, Clo-Clo opens her heart to him, her confessions evoking our sympathy. She reveals that she loves Carlos Domingo, a poor boy who can never give her what she and her family need: money. Since the cafe dancer is the sole support of her mother and younger siblings, she knows what it is like to be poor and does not want to make a career of it. When the older gentleman asks where her true feelings lie, she answers, "Feelings don't buy houses and pay for rent and help bring up kids and buy clothes for them." The man tells her to follow her heart, and everything else will take care of itself. The man hands her a hundred dollar bill: "For your mother, brother, and sister." When Clo-Clo good-naturedly replies, "What about me?" the man answers, "You'll get *your* money from your husband, Carlos." Clo-Clo's smile tells us it is more than just the money that is making her happy; she has decided to follow her heart.

With the above scene putting Clo-Clo in a very sympathetic light, we realize that now that we want her to live, we know she is going to die. Jubilant, Clo-Clo goes out into the night. As she passes Maria the fotune-teller, the latter asks, "Did the elderly man give you a lot of money?" Clo-Clo shows her the hundred-dollar bill, and Maria picks the ace of spades, announcing, "Something black is on its way to you."

For the first time Clo-Clo is bothered by these predictions. "Walk a little way with me," she begs Maria. Although Maria agrees to accompany her for part of the way, Clo-Clo must make the remainder of her trip alone. During her solo walk, she is offered a ride by a passing motorist, and she is ready to accept the lift until she sees the car is black. She hurries away, remembering the words of Maria's prophecy. While she travels along deserted streets, the soundtrack is uncluttered by score music, relying instead upon an assortment of ominous sounds amplified in the night air. The Clo-Clo we see now no longer walks with confident strides. She is without her bravado and reckless good cheer; her castanets are silent. Before, she appeared to have an aura of protection, but things have changed and what we see now is her utter vulnerability. What we see is her transition from survivor to victim.

Clo-Clo does make it home, only to discover that her prize $100 bill has

"The Procession" from *The Leopard Man.*

been lost en route. Our first visit into her home allows us to get an even more sympathetic perspective of the young woman. The dancer we once believed was a morally bankrupt golddigger is a well-appreciated member of a loving family; there is much goodwill in this household and it is plain that Clo-Clo's homelife is preferable to that of either of the film's previous victims. It is with great reluctance that she goes back out into the night to retrieve her prize.

For a while, along the darkened streets, it is deadly quiet. Then we hear the sound of footsteps mixing in with the tapping of Clo-Clo's heels. The woman believes it to be Carlos and calls out his name. She takes out her compact and applies makeup and lipstick, her cigarette dropping from her mouth as she does so. (The script would have us believe, rather lamely, that the application of makeup is Clo-Clo's typical behavior whenever she suspects her lover is nearby.) But Clo-Clo's terrified close-up reveals that it is not Carlos, after all; while she screams, we cut to a shot of the ground, framing the dropped compact and the still-burning cigarette.

As the film rushes to a conclusion, our suspicions that Dr. Galbraith is behind the deaths of Consuelo and Clo-Clo are confirmed, especially when Charlie's leopard (responsible for Teresa's death only) is found in the desert, riddled with bullet holes (shot by Galbraith, who neglected to report it). Galbraith had tipped his hand earlier, when he said the killer must have access to a leopard's fur and claws. Jerry and Kiki devise a plan to "turn the tables" on the killer by subjecting the museum curator to a series of back-from-the-dead ruses to make him panic and confess.

As Galbraith walks past the cemetery gate that evening, he hears a woman's voice within, pleading for help. This has its unnerving effect upon the curator, who, walking on, begins to hear the sound of castanets. A lit cigarette falls at his feet, thrown from somewhere; but there is no one about.

Kiki visits Galbraith at the museum (where he is seen dusting off an artifact in a torpid, unconvincing fashion). Kiki explains that she has come to the museum after-hours to see "the procession" from the window—a good view, we are told. The procession is a yearly event where a series of black-clad paraders (who look like a reversal of the KKK) get in costume to commemorate the Indian massacre site upon which the town is built. It is a celebration of death.

Kiki wants to turn off the lights for a clearer exterior view, but Galbraith fears the dark this night; apparently, he has difficulty suppressing his urge to kill when the lights are out. After a pall of silence, Kiki drops one of her castanets (a stupid mistake), and the masquerade is over. Jerry and Raoul (Consuelo's boyfriend) burst upon the scene.

A quick chase ends with the three men becoming entwined in the procession, where Raoul, sporting a pistol, urges the curator to the sidelines. Galbraith reveals no motive for the crimes except the pleasure of killing. Lewton and Ardel Wray tread the cinematic territory established by Fritz Lang's *M* when Galbraith reveals, "You don't know what it means to be tormented this way. I didn't want to kill, but I had to." When Galbraith, lost in his reverie of his first kill, begins describing Consuelo's flesh in loving detail (presumably, to make the men understand how difficult it was to resist temptation), Raoul shoots him dead with the pistol.

The Leopard Man is often considered an inferior Lewton film because it does not possess the unity of its two predecessors. Yet, ask any classic horror film fanatic about his favorite 1940s terror sequence and the chances are good that *The Leopard Man*'s blood-under-the-door scene will be cited. It is, along with *Psycho*'s shower scene, one of the most written-about horror movie sequences of all time. Granted, *The Leopard Man*'s aspirations are not justly served by the film's overabundance of static scenes and gaping narrative flaws, but Lewton's third film is so extraordinary on other counts that these shortcomings are easy to forgive. Obviously, the Lewton/Tourneur/Robson team overextended themselves, as *The Leopard Man* is too ambitious for its own good. However disjointed and episodic the film may be, though, it leaves such an indelible impression upon anyone who sees it that it should no longer be denied its place as a classic example of the genre. If *The Leopard Man* is a "second-rate Lewton film," then we can sit back in wonder at just how good a second-rate Lewton film can be.

One of the reasons *The Leopard Man* is often characterized as a misfire hinges upon the regrets of its makers; neither Tourneur nor Lewton were pleased with the results. Both disclaimed the film as a miscalculation.

There's a miss for every hit in *The Leopard Man*'s scant 66 minutes; the script, the direction, the performances, even the editing, rise and dip between the brilliant and the mundane. Such inconsistency is likely the result of the obvious commitment to experimentation in this film. Some things work and some things do not.

It does not work when Tourneur and Lewton try to mix comedy and chills with the leopard's first appearance. As a lame joke, Jerry Manning lets the leopard on a leash precede him through Kiki's apartment door, and this results in screaming fits by the women within. It is not funny, it is not scary, and it makes Kiki Walker (Lewton's female survivor prototype) look stupid. Robson includes on the soundtrack a feline hiss that sounds suspiciously like the air brakes of a bus. It is all for naught.

Without attributing the blame to any particular member of the filmmaking team, one can say that the above scene is dreadfully misguided. Not only is it entirely pointless, but it is also detrimental to the film's purpose. We are given the opportunity to see that this is not a very formidable-looking creature (the cat is not quite up to knee level), especially when presented on a leash. Not a cat one would touch noses with, mind you, but it is nothing like the ferocious beast we see in our imagination as Teresa is killed against the front door of her home. For most viewers, it is difficult to believe that the monster behind the locked door is the same well-mannered creature Kiki held on a leash just hours before.

Unlike *Cat People,* which established the ferocity of its felines in the opening scene, *The Leopard Man* loses credibility because of the offhanded way in which it introduces the focus of its terror. In essence, it is a film that shoots itself in the foot in the first reel.

The reason why so many viewers remember the harrowing Teresa sequence is because it touches a primal chord in all of us. The archetype of the mean-spirited mother (or stepmother) is the stuff of folktales, and Señora Delgado is one of the poorest examples of parenthood this side of Hansel and Gretel. Author J.P. Telotte *(Dreams of Darkness)* sees avarice as the prime causal factor for the film's tragedies: "An economic determinant is clearly enunciated . . . when Teresa Delgado's mother forces her to go to the grocery . . . lest the neighbors think they are too poor to provide the usual tortillas for her father's dinner."

But it may be that Señora Delgado is just a mean woman, plain and simple, one whose lack of concern for her child's safety triggers an atavistic fear. Tom Conway, as Dr. Judd in *Cat People,* could probably make a few profound comments about childhood fears of abandonment. Teresa's walk in the dark continues to work so well because it never ceases to disturb the inner child within us all. The sequence's only major flaw is that it comes too early and tends to make the rest of the film anticlimactic. It's a hard act to follow.

An antecedent for the blood-under-the-door shot can be found in Maurice Tourneur's 1912 French film, *Le Système du Docteur Goudron et du Professeur Plume* (see Chapter Two), while the Lewton set piece is itself the antecedent for the terrifying milkmaid scene in Mario Bava's *Black Sunday* (1960). A more interesting comparison, however, could be made between the Teresa set piece and its antithesis, the opening sequence of Fritz Lang's *M* (1931).

In Lang's film, a hardworking mother becomes painfully aware of her daughter's continued absence, especially after hearing the neighborhood children's grim song about the local child murderer, still at large. Here the mother, unlike Señora Delgado, is very concerned for her child's safety. She calls her daughter's name again and again—"Elsie! . . . Elsie! . . . Elsie!"—while we look at an empty place-setting on the table, a tenement stairwell, a maze of hanging laundry, all of these offering little answer to the woman's heartrending cries. Lang's approach differs from Tourneur's in that we only get an occasional glimpse of the victim (wandering the sidewalks, bouncing her ball against the wanted poster of the very man who befriends her). The primary focus of attention, the source of our sympathetic fear, is the mother, not the girl. This sequence in *M*, which starts with the children's rhyme and ends with the balloon in the powerlines, makes an audience identify with a mother's deepest fears.

Teresa's fate in *The Leopard Man* does not mine its thrills from parental nightmares, but from more primal fears: being abandoned by loved ones, being thrown out into the cold, being alone in the dark. Vulnerability and isolation. But as different as they may appear to be, the Lewton and Lang sequences strike within us a very similar chord of fear, a similar frisson, one which we feel deep in our gut. It is nothing less than remarkable that two classic set pieces of terror can remain so vibrant using only the most modest of cinematic tools: suggestion.

One element of *Leopard* that is terribly unconvincing is the way Jerry and Kiki continually try to outdo one another with the tough exterior routine (on separate occasions, each of them secretly passes money to the Delgado family). Jerry feels one has to have a hard skin to make it in this world, and his girlfriend is inclined to prove that two can play at anything. But all this business of bearing a calloused front is merely given script service, and while it works in nicely with Lewton's recurring motif (that things are not as they appear to be), it is not developed enough to have any meaningful impact upon an audience.

The Leopard Man's second scare sequence, Consuelo's cemetery escapade, has all the right ingredients but none of the logic required to make the scene work. Perhaps some significant details were lost in the editing.

Whatever the reason, the sequence lacks surety of purpose. The irony is laid on fairly thick when we discover that Consuelo is celebrating her birthday; it is painful to see her so happy, considering the expected outcome of her cemetery rendezvous. It is interesting to note the way Consuelo's walk contrasts with the film's earlier episode of terror. This time the victim will have an overprotective mother (rather than an indifferent one) who is wealthy (rather than poor). In direct opposition to the Teresa sequence, it is the mother who is reluctant to have her daughter venturing out into the town, while it is the daughter who has made the trip a matter of urgency. It was a mistake to create a family so different from Teresa's without making dramatic use of those differences. For instance, if the film chose to focus on the concerned parent (as Lang did in the opening reel of *M*), the camera remaining with Señora Contrera instead of following her doomed daughter into the street, the results could have produced the kind of tension the sequence needs.

As it is, Consuelo's terror sequence is wonderfully atmospheric, but oddly unsatisfying. There are too many unanswered questions. Consuelo's behavior appears to defy logic. Why does she wait so long in the cemetery? Where was Raoul, anyway? What did the lit cigarette on the bench mean? Why did the mysterious good samaritan wait until the morning before returning with the ladder? What did the bending branch mean just before Consuelo was killed? Did it mean that the killer, Dr. Galbraith, was jumping off a tree branch?

Unlikely coincidences abound as the film madly rushes to a finish. Kiki and Jerry's plan of spooking the mild-mannered killer just does not wash. Galbraith chooses to stroll by the locked cemetery gates during a time when Kiki just happens to be planted behind those doors pleading for help. How long was Kiki waiting there? We hope she did not spend more than one dark, lonely night there, awaiting the footsteps of a man she could not see. Kiki must have pole-vaulted over the cemetery wall to quickly plant herself some paces ahead on the curator's route to let him hear the sounds of her castanets. What the thrown cigarette is supposed to mean is anybody's guess. Is it a connection to the cigarette that falls from Clo-Clo's mouth before she dies, or does it relate to the lit cigarette on the cemetery bench prior to Consuelo's death? Assuming it to be the former, we should be reminded that the insert shot of Clo-Clo's burning cigarette was there for the audience's benefit. Surely the woman's dropped cigarette should not have been of any concern to a murderer-at-work; chances are, he would not have noticed it. Even if he did, how did Kiki and Jerry know that the sight of a burning cigarette would shake him up? These rather petty lapses in logic may be excused in some quarters, but they surely offer nothing to the integrity of the film. The enigmatic use of cigarettes as significant details in *The Leopard Man* is inexcusably mismanaged.

Dr. Galbraith, who appears to be a man who would not hurt a fly, comes from the "least-likely" school of movie culprits. When we consider that actor James Bell is about as ferocious as Wally Cox, it makes us wonder what made Clo-Clo (who was more than an even match for this character) become so terrified. It is possible (though nowhere in the film is it stated) that Galbraith actually wears a leopard skin and claws when he kills, which may be why his two victims scream upon seeing him (this being at least more acceptable than the notion that anyone would scream at the sight of James Bell). But then again, if he does don a leopard skin and clawed gloves, he must resemble one of those funny-looking tribal villains in RKO's 1946 *Tarzan and the Leopard Woman* and surely that would more likely provoke a guffaw than a scream.

Rather than respond as real human beings do, Jerry and Kiki seem governed by the whims of the script during the film's final 10 minutes. Oddly, we are never quite sure what Jerry's part in the entrapment plan actually is. We assume he is close by while Kiki pretends to be Galbraith's victims, but Jerry's delayed rescue, suddenly with Raoul as his accomplice, suggests he was elsewhere.

The procession adds a nice atmospheric touch, but its inclusion seems forced and extraneous. Kiki's excuse for being in the museum—to get a better view of 30 men in black hoods parading into the desert night—is risable; the procession is such a nonevent that it's hard to imagine someone being a deliberate spectator, let alone needing a better viewpoint. We can see Galbraith's anticlimactic death coming a mile away, Raoul holding the gun while the killer reminisces about murdering Consuelo. Bang!

The Leopard Man's performances are mostly very good. Margaret Landry, as the doomed Teresa Delgado, is excellent in the role no one ever forgets. Also excellent are Jean Brooks (Kiki), Margo (Clo-Clo), and Kate Lawson (Señora Delgado). By this time, Lewton had begun to assemble his own fine stable of players from the contracted actors on the RKO lot; many of *The Leopard Man*'s performers (Jean Brooks, Isobel Jewell, Ben Bard, Russell Wade, Tola Nesmith) would make numerous appearances in Lewton films.

Less impressive are the two major male roles. James Bell (Dr. Maxwell from *Zombie*) as Dr. Galbraith, is a slight improvement over his last Lewton role, but he is not a particularly convincing psycho killer. The bigger misfire, however, would have to be Dennis O'Keefe's superfluous male lead. Bland and forgettable, O'Keefe's character simply has too little to do, which is why nothing he says or does seems convincing. He's just an unnecessary generic fixture stuck in a film that is really about four women in peril (three victims, one survivor), none of whom particularly benefits from his presence. Jerry's two contributions to the plot—renting the leopard and rescuing the heroine—are slight; with a few minor alterations, the film could have done just as easily without him. This is no reflection on actor O'Keefe, however, who has shown flair in other performances, most notably *Brewster's Millions* (1945).

Although not nearly as consistent as the first two Lewton films, *The Leopard Man* possesses a power that is difficult to refute. It has long had a reputation for being mean-spirited, but what is often misinterpreted as a melange of "sadistic voyeurism" (tracking the cruel deaths of three sympathetic victims) is really a courageous essay in the random nature of death. *Leopard's* alleged cruel streak is just another deceptive appearance, for the film has a lot of heart. It is Lewton's own Blakean treatise on the tiger and the lamb. Wartime audiences may not have liked *Leopard's* downbeat message—that the young and the innocent also die—but it was an important one for them to grasp.

In *Dreams of Darkness,* J.P. Telotte observes, "In each situation an individual leaves the safety of her home to wander through a circuitous, ultimately imprisoning world within which there lurks sudden death."

Although what lurks is initially a leopard, and later a museum curator, the film is more accurately about death in all its forms, with Clo-Clo, ace of spades in hand, spreading the dark contagion. In *Hollywood from Vietnam to Reagan,* Robin Wood asserts:

> The best of the [Lewton] series are concerned with the idea that no one escapes contamination. Accordingly, the concept of the Monster becomes diffused through the film (closely linked to the celebrated Lewton emphasis on atmosphere, rather than overt shock) and no longer identified with a single figure.

Jacques Tourneur's major contribution to the Lewton formula is the way he uses camera direction, composition, and lighting to convey the presence of an unstoppable dark force, a motif that would continue in Tourneur's post–Lewton films. Of all three Lewton/Tourneur films, *The Leopard Man* makes the most extensive use of this unstoppable dark force motif; in some ways, the film is a dress rehearsal for *The Curse of the Demon,* Tourneur's masterful 1957 Lewton homage.

The Leopard Man has the appearance of a non-supernatural thriller, but a straight mystery should not be as frightening as this film is. The leopard on the leash is not scary, and, surely, James Bell is not scary. Then what is? Answer: the larger-than-life terror on the other side of Señora Delgado's door; it is the darkest of all unstoppable forces, the one from which none of us escapes.

The film further accents our fear of the great unknown by suggesting that every death is predestined, a final calendar page awaiting each of us. Not only is Clo-Clo's death foretold by the fortune-teller, but the audience catches the smell of death at the very beginning of each of the three Lewton walks, all of which end in tragedy. Teresa's death is foretold by her brother in words ("They're big and they jump on you") and hand shadows. Consuelo is the girl who tells her mother, "I must go to the cemetery; it's my birthday." And

Clo-Clo, whose doom is foretold in the first reel, knows that good fortune (money) will immediately precede her death ("something black").

When *The Leopard Man* hit the theaters in May 1943, *The New York Times*'s movie critic, Bosley Crowther, called it a "half-baked effort," and most of the other newspaper critics followed suit. At the time, *The New Republic*'s Manny Farber was one of the few critics to champion the film, calling it an "early peak example" of Lewton's ability to tell a story without being dominated by the conventions of the form.

Many of the genre critics have also been grudging in their praise. Carlos Clarens (*An Illustrated History of the Horror Film*) observes that "the formula shows through in the mechanical repetition of the murders," while Ed Naha (*Horrors—From Screen to Scream*) declares, "Moments of sheer terror and utter boredom clash in this well-made Val Lewton melodrama. . . . Some of the script is utterly useless . . . [a] sparse exercise in sadism."

Many of the more recent genre critics seem to be giving the film its due. Phil Hardy (*Encyclopedia of Horror Movies*) says: "*The Leopard Man* was received as a disappointment after the hauntingly graceful horrors of [*Cat People* and *I Walked with a Zombie*]. . . . Yet it now looks like a fascinating by-product of the then embryonic noir genre." According to *The Penguin Encyclopedia of Horror and the Supernatural:*

> *The Leopard Man* is less well-liked by Lewton's sympathetic critics than Tourneur's other films for the unit, perhaps because its very effective use of surprisingly explicit violence and horror goes against Lewton's well known and much admired taste for suggestion. But, as a whole, the film stands up better than *The Cat People* or *I Walked with a Zombie*. The script has its passages of purple poetry, but the performances . . . are far less stiff than those in the earlier films, and the moments of actual horror really do make the suspense scenes scarier than the merely suggestive stalkings of *The Cat People.*

In *Guide for the Film Fanatic*, Danny Peary says: "Some of the dialogue is a bit clunky, and the finale . . . is hurried, but this may be Lewton's and director Jacques Tourneur's creepiest film. . . . With the exception of *The Seventh Victim*, this is the most philosophical and exciting of Lewton's films."

More recently, in his fascinating 1992 collection of essays, *Cut: Horror Writers on Horror Films,* Christopher Golden reveals an unusual number of Lewton aficionados among the best-selling writers of modern horror fiction. Britisher Ramsey Campbell discusses *The Leopard Man,* as does Charles L. Grant (who calls the blood-under-the-door sequence "one of the most famous scenes in cinematic horror"). In Ronald V. Borst's gorgeous showcase of fantastic film movie posters, *Graven Images* (1992), Harlan Ellison includes a marvelously vivid verbal reenactment of Teresa's walk in the dark.

It is unfortunate that Jacques Tourneur's last film for the Lewton unit was not everything it could have been, but it was good enough to continually elicit the attention of three generations of horror fans. We sometimes count our blessings in small doses.

Tourneur was off to "A" pictures as a reward for his *Cat People* success. According to Tourneur, "We were making so much money on our films together that the studio said, 'We'll make twice as much money if we separate them.' So they pulled us apart. It was a mistake: we belonged together."

Although Lewton's superiors were not demonstrative in their appreciation of him, they apparently believed he had more clout than Orson Welles. While Lewton was preparing *Leopard* to go before the camera, Welles was back at RKO to finish his authorized release of *Journey Into Fear* (with a new ending). When the Welles film finally fell into the hands of RKO executives, they marketed it in the guise of one of Lewton's feline thrillers. Since *Journey Into Fear* included a production number with Dolores Del Rio dressed in a cat costume, RKO publicity latched onto this minor aspect of the film and designed lobby posters featuring Del Rio, in her leopard outfit, next to a looming close-up of Welles's menacing mug. In bold print, the ad promises: "Welles and Del Rio Together! As Terror Man vs. Leopard Woman!"

NINE

The Seventh Victim

His was a divided character. On one hand, he was an insecure man who tended to chop himself down, and yet he was a proud man too. . . . He was a man of great likes and dislikes and a man of even greater loyalty to his people; in his eyes, they could do no wrong.

—Mark Robson
from *The Reality of Terror*, by Joel E. Siegel

Once again the front office instructed Lewton to build a film around a title, a task tantamount to coordinating an entire suit of clothes to fit the choice of tie clip. Nevertheless, as far as film titles go, *The Seventh Victim* was decidedly less lurid than its three predecessors. Things were looking up. Change was in the air.

Bolstered by his successful debut and the promise of the upcoming April release of *I Walked with a Zombie,* Lewton felt secure enough to consider buying a home. By this time real estate prices on the southern California coast had plummeted for fear of Japanese attack. Families evacuated, often not waiting to sell before moving to safer locations, and many coastline houses remained vacant.

Jack Holt (the actor who played one of Oliver Reed's workmates in *Cat People*) had been walking on egg shells in his Pacific Palisades ranch house (on Corsica Drive) ever since the Pearl Harbor attack. Although Holt had invested an extraordinary amount of time and money on the house, having built it himself (fully equipped with maid's quarters, a four-car garage, and surrounded by acres of gardens landscaped with shrubbery, rosebushes, and fruit trees), his paranoia about Japanese attack got the better of him. Holt was so willing to get the property off his hands that Lewton was able to buy it for a song. With a daughter at the dawn of her teenage years and a son in elementary school, Val and Ruth Lewton for the first time in their marriage enjoyed the stability of their own home.

Unfortunately, stability is something Lewton did not feel at the studio. By the time *Zombie* hit the theaters, the studio executives were already praising another man-of-the-hour. Like Lewton, Edward Dmytryk was of Ukrainian descent. Like Jacques Tourneur, Mark Robson, and Robert Wise, Dmytryk served as an editor before directing his first film (in Dmytryk's case, *The Hawk* in 1935). After directing a number of low-budget series films for Columbia, including *The Devil Commands* (the best of Columbia's Boris Karloff/Mad Doctor series) in 1941 and above average entries in the "Boston Blackie" and "Lone Wolf" detective series, Dmytryk joined the "B" unit ranks at RKO in 1942, close to the time that Lewton went on the RKO payroll. If Lewton had not been so adamant about choosing Jacques Tourneur, the front office would probably have encouraged Dmytryk, as an experienced horror film director, for the early Lewton entries.

Instead, while Lewton and Tourneur worked on their first two features, Dmytryk directed three RKO "B" films—*Seven Miles to Alcatraz, Hitler's Children,* and *The Falcon Strikes Back*—before being loaned to Universal for *Captive Wild Woman,* a film which shared some superficial common ground with *Cat People.* When Dmytryk returned to RKO and buried himself in a new project called *Behind the Rising Sun,* his concentration was interrupted by sudden fame. *Hitler's Children* was released in the early months of 1943, preceding *I Walked with a Zombie* by weeks, and it became a towering success, making millions (reportedly, $3,355,000 in film rentals) and taking some of the shine off Lewton's magical debut.

To Lewton's credit, he did not begrudge Dmytryk his success, and the two filmmakers had a mutual respect for one another. The friendly rivalry between them, however, pressured Lewton to work harder and faster. Because of his assembly-line grind, he had to rotate his scriptwriters—DeWitt Bodeen, Ardel Wray, and newcomer, Charles O'Neal—to serve a string of overlapping projects. This time Lewton assigned the honors to DeWitt Bodeen; his original treatment took place near a southern California oil field and centered around an orphaned girl from Los Angeles who, after discovering she was to be the seventh victim of a murderer, had to spend the remainder of the plot searching for the identity of the serial killer.

Lewton toyed with the idea, and then a month or two later he contacted Bodeen (who was then doing research in Tarrytown, New York, for the upcoming *The Curse of the Cat People*). According to Bodeen:

> [Val] wrote to me and said: "When you come back you're going right on to a new story for *The Seventh Victim* because we've discarded the one you originally wrote and I've already put Charles O'Neal on it and you'll be working with him." . . . I had an inkling of what it was to be about because he also said in another letter to me: "See if it's possible for you to get to a devil-worshipping society meeting." So I got to one through RKO because they had a marvelous office there in New York. I went to them and said, is there any chance of me going to a devil-worshippers' meeting and they started laughing,

> but they called back and said yes, it had been arranged. But I would have to go under a pseydonym. The society would be glad to have me but I wouldn't be able to say anything—just sit there and observe. and I must say that they were exactly like the devil-worshippers in *Rosemary's Baby*. It was even in the same neighbourhood on the West Side that they used in that film. It was during the war and I would have hated to be Hitler with all the spells they were working against him. They were mostly old people and they were casting these spells while they knitted and crocheted. A bunch of tea-drinking old ladies and gentlemen sitting there muttering imprecations against Hitler. I made use of the experience in that the devil-worshippers in *The Seventh Victim* were very ordinary people who had one basic flaw, an Achilles heel which has turned them against good and towards evil. This is the one thing I got out of the meeting [John Brosnan, *The Horror People*].

When the release of *I Walked with a Zombie* proved that his success was no fluke, Lewton was called to attend a meeting with Charles Koerner and other RKO executives. Koerner and company had already broken the news to Lewton about Jacques Tourneur's promotion to "A" films; the meeting had been arranged to make it clear to Lewton that, as the result of his impressive box-office returns, he would also be rewarded. *The Seventh Victim*, they announced, would be given an "A" budget production. Lewton was jubilant, this being precisely the moment he had eagerly anticipated; his promotion to "A" pictures. So he believed.

Time passed while Bodeen and O'Neal completed *The Seventh Victim*'s script, now written with an "A" budget running time in mind. Things ran smoothly until Lewton announced to the executive board that Mark Robson would make his directorial debut with *The Seventh Victim*. The board was aghast. How could anyone dare entrust an "A" budget to a novice director? No one started at the top; they paid their dues directing low budget fare, as Jacques Tourneur and Edward Dmytryk did before they were promoted to "A" pictures.

Lewton, for whom loyalty was a matter of honor, remained adamant in his choice, even days later. Finally, the front office delivered the blow: either drop Robson or bid farewell to the escalated budget (and, thereby, the hike in his salary). Lewton chose Robson, and the rest is history.

Casting his fate to the wind, Lewton assembled his performers and crew. John Lockert was assigned the editing position left vacant by Robson; Nicholas Musuraca was secured as director of photography. The staff also included art directors D'Agostino and Keller, set director Darrell Silvera, assistant director William Dorfman, and composer Roy Webb. Lewton brought back a number of performers from his previous film (Jean Brooks, Isobel Jewel, Margaret Sylva, Ben Bard, and Tola Nesmith) and filled out the cast with two performers from his earlier films: Tom Conway and Elizabeth Russell. For the lead character of Mary Gibson, Lewton obtained the services of a young actress who, thanks to him, had just changed her name from Janet

7th VICTIM
A girl alone, trapped on the x-marked spot by a high-hat killer... matching her beauty and wiles against his brawn and wits in the most dangerous game of all—a gamble with life itself at stake!

Preproduction ad for *The Seventh Victim*.

Cole to Kim Hunter. In *Science Fiction Stars and Horror Heroes,* Kim Hunter told author Tom Weaver:

> Val Lewton knew me because he had been in charge of the screen test that got me my contract with David O. Selznick, and Jacques Tourneur had directed it. In fact, Tourneur and Val were around when Selznick said my name had to be changed. Val had worked for David during the time of *Gone*

> with the Wind, and Val was assigned to get audience comments during the intermission. He didn't want to do it, and what he finally ended up doing was making up a list of comments and inventing names to go with them. David later found out what Val had done, and when he sent me over to see Val at RKO, he said, "I'm sending you to a man who's very good at making up names!"

For the romantic male lead, Lewton selected another relative newcomer, Hugh Beaumont (to be later immortalized by his performace as Ward Clever in the long-running *Leave It to Beaver* television series). Lewton also enlisted the talents of Erford Gage, who had played in Edward Dmytryk's *Seven Miles to Alcatraz* and *Hitler's Children.*

Shooting began on *The Seventh Victim* on May 5, 1943, and was completed on May 29, 1943. At the time, Universal was busy completing its lavish Technicolor remake of *Phantom of the Opera.* One can only wonder how Lewton felt about his own meager unit when the *Phantom* remake boasted a budget nearly $2 million, which was more than the combined cost of all eleven of Lewton's RKO films.

As if that were not enough, Universal would soon be releasing another expensive genre production, *Flesh and Fantasy,* a compilation of three macabre stories (all helmed by acclaimed French director, Julien Duvivier). When Duvivier's film was released, Universal set aside $250,000 (twice the cost of the average Lewton production) merely to promote it. Lewton must have thought twice about his decision to remain in low-budget production when he saw the level of promotion given to *The Seventh Victim* after it opened in September and failed to draw the crowds. RKO's promotional department refused to part with a cent but instead offered this dandy at-your-own-expense suggestion to theater owners:

> "On a small table in your lobby, display a statue, a bust and a head of a woman. Wherever the skin shows on the statue, mold small spots out of chewing gum or candle grease to resemble goose pimples. Place a card nearby reading 'Even this marble developed goose pimples after seeing *The Seventh Victim*'" [Siegel, *The Reality of Terror.*]

It is apparent from the final print's disjointed narrative that *The Seventh Victim*'s script was written with an "A" budget running time in mind. This clearly accounts for a number of narrative gaps in the release print. The proposed screenplay included four key scenes that never made the release print. According to DeWitt Bodeen and Val Edwin Lewton, these scenes were shot for the film and later edited out to conform to a "B" budget running time.

Regardless of its lost footage, *The Seventh Victim* is recognized as a Lewton masterpiece, on a par with *I Walked with a Zombie,* by some horror film critics. It also gained a reputation in England. According to Mark Robson:

> *[The Seventh Victim]* achieved some kind of notoriety in England after the war, as I discovered when John and Roy Boulting came out here about that

> time, wanting to meet the fellow who had directed it. They used to bicycle a print of *The Seventh Victim* around London, among them Carol Reed and Cavalcanti and people like that, thinking it an advanced, weird form of filmmaking [Higham and Greenberg, *The Celluloid Muse*].

Although several Lewton films reveal the producer's world vision, *The Seventh Victim* is purportedly Lewton's most personal work. As DeWitt Bodeen explained (in John Brosnan's *The Horror People*): "There is a lot of Val in *The Seventh Victim* . . . as it came out on the screen, because it's a reflection, really, of the happiest time of his life—when he was living in New York City and working on a newspaper and as a freelance writer. He was mad about Greenwich Village and a lot of the film takes place there."

Poetry plays as major a role in *The Seventh Victim* as percussion did in *The Leopard Man*. Verse is frequently recited by the film's characters, one of whom is a published poet, and most of the action takes place in and around Greenwich Village, New York, a long-lost Bohemia for artists, writers, and, yes, poets. Following the opening credits, there appears an epigraph from John Donne's first Holy Sonnet: "I run to Death and Death meets me as fast, and all my Pleasures are like Yesterday."

We are in Highcliffe Academy (actually the interior of the RKO's *Magnificent Ambersons* mansion), a girl's boarding school. Highcliffe is an austere sanctuary run and attended by those who prefer to turn their backs upon the harsh realities of New York City streets. An older student, Mary Gibson (Kim Hunter), confers with Miss Lowood (Tola Nesmith) about a lapse in tuition payment. Mary's previous means of support had been her older sister, Jacqueline, whose whereabouts suddenly seems to be a mystery. Miss Lowood offers Mary a teaching job, but the girl is convinced that such idyllic surroundings would offer little comfort if something had happened to her sister. (Miss Lowood's name is a deliberate nod to Charlotte Brontë's *Jane Eyre* [Jane attended Lowood School and was also asked to stay on as a teacher].)

When Mary leaves the office, Miss Gilchrist (Eve March), a teacher who apparently doubles as Miss Lowood's handmaiden, accompanies the girl to the door for some personal advice, encouraging Mary to leave the school and never come back, no matter how things are resolved concerning her sister's whereabouts. The woman confesses that she too was like Mary many years ago but that instead of bravely going out into society, she made the safe, and cowardly, decision to stay within the confines of Highcliffe.

Mary packs and leaves via the elaborate staircase, and off-camera we hear the recitation of a stanza of Oliver Wendell Holmes's "The Chambered Nautilus," The first line of which is "Leave thy low-vaunted past!" The grandfather clock near the front door chimes, and Mary touches it lovingly, letting us know that she is serious about leaving all behind.

Making a visit to La Sagesse, the cosmetic company owned by her sister, Mary speaks to the suspicously cold Mrs. Redi (Mary Newton), who informs

Poet Jason Hoag (Erford Gage) and Mary Gibson (Kim Hunter) outside Dante Restaurant.

Mary that she herself bought the company from Jacqueline eight months before. After speaking to Frances Fallon (Isobel Jewell), a La Sagesse employee and a close friend of Jacqueline's, Mary gets a clue to her sister's whereabouts. She goes to the Dante Restaurant in Greenwich Village (a place her sister had been known to frequent) and questions the owners of the establishment, an Italian couple who own the building and rent the upstairs rooms. They tell her that Jacqueline, accompanied by a gentleman, had long ago rented an upstairs room without ever having moved in; she just pays the rent to keep it empty. Mary convinces the owners to open the empty apartment.

At the top of the stairs, we see Mimi (Elizabeth Russell), a sickly woman in a bathrobe (both obviously the worse for wear); Mimi leaves one room and enters another and we can only speculate upon her curious activities.

What Mary sees, when Jacqueline's door is opened, is provided by a point of view shot of an empty apartment in the middle of which is a single wooden chair. The camera begins a slow tilt up from the chair, revealing, directly above, a hangman's noose.

Local poet Jason Hoag (Erford Gage), a Dante Restaurant regular, gives Mary some cryptic advice, suggesting that perhaps she does not really want to find her sister. Mary goes to the missing person's bureau and comes up empty-handed. As she is about to leave, she is accosted by a sleazy private dick, Irving

August (Lou Lubin), who wants to take on her missing person's case. August, who is clearly missing at least one row of teeth, tells Mary that, if hired, he would check all the places, including the morgue. Rather than hire him, Mary goes to the morgue herself. There she gets a man's name as a lead, and proceeding to a particular law firm, asks to see Gregory Ward, one of the lawyers working there. She meets Ward (Hugh Beaumont), who turns out to be Jacqueline's lover; he, too, has been searching everywhere for the missing woman.

The film's credibility plummets as composer Webb's strings soar and Beaumont (in his indubitable Ward Cleaver mode) spouts: "A man would look for her everywhere. There's something exciting and unforgettable about Jacqueline, something you never quite get hold of, something that keeps a man following her." Dialogue such as this may provide some ingenious foreshadowing, but precious little else. Ward admits he helped Jacqueline rent the room, and he is well aware of what lies therein: "Your sister had a feeling about life—that it wasn't worth living unless one could end it." When Mary asks if he is worried about a grim outcome, he glibly answers, "People who commit suicide never talk about it." He describes Jacqueline as living "in a world of her own fancy . . . she didn't know what the truth was."

Eventually, Mary does take on the help of Mr. August, a decision that provides *The Seventh Victim* with one of its most memorable fright sequences. August's investigation leads him to believe Jacqueline is being held prisoner in a locked room in La Sagesse. Mary accompanies August to the cosmetic company during the after hours, setting up our first Lewton walk.

Mary and August go about their breaking and entering with great trepidation, each of them a wealth of half-hearted encouragement. Before they get too far, August is unnerved by the amount of determination Mary seems to have, despite her obvious fear, and he confesses, "I don't know if I want to go with you or not." August picks the lock, and they nudge each other ahead. The small cosmetic plant has a salon front and offices; its darkened hallways and irregular shadows offer additional tension to an already tense scene. A clock ticks loudly in the hushed hallway, the kind of intensification of sound one hears when frightened and alone.

Edgy and reluctant, the two enter the darkened corridor. August wants to turn back and forget the whole business, but Mary manipulates him with verbal alternatives: "No, we can stay and see what's in the door at the end of the hall." August says, "No, let's leave." But Mary is relentlessly cajoling: "You can go down the hall and open the door, Mr. August. It's only a little way." A quiet dare from such a vulnerable young girl.

August goes ahead, moving stealthily in the dark, aiming for the door at the far end. He reaches the doorknob, opens the door. Cut to Mary, nearly a silhouette against the plate glass, through which we can observe a well-lit hallway in the adjoining portion of the office building and a night watchman entering through a door. Mary sees this and quietly freezes. And waits. The watchman passes into another part of the building, and Mary gives a sigh of relief.

August exits the mysterious locked room, his investigation a dead end, it would seem. Mary sees him walking in the dark and meets him halfway, whispering of their danger and of the night watchman. But August ignores her and walks past in a slow, oddly deliberate, fashion, clutching his stomach with both hands. Mary continues her warning, her words trailing off as she realizes something is not right. August drops to the floor, extending an arm as he falls; Mary, looking at his immobile form, sees his hand covered with blood. Was not that the handle of a pair of scissors between his hands, just before he fell? As frightened as she is, Mary is far removed from the hysterical scream queens who typified horror movies of the period.

Mary is sheltered and innocent, but she is not stupid. Her shyness makes her reserved and hesitant, but her intelligence accounts for her resourcefulness. This combination of brains and courage is typical of a Lewton heroine. Mary does not scream for help, even though the watchman is within hearing distance. Instead, she sneaks out the way she came and hurries to a subway. In the subway car, Mary takes solace in her safety, disturbed as her thoughts may be. She is still sitting in a blue funk (a lap-dissolve having signaled a passage of time) when she realizes that she has just ridden to the end of the line and back, and here she is, back to where she started. She sits tight, waiting for the subway to move.

Three drunken men come aboard and sit across from Mary. Two of them are dressed for a formal event, apparently on their way home from some high society bash. One of the drunks, the underdressed middle man, appears to have drunk himself into a stupor. Plainly unconscious, he is supported by his companions, both of whom pay special attention to the hat they keep replacing on their silent partner's head, on his face, actually. They do not recognize Mary—why should they?—but her eyes are drawn to the man in the middle, a very dead Mr. August. Suddenly, the two men appear to be cold sober.

She walks into a forward car for help, where she manages to locate a conductor and tells him that he has a murdered man aboard his subway. By then the train has come to another stop and all three men have vanished. (In *Reality of Terror*, Siegel informs us that the preceding sequence "[stemmed] from a similar incident which Lewton once observed in Greenwich Village.")

Although August, it turns out, was correct in the whereabouts of Jacqueline, it is through Dr. Judd (Tom Conway) that Mary finally becomes reunited with her sister. Dr. Judd, the psychiatrist, appears to be the very same Dr. Judd from *Cat People*, the one Irena killed. Apparently, *Victim*'s narrative must precede that of *Cat People*. One wonders how much ambivalence the viewers were expected to feel when Lewton and Bodeen resurrected their dead villain and turned him into a pompous and unsympathetic hero.

Dr. Judd, Jacqueline's therapist, arranges an unnecessarily mysterious, and ridiculously brief, meeting in a hotel room between the two sisters which only leaves the viewer adrift in a sea of confusion. Meanwhile, Jason Hoag tries to come to Mary's aid by doing some research. Along the way he has a run-in with Judd, who is effete and vicious. Judd throws several cheap shots at Hoag, calling him a washed-up writer. We also find out that Gregory Ward is really Jacqueline's husband (though why he had kept this fact hidden from Mary is anyone's guess).

Eventually, Hoag comes up with a lead and brings Ward and Mary to a party given by Natalie Cortez (Evelyn Brent), a member of a devil cult operating in Manhattan. The cultured, elite, and apparently wealthy Palladists are quite civil, even friendly, to their uninvited guests. The atmosphere of the event seems like that of a ritzy cocktail party. For some reason or another, Dr. Judd is already in attendance at the gathering. Mrs. Redi, Jacqueline's old business partner, is also there and appears to be the key organizer of the group. No one at the party admits to knowing anything about Jacqueline's disappearance, though there are implications that she was formerly a member of their group. Our protagonists discover that the Palladists make use of a symbol that is identical to the logo for the La Sagesse cosmetics company, which, they realize, is a front for the cult's activities.

Later, in a scene anticipating Hitchcock's *Psycho,* Mary is home showering when a dark figure of a woman, her distorted catlike silhouette seen through the translucent shower curtain, boldly enters the privacy of Mary's bathroom. Mary shuts off the shower and stands frozen, the shower head still dribbling water on her bare shoulders. The voice reveals the identity of the intruder. It is Mrs. Redi, who tells Mary to leave well enough alone and go back to Highcliffe Academy where she belongs.

As the film progresses, a few pieces fall together. It seems that, having betrayed her oath of secrecy, Jacqueline had wanted to end her association with the Palladists, and this is the reason why she was confined (for "safekeeping") in the back room of La Sagesse. Like the six previous betrayers of the cult, Jacqueline was marked for death—preferably by her own hand, but otherwise by a hired assassin. The Palladists, curiously enough, have taken a vow of nonviolence.

Earlier, when August broke into the locked room at La Sagesse, Jacqueline, thinking him an assassin, stabbed him with the scissors. After she mortally wounded August, Judd somehow (his methods are never made clear) managed to whisk Jacqueline to safety, and with Ward's money, set her up in a hotel room. Finally, through Judd's peculiar form of altruism, Jacqueline is reunited with her husband and sister and given some ineffectual sanctuary in Mary's room above Dante's Restaurant, just down the hall from her own sparsely furnished rented room.

The Palladists succeed in getting their hands upon Jacqueline. (A kidnapping scene may have been filmed and omitted from the release print. Joel Siegel explains that one missing scene showed Judd meeting with the cult, on which occasion he accidentally reveals Jacqueline's whereabouts.)

After the kidnapping, it is back to the La Sagesse headquarters, where the Palladists try to talk Jacqueline into drinking some poisoned wine. The tension builds as the Palladists encourage her: "Drink the poison! You always talked about how much you've wanted to end your life." They know about the noose in the apartment.

But Jacqueline's beloved coworker, the dim-but-loyal Francis Fallon (Isabel Jewell), can no longer put up with the strain; on the brink of collapse—doing anything to get it over with—Francis screams, "Go on, drink the wine! Do it!" only to recant and slap the glass away from Jacqueline begins to follow her advice. There are some tense moments before Francis intervenes: we see assorted close-ups of the Palladists, each of them lurching in anticipation as Jacqueline takes forever to raise the glass to her lips.

Jacqueline, released by the Palladists at midnight, has a long walk ahead of her. Although her release may look like a good turn, the Palladists are merely giving Jacqueline a head start before sending their hired assassin on her trail. Leaving her captors behind, she scans the ominous view before her of a street dimly lit by the round sphere of a lamppost (capturing much of the stark beauty of Tourneur/de Grasse's urban pictorialism in *The Leopard Man*). Jacqueline walks past the darkened vestibules of apartment houses on her way to a busier part of town. Things are too quiet as Jacqueline continues her tentative steps.

Robson directs the sequence of Jacqueline's walk with considerable flair. The low-key hum of distant city noises is interrupted by a loud crash that turns out to be the lid of a garbage can (an effective "bus") knocked to the ground by an underfed dog. Jacqueline cautiously resumes her journey, halting in her steps when she sees the shadow of a man being cast from around the corner of the building she approaches. As she moves to the middle of the street, she discovers the shadow's source to be not one, but two people, a man and a woman who are doing nothing more sinister than necking. Whatever plans the amorous couple have for the evening, it is doubtful that helping a woman in distress is one of them.

When Jacqueline passes the stoop of another building, she stops and looks up into the blackened entranceway. Could there be someone standing there? Sure enough, a face slowly peeks out of the shadows. Jacqueline hurries out of the frame while a sinister man walks down the steps in hot pursuit. We cut to Jacqueline's quickened pace as she moves down a relatively populated street in the business district, the closed stores, their display windows deceptively bright, offering no refuge. To every passerby who meets her desperate glance, she gives a beseeching look, but with the stranger on her tail, closing in, she has not the time to voice her fears. A shot of her legs—she

The Palladists urge Jacqueline (Jean Brooks) to take her own life.

is running now—is followed by a match cut to the assassin's legs, running in pursuit.

About to cross the street, Jacqueline leans against a mailbox and then steps off the curb as Robson delivers the sequence's second "bus": a screech of brakes as a taxi almost hits her. Terrified, she crosses the street and ducks into an alleyway, where she finds a dark building nook to hide in while the assassin runs past her.

Continuing her walk, Jacqueline passes the back exit of a theater and hears the music and merriment from within that offers nothing more than an ironic counterpoint to her terror. Mounting dread spurring her on, Jacqueline sets off in another direction. Hearing footsteps, she freezes against the dark side of a building as she extends her hand along the wall to her left. A close-up of her reaching hand is followed by a shot of the assassin standing a breath away, looking like he has been there for a while, enjoying an intimate moment with his victim. A close shot of his hand reveals a switchblade; the image holds as the blade springs open. The assassin reaches out and grabs her wrist. As she resists, trying to tug herself away, loud, braying laughter punctuates the night, causing the killer to release his grip.

We cut to the theater's backstage exit, where the double doors burst open with light and commotion. Cast members, still in costume, pour out the door and into the street, laughing and chattering, beginning their search for the nearest watering hole. In their enthusiasm, they sweep up Jacqueline like a carnival prize. "I need help, there's a man following me," she says. "I shouldn't wonder," one man answers in admiration.

Eventually, Jacqueline arrives safely at her destination, the Dante's Restaurant building. She goes up the interior stairs and comes upon Mimi, characteristically unkempt, dressed in a housecoat. In a curious exchange:

> "Who are you?" Jacqueline asks.
> "I'm Mimi, I'm dying. I've been so quiet, ever so quiet. But it still keeps coming. I rest and rest and still I'm dying."
> "I've always wanted to die," Jacqueline confesses.
> "I'm afraid," says Mimi, "but I'm tired of being afraid and waiting."
> "Why wait?"
> "I'm not going to wait. I'm going out to laugh and dance and do the things I used to do."
> "And then . . . ?" inquires Jacqueline.
> "I don't know."
> "You will die," Jacqueline adds, as if pronouncing sentence.

To Jacqueline, clinging to the vestiges of life when all self-esteem is gone is a fate worse than death. She opens her apartment door, exposing the noose to our view, and enters.

The Seventh Victim's final chill is somewhat undermined by the conventions of a neat wrap-up. The parallel action that follows the Jacqueline/Mimi scene is flat and unsatisfying, little more than feeble exposition. There is a limp scene where Hoag and Judd confront the Palladists and make the cult members feel ashamed of their action by the recitation of a few lines from the Lord's Prayer. We should be thankful that some of this scene did not make the release print. Reportedly, it was longer and made use of the entire prayer rather than the two lines featured in its final form. To whatever purpose, the prayer scene is artificial and obligatory, like the T-square cross from *Cat People*, an artifact from a tradition-bound Universal chiller.

Equally unconvincing is the scene where Hoag realizes that Judd has been his friend all along, that his insensitive remarks were only his way of prodding the poet into finding some sense of renewed purpose. Next we have a scene with Mary and Ward in which they admit their affection for one another but are paralyzed by responsibilities to Jacqueline. Ward's bland personality, along with his intellectualized banter about life and love, makes us wonder if he is capable of feeling passion for anyone or anything.

Strangely, by this point in the film we have little concern for any of the remaining characters. After Jacqueline's terrifying experiences, everything they do seems incidental. Judd and Hoag can jump in the East River for all the help they've really given Jacqueline. Suddenly, even *The Seventh Victim*'s main character, Mary, becomes less important, her callow romance with Ward bordering on the trivial. These artificial wrap-up scenes between Judd and Hoag, Ward and Mary, are merely perfunctory and add nothing positive to the film. Paradoxically, our main concern is Jacqueline, a character who, given her brief screen time, is little more to us than a stranger off the street.

We cut back to Mimi, coming out of her apartment, overdressed in a sleek satin outfit. Mimi walks past Jacqueline's room and, as she is about to descend the staircase, hears a dull thud coming from behind Jacqueline's locked door. It is the noise a wooden chair would make if it were kicked over on its side. Mimi, with only a second's hesitation at the sound, continues her way down the stairs, bringing us full circle to the stairway image that begins the film. Jacqueline's voice-over (a repetition of the film's opening epigraph) accompanies Mimi's descent: "I run to the death and death meets me as fast,/ And all my pleasures are like yesterday."

The belief that Val Lewton was the prime author of his films is given persuasive support by one viewing of *The Seventh Victim,* the first of the series without Tourneur directing. Tourneur adherents, some of whom consider their favored director as the prime motivator of the "Lewton touch," have vaguely alluded to ways in which Mark Robson's direction of *The Seventh Victim* is noticeably inferior to Tourneur's direction of the first three films.

Regardless of one's point of view on this matter, it is easier to see more similarities than differences between Robson's directing debut and the three Lewton films that preceded his. Robson is often overlooked as one of the prime collaborators of the Lewton formula, but his contributions were considerable. The Wellesian influences upon the editing and the soundtrack of the first Lewton/Tourneur films came by way of Mark Robson. Robson not only invented the Lewton "bus," but his editing was also fundamental to the development of the Lewton walk.

Robson's impressive direction of *The Seventh Victim* is so much in the tradition of the three Tourneur films that it makes us think twice about how much impact Robson may have had upon the success of *Cat People, I Walked with a Zombie,* and *The Leopard Man.* Since an editor studies a film scene by scene, shot by shot, foot by foot, we can appreciate Lewton's wisdom in holding out for Robson as Tourneur's successor. It stands to reason that Robson would have been the best man to emulate the style defined by the Tourneur films because he was himself one of the creators of that style. Robson certainly rose to the occasion; *The Seventh Victim* is one of the most auspicious directing debuts in "B" movie history, even better than Tourneur's entertaining debut feature, *They All Come Out.*

Although somewhat formularized by this stage of the series, the Lewton walk was nevertheless a thriving and sturdy device (which explains why it is still in common use today). To Robson's credit, his execution of the climactic walk sequence in *The Seventh Victim* was surprisingly successful—especially so, given his lack of directorial experience. Roy Webb's musical score for this sequence is quite understated, when not entirely absent; rather than use a strong theme to accompany the chills, Webb relies upon single chords and ominous strains of dissonance that create an effect not unlike the characteristic work of Bernard Herrmann. Jacqueline's homeward journey is peerless in its fright quotient, providing the longest and most dynamic Lewton walk in the entire RKO series.

The Seventh Victim moves too quickly during its opening reel and lacks the coherence and unity of the Tourneur films; it is, nonetheless, a brilliant sum of parts, many of which are as striking as anything in the Lewton oeuvre. No doubt this is why it captured the imagination of English directors like Cavalcanti, Carol Reed, and Michael Powell. The wayward plot, an uneasy mixture of intrigue and confusion, anticipates such paranoid and difficult-to-follow noir classics as Edward Dmytryk's *Murder, My Sweet* (1944), Howard Hawk's *The Big Sleep* (1946), and Jacques Tourneur's *Out of the Past* (1947). Despite its narrative flaws, *The Seventh Victim* has the reputation of being the darkest and most provocative of all Lewton films. It is a brave vision, one that obviously does not pander to ticket buyers, and it is well worth the repeated viewings it takes to fully appreciate its power.

In his *Guide for the Film Fanatic,* Dan Peary says:

> This spooky noir horror film . . . is a complete original, a cult film in England way back in the forties. It features bizarre and sinister characters (ie., a one-armed female devil-worshipper who plays piano), smart, strong-willed women, and several scary scenes. . . . The double suicide that ends the film is perhaps the most baffling, depressing moment in all horror films.

Peary's positive assessment is echoed by many horror critics and Lewton aficionados, but almost all of the praise for *The Seventh Victim* is the result of reevaluation. Carlos Clarens considered it Lewton's masterpiece: "Rarely has a film succeeded so well in capturing the nocturnal menace of a large city, the terror underneath the everyday, the suggestion of hidden evil . . . a hauntingly oppressive work." In his *The Golden Age of B Movies,* Doug McClelland is a little more hyperbolic in his praise: "*The Seventh Victim* . . . remains one of the most absorbing creative chillers of any day. As an adventure in stylish diabolism, real or unreal, it makes *Rosemary's Baby* look like *Blondie's Blessed Event.*"

Such modern-day plaudits aside, when *The Seventh Victim* was released, it did little to soften the stone-cold hearts in the RKO front office. According to *The RKO Story,* "Robson . . . displayed a flair for suspense and a feel for shuddery atmosphere, but revealed his inexperience by muddying the narrative with multiple confusions. Befuddled audiences decided the picture was horrible rather than horrific and made it the least successful of Lewton's initial cycle." Critics of the day were not any kinder. *The New York Times*'s Bosley Crowther thought the film "might make more sense if it was run backward," and *The New York Tribune*'s Howard Barnes said it put him to sleep.

It is easy to understand the reaction of 1943 audiences. Lewton's masterwork of negation is unremittingly downbeat and not at all the kind of entertainment moviegoers sought during the war.

Yet, in a great number of ways, *The Seventh Victim* is typical Lewton and not all that different philosophically from the three films that preceded it. *Victim's* nihilism echoes the dark themes already found in *Cat People* (where no one can prevent Irena Dubrovna's tragic fate), in *I Walked with a Zombie* (where a man kills his lover and himself), and finally in *The Leopard Man* (where death stalks the innocent for no rhyme or reason). None of these films were upbeat, and yet they were all bigger crowd-pleasers than *The Seventh Victim.*

Unlike the Tourneur films, *The Seventh Victim* offered nothing that the publicity department could tag as a monster for their poster ads, no feline terrors or even the suggestion of supernatural menace. There is no magic or witchery in this cult; they just seem to be a lot of kooks with time on their hands and money in their pockets. Their sociopathic behavior—kidnapping, disposing of bodies, hiring of assassins—is more criminal than diabolical. A mere hired assassin was the stuff of crime movies, not horror films. Nonetheless, RKO's publicity department made the most of what they had, putting the assassin's giant knife-wielding hand in the foreground of the lobby poster.

One can understand why audiences were baffled. Much of *The Seventh Victim's* vital information is revealed verbally in such an offhanded manner, with so many characters well versed in the art of lying, that we are never quite sure who or what to believe. When we are informed of the circumstances behind August's death in such an anticlimactic way, we tend to grow suspicious of our source of information and keep expecting the actual circumstances of August's demise to be revealed later in a more dramatic dénouement. When no other explanation for August's death is forthcoming, we are disappointed that this piece of the puzzle had been so casually tossed upon the table rather than carefully fitted into place.

Surely the film's oily protagonist, Dr. Judd, had a large number of 1943 theatergoers scratching their heads. Judd is too cold a character to make anyone feel he is motivated by benevolence. He is the film's premier red herring, generating little warmth when he tells a receptionist that he will not help her alcoholic father because "dipsomania is entirely too sordid" for him to take on. Jason Hoag may be a pretentious schnook, but Judd's boorishness is absolutely insufferable. Obviously, Judd relishes the needling he gives Hoag. Why should anyone be convinced, later on in the story, that he really had the poet's best interests at heart?

(An uncanny parallel to the Judd/Hoag party scene can be found in Phil Kaufman's 1978 remake of *Invasion of the Body Snatchers.* Jeff Goldblum plays a has-been poet whose chief nemesis is Leonard Nimoy's trendy psychiatrist who, like Judd, writes best-selling self-help books. In the Kaufman film, the psychiatrist berates the poet publicly at a cocktail gathering. There is nothing that resembles this scene in Don Siegel's original *Invasion of the Body Snatchers.*)

Judd's relationships with a variety of screen characters are nebulous or misleading. According to the explanations given in the film, Dr. Judd went to Gregory Ward after Jacqueline disappeared and told Ward that she was in danger and in need of money. It seems that Ward gave Judd money but could not coerce the psychiatrist to tell him of his wife's whereabouts. Then we find that the money was used to finance Jacqueline's hotel room (not the one with the noose, another one). None of this seems to carry much logic.

For some unexplained reason, Dr. Judd is in attendance at the Palladist party that Mary, Ward, and Hoag crash. Presumably, Judd is an enemy to this group since he is working on Jacqueline's behalf. In fact, the reason for Jacqueline's disappearance and simultaneous falling-out with the Palladists stems from her revelations to Dr. Judd of the cult's secret activities. All this makes the party scene a curious one, especially when Judd is so chummy, even on a first name basis, with nearly everyone in the room.

At the party, we hear one of the guests say that Jacqueline has "taken up" with Judd, though we are never quite sure what this implies. In *Dreams of Darkness,* J.P. Telotte suggests that Judd is Jacqueline's adulterous lover. But if, as Telotte suggests, Jacqueline has "taken up" with Judd, one wonders why Judd asked Ward for money. In an adulterous relationship, one usually does not ask the husband to finance the trysting place. Judd being the successful psychiatrist he purports to be, his hourly rates and book royalties should be adequate to support an ongoing affair. Although adultery is in keeping with the lecherous Dr. Judd we know from *Cat People,* apart from the secrecy that surrounds his odd relationship with Jacqueline, there is little in *The Seventh Victim* to lend support to Telotte's claim.

In a 1992 interview with the author, Val Edwin Lewton stressed that his father's scrips left little to chance and that *The Seventh Victim*'s continuity suffered from the extensive cutting the film was given:

> His scripts were very specific about set design, camera direction, and also what you usually left to an editor—dissolves, cuts, and so on. Much of the confusion in *The Seventh Victim* would have been eliminated if scenes weren't cut. There was a final scene, after the woman hanged herself, that was just a horrible rehash, and it was wisely cut. It's a great ending, with the final scene taken out, but that last shot (when we hear the chair fall) needs to hold for another four or five seconds, just enough time to let it sink in. But it doesn't. The movie just ends, and the reason was because they couldn't go back to reshoot it. I just wish they could have held that one shot.

Jean Brooks gives an extremely memorable performance as the doomed Jacqueline. With a minimum of screen time, Brooks manages to run away with the film; Gregory Ward's comment, "Once you see her, you never forget

Tom Conway (Dr. Judd).

her," is a fairly accurate assessment of her presence and appearance. Jacqueline's straight black hair, her dark lipstick contrasting with her pale complexion, and a wardrobe whose central theme is black, not only expresses negation, but also anticipates the look of the Greenwich Village beatniks of the late 1950s.

Kim Hunter is also quite good in her understated role. The actress's quiet vulnerability puts her in good stead in many scenes, where she comes across as earnest and convincing. Hunter particularly shines in the sequence where she and August break into the La Sagesse company; her manipulation of August is wholly unexpected, as is her ability to keep her head in a crisis. Hunter's performance, in a role that is a refreshing change of pace from the catalog of standard horror heroines, lends a degree of integrity rare in low-budget thrillers.

Elizabeth Russell's role as Mimi is so minute one is tempted to overlook her performance, but like her other small roles in Lewton films (notably, her brief but powerful cameo in *Cat People*), Russell's Mimi is one of the most memorable (and pathetic) characters in the film. Although we know little to nothing about Mimi's character, all indications suggest a prostitute, or "B-girl," stricken by a fatal disease, perhaps one not uncommon to her life-style.

The Seventh Victim is, of course, open to all levels of interpretation; a principal reason why the Lewton films have garnered so much attention over the past 50 years is that they hold up well to this kind of critical scrutiny. Several critics, including J.P. Telotte (in *Dreams of Darkness*), have commented upon Lewton's preoccupation with duality and the many examples in the Lewton universe of "doubling."

Some "doubles" stand in opposition to one another—flip sides, if you will—held together by a common bond. In *Cat People,* we have the mystical Irena and the practical Alice bound together by their interest in Oliver. In *I Walked with a Zombie,* we have the vibrant Betsy and the comatose Jessica Holland, the common bond being Paul Holland. In the same film, we have the responsible stoic, Paul, pitted against his stepbrother, the irresponsible and overly emotional Wesley. In *The Leopard Man,* Teresa Delgado's callously indifferent family serves to counterpoint Consuelo's overprotective family, the link, of course, being that both families are victimized by the killer. In *The Seventh Victim,* we have sisters who fall in love with the same man; one sister, Mary, is innocent and optimistic, the other, Jacqueline, is worldly and despairing. In the same film, we also have Jason Hoag, an emotional and romantic poet, pitted against Dr. Judd, a cold intellectual living by reason and hard logic. Both men have to some extent abandoned their calling. The unproductive Hoag is a washed-up poet who no longer publishes, while Judd has given up his psychiatry practice to concentrate on publishing books (his professional relationship with Jacqueline is presumably a rarity—"I don't practice anymore. I find it easier to write about mental illness and leave the care to others"). Numerous examples of this kind of doubling can be found in subsequent Lewton films as well.

Another kind of doubling occurs when two characters, often a generation apart, symbolize a younger and an older version of a prototype. For example, we get the impression in *The Seventh Victim* that if Mary turned her back upon the world and chose to teach at Highcliffe Academy, she would end up a frustrated nonentity like her alter ego, Miss Gilchrist. But if Mary allowed herself the other extreme and followed a recklessly hedonistic lifestyle, she would become like her used-up sister, Jacqueline. Although the character of Gregory Ward is thinly conceived, he is also placed between two extremes. If his law career continues to encourage him to live "by the book," he will become another Dr. Judd; on the other hand, if he spends his life merely following his heart, he will turn into another shiftless dreamer, just like Jason

Hoag. Mimi and Jacqueline are also soulmates in this sense. Jacqueline could go on living, but her hedonism would turn her into another Mimi eventually. Jacqueline, of course, chooses to leave behind a beautiful corpse. Lewton would make extensive use of this particular form of doubling in upcoming films like *The Ghost Ship, Curse of the Cat People, Youth Runs Wild,* and *The Body Snatcher.*

In Lewton films, the theme of duality is often reflected in individual characters as well, especially those with alter egos (Irena in *Cat People*, Mrs. Rand in *I Walked with a Zombie,* and Dr. Galbraith in *The Leopard Man*). Sometimes a subtler sense of duality was used simply to shade a role and add a complex, realistic edge to a screen character who might otherwise have been a mere stereotype. Consider some of the characters who surprise us when we think we have them pegged. Alice, in *The Cat People,* seems to be a very supportive friend to Oliver, but she deliberately does things to undermine his relationship with Irena. Betsy, in *I Walked with a Zombie,* is a rational person, one who does not believe in witchcraft, yet she takes Jessica Holland to voodoo witchdoctors. Teresa's mother, in *The Leopard Man,* appears incredibly hard-hearted, but her turnabout concern and desperation in the moment of peril is heartrending, and so is her grief at the loss of her daughter. In *The Seventh Victim,* the benevolent Mary becomes cruelly manipulative when she urges August to continue with his search for Jacqueline, a bit of advice that results in his death. In the same film, it is Jacqueline's best friend, Frances Fallon, who begs her to drink the poison. Such unexpected and seemingly paradoxical behavior actually makes a screen character more realistic; only stereotypes are consistent.

These matters aside, the narrative of *The Seventh Victim* has a peculiar overabundance of sleuths, both professional and amateur. Mary and Jacqueline's brief reunion in the hotel room ends with two detectives, each employed by Ward, arriving upon the scene. This means that the film has three detectives—one dead, two alive—and four amateur sleuths: a psychiatrist, a poet, a lawyer, and a schoolgirl. Seven people pooling their efforts to help the seventh victim. Given the symmetrical construction of so many of the Lewton films, one shouldn't be surprised if Lewton and Bodeen were reaching for some irony with the traditionally lucky number. If so, it was probably lost upon a 1943 audience in search of a horror film. Or anybody else, for that matter.

Like *I Walked with a Zombie* and *The Leopard Man, The Seventh Victim*'s main focus is death: *Zombie* is about those who court Death, *Leopard* is about those who are marked for death, and *Victim* is about those who, in John Donne's words, "run to death." In a 1992 interview, Val Edwin Lewton told the author, "I think my father was really very pessimistic, and I think that comes out in his films. They may look cheerful and hopeful enough, but I think the real effect behind them was a deep dark pessimism and hopelessness. This whole dialogue of death, he was obsessed with it."

The Seventh Victim is a film where numerous people collaborate their efforts to save a woman who is beyond their help. During the woman's long walk home, the only people sympathetic to her plight are watching her on a movie screen. And as her final minutes tick away, there is nothing anyone can do: "I run to death and death meets me as fast,/ And all my pleasures are like yesterday."

TEN

The Ghost Ship

> ***For all his love of the sea, Val was never wholly at ease on the Nina [Lewton's boat]. He wasn't particularly good at athletics, but felt that he ought to be. I suppose it was all part of his extreme romanticism. He liked to see himself as a lumberjack cutting down trees or as a sailor guiding his ship around the Horn. He always seemed a bit nervous when we were on the boat. One had the feeling that his yachtsman was an uncertain self-creation, for he lacked the ease of the person to whom physical things came naturally.***
>
> —Alan Napier
> from *The Reality of Terror,* by Joel Siegel

Val Lewton's behavior reflected the kind of duality that was perfectly in keeping with the nature of so many of his screen characters. On the one hand, we have the elevated, arcane, extremely literate raconteur, and on the other hand we have the failed sportsman who fancied himself in the proper Hemingway mold. One side of Lewton was generous, diplomatic, modest, witty, and self-deprecating (he enjoyed telling friends that his "associate producer" title was usually shortened to "ass prod"). Yet, there was another side to Lewton, one that was grudging, authoritarian, self-important, petty, humorless, and pedantic. On some occasions, Lewton took pride in the ways he managed to outsmart the front office, accepting the challenges that came with taking intelligent artistic detours from the conventional boundaries suggested by his superiors. At other times, when he felt beaten, he would bemoan his ongoing plight concerning studio interference. As Mark Robson had once put it, he was "someone who needed an enemy."

One part of him was warm, friendly, and outgoing; yet the same man could be reserved, reclusive, and paranoid. He had a fondness for the underdog; he wanted to lend a helping hand—as long as a handshake was not part of the bargain.

According to his daughter, the late Nina Lewton Druckman, Lewton was not an easy man to get along with:

> As a father, he was a strange combination of gentleness and authoritarianism. He would never think of asserting himself with a waiter or a garage attendant, the sort of person that people usually assert themselves with. In fact, he was just the opposite; a waiter could throw cold soup in his face and he'd never say or do anything. He was wonderful to the people who worked for him and generous to a fault—Mother would have to hide the checkbook. But he never liked the people he worked for. He never kowtowed to them, but he was afraid of them, afraid of being without a job. . . .

In a 1992 interview, Val Edwin Lewton told the author: "He had a terrible temper, and he could turn on you on a dime. You never knew what he was going to do. He wasn't physically violent, but he didn't need to be. I think he always had that temper but it got worse as he got more frustrated, but he kept sailing his boat and building furniture. He was always doing something," Lewton added. "He was an insomniac; he couldn't sleep so he would stay up late at night tying knots and rolling his own cigarettes. Because of his working hours, I usually didn't see too much of him during the week, although on weekends I would go sailing with him on the boat, or else he'd set up a little shop for me, and we would do some projects together."

Although *The Seventh Victim* has often been cited as Lewton's most personal work, much of the producer can also be found in his fifth film, *The Ghost Ship*. This story about a demented sea captain obsessed with authority and petty details seems to bear a significant relevance to Lewton's own seafaring attitudes. Others may argue that Lewton more likely envisioned *The Ghost Ship*'s Captain Stone as a parallel to the authority-conscious RKO executives. Both views are probably correct; Lewton, who revised the script and rewrote many lines of dialogue, may have been thinking he was lashing out at his superiors, but through the process of dissociation, he was also providing us with a villain who possessed some negative traits not unlike his own.

In its production history, *The Ghost Ship* traveled a wayward course. Lewton had been dragging his feet on his upcoming *Curse of the Cat People*, a film announced to the trade papers as early as February 17, 1943. As *Leopard*'s production was concluding, the March 10 *Hollywood Reporter* announced, "After the sensational success of *Cat People*, RKO announced yesterday the purchase of two new horror stories: 'The Amorous Ghost' and 'The Screaming Skull.'"

By the time shooting started on *The Seventh Victim*, Lewton was hoping to expand his cinematic horizons; in May his plan was to turn *The Amorous Ghost* into a comic-fantasy-romance wherein Casanova is allowed to come back to earth for 12 hours, during which time he falls in love with a modern

Not one, not two, not three . . . but ALL of the famous creeper characters you ever heard of, plus some new ones, in the wildest nightmare of terror thrills that mind can imagine! . . Cat People, Zombies, Leopard Men, beast-women and bat-men, blood-curdlers by the dozen . . . all in a merger of monsters that will make anything else in this line look like a Sunday School picnic!
"THEY
CREEP
BY
NIGHT"

Rare preproduction ad for the never-made Lewton "monster rally," ***They Creep by Night*** **(courtesy of Gary Svehla).**

girl he meets at a masquerade. Lewton already believed he had the perfect choice for Casanova: Tom Conway.

The May 12 *Hollywood Reporter* announced that *Curse of the Cat People* had been postponed till September because of the temporary unavailability of three of the original film's cast members (Kent Smith, Simone Simon, and Jane Randolph, all of whom were returning for the sequel). Meanwhile, another film had to fill the gap.

The producer discussed his idea for *The Amorous Ghost* with his superiors, but they were lukewarm to a comedy produced by a man they had hired to make horror films. In the meantime, Charles Koerner urged Lewton to tackle a much more expedient alternative to his overly ambitious costume fantasy.

RKO had built a huge ship set for the Lew Landers-directed *Pacific Liner* in 1939. Since the ship set was still standing, it seemed reasonable that Lewton could design a horror thriller taking place on a boat. "Call it *The Ghost Ship*," insisted Koerner. Lewton was also to provide a suitable role for long-time contractee Richard Dix, since the aging actor owed RKO one more picture before his contract lapsed. On June 7, about a week after *Victim's* shooting was completed, the *Hollywood Reporter* announced *The Ghost Ship* as Val Lewton's new RKO project.

(For a while, *The Amorous Ghost* maintained its status as an active project, but the front office wanted to hedge their bets in attracting a horror audience. Within weeks it was announced in the *Hollywood Reporter:* "Tom Conway is set for the top spot in Lewton's *Amorous Ghost,* which RKO will send out with *The Screaming Skull* as a dual shocker saga. There will be a different director on each yarn, one of which is played for spook comedy, the other for sheet shock." Although the two-for-one feature officially remained in the works for several months, it was eventually dropped. However tempting a Lewton *Screaming Skull* might have been, genre fans should probably be grateful that *The Amorous Ghost* was discarded by RKO. Although the producer was known for his good sense of humor [sardonic ironies and witty dialogue greatly enhance *The Body Snatcher* and *Bedlam*], he was seldom successful with deliberate comedy.)

Leo Mittler was assigned the short story treatment of *The Ghost Ship,* based on Lewton's original idea for the film. Mittler's treatment was then given to Lewton's old friend and fellow reporter/novelist, Donald Henderson Clarke, who had moved to Hollywood in the hopes of becoming a screenwriter.

That summer, the RKO producer was working on the scripts of two films—*The Ghost Ship* and *Curse of the Cat People* (both based on his original stories)—while laying plays for three more films. In addition to the two-for-one film *(Amorous Ghost/Screaming Skull),* the *Hollywood Reporter* announced other Lewton films in the works: a nonhorror *Are These Our Children?* (with Edward Dmytryk coproducing) and, believe it or not, a monster rally called *They Creep by Night.*

The idea of a Val Lewton monster rally sounds so preposterous that one would suspect that the *Hollywood Reporter* was guilty of fabricating a scoop. The fact is, however, that RKO was quite serious about the never-produced *They Creep by Night;* the publicity department went so far as to design a preproduction ad for the film. The colorful poster shows a stylish melange of horror images (bats, zombies, a man holding a bloody dagger, another man swinging an axe, a woman's horrified face), and its caption reads: "Not one, not two, not three . . . but all of the famous creeper characters you ever heard of, plus some new ones, in the wildest nightmare of terror thrills that mind can imagine! . . . Cat People, Zombies, Leopard Men; beast-women and batmen; blood curdlers by the dozen . . . all in a merger of monsters that will make anything else in this line look like a Sunday School picnic!" One can only imagine Lewton's gaping expression when he caught a glimpse of this piece of work.

Ironically, while RKO was trying to get Lewton to make horror films of a more conventional nature, other studios, Universal included, were beginning to take their horror cues from Lewton films. In June, Universal planned a number of "B" unit psychological thrillers in conjunction with Simon and Schuster's popular "Inner Sanctum" mysteries. Hoping for the kind of continuity that made the Lewton films such a success, Universal appointed one man, Ben Pivar, as the associate producer of the entire series. Basically, the six "Inner Sanctum" films were designed as horror films without the monsters, but if Universal was hoping to give the Lewton films a run for their money, they were mistaken. Even with the use of Lewton's part-time dialogue contributor, Edward Dein, and a sense of continuity provided by Reginald LeBorg's direction for the first three offerings (*Calling Dr. Death, Weird Woman,* and *Dead Man's Eyes*), the "Inner Sanctum" films were a far cry from those produced by the Lewton unit.

Monogram whipped up *Revenge of the Zombies* (1943) in the wake of *I Walked with a Zombie*'s unusual success. Columbia's *Cry of the Werewolf* (released in early 1944) would be a conscious imitation of *Cat People,* complete with a lady shape-shifter and offscreen transformations—though with nothing more than tepid results. Better yet was Paramount's superior ghost story, *The Uninvited,* an "A" budget Lewtonesque horror opus of the highest order.

RKO seemed terribly misguided to demand conventional genre films while rival studios had already recognized the future of horror cinema in the films of Val Lewton. And yet, rather paradoxically, had Lewton been given the respect and the autonomy he deserved, genre fans could well be stuck with dubious, ill-advised efforts like *The Amorous Ghost* instead of maverick classics like *The Ghost Ship* or *Curse of the Cat People.*

The Ghost Ship's script completed, cameras were ready to roll on August 3, 1943. Thirteen days later the *Hollywood Reporter* announced: "Dr. Jared Criswell, former pastor of the Fifth Avenue Spiritualist Church of New York City, arrives today to serve as technical consultant on *The Ghost Ship.* Criswell is an authority on psychic phenomena and ESP and will apply his theories to members of the cast."

The role of Tom Merriam, the third officer, was assigned to Russell Wade (the disembodied voice on the other side of the cemetery wall in *The Leopard Man*); Richard Dix was given the plum role of the deranged Captain Stone. Returning from previous Lewton films were Edith Barrett, Ben Bard, Dewey Robinson, Charles Lung, and Sir Lancelot. Making their Lewton film debut were Skelton Knaggs, Edmund Glover, and future noir tough guy, Lawrence Tierney, something of a Lewton discovery in this, his first motion picture.

In Michael and Cheryl Murphy's 1990 interview with Tierney (in *Psychotronic,* issue 8) the rough-and-tumble actor said the following:

> Val Lewton was a very wonderful, kind, talented and a gentle man. And he was a real nice guy. He liked me, he got a kick out of me. When I first came [to Hollywood] I carried the Brooklyn accent and I'd say, "Doity Poiple Boids," and all that stuff and I amused him very much. I was young. I was about 23.

> He kept telling me, "Where do I know you from, where do I know you from, where do I know you from?" . . . So about 2 or 3 weeks later I'm walking down the studio lot and from his office up on the third floor he hollered out, "Lawrence, Lawrence!" and I said, "Who is it?" and he said, "It's Val Lewton, come on up." So I went up and he said, "Now I know where I know you from." And he had two books in front of him. A Sears and Roebuck catalogue and a Montgomery Ward catalogue. I had done a lot of modeling before I got into the business, so there were old pictures of me in bathing suits, hats and jackets, suits. So that's where he said he saw my face many times, "It's my hobby to buy things from the Sears and Roebuck catalogue." So we became friends after that. Then he was doing a picture called *The Ghost Ship*. He gave me the part of Louie.

Mark Robson was again chosen to direct. Ruby Rosenberg worked as his assistant, John Lockert served as editor, and Nicholas Musuraca was retained as the director of photography. The art directors and set decorators remained the same, with the addition of Claude Carpenter in the latter capacity. Roy Webb again provided the score.

With the production under wraps on August 28, 1943, *The Ghost Ship* was put into general release in late December, coming as a most peculiar Christmas offering. Although some of the reviews were indifferent, other notable critics—James Agee, Manny Farber, on occasion even *New York Times*'s Bosley Crowther—were making a habit of championing Lewton's cause. Said Crowther, "[*The Ghost Ship* is] a nice little package of morbidity all wrapped around in gloom."

The Ghost Ship opens with a blind seaport street-singer (Alec Craig) warning neophyte officer Tom Merriam (Russell Wade) not to board the *Altair*; an unhappy fate awaits him there. Tom ignores the advice and going aboard, sees Pollo (Skelton Knaggs), a mute Finn, sharpening a formidable-looking knife.

In voice-over, we hear Pollo's thoughts; his eloquent, even poetic, remarks belie our expectations of him. Once again, appearances are deceiving. Pollo, a frightfully homely leprechaun with a knife, reveals perceptions that verge on the omniscient, his cryptic musings seeming to hover in the damp, misty air: "I see the white steel thirsting for blood and the blood running to meet it. I am a Finn and my soul is in my hand here, white and cold and knowing all things." (Pollo's opening lines sound like an odd variation of *Victim*'s Donne quote.) Henceforth, Pollo will provide mystical commentary to the story's proceedings, functioning as a one-man Greek chorus (thus serving the function of the calypso singer in *Zombie* and the fortune-teller in *The Leopard Man*).

Tom Merriam meets Captain Stone (Richard Dix), who is uncommonly friendly; Stone sees Merriam as a younger version of himself. But Tom does not quite know what to make of Stone's bewildering statements and overly friendly manner. We understand his puzzlement because the Captain exudes a degree of warmth that is embarrasingly overfamiliar, especially upon a first meeting.

Captain Stone tells Tom, "Your history could have been my own at your age—orphaned, serious, ambitious." Later, he claims he found in Tom, "a man who'd think as I think." At one point, when Merriam is about to kill a moth, the Captain stops him and, without losing his smile, declares, "You haven't the right to kill that moth; its safety doesn't depend on you." It is only later in the film that we realize the full gravity of Stone's remark.

Tom is then brought to his living quarters while a crewman fills him in on previously unmentioned details: the new officer's room and bed have not been made since its last occupant, the man he is replacing, suffered violent convulsions and died. When Tom asks what happened, the crewman answers, "Oh, I don't know. He didn't want to die; he was always telling funny stories."

During roll call the next day, a dead sailor is discovered lying on the deck. The Captain appears unmoved by the incident and orders the men to go about their business, but the Finn's voice-over, baiting the audience, shows that at least one person has not taken this death lightly: "With his blood we have bought passage. There will be the agony of dying and another death before we come to land again."

Tom meets Sparks (Edmund Glover), the radio operator, and the two get along instantly. Sparks is the first normal person Tom has met since boarding ship. Although the two are fast friends, Sparks is reluctant to read anything sinister in the latest death, nor in the demise of Tom's predecessor. At least not yet.

An excellent set piece early in the film showcases Robson's underrated directorial skill. Robson creates a dynamic sense of menace from a physical object: a massive giant hook hanging upon an enormous chain, pendulumlike, inches above the deck.

When Tom realizes the unrestrained hook could prove hazardous in rough seas and ought be secured, he reports to the Captain, who disagrees vehemently, saying that a line would mar its fresh coat of paint. "I like a neat ship," he says. Later, when the waves get choppy and the massive pendulum begins moving in a slight arc, Tom informs Stone of the imminent danger. But the Captain only grows belligerent: "If you wish to discuss the hook, I've already given you my considerate opinion of the danger involved."

Thus the hook remains unattended and unsecured. In the middle of the night, after the seas become rough, the swinging hook gains momentum and moves in a wider arc, relentlessly crashing against cabin walls, life boats, anything in its path. The men arrive on deck to curtail further destruction and wind up putting themselves in peril of life and limb. In a tightly directed, genuinely exciting scene, the monstrous hook sways back and forth in a direct path toward the camera, making one wonder how cinematographer, Nicholas Musuraca, kept his camera (and head) intact during the shooting. (It would have made a marvelous 3-D set piece, had the process been available at the time.) The lighting is also used to great advantage, the shadows and fog accenting the terror. Half the time the swinging hook is so hidden in darkness that aside from the loud creak of its sway, there is no telling which direction it will take. After some harrowing close calls, the crew manages to get a tow on the chain.

When Tom later voices his complaint about the hook incident, the Captain delivers another round of nebulous remarks:

> "I told you that you had no right to kill that moth. That it's safety did not depend on you. But I have the right to do what I want with the men because their safety does depend on me. I stand ready any hour of the day or night to give my life for their safety and the safety of this vessel. Because I do, I have certain rights of risks over them. Do you understand? . . . It's the first thing you must learn about authority."

Because he wants to like the Captain and sees him as a father figure, Merriam gives him the benefit of the doubt, telling Sparks, "he's the first older man who's ever treated me like a friend." Sparks uses the opportunity to take potshots at the Captain's credibility, if not his sanity.

The next incident of Stone's erratic behavior comes when one of the seamen is stricken with appendicitis. Captain Stone, Tom, and Sparks are in the cabin preparing for an emergency appendectomy. Sparks gets a mainland surgeon on the radio so that the Captain can perform the operation step-by-step, according to the radio's running instructions. The scene is played to squeamish effect, mounting its intensity upon the blood we do not see.

As the incision is about to be made, there's a close-up of the Captain's nervous face and then a cut to a shot of the scalpel poised in a cutting position above the patient's abdomen. Reaction shots from Sparks and Tom, both beginning to feel the tension of the moment. The Captain remains frozen, and the radio surgeon's instructions go unheeded. Another shot of the scalpel, the hand is shaking a bit. Alternate shots of Tom and Sparks, of the Captain's sweating face and shifting eyes. The radio surgeon gives further instructions, assuming by now that the incision has been made. Finally Tom takes over, performing the surgery off camera, as alternate shots of the men reflect their queasiness.

Later, the Captain attempts to give Tom an explanation: "I'm not afraid of anything but failure." Since he is a sea captain and not a doctor, he explains, there was no reason why he should have risked failure by assuming the duties of a doctor. Tom is still doing his best to give Stone the benefit of the doubt, but when he tells Sparks of the Captain's lame explanation, Sparks becomes cynical, ever the critic when it comes to discussing the Captain's idiosyncracies.

One of the sailors, Louie (Lawrence Tierney), sees the Captain to voice

A poster for *The Ghost Ship*. Notice that Skelton Knaggs is portrayed as a menacing figure. The woman at top right corner is also not Edith Barrett.

a complaint. His words are given a cold reception, and a veiled threat simmers under the Stone's cool response: "There are captains who might hold this against you, Louie."

It is not long before we find Louie cleaning the empty chain locker. The men call down the shaft, asking him if he is finished. He gives the okay before discovering that his escape hatch has been shut and locked (either by accident or design, by Captain Stone). The men let the massive chain slide down the shaft, and Louie's panicked cries are inaudible over the racket as the chain piles up at his feet, getting higher and higher. The men on deck continue to feed the chain into storage as Louie's terror mounts, with the stack of heavy links growing before him, competing for his height, knocking him unconscious, and crushing him to a pulp.

When Tom discovers the body and tells the Captain, the latter appears unshaken by the incident, saying that Louie was a troublemaker, anyway, and the *Altair* was better off without him. The Captain's reaction leads Tom to say: "This is what you meant when you said you had rights over the lives of the crew." Outraged, Tom reports the events to Sparks, who is now quick to recant his former criticism of the Captain. Sparks, suddenly a man who minds his own business and does not wish to make trouble, tells Tom he is imagining things. Bowns (Ben Bard), the next in command, reacts to Tom's story as if he were listening to the ramblings of an idiot.

The boat pulls into port at San Sebastian (presumably, a nod to the island setting of *I Walked with a Zombie*), and Tom registers his complaints with Roberts (Boyd Davis), the head of the shipping office. Roberts, an old friend of Captain Stone, is incredulous. In an attempt to debunk Tom's story, Roberts makes an official investigation of the charge. The crew members are summoned, and all speak in favor of the Captain, though they also confess a fondness for Tom. None of them can understand Tom's behavior, including the benevolent Jamaican crewman, Billy Radd (Sir Lancelot). One man, speaking on Stone's behalf, says, "All I know is that the Captain saved my life once and for that I will always be grateful." He speaks of his appendectomy, the operation Tom and Sparks has sworn to keep secret in deference to the Captain. When Tom walks out, the Captain says, "I'm sorry this had to happen, Tom."

Deciding he is through with the *Altair,* Tom informs the authorities that he will not board her again. This is accepted and granted as a reasonable request. After the investigation, the Captain has a long talk with Roberts, telling his old friend that something is not right with his life these days. Stone fears the isolation he has come to know and has lately found reason to question his own competence. Roberts dismisses this as the result of overwork. Roberts's sister Ellen (Edith Barrett), an old flame of the Captain's, then becomes the topic of conversation.

Meanwhile, Tom is given a lift in Ellen's carriage. She tells him how much he and the Captain have in common. Ellen promises to fix Tom up with her younger sister.

Captain Stone meets Ellen, who tells him she is free (apparently from a previous marriage), but the Captain does not want to marry. He fears for his sanity, telling her of his experience of once watching a sea captain, his mentor, lose his mind, and how much he had now come to identify with his unbalanced predecessor. Stone tells Ellen, "I don't know myself. . . . I don't control my thoughts, my actions. . . . I've done things I couldn't remember doing." He reveals he almost lost control during the hearing, when he felt like hurting Tom. "People seem to be turning against me, the boy, some of the crew; I feel their dislike, their distrust." Ellen dismisses this and encourages the Captain to find other hobbies, other interests. Stone answers, "There are no new interests. Just authority. Authority."

That night Tom comes upon some of his crewmen in the middle of a brawl and is knocked unconscious. The crewmen, not knowing of Tom's decision to quit the *Altair,* carry him to his old cabin aboard ship. When Tom comes to, the boat is already out to sea. The Captain has a meeting with Tom and is barely able to control his rage. Nonetheless, he feigns civility and informs his former third officer that he will be treated as a privileged guest of the *Altair.* As Tom fumbles with his thanks and turns to leave, Captain Stone adds, "There are captains who might hold this against you."

Tom walks back to his cabin. He knows now that Stone intends to kill him. En route, members of the crew ignore him, not wanting to get involved with his crazy ideas. When he gets to his cabin, he notices the lock has been taken off his door. He goes to the radio cabin, but all he gets from his buddy Sparks is, "Don't come in here, fella." Tom wants to use the radio to call for help but learns that no wireless messages are to be sent out without the Captain's prior approval.

That night Tom is alone in his cabin. He is understandably restless, and the room, engulfed by large patches of darkness, is haunted by his apprehensions. He tosses and turns, keeping an eye open for intruders, not daring to fall asleep. No sooner does he start to doze than he is awakened by a loud crash from within his room (a rather miscalculated attempt to create a "bus"), nothing more than his ceramic pitcher falling off his night table. Thereafter, Tom is teased into paranoia by little things, the unfastened porthole cover making a gentle, syncopated clanging sound, the unsecured door breathing open a few fractions of an inch with a seaward rush of wind now and again.

Not being able to endure this state of apprehension a minute longer, Tom decides to confront Captain Stone. He steals up to the Captain's deck, which is dark and apparently deserted. After a little snooping, he stops short, feeling the cold barrel of Captain Stone's gun pressed to his back. The Captain treats Tom like a captured criminal, telling him, "Authority cannot be questioned."

Rather than throw him in the brig for trespassing, Stone releases his captive, saying, "There is not a man in the crew who will believe you or help you. They are too lazy, too cowardly, too disinterested. This was my lesson to you, that men are worthless cattle and a few men are given authority to drive them." Tom will not buy into this brand of cynicism, even at the point of a gun, and walks out. But the Lewton universe is once again full of human beings who are indifferent to the plight of someone in danger. When Tom asks for help, the men warn him to stay away and not provoke trouble.

That night Sparks receives a radio message and takes it to the Captain. The message is from Roberts, made at the request of his sister, Ellen; it concerns the whereabouts of Tom Merriam, who seems to have vanished from San Sebastian. The Captain hands Sparks his written response which claims that Merriam never came aboard the *Altair*.

We see Pollo's profile while he sits upon deck watching Tom as he is ignored by the crewmen. We hear the Finn's thoughts: "This is another man I can never know because I cannot talk with him. I am cut off from other men in my silence. I can hear things they never hear, know things they never know. . . . I know this man's trouble. I've seen the Captain's hatred. I know and I will watch."

Tom goes to his room and finds Sparks sitting on the bed with a paper in his hand, smiling. He now believes Tom's story and plans to show the

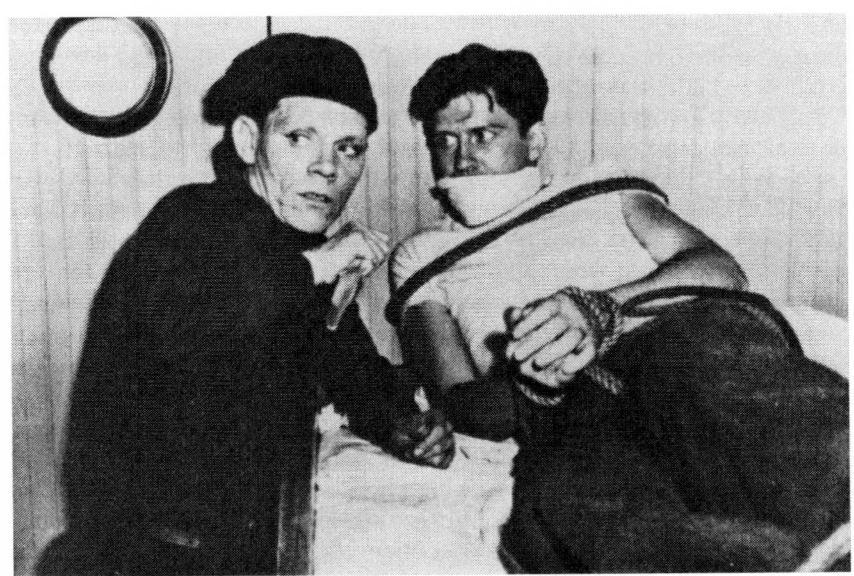

Pollo the Finn (Skelton Knaggs) comes to the rescue.

Captain's bogus radio message to the other officers. Unfortunately, after he leaves to do so, he is apprehended by Stone. Sparks drops the message, apparently on purpose, and is led to the Captain's deck. The Finn picks up the incriminating radio message.

Time passes and the Captain pays Tom a call. He needs help in sending a radio message, he says. Although agreeable, Tom asks why Sparks cannot send the message, and the Captain tells him he will understand in a little while. Tom accompanies Stone and sits down at the radio, only to see that the message is to inform authorities that radio operator Sparks was lost overboard.

Tom is enraged: "You know you killed him!" he shouts and attacks the Captain. The two grapple until crew members come to Stone's aid. Tom is restrained, his hands bound, mouth gagged. He is removed to his quarters, where the Captain gives the second officer a syringe filled with a sedative to administer to Tom. Tom struggles and tries to yell through his gag. He thinks what we think: that the syringe is filled with poison. But it really is a sedative, so Tom simply nods off. The others go about their business.

Meanwhile the Finn brings the message to the second officer, who is in a room full of crew mates. The second officer tells his men, "There might be something in what the boy says." But the Captain is at the porthole overhearing the conversation, which ends with "if the boy is right. . . ." This last remark echoes in his head as he walks to his quarters and notices the motto written on a plaque decorating his wall: "Who Does Not Heed the Rudder Shall Meet the Rock." In a mad fury, Captain Stone pulls the wooden plaque down and breaks it in half; then, selecting a large knife from a rack, he storms over the Tom's room. Tom becomes conscious as the crazed Captain invades his cabin knife-in-hand. Just as suddenly, the Finn bursts into the room with his own knife, and steel clashes as the two men confront one another, fencing with their short blades. Rather ingeniously, the knife fight is not accompanied with a rousing action score; instead, during the entire scene we hear Billy Radd's sea chanty being sung from somewhere above deck. The inclusion of this very inappropriate source music adds a genuinely ironic touch to the proceedings; here Tom is bound and gagged, his life depending solely upon the gnomish little Finn while elsewhere people go about their business making merry. This sort of counterpointing during times of danger is typical of Lewton.

Also in typical Lewton fashion, the fight is staged in a darkened room (a stylistic device already used in *Cat People* and soon to be included in *The Body Snatcher*) so we have trouble discerning who is getting the upper hand. There are numerous cutbacks to Tom Merriam's gagged and desperately bobbing head. Although, technically, the execution of this fight is not entirely successful, the scene is notable for the uncharacteristic amount of bloodletting shown to the audience. There is a brief but graphic shot of the Captain's abdomen bloodied from the plunging of the Finn's knife. In one excruciating close-up, the Finn wraps his hand around the Captain's blade; as the latter twists the blade to loosen it from his opponent's grip, the Finn's blood begins to run between his clenched fingers. Finally, the crew arrives, alerted by the ruckus, to see the Finn make his fatal stab.

We end with the Finn's voiceover: "The boy is safe and his belief in men and man's essential goodness is preserved." All is in order. In one last shot we see Tom at the dock of a seaport, greeted by a silhouette of a woman who has been asked to meet him there. It is Ellen's younger sister, who remains a silhouette as the two shadows walk off together. Unlike *The Seventh Victim*'s fatalistic ending, *The Ghost Ship*'s conclusion is decidedly upbeat; Tom's meeting with Ellen's sister signals a break in the pattern, which is to say he will not become an authority-obsessed mirror image of Captain Stone.

The Ghost Ship is one of the most accessible, consistently engaging, and dramatically sustained films of the entire Lewton series. We are not challenged by serpentine plot twists *(Victim)* or eccentric narrative structures *(Zombie, Leopard)*. It may not reach the heights of terror achieved by any of its four Lewton predecessors, but *The Ghost Ship* works wonderfully well, providing in its short running time of 69 minutes something deliberately different from the other films in the series.

The Ghost Ship is the only Lewton horror film in which not a single female is threatened. In an almost exclusively male cast (Edith Barrett [Ellen

Roberts] and Shirley O'Hara [a woman's silhouette only] are the only actresses employed). It is a man who is this time targeted for doom. No other Lewton film is set within such a strongly masculine milieu; nor is there another film in the series that has so much to say about man's obsession with authority. It is not surprising that *The Ghost Ship* exhibits a preoccupation with weapons, considering their Freudian associations with the male sex; guns and knives are repeatedly shown, as well as an assortment of weaponlike instruments (pointed net-weaving tools, scalpels, syringes, etc.).

The Ghost Ship is unique among the series for its single-minded focus; the plight of its protagonist is the narrative's sole concern. Thankfully, Russell Wade escapes the fate of so many of the Lewton films' handsome, colorless, and sometimes forgettable male leads: he does not have to play second banana to a heroine in distress. Tom Merriam is a protagonist in the Hitchcock and Lang tradition: an innocent man caught in a trap. Or as Captain Stone might phrase it, a moth caught in a lampshade.

Merriam becomes an outsider and, as such, can expect little help from his fellow men. Since most of his odd conversations with the Captain are private, with only the audience bearing witness to the enigmatic discourse, the viewer is made to feel a special kinship with the young officer. In *Dreams of Darkness,* J.P. Telotte makes some canny observations about *The Ghost Ship*'s protagonist:

> Despite his complex perspective, as both an outsider and, due to the Captain's initial fondness for him, a privileged participant in events, Tom Merriam seems an equally unlikely candidate to bear the film's moral weight. He is an orphan, a stranger in this world about to join his first ship and learn about the problems of the seafaring life. In effect, he seems the archetypal innocent, eager to learn and clearly with much to learn—about human behavior as well as about the sea.

One of *The Ghost Ship*'s greatest assets is Richard Dix's marvelous turn in the role of Captain Stone, who, like a typical Hitchcock villain, is much more complex than the flatly drawn evil stereotypes that populated so many of the Hollywood films of the 1940s. Captain Stone has friends and even a fiancée; more importantly, he is bewildered and disturbed by his thoughts and actions. Dix's understated performance is particularly gratifying because the veteran actor often tended toward a flamboyant style (most critics agree that Dix's hammy performance was the main liability of *Cimarron* [1931]). There is something strangely engaging about Dix's portrayal of a homicidal maniac. He imbues the role with an uncanny blend of pathos and murderous glee; his face mirrors his lack of emotional control as he behaves like a father enraged by his son's disgraceful behavior, the father/son motif providing another subtext for interpretation.

Captain Stone's character (and subsequent breakdown) actually anticipates a more famous fictional counterpart: Captain Queeg, in Herman

Wouk's 1951 novel (and play), *The Caine Mutiny*. Although Wouk's captain is no killer, Stone and Queeg would make a good comparative case study. The similarities between the two authority-obsessed characters become more apparent when the Lewton film is compared to Edward Dmytryk's 1954 film adaptation of *The Caine Mutiny* (with Humphrey Bogart in the Queeg role).

Both Stone and Queeg lose their grips on reality while failing to live up to their professional responsibilities; neither character holds himself to blame for his own incompetence. In fact, some of the parallels between *The Caine Mutiny* and *The Ghost Ship* are so surprising that one wonders whether Wouk had seen the Lewton/Robson film sometime during his World War II service in the U.S. Navy. If Captain Stone foreshadows Queeg, then Tom Merriam anticipates the novel's main character, the neophyte officer Willie Keith. *Ghost*'s Sparks, on the other hand, becomes the prototype for the novel's communications officer, Tom Keefer (who, as a self-appointed amateur psychologist, constantly alludes to Captain Queeg's aberrations). Aside from their both being radio men, Keefer (played by Fred MacMurray in the Dmytryk film) and Sparks are also spineless troublemakers who fail to support their convictions once the going gets tough.

Although *The Ghost Ship* makes strident efforts to veer away from the RKO team's established formula, it never stops being what we expect a Lewton film to be. A large part of Lewton's reputation for horror is based upon that which occurs offscreen (a prototypical example being Jacqueline's suicide in *Victim*), but *Ghost* reveals that Lewton was obviously not opposed to showing an occasional grisly shot (though nowhere does Robson's use of gore come close to matching the impact of Tourneur's blood-under-the-door scene in *Leopard*). For a Lewton film, *The Ghost Ship* may be uncharacteristically graphic, but its hold upon the audience is a direct result of the less-is-more approach typified by the series.

Far and away the film's most squeamish scene, the amateur appendectomy, is accomplished without the audience seeing a drop of blood. The scene is remarkably clever in its method of manipulation; that nobody in the cabin is a qualified surgeon only adds to our total involvement. Since Stone is not a surgeon, an entire audience of nonsurgeons identify with him; ultimately, the hand holding the scalpel becomes our own hand. As the Captain hesitates to make the incision, with each minute's delay increasing his patient's chances of death, the tension becomes so nerve-wracking that in spite of our squeamishness, we would guide his shaking hand and perform the operation ourselves if it were possible. No wonder we are so relieved when Merriam takes over, the camera lingering upon his face—his subtle expressions of disgust mirroring our own—as his hands go about the task of performing surgery. We never need to see the incision because Robson's direction has already forced us to imagine it, to feel it, in every detail and from both ends of the scalpel.

Like all four of its Lewton predecessors, *The Ghost Ship* makes extensive use of the theme of predestination; the Finn's prophetic remarks, like those of the fortune-teller in *Leopard,* lend a supernatural flavor to what would otherwise be a straight thriller. Anticipating the noir dictums of the postwar years, these "supernatural prophecies" illustrate fate's irreversibility. If these prophecies resemble the oracles of Greek tragedy, one should not be surprised; Greek tragedy provided a prime inspiration for noir's dark vision.

The following observation by J.P. Telotte *(Dreams of Darkness)* expresses the film's particularly cynical view of predestination:

> The "Altair" regularly carries sheep and wool as its cargo, and the ship virtually reeks with the smell of sheep. Upon reaching port in San Sebastian, [Merriam's] hopes for success ashore are undercut, as he is repeatedly framed in long shots with groups of sheep being herded through the city streets. Ultimately, it is the casual, even stolid manner in which the crew accept the series of mysterious deaths in their midst that underscores this group characterization. Besides reinforcing their fundamental estrangement from each other, their animallike placidity also demonstrates how much they are like lambs to the slaughter.

As mentioned earlier in the chapter, *The Ghost Ship* is one of Lewton's more personal works. If Lewton saw himself as Tom Merriam, the script would seem to echo his frustrations over being exploited by David O. Selznick or, more recently, by his RKO superiors. But Lewton may have also seen himself in the character of Captain Stone. Lewton's overly authoritative (and decidedly petty) yacht behavior comes through loud and clear when we see Captain Stone walking about with inflated pride, telling Merriam that there is nothing more important than a "neat ship." We can see Lewton's own reticence in coping with on-board emergencies when Captain Stone's shaking hand refuses to respond to the radio instructions. We can also still see something of Lewton in the Captain's paranoid fears of losing authority.

Ironically, the unhappy fate of Lewton's fifth production serves to illustrate the dangers of being a movie producer. Sometime during the summer of 1943, about a month or two before *Ghost* went into production, an unsolicited story and play had been delivered to Lewton's offices. Not giving them enough time to gather dust, Verna De Mots returned the manuscripts to the writers. This seemingly insignificant occurrence would come back to haunt the Lewton/Robson with an impact greater than any seaworthy spectre.

Shortly after the film was released, RKO was hit with a lawsuit. The plaintiffs were Samuel R. Golding and Norbert Faulkner, who claimed that *The Ghost Ship* was based on a play they had written, a play which Lewton had in his possession while he was fashioning the script of said film.

The Ghost Ship clearly was derivative, but its script (by Leo Mittler, Donald Henderson Clarke, and Val Lewton) had more in common with Jack

London and Joseph Conrad than it did with any unsolicited play dropped off at Lewton's office. Its more obvious resemblance is to London's *The Sea Wolf,* a novel about a crazed-but-brilliant sea captain (Wolf Larsen) who, drunk with his own power of authority and haunted by his own personal demons, helms a ship called "The Ghost." Joseph Conrad's *The Secret Sharer* has also been noted as a possible source of inspiration.

The plaintiffs were suing for $50,000, but were willing to settle for a mere $700. Lewton remained adamant, proclaiming his innocence and refusing to settle. Because the wheels of justice turn slowly, the pending suit against RKO did not go to trial until August 27, 1945.

Although Lewton held to the idea that the innocent would prevail, it is unfortunate that he did not heed one of the precepts of his own films, that the innocent also suffer, for he was understandably taken aback when the court ruled for the plaintiff and RKO was forced to pay damages of $25,000. They also lost the rights to exhibit the film. This expense on top of the lawyers' fees amounted to the closer side of $30,000; in addition, the studio lost all future booking residuals (Lewton films were used as double-bill fodder through the late 1940s and into the early 1950s) as well as the rights to sell the film to the television medium. (To think that the matter could have been settled for a mere $700.) As far as "clearing his name" was concerned, surely the trial besmirched Lewton's character more than any out-of-court settlement would have. Lewton never did understand how such an injustice could have occurred.

Aside from whatever narrative parallels may have existed between Lewton's film and other works of fiction (i.e., *The Sea Wolf, The Secret Sharer, The Caine Mutiny,* or the unsolicited play by Samuel R. Golding and Norbert Faulkner), Mark Robson's cinematic antecedent for *The Ghost Ship* was his first solo editing credit: Orson Welles's *Journey into Fear,* which Robson had edited just prior to his being assigned to the Lewton unit.

Welles did much more than inadvertently provide Lewton with an opportunity to make films for RKO. He served as a directorial model for his editing team, and the lessons Robert Wise and Mark Robson learned with Welles found their way into the Lewton films. *Citizen Kane,* of course, had an enormous influence upon the 1940s film noir cycle, but the Orson Welles film that most closely resembles the work of Val Lewton (and *Ghost Ship* in particular) was *Journey into Fear.* It was not only Robson's dress rehearsal for *The Ghost Ship*; it was also the inspiration for some of the editing techniques that came to be identified with the Lewton formula. In fact, the appropriately named *Journey into Fear* contains a pre–*Cat People* variation of Lewton's most celebrated terror technique, the "bus."

Although Norman Foster was *Journey*'s credited director, most film scholars accede that its direction was a collaborative effort between Foster and Welles, with the latter calling the shots. The film was completed and edited while Welles was in Brazil, wrestling with an unmanageable and unreleasable *It's All True. Journey* was previewed in October 1942, shortly before Welles arrived back in the States, aghast at his discovery that the film had not been given a proper ending. Using his RKO contract as a club, *Journey* being the final film in the three-picture agreement, Welles managed to pull the film from distribution (with $25,000 already invested in release prints) and reshoot the final sequence (he also added Joseph Cotten's voice-over narration as a framing device). Robson's services were not required for Welles's fix-up.

While Welles was working on his authorized version of *Journey,* the talk of the studio was the phenomenonal success of *Cat People.* When the revamped *Journey* was released in March 1943, the newspaper ads promised to pit "Terror Man" (Welles) in some standoff battle with "Leopard Woman" (Delores Del Rio), though these two "major contestants" are never even seen in the same room together. It is curious that Welles should be billed "Terror Man," because he had turned down the roles of Quasimodo and Dr. Jekyll/Hyde in order to avoid being typecast as a horror actor. Welles had done nothing with *Kane* or *Ambersons* to warrant the publicity department's peculiar label. But the public knew why Welles was billed as the "Terror Man": because the boy wonder of the air waves had terrified a nation with a 1938 radio broadcast. Little did RKO publicity realize that marketing *Journey into Fear* as an ersatz Lewton chiller was not as misleading as they intended it to be.

Most of *Journey* takes place aboard a cargo boat traveling the Black Sea (making Lewtonphiles wonder if the boat is ever within sight of the producer's Yalta homeland). The Eric Ambler story was a rather minor espionage tale which in itself is nothing like the plot of *The Ghost Ship.* However, in the hands of Orson Welles, Ambler's novel was used primarily to create a spooky, expressionistic atmosphere aboard deck. Their plot differences notwithstanding, the Welles film and the Lewton/Robson film have a very similar look (in fact, both films make use of the same portside set). Aside from Robson's connecting threads, *Journey* and *Ghost* share other RKO/Lewton traits: Albert D'Agostino's art direction, Darrell Silvera's set decoration, Vernon L. Walker's special effects, and Roy Webb's musical score. *The Ghost Ship*'s visuals certainly have more in common with *Journey into Fear* than they do with Michael Curtiz's equally expressionistic *Sea Wolf* (1941).

Journey's German émigré photographer, Karl Struss, had previously displayed expressionistic flourishes in Paramount's early–1930s classic horror opuses, *Dr. Jekyll and Mr. Hyde* and *Island of Lost Souls.* Struss would also photograph *Tarzan and the Leopard Woman* (1946), which was given yet another Lewton-bandwagon marketing ploy from RKO.

Journey's protagonist, Howard Graham (Joseph Cotten), is a confused and frightened American ammunitions executive who is separated from his wife in Turkey. The authorities show him a photograph of a man who has been hired to kill him. Via a complicated plot, Graham winds up sharing passage with an odd combination of humans and livestock on a most unfriendly Turkish cargo boat, all in an effort to avoid the hired killer. When the boat is out to sea, Graham recognizes the face of one of the passengers—from a photograph.

And this is where *Journey* and *Ghost* converge. Graham knows he is marked for death, but when he asks for help, the captain (who does not speak English) only laughs—continuously, in fact. Graham retires to his private cabin, but when he reaches under the mattress for the gun he brought as protection, he finds it missing. The paranoia becomes as palpable as the night air as Graham moves about the ship, looking for some kind of sanctuary and getting no help from an amused crew.

In one scene, Graham walks down a dark chamber, and we see a black form creeping out of the shadows to follow, coming closer, and now upon him, ready to jab something into his back: "Bang!" the captain yells, pulling his forefinger away from Graham's back, as he breaks into paroxysms of foolish laughter over the unfunny practical joke. One can easily imagine Robson being impressed by this early "bus"-like device while editing *Journey into Fear* and then putting the false scare effect into more dynamic practice in the Lewton films. If the Lewton "bus" is nothing more than a stylishly executed false scare, then it is fitting that Robson's "invention" was inspired by the boy wonder who, via his infamous radio broadcast, turned the false scare into a national event.

Modern film critics, many of them horror specialists, hold mostly favorable opinions of *The Ghost Ship*. Although some are reserved in their praise for the film, they unanimously agree upon the effectiveness of Richard Dix's performance. Phil Hardy, in *The Encyclopedia of Horror Movies,* calls the film, "Elegantly crafted with handsome sets, making evocative use of a sea-shanty score, and sketching a Hitchcockian transference-of-guilt theme, the film has little real horror unless one sees the giant hook which breaks loose during a storm and has to be subdued, as a monster threatening the crew." *The RKO Story* calls the film "another tightly coiled and penetrating study of psychological impairment. . . . In his final role for the studio, Richard Dix played a heavy for the first time in his career and contributed a potent, unnerving performance under Mark Robson's controlled direction." The *Penguin Encyclopedia of Horror and the Supernatural* asserts: "*The Ghost Ship* is, in fact, more personal than some of Lewton's better-known films. . . . Besides its atmosphere of menace and desolation and the variation that later scenes play on Lewton's theme of death in life, . . . *The Ghost Ship* is notable for Dix's restrained performance, at a time when Hollywood usually treated psychosis as an excuse for histrionics."

But *The Ghost Ship* is still officially a lost film. In the 1950s, a package of the Lewton films was sold to television; the opening RKO logos were cut and replaced by "C & C Television Films." Although *The Ghost Ship* somehow managed to make its way to television with the "C & C" batch, the film was shortly thereafter withdrawn from circulation. Only pirated (and usually inferior) videotapes of rare 16 mm C & C Television prints of the film exist today.

How curious that the mighty power of William Randolph Hearst could not wrest RKO's *Citizen Kane* from the grip of Orson Welles, while a couple of would-be scriptwriters managed to impound and bury a modest, uncontroversial thriller, making it virtually unavailable for a half century. One can only hope that some day this hostage horror film will finally be given widespread and legal release. Until that time comes, however, *The Ghost Ship,* like the *Flying Dutchman,* will maintain its elusive course: heard about, but seldom seen.

ELEVEN

The Curse of the Cat People

> ***His philosophy, in addition to scaring the wits out of people, was that he had a responsibility to the millions who saw our pictures. He aimed at more than mere exploitable crook shows, and wanted their impact to result from legitimate psychological conflicts. Lewton's pictures were cheaply made, but not cheap.***
>
> —ROBERT WISE
> *Films in Review,*
> January 1963

Robert Wise had been a friend and frequent guest of the Lewtons even before he was signed to edit the "dreaded sequel" to *Cat People*. Mark Robson was in his last two days of shooting on the ill-fated *Ghost Ship* when the sixth Lewton film, *The Curse of the Cat People,* went into production. The front office—namely Charles Koerner and "B" unit head Sid Rogell (who had replaced Lew Ostrow)—had provided the highly exploitable title, much to Lewton's chagrin. Actually, the studio brass had been encouraging the *Cat People* sequel for close to a year, and Lewton's numerous delays over research, scripting, and the procurement of key cast members (from the original film) could no longer forestall the inevitable.

In a 1991 interview with the author, Robert Wise said, "Val, being the kind of man he was, hated the idea of something called *The Curse of the Cat People.* That was the front office's idea, a sequel to match the commercial success of the first picture. Val resisted for ages and ages and finally he had to give in, and they just insisted they wanted a picture called, *The Curse of the Cat People.*"

But Lewton also enjoyed the challenge that came with turning a sow's ear title into a worthwhile movie. He met that challenge with *The Curse of the Cat People* which ultimately became a personal triumph for the RKO producer. To an extent, Lewton had to play by the rules; he had to deliver a production that met the marketing standards of a horror film. At the same time, he needed to feel he had the upper hand with his superiors. Remember, this was the man who could talk himself into believing that something as innoc-

A less lurid, but equally misleading, RKO ad.

uous as an odd-colored tie or a particular kind of floral bouquet was tantamount to a glove across the face.

Ironically, studio interference did stimulate Lewton's creative talents because he continually had to find new ways of circumventing his superiors' instructions. Lewton avenged himself by achieving excellence and box-office success even while he ignored most of the suggestions that came from above. Outside of having to give in on the often ludicrous titles, Lewton consistently maintained a level of artistic independence, and, as his films attest, he did it in grand fashion. When *The Curse of the Cat People* was released, its title was declared ill-chosen by every film reviewer in the nation; and, yet, the film itself was heralded by scores of movie critics and caught the attention of universities, psychological circles, and parent groups. It is probable that Lewton, in a Walter Mitty–like reverie, envisioned this triumph as a glorious slap in the face to Sid Rogell.

Lewton proposed to make a film that was only peripherally related to *Cat People*; his employment of much of the same cast primarily served as a cover to placate the front office about the film's official status as a sequel. In reality, *Curse* was as different from its predecessor as a sequel could get. Robert Wise told the author: "Val sat down and wrote a lovely story that could be called *The Curse of the Cat People* because he had some of the same characters from the first film in the second film. Actually what it was was a most interesting study in child psychology. And that's how Val managed to make something he could live with that would still carry that title."

What Lewton provided was a sequel removed from its source. The setting was the country (rather than the city), the central focus a young girl (rather than a tragic woman), Alice and Oliver were now parents (rather than workmates), and the character of Irena was warm and benevolent (rather than alternately pathetic and menacing). Lewton only retained elements of the original film so long as they suited the purpose of his new story. There is no real curse in the film, unless we refer to the couple's unpleasant memories. No doubt to Lewton the film's only curse was its title.

Because Robson would be busy finishing *The Ghost Ship*, Lewton was forced to search for another director for the *Cat People* sequel. After writing his own version of the story, which included autobiographical touches from his own childhood, Lewton sent DeWitt Bodeen to Tarrytown, New York (a few miles north of Lewton's Port Chester home) for purposes of research. Robert Wise, who had just finished editing RKO's noirish *The Fallen Sparrow*, was chosen to edit *Curse*, while a newcomer with documentary experience, Gunther Von Fritsch, was signed on as director. Production commenced on August 26, 1943, this time with a shooting schedule of a mere 18 days. According to DeWitt Bodeen:

> *Curse of the Cat People,* the last of his films that I worked on, was Val's conception entirely. When he was given the assignment to make the sequel ... he groaned because he was told to call it *The Curse of the Cat People* [without success, Lewton hoped to persuade the front office to let him change the title to the equally uninspired *Amy and Her Friend*—Ed.]. So he said: "What I'm going to do is make a very delicate story of a child who is on the verge of insanity because she lives in a fantasy world." I would say that my most important contribution to the story was the old lady, played by Julia Dean. Val was quite tenacious about nobody touching that character in the script. ... In a way I was responsible for Miss Dean getting the part because a number of character actresses were considered, but I suggested to the casting director that Val come and see Miss Dean at tea. There was an important sequence in the film concerning a tea party and I thought if Val could see the way she pours tea he would want her. And so Gunther von Fritsch, Val and I went to tea with her and a few days later he came to me and said: "You'll be glad to know she's got the part." [Brosnan, *The Horror People.*]

(Julia Dean [1878–1952] had been a well-known American stage actress whose career blossomed shortly after the turn of the century. Previous to *Curse,* her last motion picture, *How Molly Made Good,* had been made in 1915. After her marvelous performance in Lewton's film, she would play character roles in several other films.)

After a few weeks Fritsch was called off the assignment. The trade papers were curious, and RKO answered queries by announcing that Fritsch had been drafted into the service. In truth, Fritsch's directing methods had been overly meticulous on *Curse;* obviously, not all directors are well suited to a high-pressured 18-day shoot. When less than half the expected shooting was completed in this period of time, Lewton suggested that Wise be allowed to finish the film. According to a 1988 interview conducted by Delbert Winans (*Midnight Marquee,* issue 37), Robert Wise reports:

> I was called on a Saturday morning to go across the street from the RKO Studios to a restaurant called "Lucy's" to meet with Lewton and Sid Rogell. ... They explained to me what they wanted to do and I was happy but hesitant. In those days we worked six days a week and I was supposed to work with Gunther that night. Rogell was a man who never mixed words; he looked at me and said, "Bob, I'm just going to tell you one thing, somebody is going to be directing that film Monday morning. It's not going to be Gunther, so what's it going to be, you or someone else?" I told him I would be there. In a way that was my break. I had been wanting a chance to direct. I had been doing some second unit directing and pick-up scenes on films I had been editing. When I look back on it, it was better for me to have short notice because I didn't have all those weeks before we started shooting to be worried about my first major project. I was nervous that Monday morning, but I knew the cast and crew because I had edited ... half of the film.

Although the final directing credit is given to both Fritsch and Wise (Fritsch's name is, in fact, billed first), Robert Wise is widely acknowledged as the primary director of the film (though he is reluctant to underplay Fritsch's role in the final product). In a 1991 interview, Robert Wise told the author:

> I would think the film is about fifty/fifty, half mine and half Gunther's. Gunther had used up his whole schedule and had only shot half of the script. Practically all of Gunther's film is in there as well as mine. There was nothing reshot, it wasn't a question of having to go in and reshoot things because the filming that Gunther had done was poor. They were happy enough with his rushes, but they just couldn't afford to let him go on at that rate and have the picture cost twice as much as the budget allowed. I was given ten days to finish the film. I did it in the ten days so I couldn't tell you now which stuff he shot or I shot. I do know that I shot all the snow scenes at the end. And with the old house all the exteriors, the interiors, the scenes with Julia Dean, all those things were mine. Maybe I did do a little more than half the film, but I want to point out that we didn't have to reshoot any of *The Curse of the Cat People.*

Robert Wise told the author in 1992, "I think that tremendous credit for the look of the film goes to Nicholas Musuraca, a fine cinematographer who was an expert at low-key lighting, and he was able to do marvelous things, particularly in black-and-white." The art directing team of D'Agostino/Keller, along with set decorators Darrell Silvera and William Stevens, again lent their expert assistance, once more with the help of existing sets from *The Magnificent Ambersons.* The film was blessed by another sumptuous Roy Webb musical score. Aside from the cast members reprising their roles (Simone Simon, Kent Smith, Jane Randolph), Lewton's "gallery of stars" included Elizabeth Russell (in the role of her career), Erford Gage, Sir Lancelot, and Eve March. The final touch was the casting of seven-year-old Ann Carter in the pivotal role of Amy Reed. Because of the switch in directors, the shooting schedule was extended, but the front office insisted that Wise shoot a few extra scenes that would make the film more exploitable. *The Curse of the Cat People* wrapped up its production on October 4, 1944, and opened in theaters in March of the following year, making it the fourth of five Lewton features completed in 1943, Lewton's most prolific year.

The film begins with a vivid, richly composed opening shot, a group of elementary school children following their teacher, Miss Callahan (Eve March), down a wooded path as the sun casts its sparkling radiance through networks of tree branches. It is our first taste of one of the more remarkable aspects of this film—the fruitful teaming of Musuraca and Wise. The texture of the photography in *Curse*'s wonderfully intricate daylit scenes is extraordinarily crisp and vivid, providing visuals that appear rooted in childhood memories. Surely we have not lately viewed the natural world with such brilliance as we see here. The close-ups of Amy, her blonde hair backlit by the sun, are especially good. Even when some of *Curse*'s exterior scenes become obviously set-bound, they possess a lyrical quality that transcends their artificial origins, much in the way that the set-bound *I Walked with a Zombie* achieved a poetic brilliance.

When the children advance to a stone bridge, Miss Callahan informs them that they are in the area of Tarrytown known as Sleepy Hollow, where they will spend the remainder of their afternoon picnic. A black cat is seen perched in a tree, and one of the young boys pretends to shoot it down.

At the picnic, the children sit in a circle on the grass and play a game, but whenever it is Amy's turn, she is off in a dream world. Her schoolmates complain, but she ignores them to go off and pursue a passing butterfly. Amy addresses the fluttering swallowtail: "Oh my beautiful. You're my friend. Come play with me." When a boy, eager to please, captures the butterfly and accidently crushes it, she slaps him in the face. Within the first two minutes, Amy has all the audience sympathy a screen character could ever hope to muster.

Amy's parents are summoned as a result of the slapping incident, and the three adults (Oliver, Alice, and Miss Callahan) discuss the nature of the offense, while Oliver expresses his particular worry: "Amy has too many fancies and too few friends." Oliver dwells on the memory of Irena and her fanciful notions, believing her diseased and overactive imagination to have been responsible for her fate. As a result, he cannot react to Amy's fantasy world in the way a normal father should; Amy's behavior touches a very tender old wound. "There's something moody, something sickly about Amy. She could almost be Irena's child," Oliver tells his wife, who counters that he thinks too much about Irena.

The scene of Amy's birthday party, which soon follows, was based upon an incident from Lewton's own childhood. In the film, it is party-time and not a single one of Amy's schoolmates have shown up, despite the assurance that the invitations were sent. As her parents remain in their preparty limbo, we cut back to Amy, who is shown waiting on the porch, wearing her party dress and looking lonely and disappointed.

Oliver finally discovers that Amy placed the invitations in a hole in an old tree in their backyard; Oliver had once told her, when she was very young, that the tree was a "magic mailbox." It's a very sad moment, as this means no one will attend Amy's party. (Strangely, Oliver does not do much to remedy the situation, even though his own misinformation was the direct cause of all the disappointment.)

But the party must go on, even if the only attendees are Amy's parents and Edward (Sir Lancelot), their houseboy. Although Amy seems chipper enough, this intimate affair is such a poor substitute for the planned festivities that it only underscores her sense of loss. She gets mixed messages on the fantasy-vs.-reality issue when she is asked to make a birthday wish and blow out the candles. It is disturbing when Amy announces her wish to be "the good girl that my Daddy wants me to be," as if her flights of fantasy are

Amy (Ann Carter) has little luck getting through to her father (Kent Smith) while he's preoccupied with his ship model.

unwholesome and her self-image that of a "bad" girl. Amy promises she will make a real effort to play with the other children.

The next day, when Amy tries to make good on her promise, her friends ignore her, feeling slighted in the belief that they were not invited to her party, despite her attempted explanation. When her friends ditch her, Amy finds herself standing alone near the spooky Farren house, an elaborate but physically neglected mansion occupied by two reclusive women reputed to be witches. (If the dwelling looks familiar, that is because it's the Amberson house from Orson Welles's second RKO production, the interior of which—take note of the impressive staircase—was also used in *Cat People* and *The Seventh Victim*.)

The voice of an old woman (Julia Dean) calls from a second story window: "Little girl! Little girl! Come into the garden." Walking past the griffinlike gargoyles that guard the front door, Amy obeys the command, and the woman throws down a handkerchief weighted by a small object. Amy is examining the gift, a finger ring tied to the corner of the handkerchief, when she is jolted by the sudden appearance of Barbara Farren (Elizabeth Russell), a younger, but infinitely more menacing, presence than the woman in the window. If looks could kill, Amy would be dead and buried.

After racing home and showing her ring to Edward (who tells her it might

Barbara Farren (Elizabeth Russell). If looks could kill, Amy would be dead and buried. (This photograph isn't from the Lewton film, but represents Russell's icy glare.)

be a magic wishing ring), Amy goes to Oliver's workshop to explain why she was not able to play with her friends. Oliver ignores his daughter's sense of urgency as he beams with pride over the wonderful ship model he has built for her. When Amy finally gets her point across, telling her father how her friends shunned her, Oliver is not a fount of sympathy: "I shouldn't be surprised. I couldn't blame them," he says, forgetting that it was not entirely Amy's fault that they did not receive the invitations.

(One wonders why Oliver does not take the responsibility of calling the children's homes, offering apology and explanation. Some parents might have even set another party date, but not Oliver, a man who would rather spend his hours in the boyish task of building boat models. Oliver is just as much at play in his own world as Amy is in hers. Their relationship appears to mirror some of the friction between Lewton and his daughter Nina. That is if we wish to see, in Oliver, Lewton the yachtsman/craftsman, the man who constructed parts for his boat in his downstairs workshop and made homemade toys for his daughter and son. But we can also see Lewton, the highly imaginative child whose wild fancies were a nuisance to his guardians, in the character of Amy.)

When Amy explains about the old lady and the ring, Oliver sharply accuses her of lying. Alice comes in to interrupt his remonstrations, and she is understandably miffed that her husband will not hear the child out. When all this leads to a heated argument, Amy begins to cry, thinking she is the cause of their discontent: "I made you fight."

Amy goes out to play in the backyard (an obvious, albeit extremely stylish, set), wearing her ring and wishing aloud for a friend. Leaves, descending like oversized snowflakes, fall from the trees while the lighting shifts. Amy's face brightens, and though we are not privileged to see what she sees, it is clear that her wish has been granted. From within the house, Edward and Oliver look out to see Amy playing in the yard, skipping along with her arm held out, as if holding someone's hand.

Alice, who does not believe in accepting gifts from strangers, sends her daughter out to return the ring, not realizing its place of origin. Edward is supposed to accompany Amy on her mission, but he is too busy vacuuming Oliver's boat models: "You went there yesterday by yourself; I suppose you can go back there by yourself today."

Amy's reticence is clearly visible as she knocks on the door of the Farren house; the moment provides us with the kind of chills we have come to expect from Lewton. When the door is opened, the young girl is greeted by the hardened countenance of Barbara Farren; Amy explains her mission. Barbara says not a word, and disquieting thoughts register in Amy's eyes as she watches the gaunt woman glide down the stairway, her face lit from below. As she descends, her gaze is fixed upon Amy. Anxiously biding her time and perhaps thinking better of her decision to come alone, Amy goes back to the front door. Discovering it to be locked, she uneasily makes her way into another room. There she is assaulted by a bizarre array of animal trophies, immortalized by taxidermy. We see a particularly grotesque bit of work, a large and vicious-looking cat holding a mangled bird in its mouth (recalling a moment in Mammoulian's *Dr. Jekyll and Mr. Hyde*). Amy backs away, only to be startled as the pages of an open book riffle from a draft.

The tension is perfect for a "bus," which is what we get with some startling laughter and a sudden burst of light. The petrified girl looks back to see a mirthful Julia Farren (Julia Dean) throwing open the drapes. The old woman turns out to be a warm and gracious, albeit somewhat garrulous, retired actress of the theater, who was once one of the stage's shining stars.

With the opening of the drapes, the atmosphere of the room takes a comforting turn. Julia Farren is decked in elaborate attire—evening dress, pearls, jewelry—which matches the interior decor of her home. But these things, the furnishings, the bric-a-brac, Julia's attire, are befitting of an earlier era, like Miss Haversham's cobwebbed wedding cake in *Great Expectations*. It is apparent that Julia Farren is preparing for her final act with the darkest of leading men.

When Amy explains her visit, Julia refuses to accept the ring. Instead, the spirited old woman reminisces about her stage experience, while Barbara stands in the adjoining threshold, staring icily at Amy. To Amy, Julia whispers: "She's always spying on me. That woman is an imposter, a liar and a cheat. My daughter, Barbara, died when she was six."

Edward arrives to bring Amy home, but she persuades him to let her stay for a story Julia is about to tell, her abbreviated-but-chilling rendition of Washington Irving's "The Legend of Sleepy Hollow." Some effective background music accompanies the tale, along with the addition of hoofbeats on the soundtrack. Amy looks scared, and we cannot blame her, especially when Julia moves closer and her face reflects light from below (like the old flashlight-under-the-chin Halloween trick). By this point, Amy is quite happy to leave.

That night while Amy is sleeping, her bedroom walls awash with moonlight and the shifting shadows of tree branches, we begin to hear Julia's creepy voice-over repeating her headless horseman story, galloping hoofs on the soundtrack coming closer, growing louder. Amy wakes with a start, the memory of her nightmare continuing to haunt her in this dark and quiet room. Her parents are downstairs with company, playing a card game. Alice halts for a moment, thinking that she has heard Amy call, and then goes back to her play. Oliver simply stares into space, his mind not on the game.

The frightened girl calls upon her imaginary friend. A woman's shadow moves along the floor and stretches across Amy's bed. A soothing female voice hums a peaceful lullaby (Irena's theme from *Cat People*). We never see the source of the shadow.

The next day Amy comes across a photograph of Irena. Alice, though a little distressed at the discovery, tries to be honest. "Her name was Irena," she says, and lets the matter drop. When Alice tells Oliver about this, he becomes so distressed that he gathers up and destroys all his souvenirs of Irena (mostly photographs). "I hope we'll never have to tell Amy about her," he says.

Oliver may claim he wishes to bury the memory of Irena, but his actions indicate that he is clearly the one most responsible for keeping her ghostly memory alive. Hereafter, when Amy's friend arrives, she is in the image of Irena, presumably because the photograph of Irena gave Amy's imaginary friend a physical identity. Out first view of Amy's imaginary friend shows her

Julia Farren (Julia Dean). A nice old lady in a spooky house. Notice stuffed cat (with a mouthful of bird) on branch, at left.

dressed in a rather erotic medieval gown (nothing at all like any of Irena's dresses in *Cat People*). A scene that never made the release print shows Amy looking at a book of fairy tales and seeing an illustration of a princess wearing the gown in question, thus reinforcing the possibility of a psychological explanation for otherwise supernatural events. Without the storybook sequence, we have no idea why the previously fashionable Irena came back wearing a medieval gown.

The relationship between Amy and Irena is nicely built, with a series of shots bridging the passage of time. In one scene, Irena helps Amy to learn her numbers (inspired by an event in Lewton's childhood); in another, Amy introduces her array of dolls to Irena. Irena's benevolence is well established and totally convincing; her character in this film is nothing like the dark persona we associate from Simone Simon's other Irena role. Indeed, apart from her accent, Simon could be a different character entirely. When asked of her origins, she says, "I come from great darkness and deep peace."

A series of dissolves show further passage of time, and it is now Christmas Eve. Amy has a number of presents for family and acquaintances, including a 25¢ ring for Julia Farren and a mysterious gift for someone she refuses to name (a pin she has purchased for Irena). A group of Christmas carolers are heard in the front yard, and Alice opens the door and invites them in. One of the carolers, a young girl a few years older than Amy, is surprised that the Reeds have not yet opened their presents: "We open our presents on Christmas Eve. That's considered proper." Amy, revealing more truth than she intends, answers, "Well, I guess we're not a very proper family."

On Christmas Day, Amy and Edward go to the Farren house to drop off Julia's present. Julia is sitting near her gruesome piece of taxidermy while Barbara is peering in from her usual threshold spot. A large unopened present looms in the foreground.

Julia is overwhelmed by the child's thoughtfulness: "It's been so long since I've had a Christmas present." Amy points out the large one that remains unopened and Julie answers, "Oh, that's from her. That woman." Julia's throwaway affection to a virtual stranger makes Barbara seethe with jealousy.

Amy leaves and we remain in this cold house with these two women. (To Elizabeth Russell's credit, the pathos she is able to achieve with a character as sinister as Barbara Farren is quite amazing.) The image of Barbara's unopened gift, and its accompanying theme of rejection, achieves the same level of poignancy as the magic mailbox episode. "Look at me mother!" Barbara tells Julia, "I am your daughter." But Julia will not even look her way. We never realized it before, but the cold, mean-spirited Barbara Farren is also a heartbroken daughter. At this point in the film, the ambivalence we feel toward both Farren women is very disturbing.

The crisis for Amy starts when she chances upon another photograph; this time it is a picture of a happy, smiling couple: Oliver and Irena. Thrilled by the discovery, Amy blurts out: "Daddy! You know my friend, too!" Oliver looks as though he has been handed a hornets' nest and tells his daughter it just is not possible that she has seen Irena. He takes Amy out to the backyard to prove her wrong. Oliver wants to know, is Irena there now? Yes, Amy admits, seeing Irena in her usual spot. Losing his temper, Oliver banishes Amy to her room.

Miss Callahan is on hand to try to talk some sense into Oliver, saying it is perfectly normal for a six-year-old to have an imaginary friend. It is then that Oliver gives her the dark details about his past life, "She [Irena] was someone who told lies to herself and believed them. . . . She killed a man and then killed herself."

Up in her bedroom, the dejected girl turns her prison into a sanctuary by summoning Irena. This spectral playmate, seemingly aware of the disharmony she has caused between the young girl and her father, announces that she must leave Amy's life. They have been friends and have had a wonderful time, "But now you must send me away." Irena makes her sad departure, but to director Wise's credit, she does not vanish courtesy of special effects, but rather by a refreshingly resourceful kind of cinematic sleight-of-hand, a spatial illusion created by the movement of the camera, followed by the back of a chair blocking the foreground. Once the camera moves past the chair, Amy's playmate is gone.

When Amy sneaks out of the house in search of Irena, she immediately goes to the back yard, but despite the young girl's beckoning calls, there is no sign of her friend. Shivering from the cold, but undaunted by the falling snow, Amy leaves the yard to continue her search elsewhere, as the storm steadily builds. Oliver, Alice, and Miss Callahan become frantic when they notice Amy's absence and call the police. Oliver and Alice discover their daughter's footsteps in the snow and begin their own pursuit; Oliver swears he will believe whatever Amy says from now on, if he can have her back, safe and warm.

Amy treads her way through snowdrift-altered paths, finding herself on the Tarrytown backroad leading to the Sleepy Hollow bridge. Her fear builds with every step as she begins crossing the bridge, and (via a reprisal of Julia Farren's voice-over) she vividly recalls the story of the headless horseman. When she is only halfway across, Amy hears the galloping of a horse, and she realizes it's not just her imagination. Petrified, she kneels down near the stone wall that flanks the bridge. The camera moves in on her horrified face as the galloping grows louder, coming closer with each breath. A shadow passes over the girl's huddled form, the shadow of an automobile whose loose tirechains, hitting the underside, approximate the sound of a galloping horse.

At the Farren house, Barbara paces like a cat in a cage. "I hate this storm," she says.

Julia remarks, "It was on a night like this that Barbara died."

"Look at me!" insists Barbara, tears beginning to well in her eyes. "I'm your daughter. You lost your memory in the accident. Can't you see that I'm your daughter?"

"You're just a poor lost woman," Julia says, with genuine pity. "You're not my Barbara."

The daughter's eyes harden even while the tears remain. "You're always worse after that little girl is here. If she comes here again, I'll kill her. . . . Yes, I'll kill her!"

The sounds of barking dogs fill the night; the police and their bloodhounds have joined the search. The storm is getting worse, and the baying of hounds only makes Amy become even more frightened. Irena is nowhere to be found. Having given up her search and sensing the danger of exposure from the storm, Amy trudges to the closest shelter within reach: the Farren house.

Mrs. Farren hears a pounding at her front door and, cane in hand, hobbles over to open it. Remembering Barbara's oath, Julia works herself into a frenzy looking for a place to hide Amy. They climb the stairs, but the strain is too much for the old woman, who, halfway up the staircase, suffers a coronary, collapses, and dies. The realization of Julia's death registers upon Amy as she looks about in desperation. Glancing over the banister, down the stairwell to the floor below, Amy sees some curtains shifting in the wind and then the shadow and then the face of Barbara Farren.

Now Barbara stands at the bottom of the stairs occupied by Amy and her dead mother: "Even my mother's last moments you've stolen from me. Come here." Amy sits tight. "Come here, I said!" Amy calls for help, first to her father and then to her imaginary friend. After an uncomfortable pause, Amy's beaming expression tells us Irena has arrived. There she is, standing at the bottom of the stairs, exactly in the place where the awful woman was standing just moments before. "My friend," Amy says adoringly, while we get another look and see Barbara, not Irena. Amy rushes down the stairs to embrace the woman. Barbara is taken aback by the strange way the girl is behaving, but it is plain that she still intends to kill her. There is a close shot of the back of Amy's head while Barbara's stiff, clutching fingers come into the frame from both sides, the hands lightly positioning themselves around Amy's neck. Amy hugs even tighter, "My friend, you've come back to me. Thank you, thank you."

Another close-up shows Barbara's hands straining, frozen with indecision, until finally, Amy's show of love, given so freely and unconditionally, works its magic upon the affection-starved woman, somehow quelling both her anger and her hate. Barbara's arms fall to Amy's back where they move to return her embrace while the woman stares ahead . . . at nothing.

Barbara's change of heart comes not a second too soon, for the search party has arrived at the Farren house. Oliver rushes to Amy's side, and Barbara walks off into the interior of the house, never to be seen again.

And all is well. Or is it? The police find Julia's body and inform headquarters. Amy goes home with her father, and both go into the backyard. "Is she in the yard now?" Oliver asks, looking at Amy. "Yes," answers Amy. "I see her, too," Oliver answers, though he never actually looks in Irena's direction. The pat, happy ending, it would seem.

The Curse of the Cat People does end with some forced optimism, but the underlying dark currents of the Farren subplot remain with us after the happy ending is long forgotten. Is everything as resolved as Oliver would have us believe? Does Oliver really see eye-to-eye with Amy? Or is he only humoring a little girl? Is it not odd that Oliver is incapable of seeing Irena when he is the only character who is truly haunted by her ghost?

As far as Barbara is concerned, the film's conclusion takes an even more grim turn. What does the future hold for her? The one scrap of affection that entered Barbara's life and softened her heart—Amy's embrace—was not even meant for her. Will Amy ever return to the Farren house to make friends with Barbara? Not likely. All probability tells us Barbara will remain a recluse until the day she dies which, given the depths of her depression, may be right around the corner.

"But the whole ending of the picture," said scriptwriter DeWitt Bodeen "is not mine at all. Val, after the preview, thought that the ending did not come off. He came up to me on the lot one day and told me that he had a new ending for it and described it to me. I said I was not very moved by it and that I didn't see the ending that way. He said: 'Well, I'm not asking you to see it, I'm going to write the ending.' Which he did and that is the ending you see on the picture" (Brosnan, *Horror People*).

In *Classics of the Horror Film,* William K. Everson reveals that "In one version of the climax . . . the ghost of the former Cat Woman played a far more positive and melodramatic role, including the unlocking of a jammed closet door to enable the child to hide from the crazed woman who seeks to kill her. In the final release version, this element was eliminated and fairy tale magic won out over prolonged suspense, a preferable solution. Despite the occasionally uneven quality throughout, one feels that this is one of those rare cases where the fussing was justified and where the final version was not a 'butchery' of what might have been."

It is curious that the links between Amy Reed and Barbara Farren remain so elusive in the finished film because they were intended to function as doubles: both characters, as a result of some degree of parental alienation, live a private, isolated existence, just like Irena Dubrovna.

But all of the film's major characters suffer from some form of isolation. Oliver lives in a world of model boats and shattered dreams (he still has not gotten over the loss of Irena). Alice's world seems like that of the conventional homemaker, but she is not happy living in the shadow of the past, having to measure up to her husband's former wife. Julia, of course, lives in the past: a Miss Haversham of the stage. Even Edward and Miss Callahan occupy isolated existences. Edward, a black man in a white world, loses himself in his work. So does Miss Callahan, a lonely spinster who fills her world with theories of education and child psychology, a woman whose adult social life appears to hinge on conferences with parents. (Miss Callahan becomes such a regular member of the Reed household, one wonders if she has in fact become a boarder.)

As is the case with most of the Lewton films, *The Curse of the Cat People* is open to many levels of interpretation. Whether one chooses to see it as a ghost story, a study in child psychology, or a psychological thriller, the film is full of symbolism, and there is enough doubling (Amy/Barbara, Julia/Oliver, Barbara/Irena, Amy/Irena, Alice/Miss Callahan, Alice/Irena) to make anyone's head spin. The film holds up to Freudian, Jungian, and feminist interpretations.

J.P. Telotte offers some fascinating observations in *Dreams of Darkness:*

> *[The Curse of the Cat People]* points up a basic similarity between grown-ups and children which the Lewton films consistently explore . . . the play in which both children and adults engage. . . . Of course, the very number

> of these games should catch our attention, especially since they point up an equally prodigious amount of playing among the adults. This side of Oliver's character receives particular emphasis, as we see him engrossed in a tiddlywinks game set out for his daughter's party, building model ships, and playing cards with Alice and another couple. In this last instance Oliver is so preoccupied with Amy's troubles that he cannot concentrate on the game and lapses into a trancelike state, just as Amy does in an earlier "play" scene. Edward's toying with Oliver's models and Julia Farren's acting and storytelling are only a few of the other forms this play activity takes. Together these activities reveal a fundamental if often unrecognized similarity between the children and grown-ups, while they also foster a feeling of just how much the fantasizing impulse lingers, almost unnoticed, in all human activities.

And, of course, there is always the film-as-autobiography perspective. In *The Reality of Terror,* Siegel asserts that the character of Amy, in part, reflects upon Lewton's own childhood: "Ruth Lewton has described her husband as a man who, as a youngster, was forced to retreat from reality into an insubstantial world of his own creation and never quite made it back to reality." This view seems quite reasonable, as does the assumption that the has-been actress, Julia Farren, is based upon Alla Nazimova, but there is a lot of Lewton to be found in Oliver Reed as well, which leads to another interesting possibility: that Oliver and Amy both represent Lewton. Amy is Lewton as a child, the little boy with the overactive imagination and the magic mailbox, while Oliver is the older Lewton, grown-up, responsible, stodgy, and unceasingly preoccupied with his work and his hobbies. Viewed in this light, the film could reflect the unresolved tensions between the two Lewtons: Val Lewton, the serious adult—a husband, a father, a hard-working film producer, a would-be yacthsman—and Val Lewton, the irresponsible boy with a boundless imagination and a fear of the dark.

Horror film fans are mixed about *The Curse of the Cat People*; some view it as one of Lewton's weaker efforts, while others (the author included) rank it among his very best. Even critics of the time held mixed opinions. Manny Farber in a 1944 issue of *The New Republic* said, "*The Curse of the Cat People* lacks sufficient life in the significance of its insights into reality, and the playing, which is on the stiff, precarious side of naturalism, doesn't compensate for the sterility with enough vitality to make it an artistic dream movie."

James Agee, in the April 1, 1944, edition of *The Nation* concurred: "This had every right to be a first-rate movie; but good as it is, it is full of dead streaks—notably the writing, directing, and playing of the parts of the parents and the kindergarten teacher—and there are quite a few failures of imagination and of taste." Agee goes on to relate the reactions of the audience with which he viewed the film, blood-thirsty horror mavens who were obviously misled by the incredibly lurid posters for the film: "And when the picture ended and it was clear beyond further suspense that anyone who had come to see a story about curses and were-cats should have stayed away, they clearly did not feel sold out; for an hour they had been captivated by the poetry and danger of childhood, and they showed it in their thorough applause." Despite Agee's somewhat qualified praise, a few months later his appreciation of the film appeared to soar; in the January 20, 1945, issue of *The Nation*, Agee states: "The best fiction films of the year, *The Curse of the Cat People* and *Youth Runs Wild*, were made by Val Lewton and his associates. I esteem them so highly because for all their unevenness their achievements are so consistently alive, limber, poetic, humane, so eager toward the possibilities of the screen, and so resolutely against the grain of all we have learned to expect from the big studios."

The Curse of the Cat People is, first of all, an absolute charmer and nothing less than top-shelf Lewton. It is extraordinarily photographed, well acted (with Ann Carter, Julia Dean, and Elizabeth Russell turning in superb performances), intelligently written, and sensitively directed (by both Wise and Fritsch). Because the focus is upon a little girl, it is a unique entry to the series. It is also refreshing in having no need for the kind of artificial romantic lead we find in many of the other Lewton films. Kent Smith's Oliver is a bland character, to be sure, but at least he is essential to the core of the film (as he was in the original).

Ann Carter's sensitive, nonstagy performance is quite remarkable (especially coming from a seven-year-old) and shows that director Wise's highly touted ability to work with child performers was something that came ready-made with his first film. "One big asset," director Wise told the author, "was the little girl, Ann Carter. I don't view my films much, but when I do screen *The Curse of the Cat People*, I'm always struck by how good she is and how consistent her performance is throughout the whole film. Ann Carter just had one of those marvelous bits of chemistry for the screen that some actors have. She just clicked on the screen and that was it. You had to be a little patient with her but you do with all children. She was very responsive and very quick. I think its too bad she didn't go on to do more work." Carter is extremely believable in her role, which is why the film's suspense is so effective and why her Lewton walk through the snow is so harrowing.

While film critics were pleasantly surprised by the humanity found in *The Curse of the Cat People*, noted psychologists and sociologists took the praise one step higher. Soon the Los Angeles Council of Social Agencies used the film as the highlight of a seminar focusing upon treatment of children in films. As related by Joel E. Siegel in *The Reality of Terror*, "Lewton and Wise appeared and were praised not only for the soundness of the film's psychological content but also for the 'intelligent and unselfconscious' handling of the Negro servant." (Lewton films displayed noncondescending and nonpatronizing attitudes toward black characters long before such examples become fashionable in the heavier hands of Elia Kazan and Stanley Kramer.)

Robert Wise told the author, "It was very interesting; when we finished the film and showed it for groups of teachers and child psychologists, they all loved it and were mad about it, but both groups said, 'What in the world was it doing with that awful title?' And of course the funny thing about it was that *The Curse of the Cat People* started with a title."

After the Los Angeles seminar, Lewton was invited to UCLA by Dr. Fearing, the head of the child psychology clinic. The film was viewed in a lecture hall full of students, and Lewton attended to provide answers to their questions as well as take part in a discussion.

A few years later, *The Curse of the Cat People* was analyzed in *The Lonely Crowd*, a book by the distinguished sociologist, David Riesman, who "single[d] out the film for its accurate and touching depiction of childhood and the anxieties which accompany this stage of life."

Time has looked favorably upon the film. *The Penguin Encyclopedia of Horror and the Supernatural* admits that "*Curse of the Cat People* isn't the horror tale its misleading title suggests, but the film is hardly a disappointment. It is richly textured, delving into the innocent fears of childhood. It's warmly remembered by those who saw it in the war years, and remains rewarding viewing today." Dan Peary, in his *Guide for the Film Fanatic*, calls it a "gem," going on to say, "This is a truly imaginative, magical little sleeper, shot through the eyes of a child with whom the filmmakers are in total sympathy. Dealing with parental neglect, a favorite Lewton theme, as well as the power of the imagination, this was probably the first horror film ever screened at child-psychology courses." Phil Hardy's *Encyclopedia of Horror Movies* calls it "not so much horror as a delicate fantasy. . . . This film takes on a much darker aspect if considered as a sequel to *Cat People* (ideally, the two films should be screened together). . . . The blood-and-thunder melodramatics of the old dark house and its two weird inhabitants are very carefully calculated to provide a rational, daylight terror against which the unfathomable mysteries of the night can be measured. It is those unseen nocturnal mysteries which hover over the film, giving it the same chilling smell of the pit as Henry James's *The Turn of the Screw*. A marvellous little film, *The Curse of the Cat People* is one of the least condescending and least sentimental forays ever made into what James Agee called 'the poetry and danger of childhood.'"

Such enthusiastic appraisals of the film are in sharp contrast to the pronounced lack of taste of RKO's publicity department when *The Curse of the Cat People* was distributed to the theaters. As might be expected, the lobby posters exploited the superfluous cat imagery that was inserted into the film at the studio's behest (a bogus attempt to foreshadow a feline terror element that does not exist in the story).

"Strange, forbidding, thrilling . . ." says one ad, followed by a caption that reads, "Slinking into the heart of a little girl who could not see the evil behind smiling lips that could snarl, and feline fingers that could rip young flesh to shreds!" On the same poster we see a ferocious panther slinking around a sultry Simone Simon who, looking like a bare-shouldered feline seductress, wears a strapless dress that is nowhere to be found in the film. Another poster announces, "The Beast Woman Haunts the Night Anew!" promising, in smaller print, "Strange Adventures in Evil . . . of the beauty who changed into a killer-beast!" Still another ad shows Irena wearing the appropriate dress featured in the film, but this time she towers over the figures of Oliver and Alice and displays curved, catlike claws for fingernails. (Strangely enough, none of the ads feature the film's most fearsome visage, that of Elizabeth Russell's character.)

With such a misleading build-up from the RKO publicity department, *The Curse of the Cat People* was bound to disappoint members of the horror crowd. That the film was able to survive such sideshow misrepresentation, however, was a testament to both its poignance and its power.

TWELVE

Youth Runs Wild and *Mademoiselle Fifi*

> ***Val was a very really person, really textured; he was good with people and very much of a liberal, a democrat concerned about people and their well being. Val liked very much to do woodwork, to make things. He had a lathe in his garage in his home, and he used to turn out spindles, and he'd make furniture, and stools, all kinds of things. He was very, very good at it. He loved people who worked with their hands. He said that men should not have manicures because he thought that was kind of "sissy"; one's hands and fingers and nails should be like men who worked in the earth, did physical work. He said he never had a manicure, and I have to tell you something, that rubbed off on me, I guess, because I myself have never had a manicure, in all my life.***
>
> —ROBERT WISE
> from a 1991 interview
> with the author

In late June 1943, with neither *The Ghost Ship* nor *The Curse of the Cat People* yet before the cameras, Lewton was finally given a green light on a nonhorror production. It had not been an easy battle, breaking out of the genre for which he was hired, especially after he had, months before, turned his back on "A" budget filmmaking in order to launch Mark Robson's directorial career. Although Lewton hated kowtowing to his superiors, he had been so persistent in his quest to make a film outside the horror genre that Koerner eventually broke down and offered him a project, albeit one with a few strings attached.

Are These Our Children? was based upon an article in *Look* magazine and had been slated as another exercise in sensationalism for the studio's director-of-the-hour, Edward Dmytryk. Koerner offered the production chores to Lewton, though it was with the understanding that the 35-year-old Dmytryk would be the associate producer, as well as the director. This did not sit well with Lewton, who was forever loyal to his group of insiders; it was only after much coercion that he finally persuaded his superiors to drop Dmytryk altogether and allow Mark Robson to replace him as director. Dmytryk went on to such RKO "A" features as *Tender Comrade* and *Murder, My Sweet* (both 1944).

Unfortunately, *Are These Our Children?* was ill-fated from the start. The production would undergo so many difficulties that Lewton would regret ever having gotten involved. The front office wanted "an exploitational picture, pure and simple, appealing only to the sensational" (as he said in a letter to his mother and sister [Siegel, *Reality of Terror]*), but Lewton was not comfortable with such a concept and began voicing his contempt for the material. Lewton, of course, was no stranger to exploitation, as his enjoyable early-1930s novels attest, but during his years with Selznick, he had come to disclaim most of his sensationalized fiction (though Ruth Lewton recently told the author that her husband had always been proud of *No Bed of Her Own* and *Yearly Lease*). By the time he joined RKO, Lewton was not interested in mere exploitation, which is precisely why he worked so hard to turn "B" budget horror films into something resembling art.

Lewton tried to drum up some enthusiasm for *Are These Our Children?* during its initial stages of development, assigning John Fante and Herbert Kline to write a treatment based upon the *Look* magazine article. (Madeleine Dmytryk—who had already done considerable research for the project when her husband, Edward, was slated to direct—would retain her name in the credits as "topical research" adviser.) In a daring move, Lewton contacted 16-year-old Ruth Clifton of Moline, Illinois, and asked her to come to Hollywood to be the technical adviser to the film. Clifton had come to national attention after spearheading a youth center movement in her hometown; the idea caught fire, and youth centers began springing up in cities all over the country. Lewton believed Clifton's participation would further the film's credibility.

As the script evolved, the front office (knowing the producer's penchant for "legitimizing" his "B" budget programmers) made it plain that they wanted *Are These Our Children?* to be a sensationalistic exposé, like Dmytryk's *Hitler's Children* and *Behind the Rising Sun*, the latter of which was currently drawing large crowds. To prove they meant business, the studio brass ordered Lewton to shape his film around actress Bonita Granville, the female lead in *Hitler's Children*. Granville, they said, would receive top billing and hopefully attract the millions of people who found her spirited performance so appealing in Dmytryk's first box-office bonanza.

Lewton rounded out the cast with an assortment of performers from his past films: Jean Brooks, Kent Smith (who had also been in *Hitler's Children*), Ben Bard, Lawrence Tierney, Elizabeth Russell, Juanita Alvarez, and Edmund Glover, as well as numerous juvenile performers. Bonita Granville may have received top billing, but the real stars of the film—in performance as well as in screen time—were the fourth- and fifth-billed newcomers, Glenn Vernon and Tessa Brind, playing the ill-fated young lovers. Tessa Brind, like Ingrid Bergman, Kim Hunter, Jennifer Jones, and Dorothy McGuire, was a David O. Selznick discovery. (As were many of Selznick's actress protegées, Tessa Brind was urged to change her name; after her appearance in the Lewton film, her professional moniker became Vanessa Brown. She played Lana Turner's sexy younger rival in *The Bad and the Beautiful* [1952].)

As production for *Are These Our Children?* was about to commence, RKO's publicity department launched a campaign bigger than any previously given to a Lewton film. Ruth Clifton's Hollywood arrival was greeted with such ballyhoos one would have thought the modest RKO film entertained ambitions of solving, single-handedly, the problems of the nation's youth. As a result of all this preproduction attention, however, *Are These Our Children?* came under the scrutiny of the State Department, which concluded that a film focusing upon internal wartime problems could be detrimental to both the security and the morale of the country. The officials' apprehension was reinforced when they discovered that the script fingered the blame for juvenile delinquency upon a national war effort whose fervency minimized time and opportunity for proper parenting. The officials tried to talk RKO out of making the film, claiming that the Axis powers would use it as fuel for propaganda about America's mismanagement of its youth.

Lewton argued that the intent of the film was to draw attention to a national problem and help bring about measures to solve it, which would do the country more good than harm. RKO decided not to pull the film from active production, but because of its controversial subject matter, Lewton was given more supervision than usual, much to his displeasure.

Shooting began on November 3, 1943. John Fante had delivered the screenplay (with some additional dialogue by Ardell Wray); Lewton had performed his customary uncredited final revision. The Office of Censorship made it clear that they would withhold the film's export license if *Are These Our Children?* "proved too inflammatory." It turned out to be Lewton's most difficult shoot yet because the front office breathed down his neck and insisted upon seeing the daily rushes. A nervewracking experience for Lewton, the film took an arduous seven weeks to shoot, longer than any Lewton production thus far. Shooting was completed on December 21, the very day *The Ghost Ship* was released. Lewton had mixed feelings about the whole ordeal, but at least he felt he had made an "honest picture."

On March 29, 1944, Lewton's exposé on juvenile delinquency, renamed *The Dangerous Age*, was previewed to a Hillstreet Theater audience. It was paired with the Danny Kaye musical comedy, *Up in Arms*; it should have been obvious that an audience coming to see a Goldwyn-produced Danny Kaye vehicle was not an appropriate testing group for the downbeat Lewton film, especially when one of *The Dangerous Age*'s sub-plots involved a teenage boy

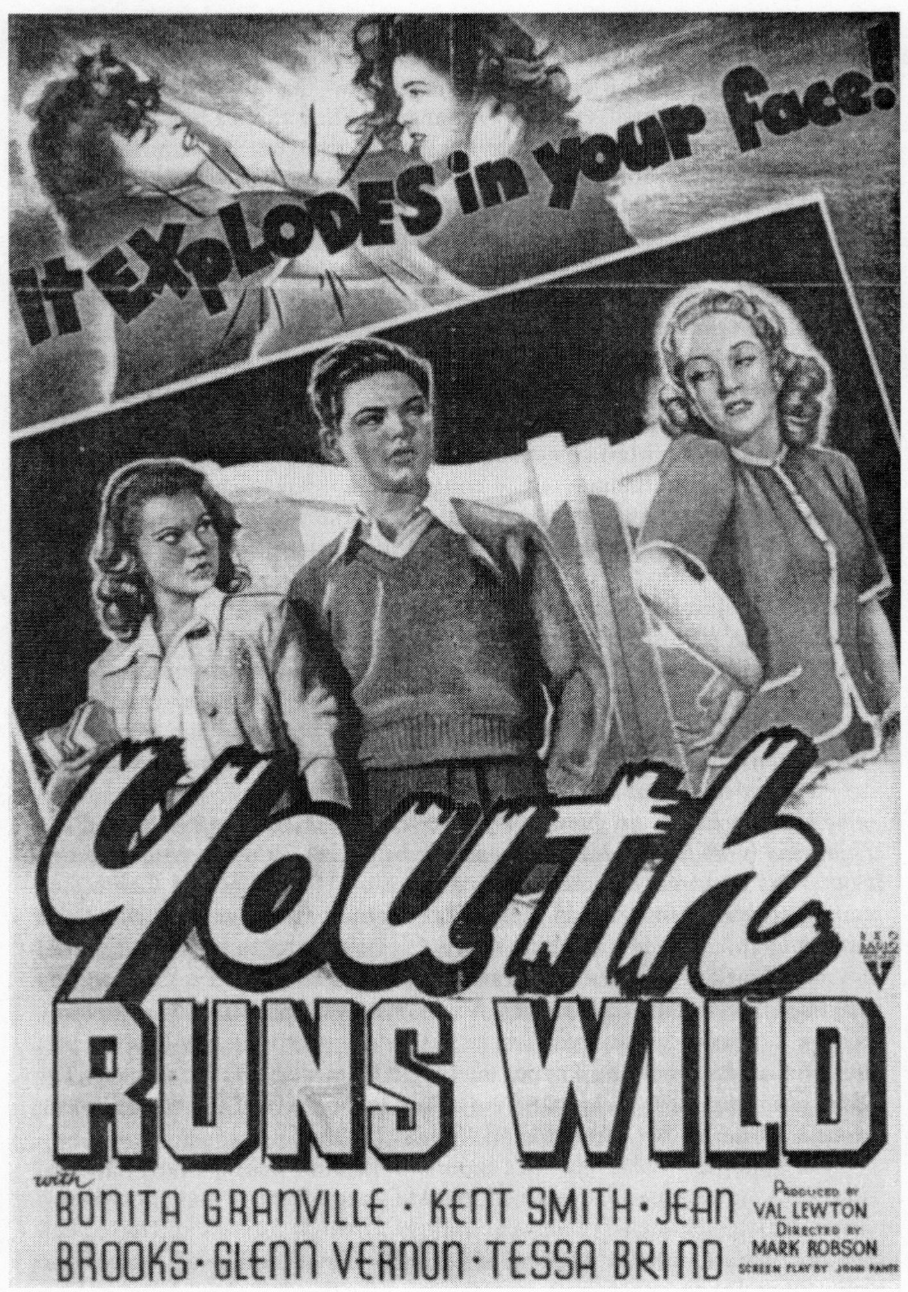

"It explodes in your face!" promised the ad for *Youth Runs Wild*.

forced to kill his abusive father. In *The Reality of Terror,* Joel E. Siegel gives a colorful account of *The Dangerous Age*'s disastrous preview, informing us that a drunk in the balcony had caused a loud ruckus in the middle of one of the film's key scenes (presumably, a scene that was instrumental to the patricide sub-plot). While the balcony audience responded with howls of laughter over the antics of the drunk, the nervous studio brass (seated downstairs) wrongly assumed the cause of the uproar to be this particular scene of the film, a scene not intended for humor. A Lewton aide reported what had caused the laughter, but the studio brass was unmoved by this explanation. Consequently, *The Dangerous Age* was yanked back to the studio for an additional five months. After extensive reshooting and reediting, the film was released in mid–September, as *Youth Runs Wild.*

The changes were considerable. Many controversial scenes were excised, and the patricide subplot was removed entirely. In addition, the studio reshot a tack-on documentary ending that offered simplistic solutions to a paramount problem. Against Lewton's wishes, the new ending proposed—in that grandiose pep-talk fashion so common in wartime newsreels—that playgrounds and youth groups could get our children back on the right track if we all worked together to make youth centers available. The rhetoric sounded very much like a wartime Red Cross pitch. Lewton asked to have his name removed from the film, but he was refused.

After the alarmingly sensational and altogether misleading opening credits, *Youth Runs Wild* delivers a montage of newspaper headlines bemoaning the current rash of juvenile delinquency, all accompanied with numerous lap-dissolves of teens running rampant, drinking, dancing, followed by shots of busy factories and belching smokestacks. We settle upon a close-up of a large street sign reading, "Keep Our Children Safe!" which noisily collapses from our view when a truck backs into it.

Mary Hauser (Jean Brooks) comes upon the scene, walking with her toddler son through a factory housing neighborhood, a place where unattended children play in the streets and make cruel remarks to Sarah Taylor (Tessa Brind) and her younger sisters, the new kids in town. Mary enters her parents' apartment and sees a chalkboard with a number of messages on it, one of them a "welcome home" greeting to Mary (the implication here being that message boards must suffice in a nation where parents—recovering from rigorous night shifts in the local defense plant—are forced to sleep during their children's waking hours).

Mary's husband, Danny (Kent Smith), wounded in the war, is about to return home—in what condition, Mary has no idea. While she is discussing this, the mail arrives with a notice for Mr. Hauser (Art Smith) about his son's truancy. He calls Frankie (Glenn Vernon), his teenage son, and while the two of them start to discuss the truancy issue, the factory whistle blows, bringing the conversation to a halt. Frankie's father and mother quickly prepare for

(Left to right) Mark Robson, Glenn Vernon, Jean Brooks, Kent Smith and Val Lewton between takes on what would come to be called _Youth Runs Wild._ (Courtesy of the Val Lewton Collection, Library of Congress.)

another night at the defense plant. The Hausers are well-meaning people; they're just burdened by an exhaustive work schedule.

The Taylor home offers a marked contrast. Here we see 15-year-old Sarah busy at endless household chores, with her unsympathetic parents working most of the day, only to play cards, drink, and carouse with coworkers for a good part of the evening. Oldest daughter Sarah is exploited as a live-in housekeeper and surrogate parent for her two younger sisters. When we first see them, the Taylor parents (Ben Bard and Elizabeth Russell) are returning home from the factory; no sooner do they get in the door than they begin barking orders at Sarah. When her father comes into the kitchen, he ignores her greeting and her presence while he washes his face and shaves near the kitchen sink. Sarah mentions that it is her birthday. No response. Only when Sarah mentions her plans for the evening (Frankie Hauser is taking her out to celebrate) does her father suddenly become animated: "No, you're staying home to watch your sisters. Your mother and I deserve time out after slaving away at the plant." Sarah's mother, her hair tied up in a factory-regulation scarf (which makes Russell look like she has cat ears), is no help; overhearing mention of Sarah's date, she shouts down the stairwell to her husband, "Fix it!" It is plain that neither of the girl's parents are in the habit of acknowledging their daughter's special day; there is not a "Happy birthday" between them, let alone a gift. (Birthdays are seldom joyous occasions for Lewton heroines. Amy Reed's birthday in *Curse* was a washout and Consuelo's birthday in *Leopard* was worse than that. Remember, on *Zombie*'s Saint Sebastian a baby's birth is an occasion to mourn.)

All the trouble in *Youth Runs Wild* starts when Sarah rebels against her parents and runs out of the house to meet Frankie. The two of them stroll the streets, passing a neon lit dime-a-dance club, where they bump into Larry Duncan (Lawrence Tierney) and his girlfriend Toddy (Bonita Granville). Larry comments to his babe, "Hey, that's a nice chick with Frankie," in that masterfully lecherous manner of Tierney's.

Frankie has been skipping school to work in Duncan's garage, a front for stolen auto parts, particularly those WWII rarities, rubber tires. (Although the release print gives us little evidence of Duncan's being mixed up with further illegal trafficking, Tierney, in an interview in *Psychotronic,* issue 8, said "in *Youth Runs Wild,* I played . . . a local bad guy peddling drugs and getting kids to do illegal things." Perhaps the drug-related incidents were left on the cutting-room floor.)

While Larry is the unsavory charmer type, Toddy is the brazen party girl with down-to-earth sensibilities, much along the lines of Rose Mahoney, the heroine of Lewton's novel, *No Bed of Her Own.* Judging by her unnatural aversion to policemen, Toddy has been in trouble before, most likely for prostitution. According to Lucy Lewton in *My Brother,* the character of Toddy was based upon Lewton's "fast-girl" from Port Chester, Olive Aldred. Lucy says, "Olive was the first of the era of wild teenagers. . . . She had red hair and drove about in a green two-seater roadster car, her hair flying and a green scarf around her neck. She made a play for Val and, for a while, Val did drive around with her. . . . Olive was used in Val's film, *Youth Runs Wild* and the novel, *No Bed of Her Own.*"

The following evening, Sarah is forced to cater to a houseful of drunken adults; it is poker night at the Taylor household and Sarah must wait table for a surly crew. When the guests arrive, she is harassed by a lecher named Bart (Jack Carrington), who directs numerous lewd comments and vulgar leers in her direction. Bart gives Sarah a friendly pinch on the behind whenever she comes by with her tray of full or empty beer bottles. Mrs. Taylor finally catches on to Bart's actions and responds by telling Sarah to take a night off and go to the movies. "My, my, what a bringdown," Bart remarks. At first, we assume the woman is finally showing a modicum of decency, but when, smiling, she tells Bart to pick on someone his own size and we cut to a glare from Mr. Taylor, we understand that Sarah has been sent to the movies to eliminate the competition.

Posters advertising *I Walked with a Zombie* bedeck the theater entrance as Sarah goes there in search of Frankie. When a ticket-taker tells her that Frankie is not in attendance (not aware that he has actually sneaked in though a side entrance), Sarah goes elsewhere, bumping into Larry and Toddy and winding up at Rocky's Cave, a nearby dance bar.

Cutting back to the movie theater, we see Frankie and a couple of his friends, Herb (Johnny Walsh) and George (Dickie Moore), sitting in the theater. In a typically self-effacing inside joke, the three bored teenagers view the Lewton/Tourneur film with such open disdain that they walk out in the middle of it. Then they hop into their jalopy and drive over to Duncan's Garage for some action. Dickens, a grizzled greasemonkey in a Jughead Jones cap, is minding the garage while his boss Larry is hitting the hotspots with Toddy. Dickens urges the three down-and-outers (with nothing to do and no money to spend) to steal some tires at the defense plant parking lot.

In the parking lot, the three boys work off the tires of one car, when the adjacent parked car captures Frankie's attention. Within it, a baby girl wails, her bruised head visible in the back window. Apparently the parents both work at the plant and a locked car in a dark parking lot is the best they can offer in childcare. There is not a false note in this grim depiction, which is what makes it so shocking; the baby is convincingly (perhaps, too convincingly) distressed.

Frankie shows his concern for the child, but Herb dismisses it, implying that there are babies in locked cars, here and there, all over the lot, and the boys continue with their business. A lineman (Edmund Glover) working on a pole in the lot spots the culprits and phones the night watchman. Alerted, the boys make their escape at the same time that Larry's car pulls onto the scene. When Larry tries to intervene (he has made a rather unconvincing turnaround and now wishes to keep Frankie out of trouble), he is wounded by one of the guard's wild gunshots and later hospitalized.

Although Frankie and his pals make a successful escape from the scene of the crime, they are picked up by the cops for breaking the speed limit. While their case is being heard, Mary's husband, Danny (Kent Smith), who has a crippled leg and must walk with a cane, turns up and speaks on the boys' behalf; seeing the wounded veteran's potential as a role model, the judge goes easy on the lads.

At this point, the film begins to flounder. Obviously, it was here that the narrative of the preview print, *The Dangerous Age,* was dismantled and reworked. It was not for the better. What began as a promising story, with interesting characters, now becomes cluttered with platitudes and rhetoric. With the softening of its punches, *Youth Runs Wild* soon degenerates into pablum. The film's more interesting characters, all of them fascinating scoundrels—Mr. and Mrs. Taylor, Bart, Larry Duncan, and Dickens—are pushed aside in favor of a number of tepid scenes focusing upon the Hauser family; as a result, Sarah, too, is relegated to an almost minor position in the story. Maybe Lewton intended us to see some duplicity in Lawrence Tierney's character, but Larry Duncan's good turn is hard to accept at face value when each of his previous scenes showed him lusting after a highschooler about 10 years his junior. Larry's heart of gold emerging so unexpectedly strikes an exceedingly false note, as do other contrived Pollyanna touches.

Mary believes, unjustifiably, that Sarah is behind Frankie's law trouble and reveals her suspicions to her mother and father. As a result, Frankie is forced to break off his relationship. The boy becomes laconic and ill-tempered, and even the good-intentioned Danny cannot bridge the rift between Frankie and his family.

Meanwhile, after a particularly nasty confrontation with her parents, Sarah leaves her innocence behind and moves in with Toddy. Soon Sarah quits school and finds herself working with her roommate as a "B-girl" in Rocky's Cave, a dive substituting for a night club.

Tragedy strikes in Frankie's neighborhood when an ice-cream truck, swerving to avoid hitting a child in the middle of the road, inadvertently plows down an entire group of children. There is a neighborhood uproar and a call for action; Mary and Danny rise to the occasion by providing a day-care center, free of charge. While Mary and Danny dedicate their efforts to the safety of the community's children, Frankie remains surly and shiftless, smoking cigarettes and hanging around. Frankie's pals, however, are greatly impressed by Danny, especially when the ex-soldier shows them the ju-jitsu he learned in basic training.

Danny and Frankie finally have their heart-to-heart, wherein they discuss Sarah's plight at Rocky's Cave. Eventually, Danny looks up Sarah and tells her Frankie still cares, but Sarah implies that she has been with other men and that she is no longer any good for Frankie. Danny passes this information along and suggests to his brother-in-law that Sarah's refusal to see Frankie is probably all for the better.

But Frankie is not about to give up. He goes to the nightclub to speak with Sarah, but in a self-sacrificing gesture, the good-girl-gone-bad tells him to go away. When he resists, he is thrown out by bouncers. Frankie enlists the aid of his two pals, and the three of them force their way into Rocky's Cave and wind up provoking a fight. One of Frankie's mates, apt ju-jitsu student that he is, throws an adversary over his shoulder. Toddy, who is nearby, is knocked to the floor in the scuffle, and her neck is broken. The unlikely accident brings all hostility to a halt, and Toddy is rushed to the hospital, where she dies. Larry, up and about now, is present at her side when she succumbs to her last breath.

Frankie and his friends are sent to a detention home for a short stretch as a result of the bar fight, but they will be all the better for it, we are told. Sarah apparently goes back home to live, though her reentry into the morally suspect Taylor household is glossed over entirely. Danny gives Sarah a pep talk detailing the accomplishments of a teenager named Ruth Clifton. While Danny continues to deliver his calculated rhetoric, we break into another

Youth running wild.

montage of documentary dissolves, introducing Ruth Clifton and her youth center program. Suddenly, Sarah is able to see the path of her future: she will follow the footsteps of Ruth Clifton, providing the film with exactly the kind of facile solution that Lewton so wanted to avoid.

Although Lewton hated the film, his loyal adherents Manny Farber and James Agee were quite taken with *Youth Runs Wild.* In his September 18, 1944, review in *The New Republic,* Manny Farber championed the film:

> In *Youth Runs Wild,* Producer Val Lewton has succeeded in making a very human, neat examination of wartime juvenile delinquency. . . . [Val Lewton's production] includes some adequate realism and some of the only thoroughly acceptable humanity to be found in movies today. . . . His pictures show a beautiful eye, memory, and a feeling for gesture and attitude. . . . I would rate Lewton as the least commercial film maker in Hollywood by about a hundred miles. Whatever spurious device you can think of for making a movie break box-office records you will find least present in [Lewton's films]. . . . They are about the only Hollywood movies in which the writing and direction try to keep in front of rather than behind the audience's intelligence.

Although James Agee, in the September 30, 1944, issue of *The Nation,* is plainly not blind to the film's flaws, he nonetheless concurs in Farber's exaltations:

> It is . . . a pleasure, and a . . . startling one, to see such a film as *Youth Runs Wild* coming out of a Hollywood studio. . . . Not even its faults are the Hollywood kind: it is gawky, diffuse, rather boyscoutish in its social attitudes (but it does have attitudes); often as not its characters go wooden (but they never turn into ivory-soap sculpture); too often the photography goes velvety (but always in earnestly striving for a real, not a false, atmosphere, and never striving for a sumptuous look). When the picture is good—and its over-all inadequacy flashes with good all through—you are seeing pretty nearly the only writing and acting and directing and photography in Hollywood which is at all concerned with what happens inside real and particular people. . . . To watch most of [the performers], you would hardly think they had ever heard of Hollywood, much less wanted to go there.

Youth Runs Wild has several things to recommend it, but one suspects Farber and Agee went a bit overboard with their praise. The two critics were obviously intent upon lionizing the Lewton name; they saw the future of cinema in the works of RKO's low-budget horror unit. At the time, no one realized how accurate they were.

But as impressed as Agee and Farber may have been at the time of its release, *Youth Runs Wild* is the most compromising entry in the Lewton series and surely the poorest film of the lot. Agee and Farber saw the film's flaws, but they were also mesmerized by the film's noble intentions, an aspect of *Youth Runs Wild* that is almost totally lost on viewers today. One can hardly believe World War II audiences were seriously moved by the film's call-for-action ending, but at least they were able to relate to its topicality.

The story of Sarah Taylor is compelling in the opening reels, misleading us to expect a tragic Lewton heroine of the first order. Midway through the film, however, it becomes apparent that Sarah's character is victimized by nothing more than vagaries of plot construction, her sudden downfall and last-minute redemption working to diminish whatever resonance her character hoped to achieve.

It's too bad that *The Dangerous Age* was not left intact after the Hillstreet Theater fiasco. One wonders whatever became of the infamous subplot; though the theme of patricide (and related familial homicides) has become something of a staple for made-for-television movies of the last decade, in 1944 it was virtually taboo.

The Dangerous Age is forever lost, and *Youth Runs Wild* is not what it should be, but it does display some inspired moments and natural performances that compensate in part for the script's improbabilities and the film's heavy-handed conclusion. *Youth Runs Wild* never came close to duplicating the box-office success of the Dmytryk exposés, but at least its themes have weathered the years more successfully. In a sense, *Youth Runs Wild* is quite timely; juvenile delinquency, youth centers, and day-care centers are subjects discussed daily in the news media, and the film's essential truth—that children need parents and role models—carries as much validity today as it did a half century ago. Although it is yet another inappropriately titled Lewton film, *Youth Runs Wild* foreshadows a later era of sensationalized juvenile delinquent films, those masterminded by, among others, Roger Corman, Samuel Arkoff, Ed Wood, and Sam Katzman.

If the unhappy fate surrounding *Youth Runs Wild* indicated that Lewton was ill-suited to make anything other than horror films, *Mademoiselle Fifi* did not prove otherwise, at least as far as RKO's front office was concerned. Right after principal shooting was completed on *Are These Our Children?* (still months before its disastrous Hillstreet Theater preview), RKO studios broke for the Christmas holiday. At the time Lewton still had every reason to be optimistic, and his ambitious plans for the new year included forging ahead with a mainstream costume drama.

Lewton hoped to make 1944 his breakthrough year. He yearned to shed his some of his horror trappings and become recognized as a producer of quality films like *Mademoiselle Fifi,* the costume drama he was fashioning as a vehicle for Simone Simon. But certain executives in the studio's front office had some New Year's resolutions of their own, and the frustrations Lewton would suffer as a result of front office mandates would mark 1944 as Lewton's nightmare year at RKO.

Sid Rogell had originally discouraged Lewton's proposed adaptation and melding of two De Maupassant stories, "Mademoiselle Fifi" and "Boule de Suif." When Koerner finally gave in to Lewton, the producer's minor victory only made Rogell more inclined to be a hindrance. Rogell gave both Lewton and his director, Robert Wise, trouble every step of the way, making numerous budget cuts—out of spite, Lewton believed—until the film was pared down to $150,000. Lewton had to voice his protests directly to Koerner before an extra $50,000 was kicked into the budget. Still, that made *Mademoiselle Fifi* a very inexpensive costume feature.

Mademoiselle Fifi would be Robert Wise's first solo directing effort; this time he would be in on the creation of a film, not merely assigned to fix up a floundering project. Lewton handed Wise detailed briefs on all his characters, descriptions he had written himself to convey the flavor of the roles. Polish émigré Josef Mischel, who had been an uncredited writer for some of the dialogue for *The Curse of the Cat People*'s opening picnic scene, was secured to write the screenplay.

All along, *Mademoiselle Fifi* had been fashioned as a vehicle for the star of *Cat People,* Simone Simon. Lewton's original intent was to have her play the role of a prostitute, though the character was changed to that of a laundress in order to please the censors (the outrage with which characters in the film view Simon's profession, however, makes it plain that something in her past is dirtier than the laundry she has washed).

Other roles were to be played by a number of Lewton newcomers, John Emery, Kurt Kreuger, and Jason Robards, Sr. (the latter soon to be a Lewton regular). Added to the cast were several of Lewton's regular stable of performers: Alan Napier, Fay Helm, Edmund Glover, Marc Cramer, Margaret Landry, and others. Peter Ruric was called in to assist Josef Mischel with the script, while Harry Wild photographed. Technical adviser Captain Cook came aboard to oversee the diagramming and building of a diligence (a horse-drawn omnibus similar to a stagecoach) designed to be an exact replica of the public transportation vehicle French people used during the Franco-Prussian War. Again, Lewton's fetish for accuracy was more obsessive than pragmatic, for much of the authenticity of such particulars was lost on an audience that simply did not care whether or not the coach was an exact replica or merely a dressed-up lunch wagon.

During *Mademoiselle Fifi*'s preproduction, Lewton and Wise studied hundreds of paintings by noted French artists—Daumier, Toulouse-Lautrec, Detaille, Delacrois, and Boutigny—to get a feeling for the era. A large standing set left over from *The Hunchback of Notre Dame* was redressed to reflect the look of the paintings by the French masters. Lewton cast some bit players simply because they had faces resembling those found in the Daumier engravings. Such attention to particulars infuriated Sid Rogell, and the tension continued to mount as the production progressed.

While Rogell and Lewton continued to lock horns, Koerner was busily establishing a new order at RKO. He reorganized the studio into three units with three executive producers in charge of these units—Sid Rogell (the head of Lewton's unit), Robert Fellows, and a fresh catch lured away from Universal, Jack Gross. In a letter to his mother and sister written later in the year (August 20, 1944), Lewton recounts those difficult and fateful days:

> The first six months of this year have been as unhappy a period as I've ever gone through. At the studio, everything seemed to go wrong. . . . I now find myself working for an abysmally ignorant and stupid gentleman called Jack Gross. . . . I had a quarrel with Rogell about the budget on *Mademoiselle Fifi*. The quarrel had been so bitter that Koerner . . . as a special favor to me, had taken me out of the Rogell unit and given me to Jack Gross. But Jack Gross is the man who has been making those Universal horror films and so had a particular grudge against me, as our pictures had shown up his films not only from an artistic viewpoint, but also from a standpoint of profits [Siegel, *The Reality of Terror*].

In a 1991 interview, Robert Wise told the author, "Jack Gross was a very nice man himself but he was far at the other end of the spectrum from Lewton in terms of background, education, taste, that kind of thing, and though Val had to work with him he did not have much respect for the man. Val had his own inimitable way of showing how he felt about Mr. Gross and that was to never call him anything but 'Mr. Gross.' He would never get on a familiar basis with him and call him Jack. It was always 'Mr. Gross' and that was to Val, in a sense, a way of putting Gross down."

Lewton and Wise began production on *Mademoiselle Fifi* on March 23, 1944. Nearly everyone directly involved rallied to the occasion and enjoyed making the film. All the actors had great respect for the project and were determined to make it show in their work, which it did. Lewton's role, as he saw it, was to maintain this spirit of good will. Robert Wise recalled:

> In those days, most producers under pressure from the front office generally took it out on their directors, which just made the situation worse. Val chose to run interference. Time and time again he was badgered to "tell Bob that he's half a day behind—go goose him up." I managed to come in two or three days late on ... *Mademoiselle Fifi* ... but Val always defended me. He'd come on the set and say, "They want me to tell you that you're behind schedule. Now go ahead and shoot the picture. I've done my job, now you do what you need to do."

Fifi's production was completed on April 22, and it was previewed on June 29 at the Academy Theater in Pasadena.

Mademoiselle Fifi was released to theaters nationally in August. As might be expected, it had a poor showing at the box office. James Agee and Manny Farber were still faithful Lewton advocates, however. In *The Nation,* Agee wrote: "I don't know of any American film which has tried to say as much, as pointedly, about the performance of the middle class in war. There is a gallant, fervent quality about the whole picture, faults and all, which gives it a peculiar kind of life and likableness, and which signifies that there is one group of men working in Hollywood who have neither lost nor taken care to conceal the purity of their hope and intention." In *Time,* Agee wrote: "With a little more time, and a little more money, it would probably have been a first-rate film. Even as it stands, it makes most of its better-barbered, better-fed competitors look like so many wax dummies in a window. . . . No other group in Hollywood, it appears, knows how to do so much with so little."

Set in occupied France during the Franco-Prussian War, *Mademoiselle Fifi* was not a particularly satisfying movie to audiences of 1944, but its message was not lost on those who followed the day-by-day plight of Nazi-occupied France. *Fifi*'s postcredit epigraph reads, "Then, as in our own time, there was occupied and unoccupied territory."

Unfortunately, many of *Mademoiselle Fifi*'s subtleties went over the heads of audiences who had grown used to Hollywood's scathing indictments of current-day enemies, like the blatant anti–Nazi/anti–Japanese propaganda spearheaded by Edward Dmytryk's *Hitler's Children* and *Behind the Rising Sun.* Even Bugs Bunny, Daffy Duck, and the Three Stooges took a more aggressive stance against the enemy in numerous Hollywood shorts than did Lewton's propaganda film in period disguise. After all, we are talking of a Hollywood where Basil Rathbone's Sherlock Holmes is plucked from his native Victorian-era setting and dropped, some two generations ahead, into a war-torn England, just to allow him to have a crack at the Nazis. It is not that audiences did not grasp Lewton's underlying anti-Axis message; they just could not figure out why a Hollywood film would choose to be anything but timely and direct in its handling of war propaganda.

But *Mademoiselle Fifi* intended to be more than a well-timed attack against the Germans. Although the film's charm and civility belie the nature of its strident attack, *Mademoiselle Fifi*'s mission was not only to lash out against the Axis Powers but, even more importantly, to expose the rampant hypocrisy that is generally found among the privileged classes of any country that is occupied by the enemy. In one sense, *Fifi* is the antithesis of its more popular cinematic cousins: Ernst Lubitsch's *To Be or Not to Be* (1942), Jean Renoir's *This Land Is Mine* (1943), Fritz Lang's *Hangmen Also Die* (1943), and Douglas Sirk's *Hitler's Madman* (1943), films which detail the Nazi occupations of, respectively, Poland, France, and (the remaining two) Czechoslovakia. Unlike *Fifi*, however, the four films mentioned are all stories of Europeans who struggle to overthrow their captors; in each case, the loss of life suffered through demonstrations of resistance is in the end redeemed by the undying spirit of the people and their unflagging pursuit of freedom. *Mademoiselle Fifi* completely jettisons this approach with its portrayal of a complacent occupied populace kowtowing to the whims of its captors.

Fifi's screenplay incorporates two separate characters, both outcast females, from two Maupassant stories: an overweight prostitute, Elizabeth Rousset, from "Boule de Suif" and Rebecca from "Mademoiselle Fifi." The first half of the film borrows heavily from the former story, while the second half works in events from the latter. Although her career of ill-repute was changed to that of a laundress, Elizabeth Rousset is retained as the name for the film's main character, played with uncommon charm by Simone Simon; it is arguably her best performance in a Lewton film.

The film opens with Prussian soldiers bullying their way about Cleresville, an occupied French town. Mounted on horses, the Prussians loom above the oppressed local citizenry, delighting in their physical superiority as they relish the insults they hurl at France and the French tradition. The Prussians find amusement in the way French citizens have become so accommodating that they allow the Prussians to share their houses, their food, and even their women.

Lieutenant von Eyrich (Kurt Kreuger) harasses the old priest (Charles Waldron) of the Cleresville church. Since the Prussian occupation, the priest has refused to ring the church bell, long ago vowing that it would remain silent until the "first blow is struck" against the nation's oppressors. When one of the impatient soldiers volunteers to ring the bell himself, von Eyrick forbids this expedient. He would rather have the French people submit to Prussian whims; Prussians should not be humbled to ring the bell themselves, he believes. The old priest craftily tells von Eyrick that because he has been officially relieved of his duties to the church, the matter is out of his hands.

A young priest, his replacement, will arrive any day, and the decision rests with him.

The film shifts its location to the town of Rouen (some leftover sets from RKO's *The Hunchback of Notre Dame* lend a degree of authenticity). It is evening, and we see the diligence loading its passengers before setting out on its journey to Cleresville. The passengers include the Count and Countess de Breville (Alan Napier and Helen Freeman), a wholesaler in wines (Jason Robards, Sr.) and his wife (Norma Varden), a manufacturer (Romaine Callender) and his wife (Fay Helm), a would-be revolutionary, Jean Cornudet (John Emery), whose reputation has lately been blemished by cowardice, and a young priest (Edmund Glover). A late arrival, Elizabeth Rousset (Simone Simon), clambers aboard and is met with immediate disdain from most of the passengers, especially the snooty trio of wives. Seeing that she is a laundress (read whore), one of the wives remarks, "They're not very particular about passengers any more." Jean Cornudet and the young priest, unlike the others, behave in a civil fashion toward Elizabeth Rousset.

The diligence is longer than a stagecoach and more rectangular, somewhat resembling a small train car on wagon wheels. From within the vehicle, the passengers while away the time with shallow talk designed to flaunt their social standing, but everyone in the coach, everyone in France, is really a prisoner in his or her own land. All their pronouncements of success and happiness, all their jitterish laughter, all their concern for class boundaries, is just desperate play. Perhaps at one time they were real people, but their fear has stolen their dignity, and now they are pompous, supercilious fools. Their semblance of happiness is driven by their fears, which is why they become joyous buffoons whenever they talk about Prussians.

One of the passengers mentions a Prussian officer who calls himself Mademoiselle Fifi, after his habit of uttering the exclamation, "Fi, fi donc!" (a rather meaningless and difficult-to-translate idiom used, in this case, as a scornful affectation of "Frenchness"). All through their conversation, the wealthier passengers continue to direct disapproving looks and remarks to Elizabeth Rousset, the laundress.

The diligence must move slowly along the snow-covered roads, occasionally halting for the benefit of the weary horses. When the passengers get out of the coach to stretch their legs during these stops, all the women except Elizabeth are assisted down by the men. As the journey continues, the passengers grow bored and hungry, and it appears that no one had thought of bringing any food. The wine wholesaler refers to an old song where a group of hungry travelers "ate the poorest of the passengers." He looks at Elizabeth and laughs.

Elizabeth, though, has had the foresight to bring a basket of chicken and a bottle of wine. As she puts a drumstick to her lips, the passengers begin to show their friendlier sides to the laundress. Elizabeth offers food to the group, and everyone is more than willing to exploit her generosity. One of the prouder women even pretends to faint from undernourishment as a pretext for getting food.

With their bellies full, the couples become very jovial, and their conversation naturally drifts to the subject of food. They talk of the Prussians' unorthodox dining habits. When one of them asks Elizabeth if she's noticed how the Germans eat, she answers, "I don't eat with the Germans. I wouldn't eat with them and I wouldn't do their laundry either. I used to watch them from the window—great pigs with their spiked helmets, and I'd wish I were a man so I could fight them." There is a passage of uncomfortable silence.

Midway in their journey, they arrive at the town of Totes, where they change horses and take rooms for the night at the inn. On this particular evening, the inn is also a stopping place for Lieutenant von Eyrick (aka Mademoiselle Fifi) and his covey of Prussian subordinates. Fifi says, "I have heard about Miss Elizabeth Rousset, the girl who dislikes the Prussians." While the passengers dine, the innkeeper informs Elizabeth that the Lieutenant wishes to speak with her in his upstairs quarters. The passengers smirk at one another as Elizabeth climbs the stairs, but they are puzzled when she comes down a short time later, wearing her most serious expression. Elizabeth remains silent about the nature of her conference.

The next morning, as the travelers prepare for their departure, the diligence driver tells them that the Lieutenant has ordered the new horses be taken from their harnesses and brought back to the stable. "Does he look greedy?" one wife asks Elizabeth, referring to Fifi. "Does he want money?"

"One can't tell that by looking at a man," Elizabeth answers.

"Haven't you looked at enough of them?" the wife retorts.

Two of the husbands go to the Lieutenant's quarters to ask the reason for their detainment. No one will leave the inn, he tells them, until Elizabeth agrees to dine with them. But Elizabeth maintains her position. The women become impatient over her stubborness, but their husbands, for a time at least, show some admiration for the girl's bravery. As the hours turn into days, however, with the Lieutenant holding to his promise, the patience of the passengers is severely tested. Elizabeth finally relents when even the sympathetic ex-revolutionary, Jean Cornudet (who appears to have fallen in love with her), reluctantly sides with the rest of the passengers. "After all," says one of the women, "you don't want us all to suffer because you were stubborn."

As soon as Elizabeth goes to the Lieutenant's quarters, the travelers bask in their merriment, all except the priest and Jean Cornudet. The wholesaler orders champagne for his companions, and they get roaring drunk. The wholesaler sneaks upstairs and leans an ear toward the Lieutenant's room. "Everything is going well," he reports to the guests downstairs, as they titter in a fashion that suggest "dining" to be a euphemism for something vastly more intimate. Later, one of the women comments, "It is only because the Lieutenant respected us that he chose her for his 'little dinner party.'"

Meanwhile, in the upstairs room, Elizabeth is forced to sing a French ditty while the Prussian Lieutenant sits in his chair smoking a cigar. He pulls her to him and kisses her, blowing a cloud of cigar smoke into her mouth. Laughing, he tells her, "That is a Prussian caress. Now you are ready for anything. But I don't want you," he says, moving back from her, "I only want to show you that when we tell you to do this, you must do this, and when we tell you to do that, you must do that . . . and all the time we despise you and your patriotism."

Elizabeth is dismissed, and the Lieutenant tells her that she and her companions are now free to leave in the morning. Hearing the good news, the diners break into a tumult of drunken cackling and braying laughter. The inebriated wife of the wholesaler crawls up the stairs on all fours singing a gross imitation of Elizabeth's lovely melody, ending her revery with "Just imagine . . . that girl holding us up for days with her fine airs . . . and now?" A self-satisfied guffaw punctuates her meaning.

To Elizabeth's credit, she is in fine spirits when the morning comes; now that it is over and done, she clearly does not mind the sacrifice she has made for the others. But when she gets into the diligence, everyone but the priest and Cornudet give her the cold shoulder, treating her with the kind of disrespect reserved for someone whose values have been compromised. Discovering this cold reception, Elizabeth sits back in silence, tears welling in her eyes.

Lieutenant von Eyrick surprises everyone by boarding the diligence himself, announcing he has matters to attend to in Cleresville; he is treated most graciously by the middle-class passengers (who seem delighted by his presence). This time the married couples are well-equipped with food and drink, and while they are generous enough to offer food to the Lieutenant, they refuse to do the same for Elizabeth. Guilt-ridden, Jean Cornudet extends a hard-boiled egg to Elizabeth, who is too upset to eat.

When the coach stops in Cleresville, three of the passengers—Elizabeth, the young priest, and von Eyrick—make their exits and go their separate ways. The married couples are visibly relieved: "Well, it's good to be rid of her . . . that creature," one of the wives says. Whereupon, the fuming Cornudet directs the driver to pull over. As he leaves, one of the passengers asks, "What business do you have in Cleresville?"

He answers, "I want to go to that little girl, kneel at her feet, and beg her forgiveness."

"Her forgiveness?" one of the women incredulously responds.

Here the film shifts to the second of the two Maupassant stories. Curiously, though the second half of the film is far more eventful, it is neither as powerful nor as interesting as the scathing indictment of middle-upper class hypocrisy that comprises the film's first half.

Elizabeth goes back to the Rousset Blanchisserie, the laundry business run by her Aunt Marie (Violet Wilson), and there she discovers that patriotism has gone the way of the wind among all classes of townspeople. Her aunt is happy having the Prussians around; it has been good for business and she has had to hire many girls to keep up with the demands of the soldiers residing in the town. When Prussians pass on horseback, Elizabeth's working companions rush to the windows to wave adoringly at them. While this disgusts Elizabeth, her aunt tells her it is only natural for young people to behave this way.

It appears that most of Cleresville's inhabitants have quite happily submitted to the yokes of their oppressors. Elizabeth's determination to retain her scruples now makes her an outcast in her own land. "The bell doesn't mean anything," she observes. "The people make friends with the Prussians. They eat and drink with them. And now, with the young priest in charge, even the bell will ring." When Cornudet comes to the laundry to beg Elizabeth's forgiveness, she is not interested in cowardly revolutionaries and sends him away.

Hoping to win her affection and to redeem himself for his past cowardice, Cornudet goes to the church to become "an apostle of silence" to help the young priest ward off the Prussians. Some of the soldiers have grown impatient with Fifi's plan and, against his orders, wish to ring the bell themselves. But the young priest intends to carry on the tradition of his predecessor: "The bell must remain silent until the first blow is struck for the freedom of France." Cornudet arms himself with a rifle and guards the church entrance.

Occupying one of the more luxurious homes, von Eyrick and his Prussian pals construct a bomb and set it on a table in an opulent dining room furnished with priceless antiques and paintings. "I merely want to show my appreciation for French art," explains the Lieutenant. The gunpowder he measures is "just enough to destroy the furnishings and leave us the room. . . . Fi, fi donc!" And with that, he and his men scurry out like a bunch of happy college pranksters and close the double doors behind them to await the blast. They revel in this activity, and it is clear that this is not the first time they have amused themselves in this manner.

Later, they remark that things have gotten dull, and they decide to throw a dinner party. One of the officers ransacks a closet and comes up with four beautiful gowns; now all they need is four beautiful young women to fill them.

One of the Prussians goes to the Rousset Blanchisserie, a prime place for the young "talent" they seek for their party. The soldier has no trouble getting four lovelies to agree to the formal dinner; the four laundresses are overjoyed with the invitation. Then he sees Elizabeth and asks her to go along. When she refuses, he threatens to have his soldiers boycott the laundry. Aunt Marie becomes upset, knowing that the drop in business would mean laying-off all the extra workers. Again, Elizabeth is asked to make a sacrifice for the benefit of others.

Meanwhile, at the church, a gathering of soldiers, noting von Eyrick's absence, work up the courage to attempt to ring the bell on their own. As they approach on horseback, Cordunet, armed with his rifle, flanks the roadway. When they persist in their approach, Cordunet shoots one of the men and makes his escape.

Back at the dinner party, the girls are treated like so many sides of beef and divided among the five officers, including Lieutenant von Eyrick who, of course, is paired with Elizabeth. For a while, the patriotic laundress accepts her plight with dignity. After dinner, however, the party escalates into a drunken orgy, the females, except for Elizabeth, its very willing participants. While the couples exchange kisses and behave with wild abandon, von Eyrick attempts to kiss his resisting partner. Incensed at her rejection, he bites her lip, drawing blood. "Why can't you behave like these other good women?" he asks. Elizabeth answers, "I'm not a good woman, or I wouldn't be here. I'm only the kind of woman the Prussians would want."

Voy Eyrick slaps her face and, as quick as an unconscious reflex, Elizabeth pulls a knife out of a roast and drives it into his chest. The party breaks into chaos, the women scream, and amidst he confusion, Elizabeth makes her escape.

From here, things become a bit rushed in an attempt to wrap up the events within the film's 69-minute running time. Elizabeth is rescued by Cordunet, and they temporarily find sanctuary in the Cleresville church. When Cordunet confesses he has failed her, she replies, "I'm not afraid—I'm happy; this is the happiest moment I've known in my life." Fugitives both, they take solace in their mutual fates. Cordunet reveals he will go to Totes where he, once again, will be a rebel with a cause.

There is a funeral for Lieutenant von Eyrick, and the priest is ordered to sound the bell when the cortege passes the church; the priest agrees to this because he realizes, unbeknownst to the Prussians, that the bell will signify that the first blow (Elizabeth's assassination of the Lieutenant) has already been struck for the freedom of France. When the bell rings at the passing of the casket, townspeople look out their windows, smiling, totally oblivious to what the bell really signifies, simply happy to hear it ringing again, never mind the reason why. All along, they have wished for the illusion of normalcy and deluded themselves into believing, as did Elizabeth's traveling companions, that they are not under the yoke of their oppressor. Now, with the ringing of the church bell, the illusion is complete. What the people of Cleresville do not realize is that they are all prostitutes to the French cause.

The obsequious inhabitants of Cleresville get exactly what they deserve. In the end, they have as much right to call themselves French patriots as that very Teutonic male chauvinist, Lieutenant von Eyrick, had to take the nickname of a French woman.

Considering the theme of oppression in *Mademoiselle Fifi,* it is likely that Lewton identified with his French heroine. Like Elizabeth, Lewton had his own oppressors—RKO's studio brass—and like his heroine, he was constantly hounded to compromise his own integrity. Moreover, Lewton may have viewed his ghetto of "B" budget horror as an apt parallel to the disreputable occupation of laundress/prostitute. Sid Rogell and Jack Gross, pressuring Lewton to conform to the accepted traditions of the horror trade, may have been telling Lewton, in a manner of speaking, to "ring the bell."

One of the most fascinating aspects of the entire Lewton series is how 11 films, helmed by three separate directors (four counting Fritsch), were able to reflect such a unified personal vision. With all due respect to Lewton's wonderful collaborators—be they directors, writers, photographers, performers, composers, or any other valued participants—Lewton was the prime author of his 11 RKO films. Although there is very little for horror fans in either *Youth Runs Wild* or *Mademoiselle Fifi,* both films strongly bear the Lewton stamp.

Val Lewton's example, as a producer auteur, has been perplexing film critics for the last 50 years. Andrew Sarris's landmark treatise to the auteur theory, *The American Cinema,* should have included Lewton within its pages—Lewton expressed as personal a vision in his body of work as any of the filmmakers given individual entries—but Sarris's book was about directors, not producers, and an auteur filmmaker who did not direct was an egg-laying mammal to the adherents of the auteur theory. Lewton's personal touches were even more highly defined than the cinematic signatures of his closest producer-as-auteur rival, David O. Selznick.

Mademoiselle Fifi is beautifully shot, expertly acted, and sensitively directed, all of which gives the film the illusion of being a much classier and higher-budget production than it actually is. Even small touches, like Wise's use of soft-edged iris shots as transitions, help give the production a glossier look. Although it is hardly a costume epic, *Mademoiselle Fifi* is handsomely mounted, and its production appears infinitely more lavish than it is. A good deal of the credit must go to Robert Wise, whose strong sense of composition and mise en scène draws the eye and keeps the film on an even keel. Wise made good use of the prevailing weather, shooting portions of *Fifi* on locations outside the RKO lot. The scenes of the diligence creeping through the snow-covered roads from one town to the next have a particularly authentic feel.

It was unfortunate, though not surprising, that *Mademoiselle Fifi* (released one month *before Youth Runs Wild*) had such limited box-office appeal. *Fifi* was more in keeping with the kind of intelligent literary adaptation Lewton yearned to make, a scaled-down version of the type of movie Selznick might have produced. The flaws of its half-baked ending notwithstanding, *Fifi* never resorts to heavy-handed proselytizing; its message maintains a subtle focus throughout, perhaps, for some viewers, at the expense of clarity. It is likely that a large number of theatergoers, like the dim inhabitants of Cleresville, missed the point of *Mademoiselle Fifi* entirely. Some, we suspect, left the theater believing that the title character was played by Simone Simon. Lewton probably felt, as he did with his surreptitious insults, that those not clever enough to understand his message deserved to bask in their own ignorance.

Fi, fi donc!

THIRTEEN

Isle of the Dead

> ***Jack Gross called Val into his office for a conference. Gross had come to RKO from Universal, where the prevailing idea of horror was a werewolf chasing a girl in a nightgown up a tree. With him in the office was a man from Exhibition named Holt who seldom, if ever, spoke. "O.K.," said Gross. "We've just signed Boris Karloff to a three-picture contract and you're going to use him for your next film." Val was not pleased.***
>
> —MARK ROBSON
> from *The Reality of Terror,* by Joel Siegel

While *Mademoiselle Fifi* was on the drawing boards during those early months of 1944, the Hollywood trade papers were buzzing with news of Boris Karloff's return to motion pictures. It was fitting, everyone thought, that Karloff was making his comeback via Universal, the studio that had elevated him to a household name. Karloff was bringing to a close his two-year hiatus from the silver screen, having just completed a long string of road shows for his sensational Broadway hit, *Arsenic and Old Lace.* Now Karloff was back and, at least for the time being, Universal had him.

Hollywood's undisputed king of horror was exactly the kind of draw Universal needed. The public had grown weary (and wary) of Universal's horror line, which, increasingly, had begun to pander to juvenile audiences. Universal's ace-in-the-hole horror actor, Lon Chaney, Jr., was so overexposed (six films a year since 1941, seven in 1944) that his limitations as an actor had become profoundly apparent. The Universal horror film formula—remember George Waggner's seven magic ingredients?—had worn quite thin since the horror film cycle got a much-needed boost from the Lewton films. Universal was now receiving formidable horror film competition from all directions, Columbia, Paramount, Fox, and, especially, RKO.

Universal's horror output in the early months of 1944 was negligible; a number of cut-rate horror sequels were forthcoming, *The Invisible Man's Revenge, Jungle Woman,* and *The Mummy's Ghost,* but such bread-and-butter

Postproduction ad.

films possessed none of the essentials needed to put Universal back in its former lead position in the horror trade. The only major horror film the studio had in the works during the first months of 1944 was Karloff's comeback film, *The Climax*. Belying its elaborate look, *The Climax*—an inappropriately titled serving of leftovers from the 1943 *The Phantom of the Opera* (using the earlier film's existing sets as well as its leading lady, Susanna Foster)—was destined to become a dismal flop. Even its beautiful Technicolor photography could not prevent *The Climax* from being a major disaster, critically and financially; Karloff's walk-through performance is still considerd one of his worst.

The actor disliked being on the set of *The Climax*, and he was discouraged that Universal only chose to see him as "Boris Karloff, the king of horror." To someone who had just received two years of curtain calls and standing ovations, going back to ground zero on a tacky *Phantom* imitation was a dire disappointment. The 56-year-old actor was under contract to the studio for 13 weeks, and Universal, wanting to make the most of his horror reputation, quickly rushed him into a second feature directly on the heels of *The Climax*. Universal believed it imperative to have Karloff's name as a drawing card for a planned monster rally called *The Devil's Brood* (released as *House of Frankenstein*), which would boast five monsters for the price of one (or so the film's poster art promised): Frankenstein's monster, the Wolf Man, Dracula, a mad scientist, and a hunchback. Universal's resident horror screenwriter, Curt Siodmak (who had opened Pandora's crypt with the first monster rally, *Frankenstein Meets the Wolfman*) had been assigned to prepare the script. Karloff, remaining adamant about his retirement from the monster role, was given the part of the film's mad scientist, Dr. Niemann.

Karloff's displeasure with his roles seriously affected the enthusiasm of his performances during his 13-week-stint at Universal. The aging actor needed a change, a lift in his career. He did not object to horror—in fact, he loved the genre—but he did object to the ridiculous way the genre was being exploited by Universal's monster-mad top brass. If Karloff were only able to connect with a kindred spirit, someone who shared his own views on how such films ought to be made . . .

Karloff signed with RKO on May 18, 1944, and was given a salary of $600 a week for each picture. Saddled with an actor whose very name stirred images of monsters, Lewton was back in the horror business. The studio execs were not going to take any more chances on Lewton's high-brow ideas (they did not need another Orson Welles). They wanted "no more messages."

Lewton did not relish the prospect of creating the kind of monster show Jack Gross wanted, but he quickly saw how wrong he was about Boris Karloff. According to Greg Mank (in *Karloff and Lugosi*), "Val Lewton—under pressure from Jack Gross—arranged for Karloff to visit RKO to meet him and Robson and Wise. For Lewton and company, it was a very pleasant surprise. "When he turned those eyes on us [said Robert Wise], and that velvety voice said, 'Good afternoon, gentlemen,' we were his, and never thought about anything else.'"

Lewton quickly saw that, horror roles aside, Karloff was also one of Hollywood's greatest character actors. A deep respect developed between the producer and the actor. As the newest addition to the Lewton unit, Karloff was in good hands; the English actor and Russian producer had more in common than either of them realized, both being well-read gentlemen with a keen interest in the high arts. They were also soulmates in their attitudes about horror, both men decrying the current state of the genre, especially the ludicrous, formula-bound Universal entries. Long before his illustrious Broadway career, Karloff had become critical of the Hollywood horror film. Actually, the English actor preferred the word "terror" to "horror" and saw the two as separate entities. The aesthetics of terror developed by the Lewton unit were in complete accordance with Karloff's own views on the subject.

A little over a year before, while *Arsenic and Old Lace* was still on Broadway, a college professor named Edmund Speare asked Karloff to edit an anthology of terror stories for the World Publishing Company. The actor, who was amazingly well-read in the field of macabre literature, happily consented, and the resulting volume, *Tales of Terror* (14 stories in all, by Poe,

Faulkner, Conrad, Blackwood, Stoker, et al.), hit the bookstores in October 1943, just in time for the Halloween trade. It became such a huge seller, going into its second and third printing within four months, that World Publishing immediately contacted Karloff for a follow-up volume.

Consider the following excerpts from Karloff's introduction to *Tales of Terror:*

> It has always grieved me professionally that the two worlds "horror" and "terror" are used indiscriminately for stories designed to stir the imagination and tingle the spine. The terms are literally poles apart in their true meaning and impact. Horror carries with it a connotation of revulsion which has nothing to do with clean terror. . . . The well-told tale of a really juicy murder, with grisly undercurrents of lust and hatred, carnage and what-have-you, topped off with intimate and gory details of how the corpse was dismembered and disposed of, and what a time the murderer had cleaning up the mess, makes exciting and even shocking reading, with a direct appeal to our morbidity and sadism. But we are not really frightened. . . . The final effect is usually one of revulsion. . . . Our hair stands becomingly on end, but our stomachs are fatally left a trifle queasy, a sensation which will linger long after our hair has returned to normal. The essential element of true terror . . . is lacking. That element is *fear.* Fear of the unknown and the unknowable. Are you afraid of the dark? You know perfectly well that you are, and you may as well admit it. . . .
>
> Go out and stand quite alone in your garden, far from your house, on a really dark, still night. Without warning every tree and bush and blade of grass is agitated by some mysterious movement coming from nowhere, and ceasing as suddenly as it began. What was it? Where did that odd sense of chill come from, and what was it that brushed your cheek? . . .
>
> The mightiest weapon of the writer of the terror tale is the *power of suggestion*—the skill to take the reader by means of that power into an atmosphere where even the incredible seems credible.

As can be deduced from all of the above, Boris Karloff's full acceptance into the Lewton fold was one of the most natural things imaginable. Although Lewton now considered himself fortunate to have Karloff as a highly qualified addition to his team, it did not exactly mean that there was smooth sailing ahead.

The origins of the first Karloff production, *Isle of the Dead,* harked back to Lewton's childhood. As a boy in his Port Chester home, he had been both fascinated and frightened by a Boecklin painting titled "Isle of the Dead." "Lewton used to enjoy scaring himself, making up gruesome stories about the painting," Greg Mank tells us in *Karloff and Lugosi.*

Use had already been made of Boecklin's painting in *I Walked with a Zombie,* where it was seen upon the wall of Jessica's meticulously decorated bedroom. Lewton reasoned that since the painting had stimulated his youthful fears, it could well serve as his muse for an entire horror thriller. Once again, he drafted the services of Ardel Wray and Josef Mischel, telling them to work up a script based on his original story, which was inspired by equal portions of the Boecklin painting and Edgar Allan Poe's "Premature Burial." Poe's widely known phobia of being buried alive had found its way into a number of his morbid tales. "Premature Burial" is not really a story as much as it is a mock report of several alleged cases of premature interment, which Poe would have us believe were fairly common.

In assembling a cast, Lewton handpicked a few of his RKO stock players, including Marc Cramer, Alan Napier, Jason Robards, Sr., and Skelton Knaggs. Of course Karloff was given star billing, and he was ably assisted by Ellen Drew (whose *The Monster and the Girl* for Paramount gave her some experience in the horror field) and Katherine Emery (whose role as the catalyptic Mrs. St. Aubin was originally slated for Rose Hobart). Helene Thimig and Ernst Dorian were chosen for small but zesty roles; both were an asset to the film. With only 11 speaking parts, *Isle of the Dead* had a smaller cast than any other film in the Lewton series.

Boris Karloff was eager to immerse himself in his role as General Pherides when production began on July 13, 1944. Perhaps the production should have been postponed a day, for if any film was beset by bad luck, it would be *Isle of the Dead.* Karloff's back problems (a chronic ailment harking back to his younger days that was further aggravated by the heavy Monster costume in the Frankenstein films) had been flaring up, probably as a result of the finale of *House of Frankenstein,* where Karloff (as Dr. Neimann) is dragged by the Monster (Glenn Strange) into a marsh full of quicksand. Karloff was already in physical anguish during the first days of *Isle*'s production, but trooper that he was, he carried on.

Unfortunately, just as *Isle* seemed to be shaping up, Karloff's affliction worsened, causing production to shut down after eight days. The actor was admitted to Good Samaritan Hospital, where his diagnosis called for a spinal operation. The July 25 issue of *The Hollywood Reporter* stated that the operation had been successfully performed and that Karloff was expected to leave the hospital in two weeks. He was scheduled to return to work on *Isle of the Dead* after another two weeks of convalescence at home. But the report came prematurely; a full month later, the August 24 *Hollywood Reporter* announced that Karloff was still in the hospital, but his release was imminent.

The temporary loss of its star led to other complications in the production of *Isle of the Dead.* By the time Karloff was out of the hospital and ready to resume work, it was well into September. By that time, several of *Isle*'s cast members were already involved in their obligations to other films. During Karloff's stay in the hospital, Lewton worked on the script of his next project, *The Body Snatcher,* which was supposed to go before the cameras on October 13 (though this scheduling was arranged before Karloff's extended health problems arrested the production of *Isle*). Because Lewton realized it was hopeless to continue with the first Karloff film until its key supporting performers were once again available, he made the decision (as reported in the October 25 issue of *The Hollywood Reporter*) that *The Body Snatcher* would be produced before *Isle of the Dead* was resumed and completed.

When production on *Isle of the Dead* was finally picked up on December 1, 1944, Lewton was in a quandary concerning its fate. It is true that, with the completed production of *The Body Snatcher,* he felt he had just delivered a sure winner, but in the interim he had lost much of his enthusiasm for the earlier Karloff project. *Isle* became a confusing mixture of alternate plans, very few of them coinciding with Lewton's original vision of the film. In a letter to his mother and sister, he called *Isle of the Dead* "a complete mess." The original script, credited to Ardell Wray and Josef Mischel, was not even used; its central character, Cathy, was totally wiped out. So were other roles.

Whatever headaches Lewton and Robson had over the alterations in *The Seventh Victim,* they were nothing compared to their frustrations over the fractured production of *Isle of the Dead. Isle* is fairly coherent, which is remarkable considering the circumstances, but the film seems haphazardly thrown together. There are dull and plodding passages and, except for its last half hour, too few of the narrative and visual hooks we have come to expect with the typical Lewton production. Although *Isle* was nearly ready for release in May 1945, Lewton decided to lead with his stronger suit, staggering the film's release until September and putting *The Body Snatcher* into the theaters first. It was a smart move.

Isle of the Dead starts off well, as do most Lewton films, imaginative openings being one of their trademarks. The first five minutes of *Isle of the Dead* are visually rich and quite promising (though it must be remembered that the opening scenes were shot before Karloff went into the hospital). A postcredit epigraph informs us: "Under conquest and oppression, the people of Greece allowed legends to degenerate into superstitions; the Goddess Aphrodite giving way to the Vorvolaka. This nightmare figure was very much alive in the minds of peasants when Greece fought the victorious war of 1912." This was the first of the Balkan Wars, where the Balkan League (Serbia, Bulgaria, Greece, and Montenegra) fought victoriously against Turkey; the war ended with the Treaty of Bucharest.

Our first shot, a close-up of a pair of hands being washed, foreshadows further events. The hands belong to General Pherides (Karloff); he and other members of the Greek army are conferring in a military tent. General Pherides (aka "the Watchdog") is dealing with Colonel Tolopedes (Sherry Hall), whose tired, emaciated soldiers arrived late to the last battle. "Even though they were late," the Colonel protests, "you won the battle! It wasn't my fault they didn't arrive in time." The General looks down at the table in front of him, as does the disgraced Colonel. A close-up of a pistol. As the Colonel picks up the gun and leaves the tent, he wears a grim, resigned expression. Moments later we hear the shot.

Oliver Davis (Marc Cramer), a Boston war correspondent, is present to witness this severe display of loyalty and disagrees with the General's methods. The General counters Oliver with, "Do you think it was easy to send Colonel Tolopedes to his death? He and I were friends." Oliver admits he does not understand the General's brand of patriotism, the kind where one would sacrifice one's own wife and child for the country's benefit. This causes Karloff to speak of his beloved wife, long dead and buried in a cemetery on a nearby island. "You think I'm a cold man, cold and brutal. If you asked her, she would never have said so." Oliver says he will visit the island cemetery the next day to put flowers on Mrs. Pherides's grave. Why wait? asks the General; they could go there immediately.

Pherides brings Oliver out of the tent, and we are given a tour of the battlefield; the effect is wonderfully atmospheric, thanks to the imaginative set design and Jack MacKenzie's photography. In a fluid tracking shot we get an all-too-short glimpse at the inexpensive but highly expressionistic soundstage fix-up; the set works amazingly well, considering that the space used was about the width of two road lanes. Muslin, attached to the shallow background of the set, simulates sky. A traveling matte passes by in the foreground, a few scattered bodies here and there, lifeless hands draping over rocks, everything dingy, the color of gunpowder and ash, all accompanied by the tortured groans of the wounded. Soldier-drawn body carts bring the dead to their resting pit. The General explains in the presence of Dr. Drossos (Ernst Dorian) that the tired soldiers must not rest, for outbreaks of septicemic plague and typhus make it imperative to bury the dead quickly. The General waxes poetic about Death: "The horseman on the pale horse; he follows the wars."

After this impressive opening sequence (which has little real connection with the rest of the film except to provide an atmospheric backdrop for the poorly motivated decision to visit the island), the seams in the patchwork script begin to show. However convenient it may be to the progression of the plot, the prospect of the General and Oliver taking time out from war (during an ensuing plague, no less) in order to row a boat to an island to put flowers on a grave borders on the preposterous. When the General reveals that it has been 15 years since his last visit, we have not the faintest idea why he should be motivated to go there now.

The island itself (a matte shot seen from the rowboat), looks beautifully idyllic and, given the nature of the title, not at all what one would expect. We see Greek ruins and what looks like the remains of a stone temple. Setting foot on the island, the men came across a statue of Cerberus, the three-headed dog of Greek mythology; the watchdog of the dead. This statue will function (as did the statue of St. Sebastian in *I Walked with a Zombie,* the floating-ball fountain in *Leopard,* and the church bell in *Fifi*) as a recurring motif; in this case the statue of Cerberus draws associations with General's own nickname, "the Watchdog." "He guards the dead," says the General, looking at the statue. "I must worry about the living."

They climb the marble steps that lead to the tomb, and when General Pherides enters the tunnel-like crypt, he discovers his wife's grave desecrated, her remains missing. Oliver and the General, having assumed the island to be deserted, hear a woman singing, her lovely, but unearthly, voice resounding through the stone chambers that lead to a passageway above. Following the source of the voice, the two men ascend to the door of an ancient stone dwelling, where they are welcomed by Albrecht (Jason Robards, Sr.), an archeologist who, upon discovering the island to be a gold mine of antiquity, has chosen to live there.

The General is outraged by the desecration of his wife's resting place. Albrecht takes the blame by saying he once encouraged the people of the island to hunt for nearby artifacts; in their zeal, they started to rob corpses as well. Albrecht has a number of house guests, travelers who have crossed over to the island to avoid the shelling of battle. We are introduced to Mr. St. Aubyn (Alan Napier), a British consul, and his pale, sickly wife (Katherine Emery). Thea (Ellen Drew), the down-to-earth Greek beauty whose singing voice we heard, is Mrs. St. Aubyn's nurse (somewhat paralleling the relationship between Betsy and Jessica in *Zombie*). Thea shows a dislike for the General; she is aware of the harm he has caused her people and refuses to serve him wine.

Not as easy on the eyes is Kyra (Helene Thimig), the disagreeable old caretaker of the house (slightly reminiscent of Eva Moore's Rebecca Femm in *The Old Dark House*); she whispers to the General that the graves were robbed to burn the remains because an evil spirit, the Vorvolaka, was residing within one of corpses. Kyra looks in the direction of Mrs. St. Aubyn and Thea, while she whispers in the General's ear: "There is one who grows stronger and another who grows weaker." When Kyra tells the General about the Vorvolaka, a female vampire of the soul whose presence brings death to those she touches, he dismisses it as nonsense.

Our final houseguest is the gnomelike Cockney drummer Robbins (Skelton Knaggs), a specialist in tinware. He has no earthly reason for being on the island other than to provide the film with its first victim. In his one and only scene, the drunken Robbins is introduced, allowed a few fragments of slurred speech (in his praise of fish 'n' chips), and then quickly given the boot. As Robbins staggers upstairs, he loses consciousness before he makes the upper landing. The others take him to his room, believing him to be merely drunk.

The General wishes to get back to his troops, but Oliver convinces him to stay the night (apparently, this leader of the Greek army will not be sorely missed). That night, Thea (who shares a room with Kyra) is awakened by the moaning of her patient, Mrs. St. Aubyn. The chiaroscuro effect—bars of moonlight covering the walls of Thea's room—recalls the look of Betsy's bedroom in *Zombie*. In fact, what follows is a reworking of a similar scene in *Zombie*. Here Thea (like Betsy in the other film) awakens from her sleep to investigate a woman's mournful cries. A creepy, tension-filled walk ensues, with Karloff's General replacing Jessica Rand as the figure in the dark. Unfortunately, as effective as this sequence is in its evocation of chills, it is merely gratuitous, doing little to delineate character or move the plot. After Thea recovers from her start at seeing the General suddenly appear in the dark hall, the two of them engage in an unconvincing dialogue about the General's harsh taxation methods.

The next morning Albrecht approaches the General: "I'd like your advice about something—a grave matter," (echoing Dr. Pretorius in *The Bride of Frankenstein*). Robbins has died in his sleep, and Pherides recognizes his prior behavior (previously dismissed as drunkenness) as possible symptoms of septicemic plague. The General quarantines the island and forbids anyone to leave, including himself. This is terrible news to Mr. and Mrs. St. Aubyn; the husband pleads, "My wife is ill and needs medical attention." But the General is unmoved. He sends for Dr. Drossos (how he does this without anyone leaving the island is one of the film's more perplexing mysteries), and, sure enough, the doctor declares Robbins a plague victim. Now even Dr. Drossos must remain quarantined on the island. "The doctor will tell you what to do," says the General, "and I will make you do it. We will fight the plague." Oliver gives Thea some flaccid wooing: "I wish you were far away," he nobly declares.

Briefly stated, the film here takes a turn in the direction of a locked door mystery or an old house thriller, our cast dying off one by one. And here's the mystery: are the characters really being picked off by the plague or is Thea (within whom may reside the Vorvolaka) really the source of the problem? This is no mystery to the audience, however, who can recognize, in Thea, the kind of plucky heroine who survives the last reel.

For a half hour or more, our narrative becomes overly talky, the tedium interrupted now and then with imaginative bridging shots (hands being washed in swirling water, dissolving to shots of Mediterranean waves crashing upon the rocky shore) telling us that time has passed and that characters are being sanitary. There is talk of the plague, of how a hot wind, blown in their direction, could kill the fleas that harbor the pestilence. When the subject of the Vorvolaka is raised and the doctor rejects it, Albrect defends the superstition as being no less believable than the doctor's strange talk of "good winds and bad winds." Here Albrecht suggests that they may as well pray to Hermes. He poses a wager: "The doctor can use his science, and I'll pray to Hermes. We'll see who dies and who is saved." The General, in his zealous support of Dr. Drossos, extends his hand to Albrecht in acceptance of the wager. They clasp hands and freeze. Albrecht announces: "You broke the doctor's first rule: no contact."

Shortly thereafter, Mrs. Aubyn confronts Kyra, telling her to stop poison-

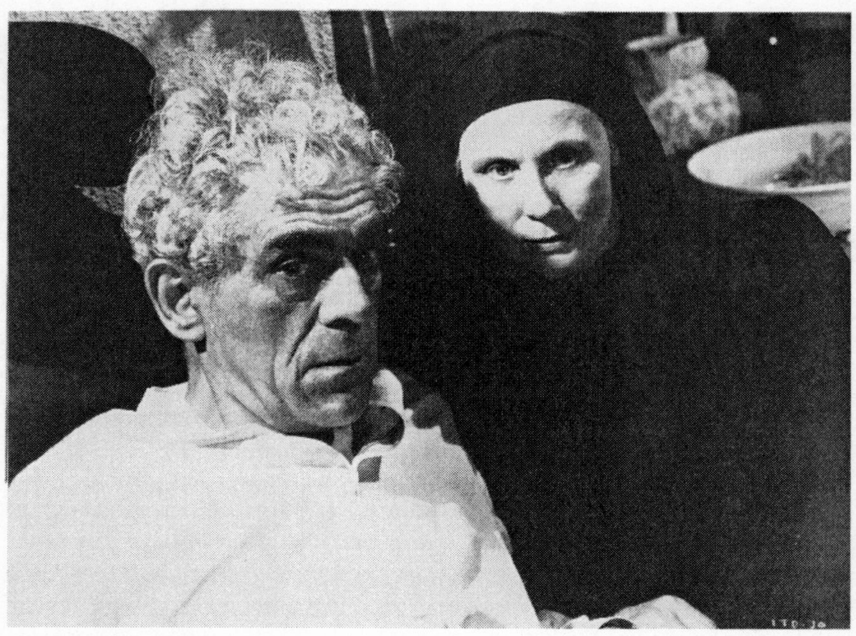

Kyra (Helene Thimig) fuels the General's paranoia with tales of the vorvolakas.

ing the General's mind about Thea. The confrontation, however, has left the woman weak. Thea goes to report the woman's condition to Mr. St. Aubyn, but discovers he is dying from the plague and wishes to hide this fact from his wife. Thea remains by his side until he dies, at which point the General barges in, finding more circumstantial evidence to support Kyra's claims that Thea is indeed the Vorvolaka.

After Mrs. St. Aubyn recovers, she hears the tragic news of her husband but insists he is not dead. Dr. Drossos assures her that, having applied the mirror-to-the-mouth test, Mr. St. Aubyn is most certainly dead.

Here we are introduced to the raison d'être for the entire film, according to Lewton's original plan. Privately, Mrs. St. Aubyn talks to the doctor, telling him that she was projecting her own fears; she, herself, suffers from deathlike cataleptic trances and lives in mortal fear of being buried alive. The grim doctor tries to reassure her, saying that, in the advent of her death, he would take every precaution to be certain of her demise. (Credibility falters during this scene when, in spite of the dangers of the plague and the concern over contact and proximity, the doctor and Mrs. St. Aubyn stand very close to each other.)

Another shot of Cerberus dissolves into waves and more handwashing before the camera settles on the ceremonial fire Albrecht has built to Hermes. The fire, built outdoors on a nearby stone dais, is confined to a small metal bowl. Dr. Drossos comes along and drops a twig into the flames. He does this to signify his surrender to Albrecht; having come down with the plague, Drossos has lost the wager. "The Greek gods are more powerful than my science," he accedes, a profound loss of reason apparently being a symptom of the dreaded plague. As is typical of a Lewton film, the most significant war waged in *Isle of the Dead* is that between reason and superstition.

Mrs. St. Aubyn shows reserves of strength as she tends to the needs of the ailing doctor, risking her own health by exposing herself to the contagion. When the chips are down, this courageous lady shows what she's made of; she's not afraid of dying, she tells her companions. (But there is one thing we know she does fear.) Mrs. St. Aubyn has the kind of dignity to mark her as a survivor, but the cards are stacked against her, and we suspect that the only thing she will survive will be her own burial.

After Drossos dies, the General's powers of reason continue to erode at an alarming rate. More and more, Kyra's warnings penetrate his fortress against superstition. He is seen feeding twigs into Hermes' fire. The General tells Thea: "I will keep you from the others . . . and, if necessary, I will make an end in the only way that we know that a Vorvolaka can be killed." (We are not sure of the methods to which he refers: a stake through the heart? a silver bullet?) He asks Thea whether she remembers her dreams, if she knows what she does in the night. Thea begins doubting herself, wondering if she (like *Cat People*'s Irena) may be a pawn to dark powers beyond her control. Since the audience is already certain that Thea is not a Vorvolaka, however, there is little dramatic power in her doubts and suspicions.

Thea goes to meet Oliver, taking a tunnel-like route through the ruins to another portion of the island, and the romantic pair begin breaking rule one: no contact. The General comes upon them and tells Oliver that he will kill Thea the first chance he gets. When Oliver, determined to get Thea off the island, goes to the rowboat that brought him across, its battered and broken hull tells him the General has been there first.

Mrs. St. Aubyn hears the General's threats against Thea and stands up for her loyal nurse. Oliver, too, pipes up: "If you do anything to harm Thea, I'll forget that we've been friends."

This quasi-friendship between Oliver and the General just does not make it. The alleged friendship between them, so often spoken of, is never convincingly developed. But that's only one of several things about the script that seems half-baked. With the numerous alterations in the screenplay, *Isle of the Dead*'s characters seldom appear clearly motivated. From this point on in the film, we are rarely given credible reasons why things happen; they just do.

While Thea tries to sleep, she hears Kyra chanting, "Vorvolaka, Vorvolaka," telling Thea of traps she has set to capture the evil spirit. Thea goes

Stark sets effectively rendered in *Isle of the Dead.*

to the room of her patient, but Mrs. St. Aubyn has died in her sleep; of course, since Thea made the discovery, the General's suspicions of her evil power are reinforced. The General becomes so unhinged by his fears that he attacks Thea, but does not get very far before Oliver intervenes. Acting as if the deranged man was a bosom friend, Oliver defends the General to Thea: "I don't know what's the matter with him; it's something up here," he points to his head. (Oliver obviously misses that sane, easygoing General Pherides, the one who ordered his good friend to commit suicide.)

After the General is subdued, Thea claims that Mrs. St. Aubyn may not be a plague victim: "She was not like the others! She fell down and hasn't moved since." A feather-at-the-mouth test follows and the results show she has stopped breathing. They all leave the room convinced of their findings, while the camera remains upon Mrs. Aubyn's corpse. In an extremely effective shot, we move in for a close-up of the woman's dead face and for just one brief moment, we see the corpse's mouth twitch.

The men carry Mrs. St. Aubyn's body in a wooden crate which they put on a marble stand in the darkened tomb (there are archways, but no formal doors in this echoing stone structure). The men leave, and the camera stays behind with the coffin, just as it stayed behind with Mrs. Aubyn's "corpse" in the earlier scene. Once again we move closer, nothing but silence accompanying our slow, even progress toward the crude casket. Then, from within, comes a woman's soft moan.

Short bits of parallel action are used to punctuate the premature burial set piece. While the cross-cutting to other characters, mostly to the General, is well intended, the parallel action is too uninspired to transcend the frustration we feel every time the camera cuts away from the tomb.

We dissolve back to a close shot of the wooden casket that places us exactly where we were when we last saw it, except time has passed and it is darker now. The camera pulls back slowly, an unwinding of the earlier shot. Then, at the farthest vantage point there is a loud scream and a simultaneous cut to a close top view of the crate; the sounds of scratching, screaming, and banging coming from under the lid continue through the shot. It is a chilling scene.

In further parallel action, the General, who is sick in bed, tells Kyra, "I'm not dead yet! She shall not harm you." Then there is another shot of Cerberus before we cut back to the coffin. We see—and hear, with acoustic precision—water dripping, drop by drop, plunk, plunk, onto the lid of the crate. We see the drops in close-up, see them collect, ready to fall, from the stone ceiling, see them land in the puddle on the lid. This time there is no jolting outcry from within, just the sounds of water drops.

We cut to Kyra warning the General, "One who dies from the Vorvolaka becomes the Vorvolaka," before returning to a close shot of the saturated coffin lid. The drops count off the moments as the water softens the wood. Then the hypnotic percussion of the drops is interrupted by a loud bang from within as the boards of the lid begin to burst upward.

A cutaway to the General shows him hearing the sound of creaking wood, shades of Roderick Usher, before we return to the open doorway of the tomb. Although we see nothing, we can hear the mad ravings of a woman: "In darkness, you shut me in. Shut in." Dressed in a white flowing gown, Mrs. St. Aubyn, now obviously insane, exits the tomb.

As we near the end of *Isle of the Dead*, we must prepare for the by-now-obligatory Lewton walk, this time taken by Thea. The reasons for her journey are pretty thin. While the survivors gather in a downstairs room (except for Kyra who is asleep upstairs), Oliver tells Thea to go to bed because her presence agitates the General, who is moaning in an adjoining room. Because Thea is not ready for bed, Oliver tells her to go outside, where it is windy, but warm, and that he will join her after the General has fallen asleep. For reasons beyond our comprehension, instead of guarding the woman he loves from the dangers of the night, Oliver chooses to stay inside to read a book and listen to Albrecht prattle about his artifacts. Oliver's audience with Albrecht establishes the existence of an ancient Greek trident which is in Albrecht's possession, and this trident will become important to the plot.

Thea goes outside and closes the door behind her. She remains standing on the step as we hear the rushing of wind and see moving shadows of branches on the house behind her. As is characteristic of most Lewton walks, there is no score music, just the wind and the melodius call of a bird, the last seeming out of place in the gloom. Thea looks into the woods; it is all very uninviting. She starts walking on a path as the wind and bird sounds mingle on the soundtrack. A screech owl shatters the night, but the "bus" comes too early in the sequence to provide a severe jolt.

As she continues, we can tell that something holds Thea's attention, but we are not sure what. Next comes an eerie female voice in a singsong pattern born of madness. Thea moves along paths, down and up stone stairways, all the while searching for the source of the voice. At times we see Mrs. St. Aubyn gliding through the woods in her flowing white dress, once crossing the path Thea has just taken, but our heroine has not yet seen her wraithlike form. Thea hesitantly walks into a tunnel-like structure, paralyzed by her fear as she suspects she is not alone. Suddenly, Mrs. St. Aubyn makes her screaming exit through the other end of the structure. The sequence ends shortly thereafter, when Thea is startled by the "bus"-like sudden appearance of Oliver. Thea tells him about the resurrected woman.

Meanwhile, Mrs. St. Aubyn, it seems, has a mission to fill. She enters the house, steals the trident from Albrecht, who is sleeping at his desk, and then approaches Kyra's bed; as the old woman awakens, the trident makes its quick, fatal descent. The mad murderess moves into a darkened corner of the bedroom and waits.

Oliver and Thea wake Albrecht, telling him that Mrs. St. Aubyn is on the loose. Oliver and Albrecht go outside to find her, but for some misguided reason, they make Thea remain in the house with the still-raving General. Thea goes to her bedroom, where Kyra lies dead under the covers of the adjoining bed, but it is too dark for her to notice the old woman's condition. She slips under the covers of her own bed. Suddenly she believes she hears something moving in the corner of her room, but decides it is her imagination and tries to sleep.

The General heads toward Thea's room to make good his vow. He enters the bedroom and, after discovering Kyra has been killed, moves toward Thea with murderous intent. From her dark hiding place, Mrs. St. Aubyn charges in and, with arms raised high, plunges the trident into the General's back. Oliver and Albrecht arrive upon the scene to see Mrs. St. Aubyn fleeing the room, her hell-bent mission completed. She runs to the edge of an island cliff and leaps to her death. This time she will not wake from her "little sleep."

Thea, still petrified, remains against the wall of her room and now, from around the corner of the bed comes the General, dragging himself along the floor with the trident in his grip, making a last attempt to kill the Vorvolaka. He dies in his efforts to reach Thea. The film ends with Albrecht paying some misbegotten tribute to the General: "In back of his madness was something simple, good. He wanted to protect us all."

Most critics agree that *Isle of the Dead* is an uneven Lewton production. It is true that the finished result is more a horror "grab bag" than a coherent, unified whole, but considering the multiple strikes against it, we can be grateful it turned out as well as it did. Its premature burial set piece is, along with the swimming pool sequence from *Cat People* and the blood-under-the-door sequence from *The Leopard Man,* among the most well-remembered horror scenes in the Lewton oeuvre.

In some instances the acting is weak and uninspired; even Karloff, in spite of his assured performance, is sometimes off the mark. As General Pherides, he shows little middle ground; one moment he is the stern officer with an iron hand, and the next moment is a fount of conviviality. All this is understandable, however, considering the uncertain evolution of the script and the fractured shooting schedule.

The other performances in *Isle of the Dead* are mostly unremarkable, although Katherine Emery does extremely well in helping Karloff carry the film. Unfortunately, she is given little opportunity for any dramatic flair once she becomes "resurrected," and her avenging angel, during the film's last reel, is a fleeting vesperal image—surely a mere ghost of her former self. Ernst Dorian, as the doctor, gives a nice reptilian edge to his role (imagine a hybrid of Edward Cianelli and Henry Daniell), but he too is not given enough screen time to make much of a difference. Certainly Helene Thimig, as Kyra, makes the most of her hooded hag role, but while she is important to the plot, her total effect is little more than that of a red herring. Ellen Drew is competent as Thea, but her character never evokes the kind of sympathy that is so often characteristic of Lewton's heroines in peril. Marc Cramer is merely a throwback to the generic leads we have seen from David Manners and Patric Knowles in the Universal horror films: a safety net for the distressed damsel. Alan Napier is, as always, his usual dignified self, though, as is often the case with his Lewton film roles, he has very little to do. Skelton Knaggs, too, is fine in his thankless cameo.

Although Jason Robards, Sr., was excellent in *Mademoiselle Fifi,* we cannot say the same about his role as Albrecht, where he appears altogether too cheerful (the plague seeming to be hardly an inconvenience) for someone in his situation. When he confesses his responsibility for the desecration of the many graves, including that of the General's wife, he talks in such inappro-

This RKO ad falsely indicated Ellen Drew as the "beautiful girl [who] will be in her coffin buried alive!"

priately pleasant tones that he might as well be giving a report on the status of his flowerbeds.

Like *I Walked with a Zombie, Isle of the Dead* is plagued by an altogether vague sense of physical space. To get to any other part of the island (according to Mark Robson's explanation in Siegel's *The Reality of Terror*), Thea must pass through the creepy stone tunnel-like enclosure, but this aspect of the film is never made clear. Robson recalled making his heroine pass through the terrifying tunnel every time she wanted to get somewhere, a neat idea, but the finished film never does anything to establish the necessity of the tunnel's use. For all we know, Thea may enjoy walking in dark tunnels. In *Isle of the Dead* it is nearly impossible to distinguish a pattern in the comings and goings of screen characters because we are never sure of the island's physical layout.

In some ways *Isle of the Dead* is a retread of *I Walked with a Zombie*. The similarities are numerous: the island locale, the air of stasis and decay, a "walking dead" woman and her heroic "nurse," the confrontation between modern science and native superstition, the recurring statue imagery, the water symbolism, and even the disorienting use of physical space. Yet—and this is rather amazing—*Isle* never seems derivative of *Zombie*.

Isle of the Dead, coming four months after the release of the critically superior and extremely popular *The Body Snatcher,* was bound to disappoint inflated expectations. A West Virginia exhibitor was quite direct in assessing the impact *Isle* had upon his theater audience: "The first part of the picture is boring, but the last part had my patrons screaming and shouting their heads off" (Paul Jensen, *Boris Karloff and His Films*).

In the September 29, 1945, issue of *The Nation,* Lewton devotee James Agee called *Isle,* "Tedious, overloaded, diffuse, and at moments arty, yet in many ways to be respected, up to its last half-hour or so; then it becomes as brutally frightening and gratifying a horror movie as I can remember." Agee concludes by recommending *The Body Snatcher* as a surer bet. Agee's favorable opinion of *Isle,* and particularly its terrifying climax, came to a fuller bloom by the time he wrote his *Time* review:

> When the shriek of the prematurely buried woman finally comes, it releases the rest of the show into a free-for-all masterpiece of increasing terror. The wild laughs, blown leaves, scrawks and tongue-swallowing of jittery night birds, and darkness in an empty room would have pleased and scared the daylights out of Poe himself. For all the film's gently dawdling beginning, horror specialist Producer Val Lewton and his colleagues have turned *Isle of the Dead* into one of the best horror movies ever made.

Although *Variety* said the film "tops all past efforts for creepiness and suspense," other reviewers were not as kind. *Motion Picture Review* stated, "it is not a well-made picture and has many faults, and all of the creators concerned in its making are at fault." A particularly scathing review (which, like it or not, was sometimes on the money) came from the November 17 *Kinematograph Weekly,* an English periodical: "Dreary modern Greek tragedy set in a weird island cemetery. . . . The picture is a vague as well as ugly essay in the supernatural, and the attempt to link its grisly tale to Greek mythology only adds to the confusion. Boris Karloff has no idea whether he is coming or going as the General, and the same applies to the rest."

Despite the mixed opinions at the time of release, *Isle of the Dead* has garnered a respectable reputation over the years and has come to be considered a minor horror classic. In *Heroes of the Horrors,* Calvin Beck concludes: "The Lewton technique of suggesting terror through continual sustained mood, instead of the more direct and commercial jolting-shock approach, is especially overpowering in *Isle.* Audiences and critics beheld something quite unique in the genre; and because it was uniquely inventive, most of the jaded and hack critics were caught off balance, some panning it (because of its deliberately slow construction) as dull and boring." William K. Everson, after giving a marvelous description of *Isle*'s premature burial sequence in the introduction to his *Classics of the Horror Film,* cites it as providing "one of the single most chilling moments in the history of the screen." Robert F. Moss, in *Karloff and Company: The Horror Film,* states: "The movie has been called a failure, but, if so, it is more interesting than most other people's successes."

Of course *Isle of the Dead* contains its share of autobiographical Lewton touches, if one wishes to play that guessing game. Lewton's obsession for historical accuracy seems to be embodied by Albrecht, who may also represent Lewton's pompous, self-important side. A younger pre–Hollywood Lewton may be found in Oliver, the New England reporter. (For the record, four Lewton films—*Cat People, Curse of the Cat People, Isle of the Dead,* and *Bedlam*—feature a character named Oliver; in each case, it appears that Lewton has drawn said character with autobiographical strokes.) But the woman in the casket may be yet another version of the producer, trapped within a genre from which he wishes to break free. General Pherides could be, depending upon one's fancy, Jack Gross, David Selznick, or even another authority-obsessed version of Lewton himself. Kyra may be Lewton's Russian nanny, the one who scared him with violent folktales and native superstitions. And perhaps we should stop here, lest we begin finding some autobiographical significance in the Cockney tin salesman played by Skelton Knaggs.

Thematically, *Isle of the Dead* has some things in common with *The Seventh Victim.* Both films use death as their central focus. To some extent, this is true with all horror films, but these two Lewton/Robson films take a more serious approach to the theme of death than the run-of-the-mill fright flick. One could pose an argument that *The Seventh Victim* and *Isle of the Dead* are two sides of the same coin. *Victim* focuses upon an acceptance of death, while *Isle* deals with its denial. In *Isle of the Dead* even those who are laid to rest deny the finality of their long sleep.

FOURTEEN

The Body Snatcher

> ***Still their unnatural burden bumped from side to side; and now the head would be laid, as if in confidence, upon their shoulders, and now the drenching sackcloth would flap icily about their faces. A creeping chill began to possess Fettes. He peered at the bundle, and it seemed somehow larger than at first. All over the countryside, and from every degree of distance, the farm dogs accompanied their passage with tragic ululations; and it grew and grew upon his mind that some unnatural miracle had been accomplished, that some nameless change had befallen the dead body, and that it was in fear of their unholy burden that the dogs were howling.***
>
> — Robert Louis Stevenson, "The Body Snatcher"

In the first months of 1944, the "period thriller" began to creep its way into the hearts of the nation's motion picture audiences. MGM's *Gaslight* and 20th Century–Fox's *The Lodger,* both released in 1944, signaled the beginning of what was to become a major, if relatively short-lived, Hollywood trend. The lavish remakes of *Dr. Jekyll and Mr. Hyde* (1941), *The Phantom of the Opera* (1943), and even *Jane Eyre* (1943), demonstrated that there was a wartime audience for thrillers that turned back the clock, but it took *Gaslight*'s remarkable popularity and *The Lodger*'s profound artistry to transform the period thriller into a viable subgenre for the remainder of the decade.

Of course, thrillers set in bygone eras, and in British or European locales, were more the rule than the exception during the horror cycle of the 1930s. The horror prototypes of that era, *Dracula, Frankenstein, Dr. Jekyll and Mr. Hyde,* offered exotic period settings as colorful and atmospheric backgrounds for their chills. During the war years, however, several of Universal's horror entries had become updated and domesticated; Lon Chaney, Jr., as Count Alucard (aka Dracula) or Kharis (aka the Mummy), suddenly found himself vacationing in the southern Gothic climes of Louisiana. Val Lewton was, himself, a strong influence upon both the Americanization and the modernization of the Hollywood creepshow during the war years, *Cat People* being the trendsetter that exemplified a profound disregard for old-world horror settings.

By 1944, however, there had been such a glut of contemporary films, often with direct or indirect references to the war effort, that period films (dramas, comedies, biopics, thrillers) offered American moviegoers a welcome respite from the troubled modern world. The period thriller, exemplified by George Cukor's *Gaslight* and John Brahm's *The Lodger,* brought back the gaslit streets, the shadows in the mist, and the footsteps in the fog, all of which seemed infinitely more comforting than the day-to-day terrors of 1944. The climate was right for Lewton's RKO horror films to follow suit. Had it not been for the popularity of the period thriller, Val Lewton would have likely had more difficulty getting a green light on a horror production set in 1830s Edinburgh.

In *Karloff and Lugosi,* author Greg Mank digs up a fascinating RKO interdepartment memo dated May 10, 1944, which was written by Lewton shortly after the front office informed him that Bela Lugosi would be added to the roster of one of the Karloff films. In the memo, Lewton informs "Mr. Gross" that subject to his approval, Robert Louis Stevenson's short story "The Body Snatcher" would be an ideal project ("for the second Karloff film") for the following five reasons:

> 1) The title seems good to us.
> 2) There is exploitation value in the use of a famous Robert Louis Stevenson classic.
> 3) There is a ninety percent chance that this is in the public domain. The legal department is now searching the title.
> 4) The characters are colorful. The background of London medical life in the 1830s is extremely interesting. The sets are limited in number but effective in type. The costumes are readily procurable and no great difficulties of any sort so far as production is concerned are evident.
> 5) There is also an excellent part for Bela Lugosi as a resurrection man.

Stevenson's original story is a mixture of fact and fiction. The factual aspects, fleeting references to "resurrectionists" Burke and Hare and their employer Dr. Knox (known in the story as Mr. K____) give Stevenson's work a degree of verisimilitude.

The notorious Burke and Hare were grave-robbers who, as history tells it, supplied Dr. Knox with remarkably fresh corpses. They committed murder 18 times for this purpose, Burke held his hand over the mouth and nose of his victims until they suffocated, while Hare assisted with numerous incidentals. When the two were caught in 1829, Hare gave king's evidence, leading to Burke's conviction and his subsequent hanging. Hare was released (though physically harassed by an outraged mob of Edinburgh rowdies), while Dr. Knox, his reputation rather miraculously sustaining the damage, eventually moved to London, where he served his profession with honor and dignity for another three decades, writing several highly influential books on anatomy. The irony wrought by the inequities of justice among the fates of these three equally culpable men, Burke, Hare, and Knox, was not lost on Lewton, who likely recognized a similar irony in the dubious art of horror filmmaking: Lewton and his directors dug the graves, while RKO executives like Sid Rogell, Jack Gross, and Charles Koerner reaped the benefits without soiling their hands.

Although Stevenson's story was not an actual account of the Burke/Hare/Knox episode, the Edinburgh-born author knew the notorious case was still common knowledge in 1884, when "The Body Snatcher" was written. In the story, Stevenson presents the fictional characters of Fettes and MacFarlane, two medical students who, in an effort to supply their school with human specimens for dissection, begin to do their own grave-robbing. In a tavern one day, a mysterious man named Gray confronts MacFarlane and displays an unusual amount of familiarity. Fettes witnesses this cryptic exchange, noticing that this "coarse, vulgar, and stupid [Gray] . . . exercised a very remarkable control over MacFarlane." When Gray orders a sumptuous meal and charges it to the tense MacFarlane, the latter's willingness to pay leads Fettes to suspect extortion. The next day MacFarlane is absent for his anatomy lectures. Then Fettes is awakened in the middle of the night by MacFarlane who needs help in delivering a body to Mr. K____. Fettes looks into the sack and sees the face of Mr. Gray.

A few nights later, on a particularly rainy evening, the two "resurrectionists" travel by carriage with their new specimen—a farmer's dead wife, wrapped in a sack—between them. During this harrowing ride (described in the Stevenson passage that begins this chapter), the men grow increasingly apprehensive. Halting the carriage, they investigate:

> And as Fettes took the lamp his companion untied the fastenings of the sack and drew down the cover from the head. The light fell very clear upon the dark, well-moulded features and smooth-shaven cheeks of a too familiar countenance, often beheld in dreams of both of these young men. A wild yell rang up into the night; each leaped from his own side into the roadway: the lamp fell, broke, and was extinguished; and the horse, terrified by this unusual commotion, bounded and went off toward Edinburgh at a gallop, bearing along with it, solo occupant of the gig, the body of the dead and long-dissected Gray."

Thus ends the Stevenson story.

After Lewton wrote his own treatment for *The Body Snatcher*, the duties of scriptwriting were given to Philip MacDonald (who by coincidence had written one of the stories that Boris Karloff included in his 1943 anthology, *Tales of Terror*). Since Karloff's stay in the hospital lasted over a month and his at-home recovery several more weeks, Lewton had time to read and reread the Stevenson story, to work and rework the Philip MacDonald script. The producer had numerous conferences with MacDonald, and the two of them created new characters (Meg, Mrs. Marsh, Georgina, and Josef) to broaden the narrative to fit the length of a feature film. Jack Gross encouraged Lewton to supply strong horror elements, and the early drafts of the screenplay were reportedly quite gruesome. "In the original script," according to Greg Mank in *Karloff and Lugosi*, "there was an episode in which the character of Mrs. MacBride, in Lewton's words, 'passes through the horrors of attempting to identify her dead son among the flotsam and jetsam of human limbs and portions on the anatomy table.'"

In adapting "The Body Snatcher" for the screen, Lewton took the characters of Fettes and MacFarlane, varied their ages, and altered their relationship, turning them into doubles along the ("if-this-goes-on") lines of *The Ghost Ship*'s Captain Stone and Tom Merriam. The Lewton/MacDonald script presented Donald Fettes as the youthful idealistic medical student who had to answer to his older counterpart, Dr. "Toddy" MacFarlane, a seasoned, worldly professor of anatomy. Gray, who remains mysterious in the Stevenson story, is given more substance in the film; he is a cabman by day and a grave-robber by night. Moreover, Gray's character is deliberately fashioned as yet another alter ego for MacFarlane.

On September 8, 1944, Lewton sent a working draft of *The Body Snatcher*'s script to the Breen Office. The response, coming near the end of the month, was:

> We have read with close attention your estimating script . . . and regret to advise that this story is unacceptable under the provisions of the code, because of the repellent nature of such matter, which has to do with grave-robbing, dissecting bodies, and pickling bodies . . . the undue gruesomeness which would unavoidably be attached to the picturization of such scenes could in no wise be approved [Greg Mank, *Karloff and Lugosi*].

Being pulled in two different directions—the horror hungry Jack Gross on one side, and the scissor-happy censors on the other—drove Lewton to distraction, though he persevered, revamping the script, broadening the romantic relationship, changing some locales, and altering much of the project's charnel house vision. When he was finished, the Breen Office, with some reservations, gave its approval.

As with all of his productions, Lewton took the responsibility of revising the final script, as usual with the intention of remaining uncredited. MacDonald, however, was so apprehensive about the film misfiring (especially since Lewton had done such extensive rewriting) that he did not want to take the blame alone and insisted that the producer include his own name in the screenplay credit as well. Lewton complied by crediting the screenplay to both MacDonald and Carlos Keith (Lewton's favored pen name).

Hoping to make the film a special event, Lewton asked Jack Gross's help in securing some moderate stars to give a boost to the film; Lewton cited *The Wolf Man* as an example of how a few recognizable names could bolster the film's drawing power. One thing was certain: Boris Karloff would play the John Gray character. Lewton and Robert Wise considered numerous candidates for the role of Dr. "Toddy" MacFarlane, the cold-hearted anatomy teacher—Albert Dekker, John Emery, George Coulouris, and even Alan Napier—though, in hindsight, it is difficult to consider anyone other than the actor they finally chose: Henry Daniell (who excelled in—and obviously relished—his villainous roles in such films as *The Sea Hawk* and *Jane Eyre*).

Daniell was RKO's only concession to Lewton's request for moderate stars. Supporting roles were chosen mostly from the ranks of studio contract players. Russell Wade, who as Tom Merriam in *Ghost Ship* had done an admirable job as the villain's innocent alter ego, was selected for the not dissimilar pivotal role of Fettes. Also cast were Rita Corday (as Mrs. Marsh). Sharyn Moffet (as young Georgina Marsh), and Edith Atwater (as MacFarlane's live-in lover, Meg). An early choice for Georgina was Ann Carter, the young actress whose natural presence in *Curse of the Cat People* provided one of the most memorable performances in a Lewton film. Robert Wise told the author in a 1991 interview, "I didn't use Ann Carter in *The Body Snatcher* because she just didn't have the right look for the little girl. I needed somebody who looked a little more wan, somebody who looked a little sickly, and Ann was too healthy for that."

Of course, Lewton and company still needed a role for Bela Lugosi, and the one written in was that of Josef (spelled "Joseph" in the final draft), MacFarlane's servant, who was made slightly humpbacked at Jack Gross's behest. At this point in his career, the drug-addicted Lugosi would take any role that came his way. Plagued with ulcers, Lugosi was being supplied with morphine under a doctor's questionable supervision.

In Tom Weaver's *Interviews with B Science Fiction and Horror Movie Makers*, Robert Clarke (who played a minor role as one of the medical students) recalls what the Hungarian actor was like on the set: "During the time that I was involved on *The Body Snatcher*, [Bela Lugosi] hardly came out of his dressing room unless the assistant director called him. They had a daybed in there, and he was flat on his back on that couch nearly all the time. He talked very little to anyone, and obviously he wasn't well at all. It was very difficult for him to perform."

Robert Wise told the author, "Bela Lugosi was not well at all during the shooting of the film. Although Boris had back problems, he was not that sick. But Bela was not very strong and I always had to nurse him through that performance. . . . Val sat down and created the part of Joseph; it didn't exist in the original first draft of that script."

The budget for *The Body Snatcher* (somewhere between $180,000 and

$200,000) was slightly higher than that reserved for the usual Lewton film and it showed. The production attracted the press, and Ezra Goodman, a columnist of *The Morning Telegraph*, visited the set and gave his readers a sense of Lewton's meticulous guiding hand:

> We proceeded to sound stage four at the studio, where *The Body Snatcher* was shooting. . . .
>
> After talking to assorted agents, writers, directors, cameramen and players, Lewton finally got around to expounding his theory of picture making. He believes that quality can be present in a low budget picture, that dramatic qualities do not need to be sacrificed if ingenuity and imagination are used, particularly in the writing of the script. Lewton pointed to the song Donna Lee had been singing as an example. Instead of building big sets to suggest the atmosphere of Edinburgh, Lewton did it by means of the evocative song the girl sang. The anatomy room he used for *The Body Snatcher* was once a set for *Experiment Perilous* and Lewton was using it for an anatomy chamber, a living room and a stable in his picture. . . . Lewton says a picture can never be too good for moviegoers and that pictures fail when they are not good but pretentious.

The exteriors for *The Body Snatcher* were primarily recycled standing sets from *The Hunchback of Notre Dame* (1939), the same film Robert Wise had edited some five years before. Musical composer Roy Webb (who had not scored the music for the previous three Lewton films) provided one of his most memorable Lewton scores, borrowing heavily from Scottish folk ballads. In addition to Webb's haunting orchestral music, a variety of folk songs ("We'd Better Bide a Wee," "When Ye Gang Awa," "Jamie," "Will Ye No Come Back Again," "Spit Song," and "Bonnie Dundee") come by way of street singers and pub quartets, a successful attempt to give the film a genuine Scottish flavor (The songs almost compensate for the film's pronounced lack of authentic Scottish dialects.)

The Lewton/RKO perennials—the D'Agostino/Keller art direction team and set decorator Darrell Silvera—were once again aboard, and they earned their money; their respective departments shine in this production. Director of photography Robert de Grasse, whose last Lewton film was *The Leopard Man,* had the opportunity here to show himself to be a formidable match for Nicholas Musuraca.

The Body Snatcher begins with some marvelously picturesque establishing shots of 1831 Edinburgh. In typical Lewton-fashion, aural textures overlap on the soundtrack, the beating of military drums counterpointing nicely with the melodious voice of a street singer. An exquisite close-up of a street singer played by 15-year-old Donna Lee approximates the effect of a portrait in oil; the shot lingers, as does her melody. Another shot, that of two shepherds guiding their sheep down a cobbled city street, rings so true that it is hard to believe it was accomplished on a Hollywood lot. Such remarkable visuals make it plain that the Lewton team's extensive study of famous paintings was starting to pay off; the shot of the shepherds tending their flock is an early nineteenth century painting come to life.

Donald Fettes (Russell Wade) is eating his lunch at a grave site in Grayfriar's Kirkyard when Mrs. McBride (perennial Irish mother Mary Gordon) comes to put flowers on her son's grave. The grave is guarded by her son's dog, Robbie, whom she feeds; the poor beast has never left his master's grave since the burial. The woman does not mind about the dog keeping its loyal vigil, however; the kirkyard needs guarding from grave-robbers, who can make a good living by supplying specimens for the nearby medical school.

We hear a hollow clip-clop of hoofbeats before we see the approach of cabman John Gray (Karloff), who delivers Mrs. Marsh (Rita Corday) and her crippled daughter Georgina (Sharyn Moffett) to the medical school run by the extraordinarily gifted surgeon, Dr. MacFarlane. Gray, wearing a worn overcoat, scarf, and dusty top hat, carries Georgina in his arms, his warmth and benevolence reflected in his words: "Come, little miss. Cabman Gray will carry you safe enough. Would you like to give my horse a little pat? He knows every little girl in Edinburgh. Someday, when you're running and playing in the streets, he'll knicker at you as we go by." When Georgina reminds him of her affliction, which prohibits her running and playing, Gray says with most genuine regret, "Hey lass, I forgot that. All the more reason for friend here to give you a hello."

Meg (Edith Atwater) answers the front door, first seeing Mrs. Marsh and then Gray, who is still carrying Georgina. A look of solemn recognition passes like a dark cloud over Meg's face when her eyes meet those of the cabman; there is a momentary hint of menace in Gray's smiling expression before he goes on his way.

Mrs. Marsh, having heard of Dr. MacFarlane's reputation, has come in the hope of having her daughter cured of her paralysis, the result of a carriage accident. But Georgina does not take to MacFarlane's cold manner, nor to the condescending way he keeps calling her "child." "Tell me where it hurts, child," he says, or when this does not work, "Child, can you at least point to where it hurts?" It is clear that the illustrious surgeon will get no cooperation from the girl. "He frightens me," whispers the girl to her mother.

"It's useless, Mum!" MacFarlane utters in frustration.

When Donald Fettes enters the building, MacFarlane wants him to try his luck with the girl. Fettes begins by talking about Georgina's chair, how he has never seen one like it, and the next thing we know Georgina graciously gives Fettes the information she had withheld from the cold, stiff-backed MacFarlane. With Fettes's assistance, MacFarlane is able to diagnose Georgina, finding a "traumatic tumor that presses on the nerve center." Surgery could remedy this, but such an operation has never been done. MacFarland would be the ideal man for the job but he flatly refuses; he has a school to run and cannot accept every hard-luck case that comes his way.

MacFarlane shows considerable flexibility when Fettes later announces he must quit his studies because he is out of money. "Nonsense, Fettes. I'll not let you quit. You're too good a man," says the doctor, appointing the student as his paid assistant. It is obvious that MacFarlane sees a younger version of himself in Fettes. Meg, the housemaid, has overheard the exchange and shows concern about Fettes's appointment. "Don't worry," explains MacFarlane after Fettes leaves the room, "it won't spoil the boy. Wasn't I assistant to Dr. Knox? Did it do me any harm?" MacFarlane gives Meg a brief peck on the cheek, and this sparks a passionate kiss and embrace from the woman. Apparently, this housemaid's services cover a wide territory.

MacFarlane takes Fettes on a tour of his new duties, bringing him downstairs. The surgeon's ongoing instructions come to an abrupt halt when he sees his servant, Joseph (Lugosi), break from an eavesdropping stance to pretend he is wiping a table, which he now does with enough vigor to make his parted hair sway. "Joseph! What the devil are you doing sneaking about like a redskin? Make a little noise, man. Let people know you're about. Otherwise, I might get the idea you're trying to spy on me."

Fettes is brought into the cellar, where the conversation turns to the subject of the human specimens the school uses for dissection. As they step behind a curtain, we hear MacFarlane explain that more subjects are needed than those they may obtain legally.

The shot of the curtain dissolves to the accompaniment of hollow hoofbeats as we shift into evening. At the cemetery where Robbie guards his master's grave, we see Gary's shadow and hear the dog's growl. Without a hitch, the shadow swings a long object—a spade or shovel—over its shoulder, and brings it crashing down. Silence.

The clip-clop of Gray's horse wakes Fettes from a restless sleep. Aware of his new duties, he opens the door to Gray, who enters with a heavy sack over his shoulder, surprised to see a new man in charge: "You'll find this specimen in good condition, as bright and lively as a thrush, not a week long gone." When the subject of payment is brought up, Gray says, "That's the soul of the business, the pay." Gray's casually delivered comment makes it clear that his crimes rest upon the shoulders (and pocketbooks) of doctors like MacFarlane, who encourage the practice of grave-robbing.

What is so notable about the Lewton/MacDonald script thus far, outside of its very colorful dialogue, is its rich characterization and its reliance upon suggestion. What we learn about characters and events we learn indirectly, thanks to Wise's savvy direction, through facial expressions, offhanded comments, shadows, and sound effects. This is exactly the method employed by the Stevenson story, where we have to infer the meaning of events by the evidence at hand. As a result, the characters of MacFarlane and Gray in the

Lewton adaptation achieve uncommon depth; we are forced to read our suspicions in their every action and remark.

MacFarlane is quickly established as the real predator of the film because whatever heinous crimes Gray commits, MacFarlane is his motivating force, the "soul of the business." Time and again MacFarlane is characterized as a beast of prey. While dissecting his subject before an audience of students, he remarks, "In an adult, this muscle can apply more than one hundred seventy-five pounds of pressure. Double that and you have the full strength of the human jaw. That, gentlemen, is to chew our food and bite our enemies." Breaking for lunch, MacFarlane, ever the carnivore, announces that he "must have a discussion with a bit of beef."

MacFarlane and Fettes go to a pub to have their meal, passing the street singer as they go. When they enter the pub, they walk over to the fireplace and warm their hands near a huge pig roasting on a spit. MacFarlane addresses the pig in his usual predatory manner, "We'll meet this fellow on fairly equal terms," when suddenly he hears another voice ring out: "A fine specimen, isn't he, Toddy MacFarlane?" It is Gray, and the meaning of his inquiry has, of course, a double edge.

The scene that follows is extremely faithful to the Stevenson story; much of its dialogue actually found its way into the script. In some ways the film improves upon its source without altering the story's intent. The provocatively written and darkly humorous verbal duels between MacFarlane and Gray provide the film with some of its more glorious moments.

When MacFarlane tells Gray not to call him "Toddy," the cabman's response is full of mystery: "I've known the time, Toddy, when you liked the name. Aye, and many a dead man who called you by it. Rough and wild ones they were, too. But sit down, Toddy, with your friends. sit down. You wouldn't want it be said of you that you refused a glass to an old friend." Reluctantly, MacFarlane and Fettes sit with Gray, who addresses the young student, "I'm a pretty bad fellow myself, but MacFarlane's the boy . . . heh, heh, heh . . . Toddy MacFarlane."

When a waiter glances over to them, Gray says, "Don't worry, waiter. I'm with my friend, the great Dr. MacFarlane. He wants to sit here with the commonality."

"I will not have you call me that name," protests the doctor under his breath.

On Mrs. Marsh's behalf, Fettes asks MacFarlane if he will operate on Georgina. When Gray overhears MacFarlane's refusal, he says, "Maybe you're afraid, Toddy. You're not as good as you make out to be. I'd like for you to do the operation. I'd like to have you prove that a lot of things I know haven't hurt Toddy MacFarlane any."

"I'll not do it, Gray."

"Oh yes, you will. You'll do it to oblige Mr. Fettes and myself. Maybe there are some private reasons between you and me that'll make you. Some long lost friend, eh Toddy?"

"It might be an interesting case," submits MacFarlane.

"That's a good boy, Toddy."

"You only want me to do it because I don't want to, that's it, isn't it, Gray?"

"Toddy hates me," Gray says in an aside to Fettes.

"Don't call me by that name!"

"D'you ever see the lads play knife?" Gray picks a knife from the table and sticks it into a loaf of bread. "Toddy'd like to do that all over my body."

"We medicals have a better way than that," Fettes interjects. "When we dislike a friend, we dissect him."

"You'll never get rid of me that way, Toddy. You and I have two bodies, aye, very different sorts of bodies, but we're closer than if we were in the same skin. For I saved that skin of yours once and you'll not forget it."

When Fettes mentions the operation the next day, MacFarlane renegs, saying he cannot be expected to be held to a promise made in drink. Besides, there are no corpses available, and one is needed before he can perform the operation. Fettes has a personal investment in this; he is beginning to fall in love with Georgina's mother.

Taking it upon himself to visit Gray, Fettes asks the street singer (Donna Lee) if she knows of his whereabouts. (She does not, but she soon will, we suspect. Since the street singer is used as a recurring image, we know her songs are numbered.)

The scene that follows, taking place within Gray's quarters, delineates its two characters rather nicely. The affable Gray is honored by the visit and bids Fettes to enter his humble home, offering the student the most comfortable chair in the room. Fettes asks about getting another specimen, and the ever-cordial Gray says he is "financially interested," but the graveyards have become well guarded after a recent episode. When Fettes leaves, he once again sees the street singer. Gray peers out his door while the young girl passes, his expression confirming our suspicions.

We dissolve to a view of the street singer walking down a deserted side street. This one-shot camera position holds as she disappears into the tunnel-like darkness of an alley. Over her song we hear the clip-clop of Gray's horse as his cab moves into the dark alley after the singer. Now the cab is also swallowed by the shadows of the narrow passageway. The shot holds, seeming to last forever as the hoofbeats and the song filter through the dark. And then the voice halts in midverse, the continuing shot revealing nothing but the silence and the darkness.

In his chambers, Fettes smiles as he hears the telltale sound of Gray's horse, unaware that his good intentions have triggered a murder: one girl's life for another girl's curse. "Sooner than we thought," says Gray, carrying his

Publicity shot of Boris Karloff as Cabman Gray.

heavy sack into the room. "A stroke of luck, you might say." When Fettes lifts the cloth and sees the face of the street singer, he is aghast: "You could not have gotten this body fairly!"

Fettes reveals his suspicions of foul play to an unsympathetic MacFarlane. "It's like Burke and Hare all over again," Fettes says, but the doctor remains undaunted, saying the girl could have been an epileptic who, to their good luck, just happened to drop dead. Joseph eavesdrops. "It was you who ordered it done," the surgeon tells Fettes. While the two men continue to argue, a wisp of the street singer's song is heard like a lilting memory over the soundtrack.

Georgina's operation is successfully performed, and MacFarlane appears to be much more jubilant now that Fettes is in full collusion with him, both having sullied their hands with Gray's misdeeds. When Gray comes to pay what he terms a social call, however, MacFarlane orders him out of the house, now and forever. The doctor says he no longer needs subjects, that his lessons in dissection will be replaced by straight lectures. "But we'll still be friends, Toddy," responds Gray, "I'll be stopping by once in a while to see you and Meg for auld lang syne."

Georgina recovers from her operation, but has not yet regained her ability to walk. The young girl is intimidated by all their expectations, especially MacFarlane's, and refuses to make a game effort. MacFarlane is so frustrated by her lack of cooperation that he drowns his sorrows at the local pub. When Gray enters the pub, Toddy is well in his cups and uncommonly friendly; he invites Gray to sit with him because he needs someone to talk to, anyone, even Gray. MacFarlane tells the cabman of the girl's operation, how she refuses to walk in spite of the surgery's apparent success. MacFarlane talks about the backbone as a series of building blocks and sets the wine glasses, one on top of the other, to illustrate his point. In sudden disgust, Gray sweeps the glasses to the floor.

> GRAY: You can't build life the way you put blocks together, Toddy. You're a fool, Toddy, and no doctor. It's only the dead ones you know.
>
> MACFARLANE: I am a doctor; I teach medicine.
>
> GRAY: Like Knox taught you? Like I taught you? In cellars, in graveyards? Did Knox teach you what makes the blood flow?
>
> MACFARLANE: The heart pumps it.
>
> GRAY: Did he tell you how thoughts come and how they go and why things are remembered—and forgot?
>
> MACFARLANE: The nerve centers of the brain.
>
> GRAY: What makes a thought start?
>
> MACFARLANE: The brain, I tell you! I know!
>
> GRAY: You don't know, you'll never know or understand, Toddy. Not from Knox or me would you learn those things. Look, look at yourself. Could you be a doctor, a healing man, with the things those eyes have seen? There's a lot of knowledge in those eyes—but no understanding. You'll not get that from me.

That the uneducated Gray—a man of the earth, shall we say?—should impart such wisdom to the reknowned Dr. MacFarlane does not at all seem foolish or contrived, thanks to the expert sparring of Karloff and Daniell, who pull off such sharply written scenes as the above with glorious panache. Nowhere have we gotten the impression that Gray is unintelligent; from the start, Gray lets Toddy know he's his equal, his double, his dark underside.

With a sudden sense of bravura, MacFarlane spouts: "I'm my own man. Why should I be afraid of you? What are you holding over me?"

Gray answers: "I'll tell you what. I stood up in the witness box and took what should have been coming to you. I ran through the streets with the mud and the stones around my ears and the mob yelling for my blood. You were afraid to face it, yes, and you're still afraid."

MacFarland counters, "No, I'm not afraid! Shout it from the housetops, but remember, they hanged Burke, they mobbed Hare, but Dr. Knox is living like a gentleman in London."

Gray responds: "Aye, there's something in what you say, Toddy. I've no wish for a rope cravat. I've never liked the smell of hemp."

That night, as Gray relaxes at home with his cat (a Lewton in-joke), Joseph pays a visit and sheepishly tries to blackmail the cabman for his murder of the street singer. But Joseph is a hopeless amateur and plays right into Gray's hands. "You say you came here of your own account?" asks Gray. "No one sent you, no one knows that you are here? . . . Well, Joseph, you shall have money. Why should you not?" Gray wears his most intoxicating smile as he pours Joseph a cup of brandy.

Joseph is terribly dimwitted, but his weak mind still senses that there is something wrong: "I have made you give me oney, but you smile. Aren't you angry?"

Gray answers: "No, Joseph, I'm not angry. Here's some more brandy."

Joseph slurps down another one while Gray continues, "I have an idea, a splendid idea. So excellent an idea that we must drink on it. You see, I admire you, Joseph. It took courage to come here and I'm looking for such a man. But drink, Joseph, drink. You and I should work together."

"You mean we would sell the bodies to the doctors together, to dig them up?"

Gray dismisses this, "There'll be no digging. The kirkyards are too well-guarded. We will, so to speak, 'Burke them.'"

JOSEPH: Burke them?

GRAY: You may have heard the chapbook singers and peddlars of verse cry their names down the street. You know:

[Gray sings] "The ruffin dogs, the hellish pair,/ The villain Burke, the meager Hare."

Eighteen people they killed and sold the bodies to Dr. Knox. Ten pounds for a large, eight for a small. That's good business.

JOSEPH: Where did they get the people?

GRAY: That was Hare's end. Oh, you should have seen him on the streets when he saw some old beldame deep in drink. How he cousined her! "Good day to you, Madame Tosspot, would you like a little glass of something, before you take your rest? Come with me to my house and you shall be my guest. You shall have quarts to drink, if you like." Ha, ha. How he cousined them. [Again, sings.] "Nor did they handle ax or knife,/ To take away

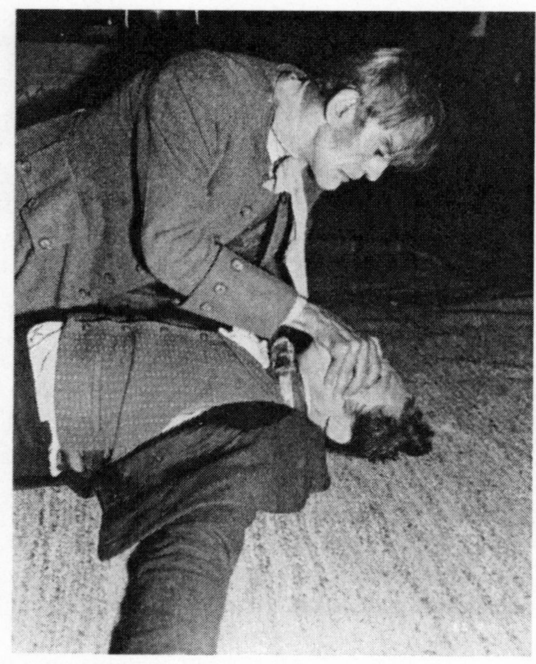

Cabman Gray (Boris Karloff) shows Joseph (Bela Lugosi) the art of "Burking."

their victim's life,/ No sooner done, than in the chest,/ They crammed their lately welcome guest."

JOSEPH: I don't understand the song. Tell me plain how they did it.

GRAY: I'll show you how they did it, Joseph, I'll show you how they "Burked" them.

Placing his hand over Joseph's face, Gray is prepared to give the ultimate demonstration. The chair falls backwards, and Gray remains on top of his struggling prey, sitting on Joseph's chest as he holds his hand tightly over the servant's mouth. When Joseph is dead, the cat comes over to Gray, purring and meowing. Gray lovingly pets his cat with his free hand, while his other is slowly lifted from Joseph's mouth.

The telltale clip-clop announces that a delivery is about to be made. Although it is an off-hour for Gray, he lets himself through the back entrance of MacFarlane's basement and passes through the dark curtain, carrying his sack over his shoulder. There is no one about. As before, we are left on the other side of the partition; we hear the splash of the body being dropped into the brine reserved for the preservation of new subjects. All the while, Gray has been humming the Burke and Hare song.

Toddy comes home to find Gray sitting down, having a chat with his old friend, Meg. In his outrage, MacFarlane tells the cabman to get out. "But I've brought you a little present, in very good condition," Gray answers. MacFarlane knows what he means and insists that he did not order a specimen. "Ah, but this is a gift," Gray insists, "a gift you'll not refuse. I wouldn't be heavy-handed. It might become known that when the great Dr. MacFarlane finds his anatomy school without subjects, he provides them himself from the midst of his own household."

After Gray exits, MacFarlane and Fettes find Joseph soaking in the brine (a ghastly shot of Lugosi immersed in a pickling barrel), and they do the only thing they can do: they dissect him, as they did the street singer. Fettes wants to go to the authorities, but MacFarlane insists he will take care of the matter.

Meg tells Fettes to leave the house and have nothing to do with the doctor. When he refuses, she comes clean: "MacFarlane was to Knox as you are to him. Do you remember the trial? Do you remember the porter who testified against Burke? They didn't tell you how that porter cried out in the witness box when the king's councillor pressed him hard. How he cried out he was shielding a gentleman of consequence. That porter was Gray and the gentleman of consequence, who couldn't swallow the shame of it, who took my last paltry savings to hire Gray, . . . was MacFarlane."

Gray comes home from the pub and, upon lighting a candle, discovers MacFarlane sitting in the shadows. Gray is surprised but undismayed as he converses with MacFarlane in his disarmingly friendly manner:

> MACFARLANE: What do you want of me, Gray?
>
> GRAY: Want of you? I want nothing of you, Toddy.
>
> MACFARLANE: Gray—I must be rid of you. You've become a cancer—a malignant, evil cancer—rotting my mind.
>
> GRAY: You've made a disease of me, eh, Toddy?
>
> MACFARLANE: There's only one cure! I must cut you out. I'll not leave here until I've finished with you, one way or another.
>
> [MacFarlane offers a bribe, saying he'll make Gray rich, setting him up nicely in some other part of the country.]
>
> GRAY: That wouldn't be half so much fun for me as to have you come here and beg.
>
> MACFARLANE: Beg! Beg of you? You crawling graveyard rat?
>
> GRAY: Aye, that is my pleasure.
>
> MACFARLAND: A pleasure to torment me?
>
> GRAY: No. A pride to know I can force you to my will. I am a small man, a humble man, and being poor I have had to do much that I did not want to do. And so long as the great Dr. MacFarlane jumps to my whistle, that long am I a man. And if I have not that, I have nothing. Then I'm only a cabman and a grave-robber. You'll never get rid of me, Toddy.

MacFarlane attacks Gray, and the two grapple among the distorted shadows of the candlelit room before they knock over their only interior source of light. (Clever use is made of the ensuing darkness: not only does it heighten the suspense by making it impossible for us to recognize the identities of the battling silhouettes, but it also effectively hides what could have been an unconvincing struggle between two stunt men.) MacFarlane and Gray roll about, toppling tables and furniture; finally one holds the other on the floor at arm's length. Occasional close-ups reveal the faces of Karloff and Daniell dipping in and out of the scant moonlight (cutaways to the hissing cat on the mantel making smooth transitions between stuntmen and principals).

Gray's hand covers his opponent's mouth in proper "Burke" fashion as he pleads: "Don't force me to kill you, Toddy. My pride is in need of you." But MacFarlane, playing possum, throws Gray off. We cannot determine who is who as one figure clobbers the other over the head with a wooden chair. One man down, the other grabs hold of a fire poker and, using it as a club, delivers a fatal blow to the head of his opponent. After another cutaway to the hissing cat, the survivor hefts his victim over his shoulder and walks out the door. The clip-clop of a horse again serves as an aural transition as we dissolve to the back entrance of the medical school. A figure carries the heavy sack into the basement. When he takes off his top hat and steps into the light, we see it is not Gray, but MacFarlane who has survived. Seeing Meg, MacFarlane victoriously announces he is rid of Gray forever. "No, Toddy, you're not rid of him."

What follows shortly thereafter is the film's most contrived scene: Georgina's recovery. Although Georgina's motivation to walk, her desire to see Gray's white horse, is established very early in the film and reinforced in other scenes, the scene with her getting out of the wheelchair and walking several feet (before realizing the miracle of her recovery, no less) strains credibility.

Overjoyed that Georgina can walk, Fettes tracks MacFarlane to the inn at Pennycooke, where the doctor has traveled to sell Gray's horse and rig. (The ironic implication is that it was MacFarlane, after all, who, driving Gray's cab, inspired Georgina to walk.) The doctor tells Fettes that Gray is out of his life, that he was persuaded to leave the area. MacFarlane waxes enthusiastic about his profession now that he is rid of Gray. While at the table, the two overhear the news of a poor farmer whose wife has just been laid to rest in Glencorse Kirkyard, and their conversation shifts to the grave matters at hand.

MacFarlane takes a keen interest in this news and convinces Fettes (a bit too easily, perhaps) that they would benefit from a trip to the out-of-the-way cemetery. Fettes offers perfunctory protest, but he is quickly persuaded. (It appears that Fettes has as much difficulty separating himself from the doctor as MacFarlane had ridding himself of Gray.)

Although MacFarlane has bragged of his experience with the spade and shovel, it is plain that, of the two men at the grave site, it is Fettes who is doing all the digging. An inch or two from the coffin lid, the surgeon finally takes over the shovel. The carriage horse tethered near the entrance of the kirkyard gate grows more skittish as metal begins striking wood; the rain and wind gather intensity as the animal snorts and whinnies, trying to pull free.

The corpse of Mrs. McCready is unearthed and put in its customary sack, the grave-robbers propping it between them on the single carriage seat. They drive home solemnly in the ungodly weather, MacFarlane taking the reins. As the bumpy ride progresses, the doctor complains, "Keep it off me, will you?" As the horse gallops homeward through the thunder and lightning, MacFarlane hears a man's voice—Gray's voice—gently beckoning, "Toddy, Toddy, Toddy!"

MacFarland stops the horse and asks if Fettes heard anything. Nothing, he says, just the wind. When they continue the journey, Gray's voice can again be heard over the sounds of the horse's gallop and the torrents of rain. Gray's voice adopts a galloping pace of its own: "Never get rid of me, never get rid of me, never get rid of me, never get rid of me, never, never, never, never."

The surgeon's face, pale and wet, mirrors his terror, and he again stops the horse: "It's changed, Fettes, I swear it's changed." Fettes climbs down and comes around with the lantern, as MacFarlane remains in his seat. "This is not a woman," the surgeon insists, "hold that lamp up! I must see her face."

MacFarlane opens the sack and sees the cabman's dead face, shiny with rain. The surgeon's terrified yells alarm the horse, causing him to bolt with MacFarlane and the carcass (but not Fettes) still aboard. Out of control, the carriage barrels down the narrow mountain road.

MacFarlane is horror-stricken as Gray's luminous form slumps against him in the bouncing vehicle. The cabman's limp body appears dead, but his flopping arms, moving haphazardly with the bumpy ride, mimic those of a living man. The cold, pale arms appear to wrap the doctor in a ghastly embrace. MacFarlane pushes Gray off and tries to get the runaway horse back under control, but Gray's limp, rain-drenched form keeps bouncing back in this mock embrace, the cabman's head even resting upon MacFarlane's shoulder from time to time. The terrified horse breaks free of the carriage as it plummets downhill, finally bouncing off the road and tumbling over an embankment. Fettes runs to the wreck, but MacFarlane is as dead as the corpse of the woman lying next to him.

As Fettes walks away, a quote from Hippocrates ends the film: "It is through error that man tries and rises. It is through tragedy he learns. All the roads of learning begin in darkness and go out into the light." And we see Fettes journeying on a dark, rainy road.

After *The Body Snatcher*'s production came to a close on November 17, 1944, Lewton received no kudos from Jack Gross. Lewton barely had time to celebrate Thanksgiving before returning to the RKO lot to resurrect and bring order to the ungainly mess that *Isle of the Dead* had become. He had under two weeks to finish the aborted project, which resumed shooting on December 1.

But if RKO's front office was slow to recognize the producer's estimable talents, other people were not. Praise for Lewton and his film would soon begin to pour in from other quarters, providing the producer with perhaps his finest hour. On Tuesday, February 13, 1945, RKO gave the trade press a special studio preview of *The Body Snatcher.* The *Hollywood Reporter* called it:

> an unqualified lulu, certain to satisfy the most ardent chill-and-thrill craver, for this is about as grisly an affair as the screen has ever ventured to offer . . . a veritable orgy of killing and grave-robbing. . . . Karloff plays the title role with a sardonic humor which makes his performance doubly effective. . . . Henry Daniell gives an excellent portrayal which carries conviction. . . . Bela Lugosi appears briefly as a sinister servant who falls victim to his own cupidity. . . . Robert Wise gives the picture distinctive direction . . . [and] for Val Lewton, this is another top production credit.

The Body Snatcher's box-office appeal was further enhanced by an uncharacteristically wise move on the part of RKO. For its official nationwide May release, Lewton's film was appropriately paired with a lively second-bill: RKO's *The Brighton Strangler,* directed by Max Nosseck (yet another East European émigré). Nosseck's film was an effective thriller starring a very good John Loder as an amnesiac theater performer who begins to take cues from his murderous stage role. Those who bought tickets for this well-matched pair of films (*TBS* and *TBS*) easily got their money's worth.

However diverting *The Brighton Strangler* may have been, it was *The Body Snatcher* that brought the house down. Easily Lewton's biggest box-office success since *Cat People,* it made history at Hollywood's Hawaii Theater, breaking all first-week attendance records. It fared almost as well at New York's Rialto Theater, whose tradition was to book all first-run horror films. John McManus announced in New York's *PM:* "After watching the worry parade of penny-dreadfuls streaming in from Universal . . . through the gory portals of the Rialto Theatre, I am compelled to the conclusion that *The Body Snatcher* is much too good for the lot of them. It is as much out of place in that company as Barnaby might be between the lurid covers of *Action Comics,* or *The Informer* in a Third Ave. saloon."

Obviously, RKO's publicity department was not banking on *The Body Snatcher*'s subtlety and taste when its lobby posters promised: "The Screen's Last Word in Shock Sensation! Graves Robbed! Corpses Carved! The Dead Despoiled!" The film's misleading trailer announced, "The Hero of Horror, Boris Karloff, joins forces with The Master of Menace, Bela Lugosi, in the Unholiest Partnership This Side of the Grave!" Such hyperbole did not acknowledge that Lugosi's role was, at best, a cameo, and that the only thing unholy about the partnership between Gray and Joseph was that it lasted all of five minutes before it was consummated in brine.

When the film opened on May 10, 1945, at Hollywood's Hawaii Theatre, a grave-robbing display was constructed in the lobby, including a "ghoul" (actor Eric Jason) who entreated live patrons to test the comfort of his coffin.

Although it was more likely the result of its gruesome and tasteless publicity (especially that poster showing Karloff dragging up a corpse of a scantily clad buxom young woman) rather than of anything in the film, *The Body Snatcher* provoked some negative reaction; it was condemned by the city of Chicago and the entire state of Ohio, as well as given a "B" rating (objectionable in part) by the Roman Catholic National Legion of Decency. This kind of notoriety can be box-office honey, however. (The British version excised some of the more horrific moments from the film's climax, removing the sections which revealed Karloff's "nudging corpse." The film was nonetheless a massive hit in Britain; its influence upon British horror cinema was felt for years to come.)

Newsweek's review described *The Body Snatcher* as "a grim duello between Daniell and Karloff. . . . Both players handle their roles with a restraint that is unusual in films of this type and budget. The climax—of itself—is a hair-raising example of genuine macabre."

("The terrifying climax," Greg Mank tells us in *Karloff and Lugosi*, "always inspired wild screaming in the audience such as movie exhibitors had not heard since the original release of *Frankenstein*.")

Much of *The Body Snatcher*'s success rests upon the shoulders of Boris Karloff. It had been the first horror film since *The Black Room* (a decade before) to treat Karloff as an actor, rather than as a calling card. The 57-year-old actor had been eager to show Hollywood what he had recently gained from the stage. Although neither *The Climax* nor *House of Frankenstein* had given him that opportunity, *The Body Snatcher* certainly did.

In a 1991 interview, Robert Wise told the author:

> Boris was very keen to do this film because he felt it gave him an opportunity to show that he could act as well as play the monster. He was fascinated by the duel between him and Henry Daniell, one of the great character actors of the time. This pleased Boris very much and he worked hard on his performance. He was not feeling well during the shooting; he had back problems, but he never let that interfere a bit and was determined to show that he could hold his own with Henry Daniell. . . . We had very good meetings with Boris before we started to shoot. Boris, as you probably know, was the opposite of what he appeared on the screen. He was very urbane, very well read, very well educated, soft-spoken, a real English gentleman. His role in *The Body Snatcher* meant a lot of him.

Karloff's performance in *The Body Snatcher* was further enhanced by the sterling talents of Henry Daniell. Daniell's memorable exercises in villainy—in films such as *The Sea Hawk* (1940), *Watch on the Rhine* (1943), *Jane Eyre* (1943), and *The Suspect* (1944)—made him a most formidable watch for

Karloff's Cabman Gray, both of them doing their best to steal the show. Interestingly, their offscreen personas were polar opposites; Karloff was a warm, personable gentleman, while Daniell was cold, detached, and self-important. Actor Robert Clarke recalls *The Body Snatcher*'s operation scene:

> "[Henry Daniell] was a smooth, accomplished and very professional actor. I was a bit overwhelmed ... by his extreme professionalism because he was a bit condescending in his attitude. The scene that we were involved with was mostly his scene—he was showing us how to perform the operation on the little girl. I had one line—'Bravo!'—and when I missed my cue, he went right by my line in his dialogue. But Bob Wise, the director, spoke up and stopped him, and said, 'Wait a minute—Bobby Clarke has a line there. Now, let's go back and start again, and let Bobby get his line in.' Unlike Karloff, Daniell was not the type to have empathy for young actors; 'aloof,' I guess would be the best word to describe him. It was his scene, we were just window-dressing, and he couldn't care less whether we were there or not" [Tom Weaver, *Interviews with B Science Fiction and Horror Movie Makers*].

Their offscreen behavior aside, Karloff and Daniell are exceptionally good in the film, as are several other members of the cast. For his small role, Bela Lugosi actually acquits himself remarkably well, proving that the actor was, indeed, capable of not chewing the scenery. Classic horror fans may identify Lugosi's Joseph with many of the actor's later, rather pathetic, small roles (like Lugosi's mute servant in *The Black Sleep* [1956]), but we need to remind ourselves that during the mid-1940s, Lugosi was still capable of giving vibrant performances in larger roles, yes, even while coping with his alcoholism and drug dependency. We often forget that Lugosi's wonderful Dracula reprise in *Abbott and Costello Meets Frankenstein* came three years after *The Body Snatcher*. Lugosi may have been wracked with physical and mental anguish during the production of the Lewton/Wise film, but his restrained, sympathetic, and totally convincing performance was not merely the result of his deterioration. There was plenty of ham left in the Hungarian actor, as subsequent film roles would show, and Lugosi's understated triumph in *The Body Snatcher* shows how effective he could still be when handled by the right filmmakers.

(Although Lugosi only played in one actual Lewton film, his next acting assignment was in *Zombies on Broadway*, RKO's comic send-up of *I Walked with a Zombie*. Like the Lewton film, this broad farce, designed as a vehicle for Wally Brown and Al Carney [RKO's cut-rate Abbott and Costello], is set on St. Sebastian; hence, there are some carryovers from the original film. Sir Lancelot and Darby Jones reprise their memorable roles and the calypso singer even does another variation of the "Fort Holland" song. Lugosi's nefarious presence, a semireprise of his Murder Legendre role in *White Zombie*, was used as an amusing foil for Brown and Carney's limp, unamusing comic antics. Although effectively produced by Ben Stoloff [under Sid

Rogell's guidance[and briskly directed by Gordon Douglas [whose 1954 *Them* would be the best of the next decade's giant bug movies], *Zombies on Broadway* is nothing more than a curio for Lewton devotees and Lugosi buffs.)

Although *The Body Snatcher*'s other performances pale in comparison to those given by Karloff and Daniell, the remainder of the cast conducts itself admirably. Edith Atwater as Meg and Donna Lee as the street singer are very memorable in small roles. Although Russell Wade (Fettes), Rita Corday (Mrs. Marsh), and Sharyn Moffett (Georgina) are good, the characters they play are rather vapid and perfunctory. Wade was much more sympathetic in *The Ghost Ship*; as Fettes, he comes across as the kind of nondescript, handsome hero that so often plagues classic horror fare. Corday's Mrs. Marsh is a sexless cypher, by far the least appealing heroine of any Lewton film. And Moffett, though often effective, never comes close to giving a juvenile performance on a par with Ann Carter's in *Curse*. (Moffett's marvelous acting in John Brahm's *The Locket*, shot the following year, shows evidence of enormous talent. Perhaps *The Body Snatcher*'s script was more confining to the young actress than her on-screen wheelchair.) Although the Lewton/MacDonald screenplay is weak in its development of Fettes, Mrs. Marsh, and Georgina, it more than makes up for it in the breadth and dimension given to the characters of Cabman Gray and Toddy MacFarlane.

Gray possesses a duality that makes him extremely complex, especially when compared to the more predictable Fettes and MacFarlane. Gray's two occupations—cabman and grave-robber—make him a transporter of bodies and whether his cargo is living or dead makes little difference to him. His pay-is-the-soul-of-the-business remark applies to his cab service just as much as it does to his grave-robbing. At times Gray appears to be a warm, generous soul; at other times he is the embodiment of pure evil. Yet, unlike the traditional Jekyll/Hyde prototype, Gray's duality is not so clearly defined because his personality does not change with his behavior. Gray is always warm, friendly, and polite, whether the person he addresses is a little girl in a wheelchair, a celebrated surgeon, or a dimwitted would-be blackmailer. However amoral Gray may be, he is a particularly ingratiating villain. Gray's moral complexity is nowhere more evident than in the scene where he strokes his pet cat while suffocating Joseph.

No matter how heinous his crimes, Gray is more likeable than Toddy MacFarlane. Although McFarlane is reputed to be a giant of medicine, most viewers agree with Georgina's perceptions of the man. The way MacFarlane compromises his profession, the way he equivocates his own culpability in matters of grave-robbing, and the way he gets other people, Gray, Meg, Fettes, and Joseph, to do his dirty work, somehow makes him appear more despicable than the murdering cabman. (This is especially significant when we consider that Gray has committed the unforgiveable cinematic act of deliberately killing a dog.)

Most of Val Lewton's films stand up well to a variety of critical approaches, and *The Body Snatcher* is no exception. Most tempting is a Jungian approach, with Fettes as the "anima" (the vital life force), MacFarlane as the "persona" (the social image), and Gray as the "shadow" (the dark underside). In accordance with Jung's three special archetypes, the film's unholy three—Fettes, MacFarlane, and Gray—could be viewed as facets of a single personality.

Fettes is the persevering idealist who wishes to become a doctor to help humanity. The "anima," according to Jung's theory, is also responsible for our sex drive and our desire for a family and the good life. Fettes associations with Mrs. Marsh and Georgina, as well as his dismay at impropriety, add support to this interpretation.

MacFarlane, the "persona," embodies social cognizance. MacFarlane is obsessed with appearances; he is a man of great reputation, a man who prizes his public image above anything else. He keeps his marriage to Meg a secret because she is too common for his public image; he doesn't even mind breaking the law—as long as his reputation is not besmirched by the crime. The doctor takes no risks as far as his public image is concerned; remember, he paid a handsome fee to keep his reputation safe those many years before.

Finally, there is Gray, man's dark underside or, in Jungian terms, the "shadow." Despite his noble white horse, Gray is the smiling face of corruption, of death and rotting corpses; he is the skeleton in MacFarlane's closet, the one skeleton MacFarlane chooses not to display in his pristine anatomy lecture hall.

The Jungian interpretation gives *The Body Snatcher* a strong sense of unity. If Fettes, MacFarlane, and Gray approximate Jung's trinity of archetypes, it means that the film is really about the inner struggle of a single man. Such a perspective would account for the tight bonds that hold these three men together. MacFarlane would like to get rid of Gray, but he cannot; even murder won't do the trick ("you'll never get rid of me"). In killing Gray, MacFarlane becomes Gray, which may explain why the surgeon has the sudden desire to rob the grave of the farmer's wife after he has already resolved to disassociate himself from the practice. In killing Gray, MacFarlane has killed himself, "William Wilson"-style; as Gray said to Toddy, "we're closer than if we were in the same skin."

Likewise, Fettes cannot seem to cut his bond with MacFarlane. He tries to leave the medical school a number of times, but MacFarlane tells him he's "too good a man" to quit. The surgeon has a tremendous hold upon the student, and, had it not been for MacFarlane's untimely end, we have every good reason to believe Fettes would have risked all else to maintain this partnership, however unholy it had become. Although Fettes professes to have had quite enough of the grave-robbing trade, MacFarlane easily gets him to partake in the film's last exhumation.

Taking an autobiographical approach, we can see a little bit of Lewton in each of the three major characters. In Fettes we can see Lewton the eager apprentice to David Selznick, the exploited student who, no matter how dirty the work gets, cannot bring himself to leave his mentor. In Toddy MacFarlane we see the astute, distant, even pretentious Lewton, the man who does not like to be touched and has trouble connecting with his daughter, the filmmaker whose behavior reflected both superiority and insecurity. And in Cabman Gray we see Lewton the horror specialist, the man who, covered in cemetery dirt, delivers the specimens that keep RKO thriving.

Whatever critical approach one takes, *The Body Snatcher* makes a fitting subject for dissection and analysis. Although a large part of the film's provocative nature is dependent upon the script, an equal measure of importance should be placed upon Robert Wise's direction. Watch the first 15 minutes of *The Body Snatcher* without sound; for a film jam-packed with dialogue, it is amazing how much of its narrative is communicated visually. Wise shows himself to be as much a storyteller as Lewton. The director's expert handling of pros like Karloff and Daniell, his subtle execution of several chilling scenes, and his ability to give a morbid subject such a high degree of class should not go unnoticed. Of his 39 directing credits, *The Body Snatcher* remains one of Robert Wise's favorite films, and we can well understand why. This was the film that convinced Wise that he was a director with promise and talent; it was also his first box-office smash.

Close to a half century after its release, *The Body Snatcher* maintains its status as a classic horror film; it comes as no surprise that the film is frequently cited as Lewton's best piece of work. Modern critics of the genre, though cognizant of its flaws, continue to praise it, and Karloff's performance is hailed to this day. Phil Hardy writes in *The Encyclopedia of Horror Movies:* "Superbly controlled and strikingly literate (to a point mistakenly criticized as excessive by several staunch admirers of Lewton productions) *The Body Snatcher* is a magnificent reworking of Stevenson's . . . short story. . . . Wise's direction is actually a model of discretion and assurance, making excellent use of de Grasse's chiaroscuro lighting and managing to bring off several memorable scenes." In *Classics of the Horror Film,* William K. Everson states that *The Body Snatcher* "is certainly equal to *Cat People,* and possibly its superior . . . one of the most literate and restrained of all horror films." In *Guide for the Film Fanatic,* Dan Peary calls it "refreshingly literate . . . the production is classy. . . . Robert Wise's depiction of the horror sequences is superb, and tasteful. Particularly spooky is the scene in which Gray kills a street singer." In *Karloff and Lugosi,* Greg Mank states: "*The Body Snatcher* reigns today as a beloved film; besides being the final Karloff and Lugosi movie, it survives as the richest, most dramatic of Lewton's RKO horrors, and, indeed, bids powerfully to be the greatest horror film of the 1940s."

Given *The Body Snatcher*'s lofty position in the pantheon of classic horror films, it is hard to ignore its weaknesses. At times the film is slow moving, even tedious, and as brilliant as portions of its script may be—particularly in those glorious stretches of dialogue between Karloff and Daniell—there is no excuse for the banal quasi-romance between Fettes and Mrs. Marsh or for the embarrassingly contrived scene that ends with Georgina getting up from her wheelchair. *The Body Snatcher* is often singled out for its wonderful dialogue, but dialogue is both its blessing and its curse. The film is so verbose that its refreshingly wordless passages stand out, etching themselves into our memories: the picturesque establishing shots, the clip-clop of Gray's horse, the death of the street singer, the murder of Joseph, and MacFarlane's death in the runaway carriage.

The Body Snatcher's most glaring liability (especially for an undisputed horror classic) is that it is not particularly scary. Although the ending strikes a chord of raw terror that easily puts it in the running for the "scariest scene *ever* in a Lewton film," this hair-raising climax is a long time coming and those characteristic Lewton staples, the "walk" and the "bus," are minimized almost to the point of nonexistence. Lewton and company must have realized their film was low on terror when they resorted to fashioning a scare sequence around the snort of a horse (a shamelessly gratuitous "bus" preceding Fettes's entrance into Gray's quarters).

Regardless of the above objections, *The Body Snatcher* was the best horror show in town, especially with the sturdy support of its playbill companion, *The Brighton Strangler*. RKO's horror double bill surpassed anything Universal had to offer in the spring of 1945.

The Body Snatcher had a profound, if belated, influence upon Britain's horror film market of the late 1950s. In 1957 Karloff would be invited to England to star in two films—*Corridors of Blood* and *The Haunted Strangler*—both of which would owe a considerable debt, in substance if not altogether in style, to *The Body Snatcher*. These two films, along with Hammer Film's milestone *Curse of Frankenstein*, would help spearhead a British period-horror cycle that would last nearly a generation. Numerous British films have been based on the exploits of Burke and Hare, the most recent being *The Doctor and the Devils* (1985). By far the best is John Gilling's 1959 entry, *The Flesh and the Fiends* (aka *Mania*).

Ironically, *The Body Snatcher*'s box-office success only reinforced the front office's notions that Lewton worked best within the genre for which he was hired. The press began to label him with such grandiose epithets as "Sultan of Shudders," "Titan of Terror," and "the Maharaja of Mayhem." Within months, *Life* magazine would give him an impressive four-page-spread profile with numerous photos of *Bedlam*, his next production. "Lewton Is a B Film Virtuoso" headlined the article.

Although it looked as if the producer's time had finally come, we must remember that in the world of Val Lewton, appearances are deceiving.

FIFTEEN

Bedlam

At present Lewton's weekly income is a modest $700, on which he supports a wife, two children, two Buicks, a dog, some chickens and such minor pleasures as woodworking and book buying. Lewton is a great reader and his house is filled with books. He can get through an average novel in 45 minutes and lifts many ideas from old plots, which he likes better than new ones. He assists in the writing of all his productions and will sum up the latest epic by saying, "It's Jane Eyre ***in a tropical setting." Lewton's bosses like his work. They are planning to give him, as soon as possible, an A picture, high-priced stars, brand-new sets and as much as a million dollars to play around with.***

—*Life* magazine (February 25, 1946) "Movie of the Week: *Bedlam*"

On July 18, 1945, the day *Bedlam* went into production, Lewton was optimistic. With *The Body Snatcher* having become box-office gold upon its release two months earlier and a completed *Isle of the Dead* finally in the can, the front office showed its appreciation by raising *Bedlam*'s budget to $350,000, making it the most expensive Lewton production yet. On top of this, the producer was given an additional eight months for postproduction, an apparent indication he was about to be taken seriously.

Unfortunately, there was little opportunity for a "Titan of Terror" or a "Maharaja of Mayhem" during the postwar forties. Truces with Germany (May 7th) and Japan (August 14th) marked the end of one era and the beginning of another, and Americans were ready to put the war years behind them. Confident that their concerted war efforts were responsible for their well-earned victory, postwar Americans (and therefore postwar Hollywood) began to entertain the belief that the nation could lick its social problems if it only dared face up to them.

And so it was realism, not fantasy, that the postwar audiences craved. In 1945, films dealing with social problems included Billy Wilder's *The Lost Weekend* (alcoholism), Irving Pichel's *A Medal for Benny* (war casualties),

Delmer Daves's *The Pride of the Marines* (blindness), and Jean Renoir's *The Southerner* (rural poverty). Such "message" or "problem" pictures would continue through the postwar years, covering such topics as civilian readjustment (William Wyler's *The Best Years of Our Lives* and Edward Dmytryk's *Till the End of Time*), racism (Elia Kazan's *Pinky* and Mark Robson's *Home of the Brave*), antisemitism (Elia Kazan's *Gentleman's Agreement* and Edward Dmytryk's *Crossfire*), more war injuries (Mark Robson's *Bright Victory* and Fred Zinnemann's *The Men*), prison reform (Jules Dassin's *Brute Force* and John Cromwell's *Caged*), and perhaps the most popular theme of all, mental illness (Alfred Hitchcock's *Spellbound*, Robert Siodmak's *The Dark Mirror*, John Brahm's *The Locket* and *Guest in the House*, Anatole Litvak's *The Snake Pit*, Fritz Lang's *Secret Beyond the Door*, Henry Hathaway's *Fourteen Hours*, Edward Dmytryk's *The Sniper*, and many, many others).

Bedlam presents an odd case, in view of the above. Although it was a message picture with a mental illness theme (and thus on the cutting edge of a lucrative trend), Jack Gross insisted that it be tailored and marketed as a horror film. Unfortunately, by the time of *Bedlam*'s April 1946 release, horror films had already fallen out of fashion.

Like *Isle of the Dead, Bedlam* was inspired by a painting, in this case Plate Eight of William Hogarth's *The Rake's Progress* series. The proposed title of the film, *Chamber of Horrors* (subtitled *A Tale of Bedlam*), made no bones about its projected market; but as he had already done with *Curse of the Cat People*, Lewton intended to make a message film in horror movie disguise.

His love for literate costume films harking back to his days with Selznick, Lewton came close to making an entirely different period horror thriller with Karloff. *The Hollywood Reporter* had over the previous months made references to a Lewton/Karloff/Wise project called *Carmilla*, purportedly a "set-in-Colonial-America vampire film." Asked what he knew about the project, Robert Wise recently told the author:

> Val came to me after I'd done *The Body Snatcher* and said he had the idea to do a horror film in color. He thought that that would be different. I can't remember just what happened with it now; we had someone come over and do a treatment; it was planned, and I had hoped to direct. I went off to do another film [*A Game of Death*, the remake of *The Most Dangerous Game*]. I was hoping to come back and do *Carmilla* with Val and then it just never developed, neither the treatment nor the script; it was just dropped and Val went on to do another film *[Bedlam]*. *Carmilla* was discussed, planned, and at least put into work as a treatment, but it never got on the boards.

(A classic vampire novella written by Anglo-Irish writer Joseph Sheridan Le Fanu [1814–1873] a year before his death, *Carmilla* has had and continues to have a lasting influence upon horror literature and horror cinema. *Carmilla* is widely known for its vision of lesbian vampirism, an aspect of the work that was heavily exploited in numerous racy vampire films in the 1960s and 1970s, at least a half dozen of which were actually based on the Le Fanu novella. For the record, *Carmilla* does not take place in America during the colonial period.)

Chamber of Horrors (aka *Bedlam*) is indeed set during Colonial times, though all its action takes place in Mother England, in and around London's St. Mary of Bethlehem Hospital for the Insane, the eighteenth century asylum more infamously known as Bedlam.

As they prepared their script, Lewton and Mark Robson studied the memoirs and letters of Casanova, Boswell, Lord Chesterfield, Nicholas de la Bretonne, and Benjamin Franklin. This is probably why *Bedlam*'s literate script is full of brilliantly droll dialogue, colorful one-liners, and irreverent quips. Boris Karloff, playing Master Sims (the head of the asylum), was once again given lines that allowed him to savor malice with the exuberance of a wine taster. *Bedlam*'s attention to period detail is at times extraordinary and results in a D'Agostino/Keller art direction that was even better than their already top-drawer work.

In addition to cowriting the screenplay, Mark Robson was also slated to direct. Lewton was lucky enough to secure the talents of Roy Webb for *Bedlam*'s musical score and to bring photographer Nicholas Musuraca back into his fold. Lewton and Robson rounded off their cast with, among others, Richard Fraser, Jason Robards, Sr., Elizabeth Russell, Billy House, Robert Clarke, Glenn Vernon (Frankie of *Youth Runs Wild*), Skelton Knaggs, singer Donna Lee (from *The Body Snatcher*), and Ellen Corby. Anna Lee (who had been the original choice for Betsy in *I Walked with a Zombie*) was well cast as Nell Bowen, *Bedlam*'s high-spirited female protagonist.

The sprightly tempered and perennially youthful Lee was not a newcomer to the motion picture world, having appeared in over thirty motion pictures (many of them British) prior to her Lewton credit: *Ebb Tide* (1932), *Mannequin* (1933), *The Man Who Lived Again* (1936, her first match with Boris Karloff), *King Solomon's Mines* (1937), *Seven Sinners* (1940), *How Green Was My Valley* (1941), *Flying Tigers* (1942), *Flesh and Fantasy* (1943), *Hangmen Also Die* (1943), and many more.

Anna Lee and her husband, director Robert Stevenson, had relocated to the United States in the late 1930s to pick up work in Hollywood. Stevenson had been the original choice to direct David Selznick's 1939 American version of *Intermezzo,* though the film was finally given to Gregory Ratoff, while Stevenson remained one of Selznick's stable of contracted directors (it was Stevenson who was assigned to the Selznick *Jane Eyre* package).

Anna Lee did not look upon her work in a small picture like *Bedlam* as a "come-down" in any sense of the word. In a 1991 interview with Tom Weaver (*Science Fiction Stars and Horror Heroes*), Lee revealed:

> After *How Green Was My Valley,* I think *Bedlam* is my favorite picture. I loved it. I knew Val Lewton quite well, because I had been close friends with

> Val and his wife Ruth—I used to go have dinner with them all the time. Val told me he was writing this story, this historical picture . . . but I forgot exactly how I became involved. I suppose it would have been Val who wanted me to do it. I know Mark Robson, the director, had other ideas; he wanted Jane Greer for the part and Val wanted me. And finally I did it, on the condition that I change my hair from blond to dark, which is nothing unusual.
>
> Boris used to get quite annoyed when people referred to it as a horror picture. He said, "It's not a horror picture, it's a *historical* picture," and he was right, absolutely dead right. . . . It was exactly what happened at St. Mary's of Bethlehem, so much so that it was not allowed to be shown in England for a long, long time. In fact, only recently have they permitted it to be shown over there.
>
> *Bedlam* was done on a very low budget, but I don't think it ever really showed . . . because it was so beautifully done.

Although Lewton's glory days at RKO were numbered, there was little indication of any downward plunge in *Bedlam*'s efficient and brisk production. Art directors and set designers renovated the standing church set used in Leo McCarey's *The Bells of St. Mary's,* ironically having it represent a quite different "St. Mary's."

When they needed a Quaker council meeting room, they found a dining room set used for Edgar Kennedy comedy shorts. With a little fixing, the austere dining room became the Quaker meeting room. Since Quakers strove for simplicity within their houses of worship, the Lewton team was able to meet two ends, historical accuracy as well as economy.

Anna Lee adds further comment about the rummage-sale spirit of *Bedlam*'s art direction: "I know that my costumes were not made for me; the green velvet riding habit that I wore was Vivien Leigh's dress, the one she makes out of curtains in *Gone with the Wind.* I was always very happy about that [laughs]. And the lovely ball gown that I wore in the gardens was Hedy Lamarr's [from Jacques Tourneur's *Experiment Perilous*]. So I wore all hand-me-downs from various actresses" (Weaver, *Science Fiction Stars and Horror Heroes*).

Robert Clarke reminisces about his *Bedlam* experience:

> We were out at the RKO-Pathé Studios in Culver City, where *Gone with the Wind* was shot, and we were on one sound stage for over a month. Mark Robson, the director, was a marvelous man, he worked so carefully with us as actors. Today, directors don't have the time to do that. I remember a scene where we were playing a card game called paroli and, being demented, instead of betting money I was betting dogs—whippets and bassets and such. Robson made practically every little move for me—"When you place a card here, you do *this,* and then *that,*" and so forth. It's been overy forty years, but I'll never forget how careful and meticulous he was. Robson, and Val Lewton, too, were both caring people, and they treated actors with respect, which is wonderful [Weaver, *Interviews with B Science Fiction and Horror Movie Makers*].

Anna Lee supports Robert Clarke's praise of *Bedlam*'s producer and director: "Val [and Mark Robson] had done such a fabulous piece of work on the script and the dialogue that it would have been tough for anyone to do a bad job, but I thought Mark did an excellent job of directing. As of the time that we made *Bedlam* Mark hadn't yet done anything really in a big way, but I know that David Selznick saw the picture and immediately wanted to sign him (Weaver, *Science Fiction Stars and Horror Heroes*).

Its shortcomings notwithstanding, *Bedlam* is an especially dignified swan song to Lewton's 11-film cycle. What other series of "B" films has had such a strong finish? Apart from its elaborate—even glossy—look, the film has engaging characters, uniformly fine performances, and several memorable sequences. Although *Bedlam*'s cast is larger than that of most films in the series, many of the surplus performers play inmates at the St. Mary of Bethlehem Asylum and are seen but briefly. While the movie is deliberately paced, its narrative is perked by the amount of interest we invest in its unusual assortment of characters.

Bedlam begins with Roy Webb's playfully baroque music playing over the RKO logo (no radio signals this time). No sooner does the logo dissolve than a loud and dissonant chord transforms the cheerful mood into one of dread. Hogarth's painting (*Bedlam,* Plate 8 *The Rake's Progress*) fills the screen: "Boris Karloff in . . . [dissolving to a different portion of the Hogarth work] *Bedlam.*" The credits play out in spirited fashion, the Hogarth visuals changing along the way, until that initial brooding chord is repeated to the cue of "Produced by Val Lewton." It's undoubtedly the classiest credit sequence in the entire Lewton series, the images well synchronized with Webb's incredibly lush period music. It seems like a special event.

A postcredit epigraph tells us that our story takes place in London in 1761 during the Age of Reason, and the epigraph is followed by an inspired establishing shot of the St. Mary of Bethlehem Hospital (a nicely done matte). The entire building and the surrounding star-filled sky are in view, but our eye is drawn (as the camera pulls in) to a very small, very distant spot of white near the top of the structure. Coming closer, we discover the wriggling patch of white to be a man in a pale shirt. He hangs off the edge of the roof, his legs flailing. In a close reverse angle, we come face to face with the man in peril as he grips the gutter like a Colonial-era Kilroy. Another man, bearing a lamp, climbs out of an eve window onto a nearby section of roof and approaches the dangling man. He places the toe of his boot directly over a set of white knuckles and grinds down. With a horrifying wail (cribbed from the *King Kong* soundtrack), the man plunges to his death.

Although this opening sequence is a genuine attention-getter, it prepares viewers to expect the kind of high-voltage thriller which *Bedlam,* despite its macabre moments, never quite becomes. This aside, the period atmosphere of this particularly eventful evening is well conceived and executed; a crane

This ad for *Bedlam* accents the horror elements of the film.

shot brings us to London's cobblestoned streets, where a coach races through the night. Along this dark thoroughfare we see torches, rectangular glass lanterns, even an open fire in the street, presumably built for warmth as well as light.

Our main character is Nell Bowen (Anna Lee), a plucky opportunist who has elevated her position in society by latching onto a generous—if portly and buffoonish—nobleman, Lord Mortimer (well played by comedian Billy House). Although Nell feigns a callous indifference to those less fortunate than she, her disdain is born of her desire to turn her back upon her own common roots. In some ways, she can be viewed as an eighteenth century version of *No Bed of Her Own*'s Rose Mahoney: a resolute heroine who wishes to keep her dignity, despite the many concessions she has made to escape her poverty. Lord Mortimer calls Nell his "protégée," which, thanks to the Breen Office, puts her duties somewhere between those of a jester and an escort. It is her responsibility to keep the nobleman amused. Apparently Mortimer's chief form of amusement is being on the receiving end of a litany of insults, for he laughs heartily everytime Nell or her talking pet cockatoo, shades of *Mad Love* and *Citizen Kane,* hurls one in his direction. Cockatoo: "Lord Mortimer is like a pig; brain small and belly big! Arrk!" Mortimer guffaws with gusto; in his white-powdered wig, he resembles Old King Cole.

Not only is Mortimer the butt of Nell's humor, but he also gets a sound roasting from the Lewton/Robson script. For example, Mortimer is outraged when he is told of the accidental death of his poet friend, young Master Colby (the man we saw fall from the roof). But Mortimer's demonstrative manner and overall pomposity only makes his rage risible, especially when, in a huff, his massive form exits the coach, causing the entire vehicle to rock ponderously back and forth. Since Mortimer is the film's primary figure of authority, one can easily imagine Lewton and Robson envisioning one or more of their RKO superiors as they fleshed out the character of the self-important nobleman.

We first meet Master Sims (Karloff) while he paces about in Lord Mortimer's waiting room, having been called to answer for Colby's fatal "accident." Mortimer's page, Pompey (Frankie Dee), a young black boy in a turban, telegraphs a message to Mortimer by making an ugly face and announcing, "I want to look like the man who is waiting."

Karloff is wonderful in his introductory scene, and his performance is an absolute joy from this moment on. In his black wig, period dress, and breeches (accenting his bowed legs), Sims is clever, vain, and extremely cordial. Sim's brand of cordiality, however, is markedly different from that of *The Body Snatcher*'s Cabman Gray. It was a testament to Karloff's craft that he could play uncommonly friendly villains in two consecutive films without having the characters be at all similar. Gray appears to be warm and genuine to everyone, friend or foe, even if it's all a deadly ruse, as in Joseph's case.

Karloff and Lewton on the set of *Bedlam*.

Although Toddy MacFarlane would disagree, Gray was, generally speaking, not a sadist; though we see nothing but Gray's shadow when the dog is killed, we do not envision the cabman taking pleasure in the deed. If that shadow in the kirkyard belonged to Master Sims, however, in our mind's eye we would know he would be grinning ear-to-ear.

Where Cabman Gray is allowed to keep his dignity, Master Sims is open to ridicule, as his introduction by little Pompey suggests. Master Sims is obviously a man who revels in cruelty; he would never elicit a smile from *The Body Snatcher*'s Georgina. If Sims does not exude any of Gray's homey charm, his flamboyant eccentricities make him an equally captivating villain. As he responds to Mortimer's half-hearted interrogation, Sims is self-effacing, even poetic. And very quick.

Mortimer accuses Sims of murdering Master Colby. But the whole incident, Sims explains in a most rational—albeit comically exaggerated—fashion, was a tragic misfortune: "Murder, m'lord? There was no murder. Colby was my guest; he chose to leave by a window before I could open the door for him . . . and then . . . then, that monstrous accident."

Nell responds: "Master Sims is writing a new dictionary where accidents are contrived, plotted and executed."

"Exactly, Mistress Bowen," responds Sims. "This was a misadventure contrived by the victim and executed by nature's law that all who lose their grip on gutters must fall."

"Do you stick to that story, Sims?" asks the stern Mortimer.

"I could never invent one half so droll: the characters of the tale, two poets, Colby and myself. But I am not only a poet but also the Apothecary General of St. Mary's of Bethelehem Hospital. My friend comes to discuss poetry; I am absent. My guards mistake him for a madman. He tries to escape from them and is killed. Like two characters from a romance."

"It's a romance that cost me twenty guineas and a night of laughter; Colby was to write a masque for the Vauxhall," the indignant lord responds, his outrage predicated upon services unrendered.

Sims offers to prepare the masque himself: "Even at the hospital, I deal in wit and laughter. . . . Are there any who have come to Bedlam and said the entertainment is not worth the tuppence they pay?"

"You do not entertain me, Master Sims," Nell responds.

"That is because you have a tender heart," answers Sims; this rankles Nell. "Most people laugh at my ugliness," continues Sims.

"It offends me," interjects Nell.

"To move a lady so beautiful in any way," rejoinders Sims.

Mortimer chuckles to see the spirited tongue of Nell so evenly matched by this masterful retort. Sims repeats his offer of taking on Colby's writing tasks, adding, "What if the masque were performed by my company of wits?" Mortimer thinks it is a splendid idea to have the "loonies" provide the entertainment.

When Sims leaves, Nell is most direct in her assessment of the man: "If you ask me, he's a stench in the nostrils, a sewer of ugliness, and a gutter brimming with slop."

"Yes," Lord Mortimer responds, "but witty!"

Bedlam's dialogue is obviously in a class of its own.

D'Agostino and Keller's art direction shines in a brief street scene following Sims's visit to Mortimer. Recalling the evocative period atmosphere of *The Body Snatcher*'s opening shots, the camera tracks through a London street, and we get a vivid amalgam of sight and sound. Here stands a street vendor and there strolls a girl (Donna Lee) singing of the virtues of the lavender she peddles. A young boy runs his stick along a wrought-iron fence, while an overloaded wagon passes by with several children hanging out the back, pointing and laughing. A dandy stops in his tracks to wonder if he is the target of the children's derision. And then we see Sims (the real source of the laughter) parading down the sidewalk, heading back to his home, the asylum.

Anna Lee's Nell Bowen is a most likeable heroine and a refreshing change from Lewton's usual wholesome run of female survivors. When, upon her next meeting with Sims, she flaunts her indifference to the plight of the

Bedlam inmates, the master apothecary invites her to seek amusement at the asylum. Nell's hard exterior is convincingly wrought, but we sense there is something fragile about her studied attitudes. (Thus, Nell becomes another of the numerous Lewton film characters who are not what they seem to be.) Nell meets Hannay, the Quaker (Richard Fraser), and scoffs at his righteousness, but she keeps coming back to him for more of the same. An unusual relationship between the pretty hedonist and the stoic Quaker soon develops. Nell responds to Hannay's religious beliefs with such quips as, "I have no time to make a show of loving kindness for my fellow men. Not in this lifetime! I have too much laughing to do."

Sims is sitting in his office trying to find a rhyme for "Lord Mortimer" when Nell makes her sudden entrance into the room; hurriedly replacing his wig, Sims acts as if he has been caught in his undershorts. Nell pays her tuppence to see "the loonies in their cages," paving the way for a memorable Lewton set piece. Nell's "walk" into the main room of the asylum is slow and creepy, with none of the Lewton team's characteristic false scares. Instead there is a gradual building of dread via a frightening point-of-view shot as we slowly approach the door to the huge room, a virtual amphitheater of babbling inmates. The door remains locked, but we hear unearthly chants and animal-like wails growing in volume with every step we take. When Sims unlocks the door and they enter this arena of lunacy, we are given a tight shot of Nell as her face reacts to the nightmarish spectacle before her. With Nell's appalled face as the central point of the frame, we pull back long and slow to view both the immensity of the room and the astonishing number of its occupants.

The set is appropriately dismal, with straw and other less identifiable debris scattered about on the stone floor. Slanted bars of light from the prisonlike windows pierce the dingy, yet spacious, confines of this one-room asylum, bending their angles as wall meets floor. There is a man playing a violin while an open book lies face down upon his head. Another man wears a duncecap. There are people moaning, milling about, picking at their tattered garments, one fellow with a looped string working out a cat's cradle, others reaching out in Nell's direction, as Sims guides her along on his tour of human derangement. Although Hogarthian in design, the impact of this scene also recalls the eccentric nightmare visions of Bosch and Bruegel.

"All in themselves and by themselves," says Sims, taking Nell from one sorry specimen to the next, all the while delighting in his commentary: "They have their world, and we have ours. Ours is a human world; theirs is a bestial world, without reason, without soul. They are animals. Some are dogs . . . these I beat. Some are pigs . . . these I let wallow in their own filth. Some are tigers . . . these I keep in cages. Some are doves . . ." and here Sims leaves his sentence unfinished, as we cut to a young woman resembling the Virgin Mary (ironically, the asylum's namesake), allowing us to draw our own sordid conclusions about what Sims does to "doves."

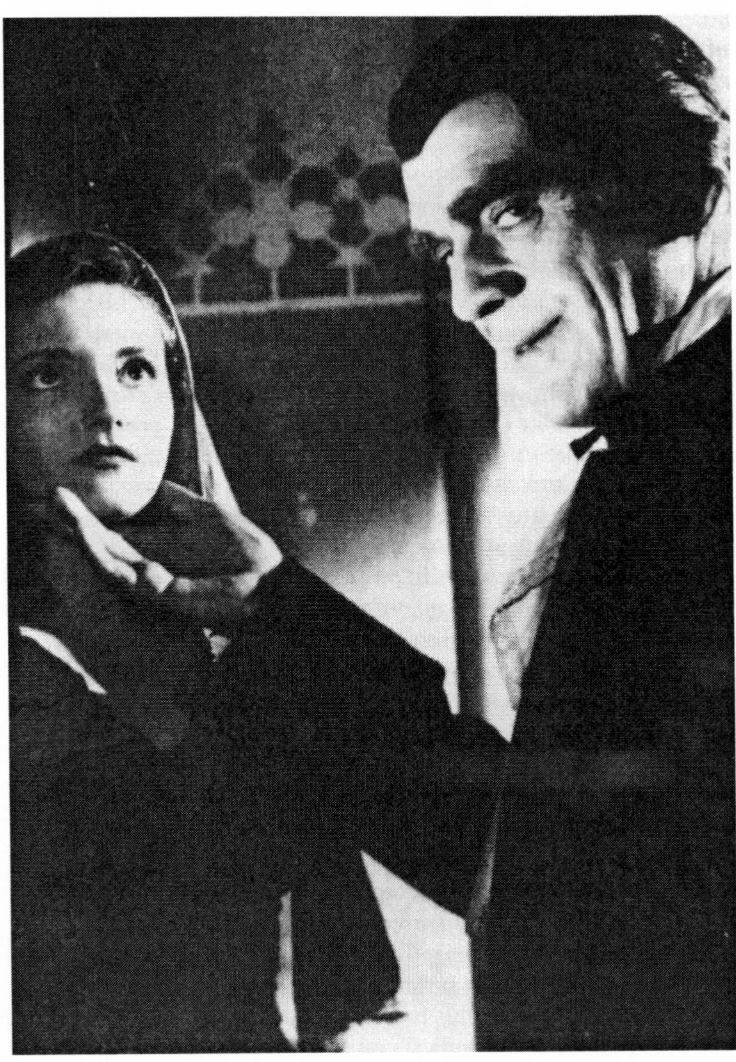

Master Sims (Karloff) presents Dorothea the Dove (Joan Newton).

Nell has had quite enough, thank you, and walks out. Amused, Sims follows and confronts her; she slaps his face and goes on her way. Hannay, who is at the asylum to attend to business matters (he is a stone mason), witnesses this event and, though a pacifist, he is impressed by Nell's fury, seeing in her reaction the evidence of her humanity. Hannay tells her that she should not have struck Sims because the inmates would have "to suffer for that blow." As the two converse, Nell tells Hannay she cares not at all for the fates of the "loonies," saying that she slapped Sims, "because I wanted to—because he was an ugly thing in a pretty world." She denies feeling pity for the inmates and prides herself in "having a heart like a flint; it may strike sparks but they are not warm enough to burn."

Another memorable *Bedlam* set piece is the Vauxhall presentation of the comic masque written by Sims. Presented outdoors in the manner of a garden party and sponsored by Lord Mortimer, the masque is attended by Tories and Whigs, the two at political loggerheads with one another. In *Dreams of Darkness*, J.P. Telotte points out, however, that the film is "historically questionable" (which is, of course, highly contrary to Lewton's usual fetish for accuracy): "Even though the Tories were out of power in England after 1714, [in *Bedlam*] they are shown in control of the government, running it for their own selfish ends and in opposition to the Whigs, who are depicted as the champions of a public or social consciousness. The Tories are personified in the fat, buffoonish Lord Mortimer, who spends his days seeking amusement from any source, while the Whigs are represented by the historical figure John Wilkes, a liberal reformer of the era."

The Vauxhall masque stays in our memories because it is so unpleasant to watch; though overdone and relentlessly smug, it is probably the most well-remembered sequence in the film (although Lord Mortimer and his friends are too easily amused by the proceedings to give the episode the credibility it deserves). The Whig contingent, represented by John Wilkes (Leland Hodgson), offers some lukewarm humanitarian rhetoric, but his very attendance at the ghastly affair suggests that his attitudes of reform are made up of words, not actions. (The Vauxhall masque anticipates Peter Weiss's 1960s play, *Marat/Sade*, and its subsequent 1966 film adaptation, directed by Peter Brook.)

In the infamous "gilded boy" scene, a youth (Glenn Vernon) is shown standing before his audience covered in gold gilt (prefiguring Shirley Eaton in *Goldfinger*). His purpose is to represent the voice of reason, and Lord Mortimer is absolutely tickled that an "idiot" should stand for reason. The boy has trouble with his lines because his body is suffocating from the gilt. "Come on, come on!" urges Sims, "I've spent all morning beating it into your head." The boy holds his throat, clearly fighting for his life, while the Vauxhall audience titters with laughter. Only Nell remains unamused by the spectacle. She hears Wilkes's comment, which is casually delivered, concerning the dangers involved in such a procedure. Yet it is only Nell who gives rise to outrage. We wonder how the party-goers can be so amused and how Wilkes, the liberal humanitarian, can look on with such disinterest.

The boy collapses, and Nell stands and shouts her protest. Sims answers (as an assistant is about to check the boy's heartbeat): "If I understand you properly, this boy is dying," (the assistant whispers something to Sims) "this boy is dead because his pores are clogged with the gilt. Since you are a stickler for the correct definition, you will grant me the legal fact that this boy died of his own exhalations. . . . You might say he poisoned himself."

The events that lead to Nell's commitment to the asylum are rather contrived. When Sims is brought before Nell and Lord Mortimer, the latter announces his plans to improve conditions at the asylum. Sims feigns approval, but expertly manipulates the nobleman, making him aware that he would suffer considerable economic loss from the reform, all for naught, since "loonies don't vote." After Mortimer changes his mind about the reform, Nell insults him and leaves his employ. She later makes a public display of her insolence by bringing her cockatoo to the marketplace so that all of London can hear it recite: "Lord Mortimer is like a pig; brain small and belly big! Arrk!"

Meanwhile, Sims is busily coaching his niece Kitty (a marvelously coquettish Elizabeth Russell) to give up her coarse ways and offer herself as Nell's replacement. Although Mortimer remains surprisingly good-natured about the abuse he has taken from Nell, Sims encourages the nobleman to teach his ex-protégée a lesson: "M'lord, we could always make her my guest." Mortimer adamantly opposes the idea: "We've been good comrades, Nell and I. I'll not do that."

Nell and Hannay come to visit Mortimer, who pulls a sword on the unarmed Quaker and becomes a laughing stock when he trips over his own feet and falls onto his daybed. When Nell laughs heartily, the indignant look on Mortimer's face suggests that he will soon be speaking to Sims.

Nell and Hannay seek John Wilkes as an ally in their quest to reform conditions at Bedlam. Sims hears of this and gets Mortimer to offer Nell a bribe, a sizable banknote which she sticks between two slices of bread. "I'll show you what I think of your money," she says, taking a bite, chewing, and swallowing.

All this leads to Nell's insanity hearing. Sims and Mortimer have a forged petition, Nell's supposed request to be incarcerated at Bedlam. The plucky protégée answers their questions with verve and confidence, a feminist heroine all the way: "I can read and write as well as any man before me . . . perhaps a little better." One man asks, "Do you know the difference between right and wrong?" Nell quips, "What's right for me is wrong for you, that much I know, and vice versa."

The interrogators are relentless, however, and their efforts finally begin to erode Nell's calm exterior, especially when they ask about her money-eating habits. When they are through asking questions, they declare her insane. Case closed.

Fade in: a close-up of Nell's frightened face framed in darkness. The din of human groans tells us what we already suspect: Nell has been made a guest at Sims's chamber of horrors. The camera pulls away from Nell. She leans against a wall, too terrified to move from a position she has held for who knows how long.

Nell (Anna Lee) is confined to Bedlam.

The screenplay's instructions for the shot are expressly followed: "The camera pulls back to display a little of the space around her. On the walls, crouching, rounded shadows can be seen moving; almost as if animals were crawling, indistinct and horrible through terrible darkness."

A sudden loud noise—the moving of the door latch, amplified by the barren stone walls—draws Nell's attention to the heavy door as it creaks open. Master Sims makes his merry approach: "We can't feed you bank notes in Bedlam," he tells her. "Perhaps you should chew on this coin," which he tries, unsuccessfully, to cram into her mouth.

Later, Nell's nerves are given a further test; the inmates, the entire mad entourage, it would seem, take to repeating her name ("Nell Bowen, Nell Bowen, Nell Bowen"), the nightmarish din of echoing voices sounding like a pronouncement of her damnation. Eventually, Nell discovers that the inmates are only mimicking the voice of a man outside who is calling her name. Several of the grotesques, huddling near the barred windows, make it their habit to listen to the world outside; whatever they hear, they repeat. Just like a room full of cockatoos.

The voice from the street belongs to Hannay. A stonemason by trade, Hannay sneaks into Bedlam by blending in with some fellow tradesmen who are delivering stone bricks for the building of an inside wall. Hannay hesitantly makes his way down the corrider leading to the inmates quarters, giving us the *Bedlam* sequence that comes closest to the conventions of the Lewton "walk." (Nicholas Musuraca's compositions during this sequence are particularly striking; so memorable is one shot that it adorns the covers of both books about Lewton, Joel E. Siegel's *The Reality of Terror* and J.P. Telotte's *Dreams of Darkness*.)

Barred cell doors line both sides of the corridor; this is the wing reserved for the most violent inmates, those not allowed to mill about in the main room. As Hannay walks by a set of bars, several pairs of hands dart out in an effort to grab him (a very effective "bus," one that prefigures similar episodes in Roman Polanski's *Repulsion* and George Romero's *Night of the Living Dead*). Pulling away from their reach, Hannay backs against a cell on the other side of the corridor, only to be startled by the laughing grimace of a maniacal inmate from that cell ("bus" number two). Hannay runs the gauntlet through numerous pairs of arms reaching out from either side before he makes it to the end of the corridor.

There are some good shocks here, but Hannay's brief Lewton walk sounds much better than it plays. Once he finds Nell and talks to her through the bars of a locked door, the moment seems to drain away all the tension inherent in Nell's plight. Hannay tells Nell that he and John Wilkes are working up a plan to expose Sims and Mortimer. Nell asks for a weapon, and in spite of his moral objections, Hannay hands over his mason's trowel.

As the days pass, Nell becomes familiar with Bedlam. She discovers a group of political prisoners ("the people of the pillar") who, like herself, have been made "guests" for no justifiable reason. "We are the wisest ones," says the Judge (John Ince), "That's why we are allowed a candle." The Judge's companions include Dan the Dog (Robert Clarke), lawyer Sidney Long (Ian Wolfe), and novelist Oliver Todd (Jason Robards, Sr.), all of whom invite Nell to play a game of paroli. As the card game progresses, Nell begins to hear the groans of a suffering inmate, and unable to concentrate on the game, she asks for the candle in order to find her way to the man in distress.

Nell approaches apprehensively, bearing her trowel as a weapon. The suffering inmate wears what might be best described as a body-shackle, his entire form constrained by straps of hammered metal; his torso bleeds from his contact with the straps. Nell bends down to rip her petticoat for a bandage, putting her trowel on the floor momentarily; a mysterious hand comes into the frame to snatch the tool. A transition in Nell's character is wrought by the events to follow, the changeover symbolically linked to the giving up of her weapon. The heroine's first act of charity, caring for the shackled man, signals her spiritual rebirth. As days pass, Nell becomes an angel of mercy, Bedlam's own version of Clara Barton, doing everything in her power to give succor to those around her.

Sims comes to visit from time to time, and he is amused that she has taken up with the asylum's upper crust, "the people of the pillar." He tells her, "The lighter elements, like scum, rise to the top." One of these chosen few is Oliver Todd (Jason Robards, Sr.), an alcoholic novelist who petitioned to have himself placed in the asylum just so he can stay away from drink, finish his novel, and thus support his family. The inmates think that Todd has become incapable of speech, but this is only a ruse; the writer simply chooses to remain silent (prefiguring Big Chief in Ken Kesey's *One Flew Over the Cuckoo's Nest*). By exercising this semblance of personal control, Todd maintains his integrity in spite of the odds. It is likely that Lewton saw something of himself in Oliver Todd.

If Todd is Lewton the novelist, another member of the "pillar" seems to be Lewton the film producer. Sidney Long shows a flipbook he has made, thumbing the pages as the pixilated drawings show Nell, the angel of mercy, in action. "If I could only get a light behind these pages," says Long, "I could throw them large as life upon the wall."

"Aye, that's not a bad notion," answers another. "One could charge admission. You could even tell the story Todd's writing that way."

The Lewton/Robson screenplay obviously alludes to RKO's own chamber of horrors. Lewton and his coworkers had jokingly dubbed their unit "the Snake Pit" during their early *Cat People* days. Given that Lewton delighted in hurling surreptitious barbs at his superiors, one can easily see Lord Mortimer as Charles Koerner and Master Sims as Jack Gross.

Bedlam's last reel has some peak moments but the events leading to the hurried climax are either farfetched or hastily inserted as a means to an end (haphazard last reels are not uncommon among Lewton films). Particularly risible is the Tom the Tiger scene. "This is your new chamber," announces Sims, indicating the cage that holds the fearsome brute, Tom the Tiger (who, played by baby-faced wrestler, Victor Holbrook, does not look especially menacing). Nell cringes and Sims taunts her further; he reasons that if she is so willing to help those in need, why shouldn't she give comfort to the caged lunatic? Challenging her sincerity, Sims dares her to enter the cage. To his surprise, she does so, and quite willingly. Sims looks on, hoping for the worst, while Nell talks to Tom soothingly and the two of them become fast friends.

Knowing that Hannay and Wilkes are working toward his ruination, Sims decides to take it out on Nell, letting her know that she will soon be given "the remedy." The inmates recoil when they hear this treatment mentioned, though the viewer can only speculate upon what is in store for Nell. Sims makes threatening advances toward the heroine, but the inmates en masse come to her aid and physically restrain the Apothecary General. Via a kangaroo court, they put him on trial.

Nell plans her escape. She discovers that the only window without bars was that from which Colby made his ill-fated escape. This window is set high out of reach, so Nell needs help from Tom the Tiger. Although the escape sequence strives for some suspense, the results are too half-hearted to be very satisfying. When Tom and Nell make it to the roof, we remember the film's opening and realize we have come full circle. Tom pulls himself up to one of the eaves and then, single-handedly (literally), attempts to assist Nell. In doing so, he becomes distracted by the sight of the moon and the stars and leaves Nell dangling precariously in his grip, before he comes to his senses and pulls her to safety.

This last ditch effort to generate some thrills falls flat. Ever since her "conversion experience," Nell seems to have been under the protection of an almost divine force, so we never really worry about her safety. Perhaps Lewton and Robson were aware of the perfunctory nature of Nell's escape because we are never given the opportunity to see the remainder of her downward journey (surely a few more hazards were forthcoming). All this is glossed over, Nell's safe deliverance being treated like a foregone conclusion; the next thing we know, she is reunited with Hannay.

More effective in mining chills is the mock trial of Master Sims. Despite continued utterances from the inmates ("Split him in half! Split him in half! Split him in half!" chants one fellow), Sims is, rather surprisingly, found "not guilty." His defense rests upon the notion that his ugliness has made him do ugly things. "Can't you understand?" Sims beseeches, "This is a great world and strong men with great advantages rule over it, and men like me are frightened, born poor and misshapen. . . . It is a great world, a world of force and pomp and power, and I was frightened at my littleness, my ugliness and my poverty." He furthers his case by saying, "I did not want to hurt you. . . . I had to be cruel. . . . I had to please those to whose favor I owe everything. . . . It is the frightened dog that bites, and I had to fawn and toady and make a mock of myself so that all I could hear was the world laughing at my ugliness. I was afraid."

That the court of inmates should accept this defense is itself evidence of their derangement. Surely Sims has gotten too much personal gratification from his torture to make these claims stick. He wants his "jury" to believe that his cruel streak is a reaction to the way he has been treated, but Sims is entirely too clever and conniving to get much sympathy as a hapless victim of society.

(*Left to right*) Karloff, Mark Robson, and Val Lewton.

Bedlam's final bid for terror is a disturbing sequence that recalls Poe as much as it does Hogarth. When Sims is set free, he backs away from his mob of inmates, not fully trusting them in their decision. However, Dorothea the Dove, who stands right behind him, is not as forgiving as the rest. She plunges the sharp end of a mason's trowel into his back.

The inmates panic, rushing about, frightened to distraction, knowing they will all have to pay for the murder. "We must hide him!" they shout. Noticing the stonemason's unfinished wall, the inmates conceal the corpse by putting it behind the partly constructed wall and finishing the job in the tradition of Poe's "The Black Cat" and "The Cask of Amontillado" or Honoré De Balzac's "La Grande Bretèche." They work the mortar and set the cut stones, building the wall up and up, covering the tight space in which they have propped Sim's body. Finally, the last stone is about to be put in place; there is a tight close-up of Sims's face through the remaining gap as they lift the last stone. Although the audience sees that Sims, having opened his eyes, is still alive, this revelation goes entirely unnoticed among the inmates. Sims appears to be on the verge of a scream when the last dense stone is lodged into place, silencing him forever.

The ending title reads: "Reforms were begun in 1773. A new hospital was erected shortly afterward, and since that time Bedlam—once a by-word for terror and mistreatment—has led the way to enlightened and sensible treatment of the mentally ill."

Bedlam was released in late April 1946 (double-billed with Robert Wise's *Game of Death*), and what Lewton first thought was a blessing, extra postproduction time, turned out to be a curse. *Bedlam* was a film in search of a vanishing audience. The seven months before the release of *Isle of the Dead* and *Bedlam* was much too long for the unit's own good. By the time Lewton's last RKO film made it to the theaters, accompanied by the studio's typically ghoulish poster art, the Hollywood horror cycle was dead, if not yet entirely buried.

Critics were impressed by *Bedlam*'s bid for quality, however, and it received the kind of praise reserved for films with a "social message." In its review of *Bedlam*, the *Motion Picture Herald* said, "It is not easy to categorize the attraction, since nothing quite like it has been seen ... [but] under whatever billing, it will make itself remembered as a powerful use of the camera to tell a story of importance."

Some of the producer's most faithful adherents, including James Agee and Manny Farber, were finding Lewton's recent literary affectations a bit tiresome, but since the RKO producer had already become in their eyes the equivalent of a Hollywood folk hero, they buffered their criticism with a liberal portion of praise.

Like *The Body Snatcher*, much of *Bedlam* is rather high-handed, its script often too literate and affected (m'lord this and m'lord that) for its own good. The lively dialogue is eminently quotable, but there is little of the visual flair that once proved a Lewton trademark. Too many of *Bedlam*'s horrific passages, especially once Nell is locked away, are offset by ponderous exposition. Nor does Nell's dramatic turnabout from hedonist to healer always work in the film's favor. Nell's redemption, an improbable plot contrivance, eliminates all that was terrifying about the asylum and makes for a limp finale. Furthermore, the heroine's metamorphosis turns her complex character into one of limited dimension, her saintliness rendering her a nonentity. Nell's previous persona may have been cold and calculating, but her pluck and reserve were admirable. In many ways, her earlier persona seems preferable to the kindhearted "angel of light" she becomes. Although our conscience tells us we should be pleased with Nell's transformation, we realize that the loss of her rebellious spirit is the price she has paid for her redemption. In the end, Nell is only slightly more interesting than the lobotomized Randall McMurphy in *One Flew Over the Cuckoo's Nest*.

Bedlam is a handsome, well-intentioned film, but its humanitarian postures are self-righteous or, at best, self-conscious. Earlier Lewton films had conveyed more sincere messages about society's wrongs in less preachy portrayals of society's victims: Irena Dubrovna *(Cat People)*, Barbara Farren *(Curse of the Cat People)*, Mimi *(The Seventh Victim)*, even Elizabeth Rousset *(Mademoiselle Fifi)*. In its attempt to be a horror film, a period thriller, a message film, as well as a wry satire of Lewton and Robson's ordeals at RKO,

Bedlam goes in too many directions at once, scattering the impact of whatever purpose it hoped to achieve.

As a message film, *Bedlam* falls short of those which popularized the trend; the sincerity of its message is difficult to accept when so much sadistic relish is written into Sims's character. It would appear that Karloff was having a field day with such a plum role, but Richard Gordon (who produced two of Karloff's more memorable films of the 1950s, *The Haunted Strangler* and *Corridors of Blood*) reports, "Boris Karloff ... was not happy with the too-irreverent approach to the subject of *Bedlam*, requiring from him a near-comic performance that was out of keeping with the theme."

If *Bedlam* makes a bid for humane and peaceful coexistence, it does so in a most ambiguous way: Sims's cruelty is given defense, the inmates are exonerated for their crime, and Hannay (our spokesperson of peace) has provided the modus operandi for Sim's death. Such ambiguous heroes and villains make *Bedlam*'s message cloudy at best. Although the film allows us to see the need for reform in mental institutions, this message is given lip-service rather than conviction. Unlike most message films of the postwar cycle, *Bedlam* is more interested in revolt than it is in reform.

Like most Lewton films, *Bedlam* has fared well with modern film critics. *The Penguin Encyclopedia of Horror and the Supernatural* goes out on a limb, saying, "There has never been a film like *Bedlam*, a horror film that is at once a reminder of the ignorance from which the human race suffers—even in progressive eras like the eighteenth-century Age of Enlightenment—and a heartfelt, humanistic work of art." Phil Hardy, however, in his *Encyclopedia of Horror Movies*, calls it a "curiously pedantic film. ... The action is less interesting than the historical detail, and suggests that Lewton was angling for a way out of B movies. ... Much too talkative (though the dialogue is good) and clumsily directed." In *Horrors—From Screen to Scream*, Ed Naha calls it "a low-keyed masterpiece of the macabre. ... Lewton presents several poignant scenes and bloodcurdling climax. ... A truly moving film, dealing frankly with a problem not often portrayed in the cinema world." In his *Guide for the Film Fanatic*, Dan Peary calls *Bedlam* "[Lewton's] most underrated film" and declares Nell Bowen "the most dynamic of Lewton's remarkable women." Peary continues: "Terrific performances by Lee and Karloff are enhanced by intelligent, witty script, offbeat supporting characters, and classy direction by Mark Robson."

Boris Karloff's career received a tremendous boost as a result of his Lewton work. Although *Bedlam* was Karloff's only film for 1946, he was given important roles in three big-budget mainstream films the next year: *The Secret Life of Walter Mitty* (produced by Samuel Goldwyn), *Lured* (Douglas Sirk's period thriller remake of Robert Siodmak's 1939 French film, *Pièges*), and *Unconquered* (a Cecil B. DeMille epic set in Colonial America).

In April 1946 (the same month *Bedlam* was released), Karloff's second terror omnibus, *And the Darkness Falls,* hit the bookstores and became another big seller. Karloff had written lengthy, charming, and impressively erudite introductions (averaging 300–400 words each) for every one of the volume's 69 selections. His biographical data for each author displayed a firm familarity with their work, often with a number of allusions to their other stories, which he had obviously also read.

After his work with Lewton was done, Karloff's career—encompassing radio, stage, screen, television, and publishing—would thrive at full throttle for the actor's remaining 24 years. In spite of his chronic back problems and incipient old age, Karloff—always the trooper—maintained his position as one of the movie industry's most visible performers. After leaving his Lewton days behind, Karloff appeared in nearly 40 more feature films, more than 100 television programs, and scores of stage and radio shows. He had his own television series, his own line of paperback horror anthologies, his own pulp magazine, even his own comic book. Karloff's death on February 2, 1969, rocked the nation like the passing of a king, a king whose territory not only included the world of horror, but also extended well beyond it.

Unfortunately, fate would not be as kind to Val Lewton.

SIXTEEN

Fellow Travelers

The term "auteur" is usually reserved for film directors but, in Val Lewton's case—because of his intense supervision and continual artistic involvement (including original story ideas and final drafts)—the crown of authorship rests upon the head of a film producer. Lewton's role remained constant throughout the 11-film RKO series, while the offices of director, scriptwriter, editor, and cinematographer continually changed hands. Plainly speaking, Lewton held it all together and kept the series going, in spite of numerous odds. Some Jacques Tourneur devotees tend to feel that Lewton has been given more credit than he deserves for the horror formula established by *Cat People,* but even they would accede that Tourneur's direction took a magnificent leap in quality once he joined the Lewton unit. By his own admission, Tourneur regretted being pulled from the unit; moreover, he looked back upon his Lewton days as the most rewarding period of his life, maintaining that *I Walked with a Zombie* was the best film he had ever made. Whatever form of magic took place in RKO's horror unit during that three-year span, it was sorely missed by everyone who left the unit for bigger and better opportunities. If Lewton did nothing more than provide the magic, it would be reason enough to insure his authorship of the series. The term "Lewtonesque" has been in use for more than a generation, and we should not be surprised to one day find it included in Webster's.

But, of course, Lewton and his collaborators did not have the world of dark cinema all to themselves. While RKO's horror unit cranked out their "B" budget horrors, similarly dark terrains in urban melodramas and psychological thrillers (both period and modern) were being explored by Lewton's cinematic contemporaries, directors such as Fritz Lang, Alfred Hitchcock, William Dieterle, Orson Welles, Edward Dmytryk, Billy Wilder, George Cukor, John Brahm, Anatole Litvak, and Robert Siodmak. (No, contrary to conventional wisdom, the RKO producer's true cinematic counterparts were not 1940s "B" movie horror meisters like Erle C. Kenton, Reginald LeBorg, Jean Yarborough, or Sam Newfield.)

The spirit of give-and-take that existed between Lewton and his fellow travelers-in-the-dark is best exemplified by the kind of symbiotic relationship that existed between Fritz Lang and Alfred Hitchcock (both of whom received their passage to Hollywood via David O. Selznick). Lang's and Hitchcock's protagonists are inextricably bound by webs of fate, either wrongly accused of crimes or trapped in circumstances over which they have no control. Paranoia reigns in the worlds of Hitchcock and Lang.

As Barry Gilliam notes in Jean-Pierre Coursodon's *American Directors, Vol. 1,* "Many of those similarities [between Lang and Hitchcock], to be sure, are superficial or coincidental, or mere consequences of the two directors' working within the same genres at the same periods and their choice of material being naturally influenced by the same trends and fashions. . . . On the most general level, Hitchcock and Lang share a very pessimistic view of human nature: they are both obsessed with the ambiguities of innocence and guilt, and they have the same fondness for the dramatic ploy of the suspected and harassed innocent fighting the world for survival."

Because Hitchcock and Lang freely borrowed from one another, we cannot be, nor do we wish to be, precise in identifying a moment from a Lewton film as being either Langian or Hitchcockian. Such a pursuit would be tantamount to solving the riddle about the chicken and the egg. There are even a few instances where both Lang and Hitchcock appear to be borrowing a thing or two from Lewton's films. *The Seventh Victim*'s corpse-disguised-as-a-living-man trick was given its Langian equivalent three years later in *Cloak and Dagger,* while the spooky climax of Lang's *Scarlet Street,* where Edward G. Robinson's mild-mannered murderer is haunted by his victims' voices, bears more than a passing resemblance to the nightmarish finale of *The Body Snatcher* (released nearly a year before Lang's film).

In David Thomson's highly opinionated but vastly entertaining *Biographical Dictionary of Film,* he contends:

> Gothic melodrama runs through [Hitchcock's] work, as does the cruel tenderness towards suffering of the women's picture. . . . Film is [Hitchcock's] world, and other film-makers his sole points of reference, especially Fritz Lang and Val Lewton (*The Testament of Dr. Mabuse* was the source of many of the English thrillers, while Lewton's sense of undisclosed horror is an essential influence on Hitchcock's stimulated voyeurism.)

Although Thomson is known for his rash opinions, there is some truth in his observations of the Lang/Hitchcock/Lewton interrelationship. While it would be ill-advised to proclaim Lewton's "B" budget films as a fount of inspiration to the crowned master of suspense, Hitchcock and Lewton did follow each other's work, and while in no way were they close, they occasionally got together socially. (Hitchcock was a dinner guest at the Lewtons' at least once according to a recent interview with Ruth Lewton, and they dined out together a number of times.) One wonders, though, if Thomson is heaping too much credit upon Lewton, as it was Lang who, in *M*'s opening reel, provided cinema with its greatest early example of "undisclosed horror." Clearly, Lang's egg came before Lewton's chicken.

Lewton's films resemble Hitchcock's more than they do Lang's. Unlike Lang, whose films had more of a masculine slant, Hitchcock and Lewton had a mutual affinity for Gothic heroines, sinister matriarchs, doomed women, and assorted other strong female characters. In addition, almost all of Lewton's villains, like Hitchcock's, go against the stereotype of pure evil. Some of Hitchcock's more genteel villains—Otto Kruger in *Saboteur,* Claude Rains in *Notorious,* James Mason in *North by Northwest,* John Dall in *Rope*—would fit in rather nicely with the Palladists in *The Seventh Victim*. Lewton's psycho-killers, Dr. Galbraith *(Leopard Man)* and Captain Stone *(Ghost Ship),* have their Hitchcock counterparts in *Shadow of a Doubt, Psycho,* and *Frenzy*.

For those familiar with *Cat People,* it is difficult not to think of Lewton's film while watching the pet shop scene in *The Birds*. In *Caligari's Children,* S.S. Prawer tells us, "the incidents involving the caged birds . . . which have no equivalent in the Daphne du Maurier story . . . are so close to the opening passages of *Cat People* that they might almost be seen as a conscious act of homage." Both Siegel and Prawer (in their respective works) make references to the pre–*Psycho* shower scene in *The Seventh Victim,* where Mary (Kim Hunter), naked, wet, and vulnerable, has her shower interrupted by the unexpected and quite bizarre intrusion of a strange woman. The silhouette of the woman, seen through the shower curtain, is our only means of identification.

Of course, such parallels may only mean that "great minds think alike," the theory upon which this chapter is predicated. It is obvious that all three filmmakers (Lang, Hitchcock, and Lewton) shared a pessimistic vision and a noir sensibility; in their films, fate is an iron-clad trap, with doom lying ahead and paranoia only a step or two behind. The motif of false appearances, which appears so frequently in the work of both Lang and Hitchcock, is also no less prevalent in the Lewton films. Putting aside the question of who influenced whom (which becomes moot after we discover, in a manner of speaking, that we have been watching three carpenters building the same house), few would deny that Lang, Hitchcock, and Lewton were kindred spirits of dark cinema.

When Lewton joined RKO in the spring of 1942, Hollywood's most beloved German émigré filmmaker was not Fritz Lang, but an actor-turned-director named William (Wilhelm) Dieterle. Dieterle, who as an actor appeared in more than 50 films, had roles in F.W. Murnau's *Faust* and Paul Leni's *Waxworks*. He directed several German films in the 1920s before coming to Hollywood, where he signed with Warners. Like his Hungarian-born Warners counterpart, Michael Curtiz, Dieterle would crank out five films a year in the early thirties before finding his niche. During the late 1930s and early 1940s, while Curtiz was coming into his own with big-budget action films (often featuring Errol Flynn or James Cagney), Dieterle was establishing an "A" budget career with a series of popular, well-mounted biographical films, often featuring Paul Muni (*The Story of Louis Pasteur, The Life of Emile Zola, Juarez*) or Edward G. Robinson (*Dr. Ehrlich's Magic Bullet, A Dispatch from Reuter's*).

Dieterle's work did not always exhibit the expressionistic flourishes one would expect from a Germanic director; like Michael Curtiz, his career was too eclectic to qualify him as a dark visionary along the lines of Lang, Hitchcock, or Lewton. Nonetheless, three of Dieterle's films—*The Hunchback of Notre Dame* (1939, RKO), *All That Money Can Buy* (1941, RKO), and *Portrait of Jennie* (1949, Selznick/RKO)—add some important pieces to our puzzle.

The Hunchback of Notre Dame is an elaborate, masterfully produced remake of the Chaney classic. It is graced by Charles Laughton's uncanny performance as Quasimodo (the role Orson Welles had turned down), solid supporting players, and a cast of thousands. Dieterle's film, which was edited by Robert Wise and Mark Robson, may have been a remake of the Thalberg/Chaney epic, but it obviously took more of its cues from the sumptuous 1935 David Selznick production, *A Tale of Two Cities* (the film that first paired Lewton with Jacques Tourneur). Leftover sets from the *Hunchback* remake also found their way into two Lewton productions (Robert Wise's *Mademoiselle Fifi*, and Mark Robson's *Bedlam*).

In *American Directors*, Vol. 1, Jean-Pierre Coursodon remarks, "Like Curtiz, [Dieterle's] imperfect command of the English Language seems to have encouraged him to develop a predominantly visual style of direction even on quite talky scripts, a quality not shared by too many directors at the time." Indeed, this "predominantly visual style" appears to have rubbed off on both Robert Wise and Mark Robson.

While not exactly a horror film, *All That Money Can Buy* (the editing team's next Dieterle opus) has some genuinely horrific moments. Coursodon tell us, "there is little doubt that Dieterle had ambitions in following in Welles's footsteps," and this is true in more ways than one since *All That Money Can Buy*, like *Citizen Kane*, was a box-office bust. Apparently audiences had trouble warming up to the deliberately artificial look of Dieterle's dark fantasy; nor were they very accepting of its rather surreal narrative techniques. Based on a 1937 story by Stephen Vincent Benet, *All That Money Can Buy* (aka *The Devil and Daniel Webster*) was an expressionistic allegory whose set-bound, storybook-in-motion approach was not unlike that of a later box-office dud, the 1955 *The Night of the Hunter* (which, by strange coincidence, was directed by Dieterle's "hunchback," Charles Laughton). *All That Money Can Buy* would be important to the story of Val Lewton if only because it provided Simone Simon (playing one of Satan's minions) with an extremely sexy pre–*Cat People* role. Her Bella Dee, the ultimate temptress, anticipates the femme fatale, one of the staples of the then still evolving world of noir cinema.

The provocative Bernard Herrmann score, the expert Wise/Robson editing, the sumptuous Van Nest Polglase art direction, the impressive Vernon L. Walker special effects, and the saucy Simone Simon performance are reasons enough to make *All That Money Can Buy* essential viewing for readers of this book, but we can go one more in pointing out that the film's less-is-more approach to terror neatly anticipates the kind of subtlety for which the Lewton films were known. While there is nothing inherently scary about Walter Huston's tongue-in-cheek performance as the devil, the dark forces he controls are quietly terrifying. The film's most memorable scene is the ghost ball, where Bella beckons legions of the dead into Jabez Stone's newly built mansion. The sight of these tattered perambulating corpses, enveloped by an eerie glow, is made even more frightening by the fact that they remain absolutely silent. Our goose bumps are given greater definition when Jabez is forced to entertain his flesh-and-blood company, none of whom can see what he sees: an adjoining room filled with the dancing dead. (This sequence had a probable influence upon Herk Harvey's 1962 low-budget cult horror classic, *Carnival of Souls*.)

Curiously enough, while Val Lewton was leaving Selznick to join RKO, William Dieterle was leaving RKO to join Selznick, working on such elaborate productions as *Duel in the Sun* as well as directing Selznick "packages" like *I'll Be Seeing You* and *Love Letters*. In 1949 Dieterle directed Selznick's rather excessive, albeit visually stunning, production of *Portrait of Jennie*, a sublimely romantic dark fantasy about a penniless painter (Joseph Cotten) and his tragic love affair with a beautiful, but peculiarly elusive, girl (Jennifer Jones) who turns out to be a ghost. Although *Jennie* is played as a haunting fantasy, rather than as a horror piece, the Selznick/Dieterle film offers a grand-scale version of the kind of darkly poetic supernatural romance that had made *Cat People* so difficult to resist eight years before. Of course, *Jennie*'s astonishing $4 million budget (four-fifths the cost of *Gone with the Wind*) puts it in an entirely different class, but the protagonist's infatuation with a mysterious, and ultimately doomed, young woman begs comparison with the romance between Oliver and Irena in *Cat People*, especially when so much of Dieterle's film is set in and around Manhattan's Central Park amid the changing of the seasons. Extravagant budget and breathtaking visuals notwithstanding, *Jennie* is really a "B" movie, its memorable but slight story hardly deserving the elaborate Selznick treatment. Its simple plot would reappear, with some variation, in low-budget sleepers like *Carnival of Souls* (1962), *Night Tide* (1963), and *Let's Scare Jessica to Death* (1971).

If German émigré film directors naturally gravitated to the darker genres (noir, horror, thrillers) of the 1940s, Orson Welles demonstrated that a filmmaker did not have to be German to be Germanic. Welles has been no stranger to this book, but our coverage has so far only extended to his early RKO career (*Citizen Kane, The Magnificent Ambersons,* and *Journey into Fear*); Welles's associations with the kind of dark cinema championed by the

Lewton team did not end after the boy wonder was "evicted" from RKO, however.

While Lewton and company were wrapping up their voodoo variation of *Jane Eyre,* Orson Welles was busily involved with 20th Century–Fox's more faithful rendition of the same. The *Jane Eyre* package that Selznick had sold to Fox included director Robert Stevenson, actress Joan Fontaine (pegged for a role not unlike her heroines in *Rebecca* and *Suspicion*), and a script by Aldous Huxley and Stevenson. As soon as Fox hired Welles (for the role of Rochester, the novel's Byronic hero), he became aggressively involved in the film's direction and production. As might be expected, Welles was determined to put his fingerprints deep into the work (even though his Fox contract only called for his services as an actor) and before long, he was bringing in some of his Mercury Theatre talent: composer Bernard Herrmann, additional screenwriter John Houseman, and actress Agnes Moorehead.

Jane Eyre, released in 1944, is a real treat for Lewtonphiles, for it is a fascinating companion piece to *I Walked with a Zombie.* Moreover, the searing presence of Henry Daniell as *Jane Eyre*'s most hateful villain is reason enough to make it a must-see for anyone who has ever taken an interest in *The Body Snatcher.* (Actually, Daniell's role in *Jane Eyre,* that of a religious martinet who runs a girl school, makes his Toddy MacFarlane character in *The Body Snatcher* seem like a nice fellow.) Obviously, the parallels between *Jane Eyre* and *Zombie* are particularly noteworthy. Creepy moments abound when Jane (Fontaine), employed as Rochester's governess, hears the strange fleeting cries of a woman (the Byronic hero's insane wife) and, leaving her bedroom, journeys through the estate's darkened hallways to investigate. Later, when Jane climbs up the stone tower, she discovers a mysterious bolted door, one that rattles and shakes from whatever is behind it that is struggling to get out. One cutaway shot, with the door enlarged in the foreground while Jane's diminished figure looks on in fear, is especially effective in raising chills.

Jane Eyre's sets and mattework are spectacular, and coupled with Herrmann's doom-laden musical signatures, the entire film has the unmistakable flavor of *Citizen Kane*'s (prenewsreel) prologue. George Barnes's photography splendidly captures the atmosphere of the Yorkshire moors. Peggy Ann Garner, as the young Jane, shows why she became the quintessential plain–Jane juvenile actress of the 1940s. Her marvelous performance is on a par with Ann Carter's in *The Curse of the Cat People* and that is saying something. A very young Elizabeth Taylor (unbilled) plays a character who befriends Garner. When Taylor contracts pneumonia as a result of Daniell's cruel methods of spiritual salvation, Jane climbs into the girl's bed to provide her with warmth and companionship. In the morning, upon waking up, Jane discovers that she has been holding the hand of a corpse. The moment is as chilling as it is moving. Despite its weak second half and some static expository scenes between Welles and Fontaine, *Jane Eyre* remains essential viewing for readers of this book.

Welles's reputation had the appeal of a poor joke during most of Lewton's RKO period. The former boy wonder floundered about from one uncompleted project to the next until he became desperate enough to compromise. After starring in Irving Pichel's heavyhanded RKO soap, *Tomorrow Is Forever,* Welles asked for a chance to again direct. At about the time that *Bedlam* was in production, Welles's new project was *The Stranger,* a fairly conservative, almost mainstream, effort. Written by Anthony Veiller and John Huston (the latter was originally slated to direct), the Sam Spiegel production intended to use Welles's capacity as an actor only (though we have heard that one before). Eventually, Spiegel gave in to Welles's desire to direct, but only if the script and editing schedule were strictly followed. Welles managed to direct with uncommon restraint.

The Stranger is a compelling film, one whose dark narrative falls somewhere between that of Hitchcock, Lang, and Lewton. Decades ahead of its time, *The Stranger* tells the story of a Nazi war criminal living incognito in a small Connecticut community. The film's plot and small-town locale make it a fascinating companion piece to Hitchcock's *Shadow of a Doubt* (the film it most resembles). *The Stranger* should please most thriller fans, and it includes several chilling moments that would seem right at home in a Lewton film. A marriage between a wholesome New England girl (Loretta Young) and an ex–Nazi college professor (Welles) may sound ludicrous on paper but, rather surprisingly, this aspect of *The Stranger* is executed with flair and credibility. Welles is especially chilling as Franz Kindler whether he is strangling an old German compatriot, making frantic efforts to hide a corpse, poisoning a pet dog, or encouraging his dear wife to climb the rickety ladder up a 124-foot clock tower. Because Kindler is also a charming and worldly man, his character evinces the same kind of duplicity that we see in the villains of Lang, Hitchcock, and, of course, Lewton.

Welles's next film (as director), *The Lady from Shanghai* (1947), was a muddled affair, an uneasy mixture of James M. Cain and James Michener, but its fun house mirror finale is justly famous, and its sweaty-faced grotesques are hard to forget. It is the least of Welles's noir films, but its nightmarish climax is guaranteed to impress. Far more satisfying and more relevant to the subject of this book was a 1949 film that Welles starred in but did not direct: Carol Reed's *The Third Man,* based on a Graham Greene novel. The on-screen reunion of *The Third Man*'s Orson Welles and Joseph Cotten harks back to the glory days of *Kane* and *Ambersons* and *Fear,* while the film's dark alleys, creepy sewers, distorted shadows, incipient paranoia, and deceptive appearances evoke the atmosphere and style of the Lewton films. Carol Reed was greatly enamored of *The Seventh Victim* (almost single-handedly elevating it to cult status in wartime England), and perhaps he saw in the Graham Greene property some of the ingredients of his favorite Lewton film: ambiguous characters, a secret organization, a missing person, and a naive protagonist. In *Caligari's Children,* S.S. Prawer tells us, "Reed's *The Third Man* is full of Lewtonesque sequences—the scene is noctunal Vienna in which the silence is startlingly broken by a clattering dustbin-lid vividly recalls a similar incident in *The Seventh Victim.*" Other cinematic antecedents for *The Third Man* include the espionage thrillers of Hitchcock and Lang as well as Welles's own *Journey into Fear,* the latter being, in some ways, a virtual dress rehearsal for Reed's film.

Oddly enough, *Touch of Evil* (1957), our final Orson Welles film of note, owes a debt to *The Third Man.* Based on Whit Masterson's novel *Badge of Evil, Touch of Evil* was the last great film noir of the post-war era. While the Welles script has a lot in common with the corruption-in-high-places plots of Fritz Lang's *The Big Heat* (1953) and Phil Karlson's *The Phenix City Story* (1955), *Touch of Evil*'s sense of xenophobia comes straight from *The Third Man.* Its Mexican bordertown setting replaces wartime Vienna, Charlton Heston replaces Joseph Cotten as the ill-fated stranger-in-a-strange-land, and a repulsive and corrupt Orson Welles replaces a charming and corrupt Orson Welles. Both films make use of labyrinthian plots and labyrinthian settings; in fact *Touch of Evil*'s track-down finale is little more than a reworking of *The Third Man*'s climax, with mazeline canals replacing mazelike sewers. While it is difficult to imagine filmmaker Orson Welles deliberately imitating anyone but himself, *Touch of Evil* contains some notably horrific moments, and its gritty atmosphere, dark imagery, and escalating paranoia are not too far removed from the urban-noir sensibilities of *The Leopard Man* and *The Seventh Victim.*

In analyzing Edward Dmytryk, Lewton's rival man of the hour at RKO, Jean-Pierre Coursodon (in *American Directors,* Vol. 2) writes, "There is a gloomy, neurotic streak to most of Dmytryk's films, particularly his more personal and memorable ones. His characters are often misanthropes, misogynists, cynics and self-haters, bent upon destroying themselves as much as others, haunted by guilt feelings and obsessive memories."

Through a series of efficient "B" budget moneymakers, Dmytryk gathered the power and autonomy that Lewton dearly wanted but was never able to grasp. Although born in Canada, Dmytryk (like Lewton) was of Ukrainian descent. After establishing his reputation as a film editor, he began to direct low-budget fare, two of his notable early efforts being *The Devil Commands* (1941) and *Captive Wild Woman* (1943).

The Devil Commands, the better of the two, is several notches above Columbia's three previous Boris Karloff "mad doctor" films, *The Man They Could Not Hang, The Man with Nine Lives,* and *Before I Hang.* Based on an excellent 1939 novel by William Sloane (with the highly provocative, vastly superior title, *The Edge of Running Water*), *The Devil Commands* may pale in comparison with its source (the book has a very high reputation), but for a

Columbia quickie, it offers much more than Karloff's usual dignified presence. Compared to the other Karloff/Columbia horror outtings, *The Devil Commands* is a darker, grimmer, more frightening film. The woman's wistful voice-over that opens the film immediately begs comparison with an earlier film, *Rebecca,* and a later one, *I Walked with a Zombie.* The setting is the Maine coast, a rather unique locale for a horror film made before the age of Stephen King. *The Devil Commands* was marketed as a straight horror film, but it really belongs in the company of a small group of pre–Lewton horror noir films: Boris Ingster's *Stranger on the Third Floor* (1940), Robert Florey's *The Face Behind the Mask* (1941), H. Bruce Humberstone's *I Wake Up Screaming* (1941), and Stuart Heisler's *Among the Living* (1941). Dmytryk's film comes fully equipped with a number of noir trappings, including a femme fatale (a phony spiritualist played by Anne Revere), a protagonist trapped by his obsessions, an angry mob (shades of Lang's *Fury* and Heisler's *Among the Living*), and an all-pervasive sense of doom.

The Devil Commands is unusually moody and atmospheric for a low-budget horror film; Dmytryk obviously tackled his dubious subject with enthusiasm. There is an earnestness in the storytelling that makes its conventional plot (about a scientist obsessed with reviving the spirit of his dead wife) surprisingly compelling. It is the first Dmytryk film to make use of the kind of chiaroscuro lighting that would become a trademark of his noir films. As such, *The Devil Commands* clearly anticipates the look and mood of the Lewton films, and while it is never more than an above average "B" film, it is distinguished by a truly horrific climax, one of the most frightening laboratory scenes of the classic horror cycle.

One suspects that Dmytryk had less freedom on the Universal lot than he did at Columbia. The publicity which accompanied *Captive Wild Woman*'s June 1943 release was clearly intended to cash in on the tremendous popularity of *Cat People*; the half-girl/half-animal motif was provocative, sexy, and very marketable. In Dmytryk's case, however, the studio did not have much of a picture to start with. Producer Ben Pivar urged Dmytryk to make extensive use of footage from an old Clyde Beatty movie, and although the director turned these lion-taming sequences into an editor's tour de force, they quickly become tiresome and take up entirely too much screen time.

Oddly enough, it was Dmytryk's nonhorror efforts at RKO that revealed his gift for dealing with horrifying subjects. Box-office bonanzas like *Hitler's Children* and *Behind the Rising Sun* (both 1943) revealed how capable Dmytryk was at imbuing his sensationalism with the kind of chills that drew theater crowds. *Hitler's Children* is an expert example of wartime propaganda. Released at exactly the right time, the film's phenomenal success preempted much of the fanfare Lewton had earned with the release of his similarly successful debut film. Upon its release, *Hitler's Children* was considered shocking and not a little risqué, particularly those scenes that showed Germany's unmarried women bearing children for the good of Nazism. Although dated and undeniably slanted, *Hitler's Children* remains a powerful and tremendously engaging anti–Nazi film. (In its attempts to chronicle the rise of Nazism in prewar Germany and the brainwashing techniques used to turn ordinarily decent human beings into fodder for the Fuehrer, Dmytryk's film is a fascinating precursor to the alien-doppelganger, sci-fi films of the 1950s [*Invaders from Mars, Invaders of the Body Snatchers,* et al.].) Our other wartime enemies were condemned in *Behind the Rising Sun,* a film which shows Japanese soldiers hurling Chinese babies in the air (on screen) and catching them on their bayonets (off screen). Both of Dmytryk's propaganda pieces are brisk, tightly directed films fraught with paranoia and numerous macabre touches. At the time of their release, they captured the imagination, as well as the outrage, of a nation at war.

As a result of his newfound success, RKO advanced Dmytryk to "A" budget productions. Among his RKO films of this period, two stand out as classic examples of film noir: *Murder, My Sweet* (1944) and *Crossfire* (1947). Although *Murder, My Sweet* (based on Raymond Chandler's *Farewell, My Lovely*) is often cited as an exemplar of the RKO noir style, the Lewton series had already provided a testing ground for much of Dmytryk's dark imagery. Moreover, *Murder, My Sweet* made use of many of the same technicians who worked on the Lewton series (among them, Harry Wild, Roy Webb, Albert S. D'Agostino, and Vernon L. Walker). Dmytryk's film bears many of film noir's definitive earmarks: a femme fatale, flashbacks with a calm but disillusioned voice-over recalling the bleak events, a seedy atmosphere of neon lights and broken spirits, a very eccentric dream sequence, and enough paranoia and deception to satisfy the darkest cynic in the house.

Raymond Chandler (along with his partners in crime, authors Dashiell Hammett, James M. Cain, and Cornell Woolrich) was one of the founding fathers of the hard-boiled crime novel. Known for their cynical first-person narratives, writers of the hard-boiled school created the literary foundation for film noir. German expressionism provided the look; America's hard-boiled crime fiction provided the substance. According to Alain Silver and Elizabeth Ward (in *Film Noir: An Encyclopedic Reference to the American Style*), "*Murder My Sweet* is a fascinating blend of the hard-boiled tradition and a hybrid form of muted expressionism . . . with a dark ambience unknown in most films of this period." The authors describe the world of *Murder, My Sweet* as a "nightmarish landscape devoid of order and ripe with chaotic images . . . an atmosphere of fear and dislocation." One comes away from *Murder, My Sweet* feeling the need for daylight, fresh air, and perhaps even a shower.

Dmytryk's other significant entry in the noir cycle, *Crossfire,* was both a film noir and a message picture. Unfortunately, the film's impact is softened by Dmytryk's efforts to play to two separate audiences (though the theatergoers, who arrived in droves, did not seem to mind). *Crossfire*'s reputation has tarnished over the years (many modern critics find it preachy and dated), but it still merits the attention of anyone interested in dark cinema. The story, told in a series of flashbacks (varying with the teller and at times covering the same ground, à la *Citizen Kane*), concerns the plight of a soldier (well-played by George Cooper) who is suspected of killing a civilian. Dmytryk makes interesting use of the "wrong man" theme, though the identity of the real murderer (Robert Ryan) is disclosed in the first reel, creating a mystery that is not so much a whodunit but a whydunit. The dénouement (that the murdered man, a Jew, was the victim of an anti–Semite) was at the time so boldly novel that the film became a word-of-mouth sensation. Although it was the first film to take a stance against anti–Semitism, *Crossfire*'s original source, a novel by future film director Richard Brooks (the husband of Lewton star Jean Brooks), had a message that is today just as timely. In the Brooks novel, the victim was a homosexual, not a Jew.

Like *Murder, My Sweet, Crossfire* is an obvious close cousin to the Lewton films. J. Roy Hunt (the cinematographer for *I Walk with a Zombie*) fills *Crossfire* with low-key lighting, skewed angles, and distorted shadows, while Roy Webb's score is filled with the musical signatures we have come to associate with his work on the Lewton series. Moreover, D'Agostino's art direction and Silvera's set decoration give the film its impeccable RKO house style. *Murder, My Sweet* and *Crossfire* are two of a trio of RKO films noir (the third being Jacques Tourneur's *Out of the Past*) that owe a considerable debt to the Lewton series.

The events of Dmytryk's life at this juncture in his directing career are historically significant. Shortly after *Crossfire* was released, Dmytryk and nine other Hollywood notables would make headlines around the world as the Hollywood Ten. While their trial was pending, the Motion Picture Association issued a statement expressing its compliance with the House UnAmerican Activities Committee (HUAC) and stating that the ten alleged Communists were discharged and would not be reemployed. Dmytryk and his producer, Adrian Scott (also one of the ten), went to England in order to continue working but were obligated to return to the U.S. to take part in assorted legal activities and public appearances. Eventually, as the Supreme Court refused to review their case, each member of the Hollywood Ten was sentenced to one year in prison. Everyone held out, except Dmytryk, who would wind up cutting his sentence in half. According to Jean-Pierre Coursodon (*American Directors*, Vol. 2):

> While serving his sentence, Dmytryk issued a formal statement denouncing the Communist party. Upon his release, he appeared before HUAC, testified that he had indeed been a party member between 1944 and 1945, and "named" a number of Hollywood people (including fellow directors Herbert Biberman, John Berry, and Jules Dassin) as having been Communists at the time. He thus became infamous among liberals as the only one of the "Ten"

who submitted to pressure in order to be able to work again in Hollywood.

The era of the Red Scare was an ugly period of American history, filled with paranoia, desperation, mob-rallying witch hunts, deception, betrayal, and tragic fates; in short, it was the world of film noir set to reality. Hollywood's German émigrés had seen it all before: the book burning, the informants, the hysteria, the pain—all in the name of love of country. The Germanic flourishes that gave definition to American film noir had, after all, originated in a land where disillusionment, hysteria, and paranoia were one's daily companions.

Dmytryk's first film after his prison pardon, *The Sniper* (Columbia, 1952), is about Eddie Miller (Arthur Franz), a pleasant, clean-cut young man who cannot resist shooting women at random with his carbine rifle. *The Sniper* was one of many Stanley Kramer message films made through the late forties and early fifties. Kramer's liberal stance also put him under the suspicions of the HUAC witchburners, but he managed to come out of it unscathed. *The Sniper* is a straightforward portrayal of its title character, a young man whose hatred of women stems from his childhood and his abusive mother. Dmytryk's film is shot in the detached, objective style of the pseudo-documentary, but so cynical and unsympathetic are its secondary characters that its central character, a sniper, comes across as the most likeable of the lot. The police are portrayed in flat, lifeless tones, their reigning emotions those of frustration and world weariness. Other characters, even Miller's victims, are not exactly model human beings. Members of the public at large, portrayed as gawking rubberneckers who appear at the scene of every killing, are a despicable cross-section of humanity. A woman brings her little girl out into the streets in the middle of the night so they can both join the crowd in looking at the bloodied corpse. Like many previous cinematic psycho-killers, Eddie Miller's homicidal rage is beyond his control. He knows he is sick and takes extreme measures to get help; he even writes notes to the police before going on a murder spree, but it is all to no avail. In some ways, *The Sniper* can be looked upon as an urban variation of *The Wolf Man*, its main character being a close parallel to Lon Chaney's Lawrence Talbot. But unlike Chaney's lycanthrope, Eddie Miller is a modern monster, one who always looks normal, just like the guy next door.

The film's most terrifying scene (actually a single continuous camera shot) is a masterpiece of understatement. A voyeuristic camera shot of a window shows a drunken woman entering her small apartment. It is an upper-story window, and because there is no tilt in the camera angle, we realize that our point of view corresponds exactly with that of someone who is, presumably, occupying the same level on an adjacent building's fire escape or outside stairwell. Although we never see him or his gun, we know that "someone" is Eddie, as he was rebuffed by the same woman earlier in the evening. The drunken woman had been abrasive and unpleasant in the barroom where she met Eddie, but now that we see her put her rag doll to bed before pouring herself another drink, we feel a rush of sympathy that only heightens our dread of the next few moments. She stands with her back to the window, hoists her drink high to propose a toast, perhaps to memories of a life gone by, and as a single chord of music builds in a crescendo, there is a thunderous blast. The woman, shot in the head, drops so swiftly we suspect she is dead before she hits the floor. The camera shot holds, the reverberations of the blast still in the air, as our attention swings back to the rag doll and the little girl to whom it once belonged.

Like his RKO colleagues Mark Robson and Robert Wise, Edward Dmytryk went on to become a major Hollywood director of the 1950s and 1960s. He was given huge budgets and brand-name stars—Humphrey Bogart, Kirk Douglas, Spencer Tracy, Clark Gable, Elizabeth Taylor, Montgomery Clift, Marlon Brando—but much of the life had gone out of his craft. His films were given gala receptions, big box office, Technicolor, and Cinemascope, but for all that had been gained, something had been lost. The critics who once championed Dmytryk's 1940 RKO efforts were now dismissing him as a hack director who had sold his soul to Hollywood. If Dmytryk did not become everything that he could have been, he nonetheless made important contributions to Hollywood's noir vision. His few examples of RKO noir not only owed a debt to the Lewton films, but they also exerted a significant influence upon the post–Lewton noir films of his RKO colleagues, Jacques Tourneur, Mark Robson, and Robert Wise.

In 1965 Dmytryk made a black-and-white thriller that recalled his RKO days. *Mirage,* shot on location in New York City, drew equal measures of inspiration from three sources: Hitchcock, Lewton, and "The Twilight Zone" television show. Although *Mirage* is overly complicated, with a fascinating plot that degenerates into stupifying mush halfway into the film, its opening scenes, taking place in an office building during a power failure (inspired by the Great New York Black Out), are what viewers remember most. Our only sources of light are the bobbing flashlight beams that turn the office building into a distorted world of dancing shadows and disembodied voices. Once seen (or not seen, as it were), *Mirage*'s first reel is seldom forgotten; if the entire film were as good as its first 15 minutes, it would be a classic of the first magnitude. Another scene, one that appears to be a deliberate homage to *Cat People,* takes place in the Central Park Zoo, where the film's romantic leads (Gregory Peck and Diane Baker) exchange cryptic comments as they direct their attention to a black leopard pacing in its cage (the only zoo animal we see, in fact). *Mirage* has a number of things in common with *The Seventh Victim:* a secret society, an inept detective, an elusive woman, a pretentious psychiatrist, hired assassins, dark streets, hotel rooms, subways, and suicide.

As its title implies, *Mirage* presents a world where nothing is quite as it appears to be.

Although Billy Wilder is often thought of as the director who makes Jack Lemmon comedies, a dark thread runs through much of the filmmaker's early work. The Austrian-born director started out as a newspaper reporter before moving to Berlin where, desperate to eke out a living, he became a professional escort. Eventually, Wilder turned to writing movie scripts and broke into Germany's filmmaking industry, where he worked with such future Hollywood emigré directors as Edgar Ulmer, Fred Zinnemann, and the Siodmak brothers, Curt and Robert. Coming to Hollywood by way of a short stay in France (as did Fritz Lang), Wilder wrote highly touted screenplays for major American films, including Lubitsch's *Bluebeard's Eighth Wife* (1938) and *Ninotchka* (1939), Mitchell Leisen's *Midnight* (1939) and *Hold Back the Dawn* (1941), and Howard Hawk's *Ball of Fire* (1941). Although Wilder's scripts had shown evidence of a smart, as well as cynical, comic touch, Wilder's directing career began to attract critical attention as the result of a small number of deadly serious films. Four of them—*Double Indemnity* (1944), *The Lost Weekend* (1945), *Sunset Boulevard* (1950), and *Ace in the Hole* (1951)—are especially recommended to fans of the Lewton films.

Double Indemnity, based on a James M. Cain novel (and adapted for the screen by Raymond Chandler), was a ground-breaking entry to the noir cycle. Dmytryk's *Murder, My Sweet* (released the same year) may have achieved the quintessential noir look, but it was *Double Indemnity* that turned dark urban melodramas into a viable Hollywood trend for the postwar years. In Barbara Stanwyck's Phyllis Dietrichson, Wilder created the archetypal "black widow" of postwar noir. Unlike the noir heroes of Hitchcock and Lang, Fred MacMurray's Walter Neff is not just an innocent bystander; he knows the difference between right and wrong, though this does not stop him from abandoning his scruples and giving in to his lover's desire to see her husband dead. Neff's better judgment falls victim to his passion for a woman, something that had not happened to previous noir protagonists, Sam Spade *(The Maltese Falcon)*, Ed Beaumont *(The Glass Key)*, or Phillip Marlowe *(Murder, My Sweet)*.

The Lost Weekend was not a film noir but an equally dark message picture. A harrowingly realistic study of the nightmares of alcoholism, Wilder's film played like a horror movie for postwar adults. Its protagonist (Ray Milland) is not beset by tragedy or hard luck, but the fact that he is given no conventional excuse (tragedy, divorce, unrequited love, rejection) for his drinking only makes the film twice as powerful. By steering clear of any particular motivation for the hero's plight, *The Lost Weekend*'s portrait of a dipsomaniac touches more viewers. For the duration of the film, we wear an alcoholic's shoes and walk the alcoholic's treadmill. Wilder's nightmare vision is as subtle as it is frightening, and the scene where Milland wakes up in the alcoholic ward is absolutely horrific.

For a number of reasons, *Sunset Boulevard* (1950) is probably the most Lewtonesque Billy Wilder film. In S.S. Prawler's *Caligari's Children,* Richard Corliss is quoted as saying:

> *Sunset Boulevard* is the definitive Hollywood horror movie. Practically everything about this final Brackett-Wilder collaboration is ghoulish. The film is narrated by a corpse that is waiting to be fished out of a swimming pool. Most of it takes place in an old dark house that opens its doors only to the walking dead. The first time our doomed hero . . . enters the house, he is mistaken for an undertaker. Soon after, another corpse is buried—that of a pet monkey, in a white coffin. Outside the house is the swimming pool, at first filled only with rats, and "the ghost of a tennis court." The only musical sound in the house is that of the wind, wheezing through the broken pipes of a huge old organ.
>
> The old man who occasionally plays it calls to mind Lon Chaney's *Phantom of the Opera*—that and other images of the Silent Era. The old man is Erich von Stroheim, playing himself as he plays the organ, with intimations of melancholia, absurdity and loss. . . . Desmond Swanson is Dracula, or perhaps the Count's older, forgotten sister, condemned to relive a former life, sucking blood from her victim.

In *Guide for the Film Fanatic,* Dan Peary notes: "Not only does the morbid, death-obsessed plot parallel 1936's *Dracula's Daughter,* but the film abounds in horror-movie references and imagery. What better locale for a 'ghost' story—about a woman long thought dead—than Hollywood, a town built on illusions and delusions, where people grow old but remain young on celluloid, where people become has-beens before they've made it."

With all references to Dracula, his sister/daughter, and the Phantom aside, Wilder's basic premise—that of an aging actress cloistered away in a spooky old mansion, reliving her past—has strong links to *The Curse of the Cat People. Sunset Boulevard* tells the story of Joe Gillis (William Holden), a destitute screenwriter who has had nothing to his credit but a couple of "B" pictures. We see Joe's ill-fortune as he goes from studio to studio, trying to sell his hackneyed screenplays. No one will bite. He owes three months rent, and he is forced to hide his car to keep it from being repossessed. He is out of money, out of luck. (Critics usually take Gillis's misfortune at face value, but the protagonist's situation also mimics the plight of the blacklisted screenwriter during the height of the Red Scare. Seen in this light, *Sunset Boulevard* could be Wilder's own personal nightmare.)

While hiding from repossessors, Gillis comes upon a dilapidated mansion. In a scene that bears a remarkable resemblance to Amy Reed's first trip to the Farren house in *The Curse of the Cat People,* Gillis is beckoned by a mysterious female voice coming from the direction of a second-story window. In both films the voice belongs to a has-been actress. Although many viewers have assumed that silent-screen star Gloria Swanson was merely playing herself as *Sunset Boulevard*'s over-the-hill actress Norma Desmond (Wilder's use of clips from Swanson's silent films reinforce this notion), the character actually bears a much closer resemblance to Alla Nazimova (who, oddly enough, was also the inspiration for *Curse*'s has-been actress, Julia Farren). It was Nazimova who completely broke away from Hollywood at the dawn of the talkies, not Swanson (who made several early talkies). Moreover, Norma Desmond repeatedly alludes to her desire to once again play Salome, but it was Nazimova whose name was forever linked with *Salome* (1923), a notorious film in its day. It was also Nazimova who was known for her bizarre gestures, her intense dramatic flourishes, her exaggerated theatrical affectations, and her mystical eccentricities, all of which appear in the character of Norma Desmond.

(Although *Sunset Boulevard*'s horror trappings are primarily those of style, rather than content, Wilder's film provided the prototype for an entire subgenre of 1960s modern Gothic thrillers [spearheaded by Robert Aldrich's 1962 film *What Ever Happened to Baby Jane?*] that cast aging Hollywood actresses as the principal sources of menace.)

Ace in the Hole (1951) was such a boldly cynical indictment of the American way that it is hard to believe it was cleared for release at the height of Hollywood's most repressive era. Shot on location in New Mexico, *Ace in the Hole* points ahead to the myriad 1950s science fiction films that would be set in the American Southwest. Released amidst the hoopla of the Rosenberg trial, *Ace in the Hole* took a scornful look at many things: the newspaper business, capitalism, the American public, corrupt self-serving politicians, and even the sacred institutions of marriage and family.

It is the story of yet another down-and-out writer, this time a reporter named Chuck Tatum (Kirk Douglas), a man so hungry for fame and a Pulitzer Prize that he exploits the news story of a man buried alive in a cave (under a mountain allegedly haunted by the angry spirits of Native Americans). Rather than arrange to have the man removed immediately (possibly within a day), Tatum convinces the local authorities that it would be good publicity for the town (and its officials) if the rescue were delayed and the news story played up for six days. In order to do this, Tatum, the town officials, and even the victim's wife, conspire to take advantage of the misfortune through the needless, but time-consuming, plan of drilling down from the top of the mountain. Unfortunately, the incessent pounding of the drill drives the victim to distraction; his inability to sleep (combined with his mental and physical anguish) wears him down to the point where he eventually develops pneumonia and dies. *Ace in the Hole* is a compelling one-of-a-kind film, though it is hardly a crowd-pleaser (which is why it lost money). The scenes in the cave focusing upon the victim (convincingly played by Richard Benedict) are appropriately eerie and effectively simulate the terrors of claustrophobia. It is easy to empathize with the doomed man—and even understand why he comes to believe in the mountain's supernatural curse—

as he sits alone in the dark, hours upon end, facing the terrors of his imagination.

Film noir was not the only dark cinematic trend of the 1940s; period thrillers had also become a staple for directors with Germanic leanings. Taking its cues from a number of theatrical psycho-romances—*Kind Lady, Love from a Stranger, Night Must Fall*—the 1940s period thriller came of age with George Cukor's *Gaslight* and John Brahm's *The Lodger* (both 1944).

The period thriller had close associations with film noir, but because the latter type of film is defined by its modern urban American setting, the period thriller (set in the past, and often upon British or European soil) is traditionally kept separate from the noir films (though the term "period noir" has lately been put to good use). In *Film Noir: An Encyclopedic Reference to the American Style*, authors Alain Silver and Elizabeth Ward tell us, "These productions, whether typed as 'Victorian,' 'atmosphere films,' or 'period melodramas,' are the genre pieces that come closest to full participation in the noir cycle."

Based on the play *Angel Street* by Patrick Hamilton, Cukor's *Gaslight* is actually a remake of a 1939 British film starring Diana Wynyard and Anton Walbrook. Leslie Halliwell's *Film and Video Guide* actually rates the British film as the superior of the two, though this original *Gaslight*, directed by Thorold Dickinson and released in America as *Angel Street*, is rarely seen today. Judging from the marvelous chills of a later Walbrook/Dickinson film, the Lewtonesque *Queen of Spades* (1949), we suspect *Angel Street* would be a film worth finding.

Cukor's *Gaslight* opens with the murder of a famous London singer. Her niece Paula (Ingrid Bergman) is so traumatized by the event that she leaves her London home to reside in Italy, where she studies voice. As time passes, Paula meets and falls in love with Gregory (Charles Boyer), whom she marries and for whom she gives up her singing. Since Paula is sole heir to her aunt's townhouse, Gregory convinces her that they should inhabit the aunt's dwelling in spite of the bad memories associated with it. After the move, however, Gregory becomes colder and more domineering. He does a number of things that are calculated to make Paula believe she is going out of her mind. Paula becomes agoraphobic and is nearly driven to the breaking point when she is rescued by the film's hero (Joseph Cotten), a man who as a boy worshipped her aunt and thus became obsessed with solving the murder case long abandoned by Scotland Yard. Gregory turns out to be the murderer of the unsolved homicide, his motivation having been some jewels hidden in the house, jewels he had not been able to get his hands on when he killed Paula's aunt.

Under the expert hand of George Cukor, *Gaslight* is highly evocative and continually absorbing; this stylish and well-acted period thriller never falters in its pace and works up some genuine suspense and exquisite period flavor.

Charles Boyer's snakelike charm, feigned concern, and ultimate cruelty—all so nicely underplayed—make him among the most despicable villains of the 1940s. Ingrid Bergman has never been more vulnerable, more beautiful, more tragic than she is here. In her debut role, Angela Lansbury, as a coarse, young, but thoroughly intimidating, housemaid (echoes of Judith Anderson in *Rebecca*), is quite marvelous. As its provocative title would indicate, *Gaslight* is rich with atmosphere; the city streets are blanketed with fog and the gaslit lampposts merely accent the fog's density. Characters walking the street have to be within arm's reach to recognize one another, voices of unseen street singers fill the air, and horsedrawn taxis telegraph the sound of clopping hoofs long before any horse is visible to the eye. Even the interiors, particularly Paula's room, with its gas-generated light mysteriously ebbing and flowing, communicate a sense of despair. Although *Gaslight* is not imitative of the Lewton films, the manner in which it builds its mounting terror from things unseen is firmly in the Lewton tradition.

Also successful, though not quite as popular as *Gaslight,* was 20th Century–Fox's superb remake of Hitchcock's *The Lodger.* If *Gaslight* had the more captivating narrative, John Brahm's *The Lodger* had the deeper, more fully sustained, period flavor. *The Lodger* and its John Brahm follow-up, *Hangover Square,* stand alone in their field. Seldom has the illusion of a period setting been so complete and on such a grand scale as it is with these two "A" budget thrillers.

John Brahm (1893–1982) was born and raised in Hamburg, Germany. Leaving Germany in the early 1930s, he gained a foothold in a Paris studio as dialogue director and film editor. Brahm had the unique distinction of making his directing debut by replacing D.W. Griffith in 1936 when a disgruntled Griffith abandoned his made-in-England remake of *Broken Blossoms.* With the British film under his belt, Brahm came to Hollywood, where he made low-budget films for Columbia; surprisingly, these programmers caught the attention of critics. One of them, *Let Us Live* (1939), was a reworking of Fritz Lang's *You Only Live Once.* Brahm made his first horror film, *The Undying Monster,* for Fox in 1942, at around the same time that Lewton was producing *Cat People.*

The Undying Monster was an adaptation of a 1922 werewolf novel by British author Jessie Douglas Kerruish. Brahm's stylish but rather uninvolving film may have been inspired by Kerruish's novel, but the feel, the look, and the plot of *The Undying Monster* indicate that its real inspiration was *The Hound of the Baskervilles* (1939), also a Fox release. Although some genre critics give the film high marks, apparently on the basis of its atmospheric sets (in many ways superior to those being used over at Universal), *The Undying Monster* is really a languorously paced mystery, with the added novelty of a genuine werewolf being included in its final dénouement.

In *American Film Directors,* Vol. 1, Jean-Pierre Coursodon calls *The Lodger:*

> an impressive achievement. . . . The film is a cinematographer's field day, a festival of weird angles, shadow effects, intricate compositions. . . . The fog is used so spectacularly as sometimes to steal the show from the star. Said [Lucien] Ballard in an interview: "I had always wanted to do fog the way I did in *The Lodger*. Before then it was always a gray haze. I did it with fog in spots, with black and white definition still coming through." To a producer who objected that fog doesn't look like that, Ballard answered, "That's the way it *should* look."

Brahm's version of *The Lodger*, unlike Hitchcock's, does not modernize the novel; instead, it includes as many historic details of the infamous Whitechapel killer as the censors would allow. *The Lodger*'s screenwriter, playwright Barre Lyndon, could not have the Ripper kill prostitutes, so the victims were euphemistically changed to dance hall actresses. Of course the killings are done offscreen, but the film is all the better for it.

Laird Cregar's performance is especially worthy; it was his first starring role. Cregar, whose imposing girth and worldly presence belied his youth, had made a chilling impression in the excellent early film noir, *I Wake Up Screaming* (1941), as a creepy cop obsessed with a young nightclub star. Equally notable was Cregar's despicable Milquetoast role in another early noir classic, *This Gun for Hire* (1942). Cregar was one of those rare performers who was able to engender sympathy in a vast string of villainous roles. As Mr. Slade, *The Lodger*'s lonely pathologist, Cregar projects a profound sense of inner tragedy. It is not difficult to understand why the film's heroine (played by Merle Oberon) would treat him kindly and why everyone in the lodging house would give him the benefit of the doubt, even as the evidence begins stacking up against him.

Cregar is given excellent support from an illustrious cast: Merle Oberon, Sir Cedric Hardwicke, George Sanders, Sara Allgood, Aubrey Mather, Queenie Leonard, Doris Lloyd, Billy Bevan, Skelton Knaggs (the inimitable), and many more. In addition, *The Lodger*'s impressive sets, including a massive dance hall theater, are filled with hundreds of extras that give the quite accurate impression that no expense was spared. The film uses no matte shots, no rear projection, no stock footage, no phony-looking inserts or establishing shots; *The Lodger* is the real thing, a thriller of high quality in all departments.

The Lodger gives us the opportunity to speculate what Lewton's period films might have looked like had he been allowed bigger budgets. For the most part, Brahm's approach to terror is more direct than Lewton's (no lonely walks or false jolts), but occasionally we see similar fear-the-dark techniques. One murder, taking place in the victim's darkened apartment, is preceded by the creak of a door and a seemingly endless pause.

Hangover Square is another John Brahm tour de force. It bears some of the same elements as its predecessor: Laird Cregar in the lead role, George Sanders in a supporting role (this time as a psychiatrist, Dr. Judd's brother, so to speak), a Barre Lyndon screenplay (this time from a novel by Patrick

Hamilton, the author of the play upon which *Gaslight* was based), and numerous standing sets from *The Lodger*. There were some changes: Joseph LaShelle replaced Lucien Ballard in the photography department (without any appreciable loss, believe it or not), Bernard Herrmann replaced composer Hugo Friedhofer (a vast improvement), Lewton veteran Alan Napier replaced Sir Cedric Hardwicke as the kindly father prototype, and Linda Darnell and Faye Marlowe took over Merle Oberon's leading lady chores. *Hangover Square* is highly derivative of its predecessor, but formula filmmaking is not necessarily artless, as the Lewton unit proved over and over again.

The film, taking place in England around the turn of the century, chronicles the story of George Harvey Bone (Cregar), a mild-mannered and distinguished musician well known for his brilliant symphonies and concerti. Because he suffers from blackouts (brought on by discordant sounds, believe it or not), Bone does not realize that he is the neighborhood serial killer, but he begins worrying once he notices the time frames of the recent homicides. He and his girlfriend, Barbara Chapman (Faye Marlowe), seek help from Dr. Middleton (Sanders), a psychologist, but unbeknownst to any of them, the "evil" George Bone has already planted false evidence to lead Middleton (and ultimately himself) astray. Relieved over his apparent innocence, George falls in love with Netta Longdon (Linda Darnell), a coarse but beautiful singer of popular songs. Although Netta already has a lover, she leads George on, convincing him to write tunes expressly for her. Eventually George discovers the ruse and, during one of his spells, kills her. The authorities put the pieces together and close in on the killer while he is giving a concert. Feeling the trap closing in, George asks Barbara to replace him on the keyboard while the visibly shaken composer confers with the police in another room. When they ask him to come along quietly, the composer hurls a burning oil lamp across the room, making his escape. A quickly spreading fire causes a panic, and everyone rushes out of the building except George, who returns to the piano, finishing the concert while flaming rafters fall down around him.

In *Guide for the Film Fanatic*, Dan Peary praises *Hangover Square*:

> Brahm's exciting, bizarre direction [is] especially impressive during the blackout sequences. Brahm wasn't afraid to use wild angles, camera distortion, swooping crane shots, even a *freeze frame!* I really love his use of darkness and light (candles and oil-lit street lamps are often evident), and how he maneuvers his stars and extras during street scenes. The streets themselves look interesting, as Brahm has the light reflect in deep puddles; one much travelled street is under construction, with dirt piled on both sides of a long ditch—I've never seen a studio set quite like it, and, more important, Brahm uses it to call attention to the disorder in Cregar's mind.

Hangover Square's most singular visual set piece centers around the events of Guy Fawkes Day. George Bone, having just strangled Netta and needing to dispose of her body, covers her face with a mask and hauls her corpse like a sack of potatoes (or one of Cabman Gray's specimens) to the Guy Fawkes celebration site. There we see an incredibly high (at least two stories) mound of effigies. Tall ladders lean against this massive mound of corpselike forms, enabling latecomers to carry their own offerings to the top of the pile. As a result of this arrangement, we see several animated bodies squirming among the lifeless ones. A large crowd circles the mound, and the entire effect recalls the nightmare visions of such painters as Bosch, Bruegel, and perhaps even Hogarth.

George is urged to hurry, for the ungainly mob is eager to set fire to the towering mass. He climbs the ladder as a crane shot captures the desperation in his face. Below him, the celebration gains speed, people running to and fro, some with torches, some pouring kerosene around the base of the pile. Netta's mask begins moving to the side, revealing the woman's face, but nobody notices. After dumping the corpse on top of the pile and getting his feet back on the ground, George backs away from the raging conflagration as flickering light illuminates his face. Obviously a part of him wishes to leave, but he does not; he just stands there watching the fire burn.

Hangover Square was Laird Cregar's last film; he died shortly after the production was completed and never saw the final cut. Anyone who has ever seen *Hangover Square* has noticed one of its strangest features: its star's weight yo-yos from scene to scene. Cregar had gone on a crash diet just before *Hangover Square* went into production and with the aid of amphetamines, the hefty actor lost an enormous amount of weight. Because Brahm's film was shot out of sequence (as most films are), Cregar's weight bounces up or down from one scene to the next. Cregar's bulky clothing and heavy overcoats hide some of the physical disparity between scenes, but nothing could be done about the actor's face, which is so visibly thinner in some scenes that we get the impression that Bone is being played by two different performers. After the shooting was done, Cregar entered the hospital to have an abdominal operation that would help him maintain his weight loss, but his heart failed during surgery and he never recovered. He was dead at age 28.

John Brahm never again matched the intensity of his two Laird Cregar classics, but he did direct some other worthwhile films. His 1947 RKO film *The Locket* should be of interest to Lewtonphiles; Brahm made good use of many of Lewton's stable of supporting performers: Sharyn Moffett (quite exceptional), Katherine Emery, Fay Helm, Helene Thimig, and, among others, Ellen Corby. *The Locket*'s screenplay (credited to Sheridan Gibney) is hard to resist. On the day of a man's wedding, a stranger (Brian Aherne) arrives to get him to call off the event, claiming the prospective bride (Laraine Day) has been married before—to him, in fact. The groom is incredulous, but the stranger tells his tale. Through flashbacks we discover that the woman in question is a pathological liar, a kleptomaniac, and probably a murderer. One of the most fascinating things about the *The Locket* is its unusual narrative frame; very much in the manner of Chinese boxes, we are given a flashback (Aherne's story), which breaks into another flashback (Robert Mitchum's story), which is followed by yet one more flashback (Day's childhood reminiscenes, with Moffett playing Day as a young girl). Brahm's film also contains what is probably the most unexpected suicide in 1940s cinema.

Apart from the above-mentioned films, Brahm's features are mostly unremarkable. When Andre de Toth's *House of Wax* (which resembled Brahm's Cregar films more closely than it did Michael Curtiz's *Mystery of the Wax Museum*) became the 3-D horror sensation of 1953, Columbia secured the talents of Vincent Price and John Brahm and made its own 3-D period thriller, *The Mad Magician*. The overall result, despite Brahm's careful direction and Price's fine performance, failed to hit the mark. The period sets are impressive, but drab. No wonderfully inaccurate fog here; in fact, there is no fog at all. *Hangover Square*'s bonfire sequence is reprised, almost shot-for-shot, with entirely lackluster results; when Price takes a room in a boarding house, it is an obvious homage to *The Lodger*, even down to identical lines of dialogue.

Brahm lived in Germany for two years before returning to Hollywood and moving into the television medium, where he appeared to ally himself with the horror/fantasy/sci-fi fields. He directed 14 "Alfred Hitchcock Presents"/"Alfred Hitchcock Hour" episodes, 12 "Twilight Zone" episodes, two "Outer Limits" episodes, and 13 episodes of "Boris Karloff's Thriller," the latter by far the most Lewtonesque television series in the history of the medium.

Anatole Litvak's impressive list of directing credits is far too eclectic to qualify him as a dark visionary. For those who like facile descriptions, imagine a blend of Val Lewton and George Cukor and one has a reasonable approximation of Anatole Litvak. Ted Sennett's *Great Movie Directors* states: "Anatole ('Tola') Litvak returned, time and again, to the theme of the woman as victim. In many of his films . . . his female characters find themselves trapped in a dire situation not of their own making."

Litvak wa born in Kiev, in the Russian Ukraine. Older than Lewton by two years, he directed films in Russia, Germany (where his assistant was Henri-Georges Clouzot), England, and France. In 1937 he came to Hollywood, where he made *The Woman I Love* for RKO. Litvak's most prolific stretch was for Warner Bros., where from 1938 through 1942, he directed *Tovarich, The Amazing Dr. Clitterhouse, The Sisters, Confessions of a Nazi Spy, Castle on the Hudson, City for Conquest, All This and Heaven Too, Out of the Fog, Blues in the Night,* and *This Above All.* When the war broke out, Litvak left Hollywood proper and joined Frank Capra in the making of the "Why We Fight" documentaries. After his Hollywood hiatus, he was back at RKO by 1947, where he disgraced himself with *That Long Night*, an expensive production that put the studio a million dollars in the red. Litvak's name should have been poison—RKO dropped him immediately—but Paramount offered him the director's post for *Sorry, Wrong Number,* and he redeemed himself.

Based on the popular radio play by Lucille Fletcher, *Sorry, Wrong Number,* starring Burt Lancaster and Barbara Stanwyck, may have been a box-office hit, but its radio-thriller source was designed for a 30-minute length. By creating a film three times as long, Litvak diminished much of the work's impact. Set in New York, the well-known plot involves a wealthy bedridden hypochondriac (Stanwyck), who picks up the telephone to overhear, via a crossed line, a conversation between two men. One of the men talks about a murder he has been paid to commit later that night on behalf of a husband who wishes to get rid of his wife and thereby come into possession of her money. The bedridden woman, not suspecting herself as the targeted victim, makes numerous calls to the police, but since she has no idea of the identity of the victim, there is nothing they can do. When Stanwyck's husband, played by Burt Lancaster, has second thoughts and calls to warn his wife to get help, it is too late. The hired assassin answers the phone, saying, "Sorry, wrong number."

Well acted and directed (if rather turgidly written), *Sorry, Wrong Number* has enough of the expressionistic ingredients of the thriller noir form to make it a close cousin to the films of Lewton and, especially, Robert Siodmak, whose work Litvak's film most closely resembles. Although it made money, primarily because of the radio play's popularity, *Sorry, Wrong Number* was able to offer no surprises; the movie audiences already knew the ending, or at least the significance of the giveaway title. (*Sorry, Wrong Number* was probably the inspiration for Richard Matheson's 1953 short story, "Long Distance Call," which in 1964 became a "Twilight Zone" episode directed by Jacques Tourneur.)

If *Sorry, Wrong Number* was marred by its predictability, Litvak's next film, *The Snake Pit* (1948, Fox), took America by complete surprise. The director's eye-opening depiction of life in a mental institution owed some debt to *Bedlam* (and to other films made by RKO's "snake pit"). The plot of Litvak's film (based on Mary Jane Ward's novel) actually bears a close resemblance to that of another Lewton movie: *Cat People.* A man becomes interested in a woman with a dark secret and a mysterious past; they enter a whirlwind romance and in spite of some reluctance on the part of the woman, they marry. Soon after, the husband discovers that his wife behaves strangely, that she becomes rigid during attempted intimacy, and the marriage remains unconsummated. The woman realizes the marriage is a mistake; because of a previous trauma, she is incapable of giving herself sexually to her husband and, in fact, fears that she might somehow bring about his death.

The above plot description fits *Cat People* and *The Snake Pit* like a pair of gloves. Imagine a version of *Cat People* where Irena's problem sheds its supernaturalism and becomes nothing more exotic than mental illness—a *Cat People* where Oliver Reed takes Dr. Judd's advice and commits Irena to a mental institution—and we would have something not entirely unlike Litvak's film. *The Snake Pit*'s smug but nice British psychiatrist, Dr. Kick (Leo Genn), is a benevolent version of *Cat People*'s Dr. Judd, while a character named Hester (Betsy Blair) functions much in the same manner as *Bedlam*'s "Dove" woman.

One of *The Snake Pit*'s strongest features is its extremely sympathetic performance by Olivia DeHavilland as Virginia Cunningham, the film's protagonist. As Virginia, DeHavilland convinces us of her insanity without losing our sympathy or empathy. She makes us understand her confusion, her paranoia, her twisted logic, and enables the viewer to believe that in every insane person, there is a voice of sanity struggling to come forth.

Litvak's experimental direction makes use of many flashbacks and shows an especial fondness for imaginative flash pans. In several memorable scenes, the camera swiftly pans across a room to generate suspense or register shock. The flashbacks are often given dynamic transitions, signaled by a pan rather than a customary shimmering dissolve; these snap transitions are marvelously effective, especially in the sodium pentothal scenes. The sequence where Virginia goes "to staff" (the last step before being released) has its *Bedlam* parallel in Nell Bowen's sanity hearing, but Lewton's sequence never comes close to achieving the dramatic intensity of Litvak's. The staff sequence in *The Snake Pit* actually contains more Lewtonesque flourishes than its parallel sequence in *Bedlam*.

In the Litvak film, the scene takes place during a thunderstorm. Virginia sits in a cold room filled with doctors and staff who scrutinize her every word, her every move. Behind her, a rain-drenched window rattles and bangs; the wind and thunder can be heard through the thick walls of the institution. We hear Virginia's thoughts overlapping her answers as she is assaulted with a barrage of questions. One interrogator wags his cigar in front of her face as he repeatedly asks her the same question, never giving her the opportunity to respond. The thunder is loud, and the banging of the window seems to mock Virginia's presence, sounding like the gavel at a court hearing. The finger-wagger has his hand close to Virginia's face, and a sense of unreality permeates the scene as the voice of the questioner becomes a faint echo. A close shot of Virginia's troubled face reveals that she is about to go over the edge.

We dissolve to a stormy sky within Virginia's mind; the flash of lightning cracks the image in half, and we know her mind has snapped. There are violent ocean waves, swirling waters; Virginia's face is within the maelstrom. She hangs off a precipice to avoid taking a long plunge into the turbulent waters below. Suddenly, her hands are gripping what looks like the rim of a bathtub. The face of one of the nurses comes into the frame, looking ill-tempered and impatient, pulling Virginia's hands from the tub rim, finally causing her fall into the metaphorical swirling waters below. In the film's most jarring moment, the camera immediately cuts to Virginia's screaming face as she lies in one of a long row of very menacing-looking therapeutic bathtubs.

Although *The Snake Pit* has lost some of its punch over the years, the film still works remarkably well for first-time viewers today. Much of it is contrived, and the ending is too pat and sentimental, but the film has a few images which last the viewer a lifetime. Although there are horrifying moments, the film's narrative can more accurately be described as that of a mystery thriller, the mystery being the reason for Virginia's insanity, the thrills coming from the mental and physical perils she experiences during her stay in the institution.

Like *Citizen Kane, The Snake Pit*'s narrative is not presented linearly but through a series of effective flashbacks, most coming from Virginia, but the first, and longest, coming from her husband, Robert Cunningham (a rather wooden Mark Stevens). The unraveling of Virginia's past is captivating as it reveals the impact of the traumas that have wrongfully made her bear the responsibilities for the deaths of the two most important men of her life, her father and her fiancé. The oversimplification given her case study (via the Frank Partos/Millen Brand screenplay) was an effort to make the film more palatable for the American public. Because of this, the ending remains weak and artificial, though nonetheless moving.

The most memorable image in the entire film is the one inherent in the film's title. When Virginia's mad harangues and aberrant behavior, all of which make perfect sense to the viewer, cause her to be incarcerated in the asylum's deepest ward, the one reserved for the most severe cases, the film takes us on a harrowing tour of human dementia. In a scene very reminiscent of Nell Bowen's first "insider's" view of Bedlam, Virginia Cunningham is surrounded by a nightmare of Hogarthian dimensions. Her horrifying visions are accompanied by the sound of mad cackling, ear-piercing shrieks, and the insectlike hum of mindless mumbling and psychotic chanting. As in the Lewton/Robson film, a long, slow pull-back shot starts with a close-up of the heroine's troubled face and then, via a crane shot, rises well beyond the confines of the building's physical limits. We hear Virginia's voice-over as we move higher still, the raving patients growing smaller and more plentiful. Now we see what look like dirt walls surrounding a writhing mass of human derangement. And we realize the significance of the film's title even before Virginia's voice-over spells it out for us; we are left with an image we will not soon forget.

Of all the filmmakers discussed in this chapter, the one whose body of work came closest to the spirit and style of the Lewton films was Robert Siodmak, one of the darkest visionaries of the 1940s. In a May 1946 issue of *Life* magazine, Siodmak was showcased in an article by Donald Marshman (who refers to the yet unnamed film noir trend as "Hollywood's profound postwar affection for morbid drama"). Marshman describes the trend:

> From January through December . . . deep shadows, clutching hands, exploding revolvers, sadistic villains and heroines tormented with deeply rooted diseases of the mind flashed across the screen in a panting display of psychoneurosis, unsublimated sex and murder most foul. Apparently delighted to pay good money for having their pants scared off, moviegoers flocked in record numbers to these spectacles.

Robert Siodmak's first directorial effort was a 1930 German silent film, *Menschen am Sonntag,* codirected by Edgar Ulmer, written by brother Curt Siodmak and Billy Wilder, and photographed by Fred Zinnemann. Marshman's account of Robert Siodmak's escape from the Nazis reveals some uncomfortable parallels to Fritz Lang's own last-minute emigration. "Realizing that Hitler was no longer a joke, Siodmak immediately left Germany for France. The Nazis came to power the next day and movie-industry Jews soon were shipped off to concentration camps."

Unlike Fritz Lang and John Brahm, who used Paris as a mere steppingstone to Hollywood, Siodmak chose to remain in France during most of the 1930s. There he established a respectable reputation as a top-notch film director, helming seven films (some with top-budget productions and casts) by 1939, the year he left for Hollywood. As Marshman tells it:

> The new arrivals found Hollywood's atmosphere almost tingling in indifference to them. Hardly anyone had heard of Siodmak's rather substantial European career, and those who had heard appeared not to care. . . . With great determination Siodmak operated out of a small apartment by telephone and bus to the major studios. In a year's time he was either asked to leave or was forcibly ejected from every studio capable of producing a two-reel comedy.

Preston Sturges, who had taken a liking to Siodmak, got him a Paramount contract by falsely claiming to have known "the great European director" for 15 years. At Paramount, Siodmak began directing "B" pictures like *West Point Widow, The Night Before My Divorce,* and *My Heart Belongs to Daddy,* but his big break came when he signed a contract with Universal. His directing debut for the studio was *Son of Dracula* (1943), the first Universal horror film to be, in William K. Everson's words, "plainly influenced by the understated methods of the Val Lewton films, and by the moods and fatalism of film noir" *(More Classics of the Horror Film).*

In a plot that seems inspired by equal measures of Bram Stoker and James M. Cain, *Son of Dracula*'s Katherine Caldwell (Louise Albritton) willingly marries Count Alucard/Dracula (Lon Chaney, Jr.) in order to exploit his supernatural powers. Once she becomes a vampire, she works to convince her old boyfriend, Frank (Robert Paige), to do away with Alucard so that she and Frank can escape with the big haul: "life eternal." The crazed and bewildered boyfriend pretends to go along with the plan, but double-crosses her with a wooden stake in the final reel. Although he survives, Frank does not enjoy the happy fate usually reserved for the typically bland horror-movie hero of the time.

Son of Dracula has a lively script (original story by Curt Siodmak, screenplay by Eric Taylor) and unexpectedly downbeat plot twists. The swamp scenes, with Katherine or Frank traversing about in the bayou (courtesy of an effective soundstage set), aspires to the kind of visual poetry seen in *I Walked with a Zombie* which, like *Son of Dracula,* also showcased the writing talents of Curt Siodmak.

As far as Universal horror films go, *Son of Dracula* was a refreshing change of pace. Because Katherine embarks willingly upon her flirtation with evil (personified by Count Dracula), she becomes a variation of noir's femme fatale. Turning themselves into smoky mists, Dracula and his bride-turned-vampire make ghostly appearances by seeping under doors or flowing through windows. For its time, this was a fresh and stylish special effect, one which made a vampire's power seem almost limitless and therefore more frightening. Also surprisingly effective is a scene where Alucard stands on his coffin and rides it across the swamp like a supernatural barge. Chaney's performance is often ridiculed by Lugosi enthusiasts, but it is oddly appropriate if we think of his role as that of a powerful thug with affectations of class, just like later Siodmak villains played by Albert Dekker *(The Killers)* and Dan Duryea *(Criss Cross).* By playing off the affections of both her lovers, Katherine is the vampiric equivalent of Ava Gardner's and Yvonne De Carlo's respective roles in *The Killers* and *Criss Cross.*

Siodmak's mainstream reputation was launched by the enthusiastic public and critical response to his next feature, *Phantom Lady* (1944). In *King of the Bs,* Tom Flinn admits to *The Phantom Lady*'s weaknesses (banal dialogue and a weak Cornell Woolrich story source), but says the film "is redeemed by the originality of the mise-en-scène and by its all-pervading style, which represents a considerable advance over the more overtly expressionistic *Stranger on the Third Floor.*"

According to Alain Silver and Elizabeth Ward (in *Film Noir*): "Siodmak and his brilliant cinematographer, Woody Bredell, have provided *The Phantom Lady* with the essential ingredients of Woolrich's world, from the desperate innocent at loose at night in New York City, a city of hot sweltering streets, to the details of threatening shadows, jazz emanating from low-class bars, and the click of high heels on the pavement." Indeed, the "click of high heels" is exactly what we get in a brilliant Siodmak set piece that mimics Jane Randolph's walk through the park in *Cat People.*

The Phantom Lady's Manhattan environment is effectively rendered in its "studio noir" setting, making it an appropriate match for either of Lewton's two New York City films, *Cat People* or *The Seventh Victim*. Its opening shot of Anne Terry (Fay Helm) sitting in a bar caused Tom Flinn to remark, "Wearing one of those improbable creations that only 1940s milliners could envisage, Miss Helm looks very much like a middle-aged neurotic left over from a Val Lewton film." Into the bar comes Scott Henderson (Alan Curtis), a civil engineer on the brink of divorce. Feeling low and discouraged, Scott picks up Anne and they have a night on the town. When he goes back home, Scott finds an apartment full of detectives and the corpse of his wife, strangled to death by his own necktie.

The plot escalates as Scott, like the hero of *Stranger on the Third Floor,* finds himself wrongly accused of murder on the basis of circumstantial evidence. He has no alibi since Anne Terry (the title character) cannot be found and other potential witnesses—a bartender, a club drummer (Elisha Cook)—have been paid off to deny ever having seen him. Scott is tried, found guilty, and is only days away from his execution when his loyal secretary Kansas (Ella Raines) decides to take matters into her own hands. Like the heroine in *Stranger on the Third Floor,* the resourceful secretary does some amateur sleuthing before settling upon a plan of action.

Kansas goes to the cocktail lounge where Scott picked up the lady with the hat. Sitting at one end of the bar, she orders a drink and then begins to stare menacingly at the bartender who lied about her boss. The effect is enormously chilling as she simply sits there, frozen, her eyes burning with accusation; actress Raines is as sexy as she is terrifying. The bartender becomes uncomfortable and self-conscious, looking over his shoulder, now and again, to see that the strange woman has not abandoned her intimidating glare. Even when he moves to the opposite end of the bar, it is to no avail. He can still see her in the mirror and that only makes matters worse, as if two women are giving him the evil eye.

Hours pass, a camera dissolve showing that the lounge has become packed and lively, but Kansas has not moved an inch, nor has she dropped her piercing gaze. More time passes, the lounge empties, and there she is, the last customer, still sitting at the end of the bar. The bartender announces the bar is closed and, getting his coat, is about to repeat his words when he discovers the woman has suddenly vanished. As he goes out into the rainy streets to make his way home, he hears the click of high heels following close behind.

What follows is a Siodmak version of a "Lewton walk," so marvelously done that it holds its own with any similar sequence from a Lewton film. Siodmak dispenses with score music, choosing rather to record the stark sounds of the city after hours and the relentless tacking of high heels. Although we know Kansas has a heart of gold, we are never privy to her plan, which is why her behavior in the lounge bewilders the viewer just as much as it does the bartender. Because the camera remains sympathetic to the bartender, the character of Kansas takes on terrifying dimensions as she continues to stalk her prey.

An equally impressive sequence has Kansas attempting to entrap the club drummer (another false witness). Kansas dresses to kill and, feigning another persona, that of any easy pickup, arranges a rendezvous with the drummer. Again Raines steals the show, though Elisha Cook, as the hedonistic drummer, offers strong competition. He takes Kansas to a private jam session in a tight smoke-filled apartment, and obviously all hopped up, he pounds his drums to an angry sax, a mad piano, and a frantic bass. Kansas acts with wild abandon (without a doubt one of the sexiest scenes of the 1940s), her gyrating body and saucy glances encouraging every note. It is amazing that this scene made it past the censors. Cook's frenzied drum solo, accompanied by some highly suggestive and quite remarkable editing, make it readily apparent that we are viewing, in simulated form, Hollywood's first on-screen orgasm. *The Phantom Lady* is a flawed film, but it has style to spare; like its 1944 companions, *Murder My Sweet* and *Double Indemnity,* it became an exemplar model for Hollywood's postwar noir cycle.

Siodmak did not fare as well with his next noir effort, *Christmas Holiday* (1944), starring Deanna Durbin and Gene Kelly. This misleadingly titled thriller disappointed anyone who was anticipating a Deanna Durbin yuletide extravaganza with song and dance. Although the film's story (scripted by *Citizen Kane*'s Herman L. Mankiewicz from a W. Somerset Maugham novel) is intriguing, actor Gene Kelly is sadly miscast as a mother-fixated murderer. Deanna Durbin, as his wife, is also cast against type but, surprisingly, she pulls it off quite well.

After the phenomenal success of George Cukor's *Gaslight,* Siodmak made preparations for his own period thriller. *The Suspect,* released in 1945, is a minor classic of its kind. Given an "A" budget and name stars, *The Suspect* was Universal's attempt to pour quality into the kind of period thriller that had taken the country by storm. Bertram Millhauser's screenplay, adapted from a novel by James Ronald, tells the story of a pleasant middle-aged banker (Charles Laughton) who is married to a shrew of a wife (Rosalind Ivan in an outstanding performance, a virtual retake of her role in *Scarlet Street*). Laughton is excellent as a decent man driven out of his marriage by his wife's intolerable harangues. Eventually he meets a young lady (Ella Raines) who is charmed by his gentle, unselfish manner. Although this extramarital relationship is kept reasonably above board, they nonetheless fall in love. Thanks to the performances of Laughton and Raines, their unlikely romance is surprisingly believable. Laughton is so endearing as the banker that we not only feel that he deserves a break, but we also understand why this beautiful young woman would find him so appealing.

When Laughton's hateful wife finds out about the relationship, she threatens to ruin Raines's reputation. Laughton retaliates by bashing his wife over the head with a cane (the murder occurring offscreen); so fervently have we allied ourselves to Laughton's character that we cannot help but take some satisfaction in his dark deed. A police inspector (Stanley Ridges) has his suspicions and begins to harass Laughton, but our loyalty remains with the endearing murderer. After Laughton and Raines get married, the inspector begins to understand the motive for the crime. Laughton's drunken no-account neighbor (Henry Daniell) also becomes suspicious and, like *The Body Snatcher*'s Joseph, makes the most of the opportunity by attempting blackmail. Little does he know that Laughton has poisoned his whiskey. In a memorably tense scene, the sudden arrival of house guests forces Laughton to temporarily dispose of Daniell's corpse by hiding it behind the couch. When the guests come through the door, guess where they sit.

After Daniell's wife is implicated in her husband's murder (the circumstantial evidence points to her sure conviction), Laughton comes forth with his confession, maintaining his integrity and clinching our affections. The film ends with a relaxed and dignified Laughton walking in the direction of Scotland Yard to turn himself in.

What is most remarkable about *The Suspect* and about Laughton's performance is the extent to which a remorseless murderer is able to remain a sympathetic character. Those who have not viewed *The Suspect* may find it odd that a murderer would be characterized as a model citizen, but such irony is precisely what makes Siodmak's film work so well. Because Laughton's character is an otherwise decent human being, one who meets with our approval, we are forced to share his guilt; by so doing, we expose the potential murderers within us all. Siodmak called the film "the best story I ever told."

The Strange Affair of Uncle Harry (1945) was an uneven thriller which, unlike most of Siodmak's work of this period, was based on a stageplay (by Thomas Job); the narrative unravels, like the play, without recourse to flashbacks. While never entirely successful, *Uncle Harry* is an interesting companion piece to *The Suspect*. The cast—George Sanders (the period thriller's most frequent performer), Ella Raines, Geraldine Fitzgerald, and others—is first rate and alone reason enough to recommend the film. Sanders (who has never been better) plays a repressed New England fabric designer who lives a dreary existence with his two spinster sisters (Geraldine Fitzgerald and Moyna Magill). The younger sister (Fitzgerald) is a jealous virago who attempts to destroy her brother's relationship with Ella Raines (a fashion expert). Sanders decides that the situation calls for a bottle of poison. The plan, as one might expect, goes awry. *Uncle Harry*'s dream ending (much along the lines of Lang's *The Woman in the Window*, released that same year) is an obvious cop-out. The producer, Joan Harrison (Hitchcock's erstwhile screenwriter), was so dissatisfied with the changes in the film's final reel that she disclaimed the film and resigned from the studio. In spite of his lack of consistency, Robert Siodmak had by 1945 become one of Universal's most well-respected directors, his carefully networked thrillers amassing more raves than the studio's Erle C. Kenton monster rallies.

In 1946, while David Selznick was putting the finishing touches on his overblown *Duel in the Sun* (his failed stab at a worthy successor to *Gone with the Wind*), his company set up a coproduction agreement with RKO that gave birth to Vanguard Films. Selznick was still securing talent for film packages sold to other studios; Vanguard Films was formed as an opportunity to add regularity to their distribution. The first Vanguard release was Robert Siodmak's *The Spiral Staircase*. For the *Staircase* package, Selznick's provisions included Siodmak (on loan from Universal), Dore Schary (producer), cast members Dorothy McGuire and Ethel Barrymore, film rights to Ethel Lina White's novel *Some Must Watch*, and a finished screenplay by Mel Dinelli. RKO provided the rest, including cinematographer Nicholas Musuraca and a number of RKO contract performers such as Lewton veterans Kent Smith and James Bell.

The Spiral Staircase, playing like a blend of Lewton, Hitchcock, and Selznick, was a smash hit. Set in a Massachusetts town early in the century, the film's heroine, Helen Capel (McGuire), is a mute servant, her inability to talk coming from a childhood trauma. Helen has good reason to worry about the killer who has been terrorizing the community; each of his victims has been a woman afflicted with some form of disability. The opening scene, where a crippled prostitute is strangled in her apartment above a movie theater, is a heart-stopper of the first degree. We see an extreme close up of the killer's eyes as he hides between the dresses in the woman's closet; when he strangles his victim, all we see are the woman's hands, growing lifeless, twitching above her head in their final moments of animation.

Staircase's conventional plot is reminiscent of the old house thrillers, with just enough psychological rhetoric to let us know it comes from the message-happy postwar years. McGuire is captivating as the heroine in distress; Elsa Lanchester is also fine as the quirky house maid. Unfortunately, George Brent, as the killer, gives his usual wooden performance. The murderer's identity is unknown through most of the film, and after a number of red herrings are introduced, the climax's pièce de résistance comes when Helen inadvertently locks up the wrong suspect and goes to the real killer for help, a situation that echoes the climax of *Phantom Lady*.

Thanks to Nicholas Musuraca, the spiral staircase scenes—with their shadowy recesses and silhouetted banisters that shift and stretch as Helen makes her descent, candle in hand—display a genuinely inspired use of light and dark and carry a vibrancy even today.

The Spiral Staircase's brooding atmosphere and expressionistic visuals are reason enough to make the film essential viewing for Lewton fans. Siodmak also includes a harrowing Lewton walk as Helen is stalked through the woods on her way to the mansion. In *Suspense in the Cinema*, Gordon Gow describes the sequence in further detail:

> Conscious of her own vulnerability, [Helen] approaches the house in trepidation, picking up a twig and rattling it along the railing to comfort

> herself with sound. The thunder and lightning are going strong as she moves through the gate and walks across the garden. A tree is in the foreground of the frame, at the left, while Helen is seen beyond it, moving from left to right. Suddenly, a great flash of lightning throws into relief the silhouette of a man who stands by the tree. Helen does not see him. She goes on into the house, and, halfway up the stairs, she pauses on a landing to look at herself in a mirror. She touches her mouth. On a higher landing, looking down toward her, is a man, most probably the same one who was lurking in the garden. We see his feet, and then an enormous close-up of one of his eyes in which Helen's face is subjectively reflected: the mouth misted, obliterated.

The arresting image of a mouthless Dorothy McGuire was the work of Vernon L. Walker, the special effects technician behind *Stranger on the Third Floor,* the entire Lewton series, and Edward Dmytryk's *Murder, My Sweet.*

For all of its pictorial splendor, *The Spiral Staircase* is never quite as satisfying as it should have been, given its talent and budget. Some of Siodmak's direction, especially in long, tedious expanses of conversation, is strictly pedestrian. The secondary characters (with the exception of Elsa Lanchester) are either bland or poorly drawn. Even Ethel Barrymore, as the killer's invalid mother, confined to her room, is little more than a head-in-a-bed until she serves a vital, if unlikely, function at the film's climax. The nurse/patient relationship between McGuire and Barrymore echoes a similar relationship between the characters played by Ellen Drew and Katherine Emery in *Isle of the Dead;* in both films, the nurse's life is saved through the intervention of her ailing patient.

The Spiral Staircase's sumptuous production sometimes tends to only accent the film's flaws; we simply expect more from an "A" film. Surprisingly, Siodmak does not make the most of Helen's affliction; he could have derived unbearable suspense from her inability to speak. Although he does exploit the heroine's helplessness to some degree, it is never enough to justify all the dramatic attention paid to her handicap and to the killer's modus operandi in the first place. When McGuire finally confronts the killer and the incipient trauma causes her to regain her ability to speak, we can only shake our heads at the marvel of it all.

Siodmak's bleak thrillers continued when he went back to his home studio, which, due to a merger, was now Universal-International. *The Dark Mirror,* a psychological thriller about twins (one good, one evil), would have been a great showcase for the talents of Olivia De Havilland if her dual performance had been more clearly drawn. Most viewers are continually confused (as are the film's subordinate characters) over the identity of a particular twin, and while such bafflement may have been intended to suit the film's purpose, it results in the audience investing little interest in either character. The twins, named Terry and Ruth, wear large pins bearing the initials "T" or "R" as an expedient for their identification (though this only distracts us from picking up whatever variation in her acting De Havilland is allowed to give either role). When Terry, the murderer, begins wearing Ruth's pin as a disguise, we realize that the switching of pins is about all that is needed to make the masquerade complete.

The Dark Mirror is Siodmak's exemplification of the doppelganger theme, a German cinematic tradition harking back to the silent versions of the Poe-inspired *The Student of Prague*. Unfortunately, Siodmak's film is riddled with gimmicks and voguish psychoanalytical trappings; though the film was popular at the time of its release, the entire plot seems preposterous today. From a psychological standpoint, *The Dark Mirror* may be more realistic in its depiction of twins than the flamboyantly disparate dual roles in *The Black Room* or *Among the Living*, but it is also less entertaining.

Siodmak's two undisputed classics are *The Killers* (1946) and *Criss Cross* (1949), both fashioned as vehicles for their leading man, newcomer Burt Lancaster. These two Universal-International films are relentlessly downbeat and taken together provide such an uncompromising noir vision that they can rightly be considered classic examples of the form.

The narrative structure of *The Killers* closely resembles the framework of *Citizen Kane* in that the main character dies minutes into the film, while his life is reconstructed, via several flashbacks, by a stranger who goes from one person to another in an effort to find meaning in the dead man's final words. As in *Citizen Kane*, the flashbacks are presented in an overlapping, nonchronological manner, like pieces of a jigsaw puzzle.

Like *Kane*, *The Killers* has a dark, wonderfully atmospheric prologue. A pair of hired killers (played to the hilt by William Conrad and Charles McGraw) comes into a small town during the night, their long, distorted shadows moving toward a local diner. They enter and shake down three people (owner, cook, and customer) to dig up information on Ole Anderson (aka the Swede, played by Lancaster). After the gunmen leave, Nick Adams, the customer, runs through backyards, vaulting fences along the way, in order to reach the Swede's apartment and warn him of the two thugs. When the Swede gets this information, however, he just lies back on his bed, saying there is nothing anyone can do. "I did something wrong once," the Swede tells Nick. Resigned to remain a sitting duck for the killers, the Swede dismisses Nick and waits in the silent darkness. The camera remains in the apartment with the Swede, as we hear the opening of the front door, followed by the sound of footsteps coming up the stairs, continuing along the hall, and stopping outside his door. There's a close-up of the Swede's blank expression as he looks at the door, waiting for it to burst open. The room's patches of darkness, the interminable silence, the terror behind a closed door, all serve as ample evidence of the tight bond between film noir and horror.

The film's prologue is a remarkably accurate translation of the entire Hemingway story (which ends before the killing), including an almost word-for-word use of the story's hard-boiled dialogue. In fact, this five-minute sequence is the most successful adaptation of Hemingway ever filmed. Of course, *The Killers* includes an additional hundred minutes with which screenwriter, Anthony Veiller, speculates upon events not contained in the Hemingway story, but his fleshing-out of the story is in keeping with the Hemingway tradition and does nothing but enhance the marvelous opening.

Since the plot is complex enough without its jigsaw-puzzle structure, it is surprising that *The Killers* was such a box-office draw. Like Dmytryk's equally complex *Murder, My Sweet*, Siodmak's film was such a visual feast that audiences did not seem to mind if they were unable to keep track of events; they recognized heroes and villains and that seemed to suffice. A major part of *The Killers* appeal was its marvelous cast: Lancaster, Ava Gardner (as one of the cycle's most memorable femmes fatale), Edmond O'Brien (as the insurance investigator), Albert Dekker (as the villain), Sam Levine (as the Swede's cop friend), Virginia Christine (as the Swede's former girlfriend), Donald McBride (as O'Brien's boss), Conrad and McGraw (as the hired killers), and literally dozens of bit parts by character actors.

The Killers is an expressionistic tour de force, probably the most flamboyantly Germanic film Siodmak ever made (and that is saying something). The predominant visual motifs are staircases and bars of confinement (both vertical and horizontal), and we see them everywhere we go. As a result of O'Brien's investigation and the flashbacks of the people that he questions, we are given a vast variety of visually rich scenes (courtesy of cinematographer, Woody Bredell) set in or around boxing rings, locker rooms, cemeteries, morgues, cheap diners, fancy restaurants, hospitals, prison cells, opulent homes, dingy apartments, rooftops, factories, parking lots, offices, movie theaters, trains, and barnyard hideouts. Given the nature of Anthony Veiller's patchwork narrative, it is difficult not to feel emotionally detached from the film's already-dead protagonist (as is also true of *Citizen Kane*), but Siodmak compensates for this by manipulating the viewer's emotions through the dynamics of lighting and composition.

Criss Cross takes an entirely different approach. Unlike *The Killers*, which was made in the studio, this second Siodmak/Lancaster film was shot mostly on location in Los Angeles. The look of the film is more realistic, though no less bleak, than its predecessor. Here we have one long flashback told from the main character's point of view, and as a result, we feel a much greater attachment to Lancaster's protagonist.

These major differences aside, *Criss Cross* has much in common with the other film. Like his doomed protagonist in *The Killers*, Lancaster plays a down-on-his-luck hero obsessed with a woman (this time played by Yvonne DeCarlo) who is the property of a gang leader (in this instance Dan Duryea). Both films have the hero taking part in a major heist (here an armored car robbery) in an effort to win the woman's affections. In each case, Lancaster, at the urging of his greedy, treacherous lover, is talked into double-crossing the gang and running away with the loot. Where *The Killers* has Lancaster gunned down in the beginning, *Criss Cross* has Lancaster gunned down in the final scene.

A frightening sequence, worthy of Lewton or Hitchcock, begins with Lancaster alone in his hospital room. Because he double-crossed the gang during the botched robbery (resulting in the bullet wound that got him into the hospital), he knows he is a sitting duck for Duryea's hired assassins. He sees some shadowy movement through the translucent glass panel above his closed door. The door opens as he holds his breath, but it is only the nurse checking in. As she attends to his needs, his arm and shoulder in a massive cast, Lancaster looks into his bureau mirror and sees the reflection of a man's shadow in the corridor. He urges the nurse to crank up his bed and, in an imaginative point of view shot, as the nurse cranks away, he gradually sees what appears to be an ordinary man seated in the corridor. The nurse tells him that the man in the hall is Mr. So-and-so, who is worried sick about his wife's car accident. Lancaster asks the mild-mannered gentleman to stand guard in his room so that he can get some sleep. They talk a while, and he seems like a nice enough fellow. But, sure enough, a few hours later Lancaster is awakened at gunpoint.

Siodmak made two other noir films worth mentioning: *Cry of the City* (1949) for 20th Century–Fox and *The File on Thelma Jordan* (1950) for Paramount. The former deals with a wounded gangster (Richard Conte), who is a cop-killer and a jewel robber, and the childhood friend (Victor Mature), now a policeman, who pursues him. The latter film, which begs comparison with Wilder's *Double Indemnity,* tells the story of a lawyer (Wendell Cory) who falls in love with a woman (Barbara Stanwyck) who leads him on a course of murder and deception.

Siodmak's last Burt Lancaster vehicle was a major departure for the director. *The Crimson Pirate* (1952), a wonderful display of Lancaster's acrobatic prowess, was produced in England for Warner Bros. and is a highly enjoyable comic-adventure, one which has long been a cult item among swashbuckler fans. Interestingly enough, *The Crimson Pirate* was a follow-up to another Warner swashbuckler starring Burt Lancaster, Jacques Tourneur's *The Flame and the Arrow* (1950).

Shortly thereafter, Siodmak, who had grown disenchanted with Hollywood during the McCarthy era, journeyed back to Europe to continue his directing career. After directing one film in France, Siodmak went back to Germany, where from 1955 to 1969, he directed 18 more films. He died there in 1973.

It would be misleading to slap a "dark visionary" label on all the filmmakers included in this chapter. Half of them—Fritz Lang, Alfred Hitchcock, Orson Welles, John Brahm, and Robert Siodmak—do deserve that epithet because they staked their filmmaking claims in dark territory. The other half, however — William Dieterle, Billy Wilder, Edward Dmytryk, George Cukor, and Anatole Litvak — made important contributions to 1940s dark cinema without actually specializing in the stuff of nightmares. Lewton, of course, was caught in the middle of both camps; the press labeled him the "Titan of Terror," but what he really desired was a more eclectic film career.

Although Val Lewton will be forever associated with the horror genre, his true contemporaries, those included in this chapter, were not horror filmmakers in the conventional sense. Neither was Lewton. Readers should be reminded that only four of the eleven Lewton films *(Cat People, I Walked with a Zombie, Isle of the Dead,* and *The Body Snatcher)* can rightly be called horror films and that even these four may be open to debate since, in each case, they leave room for a rational explanation for their suggested supernaturalism. While the conventional horror specialists of the 1930s and 1940s tried to terrorize their audiences with visions of monsters and supernatural beings, Lewton and his fellow travelers allowed their audiences to find terror in the commonplace.

SEVENTEEN

The Sincerest Form of Flattery

Although a few of the films discussed in the previous chapter—Anatole Litvak's *The Snake Pit* and Robert Siodmak's *Phantom Lady* and *The Spiral Staircase*—treaded dangerously close to plagiarism (insofar as the Lewton style was concerned), even these were a far cry from the rather blatant Lewton facsimiles that tried, with varying success, to capitalize on the popularity of the RKO series.

Because the previous chapter limited its focus to a select number of Lewton's "fellow travelers" (the most significant 10), we missed several solidly effective dark thrillers of a similar caliber to those already discussed. It should be noted that other significant films in the noir cycle—*Fallen Sparrow* (1943, Richard Wallace), *Laura* (1944, Otto Preminger), *Detour* (1945, Edgar Ulmer), *Black Angel* (1946, Roy William Neill), *Crack-Up* (1946, Irving Reis), *Kiss of Death* (1947, Henry Hathaway), *Nightmare Alley* (1947, Edmund Goulding), *The Unsuspected* (1947, Michael Curtiz), *The Web* (Michael Gordon), et al.—shared the same milieu as the Lewton films without deliberately imitating them.

Take *Fallen Sparrow,* for example. Richard Wallace's 1943 film is about an American mercenary (played by John Garfield) who, after being tortured by the enemy, escapes from captivity and suffers a mental collapse. From this point on, he begins to have terrifying flashbacks of his painful ordeal. These harrowing moments occur mostly when he is alone; they are signaled by aural hallucinations of his captor's dragging leg. The room grows dark; Garfield begins to sweat profusely and out of desperation reaches for the closest available liquor. During one of his spells, he begins to hear the amplified sound of water drops coming from his kitchen faucet, mimicking the Chinese water torture he endured in captivity. His inability to escape the symptoms of his encroaching madness is effectively and frighteningly rendered throughout the film.

But Wallace's film complements, rather than imitates, the Lewton series. If RKO's *The Fallen Sparrow* has the flavor of a Lewton film, we should not be surprised, since it is graced by Albert D'Agostino's art direction, Darrell Silvera's set decorations, Vernon Walker's special effects, Nicholas Musuraca's photography, Roy Webb's musical score, and Robert Wise's editing. Like *The Seventh Victim,* Wallace's film takes place in Manhattan and employs many of the same sets: the ornate staircase (originally from *The Magnificent Ambersons*), the beauty salon, apartment exteriors and interiors, and the Italian restaurant. Both films also feature appearances by Hugh Beaumont and Erford Gage. One might be tempted to claim that Richard Wallace's film mimics *The Seventh Victim,* but these two films were nearly concurrent productions.

William Castle's *When Strangers Marry* (Monogram, 1944), on the other hand, wears its Lewton influences on its sleeve. Castle's film does mimic *The Seventh Victim* (and, to some extent, *Cat People*), and what is most surprising is that the results are very effective. Castle's film became a "B" movie sleeper and quickly captured a cult of fans, including a very impressed Orson Welles, who said (in his New York *Graphic* column, "Orson Welles's Almanac"), "Making allowances for its bargain-price budget, I think you'll agree with me that it's one of the most gripping and effective pictures of the year. It isn't as slick as *Double Indemnity* or as glossy as *Laura,* but it's better acted and better directed by William Castle than either." (Welles's enthusiasm for Castle's talent led to their collaborative effort, *The Lady from Shanghai* [Welles directed, Castle coproduced].)

In *Time* magazine, James Agee wrote:

> I want to add to Orson Welles and Manny Farber my own respect for the Monogram melodrama, *When Strangers Marry.* I have seldom for years now seen one hour so energetically and sensibly used in a film. . . . I can no longer feel by any means so hopeless as I have lately that it is possible to make pictures in Hollywood that are worth making. When I think even no further than William Castle who made this and of the Val Lewton contingent, I know there are enough people out there of real ability to turn the whole place upside-down.

When Strangers Marry, like two other 1944 noir landmarks, *Phantom Lady* and *Murder, My Sweet,* is a triumph of style over substance. The film is an obvious combination of *Love from a Stranger, Suspicion,* and *The Seventh Victim* (Castle and Philip Yordan had two weeks to collaborate upon a screenplay). Castle plainly lost no sleep over his blatant use of Hitchcock's famous "screaming woman/train whistle" match-cut (from *The Thirty-Nine Steps*) so we need not be surprised by his conspicuous application of the Lewton style, including such Lewton signatures as the "walk" and the "bus."

Kim Hunter plays Millie Baxter, a virtual reprise of her naive-but-resourceful heroine Mary in *The Seventh Victim.* This time the missing person in Millie's husband, Paul (Dean Jagger), a man she hardly knows (they took their wedding vows after their third meeting). Millie has not seen her husband since the ceremony, though she was supposed to meet him at a hotel in Greenwich Village. When he does not put in an appearance, she bumps into her former beau, Fred (Robert Mitchum), who is surprised (and disappointed) by her whirlwind marriage. Fred helps Millie look for her husband; the two of them check in with the missing person's bureau but come up empty-handed. Husband Paul eventually turns up, but he appears distant and troubled. As the plot progresses (with some narrative twists and Lewtonesque terror set pieces), Millie comes to suspect her husband may be a murderer; her deepest fears are confirmed when the police, during his absence, come looking for him. (We will refrain from giving away the surprise ending.)

Anyone who associates William Castle's name with the gimmicky horror films of the late 1950s and early 1960s will be surprised by his almost visionary direction here. In one memorable scene, Millie waits in her dark hotel room, hearing mysterious footsteps and assorted chill-inducing sounds. She nearly jumps out of her skin when a sudden blast of jazz music comes from the nightclub across the street. She lifts the shade, and a neon sign bathes her room in eerie, intermittent light. Later, Millie takes a Lewtonesque walk along the dark city streets; cutting through the park, she begins to fear she is being followed.

When Strangers Marry was only one of many Lewton facsimiles that began showing up in theaters as early as 1943. The ground-breaking success of *Cat People* suddenly made it fashionable to accent the unseen and, in many instances, to make obvious use of Lewton's terror tactics.

Actually, William Castle had already been successful in capturing the adventurous low-budget spirit of the Lewton films months earlier with his resourceful direction of the initial film in Columbia's "Whistler" series. The first entry, *The Whistler,* involves a man (Richard Dix) who takes out a contract on his own life and then, a little too late, changes his mind. According to Castle's autobiography *(Step Right Up! I'm Gonna Scare the Pants Off America),* "*The Whistler* . . . was one of the most terrifying screenplays I'd ever read. A little after midnight, I called [Harry] Cohn at home. 'It's horrific, Mr. Cohn. . . . Exactly what I've been waiting for . . . I'll scare the shit out of audiences.'"

Based on a popular radio show, the "Whistler" series did not include recurring characters, nor was it a detective series. The "Whistler" character was nothing more than a shadow of a mysterious figure ("I am the Whistler, and I know many things") who introduced the story and occasionally reappeared to bridge gaps between scenes. Richard Dix (just off *The Ghost Ship*) was the star of seven of the eight films; sometimes he played a villain, sometimes a hero, often his character was a little of both. Each entry ran about an hour, and although only four were directed by Castle, all eight are well worth seeing and a few of them are examples of budget filmmaking at its very best. The series provided a wonderful showcase for Dix's range of talents, and the scripts (several based on Cornell Woolrich stories) were intelligent and full of surprises. The "Whistler" series ran from 1944 to 1948, and though they were designed as second-bill fodder, they were at times preferable to the feature films with which they played. The remaining titles are *Mark of the Whistler* (1944, William Castle), *Power of the Whistler* (1945, Lew Landers), *Voice of the Whistler* (1945, William Castle), *The Mysterious Intruder* (1946, William Castle), *Secret of the Whistler* (1946, George Sherman), *The 13th Hour* (1947, William Clemens), and *The Return of the Whistler* (1948, Ross Lederman).

Mark of the Whistler, a particularly good entry based on a Woolrich source, is about a tramp (Dix) who claims a dormant trust fund by impersonating the long-lost owner only to discover that the man he impersonates has made some deadly enemies. In *Power of the Whistler,* a woman helps an amiable amnesiac (Dix) regain his identity; when she succeeds, he remembers exactly who he is: an escaped psycho-killer. *The Voice of the Whistler,* with its haunting lighthouse setting (anticipating the climax of Dieterle's *Portrait of Jennie*), is as moody, atmospheric, and unpredictable as a 1940s "B" film is likely to be, which means it's an absolute joy. *Secret of the Whistler* is about an insane artist (Dix) whose second wife begins to wonder how her predecessor died. Although the "Whistler" films were not always derivative of the Lewton style, their less-is-more approach captured the innovative spirit of the Lewton cycle better than any other 1940s "B" film series.

Much more overt signs of Lewton influence could be found in Columbia's three horror entries for 1944: *Return of the Vampire, Cry of the Werewolf,* and *Soul of a Monster.*

Although *The Return of the Vampire,* a film that contains both a vampire and a werewolf, seems like an unlikely candidate for a Lewton facsimile—it was clearly designed to cash in on Universal's first monster rally, *Frankenstein Meets the Wolfman*—director Lew Landers hedged his bets by drawing an equal amount of inspiration from the Lewton films. Like *Son of Dracula,* Landers's film (written by Samuel Ornitz, later to become one of the infamous Hollywood Ten) also attempted to update the vampire legend, all the while employing a remarkably rich atmosphere of menace and mystery to offset its modern backdrop. Bela Lugosi is cast as Count Armand Tesla, a Romanian author whose obsession with vampires has turned him into one of the undead.

The vampire's face is not shown in the first part of the film; we see him from behind or in looming shadows (Lugosi's voice is a dead giveaway to any breathing member of the audience, however). Billows of fog precede his appearance like a portable storm cloud, and the entire effect is more striking than one would imagine, giving this vampire a mystical edge much in keeping with Count Alucard in *Son of Dracula.* At one point, when Tesla visits one of his victims in her mansion's library, the entire floor of the interior set is covered with flowing mist, lending a decidedly eerie quality to what could otherwise be a static moment.

According to producer Sam White (courtesy of Richard Bojarski's *The Films of Bela Lugosi*), "The film cost approximately $75,000 and grossed for

Columbia close to half a million dollars." It's true that certain aspects of the film appear shoddy, but it definitely looks as if it cost more than the amount White quoted (which is about half the cost of the average Lewton film). The visuals in certain sequences are breathtaking, as in the scene when the ghostly vampire victim (played by Nina Foch), dressed in a white, flowing gown, wanders through the fog-shrouded cemetery. The composition and mood of this sequence appears to be directly cribbed from Jessica's night walk in Lewton's *I Walked with a Zombie*. The sets—fully equipped with some stunning foreground scenery—are exceptional, and the camerawork by John Stumar and L.W. O'Connell is amazingly fluid and succeeds in capturing the kind of visual poetry for which the Lewton films were praised. The film's finale, with the doomed werewolf finding a rosary crucifix in the cemetery rubble and gaining religion and God's strength, may sound ludicrous, but its intent is more sincere and genuinely moving than Lewton's bid for the same effect in the Lord's Prayer sequence from *The Seventh Victim*. A werewolf ruminating upon a crucifix he holds in his hairy paw is about as bold and compelling an image as anyone can expect in a 1940s horror film.

Less successful was Columbia's far more obvious venture into Lewton territory, the provocatively titled *Cry of the Werewolf*. With direction by Henry Levin and a screenplay by Griffin Jay (who wrote three of Universal's "Mummy" sequels) and Charles O'Neal (who had collaborated with DeWitt Bodeen on *The Seventh Victim*), we have every reason to hope that *Cry of the Werewolf* would be at least diverting entertainment. It is not.

The performances range from good (Fritz Leiber, Nina Foch, Ivan Triesault, Blanche Yurka) to barely competent (Osa Massen, Barton MacLane, John Abbott) to plain awful (especially Steven Crane, the romantic lead). *Cry of the Werewolf* focuses upon the Trioga gypsies, who, having somehow transplanted themselves from Transylvania to New Orleans, ride about in horse-drawn wagons exactly like the scores of European gypsies seen in Universal's horror entries. Things become even more difficult to swallow when it is revealed that the Trioga gypsies have a secret altar in the basement of one of the French Quarter's ornate mansions. The mansion itself has been turned into a kind of horror museum, one whose principal attraction is the artifacts of Maria La Tour, the "well-known" Trioga lycanthrope. (Someone should have told the screenwriters that the name La Tour hardly sounded Transylvanian.)

Nina Foch (playing Maria La Tour's daughter Celeste) has a wealth of exotic presence (she resembles a feline Ellen Barkin), but she is hardly given any screen time (which is curious, considering her top billing). Instead, we spend the majority of the film cavorting with the romantic pair, Steven Crane and Osa Massen; that is, when we are not being exposed to museum interpreter John Abbott's endless schtick about the La Tour family curse or to the unfunny comic relief from policeman Barton MacLane and his crazy cop cohorts.

The film's similarities to *Cat People* are fairly obvious. In addition to its portrayal of a female shape-shifter, the use of offscreen killings, transformations in shadow (from woman to wolf), underlit sets, walks in the dark, shots of running legs, scared cats, and dead sheep, and a demonstrative use of sound to signify menace are enough to tell us that *Cry of the Werewolf*'s resemblance to Lewton's film is more than sheer coincidence. The presence of voodoo-styled "death dolls" and "love dolls" indicates that the screenwriters were not above throwing in an ingredient or two from *I Walked with a Zombie*.

Things are already off to a bad start when the opening credits sequence reveals the film's "werewolf" (never looking like anything more than a German shepherd). The creature is supposed to appear menacing as it chews away on who-knows-what, but on closer examination, we can see a rubberband looped around the animal's muzzle, making us realize that the chewing motions are nothing more than the poor animal's unsuccessful attempts to break free of its elastic restraint.

The on-screen transformation during *Cry of the Werewolf*'s climax is incredibly shoddy, especially when compared to the first-rate werewolf transformations in *The Return of the Vampire*. A shot of Celeste La Tour's arm, dripping blood from a bullet wound, dissolves with one fell swoop into the bloody forepaw of a wolf; needless to say, the wolf is not wearing Celeste's dress. After it is shot dead, the wolf resumes (in another single dissolve) its former shape, alas, fully clothed. After he and his buddies witness the transformation, MacLane announces, "You've just seen something you'll be able to tell your children about."

(*Cry of the Werewolf*'s director, Henry Levin, may not have satisfied horror fans, but apparently he satisfied Columbia mogul Harry Cohn. Hot on the heels of its own "Whistler" series, Columbia started another low-budget thriller series inspired by a radio show, "I Love a Mystery," and appointed Levin as the director. The radio show which inspired the Levin/Columbia series was somewhat of a misnomer since most of the scripts accented horror, not mystery [although the show's regulars were indeed detectives]. Although the series was not particularly successful [only three films were made], it borrowed heavily from the Lewton tradition in both style and content. The first entry, *I Love a Mystery* [1945], considered the best of the three, concerns a man who fears decapitation when he refuses to sell his head to a secret oriental society. The horrific elements of *The Devil's Mask* [1946] include shrunken heads, voices from the grave, and a killer leopard unleashed by a taxidermist. *The Unknown* [1946], the last and worst in the series, involves grave-robbers, a haunted mansion, and a deranged mother. As in *Cry of the Werewolf*, Levin attempted to accent the unseen but, again, with negligible results. This was the same Henry Levin who in 1959 directed *Journey to the Center of the Earth* with considerable elan.)

Columbia was more successful in capturing some of the Lewton magic with an odd little horror programmer called *The Soul of the Monster* (1944), directed by Will Jason. The original screenplay by Edward Dein (who had written some "additional dialogue" for *The Leopard Man*) appeared to draw its inspiration from two directions: the Lewton films and *All That Money Can Buy*. George Macready (a sinister-looking actor with a large facial scar) plays Dr. Winson, a selfless benefactor of mankind now on his death bed. His wife, Ann (Jeanne Bates), refuses to be consoled by their devoutly religious friend, Fred Stevens (Erik Rolf) and, casting her faith to the wind, prays to Satan for the life of her husband. An imaginative shot of Ann, taken from within her flaming hearth, lets the audience know that her prayers have been heard. We dissolve to a tracking shot of a well-dressed woman (Rose Hobart) walking down the street with a determined stride. She turns to cross the road, keeping the same pace, not even bothering to look for oncoming traffic, and, sure enough, an elderly couple in a car plow right over her. At least they think they do, but when they investigate, there is no sign of her mangled corpse. Instead, we see the woman on the other side of the street, still walking, without a scratch on her. Following her journey along the city's nocturnal streets (which is presented with some nicely skewed camera angles), we see that the woman is a magnet for a series of improbable accidents (falling objects, electrical explosions, broken and sputtering powerlines) that appear to greet her at every turn. Remaining unscathed, she finds her way to Dr. Winson's house and, to the amazement of everyone present, restores the dying man's health.

Ann is overjoyed, but she soon discovers that her husband has changed. No longer his benevolent self, he is prone to violence, going so far as to hurl his hedge clippers at his beloved dog. From this point on, the film plays like a precursor to *I Married a Monster from Outer Space* (1958), with Ann not knowing what to make of the changes in her husband. Lilyan Gregg, the strange woman who orchestrated the recovery, can apparently telegraph her hypnotic commands from anywhere in the city, and she begins to send Winsom on a series of evil deeds. In a nicely photographed sequence that neatly mimics a Lewton walk, Winsom stalks his devout friend Fred with an icepick. The cross-cutting between the pursuer and the pursued is done in typical Lewton fashion, with numerous leg-only shots and lots of stark urban imagery, even an effective "bus" or two.

Unfortunately, *The Soul of a Monster*'s effectively wrought (if somewhat overdone) Lewtonesque touches cannot make up for the rest of the film's inadequacies. Edward Dein's allegorical script strives too hard for profundity, and Will Jason's direction, while effective in the strictly visual sequences (probably the handiwork of ace cinematographer Burnett Guffey), is hopelessly stilted during scenes where performers must exchange dialogue. Although the film is also self-consciously artistic, it is easy to forgive such pretensions in low-budget horror films that are not obligated to be anything more than "finished on Tuesday." Although this little-known film has been mercilessly panned by just about everyone who has bothered to write about it, we find it to be a rather compelling failure.

Like Columbia's two anthologies of "B" weirdies based on a popular radio series, Universal had its own radio show spin-off: the "Inner Sanctum." Where Columbia's far superior "Whistler" series provided shifting roles for Richard Dix, Universal's "Inner Sanctum" series did the same thing for Lon Chaney. Unfortunately, Chaney was clearly out of his element when he was asked to play, primarily, a series of intellectuals: a noted neurologist *(Calling Dr. Death)*, a celebrated college professor *(Weird Woman)*, a brilliant painter *(Dead Man's Eyes)*, a hypnotist *(Frozen Ghost)*, a chemist *(Strange Confession)*, and a lawyer *(Pillow of Death)*. Richard Dix was by no means a Method actor but he lent a credibility to his remarkably diverse assortment of roles for the "Whistler" series, a credibility Chaney could in no way achieve with the erudite characters he was asked to portray in the "Inner Sanctum" series.

Weird Woman (1944), the series entry that bears the most Lewton influence, is probably the best of the lot, a modest distinction to be sure. What makes *Weird Woman* especially worthy of note is that it is the first film adaptation of the 1943 novel of subtle terror, *Conjure Wife*, written by Fritz Leiber, Jr. Directed by Reginald LeBorg, *Weird Woman* is an enjoyable but pedestrian quickie with some laughable dialogue and a number of implausible situations. Chaney is a major liability, but the rest of the cast is very good: Evelyn Ankers, Anne Gwynn, Ralph Morgan, Lois Collier, and the marvelous Elizabeth Russell.

LeBorg's film has less to do with Leiber's fine novel than it does with two Lewton films, *Cat People* and *I Walked with a Zombie*. Ironically, had it been more faithful to the book (as was its excellent 1962 remake, *Burn, Witch, Burn*), *Weird Woman* would have had better luck approximating the style of a Lewton film. Chaney plays Professor Norman Reed (Norman Saylor in the novel), a scholar/explorer of anthropology and mythology. In keeping with many of the intellectuals in the Lewton films (especially Dr. Judd), Norman regards reason as man's only weapon against superstition. Like Oliver Reed (his *Cat People* namesake), Norman has just married an exotic woman, in this case Paula Clayton (Anne Gwynn), who, having been brought up among native islanders, has learned the powers of white magic. Because Norman's marriage has thwarted the romantic designs of his work associate, Illona Carr (Evelyn Ankers), she becomes vicious and manipulative and begins plotting revenge. (There is no such romantic triangle in the Leiber novel, in which Mrs. Carr is 70 years old, so we can only speculate that the idea originated elsewhere, the probable source being *Cat People*.)

Like Irena Dubrovna, Paula Clayton is on the outside of her husband's circle of friends and is subject to their incessant curiosity. After Norman discovers that his wife has been protecting him from his enemies with the use of magic charms, he burns all her superstitious paraphenalia. As a result, misfortune begins to dog his heels. Illona attempts to destroy his reputation by orchestrating another professor's suicide and making Norman bear the brunt of the blame. The victim's virago wife, nicely played by Elizabeth Russell, agrees to conspire to turn the tables upon Illona. Pretending to have received a prophetic vision in a dream, Russell convinces Illona that the latter will die of strangulation in exactly 13 days. Illona becomes unhinged, has nightmares, and ultimately (on the 13th day) falls from a porch into a grape arbor and is fatally hanged in a noose of vines.

The authors of *Universal Horrors*, Michael Brunas, John Brunas, and Tom Weaver, note some Lewton affectations in other films from the studio during this time. In discussing the 1944 *Jungle Woman* (directed by Reginald LeBorg and written by Edward Dein *[Soul of a Monster]*), the authors observe: "LeBorg resolved to turn *Jungle Woman* into a Lewtonesque exercise, stressing atmosphere rather than physical terror. . . . As a result, Paula is not seen in her bestial stage until the 'shock' finale. . . . The famous scene in *Cat People* of Simone Simon stalking Jane Randolph down a dimly-lit city street is recreated with Lois Collier being pursued through the forest by Acquanetta, who assumes a preposterous Frankenstein-like stance. . . . *Jungle Woman* fails miserably in its feeble attempts at being an atmospheric, stylish thriller of the Val Lewton school."

Universal's *The Cat Creeps* (1946), coming at the tail end of the horror cycle, tried to upgrade its tiresome old house plot by injecting some Lewton elements into the mix. This Erle C. Kenton film wastes the talents of a capable cast, among them such "B" film dignitaries as Noah Beary, Jr., Lois Collier, Paul Kelly, Douglas Dumbrille, Rose Hobart, and Jonathan Hale. As the authors of *Universal Horrors* comment:

> Probably the oddest element in the picture is the strange character played by Iris Clive. "Kyra Goran" seems to appear supernaturally on the island, full of dreary prattle about spirits and cats. Parallels with characters from Val Lewton's *Cat People* are immediately apparent: Kyra initially speaks in an unrecognizable tongue (reminiscent of Elizabeth Russell's brief *Cat People* scene) and makes obtuse references to a cat-worshipping race. Since *The Cat Creeps* was co-written by Edward Dein . . . it seems safe to say that the Kyra character was part of Dein's contribution.

The poster art for *The Cat Creeps* was uncannily similar to that for *Cat People, The Leopard Man,* and *Curse of the Cat People.* One ad shows a soft, curvy design in its graphics and a cartoonish but darkly menacing black cat (resembling the animated "dream cats" in *Cat People*). "It Will Scare You Out of Your Skin," promises the ad. Although *The Cat Creeps* does not live up to its ad campaign, the production is nicely lit and well photographed, thanks to the expert hand of cinematographer George Robinson, but good camerawork cannot save a bad film. *The Cat Creeps* (which is not nearly as stylish or as entertaining as *Soul of a Monster*) may capture some of the look of the RKO films, but, curiously, it makes little use of Lewton's characteristic scare tactics. Kenton's film is an uneasy mixture of comedy, old house mystery, and psychological thriller, with a dose of Lewton mysticism thrown in for good measure. Obviously the film does not know what it wants to be, but successful it is not. All told, Universal's only notable ventures into Lewton territory were those masterminded by Robert Siodmak (see Chapter 16).

The classiest Lewtonesque productions of the 1940s came from Paramount and Warner Bros., two major studios that conspicuously avoided the horror genre during most of the decade.

Paramount's "A" budget *The Uninvited* (1944) still holds the honors as being the best ghost movie of the 1940s. While *The Uninvited* took many of its quiet horror cues from the Lewton series (including the presence of Lewton perennial, Elizabeth Russell, almost unrecognizable as one of the ghosts), it would in turn become an influential model for future ghost films. Directed by Lewis Allen and expertly photographed by Charles Lang, *The Uninvited* is one of the most handsomely produced ghost movies ever made. Based upon *Uneasy Freehold,* a popular novel by Dorothy Macardle, Allen's film has some glorious moments and some marvelous supernatural ingredients, including disembodied voices, a nifty seance, ouija boards, cold spots, wilting flowers, a ghost-sensitive dog, doors that open for no reason, and a number of very impressive ghost effects. The art direction and the mattework are impeccable; so is the Victor Young score, which yielded a hit song in the form of its piano piece "Stella by Starlight," an appropriately haunting tune. The film was also produced by Billy Wilder's longtime partner, Charles Brackett.

Ray Milland and Ruth Hussey play Roderick and Pamela Fitzgerald, a brother and sister who rent a house on the coast of Cornwall. Roderick, a pianist/composer, believes the house to be a perfect place to work in solitude until he discovers that he and his sister are not the dwelling's only occupants. Their neighbor Commander Beech (Donald Crisp), the owner of the house, is reluctant to divulge its mysterious history until his adopted daughter, Stella Meredith (Gail Russell), becomes entangled with the female spirits that haunt the premises. Roderick falls in love with the moody Stella and even composes a song for her, but their romance undergoes some serious strain when a malevolent spirit possesses the young woman and orchestrates her near suicide. A doctor (Alan Napier) is consulted, and finally a medium (Cornelia Otis Skinner), before we discover the true identity of the female spirits (one good, one bad) and their connection with Stella.

The Uninvited is imperative viewing for Lewton fans. Few horror films of the time were as successful in their exploitation of the unseen. Indeed, *The Uninvited*'s malevolent ghost, played by Elizabeth Russell, is rendered into nothing more than a swirl of diaphanous ectoplasm; our only clear glimpse of the actress can be found in the creepy oil portrait that adorns one of the walls of the house.

The screenplay by Frank Partos and Dodie Smith tends to overintellectualize its subject matter; what should have played upon our primal fears—the presence of some genuinely frightening female apparitions—is often turned into a mere exercise in deduction. In an all-too-civilized fashion, terror is pushed aside in favor of puzzle-solving. Fortunately, *The Uninvited* is so sincere in its approach to the supernatural that we can forgive many of its weaknesses.

Lewis Allen's directorial debut was also the first showcase for the fragile talents of Gail Russell, one of the most vulnerable and beautiful actresses ever to step in front of a camera. Russell was an apt choice for a horror film heroine, as she was already haunted by her own demons. Her screen persona suggested an aura of tragedy, and her performances barely disguised the anguish and torment that carried over from her personal life. Gail Russell hated acting and was so petrified by the prospect of going before the cameras that she drank heavily to overcome her phobia. *The Uninvited* made Russell a star, but she was already buckling under the pressure and suffered her first breakdown shortly after the film finished production. Stagefright and alcoholism would continue to plague the actress for the remainder of her erratic career. She would be found dead in 1961, her apartment littered with empty vodka bottles. Shortly before her death, the 37-year-old Russell had been asked to comment upon her turbulent career: "I didn't believe I had any talent. I didn't know how to have fun. I was afraid. I don't exactly know of what—of life, I guess" (Kirk Crivello, *Fallen Angels*).

Paramount followed up *The Uninvited* with the similarly titled *The Unseen* (1945), again directed by Lewis Allen and starring Gail Russell. This eccentric old house variation, scripted by Raymond Chandler and produced by John Houseman (Orson Welles's ex–Mercury Theatre partner), may have failed to produce the chills of its predecessor, but it had plenty of atmosphere and it provided a thoroughly unique New England setting for its mysterious proceedings.

Joel McCrea plays a widower with two troublesome children living in a small Massachusetts city. A young woman (Gail Russell) answers his ad for a nanny only to find in McCrea a Rochester-like Byronic hero. The children prove to be a handful for Russell; the little girl is likeable enough, but her brother is a terror, having pledged his loyalty to the last nanny before she was mysteriously discharged. Murders begin to occur in the alley near the house, and there seems to be a connection between the little boy and the murderer.

The Unseen is a combination of many things. At times it plays like an uncredited adaptation of Henry James's *The Turn of the Screw*; at other times it appears to be yet another updating of *Jane Eyre*. Elements from *Rebecca* and *Gaslight* also find their way into the mix, as well as a number of Lewtonesque flourishes. Unfortunately, *The Unseen* is tugged in too many directions, as its muddled narrative attests. Director Allen must have been infatuated with

Russell's screen presence and, especially, her rather self-conscious gait because she is almost always shown in motion, walking somewhere, from one part of the house to another, the camera tracking every step. There are times when the actress seems as bewildered as the character she plays, and one cannot help but wonder what is going through her mind. A stodgy Joel McCrea is way out of his depth as a Byronic hero; since he was never an actor to exude intellect and gentility, his ill-tempered and unjustified harassment of Russell gives him all the appeal of a surly, not-too-bright blowhard.

The Unseen is dark, moody, and evocative, but the Chandler script is almost indeciferable. The film's wonderfully Lewtonesque title is but an empty promise. As such, it is a seldom-seen curio which serves nicely as a showcase for Gail Russell's dark beauty, but never succeeds in being more than slightly diverting.

Several notches better was Paramount's *The Night Has a Thousand Eyes* (1948), directed by John Farrow and scripted by Barre Lyndon (from a Cornell Woolrich novel). Farrow's film captures the dark mood of the RKO series and begs comparison with two of Lewton's most doom-laden films: *The Leopard Man* (also based on a Woolrich novel) and *The Seventh Victim*. As was the case with Clo-Clo in *The Leopard Man,* the heroine in Farrow's film (once again Gail Russell) has her fortune told by a mystic (Edward G. Robinson). But more like Jacqueline in *The Seventh Victim* (whose decree of doom is less formalized, but no less certain), Russell's Jean Courtland in *Thousand Eyes* is more inclined to "run to Death and have Death meet her as fast." Jean's aborted attempt to throw herself in front of a train in the film's spooky opening scene seems to pick up where Clarence Brown's *Anna Karenina* left off.

In *Film Noir,* Alain Silver and Elizabeth Ward remark: "It is precisely the feeling of doom throughout *[The Night Has a Thousand Eyes]* that separates it from most mysteries. . . . There is never any doubt that [the prediction is] authentic. In a noir sense, man cannot control or rationalize the future. Life is pathetic for the seer, who is helpless and useless despite his efforts to avoid tragedy. . . . *The Night Has a Thousand Eyes* depicts the noir universe at its darkest. The night itself is the enemy, and the stars fatally oversee every misadventure."

Of course, a film based on a Cornell Woolrich source was bound to be in the Lewton tradition. The novel *The Night Has a Thousand Eyes* was included as an entry in *Horror: 100 Best Books* (edited by Stephen Jones and Kim Newman, 1988), and Maxim Jakubowski's essay seems to indicate Woolrich was a literary equivalent to Lewton and his team:

> Many of Cornell Woolrich's masterly romans noirs contain horrific or fatalistic elements, but only *Night Has a Thousand Eyes* actually involves the supernatural. . . . The horror and fantasy element never becomes explicit, and gains in credible terror by confronting everyday people with whom the reader can easily identify. Indeed, what you only guess at, what you never see,

> is psychologically all the more frightening; a lesson that few horror filmmakers since Val Lewton and Jacques Tourneur have learned well.

In 1946, just as all the other studios were abandoning the horror genre, Warner Bros. released one of the decade's most original horror films, Robert Florey's *The Beast with Five Fingers.* Although most classic horror fans are eternally grateful for this spirited latecomer, a little of the credit for its inception should go to Boris Karloff; he had included William Fryer Harvey's little-known 1928 story, "The Beast with Five Fingers," in his best-selling 1943 anthology, *Tales of Terror,* thus bringing it to the attention of Hollywood's horror mavens.

Screenwriter Curt Siodmak deviated considerably from his W.F. Harvey source by allowing the supernatural elements to remain ambiguous. Unlike Siodmak's script, the Harvey story has nothing to do with Italy, pianists, wills, astrology, or mad hallucinations. The creeping hand of the short story (making its first entrance sliding down a bannister) is witnessed by several people rather than being, as in the film, the figment of a crazed imagination. Disregarding most of the story's content, Siodmak retained the principal menace of a crawling hand and fashioned a bizarre Hollywood thriller, bringing together his experience with both schools of horror filmmaking: Universal's and Lewton's.

Siodmak's basic story frame was that of the old house chiller, replete with such tried-and-true ingredients as the reading of a will, violent thunderstorms, sinister characters, murder, parapsychology, pianos that play in the night, and the typical cheat ending so characteristic of the form: the tidy dénouement reveals a logical, though highly improbable, explanation for the film's fantastic events. Also thrown into the mix are a pair of typically bland romantic leads (in this case Robert Alda and Andrea King), as well as the obligatory local police commissioner (J. Carrol Naish doing his Chico Marx accent) to investigate the scene of the crime. Such hackneyed elements from an outmoded subgenre would lead anyone to expect the worst, but somehow the film nearly transcends the cinematic clichés from which it was fashioned. *The Beast with Five Fingers* is the quintessential old house film of the 1940s, the ultimate clutching-hand thriller.

Florey's direction may be off the mark during the treacly romance scenes and static during some stretches of exposition, but the terror sequences are directed with the aplomb of a horror master. Never before in his macabre films had Florey shown as much muscle as he exhibits here. If the entire film were on the level of its scare scenes, *The Beast with Five Fingers* would have been a horror classic of the first order. Putting aside Florey's rather sudden panache for terror, the film is bolstered by a marvelously flamboyant performance by Peter Lorre. His character Hilary, an eccentric secretary/astrologist, is an ingenious creation; like the child-killer in *M,* Hilary is able to evoke sympathy with an otherwise villainous role. Lorre comes across as forlorn and misguided, a frightened little boy possessive of his toys (astrology books, in this case) and an unrepentant tattle-tale. Although he is not the kind of little boy people are apt to like, it is impossible to avoid empathizing with him, especially in the final scenes.

The unconvincing and needless Italian locale was probably encouraged by Florey in an effort to give the film some "European class." The village scenes, featuring mostly local color and native shenanigans, are superfluous to the main concerns of the script and are completely dropped after the first reel. Most of the action takes place in and around the villa of the wealthy pianist Francis Ingram (strongly played by Victor Francen), who has only one functioning hand. The villa scenes (interiors and exteriors both) are full of genuinely spooky atmosphere and low-key expressionistic photography that give the film the feel of a more elaborate, but equally claustrophobic, *Isle of the Dead.* In fact, *Beast*'s Julia Holden (Andrea King) is a lot like Ellen Drew's character in *Isle.* Accused of being a witch by the villagers, Julie falls under suspicion when the invalid she has been hired to care for suddenly dies. Although the primary horror device in both films is the resurrection of the dead, in *The Beast with Five Fingers* it is only a portion of the corpse that comes back to pay a call.

Florey's film takes about 20 minutes to hook its audience, and our interest peaks with our first glimpse of Hilary (the brooding Max Steiner score offers a beautifully wistful lietmotif whenever the film centers on Lorre's character). The pianist Ingram (recalling Mrs. Cortez in *The Seventh Victim*), has gathered his associates together to witness the signing of his new will, but the identities of his beneficiaries remain undisclosed until his death. At the end of the tense evening, Ingram has a heated confrontation with Hilary wherein Ingram attempts to strangle the astrologer with his one good arm.

That night, while in his bedroom during a storm, Ingram wakes from a nightmare; his desperate calls to Julie go unheeded, answered only by the shrieking winds, driving rain, rattling windows, and occasional bursts of thunder. The shadows of windswept trees dance upon the walls surrounding him while the air becomes thick with menace. The accent on the unseen, combined with Francen's moving portrayal of a frightened and helpless man, results in a spinetingling set piece in the Lewton tradition.

In a panic, Ingram gets into his wheelchair, barrels his way out of his room onto the upper landing, and begins moving down the narrow passageway. Courtesy of an ingenious point-of-view shot, the camera hurries past the bannister rails (which impede our vision of the lower floor), making us feel trapped in Ingram's wheelchair. When Ingram gets near the edge of the ornate winding staircase, he begins hallucinating, and via his point-of-view, we see his vision beginning to distort. Ingram's backward glance down the long shimmery hallway heightens the terror. In his frenzy to escape the demons of his own imagination, Ingram, wheelchair and all, tumbles down the stairs to his death.

After the funeral, the relatives become aghast when the will is read, and Julie is pronounced the sole recipient of Ingram's wealth. When it looks like someone has broken into the family vault, the relatives investigate. Upon opening Ingram's casket, they find the pianist's paralyzed hand gripping a sharp knife; the other hand, the working one, is gone, cut off at the wrist.

That night the villa's inhabitants hear Ingram's first posthumous piano recital. They also find Ingram's lawyer, mysteriously strangled by one hand. The police commissioner finds Ingram's fingerprints on the piano, the broken crypt window, and elsewhere about the house. J. Carrol Naish's commissioner delivers this priceless Curt Siodmak line: "In my mind there is no doubt the hand is walking around."

Sitting alone in his library in the middle of the night, poring over his books on astrology, Hilary hears a faint scuttling sound. This is followed by other Lewtonesque flourishes: a book falling, the hearth fire's sudden crackle, the window curtains undulating in the breeze. Cinematographer Wesley Anderson achieves some remarkable compositions using extreme close-ups of Lorre's frightened face, lit from below. In a state of fearful ambivalence, Hilary remains seated while the lid of the small box on his desk opens up and Ingram's hand creeps out like a blond tarantula. Capturing the hand and locking it in a desk drawer, Hilary goes for help, but when he returns with witnesses, the hand is gone.

Like a macabre version of an Abbott and Costello routine, the hand continues to make numerous appearances, always when Hilary is alone. In one scene, he recaptures the hand and embracing it to his chest like a beloved pet, walks across the room and drops it onto his desk. In one of the most shockingly graphic scenes in classic horror film history, Hilary holds the creature to the desktop with one hand, reaches in a drawer with the other, pulls out a hammer, a large nail, and, whack, whack, whack, nails the hand palm-down onto the desktop. Of course by the time Hilary is able to gather some more witnesses, the hand is gone; only the nail remains, half-driven into the desk.

(The special effects are surprisingly sophisticated. In most instances a live actor's hand is "cut off" at the wrist through the use of blue-screen effects; in shots where the wrist is exposed to be camera, a realistic cross-section (revealing bone and muscle) is superimposed upon the illusory stump of the actor's hand. It is remarkable that the above scene was not eliminated by the censors. The Production Code would never have tolerated a shot of a wooden stake being driven into the heart of a dummy in a coffin, but the hammering of a nail into the top of a writhing human hand was somehow permissible, in spite of the religious significance associated with this manner of impalement.)

Eventually, it becomes clear that Hilary is the one who murdered the lawyer and that he has talked himself into believing his own fabricated evidence concerning the resurrection of Ingram's hand. In the film's final fright set piece, Hilary throws the hand into the burning hearth, laughing hysterically, as only Lorre can. When the blackened hand creeps out of the fire, Hilary remains frozen in place, defeated. Charred and smoking, but still wearing the ring, the beast begins its spidery ascent up Hilary's chest, to his neck, and finally around his throat. A lethal embrace.

The film's final minutes, unfortunately, are reserved for the improbable old house-style dénouement. The piano playing, we are shown, was done with the use of a record and hidden phonograph. In the world of the old house films, the villain always seems to live in a Rube Goldberg universe. Some of the explanations are difficult to swallow, however, especially when they defy logic and manage to sidestep physical law. Once we know that there was nothing supernatural behind any of this, we feel absolutely compelled to look for further loopholes. And we find plenty of them. In order to detour this line of thinking, the Florey/Siodmak team dismantles the whole import of the film with some lame humor. After a bit of nonsense where a housemaid becomes hysterical over a dropped glove, Naish steps out of character to talk directly to the audience, all the while pretending to be attacked by, alas, his own hand.

The Beast with Five Fingers presents some of the most arresting images of the entire 1940s horror film cycle and then deliberately pulls the rug out from under itself with some indefensible self-mockery. This aside, Florey's film is still the best crawling-hand movie ever made (and other examples of the odd subgenre, including a *Thriller* episode and an Oliver Stone film, actually number more than ten fingers). *Beast* shows an obvious affinity with the look, style, even the content, of the Lewton films. Because the film has a "monster" that refuses to stay off-camera, some may question its status as Lewtonesque cinema, but even though the hand is shown, the film maintains its sense of undisclosed horror. After all, there is nothing inherently frightening about a human hand, so it must be something else, namely the dark force behind it, that we find so terrifying.

The Two Mrs. Carrolls and *Cry Wolf,* two macabre offerings released by Warner Bros. in 1947, were basically "B" films with big name stars and modest "A" budget trappings. Both were directed by Peter Godfrey and fashioned as vehicles for Barbara Stanwyck. Neither film was well received at the time, and they remain only of minor interest to most people today, but classic horror fans will enjoy viewing them as a Lewton scavenger hunt.

The Two Mrs. Carrolls, the better of the pair, was actually shot in 1945 and withheld from release for two years. Playing like a combinaton of *Suspicion* and *The Picture of Dorian Gray,* Peter Godfrey's film provides us with the rare opportunity of seeing Humphrey Bogart play a modern Bluebeard. Bogart plays Geoffrey Carroll, a mentally unstable artist who completes a portrait of his wife as "The Angel of Death" just before he slowly murders her by poisoning her milk. His affair with another woman, Sally (Stanwyck), provides the impetus for such action. Sally becomes the second Mrs. Carroll, but Geoffrey's precocious 10-year-old daughter, Beatrice (*Curse of the Cat People*'s Ann Carter), drops casual remarks (about her late mother's slow illness) that make Sally suspicious. Meanwhile, Geoffrey has trouble finding inspiration for his work. After he falls in love with a neighbor, Cecily Latham (Alexis Smith), he again finds his artistic muse. Locked in his studio, he works feverishly, refusing to show his new masterpiece to anyone until it is completed. Meanwhile, Sally grows sicker day by day, her husband doing everything he can to make her comfortable, even delivering warm milk to her bedside every night.

Although it is nicely produced by Mark Hellinger, with a rich musical score by Franz Waxman, *The Two Mrs. Carrolls* is too derivative of earlier thrillers to be of any great merit. Barbara Stanwyck steals the show, although a very sexy Alexis Smith is also memorable. Bogart, who was always excellent as a vicious psychopath, is miscast as the charming lady-killer. Ann Carter has a sizable role, but her performance is rather affected, even for the precociousness written into her character. The film's one set piece of raw terror—when Sally and Beatrice unlock the studio door and finally look upon Geoffrey's new version of "The Angel of Death"—delivers enough shudders for two horror movies.

Cry Wolf is another ersatz horror film directed by Peter Godfrey. The appeal of its two stars (Errol Flynn and Barbara Stanwyck), the classy production, the Germanic lighting and photography (by Carl Guthrie), and the deliberate nods to Lewton ("walks" and "buses" abound) make one wonder why the film is so often overlooked by horror film surveys. Although *Cry Wolf* is not very good, the prospect of seeing Flynn and Stanwyck working together in anything resembling a horror film is reason enough to lift this entry above the commonplace. Stanwyck's plucky character in *Cry Wolf* is in keeping with the strong, independent heroines of the Lewton films, while Errol Flynn, playing the reserved British intellectual, is not unlike a Warner Bros. variation of Tom Conway. Helene Thimig (who played the old woman, Kyra, in *Isle of the Dead*) also makes an appearance here, as does Richard Basehart as a crazed killer. *Cry Wolf* treads overly familiar territory (it is yet another old house variation) and suffers from a limp ending, but it remains enjoyable if only for its production frills. We have major stars, peerless photography, impressive sets and art direction, and a ripping good score by Franz Waxman.

Sandra Marshall (Barbara Stanwyck) comes to an opulent, if physically neglected, estate and claims to be the wife of the recently deceased Jim Caldwell (who, heretofore, was believed unmarried). Mark Caldwell (Errol Flynn), an uncle of the deceased and executor of his estate, believes she is an imposter looking for a slice of the inheritance. Unwilling to leave peaceably, Sandra is given a room in the estate while the will undergoes examination. She develops a close relationship with Julie (Jim's rebellious sister), who warns her about screams in the night and other mysterious occurrences. Mention is made of a laboratory in the back of the mansion, the suspicious work therein being kept under lock and key. Julie also suspects that Jim may be alive, functioning as a guinea pig in laboratory experiments. And so Sandra does a little sleuthing in the hopes of unraveling the estate's dark secret.

The captivating first half hour of *Cry Wolf* shows a lot of promise. Stanwyck's enigmatic character, a coarse, wisecracking gold-digger, is interesting, and for a while we have hopes for another great Stanwyck femme fatale. Her character makes an unconvincing turnaround, however, once she starts playing Nancy Drew. Initially Flynn is surprisingly good as the Byronic hero hiding the family curse, but his romantic interludes with Stanwyck in the film's final scenes are laughably inappropriate. Flynn and Stanwyck are hopelessly ill-matched. Catherine Turney, the scriptwriter, should have been taken aside for including the following line as a suitable break-the-ice romantic pitch for Flynn: "I'd like to probe behind that sphinx-like exterior of yours."

Cry Wolf's Lewtonesque moments come off rather nicely though. The creepy mansion is a beautifully rendered house of shadows that adds immeasurably to the effectiveness of the film's shuddery moments. In one effective Lewton walk (this one indoors), Sandra steals her way to the laboratory, passing through shadowy corridors, even riding a dumbwaiter to another floor. During her travels, we hear a clock's exaggerated ticking that is soon accompanied by a hypnotic shot of its swinging pendulum as an atmosphere of quiet menace builds and builds. Sandra's near-collision with a water cooler—a very effective Lewton "bus"—is enough to lift any absorbed viewer out of his seat. When Sandra starts climbing the ornate rooftop of the mansion in an effort to reach the lab, it is difficult not to be reminded of the climax of *Bedlam*. *Cry Wolf*'s other walk is through the spooky woods after Sandra is thrown from her horse. As she makes her way through the forest, the common forest sounds—the chirps of the birds, the rustle of the brush, the whisper of the wind—become the harbingers of imminent peril. As the tension peaks, a covey of pigeons take flight, causing another hair-raising jolt.

Because the film is, in part, yet another variation of *Jane Eyre*, *Cry Wolf* has some qualities in common with *I Walked with a Zombie*. At one point in the film, Caldwell tells Sandra of the sea, its perils and corruption, echoing a similar monologue by Paul Holland (Tom Conway) in the Lewton film. Although *Cry Wolf* completely skirts the use of supernatural elements, its dreaded family secret also involves the living dead. The script's use of a feigned death (Jim Caldwell) as a cover for mental illness (he has become a violent lunatic) is cribbed directly from the pages of the Charlotte Brontë novel.

Some of the more adventurous Lewtonesque films of the 1940s were released by smaller studios. Three such films—Republic's *The Woman Who Came Back* (1945), UA's release of Sol Lesser's independently produced *The*

Red House (1947), and Eagle-Lion's *The Amazing Mr. X* (1948, aka *The Spiritualist*)—warrant a little of our attention.

Republic made budget serials and Westerns with considerable verve, but the studio's fitful attempts to capitalize on the horror craze—*The Vampire's Ghost* (1945), *Valley of the Zombies, The Catman of Paris* (both 1946)—were usually dreadfully misguided. The one exception to the dreariness of Republic's scant horror output was *The Woman Who Came Back,* directed by Walter Colmes. In *The Encyclopedia of Horror Movies,* author Phil Hardy calls *The Woman Who Came Back* "a strikingly intelligent film. . . . Obviously a disciple of the methods initiated by Val Lewton in *Cat People,* Colmes works by suggestion throughout, not least in the fine opening sequences."

However derivative the film may be, it is apparent that Walter Colmes, whose direction shows surprising ingenuity, was serious about making a good horror film. Nancy Kelly's strong lead performance indicates that she took this odd little project seriously as well; Kelly is engaging throughout, showing hardly a hint of her later tendency to chew scenery (i.e., her over-the-top performance as the harried mother in *The Bad Seed* [1956]).

Set in the mythical Massachusetts town of Eben Rock, a location supposedly associated with Puritan witchhunts, the film's memorable opening scene shows Lorna (Nancy Kelly) returning home by bus after a long-delayed mysterious absence. An old woman and a dog flank the road, forcing the crowded bus to a stop; the woman, a hag with a frightful face (partially hidden under a black veil), climbs aboard and offers the bus driver a Colonial banknote. Taking a seat next to Lorna, she begins spouting seventeenth century–style gibberish about Eben Rock's historical infamy. Distracted, the bus driver loses control of the vehicle, which plunges over a cliff and into a lake. Lorna is the only survivor of the accident (her miraculous survival prefigures a somewhat similar scene in Herk Harvey's 1962 cult classic, *Carnival of Souls*). The shots of the men combing the lake are especially ghoulish, with the hillside covered with shrouded corpses. Lorna gives her version of the accident, but when the old woman's body is not among the many found, the townspeople grow suspicious. Lorna is reunited with her old boyfriend, Matt Adams (John Loder), a local doctor who takes a room above the Pilgrim's Tavern. This is all poor timing for Ruth (Ruth Ford) who manages the tavern and has dibs on Matt's affections. Events of Lorna's mysterious past (undisclosed to the audience) lead the townspeople to believe she is cursed. Lorna is prone to agree, given the strange things that have been happening to her (she sees the witch's face in her own reflection and her boxed flowers wilt and die in a matter of minutes).

Lorna makes a trip to the church basement one night, her actions showing as much spunk as those of the typical Lewton heroine. (Like *Cat People*'s Irena, Lorna claims she has a "fondness for the night.") The journey to the church is fashioned as an effective Lewton walk, culminating in a creepy set

Nancy Kelly as Lorna, *The Woman Who Came Back.*

piece obviously inspired by *Cat People*'s swimming pool sequence. Lorna walks her way into the dark basement, candle in hand. A series of taxidermic animal trophies — a cat, an owl, a fox — border an upper shelf of the basement wall. Amidst the flickering candlelight and surrounding darkness, Lorna continues her search for a rare document detailing Ebon Rock's past, but when she accomplishes this and is prepared to leave, she sees the silhouette of a dog blocking her only exit.

Director Colmes shows some flair for the macabre. At one point, we see an assortment of grotesque faces through the flames of a fireplace, only to find that these monstrous visages are nothing more than children in amazingly elaborate Halloween masks (a "bus"-like device that anticipates a very similar moment in Jacques Tourneur's 1957 Lewton homage, *Curse of the Demon*). In another of the film's terror set pieces, Lorna is alone in her huge mansion during a violent thunderstorm. The power lines are down, and she sits near the fireplace reading a book on ancient superstitions; all the while, her morbid imagination is fed by the howling wind, the falling rain, and the banging shutters. After securing the shutters, Lorna goes back to her chair to find that her book has somehow found its way onto the burning hearth. The flickering light sources of the candles and the hearth accent Lorna's building dread as she looks about the darkened room, knowing that she is no longer alone. On the wall, framed by the fire's undulating light, is the immobile shadow of a large dog. For a moment or two, Lorna thinks the shadow is an illusion made by some innocuous object, a piece of furniture or a lamp—until it moves away.

Oddly enough, one of the memorable "walks" occurs on a bright Sunday morning, while Lorna is making her way down a busy neighborhood street. In a long, uninterrupted tracking shot, she passes numerous people and overhears bits and pieces of their conversations about witches and curses. Because this shot is totally free of score music, the normal sounds of a Sunday morning—a lawn mower cutting grass, birds singing, people talking, laughing—become tinged with menace.

Unfortunately, the last five or 10 minutes of *The Woman Who Came Back* (like those of *The Beast with Five Fingers*) come close to sabotaging whatever power the film possesses. The old woman's body is discovered; it was dragged out of the water and pulled under a bush, presumably by the dog. It turns out that the strange woman was only a lunatic obsessed with local history who escaped from the nearby asylum. The dog is, after all, only a dog. And, of course, this means that Lorna is not a witch. (However, this does not answer such questions as: How did the flowers wilt? Why was the dog so preoccupied with Lorna and how did it manage to throw a book onto the fire?)

Although *The Woman Who Came Back* has some serious flaws, it is a more dignified attempt to duplicate the Lewton style than, say, *Cry of the Werewolf, Weird Woman,* or *The Cat Creeps.* While the Republic film suffers from a limited budget, too many loose ends, and some trite special effects, it should be recognized as a sincere effort by one of the few directors who appeared to have some genuine understanding of the Lewton style. Walter Colmes had previously written for radio, which explains why he was so adept at using sound so suggestively. *The Woman Who Came Back* was his only horror film.

One of the more avant-garde horror films of the decade was *The Red House,* a 1947 Sol Lesser production written and directed by Delmer Daves and released by United Artists. For the uninitiated, this film is a solid find; it is continually glossed over in surveys of the genre, probably because it so defies pigeon-holing as a horror film. (Good prints of *The Red House* have been unavailable for a number of years; as of this writing, a print with a clean soundtrack does not seem to exist.)

There were only a mere handful of critics who used the word "horror" in their reviews of *The Red House.* A.H. Weiler's March 17, 1947, review in *The New York Times* states: "It's been a long time since the Hollywood artisans have turned out an adult horror number. *The Red House* is just such an edifying offering, which should supply horror-hungry audiences with the chills of the month." The *New York Herald-Tribune*'s Otis Guernsey, Jr., like most other reviewers, sidestepped the use of the "H" word: "a moody hair-raiser of a melodrama . . . a taut and steady item of menacing make-believe." In *The United Artists Story*, Ronald Bergen reports that *The Red House* "often had 'full house' signs outside theatres."

The Red House was, without question, the most regional Hollywood horror film made in the 1940s. Guernsey's review did manage to shed some light on one of the things that make *The Red House* so captivating: "Daves's direction has brought the scenery so much to life that it becomes the most important character of the piece." The film seems to be shot entirely on location in some rural community with plenty of forest; the state is never specified and from the looks of things *The Red House*'s Piny Ridge setting could be "Anywhere, USA." The underproduced, even amateurish, feel of Daves's film, including the director's extensive use of unfamiliar faces, lends it an odd kind of authenticity that reminds one of Jean Renoir's exceedingly offbeat American films, *Swamp Water* and *The Southerner*.

The Red House, the tale of a haunted forest set somewhere in rural America, conveys the flavor of national folklore. Daves's earthy script uncannily anticipates the kind of rural horror story that would one day be popularized by Stephen King and the myriad other talented horror writers who followed in his wake.

Pete Morgan (Edward G. Robinson), a moody farmer, lives a secluded life with his sister Ellen (Judith Anderson) and his adopted daughter Meg (Allene Roberts). Some 15 years earlier, Meg's parents mysteriously vanished. Pete, whose crippled leg is getting worse, hires Meg's high school classmate, Nath Storm (Lon McCallister), to help work the farm. As Nath is about to walk home that first night and announces his plan to take a shortcut through the Oxhead Woods, Pete becomes agitated and demands that the boy go nowhere near the Oxhead Woods. Nath takes Pete's warnings as something of a dare and, though he is not really familiar with the area, refuses to alter his plans. The wind is blowing, and as Pete and Nath address each other outdoors, they must shout to be heard over the howling gusts. Pete yells that in Oxhead Woods there will be no protection from "The Red House and the screams in the night." Nath calls back, "I'll just give it a good go-round" and continues upon his homeward path.

This Lewton walk is altogether terrifying. It starts with an ominous shot of Nath's departure, his figure growing smaller as he walks into the barren field and becomes engulfed in its swirling sea of high grass. While Pete continues to shout his desperate warnings, they are all but drowned out by ferocious winds. (The use of wind machines [and/or airplane engines] going full tilt prefigures a similarly effective use of artificial wind in Jacques Tourneur's *Curse of the Demon*.)

As Nath breaks into the thick forest en route to Oxhead Woods, composer Miklos Rosza adds some spooky atonal flourishes which approximate the screams Nath has been warned about. The camera continues to track

Nath; he stops, now and again, unsure of himself, the wind-swept forest alive with menace. Finally, a sign "Trespass at Your Own Risk" marks the edge of Oxhead Woods; the camera pulls in on the sign and a scream swells on the soundtrack. When Nath enters Oxhead Woods, his fears intensify. The screams are real now, or seem to be. Nath goes a little farther before turning about-face and scrambling back to the Morgan farm like a frightened animal, as the camera tracks his frenzied flight along the way. He runs for shelter to Pete's barn; the camera pulls in for a lengthy close-up as his face continues to reflect a battle between clear thinking and primal fears.

Delmer Daves certainly pressed his luck with the Breen Office; Nath's girlfriend Tibby (an astonishingly sensual Julie London) is the most wanton highschooler ever portrayed on the '40s screen. When Nath asks her if he should wear his swimming trunks when they meet at an isolated swimming spot, Tibby answers, "No, just bring them; we can change at the reservoir, just the two of us," her saucy smile making everything perfectly clear. Julie London's off-color innuendos, seductive glances, and slinky man-hungry demeanor had to have raised a few eyebrows (to say the least) in 1947; *The Red House*'s provocative sexual content was no doubt a significant factor in the film's ability to draw big crowds. In fact, even in the midst of today's more liberal climes, *The Red House* remains a very sexy film.

Tibby's suspicions are aroused when Nath starts working at the Morgan farm, especially when she sees Nath and Meg waiting at the same bus stop (indicating that Nath has spent a night away from home). As the bus approaches, some of its passengers are already whistling out the windows, laughing and hurling one-liners about the obvious implication. Upon boarding the bus, Nath gets a few more good-natured verbal jabs and shrugs them off with a smile. At that moment we understand exactly why Nath is so popular and also why Tibby is not the slightest bit amused. There is an unexpected honesty in this entire scene.

What Nath does not know is that whenever he is not around, Tibby takes up with Teller (Rory Calhoun), a high school dropout several years her senior. Teller is the town's resident ne'er-do-well, who, ostracized by the community, lives a hedonistic backwoods existence. Teller lecherously informs Tibby: "I learned plenty of things they don't teach in school." Although Tibby often exhibits a feigned disregard for Teller, there is an obvious familiarity in their verbal sparring that makes it evident that something has been going on between these two long before the opening reel. "Who are you kidding!" Teller tells Tibby. "You can fool around with your pretty boy, Nath Storm, as much as you like, but when you decide on a man, you come to me." When Nath finds them together and knocks Teller down with a surprise punch, Tibby runs to Teller's side to give him a lingering open-mouthed kiss. After she breaks for some air, her face flushed with passion, Tibby turns her head to look at Nath, who is agape with disbelief. So ends Nath's long romance with Tibby.

The dark secret associated with the Red House of Oxhead Woods concerns Pete, Meg's parents, and a two-year-old Meg, whose memory of that fateful evening has become repressed. When Nath begins showing an interest in Meg, Pete becomes unhinged. Freudian themes abound as Pete's jealous rage leads him to say things that make little sense. One night he calls Meg by her mother's name. When Meg confesses this to Ellen, the latter vehemently asks: "Did Pete ever lay his hands upon you?" Robinson's character becomes increasingly deranged. By the film's climax, Pete is thoroughly insane, reenacting the events of that horrible night 15 years before and putting Meg's life in peril.

Although *The Red House* bears little resemblance to any specific Lewton film, it successfully carries forward the Lewton tradition. Seldom has the unseen become as palpable a threatening force as it is here. Like many popular folktales, *The Red House* has what appears to be a fully developed Freudian subtext replete with sexual symbolism and Oedipal/Electral situations. Even the relationship between Pete and his sister leaves room for much speculation. So does the relationship between Nath and his single mother (their lengthy kiss still raises eyebrows).

The performances are all fine, including those of the younger actors. Twenty-four-year-old Lon McCallister (with his 40-year-old hairline) is a bit hokey, but we know the kind of person he is the minute we lay eyes on him. Allene Roberts also gives a captivating performance as the pretty wallflower, Meg. Looking a little like an anemic Teresa Wright, Roberts is convincing in her fey performance, and, as with McCallister, we have her pegged immediately: a decent, shy girl who will grow up to be a beautiful woman. Julie London, as Tibby, is simply a wonder to behold, and her type convinces us that some things never change. Rory Calhoun lends an excellent black sheep presence to his role as Teller. All four of the younger performers behave like real people, something not common in 1940s depictions of teenagers or young adults. Whatever praise James Agee and Manny Farber gave the sincerity of the young performers in Lewton's *Youth Runs Wild* should go double for *The Red House*'s youthful cast.

Finally, there are the fine performances by Edward G. Robinson and Judith Anderson. Robinson has always been outstanding in introverted roles where he was cast against type. In *The Red House,* a dark, brooding cloud seems to hover over the actor, casting a shadow upon his face, his movements, even his speech. Robinson never goes overboard with this meaty role, though the temptation for excess would not have been so easily resisted by lesser actors. Judith Anderson is such a perfect match for Robinson that we keep forgetting they are brother and sister, not man and wife. Anderson beautifully underscores the mystery of Pete Morgan; she is continually worried about something she refuses to talk about, and she makes cryptic statements or overreacts to things in which only she sees some dark significance.

The Red House is not an unqualified masterpiece. The ending is a letdown, especially after such a supreme buildup, but the story's supernatural elements are debunked without insulting the viewer's intelligence. At least there are no lapses in logic when the secret is unveiled. If the screams in the night were nothing more than the hauntings of a deranged mind or the wild fancies of an impressionable high schooler, *The Red House* nicely upholds Lewton's rudimentary principle of terror: nothing is more frightening than our own powers of imagination.

Eagle-Lion's *The Amazing Mr. X* (1948), a marvelously atmospheric but extremely minor "B" quickie, is not nearly as good as *The Woman Who Came Back* or *The Red House* but, like them, it deliberately strives to be unique. Directed by Bernard Vorhaus, *The Amazing Mr. X* is yet one more noirish thriller that centers around a spiritualist, putting the film in the company with *The Devil Commands, The Leopard Man, Flesh and Fantasy, Nightmare Alley,* and *The Night Has a Thousand Eyes.*

Lynn Bari plays Christine Faver, a wealthy widow who lives in a massive and incredibly ornate seaside estate with her sister, Janet Burke (Cathy O'Donnell). Janet has been urging her lonely older sister to remarry, but Christine resists the idea, even though she has a ready-and-willing suitor, Martin Abbott (Richard Carlson). Christine has often been haunted by the memory of her composer husband, Paul, but lately it is more than a memory that haunts her. That night, as she walks along the beach to meet Martin, Christine hears the breathy voice of her dead husband repeatedly calling her name, his voice blending with the sounds of the surf. The tension mounts as Christine hurries away, trying to escape from Paul's seemingly omniscient presence as the camera makes numerous cutaways to ocean waves beating against the rocks. The loud shriek of a bird (acting as a Lewton "bus") punctuates Christine's terror as she suddenly finds herself face-to-face with a stranger. Alexis (Turhan Bey) introduces himself; he is a psychic consultant and his remarks about Christine's private life offer evidence of his mind-reading talents.

Days pass and Christine continues to be haunted by the spirit of her husband. His favorite piano piece begins playing on the phonograph, and the double doors in her bedroom, leading to the elaborate balcony, open on their own. Matt's picture falls off Christine's night table, and when she reaches to pick it up, it has turned into a picture of Paul. An apparition of Christine's wedding dress comes out of the closet and weaving through the air like a wraith, follows her about until she becomes hysterical.

Finally, seeing no alternative but to employ the services of a psychic consultant, Christine goes to Alexis's eccentric-looking cottage which, unbeknownst to her, is rigged with two-way mirrors and phony contraptions. A squawking crow flies about at will within Alexis's mystical headquarters. Alexis is more than happy to be of service. Meanwhile, the spiritualist's plan is revealed to the audience. All along he has had a confederate, Christine's housemaid, to help rig the estate so that he could perform some supernatural hocus pocus. The aim of Alexis's scam is to soak the unsuspecting woman of her riches by pretending to be her dead husband.

But what Alexis does not know is that Paul Favor is still alive; his death had been a hoax orchestrated to give him the perfect alibi when he eventually returned to kill Christine and take her money. Paul (Donald Curtis) confronts Alexis and, having him over a barrel, begins to dictate the rules of the scam. Reluctantly, Alexis goes along, continuing to meet with Christine and, in the process, falling in love with her sister Janet. The more his affections grow, the less Alexis likes his situation. In the climax, when Paul is about to kill Christine, Alexis interferes but is shot and left for dead. Using the tricks of his trade, the fatally wounded Alexis then saves the day by pretending to be his own vengeful dead spirit.

Director Bernard Vorhaus's chief claim to fame was a series of middling John Wayne Westerns for Republic in the early forties. Although one suspects he may have felt out of his element with a horror film, it is gratifying to see (especially under such severe budgetary restrictions) that Vorhaus has some enthusiasm for his material.

Cinematographer John Alton captures some exquisite ocean imagery (day and night), some of it reminiscient of J. Roy Hunt's work in *I Walked with a Zombie*. In the interior scenes (especially those taking place within Alexis's weird dwelling), Alton achieves impressive compositions with unusual angles (in one instance the seance is shot from underneath a glass table). In fact, light and shadow are put to such flamboyant use that Alton's visuals are nearly as gimmicky as Alexis's bag of supernatural tricks. The film's final scene, where the dying Alexis bids his pet crow to fly out to sea, is much more moving than it has any right to be.

The Amazing Mr. X is no minor classic, but its inventiveness and visual splendor are worth some recognition. Although the performances are not particularly convincing, there is an earnestness to the production that is difficult to dislike. This low-budget Lewton imitation at least deserves a B-minus for having its heart in the right place.

By the end of the decade, even RKO studios, finally seeing the light, had begun to draw inspiration from the Lewton films. RKO's 1949 sleeper, *The Window*, is a masterful thriller in the Lewton tradition. Based on a Cornell Woolrich novel, the film clearly reflected the paranoia of the times, especially in its assertion that murderers (or other "undesirables") may look as normal as the people next door. Shot on location in a run-down neighborhood in New York City, this variation of "The Boy Who Cried Wolf" fable concerns a fanciful boy named Tommy (Bobby Driscoll) who witnesses a murder committed in the apartment above his own. When he tells his parents that the Kellersons, a seemingly normal married couple, have just stabbed a man to death with a pair of scissors, the parents (played by Arthur Kennedy and Barbara Hale) think it is another of his typically wild stories. Tommy goes to the police, who investigate but come up with nothing. Finding out about her son's police call, Tommy's mother drags the boy upstairs to apologize to the Kellersons (chillingly played by Paul Stewart and Ruth Roman). Alerted to the dangers of discovery, the Kellersons thus collaborate upon a plan that will keep the boy forever quiet.

The Window, directed by Ted Tetzlaff, may not be horror film in the conventional sense, but aside from being genuinely terrifying, it seems like a wayward child of the Lewton oeuvre. The RKO house style, the Roy Webb score, the wildly expressionistic cinematography, the Cornell Woolrich source, are all good reasons to characterize *The Window* as a thriller in the Lewton vein. Like *The Curse of the Cat People,* Tetzlaff's film focuses upon a child with an overly active imagination, a child whose parents grow increasingly impatient with wild fabrications and fanciful tales. The primal fear generated by Tetzlaff's film often recalls the terror of *The Leopard Man*'s most famous sequence, where the mother, refusing to take her daughter's fears seriously, locks her out of the house. In *The Window,* the father does the reverse and, before going off to his night shift factory job, nearly seals his son's doom by locking the boy in, rather than out. Not only is Tommy locked in his room, but his father also nails the windows shut, leaving Tommy all alone in a cozy firetrap for the next eight hours.

The Kellersons break in and kidnap Tommy, but he escapes. After an exciting chase through dark city streets, subways stations, and back alleys, the Kellersons recapture Tommy who, screaming for help, attracts the attention of a nearby policeman. The Kellersons are suddenly the prototypically wholesome Mom and Dad, misleading the cop to think their "son" is only screaming to get out of a spanking. "Yell all you want, young man," Mrs. Kellerman says in her best Harriet Nelson impression, "that's not going to stop your father from giving you the spanking you deserve."

The Window may have starred a child actor (Bobby Driscoll was already under contract with Disney studios), but Tetzlaff's popular film was obviously fashioned for a purely adult audience. As Fritz Lang's *M* did 18 years before, *The Window* caused adults to come face to face with one of their darkest, most unthinkable fears: that even their children were not safe from murderers within their midst. The film's tense climax takes place in an abandoned and gutted apartment building, one with enough twisted shadows and chiaroscuro effects to rival the expressionism of *Caligari*. The Kellermans chase Tommy through the dilapidated building, around torn walls, hazardous stairwells, and assorted rubble. The boy moves from one hiding place to another, finally choosing a partially standing closet; light shines through the bare slats of one of the closet walls onto Tommy's anxious face as he watches Kellerson come closer. The boy backs up a bit, away from the door he expects will be pulled open at any moment, and nearly falls over something on the floor behind him. Tommy's point-of-view shot, of the shoes and legs of the man he saw murdered, delivers the kind of frisson horror fans dream about.

Children were the targeted audience for the most unusual Lewton imitation of the late 1940s. In early October 1949 (with a Halloween audience in mind), RKO released Walt Disney's animated *The Adventures of Ichabod and Mr. Toad.* The *Legend of Sleepy Hollow* segment of this two-for-one cartoon feature may have gotten its prime inspiration from the Washington Irving story, but the way it delivered its chills was pure Lewton. Someone among *Ichabod and Toad*'s three directors and six storywriters must have remembered the Sleepy Hollow sequence from *The Curse of the Cat People;* most likely, this particular Lewton film (and possibly others, all available through RKO) was screened by the Disney team. The Lewton touch is unmistakably present in the animated film.

After Ichabod leaves the Halloween party, the chills begin. Ichabod reluctantly rides his sluggish horse into the dark forest, hearing the plaintive cries of the wind and the intrusive creaking of trees rubbing against one another in the shifting breeze. There is the occasional shriek of a bird. (Disney eliminates or limits the score music through this portion of the sequence.) Ichabod whistles in an attempt to brace himself against his darkest fears, Bram Bones's Halloween story about the Headless Horseman still fresh in his mind. Soon all we hear is Ichabod's whistling, the accompanying sounds of the wind, and the slow cadence of the horse's hoofbeats (the latter recalling the sound of Cabman Gray's horse in *The Body Snatcher*). A sharp scream echoes through the night, and Ichabod sees before him a grotesque hooded ghost with glowing eyes and outstretched skeletal arms. Before our hero can recover from his paralysis of fright, the moon peeks out from behind a passing cloud, revealing the spectre to be nothing more than a dead tree, its eyes two white moths now flying in different directions.

Although Ichabod is temporarily relieved, he soon becomes again intimidated by the sights and sounds around him. Everywhere he looks he sees menacing images. The clouds in the sky look like two dark hands ready to strangle the moon. Ichabod's paranoia increases as he begins to imagine the chanting of his name ("Ichabod, Ichabod, Ichabod") in the sounds of crickets and frogs. The baleful moans of a women's choir fill the air, but as our hero passes, we see the source of the ghostly sound: the hollow chambers of swamp reeds catching the wind.

Disney's haunted forest is a place of dark poetry for those with the courage to appreciate it (reportedly, many children in the audience were terrified, some becoming hysterical). Ichabod's passing flushes out a crow, and the bird flies into the sky, its cries carrying into the night what seems to be a fading repetition of a single word: "Beware, beware, beware." Ichabod hears the galloping hoofs of what he assumes to be the approach of the Headless

Horseman, but it is only another Lewton "bus," here caused by a row of wind-driven cattails thumping against a hollow log (paralleling the tire chains of *Curse*). (It should be mentioned that nowhere in the Irving story is there any false scare associated with the sound of a galloping horse.) The Lewton approach to terror continues until Ichabod meets up with the Headless Horseman, at which time the sequence shifts into a lengthy chase (drawing inspiration from the kind of sight gags popularized by Mack Sennett) that is as exhilarating as it is funny.

Although most of the 1940s Lewton facsimiles came from Hollywood, there were a few from the British film industry as well. The 1945 omnibus of horror, *Dead of Night* (produced at Britain's Ealing Studios and based on stories by E.F. Benson and H.G. Wells), had marked the lifting of a ten-year national moratorium on horror movies. Although *Dead of Night*'s approach to terror had more in common with the Lewton films than it did with the conventional Universal monster opuses, in all fairness it must be said that the British horror omnibus also owed considerable debt to Jules Duvivier's 1943 *Flesh and Fantasy*, an uncharacteristic Universal release with a decidedly European flair.

At least one of *Dead of Night*'s four directors, Alberto Cavalcanti (a Brazilian director working in England), had participated in the cult of young British filmmakers who pedaled a single print of Lewton's *The Seventh Victim* all over London during the war. It was Cavalcanti who directed two of *Dead of Night*'s vignettes, including the famous sequence about the mad ventriloquist. In *Classics of the Horror Film*, William K. Everson writes: "Like the Val Lewton films which certainly influenced it, *Dead of Night* avoids outright statement and concentrates on suggestion, using a skeptical psychiatrist as a figure of reason and scientific fact who, finally, cannot prevail against the unexplained forces of the supernatural. . . . The horror creeps up on the audience slowly, engulfing it; the terror by implication only."

As in the later British horror compilations (produced in the '60s and '70s by Amicus), *Dead of Night*'s five stories are given a framing device. The big difference between this film and the Amicus pictures, however, is that here the framing device is as terrifying as any of the horror vignettes. Mervyn Johns plays a neurotic architect who is summoned to the country house about which he has been dreaming. When he tells the owner and nearby guests about his dream—going so far as to correctly predict what some of the people are about to say—the fascinated guests (including a psychiatrist) respond by sharing their own experiences with the supernatural. Before they break into their own stories, the architect informs them that his dream turns into a nightmare shortly after the arrival of another guest, a woman.

The vignettes range in quality and intent, one of them (the H.G. Wells segment) is even played for laughs. The first segment, based on "The Bus Conductor" by E.F. Benson, tells the story of a race car driver who is hospitalized after his car crashes. Alone in his hospital room, the patient looks out his window and sees a horse-drawn hearse; with an inviting smile, the hearse driver looks directly into the patient's eyes and announces, "Room for one more!" After being released from the hospital, the man is about to get on a bus until he recognizes the smiling driver: "Room for one more!" He refrains from boarding the vehicle and is thereby spared from a catastrophic accident that kills every passenger. The other Benson story, "The Room in the Tower" (directed by Cavalcanti) is developed into a short but remarkably eerie vignette about a young girl who encounters the ghost of a murdered little boy.

The best two vignettes were original stories by screenwriters T.E.B. Clarke, John Baines, and Angus MacPhail. The mirror sequence, directed by Robert Hamer, is an effective tale about a woman who buys her husband an antique mirror that is capable of reflecting visions from the previous owner's past. The husband becomes obsessed with the mirror while his wife investigates the antique's background and discovers that the previous owner had strangled his wife in the presence of the mirror. In *Classics of the Horror Film,* author William K. Everson calls the mirror sequence, "perhaps the single most effective ghost story ever brought to the screen."

Best of all is the last segment, directed by Cavalcanti. This masterpiece of psychological terror concerns a psychotic ventriloquist (Michael Redgrave) whose dummy, Hugo, begins to exhibit independent behavior. As Hugo continues to take on a mind of his own, making insulting remarks to whomever he pleases, the ventriloquist must bear the brunt of the dummy's actions. On one occasion, Hugo's barbed retort leads to the ventriloquist getting punched in the jaw. When Hugo prefers the company of a visiting American ventriloquist, Redgrave's mind snaps. Thereafter Hugo is capable of anything, including walking about on his own and biting the hand of his master. After Redgrave shoots the American ventriloquist, he finds himself in a padded cell, only able to converse with Hugo's voice.

Finally, with all the stories told, the architect's prediction comes true when a female guest arrives late. The nightmare is about to begin. The architect (like the man in the mirror) suddenly feels compelled to strangle someone, and the psychiatrist is the closest at hand. Here the editing reaches a frenzied pace as the architect runs through the house while characters from the various stories (including a perambulating Hugo) keep popping up in ghastly corpselike makeup everywhere he turns. As these apparations converge upon him, the architect lies on the floor screaming.

He wakes up in his bed, his wife by his side. He tells her of his dream as he prepares himself for work. Dismissing the dream, he gets in his car and drives to his next assignment. When, within sight of his destination, he puts on the brakes and, dumbfounded, sees a very familiar country house, we realize that we have made a perfect loop back to the movie's first image.

The next year Lewtonesque moments turned up in a number of British films, including *Green for Danger* (Sidney Gilliat) and, especially, *Great Expectations* (David Lean). Hands down, the most frightening 1946 British film was Michael Powell's adaptation of Rumer Godden's novel, *Black Narcissus.* This story of a group of Anglo-Catholic nuns who are sent to a makeshift convent high in the Himalayas builds its terror gradually. For its first hour *Black Narcissus* is an absorbing and compelling drama-adventure about cultural and spiritual clashes amidst an exotic setting; it seems to be anything but a horror film until, as its title implies, things take a decidedly dark turn.

An extraordinarily beautiful and altogether terrifying film, *Black Narcissus* continues to be overlooked by genre critics ("A horror film in a convent?"). Make no mistake: while *Black Narcissus*'s charm, class, and breathtaking Technicolor photography belie its horror associations, its last reel has delivered raw terror to many an unsuspecting viewer. Deborah Kerr is superb as the young Mother Superior, and Kathleen Byron, as the increasingly mad Sister Ruth, is simply unforgettable. Everything goes wrong at this convent, and Sister Ruth's plunge into dementia provides an apt symbol for Christianity's downfall amidst the rugged climes of the Himalayas. As Sister Ruth's breakdown takes its gradual course, we see her creeping around corners, spying on her workmates, becoming increasingly more insubordinate. Finally, the woman tears off her nun's habit, dons a slinky, sexy dress, adorns her face with makeup and lipstick, and goes out on the prowl. Leaving the convent, Ruth embarks upon an eerie walk ("bus" included) through a summer forest filled with the beat of native drums. When Ruth returns to the convent (intent upon murdering the Mother Superior), her wraithlike form blends into the dark surroundings, recalling the image of the mad woman in *Isle of the Dead.* Our last look at Sister Ruth, just as she is about to pounce upon her victim, provides us with as horrific an image as any from *Carnival of Souls* or *Night of the Living Dead.*

Reportedly, the Lewton influence can be found in three other British films: *House of Darkness* (Oswald Mitchell, 1947), *The Fatal Night* (Mario Zampi, 1948), and *Dark Interval* (Charles Saunders, 1950). Although none of these titles were available at the time of this writing, *The Fatal Night* sounds particularly appetizing. According to Phil Hardy's *Encyclopedia of the Horror Movies,* the story is about two impoverished Englishmen who con a wealthy American into accepting a bet that forces him to spend a night alone in a haunted room. Hardy reports, "Locked in with a candle, a match and a loaded revolver, the healthily skeptical American happily settles down to read the (thoughtfully provided) history of the haunting which tells of a gruesome murder involving two women. But when his candle blows out, his imagination starts to work, the ghastly apparitions begin, and he empties his revolver to absolutely no effect. . . . The neat little yarn is all the more effective in that it makes no bones about the con from the outset, then shades gradually into areas of ambiguity where some of the macabre visions must be either real or a product of the terrified imagination."

It is curious that Phil Hardy's encyclopedia includes no entry for *The Queen of Spades* (1948); this oft-neglected dark fantasy directed by Thorold Dickinson is imperative viewing for any fan of the Lewton series. *The Queen of Spades* is the most Lewtonesque British chiller of the 1940s for three good reasons: its Russian source of inspiration (a novel by Alexander Pushkin), its remarkably literate (if occasionally verbose) script, and its subtle, psychological approach to the building of terror.

Horror writer Robert Bloch once wrote a memorable article called "Calling Dr. Caligari" that appeared in the summer 1953 issue of a small press quarterly called *Fantastic Worlds* (the article gained more attention 10 years later when it was reprinted in Forrest J. Ackeman's *Famous Monsters of Filmland*). In "Calling Dr. Caligari," Bloch chose his top 15 moments of "pure horror" in the cinema; the 15 films that provided these superlative set pieces of terror (and this was 1953, remember) were *Cat People, Mad Love, The Stranger on the Third Floor, The Cabinet of Dr. Caligari, Waxworks, King Kong, The Phantom of the Opera, Freaks, Mystery of the Wax Museum, The Mad Doctor, Dead of Night, The Uninvited, Dracula, Great Expectations,* and *The Queen of Spades.* (Not too surprisingly, all but one of these films *[The Mad Doctor]* have been mentioned in this volume.)

The Queen of Spades surely deserves its place on Bloch's "pure horror" list. The Rodney Ackland/Arthur Boys script tells the story of Surovin (Anton Walbrook), an ambitious soldier who is willing to do anything to elevate his position in Russian society. He goes to a bookstore and comes across a dusty volume, whereupon a weird shopkeeper (looking like he stepped out of an E.C. horror comic book) announces:

> This is a very rare book. I wouldn't recommend it to everyone. Tells of strange things that some say are better left alone. . . . There are plenty of people who believe in things neither looked for nor heard of. What means these premonitions, these hauntings, these apparitions, these tales of horror? Believe me, there are things to be seen the eye has not seen and things to be heard that the ear hasn't heard. Who knows what you may learn from it? Why you might end up gaining a fortune or losing your precious soul. [Cackling laughter]

Surovin looks at the title page of the book: *The Strange Secrets of the Count de Saint Germain* ("Containing the true stories of people who sold their souls in return for wealth, power or influence"). Bringing the book back to his modest apartment, he begins reading Chapter Four, "The Secret of the Cards," which tells the story via flashback of Countess R— —, a local aristocrat who 60 years before made such a pact in exchange for the winning cards of three consecutive hands of faro. In order to hold up her end of the bargain, Countess R— — must visit the God-forsaken Dulgaruky Palace, which is surrounded by a huge imposing wall adorned with facsimiles of human skulls. The palace and surrounding wall look as if they had been built by an earlier race (like the "old ones" from H.P. Lovecraft's Cthulhu Mythos). Within the palace the murky hallways are dark and menacing. The young Countess makes her way to a certain door, but when she opens it there is nothing but a black void. She screams and a match cut shows the neighing horses awaiting her outside the wall. Next we see an alchemy laboratory, where the hands of a man who remains faceless are busily creating a small wax effigy of the Countess. There are other such wax figures displayed about the room, all of them representing people who have previously given up their souls for wealth and fame. When the Countess leaves the Dulgaruky Palace, the camera simply tracks her long shadow stretching before her on the ground. Surovin closes the book.

Knowing that the woman is still alive, but very unapproachable (and in her eighties), Surovin plots to gain access to her estate. He begins by wooing the Countess's young nurse/companion, Lizavetta (Yvonne Mitchell), whenever he sees her at the market, and he quickly wins her heart. Soon they begin meeting in secret.

Countess R— — (wonderfully played by Dame Edith Evans) is now a hateful, doddering old woman; she is so frightened of dying that she takes it out on everyone around her, especially Lizavetta. She is constantly nodding off in her chair and refuses to be put to bed for fear of dying in her sleep. She has a crippled leg, and every time she walks we hear the shuffle of her crinoline skirt and the thumping of her cane.

One night while Surovin is secretly in the mansion (on the pretext of a romantic tryst with Lizavetta), he steals his way up to the Countess's room, finds her sleeping in a chair, wakes her, and pleads for the secret of the cards. The Countess looks at him in disbelief and says not a word. Desperate, Surovin puts a gun to her head and demands the secret, telling her, "I'll take your sin upon my own soul." The frightened woman has a coronary, slumps in her chair, and dies. The Countess's death-mask visage is a frightful one, her mouth open, her eyes wide. The baleful howl of a wolf is heard, followed by a chorus of barking dogs. Next there is an extreme close-up of the Countess's dead eyes filling the screen, staring in the soldier's direction, accusingly. Surovin runs downstairs and, no longer interested in maintaining his romantic masquerade, tells Lizavetta everything; though she can no longer stand the sight of him, she lays out his avenue of escape.

Surovin must go back to the Countess's room to make use of her secret exit, but he dreads having to see her face, her dead eyes, once again. He reaches the woman's room, and no sooner is he through the door than he is again confronted by the rictus stare of the Countess, which sears itself into his memory. Successful in his escape, Surovin heads back to his apartment, opens his mysterious book, and reads a chapter called "The Dead Shall Give Up Their Secrets."

The next day he attends the Countess's wake, waiting in line as some ancient women pay their last respects. Surovin finally gets his turn and, bending over toward the corpse's face as if to kiss it, asks one more time for the secret of the cards. The corpse's immobile face fills the screen as the camera takes Surovin's point-of-view. The camera holds and holds and then the Countess's eyes snap open. Surovin screams, making a spectacle of himself. As he runs out the door, onlookers are baffled. The corpse's eyes are closed.

Surovin retreats to his apartment. Visibly shaken, he tries to compose himself. He almost succeeds until he hears in the hall outside his apartment door a sound he recognizes: the shuffling of a crinoline skirt and the tapping of a cane. He rallies the courage to investigate, but there is nothing in the hall. The shuffling and tapping are now heard near the window, and a woman's shadow is silhouetted against the curtain; Surovin pulls the curtain to one side and sees nothing. Suddenly his apartment is filled with fierce swirling winds; objects fly about the room—bedcovers, papers, clothing, even books—a veritable indoor tornado, causing the room to go into complete disarray. Just as suddenly, the wind halts and things snap back to normal, as if the entire phenomenon was a wild hallucination or a dream. All is quiet, with everything back in its proper place, neat and tidy.

The dead woman's disembodied voice finally reveals the secret of the cards, the three winning cards being a three, a seven, and an ace, all of them spades. Surovin is a nervous wreck when he challenges a rival to a game of faro. He puts up his entire savings, as well as some money he has stolen, and wins the first game with a three of spades. Doubling the stakes, he wins the second game with a seven of spades. One last time he doubles the stakes and loses to the queen of spades. His mind snaps, and he bellows out a tortured scream. A montage of ghastly images, including a kaleidoscopic vision of the Countess's eyes, blasts his sight. Surovin is carried away, hopelessly insane. He will spend the rest of his life in an asylum muttering "Three, seven, ace, three, seven, queen!"

The Queen of Spades is one of the best-acted horror films of the 1940s. Anton Walbrook is absolutely brilliant, especially in the terror scenes, and his performance rises to magnificent heights during the nervewracking faro game. Walbrook's portrayal of Surovin should have been heralded over the past several decades as one of the great horror film performances. Instead, it's been completely ignored. (It isn't as if Walbrook was a stranger to the genre. he was in the original version of *Gaslight* [1939, also directed by Thorold Dickinson], and, before that, as Anton Wohlbrueck, he played the lead role in Germany's 1935 version of *The Student of Prague.*) Edith Evans is also wonderful as the morally bankrupt hag in aristocratic clothes, terrified by the certainty of her own death. Also fine are Yvonne Mitchell, Ronald Howard, and Anthony Dawson. Dawson, who plays the Countess's nephew, would play a male variation of the Countess in *Curse of the Were-*

wolf, a 1960 Hammer film that was obviously influenced by *The Queen of Spades.*

Thorold Dickinson's direction is first rate. So are Georges Auric's musical score (Auric had been *Dead of Night*'s composer), Jack Clayton's art direction, and Otto Heller's photography. It is anybody's guess why *The Queen of Spades* is overlooked by the vast majority of horror film surveys. If genre scholars can embrace such nonsupernatural entries as *The Tower of London, The Seventh Victim,* and *Bedlam* as three of their own, one wonders why they continue to ignore such a classy supernatural fright fest as *The Queen of Spades.*

In 1950 the horror film was virtually nonexistent, but mimicking its legion of perambulating zombies and resurrected corpses, the genre simply refused to remain in its grave. Although no one knew it at the time, within a year the horror film would be reborn in a new guise and its metamorphosis would be spearheaded by the most influential of all the postwar Lewton homages.

As space operas like *Rocketship XM* and *Destination Moon* captivated a new generation of theatergoers, auteur director Howard Hawks was bridging the gap between two genres: science fiction and horror. The sci-fi/horror hybrid, which was born with Hawks's film *The Thing from Another World,* remains as viable a cinematic form today as it was during its inception two generations ago.

Although Howard Hawks maintained his personal vision in a variety of genres, he also took his cues from other filmmakers. Hawks's career is full of homages to other filmmakers: *Ball of Fire* (Frank Capra), *Red River* (John Ford), *Sergeant York* (William Dieterle), *To Have and Have Not* (Michael Curtiz), *The Big Sleep* (Edward Dmytryk), *I Was a Male War Bride* (Billy Wilder), *Gentlemen Prefer Blondes* (George Cukor), and so on. Somehow Hawks was able to emulate other filmmakers without sacrificing his personal vision. In 1950 he was on the RKO lot, preparing a film that would exploit an audience's fear of the unseen.

Hawks took his typical adventure film stance in his provision of many men (and one or two women) working together for a common cause, once again using the people-in-peril motif to champion his ethos of professionalism. In *The Thing,* Hawks eschewed his usual big-star-as-leader approach (usually reserved for Cary Grant, Humphrey Bogart, Gary Cooper, or John Wayne) by casting second-string supporting player Kenneth Tobey in the lead role. By avoiding star performers, Hawks was able to provide the purest example of his "group" aesthetic ever filmed. Although *The Thing*'s direction is credited to Christian Nyby (Hawk's editor), most film historians contend that Hawks (who is only credited as producer) is the prime author of the film. (In *Filmgoer's Companion,* Leslie Halliwell tells us, "there were also rumours that Orson Welles had a hand.") It is worth noting that Hawks's hands-on involvement as a producer very much echoed Lewton's own approach to film production. Whether or not Hawks made a study of the RKO horror films at his disposal in the studio vaults, it is certain that in giving *The Thing* its frightening edge, he borrowed heavily from Lewton's politics of terror.

We make no attempt to rival the reams of coverage already given to *The Thing.* It remains one of the best and most famous applications of the undisclosed horror approach. By keeping the alien off camera, Hawks avoids our getting a good look at the laughable Karloff-in-a-space-suit costume that James Arness wears. We see the Thing through blocks of ice and raging blizzard conditions, as a shadow on the wall and as an impression in the ice, we see it covered in kerosene flames and juggling blinding arcs of electricity amidst the black smoke of burnt vegetable matter, but at no time do we ever get a clear view of the creature. The film's most horrifying confrontation with the Thing, the infamous greenhouse door scene, gives us our first direct look at the creature, but so brief is our glimpse that its appearance is once again left to the imagination.

The Thing's resurrection from the block of ice, the result of an ill-advised placement of an electric blanket, is played in grand Lewton fashion, in a manner not entirely unlike the resurrection scene in *Isle of the Dead.* The atmosphere of Hawks's film is dark and claustrophobic; the feelings we get are those of entrapment. Hawks has his characters speak in hushed tones during moments of extreme tension, just as Tourneur an Robson did in their direction of the Lewton films. He even throws in a frightening Lewton "bus" (the dead sled dog in the greenhouse locker). Like a ripping good horror radio play, the film's suspense is bolstered by an imaginative use of sound; we hear geiger counters, ominous crashes, fierce winds, radios, ventilating fans, airplane engines, thermite bomb blasts, electric arcs, gunfire, barking dogs, unearthly howls, and the staccato delivery of the urgent dialogue. If that is not enough, there is always Dimitri Tiomkin's transcendent score, one of the very best and most recognizable pieces of horror music in cinema history.

The Thing is embellished with an enormous amount of scientific jargon and military repartee that is used to establish the interactions of the group and to create conflict between scientific pursuit and military bureaucracy. Charles Lederer's script likely breaks the record for the amount of dialogue jammed into a 90-minute film, and yet, as a result of Hawks's characteristic overlapping banter, this steady stream of words is, paradoxically, largely responsible for much of the film's suspense.

Although *The Thing* is considered a science fiction classic, Hawks was obviously more interested in its horror aspects than he was in its science fiction trappings. Surely that was the attitude of RKO's publicity department, whose posters prefaced the film's title with the bold question: "Natural or Supernatural?" Hawks wanted a horror film that would exploit the xenophobia of a nation, and that is exactly what he delivered. The arctic location and its proximity to Russia took the Cold War into consideration (the original John

W. Campbell novelette is set in the Antarctic). Could it be that Hawks's alien represents Communism? Some may have thought so; the alien's one friend, Dr. Carrington, is the only one who wears a furry Russian hat.

Charles Lederer's screenplay was not faithful to the John W. Campbell novella, *Who Goes There,* upon which it was based. Rather than involve himself with the exhaustive special effects that would have been needed to accurately portray Campbell's shape-shifting alien, Lederer and Hawks chose the less-is-more approach, drawing associations from numerous classic horror films. Not only was the creature made to resemble Karloff's Frankenstein monster, but Hawks mined further horror movie associations by turning the alien into a blood-drinking vampire.

Often imitated but seldom equaled, Hawks's film set a sci-fi/horror precedent with its "last stand" climax, making use of a suspense formula that would become fairly commonplace within the genre. A carryover from the Western and the war film, the "last stand" approach confines our protagonists to a shelter that is under attack by an enemy/alien force. Later examples of this genre prototype include *Field Without a Face* (1958), *The Killer Shrews* (1959), *Day of the Triffids* (1963), *The Birds* (1962), *Island of Terror* (1966), *Night of the Living Dead,* (1968), and countless others.

When it becomes clear how much influence *The Thing* has had upon the cinema of the fantastic, only then can we begin to appreciate the scope of Val Lewton's legacy. The film's roving reporter, Ned Scott, said it best: "The mind boggles."

The Thing began playing the theaters in April 1951; had it been released just a few weeks earlier, Val Lewton might have had the opportunity to see it.

EIGHTEEN

Closed Doors

I didn't see Val a lot during his last two or three years; we just didn't run into each other. But after he made his success at RKO with his high-quality horror films, he kept being urged by some of his working associates to move up, move out and get away from the B-pictures and do A-pictures. . . . I think Val was frustrated by this encouragement to move up to the A pictures when he was really happiest doing what he was doing. He felt more fulfilled doing his small horror films. That was when he felt most productive and most creative.

—Robert Wise
(from a 1991 interview
with the author)

If producing the RKO series had been artistically gratifying, it had never been easy. Still, there were darker days ahead. Val Lewton, the man who built his reputation upon fear, was about to experience the ultimate earthly nightmare: unending frustration.

The year 1945 had gotten off to a grim start when Lewton's only front office ally, Charles Koerner, took ill and died of leukemia on February 2, 1945. Koerner had been temporarily replaced by corporate president, N. Peter Rathvon, until a qualified successor could be found. In spite of the inner turmoil at RKO, the very successful May 1945 release of *The Body Snatcher* gave every indication that, for Lewton, the worm had finally turned. And then, just days before *Bedlam* was to go into production, Lewton's good cheer was checked by the sudden death of his aunt, Alla Nazimova. Nazimova had briefly returned to motion pictures in 1940, turning in fine performances in character roles in *Escape* (1940), *Blood and Sand* (1941), *In Our Time* (1944), *The Bridge of San Luis Rey* (1944), and *Since You Went Away* (1944), the latter scripted and produced by David Selznick. During her brief but celebrated comeback, she occasionally visited Lewton's RKO office. Nazimova had never been happy about her nephew working in the horror ghetto (when offered a private screening of *Cat People*, she declined), but the two of them had maintained a good relationship over the years and Lewton was deeply affected by her passing.

Although the death of his aunt had a sobering effect upon the RKO producer, for a while his future continued to look bright. By July 1945, with *Bedlam* in production and a *Life* magazine article in the works, it appeared that Lewton was finally about to reap the benefits of success: enough money upon which to live comfortably and enough power to make the films he wanted to make. The trade press was already buzzing with news of Lewton's upcoming RKO productions. One of the proposed projects, *Die Gently Stranger,* was to be a suspense thriller based on a novel by Russian writer David Tutaeff. In a July issue of the *Hollywood Reporter,* Lewton announced: "Water is the menace. We are using the average person's fear of the awe-inspiring ocean and of being lost in a fog as a motivating force. One of our situations finds a lone oarsman completely cut off from everything he understands, and the result, I hope, will be psychological horror at its best."

Lewton was also slated to produce RKO's joint efforts with the British J. Arthur Rank group, including *If This Be Known,* a murder mystery with Dick Powell, and *Father Malachy's Miracle,* a story about a Roman Catholic priest which, like *The Body Snatcher,* was set in Edinburgh. According to the *Hollywood Reporter,* "*Father Malachy's Miracle* comes off the RKO shelf and will be produced by Lewton. Since Barry Fitzgerald, who was being paged for the title role, declined, Lewton is rewriting the script to minimize the priest role and building up the male romantic lead."

The oddest of Lewton's proposed projects was *The Lawyer,* a big-budget musical (based on a play by Ferenc Molnar) that was scheduled to go into production immediately following the shooting of *Bedlam.* By then, however, Lewton's RKO career had begun to slip into a limbo of perpetual misfortune. The producer's temporary good standing with the front office suffered considerable duress when on August 26, 1945, a little over a week after *Bedlam* was under wraps, the plagiarism case against *The Ghost Ship* came to trial (see Chapter Ten), ending in a victory for the plaintiffs. That Lewton was poised to make a movie called *The Lawyer* during this juncture in his career must have been a bitter pill to swallow. To compound the irony, *The Lawyer* was itself destined to become entangled in legalities over film rights, causing numerous postponements. The film was scheduled to go into production on December 18, 1945, with director William Cameron Menzies at the helm, when litigation over film rights brought further delay. Menzies left for greener pastures while Lewton waited for the courts to determine the film's fate. On February 26, 1946 (two months before *Bedlam*'s release), the *Hollywood Reporter* announced: "RKO's *The Lawyer* has been put back on production schedule with an expanded budget and will be produced as an 'A' feature by Val Lewton."

While Lewton was facing one frustration after another at RKO, the

Val Lewton.

February 25, 1946, issue of *Life* magazine hit the stands. In the four-page spread on *Bedlam,* Lewton made his livelihood at the studio seem like a lark:

> No grisly stuff for us. No masklike faces hardly human, with gnashing teeth and hair standing on end. No creaking physical manifestations. No horror piled on horror. You can't keep up horror that's long sustained. It becomes something to laugh at. But take a sweet love story, or a story of sexual

> antagonisms, about people like the rest of us, not freaks, and cut in your horror here and there by suggestion, and you've got something. . . . Our formula is simple. A love story, three scenes of suggested horror and one of actual violence. Fadeout. It's all over in less than 70 minutes.

Unfortunately, Lewton's rather belated time in the spotlight was over almost as quickly. In March, Lewton announced to the press that *The Lawyer,* now retitled *The Biggest Thief of Paris,* was set to begin production in November. Although he busied himself with some Selznick-like attention to the proper plump weight of the can-can dancers, such concerns proved futile; within a month or two, RKO jettisoned the project. The same fate awaited Lewton's "psychological horror" opus, *Die Gently Stranger.*

And then there were the J. Arthur Rank/RKO plans. Although the original plans called for Lewton to journey to London, bringing with him a director, writer, cutter, and unit business manager, the chaos of reorganization within RKO prohibited such an adventurous endeavor. As a result, the proposed RKO/Rank projects (*If This Be Known* and *Father Malachy's Miracle*) were abandoned. (Later in the year Rank would release Michael Powell's *Black Narcissus.*)

But by this time Lewton had another promising prospect on the back burner. In September 1945, the *Hollywood Report* had announced that Val Lewton's next RKO project, scheduled to go into production in early 1946, was to be a pirate saga called *Blackbeard,* starring Boris Karloff in the title role. For a while, Lewton, Ardel Wray, and Mark Robson were engaged in collaborating upon an original script for the film (presumably with Robson slated to direct), but plans for *Blackbeard* remained in limbo and the project was subsequently dropped.

Meanwhile, RKO was in an unruly state of affairs. Charles Koerner's temporary replacement, N. Peter Rathvon, was not much help in alleviating the daily crises that seemed to plague the studio during his 1946 tenure. According to DeWitt Bodeen, "Val became rather paranoid later [in his life] but he really did have opposition at the studio, especially after Mr. Koerner died. . . . The people who came in then as heads of production were rather antagonistic towards him. Val certainly *thought* they were" (Brosnan, *The Horror People*).

In spite of his friction with the front office and his frustration over aborted projects, Lewton was able to live quite comfortably on $700-a-week. By this time, according to Lucy Lewton's account in *My Brother,* the Lewtons' hired help included in addition to Minnie, their long-term housemaid, "a gardener who doubled as a chauffeur, a laundress and two maids." Lucy tells of her brother's attendance at a celebrity lunch at Hearst's Castle in San Simeon:

> Wives were not invited. Val got Ruth to buy him (or rent) a formal full dress suit, shirt and studs. He was put up in a cottage on the estate, having a big

> double bed in which it was said Cardinal Richelieu had died. Val appeared at the luncheon in the long baronial hall, dressed in his formal attire only to find that the other guests wore jeans and checked shirts, ranch costumes. And the lunch table was set with informal checked table cloth, the food was hamburgers and ketchup.

In a 1992 interview with the author, Val Edwin Lewton offered some recollections of his childhood during those post–*Bedlam* years:

> I didn't see my father's movies until around the time of *Bedlam*. Early on I wasn't allowed to see them because they were considered too violent, too exciting. It was at around this time that I remember going to the studio and looking at the *Bedlam* set. I also remember watching another unit shoot *The Spanish Main* with Maureen O'Hara. (I was impressed by the fact that she couldn't remember her lines, and they kept shooting the damn thing over and over.)
>
> I also can recall how much my father enjoyed watching films. There were times he would watch movies all day at work, then come home, and we'd all go out to a movie theater. He was a terrific fan and he told me he "dreamed movies," that his dreams had cuts and fades, closeups and the whole bit.
>
> He loved comics, too, and was always reading them; "Terry and the Pirates" was a favorite of his. He believed that comics were a precursor to the movies. I clearly remember him talking about this, telling me he learned so much about movies by the way the comic artists moved from one scene to another.
>
> On weekends we'd go down to the boat with my mother and sail. Sometimes they would have parties, and we'd have a lot of different guests. Jacques [Tourneur] was often there, and he would bring people over sometimes; I can remember Burt Lancaster. Peter Viertel, who was much younger than my father, was often there; so was Alan Napier. I remember going skiing with the Napiers; they had a cabin up at Arrowhead or Big Bear. And then there were a lot of people who just hung around: Tommy Gries, Josef and Florence Mischel, sometimes Mark Robson or Robert Wise. Fred Zinnemann was a good friend, too.
>
> But my father's career wasn't going very well, so it wasn't an entirely happy time. He felt alienated and depressed, and he was having trouble getting his projects off the ground.

Because he had not been able to produce a film in nearly a year, Lewton compensated by working with his hands. He was fond of carpentry, and, using a lathe, he made an assortment of toys and furniture pieces. When his boat was destroyed from a fire (as a result of someone's carelessly thrown cigarette), he set about building a new one, spending weeks trying to carve a one-piece keel. In *My Brother*, Lucy Lewton tells of the time his wife "came to see how Val was getting along and found him in tears. 'The keel broke—now it will not be a one-piece keel!'" Even Lewton's pastimes, driven by his dire need for some sense of achievement, were becoming exercises in frustration.

Finally, a most promising RKO project was beginning to gel: *Not So Blind*, based on a thriller novel by Mitchell Wilson. Better yet, the film was to be directed by Jean Renoir, a filmmaker with a visual style not unlike the great French pictorialist, Maurice Tourneur. Renoir had come to Hollywood shortly after the war broke out in Europe and had directed such maverick but critically praised films as *Swamp Water, This Land Is Mine, The Southerner,* and *Diary of a Chambermaid. Not So Blind,* Renoir's fifth American film—now retitled *Desperate Woman* and categorized as a "psychological thriller"—was a project for which Val Lewton was particularly well suited. Renoir came to Lewton's house several times; the two of them were kindred spirits from the start. They collaborated on casting and finally came up with Joan Bennett, Robert Ryan, Charles Bickford, and Ann Richards. *Desperate Woman* was set to begin shooting in October 1946, and Lewton was eager to begin working again. When October came around, however, the Renoir film had been postponed to November; in November it was pushed ahead to the spring.

Fate intervened, and a few days after the November postponement, Lewton began feeling ill. Although his illness was first diagnosed as exhaustion, it was later discovered that Lewton had suffered a mild heart attack. For a time, he was required to limit his activities and take time off from work. When he finally returned to his regular routine at RKO, however, he discovered that his time away had further diminished his reputation among his studio peers and he became increasingly disillusioned.

DeWitt Bodeen recalls: "When he had that first heart attack I was working with Harriet Parson's unit . . . on *The Enchanted Cottage*. Later I went to see him at his office, when they had moved to the ground floor . . . and he was very sad-looking. He grew worse and worse as time went by. His feelings of persecution increased" (Brosnan, *Horror People*).

(*Desperate Woman,* having undergone another title change, was eventually made and released in 1947 as *Woman on the Beach*. It turned out to be Renoir's last American film and the only one among his five to provoke critical scorn. Jack Gross was credited as executive producer.)

As Lewton recovered, he resolved to be done with RKO. Putting out some feelers, he received in the first days of 1947 a fabulous offer from Buddy DeSylva, head of production at Paramount. Lewton still had some clout, and his contract was unusual in that it guaranteed two years salary instead of the customary 13–24 weeks. What's more, the producer's Paramount salary was twice the amount of his RKO earnings. How could he refuse such an offer? What could go wrong?

The first thing Lewton tried to do was to move some members of his RKO unit over to Paramount. Unfortunately, the latter studio had its own employees tagged for Lewton's supervision. All Lewton could manage was the transferral of his loyal secretary, Verna De Mots. In *The Reality of Terror,* Joel E. Siegel mentions the "melancholy farewell party at RKO at which the producer was given an elegantly bound set of screenplays of the eleven films he had made there."

With the salary increase and the guarantee of "A" budget features, Lewton eagerly threw himself into his work. Drawing inspiration from his days with Selznick (as well as from David Lean's critically acclaimed 1946 release, *Great Expectations*), Lewton began to prepare an adaptation of one of his favorite Dickens novels, *The Cricket and the Hearth*. Although the novel proved difficult to script, he felt that his work on Selznick's two Dickens adaptations, *David Copperfield* and *A Tale of Two Cities*, made him well suited for the job; at the end of six months' toil, Lewton finally completed what he believed to be an inspired screenplay. Almost as soon as he submitted it, however, Paramount shelved the project, perhaps feeling that David Lean (whose *Oliver Twist* was in the works) already had the corner on the Dickens market. (Lewton was well aware of the British director's work; David Lean was at the time one of his favorite film directors. In a 1991 interview, Robert Wise told the author, "I remember very distinctly the six of us—Val and his wife, Mark Robson and his wife, myself and my wife—going to see David Lean's *Brief Encounter* (1945) not too long after the war and how impressed and moved we were by that film. We all went next door to a delicatessen and sat and talked about it for an hour or so.")

Lewton felt that in order to save face and maintain his credibility, he needed to get the ball rolling on another project immediately. To his great dismay, he discovered that the well-earned salary he had been pulling at Paramount (over the six months that he struggled with the Dickens script) would be charged against the budget of his first production. Hurriedly, Lewton reached for a novel by Yolanda Forbes called *Make You a Fine Wife*. He may have seen, in the Forbes novel, an opportunity to produce something like *Brief Encounter*; whatever the reason for his choice, the film (retitled *My Own True Love*) would turn out to be a painful ordeal. Lewton veteran Josef Mischel had collaborated with Ted Strauss on a screenplay, and Compton Bennett, who had been responsible for the acclaimed 1945 British release, *The Seventh Veil*, was to direct. British actress Phyllis Calvert headed the cast, assisted by a distinguished array of other performers, including Melvyn Douglas, Wanda Hendrix, Binnie Barnes, Arthur Shields, Phyllis Morris, and Lewton-vet Alan Napier. But the production was ill-fated from the start.

Suffice it to say that everything that *could* go wrong *did* go wrong. At Paramount, Lewton was a stranger in a strange land. No longer did he have his handpicked employees surrounding him; no longer was there that special communal spirit that characterized Lewton's previous productions at RKO. *My Own True Love* became Lewton's most unwieldy project, its already inflated budget growing by the day as the producer unsuccessfully tried to surmount difficulties concerning script, set design, costumes, shooting schedule, and, most particularly, leading lady, Phyllis Calvert, who, after an altercation with Lewton, walked off the set. It was a troubled production.

Paramount did not know what to do with this misfire. It took the studio a full year to get up the courage to release it; when they did, in September 1948, *My Own True Love* became the first Lewton film ever to lose money. During a year when Paramount was releasing such respectable psychological thrillers as *Sorry, Wrong Number* (Anatole Litvak), *The Big Clock* (John Farrow), *So Evil My Love* (Lewis Allen), and *The Accused* (William Dieterle), the best Lewton was able to deliver was the limp drama *My Own True Love.*

The soap opera plot involves a romance between a London widower and a concentration camp survivor; their relationship is interrupted when the widower's son returns from the war with an amputated leg. The son misreads the woman's concern for him and the friction begins.

While *My Own True Love* was still in postproduction, Lewton devoted time to a project he hoped would reestablish his credibility: *Sainted Sisters,* a comedy (based on an unproduced play) which was set to star Betty Hutton and Diana Lynn. To Lewton's chagrin, the front office relieved him of the property, giving it to William Russell, who went on to film *Sainted Sisters* with Veronica Lake and Joan Caulfield.

His frustration peaking, Lewton hoped to score with another proposal, *A Mask for Lucrezia,* about the youth of Lucrezia Borgia. This was a project he had become excited about, having already commissioned Josef Mischel and Ardel Wray to write the screenplay. Lewton wanted the picture to stay small, to be a character study rather than a period epic. By midfall 1946, however, the Mischel/Wray script did not appeal to the front office, and the property was shelved. Out of desperation, Lewton unsuccessful pleaded for an extra few months to rework the script to his employers' satisfaction.

Paulette Goddard, under contract with Paramount, managed to get a look at Lewton's finished screenplay and demanded to be in *A Mask for Lucrezia.* Lewton had found an ally in Goddard, who had script approval written into her contract and was therefore able to call her terms. But, as it turned out, Paramount wanted the script, but not Lewton's capacity as a producer. Finally, a settlement was reached wherein Lewton relinquished the screenplay, being guaranteed full pay through July 1948 as well as a free option on his *Cricket and the Hearth* rights (so long as he acted within six months of his official termination at Paramount). Lewton was relieved at the prospect of putting Paramount behind him; he packed up and left the studio in March 1948, six months before the release of *My Own True Love.* Fortunately, he would not have to endure the icy glares and flip comments of the Paramount executives while his movie fizzled in every major city in the country. (Lewton's *Lucrezia* script would be revamped by Cyril Hume and Michael Hogan. The resulting film was released in 1948 as *Bride of Vengeance.* Lewton received no credit for his efforts.)

With time on his hands, Lewton began to give serious attention to his pipe dream of one day setting up an independent production unit. He and Mark Robson, while working together on *Blackbeard,* had discussed the prospects of such a venture, and now the out-of-work director was once again showing great interest. Their plan was to attract established talent, deferring salaries until after the film had begun to bring in receipts. Lewton's rationale (stated in a letter to his mother and sister) was this: "All we gamble with is our time and such talents as we are supposed to have. Our whole idea is to make small, good films, not in any sense arty, but with a little more meat than the ordinary Hollywood product" (Siegel, *The Reality of Terror*).

In the meantime, however, the inactive producer needed a source of income. In July, when his Paramount stipend had run its course, Lewton sought work at MGM. He reminded them of his associations with David O. Selznick, brought them up-to-date with his RKO track record, was granted an interview with Louis B. Mayer, and was hired as a studio producer.

Unfortunately, Lewton felt no less alienated at MGM than he did at Paramount. In a July 26, 1948, letter to his mother and sister (included in Siegel's *The Reality of Terror*), Lewton tried to show enthusiasm for his new position, but his report that no one had spoken to him during the entire three weeks he had so far been at MGM was hardly encouraging news. Lewton tried to sound optimistic about his future as an independent filmmaker but the general tone of his letter, overall, reflected a sense of quiet desperation.

At MGM, Lewton immersed himself in an adaptation of Joseph Hergesheimer's *Wild Oranges*, a bittersweet romance taking place in Connecticut, with several scenes aboard a yacht. Many months later, once again in a letter to his mother and sister, Lewton expressed further disgruntlement:

> You ask me for details of my work and I just can't give you any. I'm waiting. And don't let anyone tell you that waiting is a pleasure just because one happens to be on payroll. You may think it cowardly of me, but I can't even write my own stuff. The whole aspect of such waiting is just too corrosive. One even begins to doubt one's own abilities. . . . My days here are undoubtedly numbered [Siegel, *The Reality of Terror*].

In late January 1949, MGM executive Dore Schary appeared with his own original story for a comedy and appointed Lewton to write the screenplay. Lewton had trouble writing a competent script for a story he did not think was any good, and the job took longer than expected. Joel E. Siegel reports that during this time, James Agee had come to MGM studios to do a *Life* article on John Huston's upcoming release, *Asphalt Jungle*. Agee, ever the Lewton adherent, visited Dore Schary's office for a chat. Toward the end of his visit, Agee added: "And, of course, you have one of the three greatest movie makers this country ever produced under contract." Schary had not the slightest notion to whom Agee was referring until he was fed Lewton's name.

Schary's story idea eventually became *Please Believe Me*, but the scripting credit went to Nathaniel Curtis. Norman Taurog directed (his relationship with Lewton went back to their Selznick days [*Adventures of Tom Sawyer*]). Lewton had high hopes at first.

As it turned out, *Please Believe Me* (released in May 1950) was a situation comedy without the comedy. Director Norman Taurog was out of his element. Taurog, a former child actor, built his directing reputation upon films fashioned for child performers, his more notable efforts in this milieu being *Skippy* (1931), *Huckleberry Finn* (1933), *Mrs. Wiggs in the Cabbage Patch* (1934), *The Adventures of Tom Sawyer* (1938), *Boy's Town* (1938), and *Young Tom Edison* (1940). Although there is not a single child in *Please Believe Me,* the adult characters behave in a most juvenile fashion.

The Lewton/Taurog film would have been more palatable as a low-budget film with a negligible cast. *Please Believe Me,* however, was Lewton's most expensive film, featuring such distinguished performers as Deborah Kerr, Robert Walker, Mark Stevens, Peter Lawford, James Whitmore, J. Carrol Naish, and Spring Byington. In a film as slight as *Please Believe Me,* this is a lot of talent to waste. Lewton was correct in feeling a certain derision for Schary's original story; *Please Believe Me*'s forced plot is founded upon a silly misunderstanding that would have been cleared up in minutes had the characters been allowed to behave like real people.

Alison Kirby (Kerr), an English working-class girl, inherits a 50,000 acre ranch from an American cowboy pen pal who is given to telling tall tales. The cowboy does own said amount of land, but all of it is worthless desert property, without the beautiful buildings and the countless head of livestock described in his correspondence. The film's opening five minutes, which conveys the above situation, is admirable in its economy and its humor. But the movie goes completely downhill after that, especially after all its principal players are introduced.

Traveling to America on an ocean-liner to claim her inheritance, Alison must fight off the affections of three wolves. One of them, Terence Keath (Walker), is a gambler in debt who, traveling with a small time gangster, Vince Maran (Whitmore), is out to marry a rich woman so that he can pay the money he owes to the gambling syndicate run by New York crime boss, Lucky Reilly (Naish). The second wolf is Jeremy Taylor (Lawford), a multimillionaire playboy who is plagued by innumerable breach-of-promise suits from scores of women to whom he has proposed. The third wolf is Matthew Kinston (Stevens), a hot-shot attorney who, representing Jeremy Taylor, is there to play watchdog over his client by keeping him away from women. Alison and Kinston fall in love, but when the latter recognizes Keath and Maran as con men, he jumps to the conclusion that Alison is part of their scam to drain money from his millionaire client. One misunderstanding follows another and confusion reigns. *Please Believe Me* tries hard to be in the same league as a Preston Sturges romp, but it does not come close. It would be wrong to say the film is especially awful, but its tiresome plot and pedestrian direction were ill-suited to either romance or comedy. It is the likeliest candidate for Lewton's worst film.

None of the Lewton films, even the very best of the RKO crop, had ever been very successful in the romance department, so it is not surprising that top-heavy romances like *My Own True Love* and *Please Believe Me* would become fairly unremarkable in Lewton's hands.

Genuine romance was flourishing in the Lewton household, however. It was around this time that Nina informed her father that she wished to marry Lee Druckman, a young man who had just graduated from college with a degree in mechanical engineering. Druckman, whose family was Jewish and did not approve of his relationship with a Catholic girl, was currently working in a bicycle store. Lewton accepted Lee, though he showed the typical reluctance of any man about to give his daughter's hand in marriage. Marriage arrangements were made, with the Druckmans' complete disapproval (a situation that somewhat paralleled Lewton's own marriage to Ruth Knapp), and the ceremony was conducted on Lewton's patio by a civil judge. Except for Lee's two sisters, none of the other Druckmans attended the wedding. In *My Brother,* Lucy Lewton informs us:

> Lee was a poor young man, he owned only one dark blue suit which was lost when the dry cleaner's shop burned down. So for the wedding he had to wear Val's suit, which was much too large for him. Val told Ruth to keep the wedding simple, "only a few guests and the family"; instead he went around [telling people], "My daughter is getting married on Saturday. Why don't you come?" The wedding ended up with 75 guests aside from the family. Ruth had to order champagne three times and borrow plates from neighbors. Knowing that Lee was a poor young man just starting out Ruth asked Val if they should perhaps give Ruth Nina a dowry, as is done in Europe for wealthy brides. Val said, "You arrange it, banks bore me." That saying, "Banks bore me," became an often used phrase in the family ever after.

By 1949 the careers of Robert Wise and Mark Robson were on the rise. After a few more "B' films for RKO, Wise had made his successful "A" budget debut with *Blood on the Moon* (1948) and was currently receiving critical plaudits for his boxing exposé, *The Set Up.* Robson (in his first film since *Bedlam*) had a huge box-office hit with *Champion* (another boxing film), produced by Stanley Kramer and starring Kirk Douglas and Arthur Kennedy. What was more, Robson had already directed a second film for Kramer, *Home of the Brave,* which was due to hit the theaters by the end of the year.

The sudden leaps and bounds made by Wise and Robson filled Lewton with a semblance of new hope. He had never forgotten his dream about being an independent filmmaker, of one day taking that brave leap that Selznick had taken when Lewton had first started working for him. Lewton must have seen the irony that came with being back at MGM, the studio that provided his first foothold in the industry. It was here that he first started to work for David O. Selznick. It was here that he first met Jacques Tourneur. And it was here that Selznick made *Anna Karenina* and *A Tale of Two Cities* before launching his independent career. In a letter to his mother and sister Lewton was enthusiastic about his future prospects with his former collaborators, Mark Robson and Robert Wise.

Like most of Lewton's plans of late, these too went sour. The triad named their company Aspen Productions. As Robson's directing credibility skyrocketed with the late-1949 release of *Home of the Brave,* a tense message film concerning issues of racism, the three men laid their plans for the first Aspen Production, which was to be a civil rights story. As much as they tried, however, none of them could come up with a shootable script. Aspen Productions continued to spin its wheels as the months passed. And then, one day, out of the blue, an agent-lawyer representing Robson and Wise visited Lewton's office to tell him he had been dropped from Aspen and replaced by Thoren Warth. Lewton was crushed. He felt betrayed by his two friends, which only caused his paranoia to worsen.

Lewton, meanwhile, remained at MGM, fulfilling his obligations until his option was dropped. Robson and Wise had their own difficulties with Aspen Productions and appeared to be making slow progress, but Lewton was in a worse position than either of his colleagues. For the first time since his arrival in Hollywood, he was entirely without a source of income.

Given his run of bad luck, one would have expected the Russian-born producer to be a sitting duck for the House Un-American Affairs Committee, but Lewton was somehow left unscathed. In a recent interview with the author, Val Edwin Lewton addressed the HUAC issue:

> It was strange that my father never got called up. He knew all those people, some of those people involved were pretty close friends. Though he stayed out of politics, he was really terrified because he was a naturalized citizen and I think he was afraid he would get in trouble. He was quite patriotic in a strange way. Because of his military school background, he had a lot of books on uniforms and warfare; he wasn't exactly a pacifist. He was liberal but not nearly as liberal as my mother. There might have been some ill-will between some of those people who were called and my father, but he never testified against anyone. Although he never got politically involved, he *was* at some of those parties. My mother talks about parties attended by Leadbelly, Alan Lomax, George and Ira Gershwin. I'd ask my mother what was going on and she'd say, "Oh you know George never stops playing piano and we couldn't talk."

At home Lewton grew restless and was prone to brood over his unjust fate. Ruth feared for his mental health and called David Selznick, who passed a few odd jobs Lewton's way. Finally, in the first months of 1950, Lewton managed to attract the interests of Universal, his old rival studio (now Universal-International) for a proposed Revolutionary War picture. After he left MGM, Lewton had kept himself busy by writing a script called *Ticonderoga.* The script, offered as an example of his work, was enough to secure the producer a job, although it was never accepted as a studio project. Instead, Lewton was given Harry Brown's novel, *Stand at Spanish Boot,* and told to produce a small-scale Technicolor Western. Lewton cowrote the screenplay with David Chandler but as usual did not take credit. The Brown novel was filmed as *War Dance* and released as *Apache Drums*. Working at Universal, Lewton was the happiest he had been since his early days at RKO.

Apache Drums, Lewton's final film, exhibits for the first time since he left RKO many of the cinematic touches we have come to expect from his work. This is a dark, spooky Western, and while the film does not always succeed, it should be commended for attempting something different with a formula-bound genre. *Apache Drums* has many conventional elements of the Western—Indians, gunfights, preachers, saloons, cavalry, gamblers—but it is not your typical oater. Although the film is officially helmed by South American director Hugo Fregonese, Lewton's hand in the production is evident throughout.

Ironically, while Howard Hawks was busy preparing *The Thing,* a sci-fi/ horror film in the Lewton tradition, Lewton was putting his finishing touches on *Apache Drums,* a Hawksian Western laced with darkness, doom, and the threat of the unseen. Even more fitting is the fact that both films (which make a fascinating double bill) were variations of the "last stand" theme.

No, *Apache Drums* is not a classic, but it is a valiant effort, an atmospheric, well-made, and intelligently scripted film. As far as "B" budget cult Westerns go, *Apache Drums* falls in a class with Alfred Werker's *Three Hours to Kill* (1954), Jack Arnold's *No Name on the Bullet* (1959), and Monte Hellman's *The Shooting* (1967). For Lewton fans, *Apache Drums* is must-see material, something that could not be said of his other post–RKO films.

Lewton's Western opens with the stark sounds of Indian drumbeats, which continue over the opening credits, sans score music. We are set in the town of Spanish Boot, circa 1880, and the hands and drums we see beneath the credits belong to the Mescalero Apaches. Our first shot starts in darkness as double doors open to let in the morning light; we are in the church that will provide the location for the film's nail-biting climax. We see a man sweeping the church, stopping his work to feed a kitten (a Lewton in-joke?). As the man bends down to pet the animal, a thunderous blast of gunfire (treated like a "bus") diverts our attention. In the saloon, a gambling gunfighter, Sam Leeds (Stephen McNally), has just killed a man in self-defense. This does not sit well with Joe Madden (Willard Parker), who functions as Spanish Boot's mayor, lawman, and resident blacksmith.

Representing authority and hard, honest work, Joe Madden wants to do away with gunfighters and gamblers, which is why he orders Sam Leeds out of town. The fact that both men are romantically interested in Sally (Coleen Gray) of course provides Madden with an ulterior motive for wanting to get rid of Leeds. Madden and the Reverend (Arthur Shields) have also closed down the brothel, buying out the enterprise and sending all the girls on their way in a wagon. Some of Lewton's dialogue is offhandedly funny (actually providing more humor than the comic romp *Please Believe Me*) and surprisingly flip in its attack upon the self-righteous. When the Reverend wishes to see Betty Careless, the local madam, he instructs the brothel's black Man Friday to, "Summon before us the laughing woman whose steps take hold on misery, whose feet lead down to death." Quickly, the other responds, "I s'pect you wanna see Miz Careless, Reverend." When the Reverend sees Betty, he says, "Woman, thy name is Babylon and abomination." "Don't call me names," she answers with a smile.

As might be expected, *Apache Drums* also exhibits Lewton's continuing obsession with authentic-sounding source music. A single Spanish guitar is played by one of the townspeople as principal characters converse. Later, we will hear the women and children singing "The Bells of St. Clements," the song Kim Hunter sang in *The Seventh Victim*. And, of course, there are the Indian drums, as omnipresent as the voodoo drums in *I Walked with a Zombie*.

The composition of the indoor shots, authentic and rich with detail, is reminiscient of Tourneur or Ford. Likewise, the exteriors are tastefully and stylishly framed, especially the early shots of the primitive town; in spite of its civic pride, it is quite evident that Spanish Boot is a far cry from a thriving community. The town is stagnant and out of touch with the rest of the civilized world (much like the protagonists' outpost in *The Thing*); it is a town where even roving professional gamblers like Sam Leeds become trapped. Sam tells Sally, "I saw my father work his heart out on a lathe in Bridgeport. He died young, he died broke. He was an honest man. I never want to be one."

When forced to leave, Leeds discovers the mutilated bodies of Betty and the girls a few miles out of town. The driver of their wagon is barely alive, but is still wearing his Derby hat. "Leave it on. They took my hair," the driver says. Leeds hears about the raging Mescaleros. While the murderous events are being described, the camera takes Leed's point of view as he gazes at the ominous cliffs surrounding him; so unearthly is the barren landscape that it resembles the terrain of another planet. "They came down out of the rocks like ghosts," reports the dying man. Thereafter, as Leeds continues his journey, panning the eerie cliffs on either side of him, his sense of unease is effectively conveyed to the audience. Although clearly within a Western context, this nervewracking trek among the silent cliffs plays like a scene from a 1950s sci-fi/horror movie. As the camera pans the landscape, it is the unseen that fills Sam Leeds and the audience with apprehension. In the midst of the tension, some falling rocks provide the equivalent of a Lewton "bus." At his camp during the night, Leeds cannot sleep; instead he paces around, becoming increasingly nervous as he hears the howls of coyotes—or Mescaleros?—and the frightened whinnying of his horse. Finally, losing all nerve, he jumps on his horse and races back to town in darkness; along the way unseen Mescaleros shoot at him.

When Leeds returns to Spanish Boot, no one will believe his story of the Indian attack. The townspeople turn into an angry mob intent on lynching him until the stagecoach rides in and confirms his report. The animosity between Sam Leeds and Joe Madden escalates as it becomes ever more apparent that the Mescaleros intend to attack the town. A spirited young cowpoke (James Best) takes it upon himself to ride for help. A few hours later he is found dead in the town well. The well is declared contaminated, while the entire town is trapped, cut off on all sides by the blood-thirsty Mescaleros. The film's illusion of entrapment is successfully conveyed without resorting to the genre convention of having hundreds, or even dozens, of Indian extras covering the mountainsides. Again, it is the unseen that propels our deepest apprehensions.

When Leeds sets out with a group of men to go after water, we can see across the flat expanse something no one else notices: a distant cloud of dust made from the charging horses of attacking Mescaleros (we do not see the Indians, just the dust). Once the danger becomes known, the men make a quick retreat, while Leeds and the Reverend stay behind to hold off the attack. Although there has been much friction between the two, the crisis bonds them in friendship. After Leeds wounds the chief, the Indians retreat (their cries and moans carrying an eerie ambience), and our protagonists are given a reprieve. While the buzzards circle above them, Sam and the Reverend travel back on foot, having a meaningful heart-to-heart conversation along the way. Seeing another dust cloud and figuring that it means the return of the Mescaleros, Sam and the Reverend consider themselves as good as dead. The stark landscape is effectively accented by Leed's remark, "Not even anything worth taking a last look at." Lucky for them the dust cloud is a rescue force from Spanish Boot.

In the film's chilling climax, the surviving men, women, and children of Spanish Boot hole up in the church as the attacking Indians set fire to the town. The night scenes in the church's candlelit interior are appropriately claustrophobic. We hear the children crying as the women try to comfort them, the frenzied drumbeats providing a constant reminder of the dark fate that awaits them. A friendly Indian, once shunned by the townsfolk and now a welcome interpreter in the crisis, explains the Mescaleros' death ritual in which some of the braves become suicidal zealots with the aid of whiskey and peyote. The church is impregnable, but there are windows, unpaned square openings high up the walls, far out of reach of those trapped inside, but entirely accessible to the wily warriors outside. Whenever there is a change in the drumbeat, according to our Indian friend, it precipitates a suicidal charge, whereupon a single Mescalero, covered in bizarre body paint comes charging through the square opening and drops down for an attack. All the braves who do this are shot by the protagonists, but as the ritual continues, the charges come in multiple numbers. Eventually, one of the braves knocks over the candles, and the church is plunged into darkness as the men fire their guns blindly, hoping they hit the right targets. The claustrophobia builds as the church windows glow with the flames of the burning town.

Apache Drums' script tries too hard to be poignant and at times verges on the preachy, but the film is surprisingly successful. What makes *Apache Drums* essential viewing for the Lewton fan is that it is a recognizable addition to his RKO oeuvre, one that indicates the amount of impact Lewton actually had upon the films directed by Tourneur, Robson, and Wise. *Apache Drums* boasts good performances, solid direction, and an intriguing narrative. What more could one want from a "B" budget Western?

Lewton was relatively happy at Universal, but he was faced with a difficult decision as soon as he began to get comfortable.

Stanley Kramer, the mogul with a message, confessed a longtime interest in the producer's RKO series, and we should not wonder why. Considering Lewton's morbid obsessions, the 11-film cycle was, curiously enough, among the most consistently humanistic bodies of work to come out of Hollywood during the war years. One would not have expected a series of downbeat horror films to be so filled with a love for mankind and particularly for the underdog. Every film in the series was involved with some form of handicap, physical or emotional, oftentimes both. It was Lewton's tendency to deal with social concerns in such a liberal manner (resisting racial and sexual stereotypes still fashionable at the time) that led James Agee to say, "I think that few people in Hollywood show in their work that they know or care half as much about movies or human beings as [Val Lewton] does." All of which explains why Lewton caught the attention of the 36-year-old boy wonder of the message film, Stanley Kramer.

Actually, Lewton had been friendly with Kramer for some time. According to author Siegel, it was Lewton who influenced Kramer to film *Cyrano de Bergerac* (1950). Kramer's independent films had formerly been released by United Artists. Following the staggering popularity of his two Mark Robson films, *Champion* and *Home of the Brave,* Kramer had signed a six-picture-a-year with Columbia. Kramer knew it would be impossible to personally produce all six, and he was interested in having Lewton work under his supervision in the production of three of them. The projects that now lay before Kramer (and possibly Lewton) included *My Six Convicts, The Fourposter, The Member of the Wedding,* and *Death of a Salesman.*

During the month of December 1950, Lewton pondered whether to stay with his sure thing at Universal or take the risk and ally himself with Kramer (who was 10 years his junior). On the night of the *Apache Drums* preview, Lewton suffered a gallstone attack and was hospitalized. During his precarious convalescence, he made up his mind to leave Universal at the end of December and get some rest and relaxation by staying at home, working his lathe, or spending time aboard the *Nina II*, where he grew increasingly more uncomfortable. Ruth knew her husband needed a rest before he began working for Kramer, and the Lewtons planned a trip to Ensenada, Mexico. Meanwhile, the producer had premonitions of his approaching death: "I think he knew that he didn't have long to live," Val Edwin Lewton recently told the author.

In Mexico, Lewton had another gallstone attack. When the vacation was over, he discovered that the Kramer deal had been altered; his salary had been reduced and his responsibilities were limited to those of an assistant producer.

Shortly after beginning work at the Kramer Company in early February 1951, Lewton suffered a second heart attack. This time he was not hospitalized. Two days later he was well enough to screen *Bedlam* for the scriptwriter of *My Six Convicts*. And then, according to Joel E. Siegel in *The Reality of Terror*:

> He returned home after the screening and went back to bed. That evening Ruth Lewton fell on a loose rug in the living room and her husband rushed in at the sound of her scream. Several minutes later he suffered another, more serious heart attack. Lewton's doctor insisted that he be hospitalized immediately, but he didn't want to go, claiming that if he went he would never return.

At the hospital, Lewton was put in an oxygen tent, where he felt claustrophobic and believed himself to be suffocating. In *My Brother*, Lucy Lewton describes the outcome:

> At first he seemed to rally, Nina [his mother] went in to see him . . . [but because she] had just been there that summer at Ruth Nina's wedding, he must have realized he was dying. . . . Val died on March 13, 1951 at Cedars of Lebanon Hospital from a heart condition. . . . The funeral was in a small chapel in Pacific Palisades. A beautiful eulogy was read by Alan Napier, an actor who was a close friend of Val and Ruth. The chapel was filled and people stood around the block, with friends, script girls, studio janitors, all of whom loved Val. . . .
>
> He was cremated and his ashes strewn in the ocean, the seas he sailed and loved so well.

Val Edwin Lewton, now an artist and a designer of exhibits in the Smithsonian, commented in a 1992 interview with the author upon the impact his father's career had upon his own work. "One of the things I got from my father was my ability to work with a group, which I do now. I think I learned something about how to encourage people, how to work with them and have a really good team. That was something my father often talked about, how he had this wonderful team and that they were like a little repertory company.

"I've seen very few people do what he did," continued Mr. Lewton, "take a title they give you and turn it into a good movie. . . . I don't think my father really knew—or could have imagined—the kind of longevity his films would have. He would not have survived in today's film business. He was not a deal maker, and he needed to work for a company; he needed all those people behind him to help him do the impossible. Another thing about him that influenced me was his frugality. He wasn't personally frugal, unfortunately, but he was frugal in terms of knowing how to reuse things, how to figure a cheaper way of doing it, shooting it in the fog or the dark so you couldn't see the details. That's rubbed off on me. If I have a show and I don't have very much money, I will concentrate on maybe three key areas, put all my efforts there and glide through the rest. It looks expensive when it really isn't, that sort of thing, little tricks.

"His scripts were interesting in that they were so complete that an amateur director, as long as he knew how to read, could have made a good film from one of them. The scripts are very literary and filled with detail in terms of the set, what it's supposed to look like, what's on the shelf; they tell exactly where the camera is in relationship to the characters. When I was a young boy I was fascinated by the scripts because they had different color paper according to each draft—pink, blue, white was the original. They continued to fascinate me as I grew older.

"My father loved films, but I think he was most passionate about stories—story-telling and literature. He loved books. He read constantly and was a very fast reader; he could read three or four books a night. He would go down to the book store and buy out all the magazines, *Sail, Home Mechanics, The Atlantic Monthly, Argosy, Field and Stream*—he had a very broad interest. He would read them all, cover to cover, and then be able to tell you exactly what was in every one of them. And he'd do that with a novel, almost perfect recall in anything he read. He loved to read, right through to the end. In fact, the last book he was reading was *From Here to Eternity*; it was on his bed when he died."

In the April 14, 1951, issue of *The Nation*, Manny Farber wrote a long eulogy upon the passing of Val Lewton. An abbreviated version of it follows:

> The death of Val (Vladimir) Lewton, Hollywood's top producer of B movies, occurred during the final voting on the year's outstanding film contributors. The proximity of these two events underlines the significant fact that Lewton's horror productions (*The Ghost Ship*, 1943; *The Body Snatcher*, 1945; *Isle of the Dead*, 1945), which always conveyed a very visual, unorthodox artistry, were never recognized as "Oscar" worthy. . . .
>
> Lewton always seemed a weirdly misplaced figure in Hollywood. He specialized in gentle, scholarly, well-wrought productions that were as modest in

their effects as his estimate of himself. . . . Having taken on the production of low-cost thrillers (budgeted under $500,000) about pretty girls who turn into man-eating cats or believe in zombies, Lewton started proving his odd idea, for a celluloid entertainer, that "a picture can never be too good for the public." . . . He seemed to have a psychological fear of creating expensive effects, so his stock-in-trade became the imparting of much of the story through such low-cost suggestions as frightening shadows. His talents were those of a mild bibliophile whose idea of "good" cinema had much to do with using quotes from Shakespeare or Donne, bridging scenes with a rare folk song, capturing climate with a description of a West Indian dish, and, in the pensive sequences, making sure a bit player wore a period mouth instead of a modern lipsticky one. Lewton's efforts not infrequently suggested a minor approximation of *Jane Eyre*.

The critics who called Lewton the "Sultan of Shudders" and "Chillmaster" missed the deliberate quality of his insipidly normal characters, who reminded one of the actors used in small-town movie ads for the local grocery or shoe store. Lewton and his scriptwriters collaborated on sincere, adult pulp stories, which gave sound bits of knowledge on subjects like zoanthropy or early English asylums while steering almost clear of formula horror. . . .

Innocuous plots . . . were fashioned with peculiar ingredients that gave them an air of genteel sensitivity and enchantment; there was the dry documenting of a bookworm, an almost delicate distrust of excitement, economical camera and sound effects, as well as fairy-tale titles and machinations. The chilling factor came from the perverse process of injecting tepid thrills into a respectable story with an eyedropper, a technique Lewton and his favorite scriptwriter, Donald Henderson Clarke, picked up during long careers writing sex shockers for drugstore bookracks. While skittering daintily away from concrete evidences of cat women or brutality, they would concentrate with the fascination of a voyeur on unimportant bric-a-brac, reflections, domestic animals, so that the camera would take on the faintly unhealthy eye of a fetishist. The morbidity came from the obsessive preoccupation with which writers and cameramen brought out the voluptuous reality of things, such as a dangerously swinging ship's hook, which was inconspicuously knocking men overboard like tenpins.

Lewton's most accomplished maneuver was making the audience think much more about his material than it warranted. Some of his devices were the usual ones of hiding information, having his people murdered offstage, or cutting into a murderous moment in a gloomy barn with a shot of a horse whinnying. He, however, hid much more of his story than any other filmmaker, and forced his crew to create drama almost abstractly with symbolic sounds, textures, and the like, which made the audience hyperconscious of sensitive craftsmanship. He imperiled his characters in situations that didn't call for outsized melodrama and permitted the use of a journalistic camera—for example, a sailor trying to make himself heard over the din of a heavy chain that is burying him inside a ship's locker. He would use a spray-shot technique that usually consisted of oozing suggestive shadows across a wall, or watching the heroine's terror on a lonely walk, and then add a homey windup of the cat woman trying to clean her conscience in a bathtub decorated with cat paws. This shorthand method allowed Lewton to ditch the laughable aspects of improbable events and give the remaining bits of material the strange authenticity of a daguerreotype.

The Leopard Man (1943) is a cleaner and much less sentimental Lewton, sticking much more to the suspense element and misdirection, using some of his favorite images, people moving in a penitential, sleepwalking manner, episodes threaded together with a dramatic sound. This fairly early peak example of his talent is a nerve-twitching whodunit giving the creepy impression that human beings and "things" are interchangeable and almost synonymous and that both are pawns of a bizarre and terrible destiny. A lot of Surrealists like Cocteau have tried for the same supernatural effects, but, whereas their scenes still seem like portraits in motion, Val Lewton's film shows a way to tell a story about people that isn't dominated by the activity, weight, size, and pace of the human figure. In one segment of the film, a small frightened senorita walks beyond the edge of the border town and then back again, while her feelings and imagination keep shifting with the camera into sagebrush, the darkness of an arroyo, crackling pebbles underfoot, and so on, until you see her thick dark blood oozing under the front door of her house. All the psychological effects, fear and so on, were transformed by Jacques Tourneur into nonhuman components of the picture as the girl waited for some noncorporeal manifestation of nature, culture, or history to gobble her up. But more important in terms of movie invention, Lewton's use of multiple focus (characters are dropped or picked up as if by chance, while the movie goes off on odd tacks trying to locate a sound or a suspicion) and his lighter-than-air sense of pace created a terrifically plastic camera style. It put the camera eye on a curiously delicate wavelength that responds to scenery as quickly as the mind, and gets inside of people instead of reacting only to surface qualities. This film still seems to be one of Hollywood's original gems—nothing impure in terms of cinema, nothing imitative about its style, and little that misses fire through a lack of craft. . . .

Lewton's distinction always came from his sense of the soundly constructed novel; his $200,000 jobs are so skillfully engineered in pace, action, and atmosphere that they have lost little of the haunting effect they had when released years ago.

NINETEEN
Jacques Tourneur

The directing career of Jacques Tourneur has inspired heated discussions among auteur critics for a number of years. Although his work has failed to generate a singular world view as clear-cut as those developed by Frank Capra, Howard Hawks, or Alfred Hitchcock, it is plain that Jacques Tourneur saw himself as a director with a personal vision. In *The Celluloid Muse,* Tourneur comments, "The director in America is slowly becoming a clerk. He does what he's told as fast as he's told . . . and that's not the way a director should work: he should stamp a film with his own personality." The big question, of course, is precisely what manner of "personality stamp" are we to find in the Jacques Tourneur oeuvre?

In his article "The Shadow Worlds of Jacques Tourneur" in *Film Comment,* Summer 1972, Robin Wood points out that Tourneur's mastery of composition and lighting made him something of a minor league John Ford. This observation may appear to hold some weight, but we must remember that when Ford directed his first film in 1917, the two most heralded film directors working in America were D.W. Griffith and Maurice Tourneur. Since Ford's brand of pictorialism combined the strengths of both of his forerunners, it stands to reason that his eye for composition would not be too dissimilar from that adopted by Maurice Tourneur's son. (Although John Ford never evinced a disposition to create a classic horror film, his examples of dark pictorialism would have suited the genre well. Imagine *Dr. Jekyll and Mr. Hyde* on the foggy, flamboyantly Germanic sets of *The Informer* [1935] or *The Mummy* set in the eerie desolation of the wind-swept sand dunes of *The Lost Patrol* [1934].)

In his article "The Parallel Worlds of Jacques Tourneur" in *Cinéfantastique,* Summer 1973, John McCarty characterizes Tourneur as a cross between Jean Renoir and Alfred Hitchcock, though he is quick to tell us: "Hitchcock and Renoir were Tourneur's contemporaries, not his mentors. Tourneur's real mentor was his father." During his stint as an editor for his father's post–Hollywood films, Tourneur had the privilege of working with one of cinema's pioneer visionaries. Ford, Renoir, and Hitchcock aside, Jacques Tourneur's closest cinematic sibling was probably Clarence Brown, the perennial MGM director who had been Maurice Tourneur's assistant and later codirector in the early 1920s. Clarence Brown and Jacques Tourneur had, in a manner of speaking, studied at the same school. According to Clarence Brown:

> [Maurice Tourneur] was a great believer in dark foregrounds. No matter where he set his camera up, he would always have a foreground. On exteriors, we used to carry branches and twigs around with us. If it was an interior, he always had a piece of the set cutting into the corner of the picture, in halftone, to give him depth. Whenever we saw a painting with an interesting lighting effect we'd copy it [Thomson, *A Biographical Dictionary of Film*].

Brown's bleak and ultimately terrifying conclusion of *Anna Karenina* exhibited a visual style that was largely the result of his apprenticeship with the elder Tourneur. (Brown directed the film for Selznick, while Jacques Tourneur and Val Lewton were on the MGM lot preparing for their second-unit work on *A Tale of Two Cities*.) Compare the conclusion of *Karenina* with the conclusion of Jacques Tourneur's *Curse of the Demon*, and you will note some startling stylistic similarities. The same goes for the titular scare sequence of Tourneur's *I Walked with a Zombie* and the spooky grave-digging set piece of Brown's *Intruder in the Dust* (1949).

Turning his back on Hollywood in 1927 (by walking off the set of MGM's unfinished *Mysterious Island*), Maurice Tourneur returned to Paris, where he continued to make films. By the sound era, however, his vitality as a motion picture director had already been eclipsed by a younger crop of filmmakers. In 1942, the year that *Cat People* was released, the 66-year-old Maurice Tourneur directed *La Main du Diable (The Devil's Hand)*, a creepy Faustian thriller in the vein of RKO's *All That Money Can't Buy* (released the year before). *La Main du Diable* was unavailable at the time of this writing, but William K. Everson's description of it in *More Classics of the Horror Film* indicates that the film would have some relevance to this volume:

> *[La Main du Diable]* was a variation on both the Faust legend and on folklore that exists in most countries. . . . Pierre Fresnay plays a struggling painter who sells his soul to the Devil in order to achieve recognition, fame, and the woman he wants. . . . The symbol of the artist's "contract" is a withered yet still living hand. He is the last in a long line of recipients down through the ages, and in order to save his soul before he dies he must seek out the identity of the man from whom the hand was stolen, and return it to his grave. The highlight of the film is a macabre gathering of the previous "owners" of the hand—all dressed in the costume of their period or their calling, and all wearing grotesque masks which they doff to tell their stories. The chronicling of their stories of death and disaster through the years—all presented in shadow and silhouette against highly stylized backgrounds—gradually brings the history of the hand up to date, at which point there is a sudden materialization of the Holy Man whose hand was stolen by the Devil. Knowing his identity, and despite opposition by the Devil, the artist is able to restore the hand to its rightful grave, although he dies in the process.

In 1949, when the 73-year-old Tourneur lost his leg in a car accident, he retired from films and spent the remaining 12 years of his life translating hard-boiled American fiction (Chandler, Cain, Woolrich, Thompson, etc.) into French. The 1950s efforts of translators like Maurice Tourneur are what prompted France's sudden interest in America's "black novels" and their cinematic counterparts: the dark, postwar urban melodramas which would eventually be christened "film noir."

In retrospect, we can see how Jacques Tourneur and Lewton were naturally suited for one another. Both of them, after emigrating to America as children, had the privilege of growing up in a household headed by one of early Hollywood's major European sensations; what's more, Maurice Tourneur and Alla Nazimova were both headstrong individualists who eventually thumbed their noses at Hollywood. Although compromise did not come easily to either Jacques Tourneur or Val Lewton, these second-generation filmmakers had livelihoods to maintain and families to feed; not being blessed with exalted Hollywood reputations, they were forced to make a virtue of necessity. It is unfortunate that the Lewton/Tourneur RKO partnership would last little more than a year because they complemented each other so well. Tourneur was not prone to balk at Lewton's extreme notions concerning details, nor would he think odd Lewton's determination to have his films capture the look of classic paintings.

The first professional partnership between Tourneur and Lewton, their second-unit work on *A Tale of Two Cities* (1935), held the promise of future collaboration, but their reunion was still several years away. After Selznick and Lewton left MGM, Tourneur remained at the studio, relegated to directing numerous short subjects, often under the Americanized name of Jack Turner.

For one particular batch of MGM one-reelers, a series called "John Nesbitt's Passing Parade," Tourneur directed a poignant 10-minute short called *The Incredible Stranger,* which concerned a mysterious man of wealth who, after having a house built to his exact specifications, moves into the little town of Bridgewood. Living alone and never speaking a word to any of the townspeople, he mail orders numerous items, including clothing, befitting a family of four. Although their curiosity is piqued, the people of Bridgewood, being continually rebuffed by the stranger's silence, give up their attempts to socialize with him. Five years later he has a stroke, and his incredible secret is revealed. In his house are full-scale wooden replicas of a woman, a boy, and a girl, all of them frozen in the middle of an action. These startlingly eerie images take on a further dimension when it is revealed that the stranger had lost his family when a fire consumed a house exactly like the one he had built in Bridgewood. In a failed attempt to save his family from the conflagration, he had lost his vocal chords from heat and smoke inhalation, which accounted for his speechlessness. All along he was just a lonely man living within his own re-creation of the past.

While *The Incredible Stranger* is not always on the mark (shot without a soundtrack, it is seriously marred by a storyteller's unappealing voice-over), the prototype of its title character, that of a stranger haunted by the past, would continually turn up in Tourneur's subsequent films.

Toward the end of 1938, MGM gave the green light to an expanded version of a Tourneur "Crime Does Not Pay" short called *They All Come Out*. Originally intended as a two-reeler, the film was lengthened to a six-reel feature for the second half of a MGM bill and released in 1939. Produced by Jack Chertok and written by John Higgins, *They All Come Out* was a respectable "B" film American debut for Tourneur that, at least in part, foreshadowed the coming of the 1940s noir form. In order to make it the "public service" movie it was intended to be, Tourneur had to yield to the platitudinous convictions of arch-conservative Louis B. Mayer. This was, after all, the start of MGM's post–Thalberg era, popularly known as the "Andy Hardy period." Tourneur may have been obliged to carry out the film's public service intent, but he managed to sidestep the heavy-handed preachy rhetoric so typical of similar MGM ventures. The prison parole board scenes, which make use of nonprofessional actors, are unusually realistic, transcending most of the stereotypes of prison parole boards in the countless crime films of the decade. Tourneur's mise-en-scène within this context is as interesting as it is unusual. Steering clear of the self-consciousness of other "Crime Does Not Pay" shorts, *They All Come Out* possesses a veracity that anticipates Louis de Rochemont's quasi-documentary approach in his series of late–1940s Fox opuses.

The first half hour of *They All Come Out* includes echoes of Fritz Lang's *You Only Live Once* and points ahead to such later on-the-run noir films as Raoul Walsh's *High Sierra* (1941), Edgar G. Ulmer's *Detour* (1945), Nicholas Ray's *They Live by Night* (1948), Felix Feist's *The Devil Thumbs a Ride* (1948), and Joseph H. Lewis's *Gun Crazy* (1949). The sturdy presence of Tom Neal as a down-and-out hitchhiker who, because of a woman, finds himself embroiled in crime, immediately brings to mind his similar role in *Detour*.

Outside of its associations with future noir efforts, *They All Come Out* also has a number of notably macabre moments. There is a bizarre exchange between a prison psychologist and the gang psycho, the latter an off-the-wall misogynist who claims he finds small women hiding inside of his coat pockets. A scene in a ward for the criminally insane is, not surprisingly, directed by Tourneur with a flair for the grotesque, achieving an atmosphere of derangement that aptly foreshadows similar scenes in the Lewton/Robson collaboration, *Bedlam*. Finally, there is an unexpectedly violent climax where Neal, held at gunpoint by bad-guy Paul Fix, turns his ignited blowtorch on his assailant's face and chest, whereupon the villain's scorched and smoking form is shown writhing on the floor.

Tourneur was elevated to occasional "B" features like *Nick Carter, Master Detective* (1939) and *Phantom Raiders* (1940) until his MGM contract ran out.

He made one "B" film for Republic (*Doctor's Don't Tell,* 1941) just before joining the Lewton outfit to direct *Cat People, I Walked with a Zombie,* and *The Leopard Man.*

Tourneur's post-Lewton career is roughly composed of three categories of films: thrillers (including horror and noir), Westerns, and adventures. Tourneur felt most comfortable working within these genres, and when he was given an assignment that was out of his element, such as his first post-Lewton film, *Days of Glory,* the results were often strained and unsatisfactory.

In *American Directors,* Vol. 1, Jean-Pierre Coursodon presents some illuminating observations about Tourneur's protagonists and the communities in which they—often rather suddenly—find themselves planted. Tourneur's tendency to chronicle the exploits of an outsider trying to cope within a foreign environment provides a continuous thread that runs through most of his work. Coursodon notes that though Tourneur's protagonists may "have conspiratorial motives of their own, [they] nevertheless fall prey to larger and more unpredictable conspiracies." Coursodon continues: "In nearly all these films, as the protagonist immerses him or herself into increasingly dangerous situations, other characters also become vulnerable because the mystery and reticence that previously protected them are broken. . . . These victims—or near victims—resemble Irena in *Cat People.*"

If the above helps to define the "Tourneur touch," however, one can only wonder why Tourneur's ghostly hand seems so prevalent in the Lewton films made after his departure from the unit. It is entirely possible that "the Tourneur touch" and "the Lewton touch" were but the fragmented halves of a single phenomenon. After Joel E. Siegel finished his impeccably researched volume, *Val Lewton: The Reality of Terror,* he set the record straight concerning the rather widespread notion that Jacques Tourneur was the single most important force behind the Lewton films. In an article called "Tourneur Remembers" in *Cinéfantastique,* Summer 1973, Siegel states:

> From all that I have learned, I don't think that a very strong case can be made for Tourneur as the prime mover of the Lewton-Tourneur pictures. . . . Jacques Tourneur is a superb film stylist and interpreter; his films for Lewton are formally far superior to those of the other Lewton directors. Later Lewton films had screenplays as sensitive and carefully crafted, but none had the visual grace and artistic delicacy which Tourneur used to make screenplays blossom as films. Later on, without Lewton's intelligent authority behind his work, Tourneur was often able to do little more than dispose of bad scripts with as much taste and tact as possible. On those few occasions when he was given a first-rate project, like *Curse of the Demon,* Tourneur rose again to the top of his form. However I think it would be a mistake to take this late, Lewtonesque classic as evidence that Tourneur was the actual guiding force behind the earlier movies. Rather, as it appears to me, Tourneur was simply returning to the kind of filmmaking which he and Lewton evolved together during their early days at RKO.

While Tourneur's post–Lewton career never reached the brand-name status of his Lewton colleagues, Mark Robson and Robert Wise, his directorial talent assured him work. The longevity of his career, amidst an incredible number of variables, is a testament to both his resilience and his expertise. Unlike Robson and Wise, whose work caught the attention of the Motion Picture Academy time and again, Tourneur had no such reputation to coast upon. With Lewton, Tourneur learned that he worked best when he possessed some degree of autonomy over his projects. For the two decades–plus of his post–Lewton career, Tourneur occupied himself with small, modestly budgeted pictures (some of them "A"'s, some of them "B"'s) at an average rate of one picture per year. He maintained his independence by refusing to stay with one particular studio; instead, he bid himself out to a wide assortment of production companies: RKO, Universal, MGM, Warner Bros., Fox, Eagle-Lion, Alllied Artists, Columbia, United Artists, and even American International.

Tourneur had the durability of a true Hollywood survivor; his career exemplifies artistry, integrity, and professionalism, perhaps at the expense of popularity. Although his films never received a portion of the mainstream fanfare that was given his two Lewton counterparts, a large number of film critics consider Tourneur the best of the three Lewton directors. It is tempting to embrace the notion that Tourneur provided the model upon which Mark Robson and Robert Wise built their own careers, but this popular assertion does not always hold water. Mark Robson made significant contributions to *Cat People, Zombie,* and *The Leopard Man*; moreover, the Wise/Robson/Welles connection must surely stand for something in the genesis of the Lewton formula. Tourneur advocates are quick to observe that *Seventh Victim* is a deliberate imitation of the three Tourneur films, but they often neglect to acknowledge the impact that Lewton and Robson had upon those first three films. Directing horror films for RKO had been as much of a learning experience for Tourneur as it had been for Robson, Wise, Bodeen, Wray, Musuraca, Webb, and, of course, Lewton himself.

Unfortunately for fans of the genre, Tourneur made fewer horror films than one would expect from a director who has gained the reputation of a horror stylist of the first rank. The three Lewton efforts and *Curse of the Demon* comprise his entire catalog of genuine horror films (and, given its lack of overt supernatural elements, *The Leopard Man* may be subject to disqualification among genre purists). Add to these Tourneur's last two films, one horror spoof (*A Comedy of Terrors,* 1963) and one flaccid, ersatz–Poe science fiction/adventure/horror hodgepodge (*War-Gods of the Deep,* 1965), and what remains of Tourneur's body of work hardly seems to justify his ironclad associations with the horror film. Tourneur's status as a horror director is largely the result of his Lewton experience; even his one non–Lewton horror masterpiece, *Curse of the Demon,* is a deliberate Lewton homage. Strangely, although his

Westerns outnumber his horror films, his reputation as a director of Westerns is obscure at best.

In *The Celluloid Muse,* Tourneur told Charles Higham and Joel Greenberg, "I believe in improvisation. I believe in instinct. I believe that when I write something, or paint . . . it's subconsciously inspired." Tourneur's intuitive approach does not pave the way for the creation of a bold personal style; unlike methodical directors like Lang and Hitchcock, who seldom left anything to chance, Tourneur believed his movies would naturally reflect his personality without his making any deliberate efforts in that direction. "I don't believe in doing everything in advance, as Hitchcock does," Tourneur says in *The Celluloid Muse.*

In Tourneur's case, flexibility was a condition reinforced by necessity; he never had the clout to achieve the autonomy of a Lang or a Hitchcock. Nor was he above an occasional gripe concerning his lot as a director. He told Higham and Greenberg in *The Celluloid Muse:* "In all these pictures, I've never had the right of final cut: the right to supervise the final editing of the film." No matter how much Tourneur had to yield to his wide variety of superiors, however, he never stopped believing in himself as an artist, even when he was forced to work under conditions that would have turned lesser directors into hacks.

One continuing thematic thread in the Tourneur films is the presence of an inescapable dark force, perhaps best epitomized by the black predator in *The Leopard Man* or the irreversible supernatural hauntings in *Curse of the Demon.* Outside of its obvious application to the supernatural curses of *Cat People* and *I Walked with a Zombie,* Tourneur's inescapable force comes in a variety of incarnations: Paul Lukas's mania in *Experiment Perilous,* the Nazi threat in *Days of Glory,* corruption and mob violence of *Canyon Passage,* a belated act of revenge in *Out of the Past,* murderous kidnappers in *Berlin Express,* a heart ailment in *Easy Living,* KKK-styled nightriders in *Stars in My Crown* (recalling the hooded entourage in *The Leopard Man*), and the chronic perils of gangs of drunken cowboys in *Wichita.* The list goes on. In the proper Lewton tradition, Tourneur allies his inescapable force with darkness, using expressionistic lighting to build an atmosphere of dread.

The typical Tourneur film contains an unusual number of night scenes, something that even holds true for his six Westerns: *Canyon Passage* (1946), *Stars in My Crown* (1950), *Way of a Gaucho* (1952), *Stranger on Horseback* (1955), *Wichita* (1955), and *Great Day in the Morning* (1956). Unlike John Ford's Westerns, which extolled the virtues of heroism within a community founded upon structure and order, Tourneur's Westerns are much more freewheeling in their approach, his protagonists more ambiguous. Compare Ford's version of Wyatt Earp (Henry Fonda in *My Darling Clementine*) with Tourneur's version (Joel McCrea in *Wichita*), and we see two distinct portrayals. Fonda's Earp is more like Tom Joad on horseback, a hero of the downtrodden, while

McCrea's Earp (historically, an earlier version of the man) is a reticent, ill-tempered, worldly protagonist. Ford's heroes act while Tourneur's heroes react.

Tourneur's adventure films, which are not remarkably different in tone from his Westerns, include *The Flame and the Arrow* (1950), *Anne of the Indies* (1951), *Appointment in Honduras* (1953), *Timbuktu* (1959), *The Giant of Marathon* (Italy, 1960), and *War-Gods of the Deep* (1965). The protagonists react in ways that defy the conventions of their usually bad reputations; thus, roving bands of outlaws or seagoing pirates exhibit more human decency than the characters who represent law and order. The most successful of the adventure films was Tourneur's first, *The Flame and the Arrow*. Swashbucklers were back in vogue in the late 1940s, no doubt because they were perfect fare for the Technicolor revolution. In *The Flame and the Arrow*, Tourneur's direction is tight and uncharacteristically fast-paced. For an adventure film of its type, *Flame*'s visuals are unusually dark, with much of the action taking place at night; when we are not under the stars in the nearby forest, we are sneaking about within damp, dimly lit medieval structures. Tourneur's film may have its ties with Michael Curtiz's *Adventures of Robin Hood* but, aside from its Technicolor photography, its look more closely resembles Rowland V. Lee's *Tower of London* or James Whale's *Man in the Iron Mask* (both 1939). Burt Lancaster plays Dardo, an Italian "Robin Hood" whose estranged wife has taken up with the village tyrant (a plot-wrinkle that recalls Lancaster's plight in Robert Siodmak's *Criss Cross*). In the climactic swordfight between Dardo and the tyrant, a candlelit chandelier drops to the floor, causing the remainder of the duel to be fought in the dark (likely a conscious nod to Tourneur's days with the Lewton unit).

It is interesting to note that while Robert Siodmak was directing Warners' *The Crimson Pirate* (1952), the Burt Lancaster follow-up to *The Flame and the Arrow*, Tourneur was working on *Anne of the Indies*, an account of Blackbeard the Pirate. Tourneur's film should not be confused with RKO's aborted Lewton/Robson/Karloff Blackbeard project (which, that same year, had been dusted off, rewritten, assigned to director Raoul Walsh, and released as *Blackbeard the Pirate*).

Despite Tourneur's affinity for outdoor pictures, his reputation today rests largely upon his thrillers, his first post–Lewton example being the 1945 RKO release, *Experiment Perilous*, a period thriller (set in 1903 New York) resembling George Cukor's *Gaslight*. Paul Lukas plays the domineering husband, Hedy Lamarr the wife he attempts to drive insane, and George Brent the psychologist who chances upon the dark proceedings. Albert Dekker outshines the rest of the cast as an eccentric Greenwich Village artist who paints his social life in broad strokes.

Based on a novel by Margaret Carpenter and scripted by Warren Duff, *Experiment Perilous* is easily one of the classier, if not altogether satisfying,

Burt Lancaster in *The Flame and the Arrow* (1950).

examples of period noir. It is the first Tourneur film to use the image of a charging train to represent the steady course of the film's dark forces, a visual motif the director would put to further use in *Berlin Express* and *Curse of the Demon.* In *Experiment Perilous,* it is the train we see first: a black locomotive charging over flooded tracks, sluicing a path through gigantic puddles and barreling into the perilous, stormy night like a thing out of control, the water-logged railroad ties shuddering as it passes over.

Unfortunately, *Experiment Perilous*'s powerhouse opening promises more than the film delivers; anyone expecting a dynamic thriller in the Lewton tradition is bound to be disappointed. *Experiment Perilous* is more complicated than it is thrilling. Curiously, although Tourneur had every reason to exploit the tactics of terror he helped invent for the Lewton films, his period thriller conspicuously avoided their use.

After the stunning opener, psychologist Dr. Bailey (George Brent) becomes embroiled in a plot concerning Cissie Bedereaux (Olive Blakenley), an eccentric lady he meets on the train. When Cissie dies unexpectedly the next night, Bailey's life becomes entangled with her brother, Nick (Paul Lukas), and Nick's wife, Aelita (Hedy Lamarr), with whom Bailey falls in love. Eventually, Bailey reads Cissie's journal and, via a flashback about Nick's childhood, we come to understand why Bedereaux is the warped individual that he is. We also are brought up to date about why Nick is trying to drive his wife insane, which has to do with his suspicions of her infidelity and the possibility that their five-year-old son might not be his. Nick claims that his son is growing more neurotic everyday as the result of his mother's growing derangement, but we soon discover the real reason for the young boy's neuroses. Bailey overhears the following private conversation between Nick and his son:

> "Ugly witches are going about their business, and the more beautiful they are when the sun is up, the blacker and uglier they become when it gets dark. And what they want are little boys like you."
>
> "Not me, Papa."
>
> "Oh no, not you. And do you know why? Because Papa knows all about witches. Papa put up magic bars to keep you safe, but it must be a secret. You mustn't tell this to your mother or Deery [the old housekeeper, played by Julia Dean]. Deery is an ugly witch, isn't she?"
>
> "Yes."
>
> "But not so dangerous as a beautiful witch. They are the really dangerous ones."
>
> "Mommy's beautiful."

By the time Bailey unravels the mystery, he finds Aelita and himself in imminent peril, as the title suggests. Nick reads significance in his son's being born nine months after his wife's supposed affair with a poet, but he is wrong; the child is his. He fakes a suicide and goes back to his mansion, where he tries to kill his wife and son by turning on the gas. Bailey appears to play out the final heroics.

Experiment Perilous has some interesting Lewton connections, though most of them appear to be nothing more than amazing coincidences. The plot element of a child being driven to nightmares by the telling of bloodcurdling nursery tales not only reflects Lewton's own childhood (the boy in the Tourneur film dreams of tigers hiding under his bed) but also finds its parallel in *Curse of the Cat People,* released just months before. (The actress who plays the storyteller in the Lewton film, Julia Dean, is on hand as the nanny in *Experiment Perilous.*) Tourneur's film also contains some elements that beg comparison to *The Seventh Victim:* the Greenwich Village setting, the presence of an obnoxious poet as a minor character, the suicide theme, and a psychologist as a major character. And finally, if the interior sets of the Bedereaux mansion look familiar to Lewton fans, it is because they were redressed and recycled for *The Body Snatcher*'s medical school

(The Bedereaux mansion is a wonder to behold; the huge upstairs landing has built-in aquariums for walls and these spew incredible amounts of water when the house explodes in the film's finale. There is also a very impressive department store set that demonstrates the same kind of fascination for accurate period detail that made Lewton the butt of jokes with RKO's front office.)

Tourneur's contribution to the period thriller trend could have benefited from more careful casting. The lead role deserves someone with more screen presence than George Brent, and Paul Lukas is not a particularly memorable villain. Hedy Lamarr is fine, considering her limitations as an actress, but she does not come close to generating the sympathy of Ingrid Bergman in *Gaslight.* The best bit of casting is Albert Dekker as Clagg the artist, but he is not given enough screen time, nor has he much bearing upon the plot once he introduces Bailey to the Bedereauxs.

Tourneur's decision to eschew the Lewton approach was ill-advised. Since so many other filmmakers borrowed freely from the techniques of terror established by the Lewton films, there is no reason why Tourneur should not have done the same. There is an excellent opportunity for a Lewton walk when Bailey realizes he is being followed, but Tourneur just passes it by. Moreover, the marvelously expressionistic exteriors draw such strong associations with the Lewton films that it only makes it more disappointing when the Tourneur film fails to deliver a single solid dose of raw terror. Tourneur's reluctance to make use of the "bus" technique suggests that he was holding no claims upon its invention (although Tourneur would feel no qualms over using this terror device several times in *Curse of the Demon*).

Also disappointing for genre fans was Tourneur's handling of the postwar spy thriller, *Berlin Express* (1948). With exteriors shot on location in Paris, Frankfort, and Berlin, and a cast that included Robert Ryan, Merle Oberon, and Paul Lukas, Tourneur's film was something of a cross between Hitchcock's *The Thirty-Nine Steps* and Lang's *Ministry of Fear. Berlin Express* also resembles Orson Welles's uneven spy thriller, *Journey into Fear,* except that Tourneur's film is set on a train instead of a boat. The film offered its director the opportunity to once again employ his stranger-in-a-strange-land motif as a backdrop for a paranoid plot where imposters and double crosses abound.

Although *Berlin Express* boasts good performances and able direction, it was bound by the limitations of its own half-baked evolution. The plan was to build a film around some location shooting in the war-torn, but very photogenic, rubble of Frankfort and Berlin. A couple of key scenes, without the principals, were shot abroad, but a large portion of the Hollywood shooting makes ample use of rear-projected moving shots of decimated cities, as characters ride by in trains, buses, and jeeps. There are some good scenes aboard the train in the first half of the film, but overall, *Berlin Express* is put together too haphazardly. Like *Experiment Perilous*, it is a grab bag of inspired moments and lost opportunities; even the talents of Curt Siodmak, who was called in to write the script, had little positive impact on the film. By the time *Berlin Express* was released, its friendly attitude toward a Russian soldier was already outdated by the onset of the Red Scare, and the naming of the Hollywood Ten.

Tourneur directed a few other minor thrillers—*Circle of Danger* (1951), *Nightfall* (1956), *The Fearmakers* (1958)—though they also failed to generate the kind of chills expected from a filmmaker so often championed as one of the horror film's premiere stylists. Although all three would be of some interest to readers of this volume, none of them can hold a candle to Tourneur's post–Lewton cult masterpiece, *Out of the Past* (1947).

Out of the Past is one of a handful of quintessential films noir, putting it in the company of Wilder's *Double Indemnity*, Dmytryk's *Murder, My Sweet*, Siodmak's *The Killers* and *Criss-Cross*, and Nicholas Ray's *They Live by Night*. The film's protagonist, Jeff Bailey (aka Markham), like the Swede in *The Killers*, has spent a number of years waiting for the past to catch up with him. Actually, *Out of the Past* is a marvelous complement to both *The Killers* and *Criss-Cross*. Each of the three features a doomed down-and-out protagonist and his ill-fated obsession with a woman who is the property of a powerful gangster; together, they almost work as a trilogy.

Tourneur's film opens with a series of dissolves beneath the credits, all from the perspective of a man behind the wheel of a moving automobile. Roy Webb underscores the visuals with music as majestic as it is ominous. Through the credit sequence, our point-of-view maintains one direction: the road ahead. Each dissolve reveals lovely morning countrysides and idyllic landscapes that bring us closer to the driver's destination, wherever that may be. Tourneur has in effect put us in the driver's seat of the "inescapable dark force" that propels the film's narrative.

Although Daniel Mainwaring's screenplay was an adaptation of his own novel *Build My Gallows High* (written under a pseudonym), the first few minutes of *Out of the Past* so closely parallel the opening scenes of *The Killers*

Robert Mitchum in a publicity still for *Out of the Past* (1947).

(released the previous year) that it verges on plagiarism. The villain's henchman, Joe Stefano (Paul Valentine), arrives in his car to call upon Jeff Bailey (Robert Mitchum), who runs a gas station in the small California town of Bridgeport. After behaving rudely to a deaf boy (Dickie Moore) who makes it plain that Jeff is not around, Joe goes across the street to a diner to pick up some information. (The Swede, the protagonist in *The Killers*, also works at a gas station; when the hired killers cannot find the Swede, they also go across the street to a diner.)

In spite of their obvious similarities, the opening passages of *The Killers* and *Out of the Past* each take a different approach. Siodmak's opening is shot at night and is intended to evoke terror; by contrast, Tourneur's film opens with an idyllic, sunny day, one that soon becomes tainted by Stefano's sudden appearance, an appearance which signals dread rather than terror. In *Past*, when Jeff and Stefano finally meet, their disarmingly friendly banter recalls the conversations between Karloff and Daniell in *The Body Snatcher*; we can only guess the meaning of their cryptic exchanges, but we know that their friendliness toward one another is pure deception and that Stefano has something on Jeff, something that forces the latter to respond to the other man's wishes.

The townspeople of Bridgeport have been suspicious of Jeff in the five years he has spent with them (their attitude recalls the relationship between the townspeople of Bridgewood and the mute title character in Tourneur's one-reeler, *The Incredible Stranger*). Bailey appears to be on friendly terms with only two people in town: the mute boy (Dickie Moore), simply called "the kid," and Ann (Virginia Huston), the latter being a local girl who loves him and never asks any questions. Jeff asks Ann to drive him to Lake Tahoe, where he is supposed to meet Stefano's boss, Whit Sterling (Kirk Douglas), with whom he has some unfinished business. Jeff loves Ann, which is why he tells her a long story that reveals his dark secret.

The flashback, told via Mitchum's wonderfully world-weary voice-over, covers a lot of geography, starting in New York where Jeff Markham (Mitchum), a private detective, is hired by a recently wounded Whit Sterling (Douglas) to track down Kathie Moffett (Jane Greer), the woman who shot Sterling and ran off with his $40,000. Jeff goes to Mexico, finds Kathie, and the two of them fall in love; she tells Jeff that she never stole any money and that she only ran away because Whit was cruel to her. Jeff accepts this, telling her, "Baby, I don't care," and the two of them live together in a variety of places in and around Los Angeles, not daring to stay put for too long for fear of being discovered. Meanwhile, Jeff's partner, Fisher (Steve Brodie), is hired by Sterling to track down Jeff and Kathie. When Fisher surprises Jeff and Kathie in their backwoods cabin, the two men break into a fight which is curtailed when Kathie pulls a gun and needlessly shoots and kills Fisher. Jeff is dumbfounded by her actions, and when his back is turned, Kathie gets in her car and drives off. Jeff checks the purse she left behind and finds a bankbook upon which is recorded a $40,000 deposit. He buries the body and gets rid of the gun. "I never saw her again," he tells Ann, as the flashback concludes.

Jeff leaves Ann and goes to Sterling's Tahoe estate. There he discovers that Kathie had run right back to Sterling after shooting Fisher because, as she claims, she was frightened and did not know what to do. In private, Kathie tells Jeff that she is actually being blackmailed for Fisher's murder, but her ex-lover is not about to be fooled a second time. Jeff and Whit Sterling act like old pals, but the latter's feigned warmth carries a deadly threat. If Jeff did one last favor it would even the score, says the well-dressed gangster. Caving in to Sterling, Jeff is obliged to go to San Francisco to steal some tax records from Eels, an accountant who used to work for Sterling.

Although he has no choice but to do as he is told, as he accepts the names and addresses of other parties in on the plan in Frisco, Jeff is now smart enough to suspect he is being set up as a patsy. From this point on in the film, he will be two steps ahead of Whit and Kathie and one step ahead of the audience. One of the things that makes *Out of the Past* such a unique viewing experience is our need to observe Jeff's every action closely, merely to guess at what he already knows. Paradoxically, although the motivation behind Jeff's behavior remains undisclosed, we develop a profound sense of intimacy with his character, as if, in our efforts to gain information, we are forever looking over his shoulder.

It is particularly gratifying to see the way Jeff reacts to the options set before him as we follow the twisted course of the film's narrative to its tragic end. He infuriates Meta Carson (Rhonda Fleming), his liaison in San Francisco, by acting inappropriately flippant when he is introduced to Eels. He takes a drink at Eels's apartment, looks at the glass, and comments aloud about the fingerprints he is leaving behind. When Meta leaves the room, Jeff tells Eels to watch his step because the two of them are part of a setup.

After ditching Meta, Jeff goes back to Eels's place and finds the man's corpse, just as he expected he would. Thinking quickly, Jeff throws the plan awry by hiding the body, his behavior echoing his earlier disposal of Fisher's body. This time, however, Jeff knows what he is doing. The missing body jams the machinery of Whit's frame-up and gives Jeff just enough time to steal back the tax records and temporarily get the upper hand on Whit and his gang. Jeff gets away and travels back to Bridgeport, but he is now hunted by the police for the murders of both Fisher and Eels. Stefano comes to kill Jeff but is, himself, killed, via the intervention of the kid (whom he should not have treated so shabbily in the opening reel). In order to clear his name, Jeff reunites with Kathie, only to discover that she has just shot and killed Sterling. Kathie wants to run away with Jeff, and he plays along, informing the police in the process. When she sees the roadblock, Kathie shoots Jeff, just before the two of them are riddled with police bullets. The film ends with Ann asking the kid if Jeff planned to run away with Kathie. Knowing it to be a necessary lie, the kid nods his head, hoping that it will help Ann get on with her life.

Although Tourneur's film was basically a "B" film with modest "A" flourishes, it quickly became a word-of-mouth success, elevating the sleepy-eyed Robert Mitchum to stardom. Mitchum's understated persona was a natural for film noir, which is why *Past* set the pace for Mitchum's many subsequent noir protagonist roles. He is extremely convincing as Jeff Bailey/Markham. Kirk Douglas is fine in an uncharacteristically understated role; Douglas and Mitchum seem to be competing for the most laid-back performance, and this works very well in the film, providing the quiet tension that lurks beneath appearances. (It would be two more years before Kirk Douglas hit the big time with Mark Robson's *Champion.*) Jane Greer's place among noir's greatest femme fatales is insured by her performance in *Out of the Past.* According to a 1992 interview (appearing in conjunction with the "American Movie Classics" cable showing of *Out of the Past*), actress Greer revealed that Tourneur had instructed her to act as impassively as possible; he wanted the audience to read whatever they imagined into her performance. Tourneur's advice brought wondrous results, providing a sterling example of the "deceptive appearances" motif that was so central to the entire Lewton catalog.

In *Out of the Past* we get the impression that nearly every character knows more than he or she is willing to tell. Because Jeff is always one step ahead of us, all we can do is trust his decisions without being privy to his plan. Jeff would like nothing more than to get married to a decent woman like Ann and spend the rest of his life fishing, pumping gas, minding his own business, and blending into the scenery. But trouble follows him, and he must react, which he does by listening to his intuition and his instinct.

Tourneur's horror reputation may lead one to falsely expect *Out of the Past* to be a creepy film noir but outside of Nicholas Musuraca's marvelous expressionistic touches and a narrative driven by the forces of doom, Tourneur's film avoids most horror/thriller conventions. There are no creaky doors or mysterious shadows or hands coming around the corner; there is no killer with a knife, no stalking presence, no voice in the dark; there are no Lewton scare tactics here and, in this particular case, the film is better without them.

What *Out of the Past* especially has in common with the Lewton films is its humanistic spirit. The downbeat ending fills us with regret, but also with hope. Jeff's behavior throughout the film (even in the flashback) never shakes our admiration for him; he is the victim of bad luck, not bad decisions. We find inspiration in the way he behaves in a crisis; like the Swede in *The Killers,* Jeff is resolved to accept the hand dealt to him. Unlike the Swede, however, Jeff is not about to go gently into his good night.

Filmed in England with Dana Andrews, Peggy Cummins, and Niall MacGinnis, *Curse of the Demon* is one of the most highly praised horror films in the history of the genre. Althrough Tourneur was reticent to employ Lewton terror tactics in the period thriller and film noir milieus, he had no compunctions about using them in his first post–Lewton horror film. *Curse of the Demon* (*Night of the Demon* in England) is a richly atmospheric film filled with dark mysticism, fine performances, brilliant photography, and intelligent dialogue. It has all the attributes of Tourneur's Lewton masterpiece *I Walked with a Zombie,* except where *Zombie* goes for subtle chills, *Demon* goes for stark terror. *Curse of the Demon* is Tourneur's crowning achievement, as well as his purest application of the "dark inescapable force," which is epitomized in the film by the following couplet from Samuel Taylor Coleridge's *The Ancient Mariner:* "Like one that on a lonesome road doth walk in fear and dread; Because he knows a frightful fiend doth close behind him tred."

Tourneur's Lewton homage tells the story of Dr. John Holden (Dana Andrews), an author who has spent his life debunking the supernatural. His travels to England lead him to investigate the mysterious death of Professor Henry Harrington, a man victimized by the black magic of Dr. Julian Karswell (Niall MacGinnis), a character who, like Poelzig in *The Black Cat,* is modeled after the infamous real-life British sorcerer, Aleister Crowley. When Harrington's niece Joanna (Peggy Cummins) brings evidence of Karswell's foul play to Holden's attention, the latter remains incredulous until it becomes impossible to refute the fearful evidence of Karswell's black magic.

As in *Out of the Past,* the opening scenes (after the credit's Stonehenge imagery) of *Demon* accent a moving force, again an automobile. This time, however, the car is traveling in the dead of night. The headlights of the vehicle do their feeble best to penetrate the darkness, their rays scattered by the evenly spaced trees lining both sides of the lonely road. We see several through-the-windshield shots from the driver's perspective, the branches of trees seeming to reach down menacingly as we pass beneath them. These shots are intermixed with shots of the driver, a thin frightened man, his body stiff and his eyes frozen on the road ahead.

When Professor Harrington, the frightened driver, makes it to Karswell's mansion, the interiors (courtesy of art director, Peter Glazier) and the crisp photography (by Ted Scaife) are most reminiscent of the RKO house style of the 1940s. Harrington beseeches Karswell to help him and, once again (as in *Past*), the brief exchange of words between the two men reveals the magnitude of things left unsaid. Harrington begs Karswell to "call it off"; Karswell asks for "the parchment" and Harrington says he has lost it. Karswell looks at the clock; it is 10 minutes before the hour. Nervously and briskly, Karswell urges Harrington to go home and tells him that everything will be fine in the morning. But, of course, we know better; so does Karswell. The dialogue by Hitchcock veteran Charles Bennett exudes as much intelligence and taste as the interiors of Karswell's mansion, Lufford Hall. We know we are in for a first-class excursion into Lewton territory.

Harrington drives home. He pulls his car into the garage, douses his headlights, walks out, and then hears it. A peculiar high-pitched sound alerts Harrington's attention to something in the sky, something that seems to sparkle and smoke, way in the distance, coming nearer. He jumps back into his car but in his panic backs into a telephone pole that comes crashing down. Sputtering live wires fall around the vehicle, filling the frame with splashes of light. Harrington tumbles out of his car and rolls on his back among writhing wires of raw current. A hooflike leg of a gigantic creature plants itself alongside the man's body, causing him to look up to see the horror that reaches down with a taloned claw, giving us our first view of the demon's indescribably ghastly face.

There has long been controversy over the early appearance of the demon. Fans of the film fall into one of three camps on this issue: those who think the appearance of the demon ruins the film, those who admit they like the demon but would alter or re-edit the demon sequences, and finally those who like the demon sequences just as they are. Jacques Tourneur and Charles Bennett came to loggerheads with producer Hal E. Chester over the demon issue as soon as the film went into production.

When Charles Bennett penned his first draft of the script, the proposed title of the project was *The Haunted* (an uncanny coincidence, given the title of Robert Wise's own upcoming Lewton homage, *The Haunting*). The original plan was to make a Lewtonesque film that would avoid the appearance of a conventional monster. Instead, Tourneur and Bennett opted to use an amorphous cloud to signal the demon's approach. Hal E. Chester, however, took a stand that would have made Sid Rogell or Jack Gross proud and insisted that Tourneur and Bennett follow the horror conventions of the day by providing the film with a visible monster. Chester's previous production credit had been the 1953 hit, *The Beast from 20,000 Fathoms*, a film that admittedly would have been nothing without its marvelous Ray Harryhausen monster.

Tourneur compromised by having his special effects team, George Blackwell and Wally Veevers, build a miniature monster model patterned after the demons of 400-year-old woodcuts. The team then collaborated with special effects photographer, S.D. Onions, to capture the most dynamic use of the creation. It should be stressed that Tourneur included brief shots of the demon at the film's conclusion only; after Tourneur delivered the film to Chester, the producer recut it and inserted additional monster footage, including the shots of the demon that open the film. To make matters worse, the newspaper ads and marquee posters all sported a close-up of the creature so that all the ticket-buyers knew the demon's face even before they took their seats.

Bennett was so upset by the way Chester reedited the film that he asked to have his name removed from the credits. Instead, Bennett's name was retained, though Hal E. Chester gave himself credit as co-scripter. In a 1975 interview (in the article *Curse of the Demon* by Ronald V. Borst and Scott MacQueen, in *Photon*, issue 29), Dana Andrews does not mince words over his resentment of Chester, calling him a "little schmuck," a "horrible little fellow, and a "little son-of-a-bitch" all within a 50-word stretch. Andrews threatened to walk off the picture, telling Chester, "I didn't come all the way over here to have the producer tell me what he thinks about directing the picture. I came because Mr. Tourneur asked me. Let the director direct the picture."

We will never see the film that Tourneur and Bennett intended, but so much of their collaborative genius is retained that, its monster footage notwithstanding, *Curse of the Demon* remains an indisputable horror film classic. If we had seen no other evidence of the demon, the moving cloud and the shot of the hoof would surely have sufficed. But, then again, we would have lost one of the horror genre's most terrifying images. Among the film's large cult following, there are those who believe that the revelation of the demon should have come only at the very end, but the most effective application of the demon's appearance, purely from a technical standpoint, is actually in the opening reel. Although many horror film historians consider the inclusion of the demon to be a mistake, Dan Peary, in *Cult Movies,* Vol. 2, makes no bones about his preference: "I am in favor of this vile creature as big as a house and ugly as sin. . . . Val Lewton's theory was to not show what takes place in the dark because it can never be more terrifying than what the viewer can imagine. But this demon is more terrifying than anything imaginable."

Although Bennett's script took several liberties with its M.R. James short-story source, "Casting the Runes," his screenplay is true to the spirit of M.R. James, and he retains many of the story's elements, including the characters of Karswell and Harrington, Lufford Hall, the Coleridge quote, the missing calendar pages, the mysterious writing, scenes aboard a train, and, of course, the parchment.

To summon hell's demon, Karswell must somehow pass a parchment inscribed with runic symbols to someone who willingly accepts it. (One can be tricked into accepting the parchment if it is hidden within an item being passed.) In a wonderful climactic scene set on a train, Holden, now thoroughly convinced of the curse, tricks Karswell into accepting the parchment. As if possessed by a life of its own, the parchment flies out of Karswell's hands, and he chases it, first down the aisle of the train coach, and then outside, as the parchment tumbles along the length of the railroad tracks, finally coming to a stop and burning to a crumbling cinder. Karswell's "time allowed" has elapsed.

What is so frightening about *Demon*'s "inescapable force" is that it not only defies physical law, but it also transcends religious doctrine. Again and again, the screenplay emphasizes that the demon is larger than Christianity since the various woodcuts featured in the film tells us this demon is central to all religions of the world. This is the grandest demon of them all, and there is no way to hide from its unwavering approach. By having a demon from hell appear in the sky, rather than coming from beneath the earth, the film rattles our conventional beliefs about heaven and hell and only serves to make its dark force more terrifying, more omnipotent, than the vast run of horror movie monsters.

In spite of the demon's appearance, Tourneur does manage to exploit the unseen in grand fashion. Holden hears the telltale sounds of menace when he is walking down a hotel corridor, and his vision is distorted by the force, as if this hell-spawn were able to melt away the very reality surrounding the protagonist. Holden surely has reason to question the order of the universe; there is writing on Karswell's calling card that only Holden can see, strange music in the air that only Holden can hear. We can easily appreciate his isolation and encroaching terror.

Spectacularly effective is the windstorm sequence during Karswell's outdoor Halloween party for the neighborhood children. Karswell, dressed as Bobo the clown while he performs magic tricks for his appreciative audience of children, looks every bit like a benign, kindly uncle, a chilling counterpoint to the evil he represents. With dozens of innocent children nearby, Karswell conjures up a windstorm to convince Holden of his supernatural powers. Karswell, however, has little control of his own black magic, and the storm gets out of hand. For the windstorm effects Tourneur used four airplane engines, and the effect is staggering. Tourneur also had truckloads of leaves fed in front of the engines so the surrounding air would be filled with debris. These efforts were well worth the trouble and expense. (Director Richard Donner must have thought so, because he imitated *Demon*'s windstorm sequence, nearly shot-for-shot, in *The Omen* [1975].)

Also notable are Holden's night walks to and from Karswell's place of residence. Still the skeptic, Holden decides to break into Lufford Hall (at Joanna's behest) for one of Karswell's books of magic spells. There is no score music, only the baleful cries of peacocks and assorted nightbirds as Holden travels through the menacing woods surrounding Lufford Hall. The woods are backlit in a variety of places, the light source just below the horizon, giving the composition an eerie, misty glow. Holden climbs through one of the mansion's open windows and walks from room to room in search of the library, all the while followed by an unseen presence: the door behind him opening just a crack, a close-up of a hand appearing on a bannister in the foreground, immediately followed by a shot of the entire room with not a soul near the bannister. When Holden finds the library, there are more peculiar happenings: a housecat turns into a leopard (shades of Tourneur's Lewton days) and a red hot fire poker turns cold the second it hits the floor.

In Tourneur's Lewton films, there was usually a way to come up with a rational explanation for bizarre events. There is no such safety valve in *Demon*, however; here magic exists and reason is out the window. Unlike his technique in the Lewton films, Tourneur does everything in his power to convince the audience that supernatural forces are at work in *Curse of the Demon* (just as Joanna Harrington does her best to convince Holden of the same).

Holden's journey back to his car is extraordinarily frightening. He stands in the backyard, framed in one of the huge squares of window-light cast upon the damp grass. Karswell turns off the lights, and Holden is now a lonely figure in the dark. Lonely, but not alone. As he walks between bushes and trees, a branch swings into his face (a startling Lewton "bus"). On the dirt path behind him, we see the impressions of invisible hoofs, one after another, following in his wake. The telltale sounds that introduced the demon in the first reel signal its approach now, and looking over his shoulder, Holden sees a fiery ball in the sky. He stands still, taking it in, until the thing in the sky starts moving in his direction. Then he runs like hell.

Curse of the Demon is full of wonderfully conceived moments: a spooky seance, a jolting on-stage demonstration of hypnosis, a memorably eerie scene in a farmhouse occupied by devil-worshippers (followed by a visit to Stonehenge), violent thunderstorms that serve to accent imagery and dialogue with sudden bursts of light and loud crashes, and hallucinations that serve as grim reminders that Holden's "time allowed" is quickly coming to an end. Above all, a sense of inexorable menace pervades the entire film, making us so jittery that we jump at the sight of children in Halloween masks. It is fitting that *Curse of the Demon*'s final shot should be a "bus" made by the sudden passing of a train, for it echoes a similar jolt in the Teresa Delgado sequence of *The Leopard Man*.

Karswell is one of cinema's more fascinating horror villains, and he is wonderfully played by Niall MacGinnis (who, incidentally, had a small role in Selznick's *Anna Karenina*). Karswell's complex persona is a far cry from the evil incarnate exuded by *The Black Cat*'s Hjalmar Poelzig. Karswell is given a likeable, though extremely dotty, mother, the addition no doubt reflecting Bennett's Hitchcock influence; like the best villains in the Hitchcock tradition, Karswell is more than an evil stereotype. He is a villain who evokes our sympathy, though never our loyalty, and we cannot help but feel sorry for him when he gets his well-deserved comeuppance in the film's climax.

Although the film is imperfect (mostly because of the shoddiness of some of its effects, including an unconvincing stuffed leopard), *Curse of the Demon* offers the genre some of its richest visual imagery. It is ironic that in 1957, while British horror was moving in the direction of the Technicolor Hammer films, Tourneur was turning back the clock with his horror entry. When Tourneur's film was released in America in 1958, it played in tandem with Hammer's *Revenge of Frankenstein*. It was, to be sure, a momentous double bill, as it clearly showed the lines of demarcation between horror films of the past (Lewton) and horror films of the future (Hammer).

Fortunately for *Curse of the Demon*'s endless array of fans, the mid–1980s video release of the Tourneur film included 13 minutes of footage shorn from its initial American release (shortened to be more easily packaged as double-bill fodder). The inclusion of this missing footage adds greater resonance to character motivation, plot development, and overall atmosphere. The scene at the Hobart family farm is a priceless restoration; the inclusion of the Stonehenge visit and missing footage from the seance are also welcome additions, as are several scenes between Karswell and his mother (played by Athene Seyler).

Unfortunately, the remainder of Tourneur's career did little to fulfill the promise of *Curse of the Demon*. Unlike his Lewton colleagues, Mark Robson and Robert Wise, Jacques Tourneur would not be embraced by the Hollywood elite. Rather, while Mark Robson assembled big-budgeted affairs *Peyton Place* (1957), *The Inn of the Sixth Happiness* (1958), and *From the Terrace* (1960), Tourneur busied himself with minor and often uneven efforts like *Nightfall, Timbucktu,* and the Italian-made *The Giant of Marathon*. While Robert Wise was making Hollywood history with *West Side Story* (1961) and *The Sound of Music* (1965), Tourneur had to be content directing ersatz–Poe quickies for American-International, like the unfunny *Comedy of Terrors* and the abyssmal *War-Gods of the Deep* (which, unbelievably, was scripted by *Curse of the Demon*'s Charles Bennett).

Jacques Tourneur died in 1977. During his last 10 years, he had a number of ideas for horror film projects, but none of them came to fruition.

The American feature films of Jacques Tourneur:

They All Came Out (MGM, 1939)
Nick Carter, Master Detective (MGM, 1939)
Phantom Raiders (MGM, 1940)
Doctor's Don't Tell (Republic, 1941)
Cat People (RKO, 1942)
I Walked with a Zombie (RKO, 1943)
The Leopard Man (RKO, 1943)
Experiment Perilous (RKO, 1944)
Days of Glory (RKO, 1944)
Canyon Passage (Univ., 1946)
Out of the Past (RKO, 1947)
Berlin Express (RKO, 1948)
Easy Living (RKO, 1949)
Stars in My Crown (MGM, 1950)
The Flame and the Arrow (WB, 1950)
Circle of Danger (Eagle-Lion, 1951)
Anne of the Indies (Fox, 1951)
Way of a Gaucho (Fox, 1952)
Appointment in Honduras (RKO, 1952)
Stranger on Horseback (Allied Artists, 1955)
Wichita (AA, 1955)
Great Day in the Morning (RKO, 1956)
Nightfall (Col., 1956)
Curse of the Demon (Col., 1958)
The Fearmakers (UA, 1958)
Timbuktu (1959)
A Comedy of Terrors (AIP, 1965)
War Gods of the Deep (AIP, 1965)

TWENTY

Mark Robson

Auteur critics tend to ignore, if not impugn, filmmakers whose respective bodies of work fail to reflect "a unified personal vision," as if talent and craftsmanship had less to do with art than the size of one's ego. Arthur Penn, once a cause célèbre as the "modern" embodiment of the auteur theory (critic Andrew Sarris called him "the American Truffaut"), has since proven to be something of an embarrassment, his 35-year directing career spawning (as of this writing) a mere dozen films, only about half of them worthwhile. In his 1975 *Biographical Dictionary of Film,* Dave Thomson fell to his knees in praise of Penn: "He is a major director, an attractive personality of antagonistic ideas and feelings, as important in the growing intellectual appreciation of American cinema in America as was Orson Welles." His praise is clearly excessive.

As is the case with many talented, if less "personal," film directors, Mark Robson and Robert Wise have not been fairly served by the precepts of auteur criticism. Neither of them deserves to be continually overlooked or denigrated by anyone professing an interest in the art of filmmaking or the history of the Hollywood industry. Of the Lewton trio of directors, Mark Robson seems to have taken the largest number of critical blows, and yet, in the same amount of time that it took Arthur Penn to direct his uneven dozen, Robson managed to direct 33 features, many more than a dozen of them being praiseworthy.

The public attended Robson's films in droves. The Academy of Motion Picture Arts and Sciences nominated 11 Mark Robson films for no less than 30 assorted categories. Robson was himself nominated for Best Director two years in a row (for *Peyton Place* and *The Inn of the Sixth Happiness*). It is doubtful that Arthur Kennedy ever had a bad word to say about Robson; Kennedy received four Oscar nominations (three as Best Supporting Actor [*Champion, Trial,* and *Peyton Place*] and one as Best Actor *[Bright Victory]*) for his performances in Mark Robson films. In 1957 *Peyton Place* was nominated for a total of nine categories, including Best Picture. While it is not our intention to extol Mark Robson as a cinematic genius (or put undue stock in Academy Award pageants), the majority of his films have compelling moments, thanks to his direction, and nearly all of them boast quality performances. Robson's best post–Lewton films could be thought-provoking and satisfying, his worst could be maudlin, trashy, and overdone; but whatever shortcomings he had as a director, Mark Robson left behind a consistently entertaining body of work.

For a time, Robson's name carried considerable clout in Hollywood. He garnered enough of a reputation to work with some of the best performers the industry had to offer: Kirk Douglas, Gloria Graham, Susan Hayward, Dana Andrews, Dorothy McGuire, Gary Cooper, Alan Ladd, Judy Holliday, Jack Lemmon, Kim Novak, William Holden, Mickey Rooney, Grace Kelly, Fredric March, Richard Widmark, Glenn Ford, Humphrey Bogart, Rod Steiger, Ava Gardner, David Niven, Lana Turner, Paul Newman, Joanne Woodward, Myrna Loy, Jose Ferrer, Ingrid Bergman, Robert Donat, Edward G. Robinson, Frank Sinatra, Trevor Howard, Anthony Quinn, Charlton Heston, Genevieve Bujold, Lee Marvin, Maximilian Schell, and Robert Shaw. Some may argue that Robson's films were carried by his performers, but this simplistic view seems to ignore the possibility that a director might have something to do with the quality of acting in his films. Performances in Robson's films range from good to excellent; almost without exception, his actors show respect for their craft and belief in their roles. However he managed it, it is apparent that Robson engendered in his cast a dedication to the project at hand.

Although Mark Robson's body of work hardly possesses what the auteurists would call a unified vision, two predominant themes continually show up in his films. One of them addresses the hazards of "selling out" to materialism or fame (which, rather ironically, is exactly what critics have accused Robson of doing). Robson's numerous attacks upon money-grubbers and fame-mongers—in *Champion, A Prize of Gold, Trial, The Harder They Fall, From the Terrace, Valley of the Dolls,* to name but a few—may have been a way of justifying his own success. The other predominant theme, one which is more closely connected to the Lewton oeuvre, concerns the destructive nature of fear. Not only is this theme employed in all five Lewton/Robson films, but it also turns up in a significant number of the director's post–Lewton films: *Champion, Home of the Brave, Edge of Doom, Bright Victory, Hell Below Zero, The Bridges at Toko-Ri, A Prize of Gold, Trial, The Harder They Fall, Peyton Place, From the Terrace, The Prize, Valley of the Dolls, Daddy's Gone a-Hunting, Earthquake,* and several others.

Although he directed within a variety of genres, Robson's cinematic mission was to infuse his films with social significance, a stance he shared with his equally eclectic ex-editing partner, Robert Wise. In Robson's body of work, social commentary finds its way into thrillers (*Edge of Doom* and *The Prize*), war films (*Home of the Brave* and *Bridges at Toko-Ri*), boxing films (*Champion* and *The Harder They Fall*), comedies (*Phffft!* and *The Little Hut*), exotic adventures *(The Inn of the Sixth Happiness* and *Nine Hours to Rama),* soap operas *(Peyton Place* and *From the Terrace),* Westerns *(Roughshod),* war-time romances *(My Foolish Heart* and *I Want You),* and, of course, message pictures *(Bright Victory* and *Trial).* Robson had a longtime interest in sociology, having been a student of political science, economics, and law before breaking into the movie industry.

Of special significance to a study of Robson are his first two post–Lewton films, *Champion* and *Home of the Brave.* They represented Robson's directorial comeback after a three-year hiatus, and they paved the way for his subsequent career within the industry. Not too surprisingly, the two films also reflected the director's Lewton roots.

About a year after Lewton's RKO horror films had come to a sudden halt, Dore Schary was appointed as Charles Koerner's official RKO replacement (a short-lived position prior to Schary's move to MGM). Robson reported in Higham and Greenberg's *The Celluloid Muse,* "[Dore Schary] had lots of friends, but he didn't seem to have the will to force me upon any of his important actors. So when the time came for them to pick up my option, I was dropped. . . . Then I did other things: started coaching actors, making tests, working on stories." Robson (sometimes accompanied by Robert Wise) also attended the classes of Maurice Kornofsky, a famous West Coast acting coach, during this time.

Stanley Kramer, longtime fan of the Lewton films, had been impressed by Robson's expertise; he approached the out-of-work director and offered him a film called *So This Is New York,* an adaptation of Ring Lardner's short story "The Big Town." Surprisingly, as desperate as Robson may have been to get back to the helm, he turned down the assignment because he did not care for the script. (Robson's behavior in this instance hardly seems to characterize him as an opportunist with a mercenary bent.) *So This Is New York* was given to novice director Richard Fleisher and released to favorable reviews in 1948.

Kramer was not deterred, however, and when he had another Carl Foreman screenplay based on another Ring Lardner story, he offered it to Robson, who this time accepted.

Champion, an astonishingly dynamic comeback for an out-of-work director, holds up very well today. The performances by Kirk Douglas and Arthur Kennedy still counterpoint each other nicely, and the script remains crisp and racy, with a number of memorable one-liners. The fight scenes are well informed and superbly edited, owing much of their success to Robson's own experience in the ring (he was a successful boxer in prep school) as well as in the cutting room. Harry Gerstad, *Champion*'s credited editor, won his only Academy Award for his work in the film, but surely Robson also had a hand in *Champion*'s powerhouse editing, especially when we consider the skeleton crews Kramer's Screen Plays Incorporated was working with at the time. It was a situation not unlike Robson's experience with Lewton, where everyone shared whatever talents they had in the spirit of collaboration.

Champion was made for under a half million dollars; Kirk Douglas turned down a $50,000 offer from MGM and chose instead to work for Kramer for $15,000 because he liked *Champion*'s script. Douglas's performance merited an Academy Award nomination, but it also sealed the tough-guy image that became synonymous with the actor's screen persona. Arthur Kennedy was nominated for Best Supporting Actor. One wonders to what extent *Champion*'s performers were coached by Robson.

In *Champion,* Robson applied much of what he had learned from his Lewton experience, including an effective rendering of a studio-bound style, with many scenes displaying the typical low-key lighting we have come to expect from the dark cinema of the late 1940s. The scene where Midge Kelly (Douglas) punches a table lamp, plunging the room into a darkness that foreshadows his own doom, displays the same kind of pithy cinematic shorthand that was so common in the Lewton films. Later, when Midge punches his crippled brother (Kennedy), a low hanging lamp is knocked askew, the swinging fixture throwing shifting patterns of darkness and light about the room, prefiguring a similar use of a hanging lamp in Hitchcock's *Psycho*.

When Midge refuses to throw a fight, he and his manager (played by Paul Stewart), fearing a confrontation with the gamblers they have double-crossed, leave the empty locker room and gaze into the empty, underlit corridors that seem to stretch forever in either direction. As Midge and his manager make a reluctant journey down one dark passageway, they see the threatening shadows of two men around a corner. Midge and Stewart separate; the latter tries to telephone for help as a shadow approaches from behind, but the unseen thug knocks him unconscious. Midge, meanwhile, enters the dark arena and, suddenly realizing he is not alone, heads toward the ring, the only well-lit location in the spacious hall. As he gets into the ring, the faceless men move like sharks in the surrounding darkness, converging from all sides, closing in. This sequence plays like a variation of the swimming pool set piece in *Cat People*.

The final bout of *Champion* is so relentlessly brutal it makes one suspect Robson was reaching for the kind of frisson delivered by the frightening climax of a classic horror movie. Although the viewers know that something ugly and inhuman lurks beneath the surface of Midge's handsome face and cocky grin, they never expect the horror that emerges in the film's climactic final bout. As Midge is pummeled in the ring, his facial injuries grow more frightful with each round (courtesy of a realistic and very graphic makeup job), and we are given the distinct impression that we are finally getting a look at the real Midge Kelly who, like a Dorian Gray of the boxing canvas, is growing uglier by the second. When Midge's mind snaps and he faces the fight audience (and the camera) in close-up, his ferocious grimace, replete with gore and battered flesh, is loathsome enough to send chills up the spine of the most jaded horror fan. Robson brings time screeching to a halt for a long, close look at one of the most horrific images to ever find its way into a mainstream Hollywood film.

Home of the Brave also has its share of chills, at least more than most people expect from a war movie. It was, in its day, a brave little picture, closer in spirit to Robson's work with Lewton than it was to any of the director's later, more extravagantly mounted, war films. Like several of its brethren (*The Lost Weekend, The Snake Pit, Caged*), *Home of the Brave* was a message film with horrific overtones. While it is not nearly as well made as *Champion*, nor is its direction as impressive, *Home of the Brave* was the first Hollywood film to deal squarely with race problems in modern America; it became a sensation among liberal-thinking Americans.

Based on a play by Arthur Laurents which used a Jewish soldier as the target of persecution, *Home of the Brave* was rewritten by Carl Foreman, who, realizing that antisemitism had already been the issue of *Crossfire* (1947) and *Gentleman's Agreement* (1948), decided to change the main character to a black man (played by James Edwards). Told in various flashbacks guided by the investigation of an Army psychiatrist, *Home of the Brave*'s pseudo-mystery narrative structure most closely resembles Litvak's *The Snake Pit*, a film which Robson was probably familiar with, given its similarity to his own *Bedlam*.

Actually, though, *Home of the Brave* is closer to *Isle of the Dead* than to any other Lewton film. The titles alone reveal a bizarre juxtaposition: *Isle of the Dead/Home of the Brave*. Both films are explorations of fear and claustrophobia centering upon a handful of people in forced isolation; as in *Isle*, fear is the fragmenting force that disrupts the unity of the group. *Home of the Brave*'s five soldiers are dropped off on an enemy-occupied island where they must remain until their designated pickup time. Their mission is to survey their location (with Edwards as the master surveyor), draw a map, and come back alive. The group is composed of a young officer (Douglas Dick), a seasoned soldier (Frank Lovejoy), a good-natured young recruit (Lloyd Bridges), a black soldier, and a bigot (Steve Brodie). The mission is told through flashback as the psychiatrist (Jeff Corey) tries to discover why the black soldier played by Edwards suffers from amnesia and trauma-induced paralysis.

Director Robson and photographer Robert De Grasse (who was behind the camera for *The Leopard Man* and *The Body Snatcher*) make the most of the harrowing mission, their atmosphere of dread being nicely served by Dmitri Tiomkin's eerie, pulsating music (which clearly anticipates the composer's score for *The Thing*). The jungle night is palpable with heat, insects, bird calls, and the cries and gunfire of the enemy, the latter always heard but never seen (the only Japanese soldier we see in the entire film is a dead one). Courage is put to the grand test as the men press on through the dank night, the camera tracking their moonlit progress through a series of bird's-eye shots that suggest the possibility of enemy snipers hiding in trees. The men must be quiet, always on guard, and if they need to talk at all, it must not exceed the level of a whisper. During a moment of tension, the soldiers are startled by the screech of a parrot, and we are reminded that Mark Robson, the self-proclaimed inventor of the Lewton "bus," is at the helm. Later, when Bridges is captured and tortured, the four remaining men hear his agonized screams piercing the night. "If he's screaming, it means he's alive," says one of the men, grasping at any form of hope. Although an "invisible enemy" had previously been maintained to great effect in John Ford's *Lost Patrol* (1934) and Tay Garnett's *Bataan* (1943), Robson's exploitation of the unseen in *Home of the Brave* is pure Lewton.

In between the two Kramer productions, Robson had been rehired by RKO at a figure which was, according to the director, about 10 or 20 times his former salary. His first film was *Roughshod,* a moody Western-noir (not without its Lewtonesque moments) in the tradition of Raoul Walsh's *Pursued* (1947), Sidney Lanier's *Station West* (1948), and Robert Wise's *Blood on the Moon* (1948). For a time, all three Robson films—*Champion, Roughshod,* and *Home of the Brave*—were playing theaters simultaneously, and before the year was out, Robson would sign up with Samuel Goldwyn Productions and release yet another film, *My Foolish Heart,* starring Dana Andrews, Susan Hayward, and Lewton-veteran, Kent Smith.

Based on a story by J.D. Salinger, *My Foolish Heart* was the first of Robson's many maudlin, but undeniably entertaining, soap operas. Since this Goldwyn production was shot on the RKO lot, Lewton fans will recognize some of the streets and buildings used in *The Seventh Victim;* indeed, much of the film's lengthy flashback takes place in and around Greenwich Village. *My Foolish Heart* seems very much like the work of a Lewton alumnus, though the connections are with the nonhorrific sides of Val Lewton. Deceptive appearances run strong throughout. Set in 1942, the year *Cat People* was released, *My Foolish Heart* is a strong companion piece to Robson's earlier *Youth Runs Wild,* the Lewton film it most closely resembles in content and spirit, if not in execution. As a film about the effects of war upon parents and children, *My Foolish Heart,* which does not pretend to be an exposé, certainly succeeds in providing more insight into the problem than the half-baked *Youth Runs Wild.* Unfortunately, *My Foolish Heart* shares its predecessor's most flagrant sin: an artificial pat ending.

Although 1949 marked a triumphant return to the director's helm for Mark Robson, he soon became disenchanted and later called his three-film stint with Goldwyn one of the worst periods of his career. He practically disowned his three Goldwyn films: *My Foolish Heart, Edge of Doom,* and *I Want You.*

Robson's first legitimate film noir, *Edge of Doom* (1950), starred Farley

Granger, Dana Andrews, Joan Evans, and Paul Stewart in a story that also has ties to *Youth Runs Wild.* Granger plays a moody, poverty-stricken youth who is too poor to marry his girl and cannot afford to get his dying mother medical care. When his father committed suicide a year before, the local church refused to bury him in consecrated ground. After his mother dies, Granger is so aghast over an elderly priest's refusal to give his mother an appropriate funeral that he loses control and murders the cleric by bludgeoning him with a crucifix. Andrews plays a sympathetic younger priest who helps bring the guilt-ridden youth to salvation and repentance. In a frightening scene reminiscent of Robson's work with Lewton, Granger (who is a floral delivery clerk) accidently confronts his victim's corpse in a funeral parlor. Ultimately, Granger winds up in prison, but not before he finds God. Silver and Ward's *The Encyclopedia of Film Noir* claims, "*Edge of Doom* captures as well as any film the hopelessness and despair of those who dwell at the bottom of society and, together with films like *The Window* and *He Ran All the Way,* uses the vertically oriented background of New York City to create a graphic sense of claustrophobia and entrapment."

I Want You was yet another problem picture. Although the title suggests a sappy romance, it is actually an allusion to the famous Army recruiting posters with the finger-pointing Uncle Sam. *I Want You* is basically a reversal of Wyler/Goldwyn's *The Best Years of Our Lives.* While Wyler's film turned its attention to the ordeals of men returning from World War II, the Irwin Shaw screenplay of Robson's film focused upon men coping with family strain prior to their entry into the Korean War. Although Robson disliked *I Want You,* the performances (by Dana Andrews, Dorothy McGuire, Farley Granger, Peggy Dow, Robert Keith, and Jim Backus) were praised by critics and the film remains an interesting artifact of early 1950s Americana.

Loaned to Universal between the productions of *Edge of Doom* and *I Want You,* Robson was happy with his respite from Goldwyn; the result was *Bright Victory* (1951), a very satisfying problem picture with an excellent Arthur Kennedy, this time as a wounded soldier who, blinded in battle, must adjust to his permanent affliction. James Edwards returns as an unstereotypical black who befriends the blind Kennedy. Kennedy, who does not know his best friend (Edwards) is black, commits the ultimate faux pas when he tells him that he heard "niggers" would soon be coming into their hospital ward. What may sound contrived works amazingly well upon the screen. So does the romance between Kennedy and Peggy Dow, which Robson directs with an uncharacteristically light hand. Robson shows considerable flair in the amount of emotion he is able to work into scenes between Kennedy and his parents (played by Will Geer and Nana Bryant). In fact, so many of the film's characters run against type, failing to be the kind of people they initially appear to be, that it serves as meaningful counterpoint to Kennedy's own blindness, an affliction which, ironically, allows him for the first time in his life to see things as they really are. Unfortunately, although it had many good things going for it, including Robson's consistent and dynamic direction (his best since *Champion*), *Bright Victory* did not do nearly as well at the box office as it should have because it was overshadowed by the glut of other problem pictures with more alluring stars.

Although Val Lewton had been nudged out of his affiliations with Aspen Productions, neither Robson nor Wise were able to gain sufficient financial support for any such independent projects during Lewton's lifetime. After two releases, Wise's *Captive City* (1952) and Robson's *Return to Paradise* (1953), Aspen Productions Inc. died its own quick death. Based on a James A. Michener book (adapted by Charles Kaufman), *Return to Paradise* (1953) hoped to capitalize on Gary Cooper's resurging career after his Oscar-winning *High Noon* portrayal. But the film, shot entirely on location in the Western Samoan Islands, was uneven. Robson, whose star appeared to be waning, gained little from his Aspen experience except a pleasant working vacation.

Unlike Jacques Tourneur, Mark Robson did not think twice about recycling elements and techniques of the Lewton films in a wide variety of genres (boxing films, war films, Westerns, films noir). One of Robson's 1954 films for Columbia, a shot-in-Britain Alan Ladd vehicle called *Hell Below Zero*, borrowed liberally from *The Ghost Ship*; Ladd's character signs on as first mate of a whaling boat (after the mysterious death of the previous first mate) and must contend with a murderous sea captain (Stanley Baker). Although this modern sea adventure (based on *The White South*, a Hammond Innes novel of modern whale hunters set near the South Pole), for the most part, proved a languorous voyage, the British performers—Stanley Baker as an engaging villain, Niall MacGinnis *(Curse of the Demon)* as a drunken ship doctor, and Jill Bennett as a female whaling captain (hardly a "Tugboat Annie" stereotype) are quite exceptional. One of *Hell Below Zero*'s high points, an exciting sea storm, is a deliberate reworking of the swinging hook set piece in Robson's earlier film.

The storm takes place at night, the tempestuous seas making the boat's cargo take on a life of its own; heavy barrels, having fallen on their sides, roll about unpredictably, threatening to knock sailors down like bowling pins. In the middle of these turbulent conditions, a ship mast breaks and comes crashing down, stopping short a few feet before hitting the deck, suspended in a sling of rope attached to the remainder of the standing mast. With the continuous lurching of the ship, the horizontal mast begins swinging back and forth across the deck, and the men are forced to duck its every sway. Robson obviously invested some time in the filming of this dynamic sequence; it works surprisingly well and in some ways improves upon the original.

Robson's biggest hit since his Stanley Kramer days was *The Bridges at Toko-Ri* (1955), a blockbuster epic that was Paramount's answer to Columbia's *The Caine Mutiny* (directed the previous year by Edward Dmytryk). *Toko-Ri* boasts a stellar cast—including William Holden, Grace Kelly, Fredric March, Mickey Rooney, Charles McGraw, and Earl Holliman—all of whom are in top form, giving further evidence of Robson's ability to generate solid performances from his stars. Holden plays a jet pilot stationed on an aircraft carrier during the height of the Korean War. He knows of his squadron's upcoming mission, to bomb the bridges at Toko-Ri, and he is quite certain that it is a mission from which he will not return. In a very effective and wonderfully acted sequence aboard the carrier, Holden sits with his squadron as his superior (McGraw) details the bridge mission. Holden, who has a wife and family, begins to feel the oncoming throes of an acute anxiety attack. His desperate attempts to stave off panic are brought home as he walks aimlessly about the ship in an effort to elude the dark cloud of terror that follows his every step. When Holden enters his cabin (it is midday) and gets into his bed—his final stronghold against the fear that threatens to engulf him—his rising terror is amplified by the normal above-deck sounds of jet engines, plane landings, and equipment drills. This remarkably claustrophobic sequence echoes similar scenes of Tom Merriam's encroaching paranoia aboard *The Ghost Ship*.

Outside of its first-rate performances, *Toko-Ri* showcases some incredible aerial photography and impressive special effects, especially during the running-the-gauntlet bombing scenes. The film climaxes with an intense, nail-biting finale: our three protagonists (Holden, Rooney, and Holliman) in enemy territory, hiding in a mazelike network of trenches while the bullets fly past their ears, facing the relentless assault of the North Koreans who, for the most part, remain unseen. Robson manages to make the Korean countryside appear bleak and threatening; his pans of the terrain are filled with menace (possibly mimicking a technique used in Lewton's *Apache Drums*).

If *Toko-Ri* was designed to appeal to the masses, MGM's *Trial* (1955) was clearly not motivated by commercialism. Not to be confused with Orson Welles's *The Trial,* a 1962 adaptation of the Franz Kafka's exercise in nihilism, Robson's *Trial* is a vastly underrated, seldom seen political thriller that just keeps on getting better and more timely as the years wear on. Set in 1947, *Trial* begins as a race picture and ends up as a fictional exposé of a Communist conspiracy of epic proportions, playing like an inspired amalgam of Robert Rossen's *All the King's Men* (1949), Clarence Brown's *Intruder in the Dust* (1949), and John Frankenheimer's *The Manchurian Candidate* (1962).

After a white girl with a heart ailment drops dead in the presence of an Hispanic boy, Angel Chavez (Rafael Campos), the latter is suspected of murder and a highly publicized trial ensues. Glenn Ford plays a law professor looking for practical courtroom experience; he approaches crack lawyer Arthur Kennedy, who has taken the Angel Chavez case. Kennedy not only accepts Ford's services, but he also insists upon appointing him as Angel Chevez's defense attorney. Ford cannot understand the wisdom of assigning a "green" lawyer to a court case of this magnitude but Kennedy is a smooth-talking, charismatic man whose charm inspires confidence, loyalty, and cooperation. He is also an up-and-coming politician, hoping to lead his grassroots coalition, the "All Peoples' Party," into the White House.

Ford accepts the case, falls in love with Kennedy's secretary and ex-lover (played by Dorothy McGuire), and finds himself the patsy for Kennedy's megalomaniac ambitions. The "All Peoples' Party" is, of course, really a front for a Communist conspiracy (the setting is 1947, the year of the Hollywood Ten). Kennedy and his party hope to build a political platform around the Angel Chavez case, exploiting the sensitive issue for their own unscrupulous ends. What the stalwart, inexperienced Ford does not realize is that his services have been obtained in the expectation that he will lose the case. According to the plan, once Angel Chavez is convicted and executed, the "All Peoples' Party" will have a martyr for its cause.

Although *Trial* displays few of the visual flourishes that were characteristic of Robson's Lewton period, the narrative, scripted by Daniel Mankiewicz from his own novel, is surely in keeping with the "deceptive appearances" motif that is central to the Lewton films. Glenn Ford is the innocent this time around, and his experience in a world founded upon deception is a veritable baptism of fire. He falls in love with another man's woman and uncovers an insidious plot. While the members of the "All Peoples' Party" are not exactly carbon copies of *The Seventh Victim*'s Palladists, they are presented in much the same manner: as ordinary folks who just happened to belong to a subversive cult. Robson's direction is suitably unflashy, providing an honesty and intelligence rare in the heavy-handed exposés of the era. While hardly a box-office success, *Trial* anticipated the substance and the style of John Frankenheimer's 1960s paranoid thrillers: *The Manchurian Candidate, Seven Days in May,* and *Seconds.*

Robson's next film, Columbia's 1956 *The Harder They Fall,* was a rugged, extremely brutal boxing exposé that had more in common with Robert Wise's *The Set-Up* than it did with the director's own previous boxing film, *Champion.* If *Trial* demonstrated that Robson was a filmmaker with integrity and intelligence, *The Harder They Fall* seemed to indicate that Robson had the potential to rival such esteemed 1950s filmmakers as Elia Kazan, Fred Zinnemann, Robert Rossen, Nicholas Ray, Richard Brooks and, of course, producer-turned-director Stanley Kramer. Clive Hirschhorn's *The Columbia Story* praises the film: "*[The Harder They Fall]* combined humour with pathos and revealed the malignancy at the core of the fight world through characterization and narrative without ever preaching. Mark Robson's direction was superb, and drew from Humphrey Bogart and Rod Steiger two sharply defined, unforgettable performances." Unfortunately, the film was too downbeat for popular tastes, and the death of actor Humphrey Bogart cast a morbid pall over theater attendance. The American public wanted to remember Bogart in his prime and feared seeing a pathetic shadow of his former self. There is nothing pathetic, however, in Bogart's excellent portrayal of a cynical, down-and-out sports writer who compromises his values for the almighty dollar; *The Harder They Fall* provided the legendary actor with a very strong final performance.

Columbia obviously intended the film as a kind of follow-up to *On the Waterfront*, a film with its own peripheral connections to the world of boxing. Like Elia Kazan's undisputed masterpiece, *The Harder They Fall* is based on a novel by Budd Schulberg; Robson's film also features a tour de force performance by *On the Waterfront*'s award-winning costar, Rod Steiger. Schulberg's novel was actually purchased by RKO years earlier for a proposed Robert Mitchum vehicle for director Edward Dmytryk—in fact, it was the film that was to follow *Crossfire*. When Dmytryk was targeted by HUAC, the Schulberg property was shelved. Close to a decade later, Columbia gave the property to Hollywood noir veteran Philip Yordan, the scriptwriter responsible for Robson's earlier *Edge of Doom* and before that, William Castle's *When Strangers Marry*. Schulberg's novel was loosely based on the career of Primo Carnera, the huge Italian prizefighter who became heavyweight boxing champion in the early 1930s (you may remember him as the anchor man in *Mighty Joe Young*'s tug-of-war). In 1934 Carnera suffered a savage defeat by Max Baer (who, in fact, here plays heavyweight champ Buddy Brannen).

The Harder They Fall charts the corruption of Eddie Willis (Bogart), an over-the-hill sports columnist who falls into the manipulative hands of Nick Benko (Steiger), the head of a crooked fight promotion syndicate. Benko hires Willis to help promote a huge Argentinian newcomer, Toro Moreno (Mike Lane), a formidable-looking, but good-hearted galoot with a glass jaw. Benko does not care if his fighter cannot fight; it is the package, not the talent, that he is selling. Willis befriends Moreno, who becomes a top contender through a series of fixed fights, courtesy of Nick Benko. Up to now, the naive Argentinian has no idea that his uninterrupted string of victories has been a sham. All this changes when one of Moreno's opponents, Gus Dundee, an unhealthy ex-champ who has no business getting back into a boxing ring, dies of a brain hemorrhage, only partially caused by Moreno's lucky punch. Plagued with guilt, the Argentinian vows he will never get in the ring again. Willis, prodded by Benko, reveals the truth behind Moreno's victories, and the boxer, wishing to prove Willis a liar, decides to fight one more time before returning to his native land. Meanwhile, Buddy Brannen (Max Baer), the cold-blooded champ, is furious about Moreno getting the credit for the "ring kill" when everyone should know it was Brannen, Dundee's previous opponent, who inflicted the serious damage. As a result of this imagined injustice, Brannen decides to beat "Killer Moreno" to a bloody pulp, and the resulting match provides one of the most graphically violent ring fights in cinema history.

Robson's film displays a smart cynicism reminiscent of Billy Wilder's bleakly satiric *Ace in the Hole*; both films detail the exploits of money-hungry predators thriving upon their innocent prey, in each case a good-natured, credulous man who fails to recognize the web of corruption surrounding him and instead sees a friend in every enemy. Robson shows his Lewton roots by including a macabre scene where an uncooperative fighter, naked and vulnerable, is pummeled in his shower stall by syndicate gang members while a mixture of blood and water runs underneath the partition and into a drain.

After such back-to-back artistic successes as *Trial* and *The Harder They Fall*, it appeared that Robson had rediscovered his post–Lewton niche: hard-hitting black and white message melodramas like *Home of the Brave* and *Champion*. Unfortunately, although Robson had exhibited an undeniable talent for topical melodrama, stark realism was not selling tickets, especially when such heavy dramas were readily available on television, courtesy of Paddy Chayevsky, Rod Serling, and Reginald Rose. Moreover, by 1957 the noir cycle had just about run its course. Much more popular were a series of Technicolor soap operas, a trend exemplified by Douglas Sirk's beautifully mounted 1956 Universal opuses *All That Heaven Allows, There's Always Tomorrow,* and *Written in the Wind.*

Taking Universal's lead, Fox began to prepare its own glossy soap opera with Mark Robson at the director's helm. Based on an undeniably trashy Grace Metalious best-seller, John Michael Hayes's compelling screenplay is actually an improvement over its source. *Peyton Place* was one of the largest moneymakers of 1957. On the basis of its infamous title, its inferior sequel, and the television series it spawned (the first nighttime soap opera), there are those who dismiss *Peyton Place* as tripe without ever having seen it. Make no mistake: Robson's contribution to the glossy soap opera trend is a much better film than its negative reputation would suggest, and it holds up enormously well today (better, in fact, than many of the more highly touted Douglas Sirk soaps for Universal-International).

Filmed on location in Camden, Maine, *Peyton Place* is graced by worthy performances from an unusually large cast: Lana Turner, Arthur Kennedy (his fourth Oscar nomination), Russ Tamblyn (an Oscar nomination, Best Supporting Actor), Lloyd Nolan (especially good as the town doctor), Betty Field, and Hope Lange are especially fine. Equally effective in major roles are relative newcomers, Diane Varsi (as the young heroine, Alison MacKenzie) and Lee Philips (extremely credible as the new high school principal who wishes to include sex education as part of the curriculum). Franz Waxman's lush musical score and William Mellor's wonderfully evocative cinematography add immeasurably to the film's sumptuous early–1940s period flavor. No expenses were spared in this Jerry Wald production, and it appears that every penny was put to good use.

Although this Mark Robson blockbuster appears far removed from Lewton territory, a subplot involving a high schooler (Hope Lange) and her sexually abusive stepfather (Arthur Kennedy) generates some effective chills, especially when Lange kills her tormenter and, with the help of her little brother, buries him in the yard as the unpleasant proceedings are accompanied by an effective cutaway to some bleating lambs huddling together near her ramshackle home. While it would be wrong to mislead the reader into thinking *Peyton Place* abounds with Lewtonesque touches, it is nonetheless one of Robson's master essays on the theme of deceptive appearances. In the town of Peyton Place, deception has become a way of life. It is a place where appearances count for everything, a place where good neighbors become vicious gossip mongers, where families become dysfunctional in their desperate efforts to maintain their veneer of normalcy.

In a 1992 interview with the author, Russ Tamblyn reminisced:

> The strongest memory I have of Mark was when we were up in Camden, Maine, shooting *Peyton Place*. It was the night before I was going to shoot the scene with Diane Varsi up on the hill. I remember we were staying on the same floor and I called her and said, "We have to do this scene tomorrow. Do you want to rehearse tonight?" I was going to go and knock on her door when the phone rang and she said, "You know, I would really like to rehearse in the woods where we're going to do the scene." And I said, "Well, it's night," and she said, "Well maybe we can get a flashlight or something." I called up Mark Robson and he loved the idea. So just Mark, Diane and myself went up into those dark woods, Mark carrying the flashlight. We went through that whole scene with Mark just holding the flashlight on us in the dark. That's one of the things I really remember about Mark, how enthusiastic he was, how much he loved rehearsing that way, going into the woods at night with a flashlight.

The Inn of the Sixth Happiness (1958), also for Fox, was another box-office triumph for Robson. Set in war-torn China during the 1930s and based upon a true story, Robson's film focused upon the life of a European missionary (played by Ingrid Bergman) who eventually leads a large group of children over the mountains to safety. Although overlong at 158 minutes, *The Inn of the Sixth Happiness* is a sensitive, absorbing, and at times adventurous tale with rich performances, especially those of Bergman, Curt Jurgens, and Robert Donat (playing a mandarin). Lewton fans should note that Ingrid Bergman's courageous walk into a rioting Chinese prison is, shot-for-shot, a reworking of Nell Bowen's initial walk into the insane asylum in *Bedlam*. The sequence is played for its chills, and as one might expect, Bergman's courage and unshakeable goodwill mollify the rage of the rioters.

With his success assured, Robson remained at Fox where, for the first time since his late 1940s hiatus, he began to slow down. Gone were the days of three, or even two, pictures a year. Robson took time off, and his work became more sporadic. From 1959 through 1962, he directed but one film. Based on a racy John O'Hara novel, *From the Terrace* (scripted by Ernest Lehman) is a talky but intriguing addition to the "corporate drama" trend of the late 1950s. Like others of its ilk—*Patterns, Executive Suite, The Sweet Smell of Success,* and *The Man in the Gray Flannel Suit*—Robson's film is an indictment of the rat race that the business world had become shortly after the postwar baby boom. Paul Newman plays the surviving son of a successful businessman (Leon Ames) who has difficulty coping with his other son's death. The father's inability to carry on with his life causes him to withdraw from his wife (Myrna Loy), who becomes an adulterous alcoholic. Lewton-veteran Elizabeth Russell plays a small role as the wife of the man Loy takes on as her lover. Estranged from his father (who evinced a preference for his lost son), Newman marries a wealthy ingénue (Joanne Woodward) and then begins to ascend the Wall Street corporate ladder, hoping to earn the respect of his father. Because Newman devotes so much time to his career, however, history begins to repeat itself.

MGM's *The Prize* (1963) was an ersatz Hitchcock political thriller with great entertainment value, if not an entirely credible script (by Ernest Lehman, based on an Irving Wallace novel). The strong cast included Paul Newman, Elke Sommer, Edward G. Robinson, Kevin McCarthy, Diane Baker, Leo G. Carroll, Virginia Christine, and *Bedlam* star Anna Lee. Selznick's former RKO appointee, Pandro S. Berman, produced. Set in Stockholm, the film is about a Nobel Prize winner (Robinson) who is kidnapped by the Communists and replaced by a double. In the effective kidnapping sequence, the dark streets, underlit sidewalks and growing paranoia echo the Central Park sequence of *Cat People*.

Much more suspenseful was *Von Ryan's Express* (Fox, 1965), an outstanding World War II actioner that became a huge box-office hit. Set primarily in Italy and based on a novel by Joseph Westheimer, Robson's film combines elements of the prisoner-of-war subgenre *(Stalag 17, The Bridge on the River Kwai, The Great Escape)* with the physical progression of Buster Keaton's silent classic, *The General*. Frank Sinatra is excellent as the wily American colonel who leads a group of allied prisoners on a daring escape via a German train heading for Switzerland. The film works up to a nail-biting finish as Von Ryan's train aims for the Switzerland border with an enemy train (and German aircraft) on its tail. The film pleased the public and the critics. Although *Von Ryan's Express* warrants little discussion here, it is one of Robson's most satisfying films, making it essential viewing for anyone who has doubts about Mark Robson's directing talents.

The remaining seven films in the Robson catalog are a varied lot and indicate that Robson's best years were already behind him. The 1960s had become dominated by a new generation of directors—Stanley Kubrick, Robert Mulligan, Sam Peckinpah, Michael Ritchie, John Frankenheimer, Arthur Penn, Peter Bogdanovich, Francis Ford Coppola, Sidney Lumet, Robert Altman, John Schlesinger, and Sidney Pollack. Robson, already a member of the old guard, could not ably compete with the innovations of this barrage of fresh talent.

Lost Command (Columbia, 1966) was a well-made, albeit routinely scripted, war drama set against Algeria's struggle for independence and concerns a group of French paratroopers who lend a hand in the guerrilla warfare. The cast—including Anthony Quinn, Alain Delon, George Segel, and Claudia Cardinale—was in fine form, and Robson's direction (of the battle scenes especially) was taut and visually dynamic.

Hoping to repeat the success of glossy soap operas like *Peyton Place* and *From the Terrace,* Robson began the highly publicized preproduction of *Valley of the Dolls*. Based on the 1966 best-selling Jacqueline Susann novel, Robson's 1967 film drew considerable attention and business (it even became a *Look* magazine cover story). The critics were quick to dismiss the film as an exercise in bad taste, but the theater public appeared in droves, making it one of the more lucrative films of 1967. Although *Valley of the Dolls* is not nearly as good as *Peyton Place,* it has a large cult following (no doubt enhanced by Russ Meyer's off–Hollywood send-up, *Beyond the Valley of the Dolls*) and is today considered a camp classic of the first magnitude.

The underrated and seldom-seen *Daddy's Gone a-Hunting* (1969, Red Lion Films a Warners release) was the closest Robson ever came to making a deliberate Lewton homage, which is why it warrants more attention than any other film covered in this chapter. Compared to the highly celebrated, more traditional Lewton homages made by Jacques Tourneur *(Curse of the Demon)* and Robert Wise *(The Haunting),* Mark Robson's all-but-forgotten *Daddy's Gone a-Hunting* cannot help but come in last. That does not make it anything less than essential viewing for Lewton fans, however.

Daddy's Gone a-Hunting (an imaginative but entirely misbegotten title for a film of this sort) was poorly marketed and barely distributed at the time of its release. Most critics who managed to see it scorned the tastelessness of its taboo theme, their scathing critical reception echoing that which was given to Michael Powell's *Peeping Tom* at the beginning of the decade. Like *Peeping Tom, Daddy's Gone a-Hunting* may have been underappreciated at the time of its release, but it forecasted the shape of thrillers to come. Upon first viewing, Robson's film may appear to have little of the flavor or flair of a Lewton film (although it is easy enough to spot Lewton in-jokes). With successive viewings, however, it becomes increasingly apparent that a Lewton alumnus is at the helm (obviously one who has just journeyed back from *The Valley of the Dolls*).

Be forewarned: the first half hour of *Daddy's Gone a-Hunting* is full of the kind of pseudo-hip 1960s flourishes that appear hopelessly lame today. But do not let these superficial qualities of the film fool you; the Lewton precept of deceptive appearances holds true for Robson's film, and what begins like a sappy romance with a ludicrous theme song soon evolves into a high-powered thriller suitable for the 1990s. The film (shot on location in San Francisco) is admittedly nasty, but by today's standards it is uncommonly subtle. Moreover, this tale of an antiabortion psychopath is as timely as today's headlines.

With a script written by future cult horror director, Larry Cohen *(It's Alive, God Told Me To,* and *Q), Daddy's Gone a-Hunting* tells the story of Kathy Palmer (Carol White) and her whirlwind romance with Kenneth Daly (Scott Hylands). Kathy lets Kenneth move into her apartment and eventually discovers that her photographer boyfriend is a shiftless, temperamental heel. The camera pays particular attention to Kathy's black cat (a deliberate Lewton nod if ever there was one), which serves as a symbol for the film's predator theme. (When Kathy and Kenneth make love, we see it as a reflection in a tight close-up of one of the cat's eyes.) We begin to suspect there is something wrong with Kenneth when we see him in Kathy's apartment, constructing a tower of books in just such a way as to make the caged parakeet accessible to the cat. "Would you like a little birdy-wirdy, you predatory little bitch?" Kenneth asks the cat. Things get worse when Kenneth refuses to keep the job Kathy had pulled some strings to get for him. When she is kicked out of her own apartment during one of Kenneth's fits of rage, Kathy ends the relationship, even though she is carrying Kenneth's baby. Against his wishes, she has an abortion.

Burying her dark past with Kenneth, Kathy moves to another part of the city and meets an up-and-coming politician, Jack (played by Paul Burke), whom she marries. Kathy is expecting Jack's child when Kenneth begins showing up in various places, on one occasion behind the white beard of a department store Santa, and eventually confronts her. Kenneth, a handsome, clean-cut type, shows no visible signs of menace or malice, which is what makes him all the more terrifying when he brings up the subject of his "murdered baby." He shows a great interest in Kathy's pregnancy, and this frightens her.

Kenneth begins to stalk Kathy, and, though his behavior remains unthreatening, she becomes increasingly unhinged, especially on those occasions when her ex-boyfriend appears and disappears in the blink of an eye. Kathy grows paranoid and begins seeing Kenneth around every corner (in one instance, she sees his face on her husband). In spite of her fears, Kathy cannot seek help; it would mean revealing her sordid past and thus diminishing Jack's chances for election.

The Lewton approach to terror is quite evident in this portion of the film, with several memorable scenes that convey Kathy's rising paranoia. When she rides a subway, she imagines Kenneth is behind every raised newspaper. She walks through a lonely parking garage where, distracted by her fears, she is nearly run over by a car. When she crosses the park at night, she hears the crunching footsteps of someone close behind (the figure seen only in shadow).

While Kathy has her baby, Kenneth befriends her husband in the hospital waiting room. Later, when Kathy and Jack are at home with the newborn, Kenneth (having gotten Jack's address at the hospital) shows up to take some baby photos. Covering her terror as best as she can, Kathy allows Kenneth to take the pictures. The next day, Kenneth tells her he wishes to see her baby dead, and since "murdering a baby" comes so easily to Kathy, he insists that she do the job herself. Kathy realizes she must come clean with Jack. She leaves the baby in the care of her live-in maid, ordering her to keep the doors locked and bolted, and ventures out to tell her husband the truth.

Meanwhile, Kenneth pays a visit to the doctor responsible for Kathy's abortion. After strangling the abortionist with a stethoscope, Kenneth disembowels him with the doctor's own "instruments of destruction" (this later bit of unpleasantness being suggested, not shown).

When Kathy and Jack rush back to their house, they find framed baby pictures covering every tabletop in sight. The housekeeper is out cold. Kathy rushes to the crib and, relieved to see the shape under the blanket, picks up and embraces the bundled corpse of her cat. Formula bottles are strewn about the kitchen floor, their contents white puddles on the linoleum. In a shot that could have come straight from a Dario Argento horror film, we see an extreme close-up of a fly trying to buzz itself free from one of the sticky white puddles of formula. The formula, unbeknownst to Kathy, has been poisoned.

It is full speed ahead from here. The film's last half hour is a tour de force of high-powered suspense, its marvelous twists and turns too numerous to detail here. The police are called in to help find the kidnapper, but of course Kenneth is way ahead of everyone. He calls Kathy, and, realizing that the police are probably listening in, he instructs the young mother to face him alone. He tells her that the baby is hungry and that she should bring some formula. Kathy is resolved to handle the situation; in fact, she is possessed of a newfound strength, one which comes from her maternal instinct to protect her child, however high the risks.

The police try to follow as Kenneth's labyrinthian instructions—from one place to another, from one phone to another—lead Kathy on a wild goose chase through San Francisco's theater district, where no one is the least bit sympathetic of her needs (recalling the last reel of *The Seventh Victim*). Kenneth's planning is so masterful that the police are soon left in the dust. We get to see just how depraved Kenneth really is when we discover he has been knocking out the baby with prescription cough medicine so that no one's suspicions are aroused by a baby's cry from the metal pet-carrier Kenneth uses for transportation purposes. In an episode reminiscent of *The Seventh Victim*'s poison scene, Robson works up some edge-of-the-seat suspense as Kenneth demands she feed the baby some formula he has secretly poisoned.

The film ends with Kenneth (pet-carrier in hand) having Kathy play a precarious game of follow-the-leader along the ledges and up the ladders of a tall building's rooftop. Although these exercises in vertigo may lack the visual grace of *Bedlam*'s roofhanging scenes, their terror quotient is much higher. Kathy is a fairly unimpressive character for most of the film, but when she becomes the resourceful heroine, the avenging mother, she quickly wins our profound admiration. It is gratifying to see the way Kathy conducts herself on the rooftop, how brave she is while walking the ledge, feeling no danger for herself while she cleverly manipulates Kenneth with her own deceptive words. During these harrowing moments, Kathy's motherhood possesses a grand power that is wholly convincing.

Kenneth is a charming psychopath in the tradition of the cinematic psychos found in *Night Must Fall* and, especially, in *Shadow of a Doubt* (in fact, a scene with a boobytrapped outdoor staircase is cribbed from the Hitchcock film). Socially adept and infinitely clever, Kenneth conceals his murderous nature most convincingly. As despicable as Kenneth may be, Hylands's performance allows us to see the pathetic workings of his mind, so that by the end of the film, he achieves a kind of twisted dignity that is entirely unexpected.

Daddy's Gone a-Hunting is bound to disappoint anyone expecting a Lewton homage as pure as *Curse of the Demon* or *The Haunting*; Robson's film is, at least superficially, more in the league of horrific thrillers like *Wait Until Dark* (1967) and *Play Misty for Me* (1970). While not a terror classic of the first magnitude, *Daddy's Gone a-Hunting* could easily find a cult following today; Robson's film deserves an audience, and given its timely plot, it is begging for a remake.

In the 1970s Robson was overshadowed by yet another batch of up-and-coming Hollywood directors: George Lucas, Steven Spielberg, Martin Scorcese, Brian DePalma, Bob Rafelson, John Boorman, et al. In order to remain in competition, Robson tackled the kind of offbeat projects in vogue with that current batch of young trendsetters, but it was all to little avail.

Happy Birthday, Wanda June (1971, Columbia) was a unique, but hopelessly stagy, adaptation of a Kurt Vonnegut play, with Rod Steiger, Susannah York, Don Murray, George Grizzard, and an outstanding William Hickey as Steiger's son. Like *Daddy's Gone a-Hunting,* it was another box-office misfire, as was Robson's next film, Universal's *Limbo* (1973). *Limbo* combines soap opera with message film and concerns the tribulations of three women whose husbands are missing in action in Vietnam (echoing, somewhat, Robert Wise's 1951 *Three Secrets*). Although competently made, with good performances from modest performers (Kathleen Nolan, Kate Jackson, and Katherine Justice), *Limbo* was destined to live the fate of its title insofar as the public was concerned.

Already in his early sixties by 1974, Robson yearned for a box-office success. Knowing his current esoteric course was a one-way ticket to obscurity, he signed with Universal to make one of the more successful entries in the slew of early–1970s disaster films epitomized by *Airport, The Poseidon Adventure,* and *The Towering Inferno.* Robson's contribution to the subgenre, *Earthquake,* was a multimillion dollar star-studded box-office winner. Although the critics were less than kind to the film, its script (by George Fox and Mario Puzo) was a cut above that of the Irwin Allen disaster spectacles. Like so many of the all-star disaster movies, the cast was primarily composed of one bonafide star presence (Charlton Heston, whose stock was falling) and an assortment of Hollywood has-beens, second-billers, and television stars: in this case, Ava Gardner, George Kennedy, Richard Roundtree, Barry Sullivan, Lloyd Nolan, Gabriel Dell, and so on. The real stars of the film were the brilliant Academy Award–nominated special effects by Frank Bredel, Jack McMasters, Albert Whitlock, Glen Robinson, and John Daheim. It was the first film to use the short-lived gimmick of "Sensurround."

Robson's swan song was the unfortunate botch-up, *Avalanche Express,* produced at Fox. Although it boasted an Abraham Polonsky script and capable performers—Lee Marvin, Robert Shaw, Maximillian Schell—*Avalanche Express* was not a very good film. Robson died shortly after production; he was 66.

Although Robson's film career was admittedly uneven, it was not as forgettable as some critics would have us believe. Mark Robson made several important contributions to cinema history. He coedited (or edited) Orson Welles's first three films *(Citizen Kane, The Magnificent Ambersons* and *Journey into Fear).* He was involved with more Lewton films than any other director (editing three and directing five), and he contributed significantly to the development of the "Lewton touch," giving it further definition with the editing innovations that led to the development of two Lewton mainstays, the "bus" and the "walk," both of which remain vibrant horror film devices to this day. Robson (in tandem with Robert Wise) also redefined the boxing film, paving the way for later hard-hitting boxing films like *Rocky* and *Raging Bull.* With *Home of the Brave, Bright Victory,* and *Trial,* Robson was also a major exponent of the race picture; he provided some of the first examples of dignified roles for black performers (James Edwards, Juan Hernandez) in Hollywood. And finally, with *Peyton Place* and *Valley of the Dolls,* Robson helped to loosen the strictures of Hollywood's Production Code.

Clearly, Mark Robson was a filmmaker who left his mark upon the Hollywood industry. If he is not a director of the first rank, his work displays a solid craftsmanship and his track record shows more wins than losses. Moreover, fine performances can be found in almost all of Robson's films, even the inferior ones. A large share of a director's expertise is his wisdom in casting a film; although he was seldom recognized for it, Robson was especially adept in this capacity. In a 1992 interview with the author, Robert Wise spoke on behalf of both Robson and himself when he said:

> Any director will tell you that 75–80% of his job is getting the right actor in the right part. And maybe some of us are more careful than others about being sure, if it's at all humanly possible, to get the right person in the right part. That's a major jump on your performance. From that time on, you can shade some, you can suggest, you can help them move a little bit, and improve. But if you have the wrong person for the part, no matter what you do, it won't work. And this applies all the way through, from your stars to your supporting roles, all the way down to your smallest bit. You need to cast even the smallest bit just as correctly because you want that whole fabric, there's a unity to it; if someone's got just a few lines and they're wrong, it'll stand out and hurt your entire picture.

He may not have been the brightest beacon of light in a sea of Hollywood mediocrity, but Mark Robson's filmmaking career had a significant impact upon the collective consciousness of a nation. Aside from his significant work with Lewton, Robson directed five superior films *(Champion, Trial, The Harder They Fall, Peyton Place,* and *Von Ryan's Express),* ten good films *(Home of the Brave, Edge of Doom, Roughshod, Bright Victory, I Want You, The Bridges at Toko-Ri, The Inn of the Sixth Happiness, From the Terrace, The Prize,* and *Daddy's Gone a-Hunting),* and an assortment of largely entertaining lesser works *(My Foolish Heart, Return to Paradise, Phffft!, Hell Below Zero, Nine Hours to Rama, Lost Command, Happy Birthday, Wanda June, Limbo, Valley of the Dolls,* and *Earthquake).* Of one thing we may be certain: history will be kinder to Mark Robson than the critics have been.

The films of Mark Robson (as director only):

The Seventh Victim (RKO, 1943)
The Ghost Ship (RKO, 1943)
Youth Runs Wild (RKO, 1943)
Isle of the Dead (RKO, 1945)
Bedlam (RKO, 1946)
Champion (UA, 1949)
Home of the Brave (UA, 1949)
Roughshod (RKO, 1949)
My Foolish Heart (RKO, 1949)
Edge of Doom (RKO, 1950)
Bright Victory (Univ., 1951)
I Want You (RKO, 1951)
Return to Paradise (UA, 1953)
Hell Below Zero (Col., 1954)
Phffft! (Col., 1954)
The Bridges at Toko-Ri (Par., 1955)
A Prize of Gold (Col., 1955)
Trial (MGM, 1955)
The Harder They Fall (Col., 1956)
The Little Hut (MGM, 1957)
Peyton Place (Fox, 1957)
The Inn of the Sixth Happiness (Fox, 1958)
From the Terrace (Fox, 1960)
Nine Hours to Rama (Fox, 1963)
The Prize (MGM, 1963)
Von Ryan's Express (Fox, 1964)
Lost Command (Col., 1966)
Valley of the Dolls (Fox, 1967)
Daddy's Gone a-Hunting (Red Lion Films/Warners, 1969)
Happy Birthday, Wanda June (Col., 1971)
Limbo (Univ., 1973)
Earthquake (Univ., 1974)
The Avalanche Express (Fox, 1979)

TWENTY-ONE

Robert Wise

As both an editor and director, Robert Wise displayed the kind of professionalism one would expect to find in a film by Howard Hawks. He did his job and did it well, without apology or complaint, confident that his earnestness would eventually be recognized. Although he was not yet 30 when he took over the directing chores on *Curse of the Cat People,* he had by that time already been on the RKO payroll for more than a decade and maintained his foothold within the studio by virtue of hard work, a positive attitude, and a strong desire to learn everything he could about the filmmaking craft.

In a 1991 interview with the author, Robert Wise spoke of his beginnings:

> After a year of college in a small school near Indianapolis, I found myself without money for a second year and I couldn't get a job in the little town of Franklin, Indiana. I had an older brother who had the wanderlust and had gone to Los Angeles five years before and gotten work at the RKO studios, on the labor gang, actually. By this time in the summer of 1933, he had worked his way up to the accounting department, and I accepted the decision by my mother and dad that I should go to L.A., to my brother, so I could get a job and earn a living. It was the height of the Depression. I was fortunate enough to get an interview with Jim Wilkinson, who was the head of the film editing department at RKO, and he happened to need a young strong kid to work in the film shipping room to carry prints of films up to the projection rooms for the executives to look at, check prints and patch leads and all that. That was my first job and that was my break, of course, getting into the editing department, because I was able to work my way up through all phases of that and finally become a film editor and on into directing.

Robert Wise never stopped being a student of film. His desire to learn, to try new techniques and work within a remarkable variety of genres, resulted in a highly eclectic body of work. Wise's zealous pursuit of versatility may have inhibited the development of a personal style, but such methods did not impede his craftsmanship or prevent him from delivering a high number of significant works.

Altogether, his films garnered 67 Academy Award nominations and 19 Oscars. Wise himself received seven nominations and four Oscars. He worked with as impressive a cast of performers as any director could hope for:

Robert Mitchum, Robert Preston, Boris Karloff, Bela Lugosi, Robert Ryan, Lawrence Tierney, Barbara Bel Geddes, Michael Rennie, Patricia Neal, William Holden, Barbara Stanwyck, James Cagney, Paul Newman, Clark Gable, Burt Lancaster, Susan Hayward, Natalie Wood, Julie Andrews, Steve McQueen, Julie Harris, George C. Scott, Eleanor Parker, Joseph Cotten, Linda Darnell, Cornel Wilde, Jeff Chandler, Richard Basehart, John Forsythe, Richard Widmark, Victor Mature, Edmund Gwenn, Richard Burton, James Mason, Robert Newton, Sterling Hayden, Fredric March, Walter Pidgeon, Shelley Winters, Walter Slezak, Claire Trevor, Brigitte Bardot, Joan Fontaine, Jean Simmons, Harry Belafonte, Gloria Graham, Shirley MacLaine, Claire Bloom, Christopher Plummer, Candice Bergen, Peter Fonda, Anne Bancroft, Gig Young, Marsha Mason, Anthony Hopkins, and others.

In *American Directors*, Vol. 2, Jean-Pierre Coursodon notes: "Wise's versatility is impressive . . . but it is *mere* versatility; no unifying vision underlies it. . . . A thematic analysis of Wise's work could dredge up little more than an occasional and not particularly significant similarity." Coursodon may feel he stands on solid ground, but his statements are predicated upon the auteur theory, which is not the only yardstick one uses in measuring the worth of a filmmaker.

The Lewton experience had a profound impact upon the subsequent careers of Jacques Tourneur, Mark Robson, and Robert Wise. Lewton trademarks—the reverence for the underdog, the focus upon humanist concerns, the alliance between danger and darkness, the depiction of fate as an unstoppable force, and, of course, the preoccupation with things unseen—permeate the postwar films of all three directors. In addition, other Lewton film characteristics, those of *content* (negative forces, doomed characters, ambiguity, paranoia, deception, predestination, nihilism, death) and of *form* (expressionistic interplay of light and dark, meticulous multilayered soundtracks, literate scripts, dynamic compositions, understated performances), seemed to have filtered into the respective works of Tourneur, Robson, and Wise. True, many of these characteristics were in keeping with the trends of the noir cycle, but let us not forget that the Lewton films were instrumental to the evolution and popularization of these very trends. In 1991 Robert Wise told the author:

> [Dark melodrama] was the prevalent style of the times and a number of films of that nature, of that texture and feeling, were being made. But certainly—I don't think there's any question about it—the experience of working with Val Lewton has had a continuing influence upon all three of us. . . . This experience with Val was one of the high points of my career.
>
> You pick some things up by a sort of osmosis, things you're really not conscious of. Val impressed me with the subtlety of his approach, the way he could get reactions and effects without going overboard and being so obvious or heavy-handed. That is something I definitely picked up from Lewton.

(Left to right) **Robert Wise, Mark Robson, Val Lewton (courtesy of the Val Lewton Collection, Library of Congress).**

Speaking of his other major influence, Orson Welles, Robert Wise told the author:

> I think one of the things I picked up most from Orson is the desire to keep my films, as much as possible, strong and dynamic. It was something Orson did very well, and I think that was always a key point with him, no matter the nature of his film. Also, the value of the soundtrack. To Orson, having come from radio, the soundtrack was very important. Although I had already been a sound effects editor and a music editor, I think working with Orson taught me the real value of the soundtrack.

Although Robert Wise's films have several things in common with those of Tourneur and Robson, his direction exhibits a greater visual preoccupation with time; more shots of clocks and watches turn up in Wise's films than in the films of either of his two Lewton counterparts. Time ticks away most insistently and threateningly in such Wise films as *A Game of Death; Criminal Court; The Set-Up; Three Secrets, The House on Telegraph Hill; The Day the Earth Stood Still; The Captive City; Executive Suite; Somebody Up There Likes Me; Run Silent, Run Deep; I Want to Live; Odds Against Tomorrow; The Sand Pebbles; The Andromeda Strain*; and *Audrey Rose*, to name but a few. If a similar employment of time can also be found in some of the films of Tourneur (*Curse of the Demon* and *Nightfall*) and Robson (*Home of the Brave* and *Hell Below Zero*), it was Wise (the sharpest editor of the three editors-turned-directors) who was most conspicuous in his use of clock imagery as a method of building suspense. (Wise would have made an interesting candidate for the direction of *High Noon*.)

Paranoia also tends to be a more predominant trait in the Wise films than it is in the bodies of work of his Lewton contemporaries. The typical Robert Wise protagonist (male or female) is threatened by conspiratorial forces, often from two opposing directions. We see this in *Blood on the Moon, The Set-Up, The House on Telegraph Hill, The Day the Earth Stood Still, The Captive City, Executive Suite, I Want to Live, The Haunting, The Sound of Music, The Hindenburg,* and several others. It is not unusual for the Wise protagonist to be victimized by friends as well as enemies. This is true with all three Lewton/Wise films, the best example being the nonhorror *Mademoiselle Fifi*, where Elizabeth Rousset (Simone Simon) is victimized by both her Prussian enemies and her fellow countrymen. Elizabeth Rousset is also the forerunner of a variety of strong, if socially improper, Robert Wise heroines found in *Born to Kill, Three Secrets, The House on Telegraph Hill, Helen of Troy,* and *I Want to Live*.

Wise's nine RKO films, from *Curse of the Cat People* to *The Set-Up*, constitute his journeyman period. It was during this period that he tested his mettle on an assortment of studio projects set before him. The second phase of the director's career consists of the 18 films he made during the 1950s—from *Two Flags West* to *Odds Against Tomorrow*. It was during this period that his growing reputation granted him mobility from studio to studio (Fox, UA, MGM Warners). The final phase—from *West Side Story* (1961) to *Rooftops* (1989), these two juvenile delinquent films serving as bookends—comprises the director's lengthy (though not particularly prolific) period of autonomy. It was a time during which Wise would produce, as well as direct, his own features.

Wise's first two post-Lewton films were lively "B" budget programmers. Though neither *A Game of Death* (a remake of *The Most Dangerous Game*, replete with stock shots from the original) or *Criminal Court* (a courtroom programmer with a narrative reminiscent of *Stranger on the Third Floor*) were especially praiseworthy, they both profited from sharp editing and sturdy performances. Considering their position as second-bill fodder, they served their purpose as diverting entertainments.

Wise's first significant post-Lewton film was *Born to Kill* (1947). Critically dismissed at the time as being just another nasty little melodrama, Wise's first "official" film noir has gained cult status over the years, thanks to dynamic direction, a cynical screenplay (by Eve Greene and Richard Macaulay [based on James Gunn's *Deadlier Than the Male*]), and marvelously offbeat performances. *Born to Kill* was notorious for being a particularly mean-spirited noir entry, but it had nothing on its even nastier Lawrence Tierney predecessor, Felix Feist's darkly comic exercise in bad taste, *The Devil Thumbs a Ride.*

Feist's one-of-a-kind cult film, *The Devil Thumbs a Ride,* set the precedent for *Born to Kill*'s amoral exuberance, as did the wild reputation, on screen and off, of its top-billed male star, Lawrence Tierney (who, around this time, was making the headlines as a hard-drinking brawler). *The Devil Thumbs a Ride* is more flamboyant than its Robert Wise follow-up, with a narrative reminiscent of Edgar Ulmer's *Detour.* In Feist's film, Tierney gets his meatiest role as the manipulative psycho-hitchhiker, a malevolent Bud Abbott who talks his happily married driver into picking up two women. Thus begins a dark odyssey ending in three deaths, two injuries, one case of forced inebriation, and a near divorce.

Compared to *Devil, Born to Kill*'s sense of depravity is almost subdued. Almost, but not quite. Barry Gifford (in his book, *The Devil Thumbs a Ride and Other Unforgettable Films*) comments:

> [Robert Wise] knew his way around low-budget horror and suspense productions. Tierney's menacing presence is as volatile here as in *Devil,* but the circumstances are slicker—no more believable, really, but more sophisticated. Again, the big lug is a squinty-eyed killer, a rock-hard devil with women, the big brute fantasy come alive in all of his horrifying glory.

Born to Kill is one of the few examples of 1940s noir where a woman, rather than a man, provides the role of the embittered, cynical, morally compromised protagonist. In a stroke of perfect casting, Claire Trevor plays the worldly heroine who goes to Reno to obtain a divorce and walks into a double murder, the handiwork of Tierney. Instead of reporting the murder and being inconvenienced by delay and further questioning, Trevor heads back to San Francisco by train. En route, she engages in some flirtatious sparring with Tierney, who is also aboard, fleeing the scene of the crime. Trevor does not know he is the killer.

In San Francisco, Tierney refuses to leave Trevor alone; he finds her living at the palatial estate of her half-sister (played by Audrey Long) and when he discovers that Trevor is already engaged to be married, he woos and marries Trevor's wealthy sister. However, this does not stop the physical relationship that develops between Tierney and Trevor, the latter captivated by the other's aggressive nature (she has yet to connect him with the murders). Even when, after a subsequent murder, Trevor manages to uncover Tierney's secret, she still cannot deny her attraction for the big guy. This amoral relationship (which recalls the bizarre romance of Richard Thorpe's *Night Must Fall*) led to some controversy. Jewell and Harbin tell us in *RKO Story:*

> Ethically-minded critics sharpened their talons and attacked *Born to Kill* with a vengeance. ... The film's climax in which both [Trevor and Tierney]

> are snuffed out ... was supposed to prove—once and for all—that crime doesn't pay, but it failed to pacify the arbiters of public morality. Much of their discomfort was based on the fact that director Robert Wise made this descent into the human cesspool damned exciting.

No less controversial than the brutal double slaying and the heroine's glib decision against reporting the crime is the implied homosexuality between Tierney and his best friend, a seedy runt played by Elisha Cook. They live together, share the same bed, and fight like man and wife, especially when Cook addresses Tierney's womanizing, warning the bigger man that all women lead to trouble.

Born to Kill is a key film in Wise's journeyman period; although it was planned as a midbudget "B" film, it was given more money and attention and released as a modest "A" feature. As might be expected, its atmospheric use of light and dark—especially in the execution of the opening reel's double murder—shows a conscious design to recapture the Lewton style. Wise also makes extensive use of provocative sounds (crickets chirping, dogs barking, sudden noises) in the building of his terror scenes (each of which is executed sans score music).

Blood on the Moon, released in 1948, elevated Wise to "A" film status. This Western vehicle for Robert Mitchum was a box-office hit and one of the best examples of Westerns-noir, an intriguing late-1940s hybrid with a decidedly adult slant. *Blood*'s closest cousin was Raoul Walsh's noirish *Pursued* (1947), also with Mitchum in the lead role. (Other examples of the Western-noir include Andre DeToth's *Ramrod* [1947], Sidney Lanfield's *Station West* [1948], and Leslie Fenton's *Whispering Smith.* The major precursor to the Western-noir form was, of course, William Wellman's *The Ox-Bow Incident* [1945]. Wellman delivered another excellent example of the subgenre in *Yellow Sky* [1948]; in 1954 he directed the most overtly Lewtonesque Western-noir, *Track of the Cat* [see following chapter], also with Robert Mitchum.)

Blood on the Moon is among the most beautifully photographed black-and-white Westerns ever made. No wonder, with Nicholas Musuraca behind the camera, trying to get as much brooding atmosphere as possible from the combination of rugged terrain and equally rugged weather. In a 1992 interview, Robert Wise told the author:

> We were down in Sodona, Arizona, for all those marvelous shots; the weather changes so fast down there. You'd be at one end of the valley to shoot something, and it would be dark and gray and rainy, and you would look at the other end of the valley and it would be sunny. So, you would pack everything up and run to the other end of the valley for another location, and by the time you got there the weather had changed. We were constantly jumping around, grabbing what we could between—and during—these stretches of bad weather. We finally got snowed out before completing all our shooting there, so we had to shoot some scenes when we got back home. A

lot of the raids and the things toward the end, outside the cabin, was done on a set.

Expressionistic lighting pervades every indoor scene; even the saloon is underlit with only a few dusty lanterns. Outdoors, under the clouded night sky, the terrain is dappled by moonlight and punctuated by a small campfire or an oil lantern. Saloon gunfights and barroom brawls are surrounded by deep shadow. Wise gives a nod to Lewton and *The Body Snatcher* when a horse's whinny is used as a "bus" during a moment of tension. *Blood* is remarkably claustrophobic for an outdoor picture, and seldom has a Western's mood been so interlocked with the prevailing weather of its setting. Wise's film has long been a favorite among Western fans, but it is also full of delights for anyone interested in Lewton or film noir.

The critics rallied in their praise for Wise's next film, *The Set-Up* (1949), which even today maintains its long-established reputation as an all-time-great boxing film. *The Set-Up* did not set the box office afire, but it did make critics speculate about Robert Wise's promising future as a director. Robert Ryan's understated performance as the sympathetic palooka, Stoker Thompson, is nothing less than remarkable; it was Ryan's favorite role (in a career that lasted three more decades) and we should not wonder why.

The Set-Up was even more cynical, more gritty, than Robson's *Champion* (released that same year). The scenes in the boxing arena reek with cigar smoke, sweat, and rubbing alcohol, while the filmed-on-location exteriors (amid bustling streets, railroad tracks, penny arcades, and tenements) are thick with carbon monoxide, coal fumes, and the smells of hamburger grease. In the world of *The Set-Up*, people are either predators or victims. The victims are the losers and the has-beens, the small-time fighters like Stoker and Gunboat Johnson (an over-the-hill fighter whose brains are scrambled). The predators seem to make up rest of the world—a cross-section of which is represented in the fight audience—or at least those who endorse the fight game. The spectators, especially, are portrayed as a vicious, bloodthirsty lot. Stoker's manager and trainer have thrown the fight for $50, but they have not told their over-the-hill boxer (who has not won a bout in years, anyway) because it would mean having to split the money three ways. After Stoker goes several brutal rounds and rallies to an exciting—and thoroughly unexpected—win, the racketeers, headed by Little Boy (the dapper crook behind the fix), decide to make Stoker pay for his mistake.

Although it is a more appropriate companion to Robson's second boxing opus, *The Harder They Fall* (1956), *The Set-Up* has numerous things in common with *Champion*, especially in their respective applications of the Lewton approach during scenes of rising terror. Rather uncannily, there was such similarity in content and style between parallel sequences in the two films that it sparked some controversy (Robert Wise told the author that the sequences were so alike that RKO, suspecting plagiarism, attempted to get an injunction against *Champion*). As did Midge Kelly in Robson's film, *The Set-Up*'s Stoker Thompson runs about the empty arena in an attempt to avoid the inevitable postfight beating. He tries to open a series of metal doors, going from one side of the menacingly dark arena to another (again, reminiscent of the swimming pool sequence in *Cat People*) until he finds an exit and hobbles through an alley, where he runs smack into Little Boy and company. Meanwhile, overlooking the alley, a party is in session; on the other side of the alley, jazz music pours out from an adjacent nightclub. Stoker is beaten, his hand broken by a brick (as this later action is being performed, we cut to the shadow of a nightclub musician in the middle of a drum roll). After the thugs leave and couples from the upstairs party come out on the balcony, they think the battered fighter stumbling around in the dark alley below is merely another drunk.

Thanks to Robert Ryan's poignant performance (quite the contrast from the exuberantly cocky Kirk Douglas in *Champion*), Stoker gains a noble dignity. Even at his fiercest and bloodiest, Stoker Thompson never becomes the "monster unleashed" of *Champion*'s Midge Kelly. The straight-shooting Stoker has a loyal wife (Audrey Totter), who, making the best of the situation, soothes the battered, beaten, and broken fighter by saying, "Tonight we both won," implying they were both victims of the fight racket, a dirty game whose only winners are those smart enough to get out.

Shot to simulate actual time, images of clocks and other timepieces are all-pervasive in *The Set-Up*, anticipating (by three years) the visuals of Zinnemann's "actual time" classic Western, *High Noon*. *The Set-Up* is one of Robert Wise's most highly regarded films, and the years have not worn down any of its hard edges. This powerful fight drama provided a strong finish to Wise's journeyman period and elevated him to the status of a dependable, hard-working director and a talent to be reckoned with.

What is most striking about Wise's 1950s films is their diversity; the director helmed an average of two films each year in a wide assortment of genres. One would expect this 18-film bumper crop to have a number of lesser showings, and there are those, but most of them were of consistently high quality.

Fox's *The House on Telegraph Hill* (1951) was an effective thriller (scripted by Elick Moll from a Dana Lyon novel) about a concentration camp victim (Valentina Cortese) who impersonates a dead fellow-inmate, a woman whose son (a baby at the time of their separation) is heir to a fortune. Supposedly a widow, the imposter marries the boy's guardian (Richard Basehart), only to find that her new husband has his own shortcut to a fortune: the poisoning of his wife and stepson. Although *The House on Telegraph Hill* was not available at the time of this writing, Robert Wise told the author, "You'll find that some of the elements of *House on Telegraph Hill*—low-key lighting, camera angles, use of the camera, editing, sound, music—go back to my early days with Lewton." Authors Silver and Ward in *Film Noir* include the following mouth-watering commentary:

> A film that borders on the Gothic, *The House on Telegraph Hill* is film noir because of the atmospheric photography of Lucien Ballard; the fatalistically romantic narration of Valentina Cortese, who tells Victoria's story in flashback; the devious characterization of Alan Spender by Richard Basehart; and the glacial performance of Fay Baker as the governess, Margaret. Additionally, the hints of sexual aberration, the intrusions of an enigmatic past, and the isolation and ultimate entrapment of the heroine in the old mansion combine the paranoia of a modern setting while exploiting certain conventions of noir-related period films such as *Gaslight* and *The Spiral Staircase*.

Robert Wise recalled the political climate in Hollywood during the time that *Telegraph Hill* was made:

> There was not a good atmosphere at all around town, and I had a number of friends—Eddie [Dmytryk], Adrian Scott—who were victimized by the Red Scare. It was a terrible time. All of us who were on the liberal side were very teed off at the studios for not having stood up for the accused because this was just a ridiculous charge, a terrible charge. There was a booklet that had a list of all the organizations that were suspect. I got a hold of the booklet, looked at it—there must have been twenty or twenty-five of these organizations—and I belonged to three or four, but I guess I didn't belong to enough for them to come smelling around me, so I didn't get a call. It was not a good time.

Wise's next feature for Fox showed an obvious disdain for the kind of xenophobic hysteria that fostered the Red Scare. It is hard to believe that *The Day the Earth Stood Still* managed to deliver its liberal message amid the oppressive political climate of 1951. The cult status of *The Day the Earth Stood Still*, one of the most beloved science fiction films ever made, was forever secured when it made its television premiere on NBC's *Saturday Night at the Movies* in the early 1960s. Mention the title of Wise's science fiction masterpiece in any crowded room, and someone is bound to spout a line or two of alien language ("Gort! Klaatu barada nikto!") memorized from the movie. (Sam Raimi's 1993 release, *Army of Darkness*, makes comic use of the "barada nikto" line.)

Robert Wise told the author:

> I've been asked many times how we managed to make *The Day the Earth Stood Still* during the McCarthy period and how we got the support of Darryl Zanuck, a right wing Republican who had been a colonel in the war and ended up a general or something, pro-military and all that. . . . And I always have to come back to the fact that, beyond anything else, Darryl was a film producer and he felt that it was one hell of a good story, loved the picture when we showed it to him, and he said, "Ship it out!" There was no concern

> expressed by him about the content of the film vis à vis the period of time we were in, the McCarthy period.

The George Pal ground-breaker, *Destination Moon* (1950), is often regarded as the progenitor of the entire 1950s science fiction cycle (which it indeed heralded), but it would be inaccurate to credit Pal's "submarine movie" set in space as a powerful influence upon the decade's science-fiction classics. The two most influential films of the early period of the science fiction cycle were *The Thing* and *The Day the Earth Stood Still.* In *The Thing,* the dignity of every human being—even that of the overzealous Dr. Carrington—is preserved and order is restored by the combined efforts of people dedicated to a cause. *The Day,* on the other hand, is a scathing indictment of humanity. In Wise's science fiction classic, panic and paranoia become man's reigning common bonds; here, the military is a trigger-happy, fear-driven force, intent upon the destruction of a blameless scapegoat.

In the Hawks film, the military may be governed by red tape, but when leadership is called for, men of action (like Kenneth Tobey's Captain Hendry) step forward and take the reins. In spite of *The Thing*'s gentle kidding of Army bureaucracy, the military is presented in a very humanistic way; the soldiers' jovial interaction with one another reveals a genuine camraderie behind their verbal jabs. On the other hand, the film's scientists are exceedingly polite to one another, which only serves to accent their stoicism, their cold regimentation, and their inability to make—or take—a joke.

Wise's film portrays the factions of science and the military in quite the opposite manner. Here, the members of the military come across as humorless, self-important, and bumbling; the men of science, however, exemplified by the Einstein-like Professor Barnhardt (Sam Jaffe), are full of warmth, good-humor, wisdom, and humility. If Klaatu possesses similar virtues, it is because he is a scientist from space.

The Day the Earth Stood Still continues to amaze first-time viewers, who expect a 1950s science fiction film to be low-budget and purely exploitative, a stereotype established by later genre entries which were aimed at children or teenagers. But *The Day* was an adult film, one whose high production costs (the total budget came close to a million dollars, a lofty sum then) made it the most elaborate science fiction film of its day. Its glossy look, its Washington, D.C., locations, and its hundreds of cast extras tell us that Wise and Zanuck intended *The Day the Earth Stood Still* to be a film of rare quality. Edward North's intelligent script, based on the Harry Bates's short story, "Farewell to the Master," showed respect for the science fiction genre. The only thing lurid or sensational about the film was its poster art, which showed a scantily clad woman being carried by Gort the robot (no such scene was even shot), while in the background a hairy monster hand holds planet earth in its grip.

The Day the Earth Stood Still was on Fox's preproduction shelf as early as 1949, when the rights to the Bates story were purchased. When Robert Wise was signed to direct, following his completion of *House on Telegraph Hill,* it was still undecided who should play Klaatu. Robert Wise told the author:

> All of us—Eddie North, the screenplay writer, Julian Blaustein, the producer, and I—thought that Claude Rains would be just right for this role. Unfortunately, he was tied up in a play in New York and we couldn't get him. About that time we were looking around trying to decide, when we got a memo from Darryl Zanuck saying, "Hey fellas, I've just come back from London, and while I was there I saw a young man on the stage, never been in any films over here. He's very interesting; I think he has a future, I signed him to a contract with Fox, and I think you should look at him for your picture." And it turned out to be Michael Rennie. That was a big break for us because here was an attractive, different-looking guy, absolutely fresh and new to the screen. Because people had never seen Rennie before, it gave a big lift to our film.

In *Twenty All-Time Great Science Fiction Films,* authors Kenneth Von Gunden and Stuart H. Stock point out that *The Day*'s Lewton influence is especially apparent in a scene where Klaatu, taking the name of Mr. Carpenter, confronts a nervous circle of boardinghouse guests. Von Gunden and Stock quote Robert Wise, who acknowledged that *The Day* "stressed the very elements emphasized by Lewton in the early forties—fear of the unknown and horror based on legitimate psychological reaction." Wise's film, however, also harkens back to his days with Orson Welles. *The Day*'s brilliantly edited first reel (its newsflash technique no doubt inspired by Welles's *War of the Worlds* broadcast) is every bit as convincing as the mock newsreel edited by Wise for *Citizen Kane.*

So many films in the 1950s sci-fi cycle tried to duplicate the pseudo-documentary look of *The Day the Earth Stood Still* that it soon became a tradition to preface any genre entry with stock shots cribbed from documentary films and accompanied by a newscaster's voice-over. Often imitated, but never duplicated, *The Day the Earth Stood Still* is one of a handful of genuine classics from the 1950s science fiction cycle, and it remains a compelling film today.

Aspen Productions, the independent company founded by Wise and Mark Robson was the force behind Wise's next film, *The Captive City* (released by UA), a suspenseful crime exposé inspired by the Kefauver investigations. Brimming with paranoia, *The Captive City* closely anticipates the narrative framework and overall mood of Don Siegel's classic alien-doppelganger film, *Invasion of the Body Snatchers* (an odd juxtaposition given that Wise had already directed a movie called *The Body Snatcher*). Like Siegel's film, *The Captive City* is a them-or-us conspiracy movie, one in which a man and a woman uncover a plot of such startling magnitude that they are forced to escape from a town whose entire populace, it would seem, has been taken over an evil force, in this case a gambling syndicate controlling the town's incredibly widespread numbers racket. While Siegel's film chronicled an "invasion from without," its Robert Wise counterpart exposed a "corruption from within" to much the same effect. Thanks to the film's taut direction, sharp editing, and deep focus photography (by Lee Garnes), *The Captive City* is an effective exercise in paranoia, one which begs comparison with such noirish 1950s entries as *The Whip Hand* (1951), *The Big Heat* (1953), *The Phenix City Story* (1955), and *Kiss Me Deadly* (1955). In several scenes, Wise flaunts his Lewton experience in his application of the unseen threat ("walks" and "buses" abound). Members of the crime syndicate are seen only in long-shot or presented as sinister voices on the phone, or as unidentifiable drivers in dark, ominous-looking automobiles.

The Captive City's opening scene of a man and woman speeding down a highway in their car, looking back for a pursuing enemy who could be anyone, is a genuine attention-grabber. A newspaper editor (John Forsythe) and his wife (Joan Camden) are the couple in distress. Marked for death, they drive all night to reach a town that they hope is "safe," and there they tell their story to an incredulous police chief. The flashback occurs as Forsythe begins to recount events to a tape recorder. The hero's story uncovers a vast conspiracy that not only involves the town's politicians and police force but also his closest friends. When he uses his newspaper to stir controversy over the unsolved death of a discredited private eye (who was guilty of not keeping his mouth shut), he finds himself the victim of harassment. His phone is tapped, he receives parking tickets as a matter of course, and he is watched or followed by a car with out-of-state plates. The gregarious police chief (played by Ray Teal, a semireprise of his crooked sheriff role from *Ace in the Hole*) is, of course, no help. Eventually, the ex-wife of the political boss behind the racket agrees to spill her guts, but when her visibly shaken husband shows up on her behalf, we realize that this vast network of corruption is more widespread than anyone dared believe. Kensington is only one of many towns controlled by the same mob. Things take a terrifying turn when our protagonists suspect that each of the surrounding towns comes fully equipped with its own carload of out-of-state hired assassins, already informed, poised, and waiting for the editor and his wife. Their only alternative is to drive nonstop to Washington, D.C., and hope their vehicle holds up.

The Captive City is not always on the mark. It could use stronger leads (Forsyth and Camden are sturdy but forgettable), a brisker pace, and a less compromising ending. All things considered, though, the film has a few surprisingly vibrant moments and some well-orchestrated chills. Lewton fans should take note.

Having walked away from a science fiction trend he helped inspire, Robert Wise created another trendsetter in 1954 with MGM's *Executive Suite*, the first of many corporate-ladder dramas which, through the 1950s, would expose the dog-eat-dog nature of big business. Later examples of this topical subgenre would include *The Man in the Gray Flannel Suit, Patterns,* and Mark Robson's *From the Terrace.* Wise's prototype, *Executive Suite,* is the purest of them all and perhaps the best. In *American Directors,* Vol. 2, Jean Pierre Coursodon says "*Executive Suite* may be, in terms of pure craftsmanship, [Wise's] masterpiece. . . . [It] may paint a somewhat naive, schematized, or romanticized picture of power struggles in the world of big business; still it is one of the more complex and dramatically satisfying ever presented by the movies." Produced by John Houseman (erstwhile Mercury Theatre companion to Orson Welles), *Executive Suite* is one of Robert Wise's most courageous films. (Ironically, Houseman's previous project had been his production of *The Bad and the Beautiful,* whose main character, Jonathan Shields, was an inspired amalgam of David Selznick and Val Lewton.)

Executive Suite is of no special interest to horror fans, but it deserves praise of the highest order. Wise gained tremendous credibility as a result of the film and its all-star cast (William Holden, Fredric March, Barbara Stanwyck, Walter Pidgeon, June Allyson, Dean Jagger, Louis Calhern, Nina Foch). Without a note of score music being heard through its entire duration, *Executive Suite* is a masterpiece of editing that moves through its narrative without any transitional devices other than quick, clean cuts. Since the narrative delivers parallel action among eight or nine characters of equal importance, Wise's film is a challenging one to follow and keeps even the most discernable viewers on their toes.

When the author asked Robert Wise what it was like working with such an all-star cast, the director replied:

> It was a pleasure. They were all very good, very professional, and I had no problem with them, even though I was considerably younger than some of them.
>
> I had an interesting experience with Freddie March. He had a very rich part, a man who was always taking his handkerchief out and wiping his hands, always nervous about what he was doing and all. And although Freddie was always an excellent actor, he sometimes had a tendency to go over the top. He had just done a film, *Death of a Salesman,* and it was not well received; he was roundly criticized for going overboard with his performance. So I didn't quite know how to handle this thing with Freddie, to be sure he didn't approach this character in the wrong way. . . . He said, "You know, Bob, when I read the script the first time I just started to think of all the marvelous business I could do with him!" And my heart was saying, oh boy, here we go.
>
> Then he said, "But then I read it again and, you know, I've come to the conclusion that the less I do the better. . . . If you find I'm getting to be too much in any scene, just come up and whisper in my ear, will you, and I'll bring it down." That's the real pro for you.

Wise did not always have good luck with his star performers. In late 1955, he was in Colorado doing a Spencer Tracy Western, *Tribute to a Bad Man,* for

MGM. In the throes of excessive heat during on-location shooting, Tracy had a number of altercations with Wise that culminated in Tracy's walking off the picture (and ending his 21-year contract with MGM). Wise told the author:

> We were at the height of the western Rockies, out in Montrose, Colorado, when Tracy, who was such a hypochondriac, finally came up. He managed to get in a few days work, but we were up about nine thousand feet and he just felt the altitude was too much for him. He was crying and beefing so much I called the studio and said, "I don't think I'll ever get this guy through the picture; I think we better close down and you better replace him." And that's what finally happened. [James] Cagney agreed to do it, and I think he did very well. He couldn't have been more of a contrast from Tracy. Spencer was a marvelous actor but, boy, was he difficult to deal with. Tracy was not very nice to his younger costars; Cagney came on and he was just as warm and lovely to the young people. Tracy and Cagney were the same age, but Cagney was a far different man as a human being.

Somebody Up There Likes Me (1956), Wise's subsequent MGM film, was an immediate success; not only did it insure the director's place among his promising postwar contemporaries—Elia Kazan, Fred Zinnemann, Richard Brooks, and, yes, Mark Robson—but it also turned Paul Newman into a full-fledged star. Like *The Harder They Fall* (Robson's 1956 boxing film), *Somebody Up There Likes Me* (the screen biography of Rocky Graziano) also drew some inspiration from Elia Kazan's masterpiece, *On the Waterfront* (1954). Ernest Lehman's script was originally fashioned to showcase the talents of James Dean. Robert Wise told the author, "The studio had given James Dean the book, which he read and liked; he agreed to do the film, dependent on the script. Ernie Lehman was writing the script but before the script was finished, Dean had that terrible accident."

How odd that Robson and Wise should each make a boxing film in 1949—itself an uncanny coincidence, given the directors' mutual origins—only to repeat the process in 1956 with an additional pair of boxing films. Even more uncanny is how each of the second pair of films tends to complement the previous boxing film of the other director. Robert Wise's 1956 boxing opus, *Somebody Up There Likes Me*, reworks the narrative approach used in Robson's *Champion* of 1949 (a cocky up-and-coming boxer as the story's main thrust), while Robson's *The Harder They Fall* (1956) comes across as a variation of Wise's 1949 film *The Set-Up* (exposing the corruption of the fight game and championing the noble dignity of the exploited "losers" who become grist for its mill). In 1949, when Wise and Robson had their first boxing "showdown," it was Robson's *Champion* that won the box office, though many critics preferred Wise's *The Set-Up*. In 1956 the situation was reversed: Wise's film won the popularity and Robson's film won the critics.

In a recent interview, Robert Wise was questioned about this remarkable juxtaposition. When asked about the 1949 pair, director Wise said, "It was just a matter of timing, that's all. I guess I knew Mark was doing a boxing film, but I can't say I knew too much about it at the time." When asked about the 1956 pair, Wise told the author, "We were always working at different places and, although we were good friends and saw each other pretty regularly when we were each preparing and working on a film, we didn't get around to see each other that much. I just knew Mark was doing something called *The Harder They Fall,* I didn't know too much about the story."

Scores of critical accolades followed the release of *I Want to Live,* the film that gave the oft-nominated Susan Hayward her only Best Actress Oscar. The United Artists release was also a huge commercial success that placed Robert Wise in the front line of marketable directors of the day. At the time, producer Walter Wanger had a personal investment in films about prisons and convicts. After having worked with some of Hollywood's pantheon directors—Fritz Lang *(You Only Live Once, Scarlet Street),* John Ford *(Stagecoach, The Long Voyage Home)* and Alfred Hitchcock *(Foreign Correspondent)*—Wanger was destined to serve a short prison sentence in the early 1950s, after shooting and wounding the agent of his wife, actress Joan Bennett. Upon his release, Wanger had a large axe to grind, but with a reputation besmirched by scandal and prison, he suddenly had little clout in the motion picture business. Major studios were uneasy about the prospects of a convicted felon wielding studio power. But Allied Artists, formerly Monogram, was not a major studio. When Wanger got his foot in the door at Allied, he hooked up with Don Siegel, and the partnership resulted in two films: *Riot in Cell Block 11* (which became the sleeper of 1954, and a major catalyst for prison reform) and *Invasion of the Body Snatchers* (a top candidate for the greatest "B" movie ever made). After his brief-but-noteworthy stint at Allied Artists, Wanger was determined to produce another prison movie (of sorts), one which was based on the trial and execution of Barbara Graham—a cardsharp, thief, prostitute, and convicted murderer. The result was *I Want to Live.*

Wanger's earnestness, Wise's documentary-like direction, and Susan Hayward's spirited performance were the three major reasons for the film's success. Wise's jazzy opening sequences (featuring the Gerry Mulligan Quartet) are notable for their skewed camera angles and their evocation of bebop/beat generation atmosphere (a couple of jazz club patrons are shown sharing a reefer). As the camera leaves the establishment and pans up to a hotel room window above the club, we are reminded of the opening of *The Set-Up.* Like Stoker Thompson, Barbara Graham has made a career at losing; she is about to be "set-up" for a crime she did not commit. Like the boxing crowd crying for Stoker's blood, *I Want to Live*'s bloodthirsty American public, fed by the sensationalism of the press, converges upon the trial and execution of Graham with morbid excitement.

The most powerful portion of *I Want to Live* is its last half hour. Here Wise makes use of a highly objective camera during a prolonged—but nonetheless riveting—execution sequence. While Graham awaits her fate, the nondescript executioners are shown doing their job, methodically pouring liquid chemicals to specified gradations within numerous containers, the very chemicals which, when mixed in the gas chamber, will prove lethal. Significantly (and wisely), the director chose not to tinge these scenes with conventional eerie lighting or ominous angles. Rather than imbue a sense of menace in an artificial manner, Wise maintains an objective, documentary-like approach, the overall effect being surprisingly chilling. Later, with the execution imminent, Wise infuses the sequence (sans score music) with so much tension that the ringing of a nearby telephone (signifying a stay of execution) carries a "bus"-like jolt.

I Want to Live shows Wise to fine advantage; he is in peak form and his direction here was among the most intelligent of his career. Seen today, *I Want to Live* is timely and compelling cinema. Although Hayward could have used some toning down, it is probable that her irritatingly boisterous approach works in the film's favor. Because her abrasive performance creates some distance between Barbara Graham and the audience, it serves to make our belated sympathy for her all the more poignant. Hayward's character achieves dignity only because she is never as unconscionable as the system that condemns her.

With his success insured, Wise became his own producer in his next UA-released opus, *Odds Against Tomorrow* (1959), a very late film noir along the lines of John Huston's *Asphalt Jungle* and Stanley Kubrick's *The Killing* (with a few dashes of Dmytryk's *Crossfire* thrown into the mix). Wise's modestly budgeted crime drama benefited from a solid cast (Harry Belafonte, Robert Ryan, Gloria Graham, Shelley Winters, Ed Begley) and a tight script (by John O. Killens and Nelson Gidding). Shot in upstate New York, *Odds Against Tomorrow* casts Robert Ryan as a racially prejudiced ex-con and Ed Begley as the disgraced law officer who talks him into a bank robbing plan. Belafonte, a nightclub singer with a wife and family, joins in because he is in debt to a loan shark who is putting the squeeze on his loved ones. Ryan plays the bigot, as he did in *Crossfire*, everything goes wrong with the carefully planned robbery, as in *The Asphalt Jungle*, and racism and treachery precipitate the dissolution of the plan, as in *The Killing*. With the cops in hot pursuit, the partners-in-crime, Ryan and Belafonte, turn against one another and shoot it out from atop two oil storage tanks. Ryan and Belafonte's gunfire ignites the tanks in an explosive climax reminiscent of *White Heat*. The next day someone sorts through the wreckage: "Which is which?" he asks, looking at the charred remains of the two corpses. "Take your pick," another man replies. So much for racism.

West Side Story was over a year in the making, and its 1961 release proved to be perfect timing. With the growth of rock 'n' roll in the late 1950s, a number of crank-'em-out Hollywood outfits (Allied Artists, American International, and Columbia's Sam Katzman unit, to name a few) had begun to lure teenagers into theaters and drive-ins with low-budget films chronicling the reckless exploits of misunderstood teenagers. Actually, the pioneer youth culture films of the era—*The Wild One* (1954), *Blackboard Jungle* (1955), and *Rebel Without a Cause* (1956)—were not fashioned for the youth trade; they were serious films made for adults. Because teenagers wound up attending the above films in droves, low-budget producers like Sam Katzman, Albert Zugsmith, and Samuel Arkoff began to churn out scores of quick-buck teen exploitation films: rock 'n' roll musicals, high school angst dramas, juvenile delinquent pics, horror and science fiction films, and, with the turn of the decade, beach party movies. This marketing trend tended to alienate most adults. The two audiences, teens and adults, seemed forever split, and the chances appeared slim that the demands of both factions could ever again be met by a single film.

West Side Story was the film that successfully bridged the generation gap. Teens loved it because they sympathized with the troubled youths depicted on the screen; adults loved it because many of them were already familiar with the critically acclaimed Broadway show, or knew they should have been. Teachers even promoted the film because it was a modern updating of Shakespeare's *Romeo and Juliet*. Based on the successful Leonard Bernstein Broadway hit (already responsible for a best-selling Broadway soundtrack), Wise's film adaptation, co-directed with Jerome Robbins, was released with a fanfare that was picked up by an entire pop culture. Indeed, in addition to the film's soundtrack LP becoming a number-one chart-buster, several of its songs—"Tonight," "America," "Maria," and "There's a Place for Us" among them—became AM radio hit covers by rock/pop outfits like "The Tokens" and "Jay and the Americans." All across America, children stopped playing "cowboys and Indians" and switched to staging "rumbles" between *West Side Story*'s rival gangs, the Jets and the Sharks, snapping their fingers as they mimicked portions of the overture. In short, *West Side Story* was a pop culture phenomenon; after the film walked away with all but one of the 11 Academy Awards for which it was nominated (including Best Picture and Best Director), its popularity soared even further. Robert Wise was suddenly the most talked about filmmaker in Hollywood.

In an effort to show he could live without spectacle and epic budgets, Wise followed *West Side Story* with a modest adaptation of William Gibson's serio-comic *Two for the Seesaw*. The results were somewhat stagy and not entirely satisfying, even with solid support from Robert Mitchum (as a tired businessman on the verge of divorce) and Shirley MacLaine (as the Greenwich Village kook who falls in love with him). After the ballyhoos of *West Side Story*, a follow-up with as low a profile as *Two for the Seesaw* was bound to disappoint, and disappoint it did.

With the misfire of *Seesaw*, following the history-making success of *West*

Side Story, Robert Wise felt the pressure to make another epic musical. For the time being, though, he resisted, determined to first express his gratitude to the producer who had given him his first directing assignment. Since 1959, Wise had had his eye on a particular property that would put him back in touch with his Lewton roots. In a 1991 interview, Wise told the author, "Lewton was the unifying force between the directing styles of Jacques, Mark, and myself because all of his films had a certain touch and a certain feeling; most of them were in the horror genre so I think they all had certain kinds of requirements: that sort of low key lighting, the kind of setups you would get, the kind of casting you would choose, the overall look of the film. Lewton's vision was very strongly imprinted on our films."

The property Wise had picked for his tribute to Val Lewton was Shirley Jackson's 1959 novel, *The Haunting of Hill House.* When Wise read Jackson's novel (while *West Side Story* was still in its preproduction phase), he quickly realized that the author's approach to terror perfectly complemented the darkly suggestive style of the Lewton films. It is very likely that Jackson had seen many of the Lewton films upon their first release; during the war years, Jackson was in her mid–20s and already displaying her active obsession for the occult—in literature and film. In the *Penguin Encyclopedia of the Horror and Supernatural,* Jack Sullivan's description of Jackson's literary style carries a familiar ring:

> [The] depiction of intense loneliness and mental disturbance in an ambiguously supernatural context became Jackson's trademark. Reversing M.R. James's dictum that a ghost story should leave a narrow "loophole" for a natural explanation, Jackson wrote stories of psychological anguish that leave a loophole for a *supernatural* explanation. The supernatural is a final dark corner in the desolate room where Jackson's isolated protagonists, usually women, find themselves.

The Haunting's plot—about a group of people who willingly spend time in a house reputed to be haunted—is an admittedly creaky contrivance, but it is surprising how many notable works of horror fiction and horror cinema have made wonderful use of this chestnut. Richard Matheson's novel *Hell House* (adapted to the screen as *The Legend of Hell House* in 1973) owes a great debt to Jackson's novel, as does William Castle's unforgettably kookie 1959 film, *The House on Haunted Hill,* a film whose title is an anagramlike reconfiguration of *The Haunting of Hill House.*

Like the later Matheson novel, Jackson's *The Haunting of Hill House* concerns a psychic investigator who, along with a few choice companions (those who are susceptible to supernatural presences), spends a few harrowing nights in a haunted mansion. Jackson's novel may have been inspired by Lewis Allen's decidedly Lewtonesque haunted house film, *The Uninvited.* While the plot contrivances between the two works differ, *The Uninvited*'s moody and morose heroine, Stella Meredeth (Gail Russell), is the probable antecedent for the ultrasensitive and deeply neurotic Eleanor Vance found in the Jackson novel. *The Haunting of Hill House* offers a number of significant parallels to *The Uninvited*—female ghosts, cold spots, mournful disembodied cries in the night—all wrapped up in a history of suicide, violent death, and murder most foul.

Filmed in black and white during a time when color was very much in vogue, *The Haunting* (a shortened version of the novel's title) was only mildly successful during its initial release. Over the years, however, Wise's film has gained a wide cult audience, even among cinephiles who are not particularly enamored of the horror genre. There are many who consider *The Haunting* to be the scariest haunted house film ever made, a veritable *Citizen Kane* of ghost films. In *Cut* (Christopher Golden's collection of horror movie essays by horror fiction writers), Nancy Holder comments in her essay "Why *The Haunting* Is So Damned Scary":

> A bare-bones synopsis of *The Haunting,* book and film, may rattle like a skeleton of tired cliches . . . but *The Haunting* does anything but rattle.
>
> Nor does it roar, and that's one of the most amazing things about it. This is a movie that never jumps out at you. In the immortal words of Stephen King, "She creeps." And creeps, and crawls, and squeezes you too tight, and doesn't let go . . . even after the last foot of film flaps off the reel. It follows you home . . . but it never quite catches you.

Because Jackson's novel celebrated an approach to terror that was virtually interchangeable with the suggestive style of the Lewton films, Wise managed to create a deliberate Lewton homage that was at the same time faithful to its literary source. Not only did Wise direct a film that bore all the Lewton trademarks (a literate script, strong female characters, expressionistic photography, low-key lighting, a dynamic multilayered soundtrack, a sense of irrevocable doom, and, of course, an accent on the unseen), but he also seasoned his cinematic tribute with numerous "walks" and "buses." Wise's use of skewed camera angles, alternating depths of field, including "fisheye" distortion, all within the interior of a massive home, recalls Orson Welles's flamboyant visuals in *Citizen Kane* and, especially, *The Magnificent Ambersons.*

Curse of the Cat People (which used the Ambersons mansion) is also echoed in *The Haunting.* In *Curse,* the character of Barbara Farren (Elizabeth Russell), a woman trapped into providing hand-and-foot service to her unappreciative invalid mother, provides a rich parallel to *The Haunting*'s Eleanor Vance (Julie Harris). It's true that scriptwriter Nelson Gidding was only following the events laid out in the Jackson novel, but this similarity was surely not lost on Robert Wise.

Eleanor's personality is nothing like that of the mean-spirited Barbara Farren; rather, Eleanor is more like a grown-up version of *Curse*'s fanciful, introspecitve, and very sensitive young protagonist, Amy Reed. Unfortunately,

Eleanor is not lucky enough to have spiritual companions as benevolent as Amy's secret friend, Irena. The spirits of Hill House mock Eleanor's existence; they write her name on the wall, and they accent the guilt she feels over her mother's death. In spite of her terror, the attachment Eleanor feels with Hill House (and the unseen forces that occupy it) is every bit as strong a bond as that between Amy and her imaginary friend.

Eleanor has been handpicked by ghost-hunter Dr. Markway (Richard Johnson) because he believes she possesses the power of telekinesis; as a young girl, Eleanor caused rocks to shower upon the roof of her home, an incident covered by the newspress. Eleanor and Dr. Markway are joined at Hill House by Theo (Claire Bloom), the manipulative telepath who befriends (and is attracted to) Eleanor. Like many of the Lewton films, Jackson's story of the supernatural also calls for a doubting Thomas. In the early Lewton films, such a character was often played by Tom Conway (in Tourneur's *Curse of the Demon* it is played by Dana Andrews). In *The Haunting,* the skeptic is Luke Sanderson (Russ Tamblyn), who completes the party of four not by virtue of his connection with the paranormal but, rather, because he is the heir to the house and wants to convince himself that the structure's dark reputation is foundless.

The Haunting evokes our most atavistic fears—those of being isolated, stalked and trapped—all conveyed with an accent on the unknown, on the dark. In fact, the housekeeper warns the four guests: "No one lives any closer than town; no one will come any closer than that. So no one will hear you if you scream. In the night. In the dark."

Most of us can remember what it was like being a frightened child in a darkened bedroom. We can remember how power of suggestion enabled the dark to play tricks with our vision and how innocuous objects—articles of clothing, blankets, toys, furniture, lamps—would be transformed into things of menace with horrifying faces, sources of terror that could only be vanquished by a light bulb or the sun's belated rays. Such primal fears of the dark are given free rein in *The Haunting,* especially when Eleanor, hearing unintelligible mumblings mixed with plaintive cries, begins to imagine a face in her bedroom wall's ornate scrollwork. When Eleanor feels her hand taken in a vicelike grip, she believes the contact comes from her bedroom companion, but Theo turns out to be nowhere near Eleanor's bed during the time of this incident, and Eleanor is left pondering the chilling question: "Whose hand was I holding?" This is a horror sequence that continues to have the most profound effect on viewers, one that is long-remembered when the spooky walks and sudden jolts of *The Haunting* have departed from memory.

In Stephen King's nonfiction *Danse Macabre,* the best-selling author reveals an appreciation for subtlety in horror fiction and film, but admits a bias against horror that is left completely to the realm of the imagination. King likens this approach to a poker player refusing to show his hand. Nonetheless, discussion of the Shirley Jackson novel and the Robert Wise film take up many pages in King's study of the horror genre. King comments:

> We never actually see whatever it is that haunts Hill House. *Something* is there, all right. . . . *Something* knocks on the wall with a sound like cannonfire. And most apropos to where we are now, this same something causes a door to bulge grotesquely inward until it looks like a great convex bubble—a sight so unusual to the eye that the mind reacts with horror . . . something is scratching at the door. In a very real way, in spite of fine acting, fine direction, and the marvelous black and white photography of David Boulton, what we have in the Wise film . . . is one of the world's few radio horror movies. Something is scratching at that ornate, paneled door, something horrible . . . but it is a door Wise elects never to open.

If *The Haunting* is guilty of frustrating some of our expectations, its sense of undisclosed terror does not make the film any less frightening. Some viewers may be frustrated never knowing whether Hill House is really haunted (the unexplained events may come from Eleanor's "self-inflicting" use of telekinisis—a subsconscious desire to punish herself for her mother's death), but, obviously, this ambiguity has not stopped the film from developing a tremendous cult following. Regardless of *The Haunting*'s open-ended quality, this author can attest that the film goes over amazingly well with modern high school audiences, and a tougher house of horror critics you will never see. Whatever it is that works so well in *The Haunting,* it remains vibrant today.

In comparing *The Haunting* with Jacques Tourneur's *Curse of the Demon,* it would be difficult to make a case for either one being superior to the other. Both are classy productions, *The Haunting* a little more so, and yet both films somehow manage to capture the flavor, the excitement, and the raw ingenuity of "B" budget filmmaking. Economy was a driving force, as both productions were shot in England primarily to save money.

In a 1991 interview, Robert Wise told the author:

> When I read Shirley Jackson's book, I immediately thought of those days with Lewton and the kind of film I felt I could get out of this, so *The Haunting* became a tribute to Val Lewton. I wanted to return to that genre of film. One thing I might mention is that it was all shot, and finished up in England. The screenplay was written just after I finished *West Side Story.* At some point or other, after United Artists kept putting it off, they gave me the right to take it someplace else. I owed MGM one more picture from the old contract I'd gotten out of, so my agent said maybe MGM would be interested and we could work that other committment off to them. So we took it over to them and they liked it and wanted to do it, but they didn't want to put over a million dollars into it at that time, and I could not get a decent budget of any kind on the picture at the MGM Culver City lot. They were just not willing to go for it. Somebody mentioned, "Well, why don't you try their English studio?" I happened to be going over to England about that time for a special showing—a command performance—of *West Side Story* for the queen in London, so I

took along a copy of the script, took it out to the people at the MGM studios and left it with them, telling them how I saw it being done. They came back with a budget of a million fifty thousand dollars. MGM said they would go for that, and so that's what took us to England to make the film.

I kept the New England background of Shirley Jackson's original story and faked some of the shooting over there. A movie like *The Haunting* is a great deal of fun for a director; you can do wonders with your lighting, your camera angles, your effects, your sound, your music. It's a rich tapestry that you can play with like mad in that kind of film, and I tried to work that to the hilt. I've had any number of people over the years say to me, "You know, Mr. Wise, you made the scariest picture I've ever seen and you never showed anything. How'd you do it?" And it goes back to Val Lewton, by the powers of suggestion.

A couple other interesting points.... Because the soundtrack of the offstage voices was so important in those sequences where the people are reacting to what's outside the door, I decided to prescore the film, like you would a musical, with a soundtrack on a playback machine and a big speaker outside the doors for the actors to react to. It made a great difference in the success of those sequences. Filming *The Haunting* was one of my favorite experiences, and I count it among one of my ten or twelve favorites of the thirty-nine films I've done. I enjoyed doing it, and I think it came off well. I'm very pleased and very proud of that one.

Mr. Wise neglected to mention, however, what manner of house was selected for *The Haunting*'s exterior scenes. In a 1992 interview, Russ Tamblyn told the author:

When Robert Wise went to England, he went to some society for haunted houses, where haunted houses are officially registered, and he found one of the oldest, dating back hundreds of years, about ten or fifteen miles outside of Stratford on Avon, and that's where we shot *The Haunting*'s exteriors. It was definitely a strange place, especially the grounds. The house, itself, had a history . . . oh, children who had been murdered, and a twelve-year-old who had committed suicide, some other woman who fell out of a window. . . . There was a bunch of stuff like that which had happened in this house, and there was a little cemetery behind it which was reported to be haunted. People had seen ghosts in this place, even those who had no idea of its reputation. The house was being used as an inn, and you could go in there and have a drink at night—it was a huge library—and the library was set up with tables. The owner—the innkeeper—asked us, "Please just do me the favor while you're here, and don't spread the word around that this place is haunted." He said he had people who had seen ghosts there—the same ghosts that people had seen for hundreds of years—without even knowing about the house's reputation.

We were boarders there for about a week while we were shooting the exteriors. . . . I never saw any ghosts—and no one else did either—but I did have a chilling experience. One night I went out for a walk in the dark, by the little cemetery about fifty yards in back of the house, and it was pitch black. I followed a path out there and decided to go out to look for a ghost. The shooting was being done in front of the house so I went in the back where

> it was so dark you could just make out the silhouette of the house. I walked way out and turned around, and I'll never forget this: I could just hear the noise of the arc lights that were in front, making this great silhouette, and all of a sudden I got this chill on the back of my neck. It was like somebody had laid a big piece of ice there, so much so that my head actually went forward. I had gone out there to look for a ghost, and I knew there was something behind me, but now that I knew it was there I didn't want to actually see it. There was a quick moment when I wondered, do I want to turn around or do I want to walk? And I just walked, walked straight back to the house. I don't know if there was a ghost there or not. But there was something ice cold on the back of my neck, I'll tell you that.

In Shirley Jackson's words (which begin and end both the novel and the film): "Within, walls continued upright, bricks met neatly, floors were firm, and doors were sensibly shut; silence lay steadily against the wood and stone of Hill House, and whatever walked there, walked alone."

The Sound of Music (1965) is still one of the most beloved motion pictures in Hollywood history, in spite of some of the critical bashing it received at the time of its release. Critics who were quick to dismiss *Music* upon its initial run were wont to eat their words once the American public began to appear in unprecedented numbers. It played movie theaters for more than a year and, in 1966, was hailed the biggest money-maker in cinema history. Although Wise's reputation further skyrocketed as a result of *The Sound of Music*'s success, some critics who had praised the director's earlier work were unimpressed with the blockbuster status of a film they considered treacly and maudlin. In retrospect, we can see that *The Sound of Music*'s success was enhanced by the political climate of the day. At the dawn of a period of American discontent, the nation's populace needed something old-fashioned and unabashedly sentimental, and Wise's film delivered a healthy dose of such medicine.

Wise followed *The Sound of Music* with *The Sand Pebbles* (1966), another hit (nominated for, but not winning, Best Picture). If *Music* had been excessively sentimental, *Pebbles* was unremittingly grim. Set in 1926 and chronicling the adventures of a U.S. Navy gunboat on the Yangtze River of China, *The Sand Pebbles* culminates in an international incident, one leading to military conflict with China. Wise's film addressed some of the political and moral issues that were on the public's mind during the days of the Vietnam conflict. In spite of several excellent scenes, Wise had some trouble sustaining tension in an overlong (three hours plus) and somewhat rambling narrative.

By 1968 the tide had turned. Hoping to repeat the success of *Music,* Wise directed the ultraextravagant Julie Andrews vehicle *Star* fashioned after the life and career of theater star Gertrude Lawrence. The film was undoubtedly ambitious (it opens with a mock newsreel à la *Citizen Kane* covering the career of Gertrude Lawrence), but its overblown budget and inordinate running time seemed to do little else but annoy critics who were just waiting for Wise's career to falter.

While *Star* failed to fill the coffers at Fox, another 1968 movie about stars, one directed by Stanley Kubrick, had become the surprise smash hit of the year for MGM. Robert Wise had always had an interest in science fiction, and 1968 was a landmark year for the genre. Franklin Schaffner's amazingly successful *Planet of the Apes* had been quickly followed and topped by Kubrick's mystical space epic, *2001, A Space Odyssey,* and the popularity of these premiere big-budget entries induced Wise to embark upon his own science fiction epic.

Michael Crichton's 1969 best-seller, *The Andromeda Strain,* seemed to be a surefire project for a director who hoped to take advantage of the resurgent interest in science fiction. With a six-and-a-half million dollar budget, *The Andromeda Strain* was one of most expensive science fiction films of its day. Taking his cues from Kubrick's *2001,* Wise avoided hiring big stars and allowed the technology conjured up by *2001*'s special effects wizard, Douglas Trumball, to take center stage. Released in March 1971, *The Andromeda Strain* opened to mixed reactions from the public and the press.

Nelson Gidding's adaptation was particularly faithful to the novel, and the film's nonstars (Arthur Hill, David Wayne, James Olson, and Kate Reid) were all very good, but the complicated script, the spare direction, and the austere production tended to split viewers into two camps: those who loved the film for its intelligent, cautionary message, and those who were numbed or befuddled by the film's leisurely pace and inaccessible script. Even *Variety,* a periodical which tends to accent the positive, admitted that "Nelson Gidding's adaptation . . . is too literal and talky, while the principal players . . . inhibit interest via pedantic and lifeless acting of overly expository sequences" (March 10, 1971).

Crichton's story of a dangerous viruslike organism that is brought to earth by a returning space probe is given a dynamic and genuinely terrifying first reel, thanks to Wise's sharp eye. The sequence where a group of scientists dressed in protective gear investigate the mysterious death of the inhabitants of a small American town in the Southwest is remarkably chilling. The scientists travel from house to house, building to building, only to find an alarming number of wide-eyed corpses of men, women, and children. The shots of the deceased, with their rictus facial expressions, are etched in the memories of viewers long after the rest of the film, with its assemblage of unknown performers and its state-of-the-art Douglas Trumball technology, becomes something of an antiseptic blur. The last reels generate some effective suspense, but the viewer's patience may be unduly tested before he reaches that point.

(The anticipated post–1968 science fiction boom proved to be something of a bust; by 1971 even Kubrick's dark masterpiece, *A Clockwork Orange,* failed to solidify any ongoing science fiction trend. One week after *Andromeda Strain* was released, a modestly budgeted science fiction film called

THX 1138 had a limited run in selected theaters. The young director of this futuristic satire, George Lucas, portrayed technology in a sterile, monochromatic fashion [this time white instead of red] that was remarkably similar to the visual austerity of *Andromeda Strain*. Putting viewers off for many of the same reasons, neither of these coldly clinical films made much of a dent in the box office.)

Two People (1973), a down-to-earth drama about an army deserter (Peter Fonda) who falls in love with a fashion model (Lindsay Wagner), is a well-acted, beautifully photographed film. That Wise would bother with such a property made it obvious that he was still interested in smaller pictures that explored the concerns of the human condition and that he had not sold his soul to the making of blockbusters. Unfortunately, *Two People* did poorly at the box office and received mixed notices from the critics. Ironically, if Wise wanted an audience, it looked like he would have to regain his blockbuster status.

Universal's *The Hindenburg* (1975) came in the wake of the disaster movie trend, as did Mark Robson's *Earthquake*, released one year before, also by Universal. The short-lived trend had been spearheaded by George Seaton's 1970 all-star epic, *Airport*, and given new life by Irwin Allen's 1972 *The Poseidon Adventure*. Unfortunately, by 1975 the market for these all-star epics of destruction had been glutted; it didn't help *The Hindenburg*'s box office when a 1971 British film, *Zeppelin*, was shipped to America just prior to the release of the Wise film, in the hope of cashing in upon the wide publicity surrounding the American production. *The Hindenberg* was fashioned as an all-star Grand Hotel-of-the-skies (like many of the airborn disaster pictures) which speculated upon circumstances of sabotage leading to the aircraft's destruction over Lakehurst, New Jersey.

The Hindenburg was deftly directed, with smart performances from George C. Scott, William Atherton, Anne Bancroft, Gig Young, Burgess Meredith, and Charles Durning. Nelson Gidding penned an intelligent script, Robert Surtess contributed some stunning photography, and David Shire composed a haunting and memorable score, particularly the transcendent opening theme. Wise even provides (à la *Citizen Kane*) a precredit mock newsreel prologue. Although Wise's film is consistently entertaining and visually quite impressive, many of the critics dismissed it as just another disaster film and the audience turnout fell short of expectations. Apparently, the disaster film crowd reasoned that there was little value for their money in a film that covered a historical disaster that was over in a matter of seconds. The finale prolongs the explosive climax—via slow motion, freeze-frames, and alternate-perspective replays—but Wise's creative manipulation of time in this sequence had a disorienting effect upon some viewers.

(During the summer that *The Hindenburg* was released, the blockbuster crowds were eating their popcorn elsewhere. The film's fiercest competition was *Jaws,* directed by the industry's umpteenth "new boy wonder," Steven Spielberg.)

Hoping to capitalize on the big-budget horror boom ushered in by adaptations of horror best-sellers such as Ira Levin's *Rosemary's Baby,* William Peter Blatty's *The Exorcist,* and Stephen King's *Carrie,* Robert Wise filmed an adaptation of Frank de Felitta's *Audrey Rose,* a 1977 UA release. Like Wise's horror films with Lewton, *Audrey Rose* feels like a well-made "B" film. Wise avoided a stellar cast and state-of-the-art special effects to make a film about ordinary people, and this aspect of *Audrey Rose* works remarkably well. In comparing it to Wise's previous horror films, *Audrey Rose* is most reminiscent of *Curse of the Cat People* (and, to a lesser extent, *Cat People*).

The film focuses upon a married Manhattan couple, Bill and Janice Templeton (played by John Beck and Marsha Mason) and their little daughter Ivy (Susan Swift), who is soon to celebrate her eleventh birthday. (In what appears to be a nod to *Cat People,* under the opening credits, the Templetons are shown visiting the Central Park Zoo.) Bill Templeton, like Oliver Reed in *Curse of the Cat People,* is a stodgy, disbelieving, and overprotective parent whose patience grows shorter by the minute.

Although the Templetons appear to be living an idyllic existence, their daughter Ivy has fallen victim to a series of nightmares; these coincide with the appearance of a mysterious bearded man, Elliot Hoover (brilliantly played by Anthony Hopkins), who appears to be stalking the little girl. These initial scenes where Hoover is perceived as a menace carry an undeniable power. Wise generates some solid suspense in grand Lewton style with several scenes, including a school-during-the-after-hours set piece that reminds one of *Cape Fear* (another variation of this scene would show up the next year in John Carpenter's *Halloween*). Lewtonesque "walks" (through rainy alleys and city streets) and "buses" (a door slamming against its chainlock, a sudden shot of a gargoyle accompanied by booming thunder, a capsized cup of tea during a moment of tense silence) are plentiful in *Audrey Rose.*

After a lengthy period of observation, Elliot Hoover makes his peaceful mission known. Although he is reticent about sounding like a lunatic, Hoover conveys his belief that young Ivy Templeton is harboring the spirit of his dead daughter, Audrey Rose (the latter having died at the very second that Ivy was born). Because Ivy is quickly approaching the age of Audrey when she died, Hoover believes the girl's life is in peril. Although Janice is open-minded about Hoover's convictions, having suspected that something was amiss in her daughter's recent behavior, her husband (the prototypical Lewton skeptic) becomes a pigheaded hindrance to Hoover's mission of mercy. As the film comes to its dark conclusion, we recognize that Templeton's behavior only pushed Ivy closer to her inevitable death.

Audrey Rose has many effective moments, but once Hopkins's character is no longer perceived as a threat, the film loses some of its momentum. De

Felitta's script becomes inexorably unpleasant as we are forced to witness the escalating stages of Ivy's distress. Susan Swift's performance is fine, but the script provides entirely too many opportunities for her character to undergo severe anguish, resulting in numerous scenes that are difficult to watch (or listen to, for that matter). Wise managed to steer clear of the graphic scenes that permeated the genre in the late 1970s, but one suspects that the director's desire to compete with the new order of Hollywood horror (ushered in by *The Exorcist* and *The Omen*) led him to become uncharacteristically grim in his depictions of Ivy's attacks. *Audrey Rose* is not in the same classic league as *The Haunting,* but it holds a fascination for fans of the Lewton films.

The runaway Hollywood hit of 1977 (the year *Audrey Rose* was released) was, of course, George Lucas's *Star Wars,* the progenitor of the first real science fiction boom since the 1950s. Just as *The Thing* and *The Day the Earth Stood Still* had served as influential early models of the 1950s science fiction cycle, the new wave of science fiction films offered a strikingly similar pair of trendsetters: Stephen Spielberg's benevolent-alien UFO movie, *Close Encounters of the Third Kind* (a 1977 equivalent of *The Day the Earth Stood Still*), and Ridley Scott's *Alien* (a 1979 equivalent of *The Thing*). These two films became primary blueprints for scores of science fiction thrillers of the '70s, '80s, and '90s. (That is, when genre moguls were not producing surprisingly effective "A" budget remakes of such first-wave classics as *The Thing, Invaders from Mars, Invasion of the Body Snatchers* [twice remade], *The Fly, The Blob,* and *Village of the Damned.*)

By 1978 Robert Wise found the burgeoning new wave of science fiction films impossible to resist and soon became involved in his own contribution to the cycle, one which drew inspiration from two ground-breaking theatrical films (Kubrick's *2001* and Lucas's *Star Wars*) and one ground-breaking television series. By now in his mid–60s, and working within a genre dominated by a new order of young filmmakers, Robert Wise directed *Star Trek,* the first theatrical film based on the cult television show.

Although it was enough of a box-office hit to spawn numerous sequels, *Star Trek*'s leisurely pace (in conjunction with its impressive, but rather long and stately, displays of simulated space travel [courtesy of Douglas Trumball and John Dykstra]), tended to put off some viewers, especially those who had expected to see Captain Kirk and company matching their strength and wits with some form of alien monster. Of course, Robert Wise had never made a monster film in his entire career, and he was not about to start doing so with *Star Trek.*

The 1979 Paramount film, produced by Gene Roddenberry (the mastermind behind the television series), reprised the cast from the TV show with the addition of two "guest star" characters pivotal to the plot: Dekker (Steve Collins) and Ilia (played, sans hair, by a captivating Persus Khambutta). The thought-provoking script, written by Harold Livingstone and based on an

Alan Dean Foster story, calls for a confrontation between the Enterprise and an unseen alien force that is as destructive as it is intelligent. Along the way there are some stunning visual effects (reminiscent of the "space warp" sequence from *2001*). Although it is never as lively as any of its sequels, *Star Trek* pleased its enormous ready-made audience of loyal "Trekkies," who were thrilled to see their television series favorites reprising their roles in a big-budget feature film.

Many people assumed *Star Trek* would be Robert Wise's swan song, but, rather unbelievably, after a 10-year hiatus, a 75-year-old Wise came back to direct *Rooftops* (1989), a choreographed "juvenile delinquent" thriller (with an accent on music) that stands somewhere between youth-oriented pop musicals like *West Side Story* and *Fame* and the gang pix directed by Walter Hill, *The Warriors* (1979) and *Streets of Fire* (1984). (Oddly enough, a recent Walter Hill film, *Trespass* [1993], appears to have drawn some inspiration from *Rooftops*.) Produced by Howard W. Koch, Jr. (for an independent outfit called New Horizons Films), Wise's film may exhibit the rock-video dynamics typical of glossy money-makers like *Flashdance* or *Dirty Dancing*, but *Rooftops* is really a "B" movie, one whose spirit recalls Mark Robson's *Youth Runs Wild* just as much as it does Wise's own *West Side Story*. With an original musical score by Michael Kamen and David A. Stewart (of Eurythmics fame), *Rooftops* was obviously fashioned for a generation that had grown up with MTV, and while the film (which had seen little theatrical release) is not always on the mark, it rented well at the video stores and satisfied the youthful audience for which it was intended. (While the style of the film appears to borrow liberally from the world of rock videos, Wise was only working within a milieu he helped create, given *West Side Story*'s tremendous influence upon such music video luminaries as Michael Jackson, Paula Abdul, and Prince.)

Shot with a largely unknown cast of capable young performers, *Rooftops* is a modest but well-made Robert Wise curio. Terence Brennan's screenplay is not always credible (he often tries a little too hard to be poignant), but the characters and dialogue are definitely out of the mainstream. In some ways, Brennan's screenplay is a throwback to Reginald Rose's teenage-angst scripts of the 1950s *(Crime in the Streets, Dino)*, while the story's setting recalls the dilapidated tenement environment of Ted Tetzlaff's *The Window* (194). *Rooftops'* climax, like that of the Tetzlaff film, takes place in a condemned and gutted apartment building (which, thanks to the photography of Theo Van De Sande, provides an optimum of expressionistic atmosphere).

Rooftops is not an outstanding film, but it is a memorable one with offbeat characters, fresh faces, silly dance numbers, exciting fight scenes, and an unpredictably tragic conclusion. Whatever its failings, *Rooftops* has its heart in the right place. Although the film's pulsating soundtrack, numerous action scenes, perfunctory romance, and drug-dealing subplot all suggest that *Rooftops* was fashioned as nothing more than a teen exploitation picture, a perceptive viewing of the film reveals that Wise and his associates had more on their minds than the making of a quick buck. *Rooftops* is hardly the comeback film one would expect from a director with as much Hollywood clout as Robert Wise. During the director's 10-year hiatus, he had become increasingly disenchanted with the kind of formula-bound profiteering that dominated the Hollywood industry in the 1980s, as he told the author:

> Film has always been, even from the very beginning, both an art and a business; we have to have the business end in order to keep making the films we hope will be artistic. What I think happened in the last fifteen or twenty years is that the business side of the equation has gotten so much larger and stronger that it outweighs the art side. We are so concerned with the biggest possible grosses that it leads us—or the business—into making the kinds of thrillers that rely upon guns and fires and flames and bullets and special effects and all that. This is what seems to draw the largest audience; it is no longer enough to simply tell a good story.
>
> You've mentioned that most of my films carry some kind of social message—and I think that's more-or-less true—but I've always treated it as a by-product of the story. To tell a good story, you have to accent people, the world they live in, the issues they're having to face. And any message—if there is one—comes out of that. That's always been very important to me, and it shows up in practically all my films, at least whenever I've had any control in selecting my projects.

A reassessment of Robert Wise's career is long overdue. His impact upon the Hollywood industry has been most significant. Had Wise not become a director, his place in Hollywood history would have been assured by virtue of his editing on *Citizen Kane* and *The Magnificent Ambersons* alone. But he went on to direct films of tremendous importance: two Lewton horror classics *(The Curse of the Cat People* and *The Body Snatcher),* one of the greatest boxing films ever made *(The Set-Up),* a groundbreaking science fiction film *(The Day the Earth Stood Still),* a trend-setting corporate ladder drama *(Executive Suite),* one of the most powerful indictments of capital punishment *(I Want to Live),* a musical that became a cultural phemonenon *(West Side Story),* the scariest ghost movie ever made *(The Haunting),* and a box-office record breaker *(The Sound of Music).* If we eliminated all of the above, Wise would still have an impressive roster of solid films: *Mademoiselle Fifi; Born to Kill; Blood on the Moon; The House on Telegraph Hill; The Captive City; Tribute to a Bad Man; Somebody Up There Likes Me; Run Silent, Run Deep; Odds Against Tomorrow*; and *The Sand Pebbles.* And even if Robert Wise's detractors failed to recognize his obvious talents as a director, they could hardly deny that Wise brought out the best in his actors.

Russ Tamblyn told the author in a 1992 interview:

> Robert Wise had one of the best qualities a director can have: he knew when to direct his actors and when to leave them alone. I learned a lot about

> directing because I worked with so many directors and can tell the difference between the good ones and the bad ones. The good ones were like traffic cops; they would point you in the right direction and tell you which way to go. The bad ones get in the car with you and try to drive it for you. They tell you how to accent your lines, what words to emphasize, and you end up imitating their rendition of the line rather than having it come from a fresh source. Robert Wise was an exception director because he understood what was really important: it's not how you say a line that counts as much as the freshness of it.
>
> Bob Wise was more businesslike than Mark [Robson], definitely, but, at the same time, he was more congenial. A little straighter, you know, a little more quiet, withdrawn on the set, but still more friendly. Mark was more fluid, he had a much broader personality, but as far as being more friendly, I know this about Bob: he's gone out of his way to help more people than I would care to count. He'd help anybody. If you look at his credentials you'll see that he has been involved in all kinds of organizations that help filmmakers. Aside from being president of the Academy of Motion Pictures Arts and Sciences, he has also been on the board of directors of all sorts of film institutes and he's offered his time and services and gone places to help peole. I became closer with Bob Wise than any other director that I've ever worked with. Even though I've long since left the performing arts [for fine arts], we still remain in touch, and I'm often invited to his testimonials and lifetime achievement awards.

Mark Robson and Robert Wise witnessed and survived the dissolution of the studio system. The filmmaking origins they shared, the polar influences of Orson Welles and Val Lewton—artistic integrity vs. creative compromise—accounts for their similarly eclectic, if sometimes uneven, directing careers. At times, their success may have worked against them, but they were not the mercenary filmmakers their detractors had them pegged as being.

Robert Wise's dedication to the industry, a professionalism tempered by a generous spirit and a genuine concern for humanity, plainly speaks for itself. Had he adhered to a particular formula of success, his critics might have been at least partially justified in their hasty assertions, but Wise, who worked within a wide variety of genres and alternated his crowd-pleasers with risky, offbeat projects, was clearly more adventurous than that. The personal and professional success Robert Wise achieved within the film industry warrants no apology.

The films of Robert Wise:

The Curse of the Cat People (RKO, 1944)
Mademoiselle Fifi (RKO, 1944)
The Body Snatcher (RKO, 1945)
A Game of Death (RKO, 1945)
Criminal Court (RKO, 1946)
Born to Kill (RKO, 1947)
Mystery in Mexico (RKO, 1948)
Blood on the Moon (RKO, 1948)
The Set-Up (RKO, 1949)
Two Flags West (Fox, 1950)
Three Secrets (WB, 1950)
The House on Telegraph Hill (Fox, 1951)

The Day the Earth Stood Still (Fox, 1951)
The Captive City (Aspen/UA, 1952)
Something for the Birds (MGM, 1952)
The Desert Rats (Fox, 1953)
Destination Gobi (Fox, 1953)
So Big (WB, 1953)
Executive Suite (MGM, 1954)
Helen of Troy (Italy, France, WB, 1955)
Tribute to a Bad Man (MGM, 1956)
Somebody Up There Likes Me (MGM, 1956)
This Could Be the Night (MGM, 1957)
Until They Sail (MGM, 1956)
Run Silent, Run Deep (UA, 1958)
I Want to Live (UA, 1958)
Odds Against Tomorrow (UA, 1959)
West Side Story (with Jerome Robbins; UA, 1961)
Two for the Seesaw (UA, 1962)
The Haunting (MGM, 1963)
The Sound of Music (Fox, 1965)
The Sand Pebbles (Fox, 1966)
Star (Fox, 1968)
The Andromeda Strain (Univ., 1971)
Two People (Univ., 1973)
The Hindenburg (Univ., 1975)
Audrey Rose (UA, 1977)
Star Trek: The Motion Picture (Par., 1979)
Rooftops (New Visions Films, 1989)

TWENTY-TWO

Dark Legacy

Shortly after Val Lewton's death, film producer John Houseman (Orson Welles's one-time "Mercury Theatre" partner) embarked upon a project about a ruthless Hollywood producer. He assigned the script to Charles Schnee, who, under Houseman's supervision, created the central character, Jonathan Shields, a composite of some very real Hollywood producers. (The year before, Billy Wilder had taken a similar approach with his creation of *Sunset Boulevard*'s Norma Desmond.) Although there may be glimpses of other Hollywood film producers in the character of Jonathan Shields, he is primarily a mixture of David Selznick and Val Lewton, leaning more toward the Selznick end.

In the completed 1952 film *The Bad and the Beautiful,* directed by Vincente Minnelli, Jonathan Shields (Kirk Douglas) is shown getting his start as a producer of low-budget films, in tandem with his friend and filmmaking partner, director Fred Emile (Barry Sullivan). Fred Emile narrates this particular flashback (there are several in the *Citizen Kane*–like narrative frame of this Houseman production), saying, "In the next few years Jonathan Shields produced eleven films for Harry Pebble. . . . We weren't really picturemakers; we were second-hand dealers, but we learned our trade. One day Harry Pebble assigned us a little horror called *The Doom of the Cat Men.*"

In the very funny scene that follows, Shields and Emile are forced to endure a pitifully bad cat-creature fashion show from the studio's inept costume department. The moth-eaten pajamalike jumpsuits are ill-fitting, but the fast-talking costume man assures Shields and Emile that a little black muslin will take care of the various gaps in the front and the back. Some of the men in costumes wear dime-store cat masks. "This material is imported," says the costume man. "We can't get it anymore. But don't let that be an obstacle." The costume man spies a cat man who is not bulging out of his costume and pulls him over to Shields and Emile: "Here's a perfect fit. This will give you the full effect. Ya see [turning the cat man around], lotsa character in the tail, plenty of fright . . . needs a little puffing up [lifting material on the cat man's shoulders] but it'll be all right—of course, you gotta visualize it in the light, you gotta use your imagination—shoulder pads, that'll straighten it right out. This'll give you the effect. It'll be good!"

In a later exchange, Shields and Emile discuss their prospects:

> SHIELDS: Look, put five men dressed like cats on the screen, and what do they look like?
> EMILE: Like five men dressed like cats.
> SHIELDS: When an audience pays to see a picture like this, what do they pay for?
> EMILE: To get the pants scared off them.
> SHIELDS: And what scares the human race more than any other single thing? [Shields goes over to the wall and turns off the light switch.]
> EMILE: The dark!
> SHIELDS: Of course, and why? Because the dark has a life of its own. In the dark all sorts of things come alive.
> EMILE: Suppose we never do show the cat men. Is that what you're thinking?
> SHIELDS: Exactly.
> EMILE: No cat men.
> SHIELDS: All right, what'll we put on the screen that'll make the backs of their necks crawl?
> EMILE: Two eyes! Shining in the dark.

Val Lewton died nearly two generations ago, but his tradition of terror continues to this day. Although he lived long enough to witness some of his impact upon the film industry, evidenced by the wide number of 1940s films that mimicked his style, Lewton's last years, tainted by bad luck and unending frustration, were spent in relative obscurity. Since his death, however, Val Lewton's cinematic spirit has been unearthed by more "resurrectionists" than could be found in all the kirkyards of Edinburgh. And like Cabman Gray, it is probable that the motion picture world will "never be rid of him, never be rid of him, never be rid of him."

The mission of this final chapter is to chart the course of Val Lewton's posthumous influence upon the motion picture industry. Because the material covers more than four decades in this single attempt to bring us up-to-date, the commentary on each title necessitates brevity. Readers are invited to do their own exploration. No doubt their viewing of the films introduced in this chapter will reveal more Lewton parallels than those discussed here, and it is entirely possible that readers may unearth some Lewtonesque films we have overlooked.

We begin with the 1950s. About a month after Val Lewton's March 14, 1951, death, *The Thing* was released, followed five months later by *The Day the Earth Stood Still.* Since these two Lewton-influenced films provided models for a wide array of imitators, we can see that our subject, at least indirectly, had a significant impact upon the entire 1950s science fiction cycle. By 1951, as the cycle was just beginning to pick up steam, the horror film still appeared to be an endangered species, though not entirely extinct. Some last ditch efforts in the genre often revealed some manner of Lewton influence. *Bride of the Gorilla,* for example, directed and scripted by Curt Siodmak, accented an unseen menace, a man who may or may not turn into a killer gorilla (it was not a good film). Shortly before Universal jumped on the science fiction bandwagon, the studio half-heartedly attempted to revive the horror trade with a pair of films: *The Strange Door* (1951, Joseph Pevney) and *The Black Castle* (1952, Nathan Juran). Although marketed as horror, these two films (each starring Boris Karloff) were really Gothic period thrillers in the fashion of earlier Karloff vehicles like *The Black Room* (1935) and *Tower of London* (1939). While the Gothic atmosphere of *The Strange Door* and *The Black Castle* bore considerable resemblance to 1930s horror, their manner of thrills more closely resembled those of Lewton's period thrillers that starred Karloff, *The Body Snatcher* and *Bedlam.* Like *The Body Snatcher, The Strange Door* was based upon a story by Robert Louis Stevenson (though its plot had more in common with *The Black Room*). Its follow-up, *The Black Castle,* was a Gothic reworking of Richard Connell's oft-filmed *The Most Dangerous Game.* Curiously, these two Gothic thrillers directed by Pevney and Juran feature Boris Karloff in benevolent character roles, while the villainy is reserved for Charles Laughton *(Door)* and Stephen McNally *(Castle).*

The Val Lewton influence could also be found in numerous straight thrillers, like RKO's 1951 entries, *Sealed Cargo* (Alfred Werker) and *The Whip Hand* (William Cameron Menzies). Whatever dark ambience Lewton and Robson had hoped to achieve within the confines of a sea vessel in *The Ghost Ship,* their efforts were brilliantly matched by a quietly terrifying (and superbly photographed) sequence in the first reels of *Sealed Cargo,* an extremely atmospheric and all-around-excellent shipboard espionage thriller directed by Alfred Werker, which, naturally, also recalls Orson Welles's *Journey into Fear.* Dana Andrews (no stranger to the films of Tourneur and Robson) plays a fishing boat captain who uncovers a Nazi plot during the early days of World War II. When Andrews and his men board a crippled, fog-enshrouded, and seemingly uninhabited ship that is listing upon a quiet sea, we are treated to a marvelous facsimile of a Lewton walk, the sequence providing enough creaks, shadows, and chills to satisfy the most ardent thriller fan. Equally dark and claustrophobic was Menzies's *The Whip Hand,* a forerunner of the aliens-among-us theme that would become a mainstay of the burgeoning science fiction cycle. Like Robert Wise's *The Captive City, The Whip Hand* is a paranoid thriller about an entire town that is taken over by an evil force, though this time that force is Communism, rather than crime. Nicholas Musuraca's expressive photography, as might be expected, contributed to *The Whip Hand*'s Lewtonesque edge.

William Cameron Menzies, an old colleague of Lewton's, had been the art director of such Selznick films as *The Adventures of Tom Sawyer* (with its richly atmospheric grave-robbing scene) and *Gone with the Wind* (where

Lewton's suggestion to include a panoramic shot of the dead and dying became a massive undertaking for Menzies's department). In 1953 Menzies directed the first official alien-doppelganger movie, and a minor classic of the form, 20th Century–Fox's *Invaders from Mars.* Until it breaks down into a frenetic display of poorly edited stock footage, Menzies's low-budget film is visually inspired and genuinely frightening. By using a young boy as its central character, Menzies's film terrifies the child in each of us, making *Invaders from Mars* a close relative to *Curse of the Cat People* and *The Window,* two other chilling films with alienated child protagonists.

The most Lewtonesque of Menzies's genre entries was probably Allied Artists' *The Maze* (1953). Released in 3-D and based upon a novel by Maurice Sandoz, *The Maze* tells the rather Lovecraftian story of a man (Richard Carlson) who mysteriously breaks his engagement to his fiancée (Veronica Hurst) after a family emergency necessitates his return to his uncle's Scottish castle. After Carlson discovers the dark secret of his ancestry, a 200-year-old relative who is kept locked and hidden in a castle tower, he cuts all ties with his former life. Undeterred, the fiancée and her aunt (Katherine Emery, *Isle of the Dead*'s walking "corpse") journey to Craven Castle and find that Carlson has aged 20 years. Although the ladies are encouraged to leave, they remain and eventually uncover the dreaded secret. Locked in their room each night, the two women hear odd shuffling sounds passing their door and, looking out a window, they see that the elaborate outdoor hedge-maze is filled with nightly activity and flickering torch light. Odd leaf-shaped footprints are discovered now and again, as well as unexplained wet spots on stairs and corridors. Eventually, after considerable application of the Lewton standby of suggested horror, the two women break out of their locked room and investigate the nightly maze ritual. The buildup is better than the revelation, as novel as it may be: Carlson's 200-year old relative, the true laird of Craven Castle, is a man-sized frog, who having never passed the embryonic froglike stage in utero, was born an amphibian. Every night he is carried to the pond (located in the middle of the maze) for a swim in his natural element. Although *The Maze* is visually inspired and effectively atmospheric, Menzies's film presents a good argument for the preference of undisclosed horror. The revelation of the giant frog undermines the sense of menace that *The Mace* worked so hard to build and, unfortunately, brings the film to a nearly laughable finale.

The year 1953 was a banner one for science fiction films, with well over 20 releases in the genre from studios great and small. Universal finally contributed to the boom with *It Came from Outer Space,* Jack Arnold's first science fiction entry, based upon a short story by Ray Bradbury, was set in the desert and was released in 3-D. Ironically, just as Universal had about given up the ghost on horror films, Warner Bros. (the studio which had shied away from the genre during the 1940s) released what was to become the most successful horror film of the early fifties, as well as the most successful 3-D movie of all time: *House of Wax* (directed by Andre De Toth). The film's major claim to fame is that it elevated its star, Vincent Price, to the status of a nearly crowned "king of horror." But *House of Wax* was also significant because it proved there was a market for horror film remakes (*House* was a remake of Curtiz's *Mystery of the Wax Museum*); clearly, there was gold to be found in modern updates of horror classics. With that in mind, Warners launched another remake, a color 3-D version of *Murders in the Rue Morgue,* directed by Roy Del Ruth and redubbed *Phantom of the Rue Morgue* (1954). The latter was a loose reworking of the Florey film, with Karl Malden chewing the scenery instead of Bela Lugosi. Unfortunately, it failed at the box office as miserably as the Universal film upon which it was based. Although *House of Wax* and *Phantom of the Rue Morgue* were purportedly remakes of early 1930s films, they more accurately reflected the styles of Val Lewton and John Brahm. Like the Lewton films, they used tension-filled walks to convey a feeling of unease and helplessness; like the Brahm films, they were meticulous in the embellishment of their period settings, providing everything from gas streetlamps and fog-laden cobblestoned streets to elaborate dance hall numbers.

One of Warners' most unusual pictures of 1954 was William Wellman's *Track of the Cat,* probably the most Lewtonesque Western ever filmed. Based on a novel by Walter Van Tilburg Clark, *Track of the Cat* is set primarily in a snowbound farmhouse in the backwoods of California. Although it was shot in Technicolor, Wellman's film is so monochromatic that one comes away from it remembering a black-and-white film. The only major deviation from the film's monochromatic look is the use of a bright red parka, one that is worn by the two characters who are marked for death. Walter Van Tilburg Clark's novel had been chosen as Robert R. McCammon's entry in *Horror: 100 Best Books* (edited by Steven Jones and Kim Newman). In his essay, McCammon introduces *Track of the Cat:*

> Mystic dreams. A half-mad, half-shaman Indian who carves portents of the future from bits of wood. Three brothers on a rite of passage that will see two of them dead and one the victor over an old, cunning evil. A snowstorm that tears at the soul, and a landscape of white mountains where crevasses lie hidden under smooth, deceptive powder. The land of the black painter, and blood on the snow. . . . Very few people know about *The Track of the Cat,* which is a horror novel dressed up in cowboy duds and riding a horse.

Although the film *Track of the Cat,* is a bit heavy-handed with its symbolism, it is a fascinating companion piece to *The Leopard Man.* Like the formidable feline in Lewton's film, Wellman's killer panther ("black painter") is the embodiment of death. "It cannot be killed," says Joe Sam, the Indian ranch hand. After his brother Arthur is killed by the black painter, Curt (Robert Mitchum) vows to destroy the animal and goes hunting for it alone, in spite of the dangers of an approaching blizzard.

Track of the Cat is every bit as fatalistic as *The Leopard Man,* with the superstitious Indian replacing the fortune-teller as the oracle of the film's grim events. The fact that we never actually see the black predator gives *Cat* a decidedly Lewtonesque slant, though this aspect likely disappointed ticket buyers, who interpreted an offscreen panther as nothing more than an inexpensive cop-out. Even the presence of teen heartthrob Tab Hunter could not save *Track of the Cat* from box-office oblivion.

Universal's single 1955 horror offering was an overt Lewton imitation. *Cult of the Cobra* is a personal favorite of author Barry Gifford, who (in *The Devil Thumbs a Ride & Other Unforgettable Films*) calls the Francis D. Lyon film a "little movie that deserves attention if only for the unexpected, perfect evocation of Greenwich Village bohemian life in the 1950s." In *Cult of the Cobra,* six soldiers (played by Richard Long, Marshall Thompson, David Janssen, Jack Kelly, William Reynolds, and Peter Norton), all old friends hailing from the same neighborhood, meet in a city in India, where their night on the town provokes the wrath of a cobra-worshipping cult. One soldier dies by a cobra bite, and his five friends are marked for death by the "cobra's curse." Back home, in Greenwich Village, one of the men (Marshall Thompson) falls in love with a mysterious and exotic woman (Faith Domergue) who has just moved into his apartment building. One by one, the woman kills three of the remaining five men by turning into a cobra (via offscreen transformations) and biting their necks.

Similarities to *Cat People* abound. Cats and dogs cringe in fear everytime Lisa is around. The sounds of ordinary things, like pressure cookers and automobile brakes, deliver jolts in the Lewton "bus" tradition. In *Cult* the transformations are suggested, primarily through shadows and through the use of a point-of-view bubble lens similar to that which was used for the alien in *It Came from Outer Space.* Barry Gifford notes, "The scene where [Lisa] stalks and kills David Janssen in his bowling alley after hours is comparable to Simone Simon tracking and terrorizing Jane Randolph in the darkened basement swimming pool in *Cat People.*"

If *Cult of the Cobra* was the most faithful Lewton homage of 1955, the film that most successfully captured the spirit and the stark terror of the Lewton series was one not packaged for the genre crowd. Charles Laughton's one and only directorial credit, the flamboyantly expressionistic *Night of the Hunter,* was a misfire by Hollywood standards and box-office receipts, but its cult status as one of the most frightening American films of the mid–1950s has long been insured. Childhood terror had been effectively explored in *The Leopard Man* and *Curse of the Cat People,* two films that probably influenced *Hunter*'s direction and script. The screenwriter who adapted Davis Grubb's novel *Night of the Hunter* was none other than one of Lewton's staunchest advocates, James Agee.

Night of the Hunter has been widely praised of late, and rightfully so.

Laughton's film eschews realism in favor of pronounced stylization (expressionistic sets and bizarre lighting); within this unusual physical context, Agee transforms the Grubb novel into the dimensions of a folktale, a modernized Grimm's fairy-tale set in middle America. Laughton's inspired direction is forcefully dynamic, going from the darkly grim to the exquisitely beautiful in one breath. Few moments from any horror film can match the frightful intensity Laughton gets from cutaways to Powell's approaching train in the first reel, a sequence that dwarfs the similarly conceived train sequence in Hitchcock's *Shadow of a Doubt* (which also appears to have had a profound influence upon *Night of the Hunter*). If beauty is effectively mixed with chills in *I Walked with a Zombie,* so it is here, most notably with Laughton's celebrated underwater shot of the dead Shelley Winters, looking like a Chinese water lily beneath the surface of the lake.

Robert Mitchum is outstanding as the crazed preacher, Harry Powell. Also remarkable is how Robert Mitchum (as detailed in Dan Peary's *Cult Movies* 3) managed to coax such wondrous performances from *Hunter*'s two juvenile leads, Billy Chapin and Sally Jane Bruce (the latter an uncanny dead ringer for *Child's Play*'s Chuckie), both of whom are every bit as natural as Amy Carter had been in *Curse of the Cat People.* Also excellent are Shelley Winters and Lillian Gish, whose characters function as poles of feminine weakness and feminine strength. Despite the looming presence of Mitchum, *Hunter* is primarily about women (survivors and victims) and the way they respond to masculine power, the film's feminist bent being another tie-in with the Lewton films.

Meanwhile, across the Atlantic suspense director Henri-Georges Clouzot was being crowned the "French Hitchcock" as a result of the fanfare that attended his 1955 release, *Les Diaboliques.* In 1952 Clouzot had made French cinema history with his nail-biting screen adaptation of *The Wages of Fear,* a property Hitchcock had turned down. In 1955 two French suspense writers, Pierre Boileau and Thomas Narcejac, both fans of Hitchcock, offered their novel *Les Diaboliques* to the British director. When Hitchcock did not show an interest, the property fell into Clouzot's lap, resulting in an international smash-hit that became one of the most often imitated thrillers of all time, one that, rather ironically, was to have an influence upon Hitchcock's *Psycho.* If Hitchcock merely appreciated *Les Diaboliques,* it is quite evident that William Castle adored it. Through the 1950s and 1960s, William Castle thrillers would repeatedly mimic the kind of brilliantly skewed plotting that made *Les Diaboliques* so memorable. Almost in anticipation of Castle's gimmick-laden features, Clouzot's film delivered, in its closing credits, an earnest plea for viewers to keep the film's surprise ending a secret.

Les Diaboliques is a superior film, one whose durability has been tested by the innumerable films that have used it as a source of inspiration. The cat-and-mouse plot focuses upon a pair of women schoolteachers who drown the megalomaniacal school principal (the husband of one and the lover of the other) in a bathtub, dispose of his body in a swimming pool, and later become unhinged when the drained pool does not produce the expected corpse. Clouzot borrows freely and successfully from all directions; while the film's characters and plot recall Lang's *The Woman in the Window* or Pabst's *Pandora's Box*, the frightening final reels take a dark detour into Lewton territory. By withholding information on the missing body, Clouzot invites his audience to speculate about their worst fears. The most nightmarish possibility (that the man is one of the walking dead) becomes increasingly difficult to dismiss with the puzzling events of late (The dead man's face shows up in the background of a freshly taken photograph, and the suit he was killed in mysteriously appears back from the dry cleaners). The building terror that leads to *Les Diaboliques*'s literally heart-stopping climax, gives every indication that Clouzot was familiar with the Lewton films. *Les Diaboliques* manipulates an audience's fear of the dark unknown and chooses to terrify us with things as innocuous as swimming pools, bathtubs, and suits of clothes.

Meanwhile, across the English Channel, a small production outfit going by the name of Hammer Films had just released *The Quatermass Xperiment.* Through the early fifties, Hammer Films (controlled by key producers Michael Carreras, Anthony Hinds, and Anthony Nelson Keys) produced a variety of contemporary dramas, mysteries, noirish thrillers, and an occasional science fiction film. In 1953 Hammer's contributions to the science fiction cycle had been two intelligent, but rather turgid, dramas directed by Terence Fisher: *The Four-Sided Triangle* and *Spaceways.* While these films sparked little interest, "The Quatermass Experiment," a 1953 BBC television serial written by Nigel Kneale, had captured the nation's imagination. In *Future Tense,* John Brosnan calls Kneale, "a writer with an uncanny knack of combining contemporary sf themes with both mythology and traditional elements of the supernatural to produce stories that tend to bypass the forebrain and work directly on unconscious fears."

Seeing the writing on the wall, Hammer secured the rights to Kneale's teleplay, and in early 1955 *The Quatermass Xperiment* went into production. Strangely, the X-for-horror British rating was no longer a deterrent to a film's success, as it was during the war years. In fact, an X-rating was now starting to guarantee large audiences; the British release of Clouzot's *Les Diaboliques* gave proof of the kind of enormous profits such a film could make. The Nigel Kneale property had been given to Val Guest, who cowrote the script and directed. Released in Britain in 1955 (and in America in 1956, with the wonderfully lurid title change, *The Creeping Unknown*), *The Quatermass Xperiment* turned out to be a top box-office draw.

Val Guest, a longtime writer/director of British cinema, who had started out as an actor, but then became a journalist and in the early 1930s, joined the writing staff of the *Hollywood Reporter.* Through the 1930s, Guest wrote numerous scripts (mostly minor comedies) before settling back in England to direct. He had already directed more than 20 films by the time he was handed the Kneale project. Guest was a craftsman (perhaps best described as a cross between Robert Wise and Jack Arnold) who prided himself on his solid and efficient work. Like Lewton, Val Guest supervised, and often rewrote, the scripts of his films. Guest condensed the Kneale teleplay (with the help of American screenwriter, Richard Landau) and reworked a few of the scenes. Since it was the custom for independent studios like Hammer to bolster their box-office scope with the inclusion of an American performer (usually one in the decline of his career), Brian Donlevy was given the role as Professor Quatermass.

Xperiment brought in over $3 million in profits and saved Hammer Films from imminent collapse. (By now this kind of success story may have a familiar ring.) *The New Statesman* praised the film for its subtle horror approach: "The film does in fact touch the imagination. Its hero, gripped by fantastic horror, hints at tragedy. What we witness in a number of scenes is much extended by what we don't quite see. . . . The result seems to be a better film than either *War of the Worlds* or *Them*." In *Keep Watching the Skies*, Bill Warren contends that *Xperiment* is the British equivalent of *The Thing*, while in *Horror People*, John Brosnan calls *Xperiment*, "Hammer's first remake of *Frankenstein*, and perhaps its best." Oddly, the respective views of Warren and Brosnan are perfectly compatible, as *The Thing* is not without its own *Frankenstein* connections.

Richard Wordsworth plays Victor Carroon, the unfortunate astronaut who, infected with an intelligent space virus, undergoes a painfully gradual transformation into a tendrilled, amorphous monster straight from the pages of H.P. Lovecraft. In part, *Xperiment*'s solid reputation rests upon this amazing performance; Wordsworth's Victor Carroon is truly one of the great horror characterizations, one that rivals Boris Karloff's celebrated mute performances in *Frankenstein* and *The Walking Dead*. The remainder of *Xperiment*'s well-deserved reputation rests upon its ability to frighten an audience, something it does quite well, particularly in a terrifying (and very Lewtonesque) zoo scene, as well as in an exceedingly creepy scene where the half-human Carroon chances upon a little girl (à la James Whale's *Frankenstein*) in a deserted shipyard. As Bill Warren notes, "The horror is almost entirely off-screen and in the mind of the viewer. When the thing walks into the zoo and slithers out later, all we ever see are vague shadows. . . . The photography is low-key, shadowy and imaginative throughout; most of the story seems to take place at night." Guest only shows us parts of the monster, a realistic close-up of an alien eye in the zoo shrubbery, a dragging tendril or two, and enough ambient atmosphere to please any Lewton fan. As Randy Palmer contends (in his March 1993 *Filmfax* article, *The Quatermass Experience*), "The most remarkable scenes in *The Quatermass Xperiment* were those involving the 'terror-by-suggestion' technique pioneered by Val Lewton in the 1940s." Nigel Kneale and Val Guest collaborated on the script of the Guest-directed follow-up, *Quatermass II* (released in America in 1957 as *Enemy from Space*), which turned out to be a remarkable British equivalent to Don Siegel's alien-doppelganger classic, *Invasion of the Body Snatchers.*

By 1957 the horror and science fiction genres had become nearly interchangeable, and both were in full bloom. In Hollywood it was the year that teenagers invaded the genres with films like *I Was a Teenage Werewolf/Frankenstein, Teenage Zombies,* and *Invasion of the Saucermen.* A wild assortment of gigantic creatures stalked the motion picture screen in 1957: robots, crabs, scorpions, praying mantises, grasshoppers, a sea snail, a zany-looking feathered bird from outer space, and even a walking tree stump. In spite of the silly turns Hollywood had taken by pandering to a younger audience, British filmmakers maintained an adult course with their genre entries. Since the British thrillers were still X-rated, there was little sense in trying to exploit the juvenile market.

Hammer's *X—the Unknown,* for example, managed to include a number of children in its cast without being remotely juvenile in its approach. Fashioned somewhat in the manner of *The Quatermass Xperiment, X—the Unknown* (directed by Leslie Norman and Joseph Walton from a Jimmy Sangster script) is a moody, genuinely spooky science fiction film, one that makes superb use of its barren English countryside locations (the latter an attribute it shares with Hammer's other 1957 science fiction/horror hit, *Quatermass II*). Also in 1957, Nigel Kneale's BBC teleplay, "The Creature," became *The Abominable Snowman of the Himalayas,* Hammer's final Guest/Kneale collaboration. While *Snowman* never rises to the heights of the first two Quartermass films, it is a highly evocative and even mystical horror film. Guest manages to accomplish a haunting sense of desolation through the dynamic use of some Swiss mountain-climbing footage shot specifically for this film. Even the studio sections, however, are well done, and the illusion of a Himalayan locale is nicely realized, thanks to some Pinewood Studio sets and props that look like they are left over from Michael Powell's *Black Narcissus,* a film that exuded the kind of bleak atmosphere Guest hoped to capture.

Snowman was not the first or the last film of its kind, but it is still the best, and most Lewtonesque, of the abominable snowman films. *Snowman*'s eerieness is accomplished with wide open spaces and the use of predominantly white compositions. Guest gets great mileage from the Lewton approach by not showing the creatures but, instead, letting us hear their lonely cries echoing over the snow-covered slopes. Because they remain offscreen, the mournful-sounding "Yeti" appear frighteningly omniscient, an illusion that is enhanced by the vast, other-worldly surroundings. A partial closeup of the Yeti's face—half-covered in shadow, its eyes reflecting keen intelligence and ageless wisdom—is artfully rendered at the film's climax.

The British film industry was instrumental in bringing about a horror film revival in 1957, and, more often than not, the year's British horror offerings showed some degree of Lewton influence. Let's not forget that Jacques Tourneur's *Curse of the Demon* was a 1957 British film. So were *Corridors of Blood* and *The Haunted Strangler*, a couple of nasty shockers whose subject matter was plainly inspired by varied elements of two Lewton films: *The Body Snatcher* and *Bedlam*. A matched pair, *Corridors* and *Strangler* were directed by Robert Day, produced by John Croydon and Richard Gordon, and, like their Lewton antecedents, fashioned as vehicles for horror icon Boris Karloff. Although they were not released in Britain until the following year (*Corridors* did not make it to the U.S. until 1961), the two Karloff films, along with Hammer's *Curse of Frankenstein* (also 1957) and Tourneur's *Curse*, defined the British horror film for the next two decades.

It is ironic that *The Body Snatcher* was censored in England, while *Bedlam* was banned altogether; compared to the more sadistic Day/Croydon pair, the Lewton films are masterpieces of subtlety. Whatever their shortcomings, the Day/Croydon films' gritty presentation of Britain's nineteenth century life-styles is second to none; the most accomplished aspect of either of these films is their portrayal of the lowest strata of English society.

The first of the pair, *Corridors of Blood* (aka *The Doctor from Seven Dials*), is set in 1820 London prior to the discovery of anesthesia. Karloff plays Dr. Thomas Bolton, a humanitarian surgeon who is the only one among his peers who believes that science can separate "the pain from the knife." Bolton is a warmhearted Toddy MacFarlane; when he uses himself as a guinea pig, thereby becoming addicted to an opium distillate, his notebook falls into the hands of a tavern full of the most corrupt hooligans imaginable. The unsavory gathering blackmails Bolton into signing death certificates for ill-begotten corpses (down-on-their-luck-wretches who have been "Burked"). The murdering body snatcher in this case is Resurrection Joe, played with chilling aplomb by Christopher Lee (before his burst to fame as Hammer's *Dracula*). Lee wears a top hat and dresses much like Cabman Gray. Resurrection Joe has none of Gray's charm, however; even the local tarts are warned to stay away from his kind.

Corridors of Blood must have seemed like an enticing venture to Karloff. Judging from its quality sets, cast, and production, it had all the potential ingredients to be another *Body Snatcher*, which is probably why the actor rose to the occasion with a vigorous, full-bodied performance (something he had not given in such sorry offerings as *Voodoo Island* [1957] and *Frankenstein 1970* [1958]). The British actor must have seen *Corridors*'s similarities to his favorite Lewton film—from its provision of street singers to a climax precipitated by an operation upon a young crippled girl. For all its appropriate ingredients, however, *Corridors of Blood*'s heavy-handed and rather sadistic approach can hardly be called Lewtonesque. While the film has many good things going for it, the chain of events that substitutes for a plot is simply a tableau of unpleasantness in which violence and debasement are the big attention getters.

The Haunted Strangler has a more ingenious plot than its companion, though Day's direction is more pedestrian. Here Karloff plays James Rankin, a dedicated writer (and family man) who is preparing a book on Edward Styles, the "Hillside Strangler" who had been executed some 20 years before. Rankin believes Styles was falsely hanged, and in his attempt to uncover the identity of the real murderer, he follows a trail that eventually leads right back upon himself. (Having permanently lost his memory close to 20 years before, Rankin married and started his life anew, at which point he took up writing.) When Rankin discovers Edward Style's knife (used to cut the victims' throats after they had been strangled) and picks it up, it triggers his transformation into the distorted, crippled killer he had once been those 20 years past. Karloff's transformation is effectively rendered with a minimum of makeup and a maximum of the actor's fearfully bizarre facial grimaces (which, rather amazingly, make Karloff's character actually look 20 years younger). In his strangler state, Karloff kills his wife, and upon regaining his alternate personality, he turns himself in. Unfortunately, no one believes such an upstanding man is capable of the crime, so he winds up in the padded cell of a mental ward before he finally breaks out and is killed in the midst of another murdering spree.

Like its Robert Day predecessor, *The Haunted Strangler* is rich in atmosphere and performance, but its script meanders rather meaninglessly between the poignant and the cruel. Its opening scene of a public hanging is most memorable, harking back to the execution scenes in Selznick's *A Tale of Two Cities*. Later in the film, when Rankin breaks into a cemetery to dig up the grave of the executed man, Day directs his variation of a Lewton walk, and, adding a couple of "buses" for good measure, he carries it off rather well. When Rankin is thrown into the padded cell and the soundtrack is brimming with the yowls and screams of his fellow lunatics, it is like witnessing some leftover bad Karma from Karloff's previous life as *Bedlam*'s apothecary general, Master Sims.

Besides Tourneur's classic Lewton homage, *The Curse of the Demon*, the most overt 1957 Lewton imitation was *Cat Girl*, a non–Hammer English film whose study in feline dementia did little to hide its *Cat People* origins. In *A Heritage of Horror*, David Pirie discusses the film's value as British social commentary, particularly in its depiction of feminine roles, but *Cat Girl* remains for most Americans a cheap set-bound Lewton imitation that never seems to fully understand its source of inspiration. Barbara Shelley's debut in the title role, however, shows a remarkable sense of presence and almost makes up for the film's many deficiencies.

The initial scenes, where Shelley's Leonora is called back to her uncle's estate to accept the family curse, parallel those of *The Maze*. Unlike *Cat People*, with its varied locations, Alfred Shaugnessy's film takes place primarily in and around the estate of the heroine's uncle. The flimsy outdoor sets are enhanced by sound effects that are suspiciously reminiscent of those used in Dana Andrew's *Curse of the Demon* "walk" sequences (to and from Karswell's mansion). The uncle's trophy room is surrounded by bizarre feline taxidermy (one specimen shows a cat ripping out the throat of a human effigy). The room recalls both *Curse of the Cat People* and *The Most Dangerous Game*, all the while anticipating *Psycho*'s fetish for taxidermy.

A major problem with *Cat Girl* is a lack of editing continuity, especially in scenes that attempt to show a connection between Leonora and the feline menace. Shelley's character does not really change into a cat; rather, an escaped spotted leopard, controlled by her repressed jealousy, does her killing for her. It is a confusing new angle. At times we feel she is seeing through the eyes of the predator, but we are never quite sure. Whenever Leonora is in one of her spells, the camera repeatedly cuts back and forth between Shelley and the escaped leopard, so they are clearly established as separate entities; yet this cross-cutting is so disorienting that it diffuses any potential suspense.

Shaughnessy seems to have screened the Lewton film several times, but somehow Tourneur's methods and motivations went entirely over his head. He repeats *Cat People*'s birdcage scene by having Shelley simply kill the bird and letting it end there, apparently not realizing that what made the original scene so shocking was Irena's deliberate actions following the bird's death. In the scene from *Cat Girl* that attempts to mimic *Cat People*'s Central Park set piece, Leonora says to her departing rival, "Why don't you take the bus?" This is immediately followed by a facsimile of *Cat People*'s famous "bus" shot except, in this instance, the sound of the bus's brakes sounds exactly like the sound of a bus's brakes. One can only wonder what Shaughnessy must have been thinking. He tries his best to duplicate the Irena/Alice pursuit—even down to the alternating shots of the women's legs—although this time, after the female predator's clicking high heels come to a sudden halt, we cut to a ludicrous shot of Leonora running barefoot. When a car hits and kills the leopard, Leonora also dies. In the film's most inspired shot, she is shown lying on her back in her shiny mackinaw, her dead eyes staring up at the sky.

Lewtonesque British horror films grew less frequent once Hammer's Technicolor offerings became international trendsetters. By 1958 Hammer had already made its first sequel, *Revenge of Frankenstein*, a film which had more in common with the Day/Karloff pair of films than it had with its own Hammer predecessor. In a most momentous American double bill, Columbia released *Revenge of Frankenstein* with *Curse of the Demon*, providing for the price of one ticket a fascinating demonstration of the dichotomy between the Lewton and Hammer cinematic styles. Outside of their occasional use of a Lewton "wallk" or "bus," these Technicolor period productions left less to the

Barbara Shelley in *Cat Girl.*

imagination than the same studio's Guest/Kneale collaborations. Hammer's decision to remake the popular classics (like those being shown across America via the "Shock Theater" television package) with the addition of color, sex, and graphic violence (bodyparts and blood being Hammer specialties) was a sure-sell idea. Consequently, the Lewton approach, which had been, after all, a respite from Universal's tried-and-true horror formula, was usually discarded in favor of the monster approach. And yet, while the deliberate Lewton homage, for the time being at least, became less prevalent, a number of erstwhile Lewton techniques—unseen menaces, spooky walks, false jolts—began to infiltrate countless horror films on both sides of the Atlantic. These techniques had become such genre conventions that they were being employed by filmmakers who did not know Val Lewton from Adam.

It was around this time that England produced four non–Hammer Guest/Kneale facsimiles: two starring Forrest Tucker (*The Trollenberg Terror* [1958—aka *The Crawling Eye*] and *Cosmic Monsters* [1958]) and two starring Marshall Thompson (*Fiend Without a Face* [1958] and *First Man into Space* [1959]). As was characteristic of their Guest/Kneale models, each of the four films kept their monsters offscreen until the final reel. These black-and-white ventures were not without merit, but none of them possessed the box-office clout of Hammer's colorful and carefully assembled late-1950s remakes of *Dracula, The Hound of the Baskervilles,* and *The Mummy.*

One 1959 British film that holds up even better than most of the Hammer films of the period is John Gilling's black-and-white *The Flesh and the Fiends,* a near-brilliant prequel to *The Body Snatcher,* covering, with considerable accuracy, the story of Burke and Hare. *The Flesh and the Fiends* has a lot in common with *Corridors of Blood,* but where Day's film is merely vicious, Gilling's ghoulish tale is, like Lewton's, darkly humorous with wonderfully quirky performances. Donald Pleasance, as Hare, gives the performance of his career, imbuing his role with enough gallows humor to rival the likes of Cabman Gray, and he is more than ably assisted by Peter Cushing as Dr. Knox and George Rose as Burke. Kudos also go to Billie Whitelaw for her wonderful turn as a cheeky prostitute. Gilling's film is far superior than either of its Day/Karloff antecedents (and infinitely superior to two later British versions, *Burke and Hare* and *The Doctor and the Devils*). *The Flesh and the Fiends* (aka *Mania*) is a must-see film for fans of *The Body Snatcher.*

Another 1959 black-and-white British horror film worthy of note is *City of the Dead* (aka *Horror Hotel*), the first film made by Amicus, the only British horror outfit ever to give Hammer a serious run for its money. A tale of witchcraft set in a small Massachusetts town, *Horror Hotel* (as it was released in America) was closer to the Lewton-inspired *The Woman Who Came Back* (1945) than it was to anything Hammer was releasing at the time. Directed by John L. Moxey, *Horror Hotel*'s eccentric minimalism prefigures the look and texture of the Corman/Poe films (especially *The Haunted Palace*). Its narrative, courtesy of screenwriter George Baxt, seems like a dress rehearsal for Sidney Hayers's 1961 *Burn, Witch, Burn* (whose screenplay Baxt also helped write). In *Heritage of Horror,* David Pirie describes John Moxey's Amicus entry as "an intriguingly expressionistic film [which] despite a few phoney transatlantic settings and accents . . . remains the English horror film which comes nearest to reproducing Val Lewton's RKO work in the 1940s and the 'City,' a New England town, consisting of a few black and rotting buildings saturated in fog and gloom, had an unusually Lovecraftian flavor." Pirie's book may be the best volume on British horror, but his pronouncement of *Horror Hotel* as the most Lewtonesque English film of the era is questionable. While it is an earnest little film, its production is more amateurish than any Lewton opus; Moxey's direction, however artful it may be, is often static and ineffectual. In spite of its spare budget, though, *Horror Hotel* does convey a strong sense of paranoia with a plot chillingly reminiscent of Shirley Jackson's "The Lottery."

The fifties closed in a frenzy of monstermania, a world-wide condition fostered by television, movies, and magazines like Forrest J. Ackerman's *Famous Monsters of Filmland.* In America, William Castle was doing his best to imitate Clouzot with the conspiratorial plots (usually written by Robb White) of such films as *Macabre* (1958), *The House on Haunted Hill* (1959), and

The Tingler (1959), all three being enjoyable blends of schlock and shock, with occasional Lewton touches. In spite of his gimmicks and crass showmanship, Castle knew how to raise goose bumps, and his late 1950s horror entries attracted huge audiences.

For the most part, American audiences were inundated with a vast variety of cheaply made horror/science fiction double-bills from Universal, American International, Allied Artists, Columbia, and UA's Bel-Air and Grammercy Productions. Certain titles—*The Blob, The Fly, I Married a Monster from Outer Space*—stood apart from the rest, seeming like major productions amid the dross of pure exploitation. Every now and then an American horror release would exploit the unseen, like the 1958 *I Bury the Living* (a well-made, low-budget thriller that seemed to borrow heavily from both Lewton and William Castle), but such instances were rare.

One of the more Lewtonesque American horror films of 1959 was *Face of Fire* (Allied Artists), an artfully directed low-budget adaptation of Stephen Crane's excellent novelette, "The Monster." *Face of Fire* is essential viewing for Lewton fans; not only did producer/director Albert Band (the father of modern-day horror meister, Charles Band) take an undisclosed-horror approach in this story about a handyman (James Whitmore) whose face is disfigured in a fire, but he also directed a difficult subject with the kind of sensitivity that could be found in the best of the Lewton series. In fact, like *Curse of the Cat People, Face of Fire* is a touching and heartfelt film that clearly transcends the genre it was marketed for. Although *Face of Fire* has some horrific touches, it is quite plain that Band was not interested in following horror film conventions. *Face of Fire* focuses upon the friendship between a doctor's son and the disfigured handyman (who walks about the town wearing a black veil); the result is atmospheric and surprisingly poignant.

To help market *Face of Fire,* the Allied Artists publicity department came up with an inappropriately lurid ad campaign, one reminiscient of those RKO used to launch the Lewton films. The posters for *Face of Fire* were covered with such titillating (and altogether misleading) lines as, "What was once a man, roamed the night in search of a woman!" or "Women shudder at the sight of him . . . but are fascinated by the thought of him!" or, finally, "Lips that once parted for his kisses now are frozen in a scream of terror!" The pressbook also suggested that theater managers "hire a rather tall man to walk about the streets with his face covered as shown in the art. Have him wear a horror type mask, available at any toy store. Have him distribute inexpensive cards bearing this copy: Mine is a 'face of fire.' . . . Please do not shy away from me. See 'Face of Fire' at the Rex Theatre."

With the decade of the sixties came an expansion of established trends. The handsome, but fairly inexpensive, Hammer films continued to thrive. Taking Hammer's lead, American-International's Roger Corman directed and produced *House of Usher* (1960), demonstrating that the English had no monopoly on period horror films shot in color. Corman's successful adaptation (scripted by Richard Matheson) ushered in a cycle of AIP Poe films that would continue for more than a decade. Like most horror films of the period, AIP's Poe films would make significant use of "walks" and "buses." Corman's Poe entries, however, seldom achieved the spirit and style of the Lewton films, in spite of such common bonds as limited budgets, literate—and occasionally longwinded—scripts, and a predilection for *Isle of the Dead*'s central theme: premature burial. Corman usually adhered to a set-bound, limited-cast formula very much like the structure of *Isle of the Dead.* Moreover, scriptwriters Richard Matheson and Charles Beaumont, both of whom contributed their talents to several of the films in the series, were longtime Lewton fans whose scripts leaned in the direction of suggested horror. Given all the above, one would expect *House of Usher* and its immediate follow-ups—*The Pit and the Pendulum* (1961), *Premature Burial* (1962), and *Tales of Terror* (1962)—to be more Lewtonesque than they actually are. Even when Jacques Tourneur was brought in to direct the ersatz-Poe features, *Comedy of Terrors* and *The City in the Sea* (aka *War Gods of the Deep*), there was, quite surprisingly, little in these films to suggest that the spirit of Lewton was alive and well at American-International.

Even the gimmicky British (black-and-white) production of *The Tell-Tale Heart* (directed by Ernest Morris for the Danzigers), released the same year as *Usher,* is closer to the spirit of Lewton than any of the AIP series entries. Morris's use of ordinary things like ticking clocks and dripping faucets to suggest the relentless beating of the murder victim's heart is more in keeping with the approach taken by Lewton's own (unofficial) Poe adaptation, *Isle of the Dead. The Tell-Tale Heart*'s murdering protagonist, sympathetically played by Lawrence Payne, is also somewhat of a reprise of Peter Lorre's character in Robert Florey's *The Beast with Five Fingers.*

When *Psycho* (1960) signaled a trend in monochromatic psychological thrillers, Hammer followed suit with Seth Holt's *Scream of Fear* (1960), a contemporary shocker that owed as much to Clouzot's *Les Diaboliques* as it did to Hitchcock's film. *Scream of Fear* (*Taste of Fear* in Britain) was the first of several black-and-white psychological thrillers of the Hitchcock/Clouzot school that would be produced by Hammer in the early 1960s; other titles included *Maniac* and *Paranoic* (both 1962), *Nightmare* (1963), and *Hysteria* (1964). Although the Hammer psycho-thrillers drew their primary inspiration from two obvious sources—*Les Diaboliques* and *Psycho*—Hammer's methods of building terror suggests a no less significant debt to the films of Val Lewton.

Another black-and-white British film, Wolf Rilla's *Village of the Damned* (1960, MGM), was reminiscent of the Val Guest/Nigel Kneale collaborations. This striking genre entry, based upon a John Wyndham novel *(The Midwich Cuckoos),* mined its thrills from a less-is-more approach, counterpointing its terror with the deceptively innocent appearance of its visible sources of menace. An unseen alien force somehow renders an entire town unconscious for a few hours, during which time the force manages to impregnate every woman in town capable of bearing a child. The babies are all born on the same night; each of the newborns (there are only 12 in the film, 60 in the novel) has blond hair, strange eyes, unusually small fingernails and weighs exactly 10 pounds. The children grow at an accelerated rate and soon exhibit special mental powers; not only are they brilliant, but they can also control the mind of any person in town. (When the children use their powers of mind control, their eyes take on an unearthly glow.) One mother, after spanking her golden-haired child, is abruptly compelled to immerse her hand into a pot of boiling water. George Sanders and Barbara Shelley are fine as the central characters, a school teacher and his wife, the latter of whom bears one of the alien children. Significantly, no attempt is made at the film's conclusion to explain how this phenomenon happened to occur. The alien force remains unseen; its methods remain unknown. At the time of *Village of the Damned*'s release, religious groups were outraged by the film's sacrilegious use of what amounted to a series of virgin births, but the film received a memorable television promotion in America, where it became MGM's sleeper hit of the year.

In 1960 Mario Bava's landmark vampire film, *Black Sunday,* a film that is as beautiful as it is terrifying, was released. Set in the Ukraine (and based on Gogol's "Vij"), *Black Sunday* includes a terror set piece that harks back to the Teresa sequence in *The Leopard Man.* In Bava's film, an innkeeper's wife forces her young daughter to go out into the night to milk a cow. The barn is a distance away and stands on the edge of a cemetery, giving Bava a splendid opportunity for the execution of a harrowing Lewton walk. Although the girl in the Bava film is more fortunate than Teresa, *Black Sunday*'s Lewtonesque set piece is one of the scariest things in the film. Lewton adherents will also wish to view Bava's *Black Sabbath* (1963), a three-in-one compilation film (narrated by Boris Karloff). Karloff performs in the longest of the three segments, an excellent adaptation of Leo Tolstoy's Russian vampire story, "The Wurdalak," but the most purely Lewtonesque segment is "A Drop of Water." Based on the story by Chekhov, it concerns a nurse who steals a ring from the grimacing corpse of a clairvoyant and then, upon going back to her dark apartment (lit primarily by the blinking light of an outdoor neon sign), believes herself to be haunted by the clairvoyant's vengeful spirit, a manifestation that is heralded by the sound of dripping tap water. Bava gets absolutely terrifying results with this story of suggested horror.

The year 1961 was another strong one for films with a Lewtonesque flair, several of them, once again, coming from Great Britain. John Gilling's *Shadow of the Cat* (double-billed in America with Hammer's *Curse of the Werewolf*) is a wonderfully old-fashioned "dark house" thriller with a most unusual protagonist: a murdered woman's cat (its eyesight approximated by numerous slightly distorted point-of-view shots). Shot in glorious black-and-white, this effective exploration of feline phobia opens with a spooky scene in which the title character (a cat, remember) witnesses the murder of a wealthy elderly woman, the victim of some conspiring relatives who hope to gain possession of the estate. The plot of Gilling's film is obviously closer to *The Cat and the Canary* than it is to *Cat People,* but George Baxt *(Horror Hotel)* contributed an especially memorable script that makes great use of the less-is-more approach. One by one, the conspirators become the victims of misfortune; whether or not the cat has actually brought a curse down upon their heads, however, is left for the viewer to decide.

A Lewtonesque slant could also be found in Michael Anderson's 1961 British thriller, *The Naked Edge,* a minor but well-made film with an overly familiar plot (in the vein of *Love from a Stranger, Suspicion, Gaslight, House on Telegraph Hill*) concerning a woman who suspects her husband is making plans to murder her. Although Deborah Kerr is fine as the wife, the husband is uncomfortably played by a miscast and unhealthy-looking Gary Cooper (in his final performance). Joseph Stefano (of *Psycho* and *Outer Limits* fame) wrote *The Naked Edge*'s intelligent script (based on the novel *First Train to Babylon* by Max Ehrlich). Although the film is seriously flawed, Edwin Hillier's eerie black-and-white photography is breathtaking, the shots of the spooky mansion interiors closely anticipating the look of Robert Wise's made-in-England Lewton homage, *The Haunting.*

Deborah Kerr gave a wonderful performance in another 1961 British film that deserves inclusion in this chapter. The understated terror of Henry James's subtle ghost novel, *The Turn of the Screw,* was given expert handling in *The Innocents,* directed by Jack Clayton. Lest we put the cart before the horse, however, it must be stated that much of what came to be known as the Lewton approach was a natural extension of the Victorian ghost story, the milieu within which Henry James worked when he penned his masterpiece of suggested horror. Kerr plays a sexually repressed governess who is given charge of a pair of young siblings wonderfully played by Martin Stephens (one of the fair-haired children in *Village of the Damned*) and Pamela Franklin (who would go on to star in the early–1970s haunted house classic, *The Legend of Hell House*). Kerr believes the children are possessed by evil spirits of the dead, the previous governess and her gardener lover (whose suggested presences can be perceived by the viewer as real or imagined). *The Innocents*' screenplay, by William Archibald, Truman Capote, and John Mortimer, is tasteful and intelligent, if slightly verbose, but the strengths of the film lie in its sensitive performances and its evocative low-key photography by Freddie Francis (soon to become a prolific horror film director).

The most satisfying of all the 1961 British films to emulate the Lewton style was Sidney Hayers's *Night of the Eagle* (released in America in 1962 as *Burn, Witch, Burn*). Based on Fritz Leiber's *Conjure Wife* (the same novel from which the slightly Lewtonesque "inner sanctum" film, *Weird Woman,* had been adapted in 1944), *Burn, Witch, Burn* is the perfect companion piece to Jacques Tourneur's *Curse of the Demon,* and their parallels go much further than their similar sounding British titles. Hayer's film deserves more space than we are able to give it here. Of the numerous examples of Lewtonesque films mentioned in this book, a trio of features filmed in Britain stand out above the rest as the purest examples of their kind: Jacques Tourneur's *Curse of the Demon,* Sidney Hayer's *Burn, Witch, Burn,* and Robert Wise's *The Haunting.* (In a perfect world, *Burn, Witch, Burn* would have been directed by Mark Robson and given lengthier coverage two chapters ago.)

Although Hayer's horror masterpiece, like *Curse of the Demon,* was largely ignored by American theatergoers, the critics were pleased and the film soon gained a cult audience when it began to play on television. Howard Thompson's July 5, 1962, review in the *New York Times* echoes the kind of enthusiasm James Agee once had for a certain RKO producer:

> Don't miss *Burn, Witch, Burn.* . . . This low-budget British import is quite the most effective "supernatural" thriller since *Village of the Damned.* For all we know it may be the best outright goose-pimpler dealing specifically with witchcraft since *I Walked with a Zombie,* with that superb Caribbean flavoring, way back in 1943. . . . Simply as a suspense yarn, blending lurid conjecture and brisk reality, growing chillier by the minute and finally whipping up an ice-cold crescendo of fright, the result is admirable. Excellently photographed (not a single frame is wasted), and cunningly directed, the incidents gather a pounding, graphic drive that is diabolically teasing. The climax is a nightmarish hair-curler but, we maintain, entirely logical within the context. . . . For blueprinting a story that gallops toward occult darkness with feet touching the ground, the two scenerists rate credit for the blunt, steadying dialogue. . . . Count on seeing a good, unholy brew, seasoned by professional hands and rising to a boil.

Burn, Witch, Burn was a project initiated by Richard Matheson and Charles Beaumont while they were riding high on the success of their numerous "Twilight Zone" adaptations for television. They collaborated on a screenplay of one of their favorite novels, *Conjure Wife,* Matheson writing the first half and Beaumont the second. They finally sold it to England's Independent Artists Productions, whereupon producer Albert Fennell handed it over to George Baxt *(Horror Hotel, The Shadow of the Cat)* for a final revision and called in Sidney Hayers to direct.

Matheson credited Lewton as being a major influence upon his writing career. In Paul Sammon's "Interview with Richard Matheson" (*Midnight Grafitti,* Fall 1992, issue 7), Matheson revealed, "I remember distinctly, when I was seventeen, seeing *Cat People* and being just incredibly impressed. I loved Val Lewton's movies. I wrote to him once, by the way, and he answered me. I told him that I had figured out his three major techniques for scaring the hell out of people. And he was delighted at the time. Robert Wise, who was one of his directors, and Mark Robson, who was also one of his directors, also replied. They said they were all three delighted that I had picked out their techniques. One was to lead your eye to one side of the screen, and while you were looking at that, something would pop out from the other side of the screen. Or they would use a long period of absolute, deadly silence. Broken, suddenly, by a noise. And it works! Even now."

Burn, Witch, Burn, released by American International as part of a double bill with *Tales of Terror* (a Corman/Poe film also scripted by Matheson), carries all the Lewton trademarks: "walks," "buses," unseen terrors, deceptive appearances, and unstoppable forces, all neatly wrapped in an intelligent, provocative script that is well served by credible performances. Janet Blair, as the film's Lewtonesque heroine, gives an unusually compelling performance, especially in the opening reels, and she is ably assisted by Peter Wyngarde (Quint in *The Innocents*) as her skeptical college professor husband (serving much the same function as Dana Andrews's doubting Thomas in *Curse of the Demon*). Sidney Hayer's dynamic direction and Reginald Wyver's moody, expressionistic photography add immeasurably to *Burn, Witch, Burn*'s exalted position among the multitude of films that have attempted to duplicate the dark magic of the Val Lewton productions.

Hollywood also had its share of Lewton-influenced films in the early 1960s. Curtis Harrington's ultra-low-budget *Night Tide* (1961), released by American International, was a moody reworking of *Cat People.* The plot concerns a sailor (Dennis Hopper) who falls in love with a mysterious Greek beauty named Mora (Linda Lawson), who happens to earn her living posing as a mermaid in a water tank for a Venice Beach, California, sideshow attraction. Like *Cat People*'s Irena, Mora believes herself to be cursed, especially when her relationships with previous boyfriends have ended in their mysterious deaths by drowning. Mora believes herself to be a descendent of the Greek sirens, the mythical women of the sea who lured men to their doom. At one point of the film, a strange woman, also of Greek descent, greets Mora as her "sister" in a scene that is a virtual replay of Elizabeth Russell's memorable cameo in *Cat People. Night Tide* has none of the polish of the Lewton films, yet it manages, within a severely limited budget, to achieve the melancholy atmosphere and dark poetry for which the Lewton films were praised.

That goes double for the off–Hollywood *Carnival of Souls* (1962), made on a shoe-string budget ($30,000) in Lawrence, Kansas, and Salt Lake City by Herk Harvey, a director of industrial films. *Carnival of Souls* tells the chilling story of a woman (Candace Hilligoss) who survives what appears to be a near collision with death when her car goes off a bridge. Piecing her life together after the accident, the woman accepts a job as a church organist several states away in Utah. As she makes the long drive, she begins to be haunted by frightening visions of a man with the face of a corpse. After establishing residence in a small boardinghouse, she continues to see the man's fearful countenance wherever she goes. She finds herself drawn to a deserted pavilion on the outskirts of town, where her visions become even more nightmarish, as they now include numerous corpselike people dancing in the structure's huge ballroom. Eventually, after several genuinely eerie sequences (and a number of effective Lewton "buses"), the audience comes to discover the dark secret that lies at the root of the moody heroine's problems.

Long considered a cult classic, *Carnival of Souls* is one of the creepiest horror films ever made. If some aspects of Harvey's meager budget (cheesy sound recording and poorly synchronized sound effects) hinder the film, other amateurish qualities of the production (static and overlong camera shots, nonprofessional actors, off-kilter editing, self-conscious artistic pretensions) actually tend to enhance the film's simulated reality with a documentary-like edge. *Carnival of Souls* is a horror film milestone in that it not only echoes the "suggested horror" approach of the Lewton films, but it also anticipates the jarring nightmare visions of George Romero's independently produced *Night of the Living Dead.*

Carnival of Souls has numerous cinematic antecedents, most of them titles already discussed: *All That Money Can Buy* (the silent "dance of the dead"), *Dead of Night* (the terrifying finale, replete with performers in corpselike makeup), and *Portrait of Jennie* (whose plot concerns a moody young woman who does not know she is really dead). The film's primary influence, however, appears to have been "The Hitch-Hiker," a 1960 episode of the "Twilight Zone," which was based on Lucille Fletcher's radio play of the same name. Fletcher, who for a time was married to composer Bernard Herrmann, wrote the play in 1940. In 1941 "The Hitch-Hiker" was broadcast on Orson Welles's "Mercury Theatre on the Air," which was when it first caught Rod Serling's attention. Serling bought the rights and, changing the male lead into a female, adapted Fletcher's radio play into a memorable teleplay, one which plays like a miniversion of Herk Harvey's cult classic. In the late 1980s, *Carnival of Souls* was restored to its original length and given a small theatrical rerelease, at which time it received the ballyhoos of critics, who hailed it as a low-budget horror masterpiece.

In 1962 the glut of psycho-thrillers included uneven low-budget entries like *Cabinet of Caligari* (a remake scripted by Robert *[Psycho]* Bloch) and *The Couch* (also from a Robert Bloch script) as well as star-studded "A" films like J. Lee Thompson's *Cape Fear.* Thompson's excellent film (remade by Martin Scorcese in 1992) makes extensive use of Lewtonesque fear tactics, including frightening "walks" and unnerving "buses." Most memorable for its Lewtonesque flourishes is a stalking sequence set in and around an elementary school. Gregory Peck plays the lawyer protagonist, but the real star of the film is Robert Mitchum, whose intimidating presence as the sadistic villain,

Max Cady, recalls his equally deranged performance in *Night of the Hunter. Cape Fear* is an extremely tense, deeply paranoid film that truly exploits an audience's fear of the dark.

The huge psycho-thriller trendsetter of 1962, however, was Robert Aldrich's *Whatever Happened to Baby Jane?* It was the first of a cycle of rather Gothic southern sagas that made flamboyant use of aging female stars, in this case Bette Davis and Joan Crawford. *Psycho* may have provided the impetus for *Baby Jane,* but Aldrich's landmark thriller actually had its cinematic antecedents in such films as *Kind Lady, Curse of the Cat People, My Name Is Julia Ross, Great Expectations, The Queen of Spades,* and especially *Sunset Boulevard* (with which *Baby Jane* shares a number of things in common). Like *Sunset Boulevard* (and, to a considerable extent, the earlier *Curse of the Cat People*), *Whatever Happened to Baby Jane?* is about an aging actress who lives a cloistered existence in an elaborate mansion whose dilapidated state reflects the condition of her life. The so-called "hag thriller" cycle initiated by *Baby Jane* would last more than a decade.

The Haunting was released in 1963, but by then deliberate Lewton homages seemed to have run their course and Wise's tribute was already something of an anomaly. To some degree, Lewton's methods were alive and well in psycho-thrillers like Hammer's *Maniac* and *Paranoiac,* as well as in American films like Francis Ford Coppola's Hammer-like *Dementia 13* (AIP), but aside from Robert Wise, few filmmakers were intent upon modeling their horror films upon a batch of "B" films made some 20 years before. *The Birds* had a pet shop scene that harked back to *Cat People,* but it otherwise had little in common with the spirit of the RKO series. Terence Fisher's *The Gorgon* was a Hammer film whose plot was not too far removed from that of *Cat People.* Two intelligent and quietly chilling 1963 British science fiction films—*Children of the Damned* (the nonsequel to *Village of the Damned*) and *The Unearthly Stranger*—also exhibited a few Lewtonesque flourishes.

While the psycho-thrillers prospered in the 1960s, the supernatural horror film tottered on the brink of uncertainty. *Witchcraft* (1964), a low-budget horror entry released by Lippert and nicely directed by Don Sharp, was somewhat in the Lewton mold (at the very least, it was reminiscent of such Lewtonesque witchcraft films as *Curse of the Demon, Horror Hotel,* and *Burn, Witch, Burn*). In 1964, Amicus (the production company behind *Horror Hotel*) also released *Dr. Terror's House of Horrors,* its first of many omnibus horror films in the *Dead of Night* tradition. Unfortunately, Amicus showed little interest in providing room for the quiet chills and long, unnerving pauses that had contributed to the success of better omnibus horror films like *Dead of Night* and *Black Sabbath.*

There was also a dearth of supernatural horror films in 1965 (Hammer's only entry was *Dracula, Prince of Darkness*), but psychological thrillers of all kinds continued to thrive, attracting even serious filmmakers like Roman

Polanski and William Wyler *(The Collector)*. Polanski's 1965 psycho-thriller, *Repulsion,* takes the genre a few steps closer to Lewton territory, especially in its sex-triggers-the-beast motif. Catherine Deneuve's character—an introverted, sexually repressed, and very sympathetic psycho-killer—is actually closer to the tragic heroines of *The Haunting, Carnival of Souls, The Snake Pit,* and *Cat People* than she is to any of the crazed older women swinging knives and axes in the typical thrillers of the day. Because *Repulsion* is such a twisted film, many viewers forget just how subtle it is, but Polanski's film gets more horror mileage from a skinned rabbit carcass than most other psycho-thrillers get from a bevy of murder scenes. At the time, Polanski had a tremendous interest in the horror genre (his upcoming 1967 vampire thriller/spoof, *The Fearless Vampire Killers,* would be his self-proclaimed homage to Hammer Films), and *Repulsion*'s influences seem to come from three directions: Clouzot, Hitchcock, and Lewton.

Old-fashioned supernatural horror came back from the dead in 1966, at least in England, where horror films had taken a turn for the better. Hammer released a solid pair of atmospheric horror films by John Gilling, *The Reptile* and *Plague of the Zombies,* both of which should be of interest to Lewton fans. Gilling, who directed the *The Flesh and the Fiends* and *Shadow of the Cat,* appeared to have an appreciation for the Lewton tradition (it was Gilling who had written the script for *The Gorgon*). *The Reptile* and *Plague of the Zombies* were shot in Cornwall (as was *Burn, Witch, Burn*), whose provocative geography and quaint, almost primitive, architecture proved well suited for supernatural horror films. *The Reptile,* a tale of Malayan curses and sexual repression, is about a doctor whose daughter turns into a snake whenever she is sexually aroused, a plot-wrinkle that is reminiscent of *Cult of the Cobra*). *Plague of the Zombies* does not have the bright sun of Saint Sebastian, but its voodoo plot is a neat reversal of *I Walked with a Zombie.* While Lewton's film took elements of an English novel *(Jane Eyre)* and transferred them to a West Indian setting, *Plague of the Zombies* transferred West Indian voodoo elements to an English setting.

Two other British horror films of 1966 are worth noting. One of them, *The Devil's Own* (aka *The Witches,* directed by Cyril Frankel), is yet another Hammer witchcraft film with a Cornwall setting. Although the presence of aging actress Joan Fontaine may lead one to suspect that Frankel's film is just another thriller in the *Baby Jane* mold, *The Devil's Own* is more firmly rooted in the Lewton tradition. Fontaine is the heroine, not the horror attraction. Although we may be misled by her 1960s teased hairdo, we have to remember that we are looking at the same actress who in *Rebecca, Jane Eyre,* and *Suspicion* established the cinematic prototype for the Gothic heroine, a prototype that had a profound influence upon the heroines of Lewton's films. Based on a Peter Curtis novel, the script of *The Devil's Own* was penned by "Quatermass's" Nigel Kneale, a writer whose past work demonstrated a profound understanding of the virtues of undisclosed horror. *The Devil's Own* also anticipates the 1974 cult film, *The Wicker Man.*

The Shuttered Room, based on an H.P. Lovecraft story, is the other 1966 British horror entry that makes good use of the less-is-more approach. Produced by a British independent and directed by David Greene, *The Shuttered Room* is one of the more flavorful Lovecraft adaptations (much better than the AIP offerings, *Die, Monster, Die* [1965] and *The Dunwich Horror* [1969]). Although we never believe that this obviously filmed-in-Britain production is set in a small town in Massachusetts, director Greene makes the most of his low budget in this earnest effort. His continual use of a subjective camera, from the monster's point of view, cleverly keeps the source of horror off-screen, so that the audience imagines something more frightening than anything the special effects department could deliver. Although actor Oliver Reed, as a motorcycle thug, is most memorable, *The Shuttered Room*'s glaring liability is its casting; Gig Young and Carole Lynley are all wrong for the lead roles. Beware of a disappointing ending.

By 1967 black-and-white cinematography appeared to be a thing of the past. Unless a film aspired to a documentary-like approach (*In Cold Blood,* for instance), it was bound to be shot in color. This was the case with Hammer's long belated third Quatermass film, *Five Million Years to Earth,* Nigel Kneale's own film adaptation of his 1959 BBC teleplay, "Quatermass and the Pit." Had it been shot in monochrome and directed by Val Guest, the third Quatermass film would likely have been the most Lewtonesque film of the series. Unfortunately, Roy Ward Baker's direction is uneven, and the film's many static scenes of exposition slow down the pace. If *Five Million Years to Earth* does not have the raw power of *The Creeping Unknown* or *Enemy from Space,* it is easily the most provocative of the series and brilliantly melds such diverse elements as Martians, witchcraft, metaphysics, evolution, and Satan. As Danny Peary tells it (in his coverage of *Five Million* in *Cult Movies* 3), "There are few shocks, but the atmosphere is intense, as in a Jacques Tourneur horror film. In fact, the night scene in which the possessed Sladden runs through the empty streets and deserted cemetery while much psychic activity takes place recalls haunting nocturnal sequences in Tourneur's British horror film, *Night of the Demon/Curse of the Demon.*"

Hammer's *The Devil Rides Out* (American title: *The Devil's Bride*), based on a Dennis Wheatley novel, is a colorful, sharply directed, expertly acted, and intelligently written satanic cult thriller that plays like a neat amalgam of *The Black Cat, The Seventh Victim,* and *Curse of the Demon.* In a manner similar to *The Black Cat,* the satanists are presented as ritual-bound, robe-clad individuals in search of a human sacrifice. As in *The Seventh Victim,* the satanists are aristocratic and effete, but otherwise quite ordinary, human beings; and, as in *Curse of the Demon,* the cult leader (well played by Charles Gray) has a nasty habit of summoning demons from hell. Briskly directed by

Terence Fisher (the king of Hammer horror directors), *The Devil's Bride* also benefits from a strong Richard Matheson script and an admirable Christopher Lee performance. Unfortunately, as captivating as the film may be, some flimsy special effects stand in for things that should have been kept in the shadows. With no disrespect to the legion of fans of *The Devil's Bride,* Fisher's decision to adorn terror scenes with cheesy superimposed menaces (particularly a giant spider) was a mistake.

Two more 1967 films need be mentioned here, one a dismal box-office flop and the other a gigantic hit. The flop was *Games,* Curtis Harrington's decadent, but largely effective, homage to *Les Diaboliques.* Harrington, once a director of experimental shorts in the late 1940s, made his feature film debut with the already-mentioned *Night Tide,* a film that captured the poetry, but not the terror, of its Lewton source of inspiration. In *Games,* Harrington demonstrated that he had effectively mastered the terror techniques of the Lewton films as well. Although *Games* is not nearly as good as Clouzot's film, Harrington shows considerable verve in his direction of his fright scenes. James Caan and Katherine Ross play the decadent couple. Simone Signoret (the catalyst of the horror to follow) is on hand to remind us of *Les Diaboliques,* while Kent Smith's presence suggests that the shadow of Lewton is not far behind.

The 1967 thriller that people attended instead of *Games* was Terence Young's *Wait Until Dark* (based on Frederick Knot's Broadway play), a film with strong ties to *The Spiral Staircase, Scream of Fear,* and any of a number of other films where physically handicapped heroines are terrorized by psycho-killers. While Dorothy McGuire was mute and Susan Strasberg was crippled, *Wait Until Dark*'s Audrey Hepburn is blind. Terence Young's film is Lewtonesque in its thematic content, if not its visual style; it has a vulnerable but resilient heroine as its central focus and it is a master essay on the theme of deceptive appearances. Do not expect Lewtonesque atmosphere, but do expect to fear the dark. Alan Arkin plays a terrific psycho (apparently a frustrated member of the actor's union, given his several disguises—all for the sake of a blind woman?). The climactic moment when Arkin (believed to be dead) leaps across the apartment, arms outstretched, provides a cinematic jolt as historic as the first Lewton "bus." We can thank *Wait Until Dark* for every psycho-killer who suffers a "false death" in the final reel. In case you have not noticed, the false death has become the modern horror film's most flagrant cliché. (A less flamboyant antecedent for the false death can also be found in *Isle of the Dead;* although Karloff's character does not leap across the room, he does drag himself along the floor, with the use of his knife, just as Arkin's character does in *Wait Until Dark.*)

Much more Lewtonesque, and deliberately so, was William Castle's production of Roman Polanski's *Rosemary's Baby* (1968). In addition to taking the director's helm, Polanski wrote the script, an adaptation of a best-selling novel by Ira Levin. Levin's novel signaled the beginning of a horror fiction boom which, thanks to William Peter Blatty's *The Exorcist* and Steven King's ground-breaking career, continues to this day. Whether or not it was Levin's conscious design, his novel about satanic practices in New York's Greenwich Village echoes *The Seventh Victim,* as well as a Charles Beaumont short story, "The New People," concerning a young couple whose overly friendly neighbors turn out to be devil worshippers. If Levin was not aware of his novel's Lewton connections, horror aficionado Roman Polanski surely was. The Polish director, whose last film had been the Hammer-inspired *Fearless Vampire Killers,* turned *Rosemary's Baby* into a subtle, quietly horrifying study of deceptive appearances. Mia Farrow and John Cassevetes are fine, but Ruth Gordon, Sidney Blackmer, and Ralph Bellamy steal the show. In its *Rosemary's Baby* entry, Phil Hardy's *Encyclopedia of Horror Movies* makes some telling observations about Polanski's approach:

> Many subtle devices are employed to involve the viewer. . . . The film's style is deliberately naturalistic, using familiar, everyday locations (telephone boxes, kitchens) as its tools of terror. Less importantly, but nevertheless essential to ensure implicit suspension of disbelief in an otherwise ludicrous set of circumstances, *Rosemary's Baby* is one of the few films (*Night of the Demon,* 1957, is another) where the artifacts and rituals of witchcraft are given credibility and where its practitioners are virtually free of caricature; the unreal, for a short while, becomes reality.

Except for an occasional rarity like *Rosemary's Baby,* Lewtonesque films were hard to come by in the late 1960s. David Lowell Rich's *Eye of the Cat* (1969) sounds appetizing to Lewton aficionados, but the film's multitude of angry housecats does not equal the terror of one unseen feline predator. Joe Stefano tries hard for some neat plot twists in a script that somewhat recalls *Shadow of the Cat* (with a dash or two of *Les Diaboliques*), but *Eye of the Cat* has all the atmosphere of a Purina ad. That same year Mark Robson made far more effective use of a single unthreatening housecat in his underrated and seldom-seen thriller, *Daddy's Gone a-Hunting.*

In the early 1970s, subtle horror films continued to be rare finds. There were some made-for-television genre entries (several by producer Dan Curtis) that tended to be a trifle old-fashioned, but they could not be otherwise in a medium that prohibited the graphic approach. Curtis Harrington had become the natural heir to the Grand Guignol thrillers in the *Baby Jane* mold: *How Awful About Allan* (made for television, 1970), *What's the Matter with Helen?* (1971), and *Who Slew Auntie Roo?* (1971). Although Harrington continued to build his terror in the Lewton tradition, he felt compelled to straddle both camps by also including gruesome shock scenes. By this time, the "walk" and the "bus" had become such horror staples, even among gore films, that it was no longer appropriate to characterize a film as Lewtonesque merely because it had a couple false scares and a walk in the dark.

It is a safe bet, though, that Lewton fans would be pleased with Clint Eastwood's directing debut, *Play Misty for Me* (1971), a moody, subtle, and genuinely frightening precursor to *Fatal Attraction* (1987). We should also recommend Don Siegel's *The Beguiled* (again 1971 and again starring Eastwood), a dark, claustrophobic Grand Guignol–Western. A Hammer film that rather uncharacteristically mined its chills from things unseen was Seth Holt's *Blood from the Mummy's Tomb* (a 1971 adaptation of Bram Stoker's *Jewel of the Seven Stars*). The female menace is not the conventional perambulating mummy the misleading title implies but the reincarnated spirit of an evil Egyptian queen. Hollywood's *Mephisto Waltz* (1971, directed by Paul Wendkos) also tried for some Lewtonesque ambience, but this cross between *Rosemary's Baby* and *The Hands of Orlac* is too confusing for anyone's taste.

Far more on the mark was *Let's Scare Jessica to Death*, a low-budget rural horror sleeper shot in Connecticut that was released by Paramount in 1971. Although this directing debut by John Hancock *(Bang the Drum Slowly)* bears a title that leads one to expect yet another Clouzot imitation, *Let's Scare Jessica to Death* is actually a moody, provocative, and beautifully photographed ghost chiller with a feminine bent. Zohra Lampert is marvelous as the haunted heroine with a history of mental illness, and Gretchen Corbett, as the strange female guest who may or may not be a ghost/vampire, is also good. Unfortunately, the same cannot be said for the two male leads (though the amateurish acting and unHollywood-like looks of Norman Jonas and Ralph Rose do lend an air of authenticity to the proceedings). If modern viewers can get past the early-1970s trappings of the film, they will discover a Lewtonesque gem in *Let's Scare Jessica to Death*.

A similarly lush and provocative rural horror atmosphere can be found in Richard Mulligan's 1972 adaptation of Thomas Tryon's *The Other*. In *The Encyclopedia of Horror Movies*, Phil Hardy states, "*The Other* is an exceptionally imaginative horror film in the Jacques Tourneur-Val Lewton vein. Low on gore but high on suggestion." Although Hardy describes the film as a cross between *To Kill a Mockingbird* (also directed by Mulligan) and *The Innocents*, *The Other* can perhaps be more accurately characterized as an "evil twin" variation of *Curse of the Cat People*. After all, this tale of a Russian family living in a small rural community in 1930s America has as its central character a fanciful child (this time a young boy) with an imaginary friend.

Curtis Harrington directed a 1973 made-for-TV film called *The Cat Creature*, a deliberate attempt to recreate the 1940s mood of the Lewton thrillers. Harrington's film was only so-so, but the presence of such 1940s performers as Gale Sondergaard, John Carradine, Key Luke, John Abbott, and, yes, Kent Smith gives some indication of *The Cat Creature*'s "B" movie roots. Two 1973 English films, *The Wicker Man* and *Don't Look Now*, were also somewhat in the Lewton mold. The first, directed by Robin Hardy and scripted by Anthony Shaffer, played like a sexy updating of Nigel Kneale's script for *The Devil's Own*. Long a cult film, the slightly overrated *Wicker Man* (in some quarters it is called the *Citizen Kane* of horror films) may make few deliberate attempts to emulate the Lewton style, but Hardy's film is a master thesis on the theme of deceptive appearances, and its witchcraft elements, island setting, bizarre rituals, and evocative photography provide some interesting contrasts to *I Walked with a Zombie*. *Don't Look Now*, based on Daphne du Maurier's novella and directed by Nicolas Roeg, is a slow-moving but extremely creepy film set in Venice. Because of its death-of-a-child theme, it is a disturbing film to endure, but the climax creates a frisson not easily forgotten. Venice is portrayed as an incredibly menacing city, filled with characters no one would wish to meet in a dark alley. One of the film's benevolent characters, a blind vacationing psychic from Britain, is frightening enough, but the identity of the film's killer is one of the most terrifying revelations in horror film history. Roeg's direction is at times self-consciously aloof, but *Don't Look Now* achieves harrowing results with the suggestive approach of du Maurier's novella.

Once *The Exorcist* made cinema history in late 1973 (for two years holding the crown as the world's champion money-maker), the market for subtle horror films would further dwindle. Months before William Friedkin's *The Exorcist* was released, however, came one more relic of a bygone era: *The Legend of Hell House* (based on Richard Matheson's *Hell House*, a reworking of Shirley Jackson's *The Haunting of Hill House*). Produced in Britain (as was *The Haunting*), *The Legend of Hell House* profits from John Hough's dynamic direction and Matheson's fascinating screenplay and demonstrates that cold terror could still be built upon nuance. As in *The Haunting*, the supernatural spirits are never seen, but their presence is frighteningly indicated in numerous ways: flying objects, mind control, possessed housecats, fierce winds, and myriad aberrant sounds. *The Legend of Hell House* is essential viewing for any reader of this volume. Director Hough and writer Matheson combined the tacky gimmickry of William Castle's *House on Haunted Hill* with the sublime terror of *The Haunting*, and the results were surprisingly effective.

The Exorcist brought about a minor horror boom, but it did not inspire many films that would qualify for inclusion here. In 1975, *Jaws* (the film that stole *The Exorcist*'s box-office crown) fostered a science fiction subgenre showcasing nature's rebellion against mankind. The monster threat varied: whales, dogs, spiders, octopuses, alligators, piranhas, grizzlies, and mutant grizzlies. One Lewtonesque oasis in the midst of this zoological nightmare was *The Premonition*, released in 1975, a one-shot independent film produced, directed, and cowritten by Robert Allen Schnitzer. In *The Encyclopedia of Horror*, Phil Hardy reports:

> *[The Premonition]* is a film which bears favourable comparison with such earlier moodpieces *[sic]* as *Night Tide* . . . and *Carnival of Souls*. . . . Strange, complex and haunting, in the Val Lewton tradition, the film draws its effect largely from suggestion as opposed to blatant horrors. Eerie and atmospheric, *The Premonition* is also graced with excellent performances.

The Omen (1976) did not deserve the box-office success it received, but it was gratifying to see that director Richard Donner had made a careful study of *Curse of the Demon*'s supernatural windstorm, even if he did copy it nearly shot-for-shot for his own essay in satanic horror. The year 1976 also saw the release of Brian De Palma's *Carrie*, an adaptation of Stephen King's first novel. *Carrie* was the first (and, in some ways, the best) of a long line of Stephen King adaptations. Although *Carrie* is not particularly Lewtonesque, its main character (reportedly inspired by *The Haunting*'s Eleanor Vance) is somewhat of an adolescent version of *Curse of the Cat People*'s alienated central character, Amy Reed. An even more accurate parallel to *Carrie*'s title character (played by Sissy Spacek) would be that of Meg Morgan (Allene Roberts) in Delmer Daves's *The Red House.*

A horror film milestone became the sleeper of 1978. Because it spawned a never-ending stream of slasher films (creating a gory subgenre that seldom had much in common with the Lewton tradition), there is a tendency to disassociate *Halloween* with the realm of the unseen. But John Carpenter's career-making smash hit, arguably the most frightening film of the 1970s, is a masterful exercise in the kind of subtle terror popularized by the Lewton films. Carpenter's film raises a generous amount of goose bumps with the suggestive approach; its menace, Michael Myers (whose adult face is never revealed), is often kept out of the frame, a tactic that only heightens the film's sense of encroaching horror. The film's nod to Howard Hawk's *The Thing* (it is what is on television that Halloween night) suggests that Carpenter was well aware of the less-is-more approach to screen terror. Although *Halloween* is, indeed, a slasher movie, it is much more subtle than people's memories of it tend to be.

Carpenter never made another film quite as good as *Halloween,* although his 1983 un-Lewtonesque remake of *The Thing* came close. *The Fog* (1979), Carpenter's other Lewton-inspired horror film, offered some marvelous seacoast atmosphere (and the best billowing fog since Brahm's *The Lodger*), but it was otherwise a disappointment. Audiences in 1979 preferred the chills in the dark to be found in Ridley Scott's *Alien,* an extremely graphic deep-space nightmare that, as paradoxical as it may sound, exploited Lewton's terror tactics to the hilt. The carnage and "on-screen monster scenes" aside, the very dramatic use of "walks" and "buses" within the claustrophic confines of the poorly lighted spaceship *Nostromo* are evidence of screenwriter Dan O'Bannon's affinity for the Lewton films. A resilient heroine as the central character and the (rather unlikely) addition of a shipboard cat (responsible for a number of "buses") are further evidence of *Alien*'s Lewton affiliations. While *Alien* is most often said to be an unofficial remake of *The Thing* (crossed with *It, the Terror from Beyond Space*), Dan O'Bannon made most particular use of the Lewton approach in his script. O'Bannon and his one-time film collaborator, John Carpenter, were longtime horror/science fiction fans who had grown up watching the genre classics of the 1930s, 1940s, and 1950s on television. They read *Famous Monsters of Filmland* and *Castle of Frankenstein* and were fully aware of their genre antecedents. While neither *Halloween* (with its own resilient heroine) or *Alien* can rightly be called pure Lewton homages, Carpenter and O'Bannon clearly drew inspiration from the Lewton films, an oeuvre they knew well.

The success of such late-seventies films as *Halloween* and *Alien* (not to mention *Star Wars* and *Close Encounters of the Third Kind*) signaled an unprecedented boom in horror, science fiction, and fantasy films (enough to glut the market of each) in the decade of the 1980s. The horror film gained some credibility with Stanley Kubrick's fascinating, but terribly uneven, box-office smash, *The Shining* (1980), based on Stephen King's third horror best-seller. Although Kubrick's film had its moments, it did not do for horror what *2001* did for science fiction.

In the early eighties, the horror genre was characterized by countless stalker/slasher/splatter films, many, if not most, of them reproducing themselves in litters of sequels. By the mid–eighties, horror cinema had more connections with men bearing knives and hatchets than it did with supernatural spooks or monsters. Even the supernatural films like the Spielberg-produced *Poltergeist* trilogy fell victim to the excesses of special effects technology. The more-is-better approach was now the rule of thumb. Joe Dante's *The Howling* (1981) and John Landis's *American Werewolf in London* (1981) renewed interest in lycanthropes, but this time (via some admittedly wondrous special effects) little would be left to the imagination. By the time Paul Schrader remade *Cat People* (1982), it seemed suitable to eschew the Lewton approach entirely and imitate *The Howling* and *American Werewolf* instead. Stephen King adaptations became a mainstay for horror cinema in the 1980s and, in spite of their popularity, most of them (with the particular exception of David Cronenberg's *The Dead Zone*) were not especially good. Wes Craven gained horror auteur status with the enormously successful *Nightmare on Elm Street* (1984). Graphic horror films reached bizarre heights (or depths) with independent horror films such as Sam Raimi's *Evil Dead* (1983), Stuart Gordon's *Re-Animator* (1985), and Jim Muro's *Street Trash* (1987). Meanwhile, George Miller's *Road Warrior* (1982) set a trend that turned science fiction away from the cerebral and into the realm of the action picture, setting the stage for James Cameron's *The Terminator* (1984) and Paul Verhoeven's *Robocop* (1987).

More horror films were released in the 1980s than in any previous decade, but considering the above trends, it is not surprising that Lewtonesque films were rare. What else would you expect from a decade where the only official remake of a Lewton film ever undertaken deliberately avoids the Lewton approach? (The remake's revamped story and setting actually bear more in common with the abyssmal Lewton imitation *Cry of the Werewolf* [1944].) Since the 1980s were responsible for twice the number of genre entries—horror, science fiction, fantasy, thrillers—of any previous decade, we can expect to find at least a handful or two that, for one reason or another, would be of interest to Lewton aficionados.

One would have expected David Lynch's *The Elephant Man* (1980) to be just the sort of project to warrant a Lewtonesque edge or two, but thanks to Freddie Francis's cinematography, Lynch's film is more accurately a chic throwback to Hammer's "Frankenstein" series (most particularly *Revenge of Frankenstein* and *Evil of Frankenstein*). *Raggedy Man* (1981), a drama/thriller directed by Jack Fisk, is a much better bet for Lewtonphiles. When *Raggedy Man* was released, there had already been such a glut of poorly made stalker films that critics could not understand why Fisk would turn a sensitive and well-acted rural drama (about a divorced mother's WWII homefront efforts as the telephone operator of a small Texas town) into something resembling a horror film. *Raggedy Man*'s intelligent and resilient central character (wonderfully played by Sissy Spacek) is much closer to the Lewton heroine than, say, the rather vapid character played by Shelley Duvall in *The Shining*. Although Fisk's subtle approach may or may not have been inspired by the Lewton films, it shares many of their qualities and makes a perfect double bill with *Face of Fire*.

Another subtle 1981 chiller that was not exactly marketed for the horror trade was Ralph L. Thomas's religious cult film, *Ticket to Heaven*, which was produced in Canada. Nick Mancuso is very effective as the sympathetic protagonist, and his rite of passage into the cult is terrifyingly accurate. In many ways, this is an eighties version of *Invasion of the Body Snatchers*, minus the conventional horror or science fiction angles (their absence only makes the film's message more frighteningly clear). The level of menace underneath the saccharine exteriors of the cult members gives viewers an undeniable emotional charge. These beatific zombies spout sickening platitudes and take part in a series of annoying camp sing-a-longs for God. Meg Foster, an actress with startling silver eyes, is well suited to her role as one of the more established cult members. Her directions for suicide (in the case of their being kidnapped by friends and family members) provides a frightful irony in light of the David Koresh/Waco 1993 catastrophe. The film does lapse into familiar territory by the final half hour, but *Ticket to Heaven* is well worth the price of admission for a true vision of hell.

Lewton fans should also be pleased by a thoroughly unique, independently produced, Colonial-era horror film from Canada, *Eyes of Fire* (1983), written and directed by Avery Crounse. Back in the early 1940s, the *Hollywood Reporter* announced that an upcoming Lewton project, *Carmilla,* was to be reworked as a Colonial-America period film. Although Lewton's adaptation of *Carmilla* was never filmed, the little-known, vastly underrated *Eyes of Fire* remains our best example of a Lewtonesque American-Colonial horror film. *Eyes of Fire* is a one-of-a-kind journey that defies almost all of our expectations. One logically assumes a Colonial-era horror film would be about witchcraft in a small New England town. While *Eyes of Fire* appears to begin in this expected fashion, 10 minutes into the film, Crounse takes us into uncharted territory (both figuratively and literally). Most of this extremely literate and wonderfully atmospheric horror thriller takes place in forests haunted by Indian spirits. *Eyes of Fire* has moments of visual poetry seldom seen in horror films of the 1980s, with cinematography by Wade Hanks that is absolutely breathtaking. Although Crounse's film deteriorates near the end (with too much screen time being given to special effects), it is still an amazing piece of work; the acting is superb and the film's authentic period flavor is beyond reproach. Films as eerie, unusual, and unpredictable as *Eyes of Fire* are far too rare to pass up. Play Crounse's film on a double bill with *The Red House,* and you may never go into the woods again.

Freddie Francis's 1985 adaptation of Dylan Thomas's play, *The Doctor and the Devils,* is recommended for die-hard *Body Snatcher* fans who wish to see yet another version of the Burke and Hare story. Otherwise, Francis's film is little more than an elaborate homage to his days at Hammer (the British studio's final feature film having been *To the Devil a Daughter* [1976]). *The Flesh and the Fiends* remains the definitive version of the Burke and Hare story.

Some effective Lewton touches can also be found in Nico Mastorakis's eerie thriller, *The Wind* (1987), an American film shot at a centuries-old seacoast dwelling in Greece. Although *The Wind* is not much more than a stylish stalker film, Mastorakis should be commended for imbuing his setting with an almost palpable sense of evil. Meg Foster (with those silver eyes) makes an excellent heroine and Wings Hauser an appropriately deranged villain. *The Wind* (released straight to video cassette) is a very minor and not entirely credible horror programmer, but its ambient atmosphere and resourceful spirit are to be admired. Recommended Greek-horror double bill: *The Wind* and *Isle of the Dead.*

Three powerful American chillers did their best to expose the evil forces lurking beneath the veneer of middle-class normality: David Lynch's *Blue Velvet* (1986), Tim Hunter's *River's Edge* (1986), and Joseph Ruben's *The Stepfather* (1987). All three films are classics of their kind, and while each film is explicit in its portrayal of violence, there are enough subtleties in these frightening exercises in deceptive appearances to please most Lewton fans.

The late eighties witnessed a sudden resurgence in voodoo-style horror films. Two of them, Alan Parker's *Angel Heart* (1987) and Wes Craven's *The Serpent and the Rainbow* (1988), should be of interest to those following the Lewton legacy. The controversial *Angel Heart* has Mickey Rourke as a most convincing derelict detective of the hard-boiled school who becomes embroiled in a twisted plot of murder, voodoo, and retribution. Parker's horror-noir recalls the bleak fictional worlds of Cornell Woolrich or Jim Thompson. *Angel Heart* is extremely violent, excessively downbeat, and ultimately depressing, but seldom has a modern horror film sustained such vague feelings of unease over nothing in particular for so long a time (static shots of fans and elevators seem to forecast some dreadful secret that we cannot quite fathom). Undisclosed horror is the driving force behind the film's narrative; unfortunately, the surprise dénouement seems a cheat. *The Serpent and the Rainbow* is equally flawed, but at times it does play like a virtual homage to several Lewton films (containing elements of *Zombie*, *Isle*, and *Bedlam*) as well as to Carl Dreyer's *Vampyr*. Based on Wade Davis's nonfiction book, Craven's *The Serpent and the Rainbow* is the 1980s equivalent of *I Walked with a Zombie*. The film's conventional zombie recalls the appearance and abject loneliness of Carrefour in the Lewton/Tourneur film. In *Serpent*'s most harrowing fright scene, the protagonist is closed in a coffin with a tarantula; when the lid comes down, the screen becomes dark. We hear the hero's body rubbing against the confining walls of the coffin, we hear his breathing and eventual screams, but we see nothing at all but the fearful dark. And the results are absolutely terrifying.

A genuinely satisfying horror film of the decade was *The Lady in White* (written, directed, and produced by Frank LaLoggia, who also composed the music). LaLoggia's film became an instant cult classic as soon as it hit the video stores in September 1988, and it is easy to see why. *The Lady in White* received limited theatrical release but like many horror classics whose reputations were established via the television medium (*Invasion of the Body Snatchers*; *Curse of the Demon*; *Burn, Witch, Burn*; *Carnival of Souls*; *The Haunting*), *Lady*'s cult status is assured. Those who view it once are usually inclined to see it again and again. Like *Curse of the Cat People* (with which *Lady* shares several elements) and *The Window*, LaLoggia's film is one of that rare breed: an adult film about children. It is also the film that most closely captures the flavor and youthful magic of Ray Bradbury's fiction (although LaLoggia's film is, paradoxically, not based upon anything Bradbury had ever written). This modestly budgeted (but gorgeous-looking) film, set in a small New Jersey town (circa 1962–1963) is a sterling evocation of lost youth and childhood terrors. LaLoggia's musical score is quite remarkable (though it gets a little ponderous near the climax), and his direction is even better. *The Lady in White*'s occasionally heavy-handed lapses (the alligator incident, the cliffhanger, and the touching—but tediously poignant—mother/daughter reunion) are easily forgiven in light of the film's perfectly realized vision of childhood in the early

1960s. The entire cast conducts itself admirably—obviously everyone believed in the project—and the ensemble acting and quirky behavior lends an air of credibility to the whole project. Considering it was LaLoggia's independently financed dreamchild, it's a miracle that *Lady in White* was made at all. That it turned out this good was an even greater miracle.

Also recommended is *Paper House,* a 1989 British import directed by Bernard Rose that was heralded by critics, at least one of whom called it "a thinking-man's *Nightmare on Elm Street.*" But Rose's adult film about children has closer associations with *Curse of the Cat People. Paper House*'s main character is a misunderstood and overly imaginative 11-year-old girl (well-played by Charlotte Burke) who retreats into a fantasy world dominated by a series of surreal dreams (involving a hand-drawn picture of a house and the occupants who live there). Although the dreams are pleasant enough at first, they take on nightmarish proportions as they begin to interfere with her waking life. Slow going, but worthwhile.

Three sexually explicit 1989 thrillers—one from Canada (Sandor Stern's *Pin*), one from England (Gordon Hessler's *Girl on a Swing*), and one from America (Phillip Badger's *The Forgotten One*)—exhibited some Lewtonesque verve. *Pin,* perhaps the best of the three, is a well-made, wonderfully atmospheric thriller about a deranged boy (David Hewlett) who develops a fixation with his father's medical dummy (named Pin). Terry O'Quinn (who was superb in the title role of *The Stepfather*) is excellent as the boy's father, a doctor who is also not playing with a full deck. *Pin* is a fascinating study of dementia that somewhat echoes the "ventriloquist segment" of *Dead of Night.* Sandor Stern's film possesses a purity of intent rare in the genre (also catch Stern's 1992 made-for-cable thriller, *Duplicates*).

Girl on a Swing is a slow-moving, though remarkably sensual, thriller/romance about an Englishman (Rupert Frazier) who, visiting Amsterdam on business, falls in love with a mysterious woman (Meg Tilly) who is reluctant to establish a relationship because of a dreadful secret in her past. Gordon Hessler's surprisingly artistic (and very European) direction is a big departure from his early-seventies style *(The Oblong Box, Scream and Scream Again, Cry of the Banshee)*. Basically, the film is a sexy reworking of *Night Tide,* including the water symbolism; as in Harrington's film, the accent is on the unseen.

The third of the 1989 trio, *The Forgotten One,* is about a single man (Terry O'Quinn) who buys a house only to discover that it is haunted by a female ghost; he soon falls in love with her and takes her to bed. The film's power disintegrates as soon as the supernatural romance begins, but until then we have some Lewtonesque filmmaking at its very best. Phillip Badger's depiction of the ghostly manifestations in the film's first half is reminiscent of such supernatural classics as *The Uninvited* and *The Haunting.* O'Quinn's home-alone reactions to the haunting provide the most realistic behavior ever exhibited by a screen character who has seen a ghost. His response to the things that go bump in the night is at once hilarious and terrifying. When he resorts to sleeping in his car, something all of us would do in his circumstances, Badger's brilliant mixture of the comic and the terrifying has a verisimilitude that recalls the famous "whistling in the dark" scene in the opening reel of John Landis's *An American Werewolf in London.* However flawed they may be, the 1989 trio of sexy horror films, *Pin, Girl on a Swing,* and *The Forgotten One,* were refreshing entries in a genre riddled by threadbare formulas and tiresome special effects.

Although it is too early in the decade to look at the 1990s with any sort of objectivity, a few early-nineties releases at least deserve a quick mention. Jerry Zucker's *Ghost* (1990) was a massive sleeper hit and a harbinger of good things to come in the horror-happy 1990s. *Ghost*'s ingenious mix of romance, horror, comedy, and tragedy combines the fantasy elements of *Topper* with the horrific suspense of the new breed of romantic psycho-thriller, all to glorious effect. Oddly, it has not spawned numerous imitations, at least not yet. Zucker creates a number of spinetingling scenes, and his ghost protagonist (well played by Patrick Swayze) is one of the genre's more sympathetic spooks.

Adrian Lynn's *Jacob's Ladder,* written by Bruce Joel Rubin (who had also written the script for *Ghost*), can best be described as a horror-noir combination of Herk Harvey's *Carnival of Souls,* Bob Clark's *Deathdream,* and Ambrose Bierce's short story, "An Occurence at Owl Creek Bridge." *Jacob's Ladder* is a film that fairly pulsates with a sense of undisclosed horror. Unfortunately, Lynn's film is also guilty of some of the same pitfalls that plagued *Angel Heart:* it is unremittingly grim, ghoulishly gruesome, unfairly misleading, and ultimately depressing.

Three 1991 romantic psycho-thrillers, Kenneth Branagh's *Dead Again,* Damien Harris's *Deceived,* and Wolfgang Petersen's *Shattered,* all fought for the same audience, but it was Branagh's impressive thriller debut that received all the fanfare. *Dead Again* was also the most Lewtonesque of the three. After coming to worldwide attention by directing (and starring in) his celebrated 1989 cinematic version of Shakespeare's *Henry V,* Kenneth Branagh (still in his mid–20s and touted as the Orson Welles of the 1990s) immediately embarked upon the kind of supernatural thriller that we have not seen since the 1940s. *Dead Again* is also a horror-noir (with an elaborate, visually stunning black-and-white flashback), but unlike *Angel Heart* and *Jacob's Ladder,* it does not try so hard to be uncompromising. So much the better, as far as Branagh's intelligent, exciting, and satisfying thriller is concerned. Who knows? Kenneth Branagh may turn out to be the next great black-and-white hope for horror cinema.

It was gratifying to see in *Silence of the Lambs* (1991) that director Jonathan Demme had learned a lesson or two from the films of Val Lewton. The chilling scene where the vulnerable-but-resilient heroine (Jodie Foster) first makes her way into the labyrinthian depths of the prison (à la *Bedlam*), en route to her first encounter with Hannibal Lector (Anthony Hopkins), is a perfect example of the modern application of the Lewton walk, while the film's gripping climax in a pitch-dark basement exhibits a direct link to the politics of terror popularized by the Lewton films.

As this volume goes to press, there is much excitement in the horror film industry. In late 1992, Francis Ford Coppola released his ambitious *Bram Stoker's Dracula,* its box-office success pointing ahead to a possible horror film renaissance. There are high expectations for Coppola's follow-up production, *Mary Shelley's Frankenstein,* to be directed by Kenneth Branagh, with Robert DeNiro as the monster. Meanwhile, Jack Nicholson has just played a werewolf in a June 1994 release called *Wolf.* Anne Rice's *Interview with a Vampire* is being given a first-class production, with direction by Neil Jordan (who helmed the 1992–93 sleeper hit, *The Crying Game*). Rice is also involved with a screenplay/novel for yet another remake of *The Bride of Frankenstein.* In addition, there is a big-budget remake of *Village of the Damned* waiting in the wings.

Meanwhile, Val Lewton's films have been given considerable attention. They are repeatedly telecast (with the exception of *The Ghost Ship*) on cable channels, including PBS stations. In the summer of 1993, a New York revival theater had a well-attended Lewton festival, playing all 11 of the RKO films. Christopher Golden's 1991 book, *Cut: Horror Writers on Horror Film,* includes essays on the horror film from 25 of the best-known modern horror novelists working today. Close to half of the entries include some appreciative reference to the films of Val Lewton. Ray Garton's essay, "On Kids and *Cat People,*" includes a passage typical of the kind of thinking echoed by several of the book's contributors:

> I think there are way too many people out there making horror movies who, first of all, have no respect for the genre, and who wouldn't know a solid story from a bowl of pudding. Some of them say they love horror, but what they really love are the special effects, the mechanics of *making* the horrors. Or maybe they just want to make a buck. They don't seem to realize that a horror story, just like any other kind of story, has to make sense. . . .
>
> While watching the original *Cat People,* we recognized the feelings that were passing back and forth between the characters. We felt for them, understood why they were doing what they were doing, and believed in them, even if, for whatever reason, we didn't like them. We believed in them so much that we believed in the things that happened to them, too, no matter how extraordinary, how impossible.

We would hazard a guess that a surprising number of genre fans find modern horror films predictable, feel much of the gore unnecessary, and, most of all, find themselves cheated out of a sincere emotional response by the shameless provision of stock characters in livestock roles. Even when an occasional slice-and-dice horror epic shows a rare concern for character development, we generally know better than to befriend cattle en route to the slaughterhouse.

So maybe the future of Hollywood horror lies in the hands of filmmakers courageous enough to give horror fans what they really want: a good, healthy scare, the kind that preys upon their imagination as much as it plays upon their nerves. Whether or not Hollywood wishes to admit it, the "Lewton touch" is alive and well. As long as horror films continue to make their audiences fear the dark, there will always be an occasional return to the purity of the Lewton approach. (As this book went to press, in fact, a remake of *Bedlam* was in the works.)

It is amazing that a small batch of low-budget films made within a three-year period more than a half century ago continues to be such a vital force within the horror milieu. The Lewton films drew their inspiration from myriad sources: traditional folktales, the Gothic novel, Russian literature, Victorian literature, German expressionism, Maurice Tourneur, Fritz Lang, 1930s horror talkies, 1930s radio, David Selznick, Alfred Hitchcock, Orson Welles, and all the talent and opportunities that existed on the RKO lot. In turn, the Lewton films have had a dramatic influence upon the horror, thriller, and science fiction genres, an influence that continues to this day. The film careers of Jacques Tourneur, Mark Robson, and Robert Wise, and the various contributions each made to the history of cinema, are, of course, also part of the Lewton legacy. So are the numerous Lewtonesque films detailed in this and earlier chapters, several of them among the greatest horror films ever made.

Val Lewton was the George Bailey of the Hollywood horror film. Like the hero of Capra's *It's a Wonderful Life,* he continually made sacrifices and endured innumerable frustrations for the sake of an ideal he believed in. He championed the underdog and protected his small "B" budget horror unit from the profiteering forces that threatened to usurp his independence. Like George Bailey, Lewton was once offered the chance to improve his lot. Instead, he turned down a career in "A" budget pictures to maintain the integrity of his small, but honest, enterprise. Although he never had the opportunity to fully appreciate how his life touched the lives of so many, his cinematic contributions and his continuing dark legacy have forever changed the course of Hollywood history.

Thank you, Val Lewton.

FILMOGRAPHY

Cat People (1942)

Production Company: RKO-Radio. Producer: Val Lewton. Director: Jacques Tourneur. Assistant Director: Doran Cox. Script: DeWitt Bodeen. Director of Photography: Nicholas Musuraca. Editor: Mark Robson. Art Directors: Albert S. D'Agostino, Walter E. Keller. Set Decorators: Darrell Silvera, Al Fields. Music: Roy Webb. Musical Director: C. Bakaleinikoff. Costumes: Renie. Sound Recordist: John L. Cass.

Simone Simon (Irena Dubrovna), Kent Smith (Oliver Reed), Tom Conway (Dr. Judd), Jane Randolph (Alice), Jack Holt (Commodore), Alan Napier (Carver), Elizabeth Dunne (Miss Plunkett), Mary Halsey (Blondie), Alec Craig (Zoo Keeper), Elizabeth Russell (Cat Woman), Dot Farley (Mrs. Agnew), Teresa Harris (Minnie), Charles Jordan (Bus Driver), Don Kerr (Taxi Driver), Betty Roadman (Mrs. Hansen).

Filmed in the RKO Studios, Hollywood, 28 July–21 August 1942. First shown in U.S.A., December 1942; G.B., April 1943. Running time: 71 min.

I Walked with a Zombie (1943)

Production Company: RKO-Radio. Producer: Val Lewton. Director: Jacques Tourneur. Assistant Director: William Dorfman. Script: Curt Siodmak, Ardel Wray. Based on a story by Inez Wallace. Director of Photography: J. Roy Hunt. Editor: Mark Robson. Art Directors: Albert S. D'Agostino, Walter E. Keller. Set Decorators: Darrell Silvera, Al Fields. Music: Roy Webb. Musical Director: C. Bakaleinikoff. Songs: "O Marie Congo" (chant); "British Grenadiers" (Calypso singer); "Fort Holland Calypso Song" (Calypso singer); "O Legba" (chant); "Walee Nan guinan" (chant). Also: Chopin's E Minor Étude (piano). Sound Recordist: John C. Grubb.

James Ellison (Wesley Rand), Frances Dee (Betsy), Tom Conway (Paul Holland), Edith Barrett (Mrs. Rand), Christine Gordon (Jessica Holland), James Bell (Dr. Maxwell), Richard Abrams (Clement), Teresa Harris (Alma), Sir Lancelot (Calypso Singer), Darby Jones (Carrefour), Martin Wilkins (Hougan), Jeni LeGon (Dancer), Jieno Moxzer (Sabreur), Arthur Walker (Ti-Joseph), Kathleen Hartfield (Dancer), Clinton Rosemond (Coachman), Alan Edmiston (Mr. Wilkens), Norman Mayes (Bayard), Melvin Williams (Baby), Vivian Dandridge (Melisse).

Filmed in the RKO Studios, Hollywood, 26 October–19 November 1942. First shown in U.S.A., April 1943; G.B., September 1943. Running time: 68 min.

The Leopard Man (1943)

Production Company: RKO-Radio. Producer: Val Lewton. Director: Jacques Tourneur. Assistant Director: William Dorfman. Script: Ardel Wray. Based on the novel *Black*

Alibi by Cornell Woolrich. Additional Dialogue: Edward Dein. Director of Photography: Robert de Grasse. Editor: Mark Robson. Art Directors: Albert S. D'Agostino, Walter E. Keller. Set Decorators: Darrell Silvera, Al Fields. Music: Roy Webb. Musical Director: C. Bakaleinikoff. Sound Recordist: John C. Grubb.

Dennis O'Keefe (Jerry Manning), Margo (Clo-Clo), Jean Brooks (Kiki Walker), Isabel Jewell (Maria), James Bell (Dr. Galbraith), Margaret Landry (Teresa Delgado), Abner Biberman (Charlie How-Come), Richard Martin (Raoul Belmonte), Tula Parma (Consuelo Contreras), Ben Bard (Chief Robles), Ariel Heath (Eloise), Fely Franquelli (Rosita), Robert Anderson (Dwight), Jacqueline De Witt (Helene), Bobby Spindola (Pedro), William Halligan (Brunton), Kate Lawson (Señora Delgado), Russell Wade (Man in Car), Jacques Lory (Philippe), Tola Nesmith (Señora Contreras), Margaret Sylva (Marta), Charles Lung (Manuel), John Dilson (Coroner), Mary Maclaren (Nun), Tom Orosco (Window Cleaner), Eliso Gamboa (Señor Delgado), Joe Dominguez (Cop), Betty Roadman (Clo-Clo's Mother), Rosa Rita Varella (Clo-Clo's Sister), John Piffle (Flower Vendor), Rene Pedrini (Frightened Waiter), Brandon Hurst (Gatekeeper), Rose Higgins (Indian Weaver), George Sherwood (Police Lieutenant), John Tettemer (Minister).

Filmed in the RKO Studios, Hollywood, 9 February–8 March 1943. First shown in U.S.A., May 1943; G.B., January 1944. Running time: 66 min.

The Seventh Victim (1943)

Production Company: RKO-Radio. Producer: Val Lewton. Director: Mark Robson. Assistant Director: William Dorfman. Script: Charles O'Neal, DeWitt Bodeen. Director of Photography: Nicholas Musuraca. Editor: John Lockert. Art Directors: Albert S. D'Agostino, Walter E. Keller. Set Directors: Darrell Silvera, Harley Miller. Music: Roy Webb. Musical Director: C. Bakaleinikoff. Costumes: Renie. Sound Recordist: John C. Grubb.

Tom Conway (Dr. Lewis Judd), Jean Brooks (Jacqueline Gibson), Isabel Jewell (Frances Fallon), Kim Hunter (Mary Gibson), Evelyn Brent (Natalie Cortez), Erford Gage (Jason Hoag), Ben Bard (Bruns), Hugh Beaumont (Gregory Ward), Chef Milani (Mr. Romari), Marguerita Sylva (Mrs. Romari), Mary Newton (Mrs. Redi), Wally Brown (Durk), Feodor Chaliapin (Leo), Eve March (Mrs. Swift), Milton Kibbee (Joseph), Marianne Mosner (Miss Rowan), Elizabeth Russell (Mimi), Joan Barclay (Gladys), William Halligan (Radeau), Lou Lubin (Irving August), Kernan Cripps (Cop), Dewey Robinson (Conductor), Lloyd Ingraham (Watchman), Ann Summers (Miss Summers), Tiny Jones (News Vendor), Sara Selby (Miss Gottschalk), Betty Roadman (Mrs. Wheeler), Eileen O'Malley and Lorna Dunn (Mothers).

Filmed in RKO Studios, Hollywood, 5–29 May 1943. First shown in U.S.A., September 1943; G.B., March 1944. Running time: 71 min.

The Ghost Ship (1943)

Production Company: RKO-Radio. Producer: Val Lewton. Director: Mark Robson. Assistant Director: Ruby Rosenberg. Script: Donald Henderson Clarke. Based on a short story by Leo Mittler. Director of Photography: Nicholas Musuraca. Editor: John

Lockert. Art Directors: Albert S. D'Agostino, Walter E. Keller. Set Directors: Darrell Silvera, Claude Carpenter. Special Effects: Vernon L. Walker. Music: Roy Webb. Musical Director: C. Bakaleinikoff. Songs: "Blow the Man Down" (sung by the Blind Beggar and Billy Radd); "Home Dearie Home," "Come to San Sebastian," "I'm Billy Radd from La Trinidad" (all sung by Billy Radd). Costumes: Edward Stevenson. Sound Recordist: Francis M. Sarver.

Richard Dix (Captain Stone), Russell Wade (Tom Merriam), Edith Barrett (Ellen Roberts), Ben Bard (Bowns), Edmund Glover (Sparks), Skelton Knaggs (Finn), Tom Burton (Benson), Steve Winston (Ausman), Robert Bice (Raphael), Lawrence Tierney (Louie), Dewey Robinson (Boats), Charles Lung (Jim), George De Normand (John), Paul Marion (Peter), Sir Lancelot (Billy Radd), Boyd Davis (Roberts), Harry Clay (McCall), Russell Owen, John Burford, Eddie Borden, Mike Lally and Charles Regan (Crew Members), Nolan Leary (Stenographer), Herbert Vigran (Chief Engineer), Shirley O'Hara (Silhouette Girl), Alec Craig (Blind Beggar), Bob Stevenson and Charles Norton (German Sailors), Norman Mayes (Carriage Driver).

Filmed in the RKO Studios, Hollywood, 3–28 August 1943. First show in U.S.A., December 1943; G.B., April 1944. Running time: 69 min.

The Curse of the Cat People (1944)

Production Company: RKO-Radio. Producer: Val Lewton. Directors: Gunther Von Fritsch, Robert Wise. Assistant Director: Harry D'Arcy. Script: DeWitt Bodeen. Director of Photography: Nicholas Musuraca. Editor: J.R. Whittredge. Art Directors: Albert S. D'Agostino, Walter E. Keller. Set Decorators: Darrell Silvera, William Stevens. Music: Roy Webb. Musical Director: C. Bakaleinikoff. Songs: "Ruben Ranzo" (sung by Edward); "It Came Upon a Midnight Clear" (sung by carolers); "Shepherds Shake Off Your Drowsy Sleep" (sung by carolers, and by Irena in a counterpoint French version). Costumes: Edward Stevenson. Sound Recordist: Francis M. Sarver. Sound Rerecordist: James G. Stewert.

Simone Simon (Irena), Kent Smith (Oliver Reed), Jane Randolph (Alice Reed), Ann Carter (Amy), Elizabeth Russell (Barbara), Julia Dean (Julia Farren), Eve March (Miss Callahan), Erford Gage (Captain of Guard), Sir Lancelot (Edward), Joel Davis (Donald), Juanita Alvarez (Lois), Charley Bates (Jack), Gloria Donovan, Ginny Wren and Linda Ann Bieber (Little Girls), Sarah Selby (Miss Plummet), Mel Sternlight (State Trooper).

Filmed in the RKO Studios, Hollywood, 26 August–4 October 1943. First shown in the U.S.A., March 1944; G.B., October 1944. Running time: 70 min.

Youth Runs Wild (1944)

Production Company: RKO-Radio. Producer: Val Lewton. Director: Mark Robson. Assistant Director: Harry D'Arcy. Script: John Fante. Story: John Fante, Herbert Kline. Inspired by a *Look* magazine picture story, "Are These Our Children?" Additional Dialogue: Ardel Wray. Director of Photography: John Mescall. Editor: John Lockert. Art Directors: Albert S. D'Agostino, Carroll Clark. Set Directors: Darrell Silvera, Ross Dowd. Special Effects: Vernon L. Walker. Music: Paul Sawtell. Musical Director: C. Bakaleinikoff. Costumes: Edward Stevenson. Sound Recordist: Frank McWhorter. Technical Advisor: Ruth Clifton. Topical Research: Madeleine Dmytryk.

Bonita Granville (Toddy), Kent Smith (Danny), Jean Brooks (Mary), Glenn Vernon (Frank), Tessa Brind (Sarah Taylor), Ben Bard (Mr. Taylor), Mary Servoss (Mrs. Hauser), Arthur Shields (Mr. Dunlop), Lawrence Tierney (Duncan), Dickie Moore (Georie Dunlop), Johnny Walsh (Herb Vigero), Rod Rodgers (Rocky), Elizabeth Russell (Mrs. Taylor), Juanita Alvarez (Lucy), Gloria Donovan (Nancy Taylor), Jack Carrington (Bart), Ida Shoemaker (Card Player), Claire Carleton (Taxi Driver), Art Smith (Mr. Hauser), Harold Barnitz (Stevie), Frank O'Connor (Cop), Rosemary La Planche and Joan Barclay (Women), Margaret Landry (Hysterical Girl), Harry Clay (Good Humor Man), George De Normand (Fireman), Danny Desmond (Eddie Wilson), Fritz Lieber (Judge), Robert Strong (Juvenile Officer), Tom Burton (Soldier with Sarah), Russell Hopton (Dickens), Chris Drake (Usher), Edmund Glover (Lineman), Lee Phelps (Fireman), Gordon Jones (Truck Driver), Harry Harvey (Watchman), Maxwell Hayes (Priest), Bud Wiser (Motor Cop).

Filmed in the RKO Studios, Hollywood, 3 November–21 December 1943. First shown in U.S.A., September 1944; G.B., May 1945. Running time: 67 min.

Mademoiselle Fifi (1944)

Production Company: RKO-Radio. Producer: Val Lewton. Director: Robert Wise. Assistant Director: Sam Ruman. Script: Josef Mischel, Peter Ruric. Based on two stories, "Boule de Suif" and "Mademoiselle Fifi," by Guy de Maupassant. Director of Photography: Harry Wild. Editor: J.R. Whittredge. Art Directors: Albert S. D'Agostino, Walter E. Keller. Set Decorators: Darrell Silvera, Al Fields. Special Effects: Vernon L. Walker. Music: Werner Heymann. Musical Director: C. Bakaleinikoff. Songs: "Three Captains" (sung in French by Elizabeth); "Drinking Song" (sung by men, in German). Costumes: Edward Stevenson. Sound Recordist: Francis M. Sarver. Sound Rerecordist: James G. Stewart.

Simone Simon (Elizabeth Rousset), John Emery (Jean Cornudet), Kurt Krueger (Lt. von Eyrick, called "Fifi"), Alan Napier (Count de Breville), Helen Freeman (Countess Wife), Romaine Callender (Manufacturer), Fay Helm (Manufacturer's Wife), Edmund Glover (Young Priest), Charles Waldronn (Cure of Cleresville), Mayo Newhall (M. Follenvie), Lillian Bronson (Mme. Follenvie), Alan Ward (Coach Driver), Daun Kennedy (The Maid), William Von Wymetal (The Major), Max Willenz (The Captain), Marc Cramer (The Lieutenant), John Good (Fritz), Allan Lee (Hostler), Frank Mayo (Sgt. at Inn), Margaret Landry (Eva), Rosemary La Planche (Amanda), Marie Lund (Helene), Margie Stewart (Pamela), Violet Wilson (Aunt Marie), Tom Burton and Steve Winston (Uhlans), Paul Marion (Devoir), Ed Allen (Soldier), Richard Drumm (German Sentry), Victor Cutler (Soldier Waiter).

Filmed in the RKO Studios, Hollywood, 23 March–22 April 1944. First shown in U.S.A., August 1944; G.B., not shown. Running time: 69 min.

Isle of the Dead (1945)

Production Company: RKO-Radio. Producer: Val Lewton. Director: Mark Robson. Assistant Director: Harry Scott. Script: Ardel Wray, Josef Mischel. Director of Photography: Jack Mackenzie. Editor: Lyle Boyer. Art Directors: Albert S. D'Agostino, Walter E. Keller. Set Decorators: Darrell Silvera, Al Greenwood. Music: Leigh Harline.

Musical Director: C. Bakaleinikoff. Song: "Greek Song" (sung by Thea). Costumes: Edward Stevenson. Sound Recordist: Jean L. Speak. Sound Re-recordist: James G. Stewart.

Boris Karloff (General), Ellen Drew (Thea), Marc Cramer (Oliver), Katherine Emery (Mrs. St. Aubyn), Helene Thimig (Kyra), Alan Napier (St. Aubyn), Jason Robards, Sr. (Albrecht), Ernst Dorian (Dr. Drossos), Skelton Knaggs (Robbins), Sherry Hall (Greek Colonel), Erick Hanson (Officer).

Filmed in the RKO Studios, Hollywood, 14–22 July and 1–12 December 1944. First shown in U.S.A., September 1945; G.B., November 1955. Running time: 71 min.

The Body Snatcher (1945)

Production Company: RKO-Radio. Executive Producer: Jack J. Gross. Producer: Val Lewton. Director: Robert Wise. Assistant Director: Harry Scott. Script: Philip MacDonald, Carlos Keith (Val Lewton). Based on the story by Robert Louis Stevenson. Director of Photography: Robert de Grasse. Editor: J.R. Whittredge. Art Directors: Albert S. D'Agostino, Walter E. Keller. Set Decorators: Darrell Silvera, John Sturtevant. Music: Roy Webb. Musical Director: C. Bakaleinikoff. Songs: "We'd Better Bide a Wee," "When Ye Gang Awa," "Jaime" and "Will Ye No Come Back Again?" (sung by Street Singer); "Spit Song" (sung by Boy); "Bonnie Dundee" (sung by quartet of men). Costumes: Renie. Sound Recordist: Bailey Fesler. Sound Re-recordist: Terry Kellum.

Boris Karloff (Gray), Bela Lugosi (Joseph), Henry Daniell (MacFarlane), Edith Atwater (Meg), Russell Wade (Fettes), Rita Corday (Mrs. Marsh), Sharyn Moffett (Georgina), Donna Lee (Street Singer), Robert Clarke (Richardson), Carl Kent (Gilchrist), Jack Welch (Boy), Larry Wheat (Salesman), Mary Gordon (Mrs. Mary McBride), Jim Moran (Horse Trader), Ina Constant (Maid), Bill Williams (Medical Student).

Filmed in the RKO Studios, Hollywood, 25 October–17 November 1944. First shown in U.S.A., May 1945; G.B., December 1945. Running time: 78 min.

Bedlam (1946)

Production Company: RKO-Radio. Executive Producer: Jack J. Gross. Producer: Val Lewton. Director: Marc Robson. Assistant Director: Doran Cox. Script: Carlos Keith (Val Lewton), Mark Robson. Suggested by William Hogarth's *Bedlam*, Plate 8, *The Rake's Progress*. Director of Photography: Nicholas Musuraca. Editor: Lyle Boyer. Art Directors: Albert S. D'Agostino, Walter E. Keller. Set Decorator: Darrell Silvera. Special Effects: Vernon L. Walker. Music: Roy Webb. Musical Director: C. Bakaleinikoff. Costumes: Edward Stevenson. Sound: Jean L. Speak, Terry Kellum.

Boris Karloff (Master Sims), Anna Lee (Nell Bowen), Billy House (Lord Mortimer), Richard Fraser (Hannay), Glenn Vernon (The Gilded Boy), Ian Wolfe (Sidney Long), Jason Robards, Sr. (Oliver Todd), Leland Hodgson (John Wilkes), Joan Newton (Dorthea the Dove), Elizabeth Russell (Mistress Sims), Victor Holbrook (Tom the Tiger), Robert Clarke (Dan the Dog), Larry Wheat (Podge), Bruce Edwards (The Warder), John Meredith (1st Maniac), John Beck (Solomon), Ellen Corby (Queen of Artichokes), John Ince (Judge), Skelton Knaggs (Varney), John Goldsworthy (Chief Commissioner), Polly Bailey (Scrub Woman), Foster Phinney (Lord Sandwich), Donna Lee and Nan Leslie

(Cockney Girls), Tom Noonan (1st Stonemason), George Holmes (2d Stonemason), Jimmy Jordan (3d Stonemason), Robert Manning (John the Footman), Frankie Dee (Pompey), Frank Pharr (2d Commissioner), Harry Harvey (John Gray), Victor Travers (Sims's Friend), James Logan (Bailiff), Betty Gillette.

Filmed in the RKO Studios, Hollywood, 18 July–17 August 1945. First shown in U.S.A., April 1946; G.B. (not shown). Running time: 79 min.

My Own True Love (1948)

Production Company: Paramount. Producer: Val Lewton. Production Manager: Curtis Mick. Director: Compton Bennett. Assistant Director: Oscar Rudolph. Script: Theodore Strauss, Josef Mischel. Based on the novel *Make You a Fine Wife,* by Yolanda Forbes. Adaptation: Arthur Kober. Director of Photography: Charles B. Lang. Editor: LeRoy Stone. Art Directors: Hans Dreier, Henry Bumstead. Set Decorators: Sam Comer, Ross Dowd. Special Effects: Gordon Jennings. Music: Robert Emmett Dolan. Costumes: Edith Head. Sound: Harry Lindgren, John Cope.

Phyllis Calvert (Joan Clews), Melvyn Douglas (Clive Heath), Wanda Hendrix (Sheila Heath), Philip Friend (Michael Heath), Binnie Barnes (Geraldine), Alan Napier (Kittredge), Arthur Shields (Iverson), Phyllis Morris (Mrs. Peach), Richard Webb (A Corporal).

Filmed in the Paramount Studios, Hollywood, July–September 1947. First shown in U.S.A., September 1948; G.B., January 1949. Running time: 84 min.

Please Believe Me (1950)

Production Company: MGM. Producer: Val Lewton. Director: Norman Taurog. Script: Nathaniel Curtis. Director of Photography: Robert Planck. Editor: Ferris Webster. Art Directors: Cedric Gibbons, Daniel B. Cathcart. Set Decorator: Edwin B. Willis. Music: Hans Salter. Sound: Douglas Shearer.

Deborah Kerr (Alison Kirbe), Robert Walker (Terence Keath), Mark Stevens (Matthew Kinston), Peter Lawford (Jeremy Taylor), James Whitmore (Vince Maran), J. Carrol Naish (Lucky Reilly), Spring Byington (Mrs. Milwright), Carol Savage (Sylvia Rumley), Drue Mallory (Beryl Robinson), George Cleveland (Mr. Cooper), Ian Wolfe (Edward Warrender), Bridget Carr (Lily Milwright), Henri Letondel (Jacques Carnet), Gaby Andre (Mme. Carnet), Leon Belasco (The Croupier).

Filmed in the MGM Studios, Hollywood, August–September 1949. First shown in U.S.A., May 1950; G.B., July 1950. Running time: 88 min.

Apache Drums (1951)

Production Company: Universal-International. Producer: Val Lewton. Director: Hugo Fregonese. Script: David Chandler. Based on a novel, *Stand at a Spanish Boot,* by Harry Brown. Director of Photography: Charles P. Boyle. Color Process: Technicolor. Editor: Milton Carruth. Art Directors: Bernard Herzbrun, Robert Clatworthy. Set Decorators: Russell A. Gausman, A. Roland Fields. Music: Hans Salter. Costumes: Bill Thomas. Sound: Leslie I. Carey, Glenn E. Anderson.

Stephen McNally (Sam Leeds), Coleen Gray (Sally), Willard Parker (Joe Madden), Arthur Shields (Reverend Griffin), James Griffith (Lt. Glidden), Armando Silvestre (Pedro-Peter), Georgia Backus (Mrs. Keon), Clarence Muse (Jehu), Ruthelma Stevens (Betty Careless), James Best (Bert Keon), Chinto Gusman (Chacho), Ray Bennett (Mr. Keon).

Filmed in the Universal Studios, Hollywood, and on location, August–September 1950. First shown in U.S.A., May 1951; G.B., June 1951. Running time: 75 min.

BIBLIOGRAPHY

Aylesworth, Thomas G., and Bowman, John S. *The World Almanac Who's Who of Film.* New York: Bison Books, 1987.

Baxter, John. *Hollywood in the Thirties.* New York: Paperback Library, 1970.

-----. *Science Fiction in the Cinema.* New York: Paperback Library, 1970.

Beck, Calvin Thomas. *Heroes of the Horrors.* New York: Macmillan, 1975.

Behlmer, Rudy. *Memo from David O. Selznick.* New York: Viking, 1972.

Bergan, Ronald. *The United Artists Story.* New York: Crown, 1986.

Bojarski, Richard. *The Films of Bela Lugosi.* Secaucus, N.J.: Citadel, 1980.

-----, and Kenneth Beals. *The Films of Boris Karloff.* Secaucus, N.J.: Citadel, 1974.

Brady, Frank. *Citizen Welles.* New York: Scribners, 1989.

Brosnan, John. *Future Tense.* New York: St. Martin's, 1978.

-----. *The Horror People.* New York: New American Library, 1976.

Brunas, Michael, John Brunas, and Tom Weaver. *Universal Horrors: The Studio's Classic Films, 1931–1946.* Jefferson, N.C.: McFarland, 1990.

Budd, Mike. *The Cabinet of Dr. Caligari, Texts, Contexts, Histories.* New Brunswick, N.J.: Rutgers University Press, 1990.

Butler, Ivan. *The Horror Film.* New York: A.S. Barnes, 1967.

Clarens, Carlos. *An Illustrated History of the Horror Film.* New York: G.P. Putnam's Sons, 1967.

Coursodon, Jean-Pierre. *American Directors,* Vols. 1 and 2. New York: McGraw-Hill, 1983.

Cross, Robin. *The Big Book of B Movies or How Low Was My Budget.* New York: St. Martin's, 1981.

Curtis, James. *James Whale.* Metuchen, N.J.: Scarecrow, 1982.

Douglas, Drake. *Horror!* Ontario, Canada: Collier Books, 1966.

Eames, John Douglas. *The MGM Story.* New York: Crown, 1975.

-----. *The Paramount Story.* New York: Crown, 1985.

Eisner, Lotte. *Fritz Lang.* New York: Da Capo, 1976.

Everson, William K. *The Bad Guys.* New York: Citadel, 1964.

-----. *Classics of the Horror Film.* Secaucus, N.J.: Citadel, 1974.

-----. *More Classics of the Horror Film.* Secaucus, N.J.: Citadel, 1986.

Finler, Joel W. *The Movie Directors Story.* New York: Crescent Books, 1985.

Frank, Alan G. *Horror Films.* New York: Spring Books, 1977.

-----. *The Movie Treasury Horror Movies.* London: Octopus Books, 1974.

Friedrich, Otto. *City of Nets.* New York: Perennial Library, 1987.

Gifford, Barry. *The Devil Thumbs a Ride and Other Unforgettable Films.* New York: Grove, 1988.

Gifford, Denis. *Karloff the Man, the Monster, the Movies.* New York: Curtis Books, 1973.

-----. *A Pictorial History of Horror Movies.* New York: Hamlyn, 1973.

Glut, Donald F. *The Dracula Book.* Metuchen, N.J.: Scarecrow, 1975.

-----. *The Frankenstein Legend.* Metuchen, N.J.: Scarecrow, 1973.

Golden, Christopher. *Cut! Horror Writers on Horror Film.* New York: Berkley Books, 1992.

Goldner, Orville, and George E. Turner. *The Making of King Kong.* New York: Ballantine Books, 1975.

Gottesman, Ronald. *Focus on Citizen Kane.* Englewood Cliffs, N.J.: Prentice-Hall, 1971.

Gow, Gordon. *Suspense in the Cinema.* New York: Paperback Library, 1971.

Halliwell, Leslie. *Halliwell's Film Guide.* New York: Charles Scribner's Sons, 1986.

-----. *Halliwell's Filmgoer's and Video Viewer's Companion.* New York: Perennial Library, 1988.

Hardy, Phil. *The Encyclopedia of Horror Movies.* New York: Harper & Row, 1986.

Higham, Charles. *The Films of Orson Welles.* Berkeley: University of California Press, 1970.

-----, and Joel Greenberg. *The Celluloid Muse: Hollywood Directors Speak.* New York: New American Library, 1969.

-----, and -----. *Hollywood in the Forties.* New York: Paperback Library, 1970.

Hirschhorn, Clive. *The Columbia Story.* New York: Crown, 1989.

-----. *The Universal Story.* New York: Crown, 1983.

-----. *The Warner Bros. Story.* New York: Crown, 1979.

Hogan, David J. *Dark Romance: Sexuality in the Horror Film.* Jefferson, N.C.: McFarland, 1986.

Humphries, Patrick. *The Films of Alfred Hitchcock.* Greenwick, Conn.: Bison Books, 1986.

Huss, Roy, and T.J. Ross. *Focus on the Horror Film.* Englewood Cliffs, N.J.: Prentice-Hall, 1972.

Hutchinson, Tom. *Horror and Fantasy in the Movies.* New York: Crescent Books, 1974.

Jensen, Paul M. *Boris Karloff and His Films.* New York: A.S. Barnes, 1974.

Jewell, Richard B., and Vernon Harbin. *The RKO Story.* New York: Arlington House, 1982.

Johnson, William. *Focus on the Science Fiction Film.* Englewood Cliffs, N.J.: Prentice-Hall, 1972.

Kaminsky, Stuart M. *Don Siegel: Director.* New York: Curtis Books, 1974.

King, Stephen. *Danse Macabre.* New York: Everest House, 1981.

Kracauer, Siegfried. *From Caligari to Hitler.* Princeton: Princeton University Press, 1947.

LaValley, Al. *Invasion of the Body Snatchers.* New Brunswick: Rutgers University Press, 1989.

Leff, Leonard J. *Hitchcock and Selznick.* New York: Weidenfeld & Nicolson, 1987.

Lentz, Harris M. *Science Fiction, Horror and Fantasy Film and Television Credits,* Vols. 1 and 2. Jefferson, N.C.: McFarland, 1983.

Lewton, Val. *No Bed of Her Own.* New York: Vanguard Books, 1932.

-----. *Yearly Lease.* New York: Vanguard Books, 1933.

Luciano, Patrick. *Them or Us.* Indianapolis: Indiana University Press, 1987.

McCarthy, Todd, and Charles Flynn. *Kings of the Bs.* New York: Dutton, 1975.

McCarty, John. *Psychos: Eighty Years of Mad Movies, Maniacs, and Murderous Deeds.* New York: St. Martin's, 1986.

McClelland, Doug. *The Golden Age of B Movies.* New York: Bonanza Books, 1978.

McGee, Mark Thomas. *Fast and Furious: The Story of American International Pictures.* Jefferson, N.C.: McFarland, 1984.

Malmstrom, Lars, and David Kushner. *The Seventh Seal: A Film by Ingmar Bergman.* New York: Simon and Schuster, 1960.

Maltin, Leonard. *Movie and Video Guide 1992.* New York: Signet, 1991.

Mank, Gregory William. *It's Alive! The Classic Cinema Saga of Frankenstein.* San Diego, Calif.: A.S. Barnes, 1981.

-----. *Karloff and Lugosi: The Story of a Haunting Collaboration.* Jefferson, N.C.: McFarland, 1990.

Miller, Don. *"B" Movies.* New York: Curtis Books, 1973.

Moore, Darrell. *The Best, Worst, and Most Unusual: Horror Films.* New York: Beekman House, 1983.

Moss, Robert F. *Karloff and Company: The Horror Film.* New York: Pyramid Communications, 1973.

Naha, Ed. *Horrors, From Screen to Scream.* New York: Avon Books, 1975.

Newman, Kim. *Nightmare Movies.* New York: Harmony Books, 1988.

Ott, Frederick W. *The Films of Fritz Lang.* Secaucus, N.J.: Citadel, 1979.

Peary, Danny. *Cult Movies.* New York: Delacorte Press, 1981.

-----. *Cult Movies 2.* New York: Delacorte Press, 1983.

-----. *Cult Movies 3.* New York: Simon and Schuster, 1988.

-----. *Guide for the Film Fanatic.* New York: Simon and Schuster, 1986.

-----. *Omni's Screen Flights/Screen Fantasies.* Garden City, N.Y.: Doubleday, 1984.

Pirie, David. *A Heritage of Horror.* New York: Avon Books, 1973.

Polan, Dana. *Power and Paranoia.* New York: Columbia University Press, 1986.

Prawer, S.S. *Caligari's Children.* New York: Da Capo, 1980.

Reemes, Dana M. *Directed by Jack Arnold.* Jefferson, N.C.: McFarland, 1988.

Sarris, Andrew. *The American Cinema, Directors and Directions 1929–1968.* New York: Dutton, 1968.

Sayre, Nora. *Running Time: Films of the Cold War.* New York: Dial Press, 1982.

Schatz, Thomas. *The Genius of the System: Hollywood Filmmaking in the Studio Era.* New York: Pantheon, 1988.

Siegel, Joel E. *Val Lewton, The Reality of Terror.* New York: Viking, 1973.

Silver, Alain, and Elizabeth Ward. *Film Noir: An Encyclopedic Reference to the American Style.* Woodstock, N.Y.: Overlook, 1979.

Skal, David J. *Hollywood Gothic.* New York: Norton, 1990.

Spoto, Donald. *The Art of Alfred Hitchcock.* Garden City, N.Y.: Doubleday, 1976.

-----. *The Dark Side of Genius: The Life of Alfred Hitchcock.* New York: Ballantine Books, 1983.

Stanley, John. *Revenge of the Creature Features Movie Guide.* Pacifica, Calif.: Creatures at Large Press, 1988.

Sullivan, Jack. *The Penguin Encyclopedia of Horror and the Supernatural.* New York: Viking Penguin, 1986.

Taylor, John Russell. *Strangers in Paradise.* New York: Holt, Rinehart and Winston, 1983.

Telotte, J.P. *The Cult Film Experience.* Austin: University of Texas Press, 1991.

-----. *Dreams of Darkness.* Chicago: University of Illinois Press, 1985.

Thomas, Bob. *Thalberg, Life and Legend.* Garden City, N.Y.: Doubleday, 1969.

Thomas, Tony, and Aubrey Solomon. *The Films of 20th Century-Fox.* Secaucus, N.J.: Citadel Press, 1979.

Thomson, David. *A Biographical Dictionary of Film.* New York: William Morrow, 1981.

Von Gunden, Kenneth, and Stuart H. Stock. *Twenty All-Time Great Science Fiction Films.* New York: Arlington House, 1982.

Waller, Gregory A. *American Horrors, Essays on the Modern American Horror Film.* Chicago: University of Illinois Press, 1987.
Warren, Bill. *Keep Watching the Skies!* Vols. 1 and 2. Jefferson, N.C.: McFarland, 1982, 1986.
Weaver, Tom. *Interviews with B Science Fiction and Horror Movie Makers.* Jefferson, N.C.: McFarland, 1988.
-----. *Science Fiction Stars and Horror Heroes.* Jefferson, N.C.: McFarland, 1991.
Weldon, Michael. *The Psychotronic Encyclopedia of Film.* New York: Ballantine Books, 1983.
Wiater, Stanley. *Dark Dreamers.* New York: Avon Books, 1990.
-----. *Dark Visions.* New York: Avon Books, 1992.
Wiene, Robert. *The Cabinet of Dr. Caligari.* London: Lorrimer, 1984.
Winter, Douglas E. *Faces of Fear.* New York: Berkley Books, 1985.
Wood, Robin. *Hitchcock's Films.* New York: Paperback Library, 1970.
-----. *Hollywood from Vietnam to Reagan.* New York: Columbia University Press, 1986.

INDEX